AMERICAN RECOVERY and REINVESTMENT ACT of 2009

P.L. 111-5

Text of P.L. 111-5 (Division B), as Signed by
the President on February 17, 2009

Conference Report, as Released on
February 12, 2009

CCH
a Wolters Kluwer business

ISBN 978-0-8080-2148-3

4025 W. Peterson Ave.
Chicago, IL 60646-6085
1 800 248 3248
www.CCHGroup.com

Printed in the United States of America

About This Publication

This CCH publication reproduces the text of Division B of the American Recovery and Reinvestment Act of 2009 (P.L. 111-5), as passed by the House and Senate on February 13, 2009, and signed by President Obama on February 17, 2009. The total $787 billion cost of the bill includes nearly $300 billion in tax relief. This report also includes the Joint Explanatory Statement (Division B) of the House and Senate Conferees, as released on February 12, 2009.

The legislation includes a new Making Work Pay Credit, enhancements to the child tax credit and first-time homebuyer credit, an alternative minimum tax (AMT) patch for 2009, and energy incentives. In addition, the legislation provides extensions for 2008 bonus depreciation and increased Code Sec. 179 expensing, a limited five-year net operating loss (NOL) carryback for small businesses, and tax relief for state and local governments. The package also contains:

1. a one-time stimulus payment of $250 to retirees, disabled individuals, social security recipients and disabled veterans;

2. a temporary increase of the earned income credit for working families with three or more children;

3. an above-the-line deduction for interest expenses and state and local taxes paid on the purchase of a new automobile;

4. an above-the-line deduction for interest expenses and state and local taxes paid on the purchase of a new automobile;

5. and a suspension of federal income tax on the first $2,400 of unemployment benefits per recipient for 2009.

About CCH, a Wolters Kluwer business

As always, CCH Tax and Accounting remains dedicated to responding to the needs of tax professionals in helping them quickly understand and work with these new laws as they take effect. Other products and tax services relating to the American Recovery and Reinvestment Act of 2009 can be found at CCH's website http://tax.cchgroup.com/legislation.

February 2009

DIVISION B—TAX, UNEMPLOY-MENT, HEALTH, STATE FIS-CAL RELIEF, AND OTHER PROVISIONS

TITLE I—TAX PROVISIONS

SEC. 1000. SHORT TITLE, ETC.

(a) SHORT TITLE.—This title may be cited as the "American Recovery and Reinvestment Tax Act of 2009".

(b) REFERENCE.—Except as otherwise expressly provided, whenever in this title an amendment or repeal is expressed in terms of an amendment to, or repeal of, a section or other provision, the reference shall be considered to be made to a section or other provision of the Internal Revenue Code of 1986.

(c) TABLE OF CONTENTS.—The table of contents for this title is as follows:

TITLE I—TAX PROVISIONS

Sec. 1000. Short title, etc.

Subtitle A—Tax Relief for Individuals and Families

PART I—GENERAL TAX RELIEF

Sec. 1001. Making work pay credit.
Sec. 1002. Temporary increase in earned income tax credit.
Sec. 1003. Temporary increase of refundable portion of child credit.
Sec. 1004. American opportunity tax credit.
Sec. 1005. Computer technology and equipment allowed as a qualified higher education expense for section 529 accounts in 2009 and 2010.
Sec. 1006. Extension of and increase in first-time homebuyer credit; waiver of requirement to repay.
Sec. 1007. Suspension of tax on portion of unemployment compensation.

Sec. 1008. Additional deduction for State sales tax and excise tax on the purchase of certain motor vehicles.

PART II—ALTERNATIVE MINIMUM TAX RELIEF

Sec. 1011. Extension of alternative minimum tax relief for nonrefundable personal credits.
Sec. 1012. Extension of increased alternative minimum tax exemption amount.

Subtitle B—Energy Incentives

PART I—RENEWABLE ENERGY INCENTIVES

Sec. 1101. Extension of credit for electricity produced from certain renewable resources.
Sec. 1102. Election of investment credit in lieu of production credit.
Sec. 1103. Repeal of certain limitations on credit for renewable energy property.
Sec. 1104. Coordination with renewable energy grants.

PART II—INCREASED ALLOCATIONS OF NEW CLEAN RENEWABLE ENERGY BONDS AND QUALIFIED ENERGY CONSERVATION BONDS

Sec. 1111. Increased limitation on issuance of new clean renewable energy bonds.
Sec. 1112. Increased limitation on issuance of qualified energy conservation bonds.

PART III—ENERGY CONSERVATION INCENTIVES

Sec. 1121. Extension and modification of credit for nonbusiness energy property.
Sec. 1122. Modification of credit for residential energy efficient property.
Sec. 1123. Temporary increase in credit for alternative fuel vehicle refueling property.

PART IV—MODIFICATION OF CREDIT FOR CARBON DIOXIDE SEQUESTRATION

Sec. 1131. Application of monitoring requirements to carbon dioxide used as a tertiary injectant.

PART V—PLUG-IN ELECTRIC DRIVE MOTOR VEHICLES

Sec. 1141. Credit for new qualified plug-in electric drive motor vehicles.
Sec. 1142. Credit for certain plug-in electric vehicles.
Sec. 1143. Conversion kits.
Sec. 1144. Treatment of alternative motor vehicle credit as a personal credit allowed against AMT.

PART VI—PARITY FOR TRANSPORTATION FRINGE BENEFITS

Sec. 1151. Increased exclusion amount for commuter transit benefits and transit passes.

Subtitle C—Tax Incentives for Business

PART I—TEMPORARY INVESTMENT INCENTIVES

Sec. 1201. Special allowance for certain property acquired during 2009.
Sec. 1202. Temporary increase in limitations on expensing of certain depreciable business assets.

PART II—SMALL BUSINESS PROVISIONS

Sec. 1211. 5-year carryback of operating losses of small businesses.
Sec. 1212. Decreased required estimated tax payments in 2009 for certain small businesses.

PART III—INCENTIVES FOR NEW JOBS

Sec. 1221. Incentives to hire unemployed veterans and disconnected youth.

PART IV—RULES RELATING TO DEBT INSTRUMENTS

Sec. 1231. Deferral and ratable inclusion of income arising from business indebtedness discharged by the reacquisition of a debt instrument.
Sec. 1232. Modifications of rules for original issue discount on certain high yield obligations.

PART V—QUALIFIED SMALL BUSINESS STOCK

Sec. 1241. Special rules applicable to qualified small business stock for 2009 and 2010.

PART VI—S CORPORATIONS

Sec. 1251. Temporary reduction in recognition period for built-in gains tax.

PART VII—RULES RELATING TO OWNERSHIP CHANGES

Sec. 1261. Clarification of regulations related to limitations on certain built-in losses following an ownership change.
Sec. 1262. Treatment of certain ownership changes for purposes of limitations on net operating loss carryforwards and certain built-in losses.

Subtitle D—Manufacturing Recovery Provisions

Sec. 1301. Temporary expansion of availability of industrial development bonds to facilities manufacturing intangible property.
Sec. 1302. Credit for investment in advanced energy facilities.

Subtitle E—Economic Recovery Tools

Sec. 1401. Recovery zone bonds.
Sec. 1402. Tribal economic development bonds.
Sec. 1403. Increase in new markets tax credit.
Sec. 1404. Coordination of low-income housing credit and low-income housing grants.

Subtitle F—Infrastructure Financing Tools

PART I—IMPROVED MARKETABILITY FOR TAX-EXEMPT BONDS

Sec. 1501. De minimis safe harbor exception for tax-exempt interest expense of financial institutions.
Sec. 1502. Modification of small issuer exception to tax-exempt interest expense allocation rules for financial institutions.

Sec. 1503. Temporary modification of alternative minimum tax limitations on tax-exempt bonds.
Sec. 1504. Modification to high speed intercity rail facility bonds.

PART II—DELAY IN APPLICATION OF WITHHOLDING TAX ON GOVERNMENT CONTRACTORS

Sec. 1511. Delay in application of withholding tax on government contractors.

PART III—TAX CREDIT BONDS FOR SCHOOLS

Sec. 1521. Qualified school construction bonds.
Sec. 1522. Extension and expansion of qualified zone academy bonds.

PART IV—BUILD AMERICA BONDS

Sec. 1531. Build America bonds.

PART V—REGULATED INVESTMENT COMPANIES ALLOWED TO PASS-THRU TAX CREDIT BOND CREDITS

Sec. 1541. Regulated investment companies allowed to pass-thru tax credit bond credits.

Subtitle G—Other Provisions

Sec. 1601. Application of certain labor standards to projects financed with certain tax-favored bonds.
Sec. 1602. Grants to States for low-income housing projects in lieu of low-income housing credit allocations for 2009.
Sec. 1603. Grants for specified energy property in lieu of tax credits.
Sec. 1604. Increase in public debt limit.

Subtitle H—Prohibition on Collection of Certain Payments Made Under the Continued Dumping and Subsidy Offset Act of 2000

Sec. 1701. Prohibition on collection of certain payments made under the Continued Dumping and Subsidy Offset Act of 2000.

Subtitle I—Trade Adjustment Assistance

Sec. 1800. Short title.

PART I—TRADE ADJUSTMENT ASSISTANCE FOR WORKERS

SUBPART A—TRADE ADJUSTMENT ASSISTANCE FOR SERVICE SECTOR WORKERS

Sec. 1801. Extension of trade adjustment assistance to service sector and public agency workers; shifts in production.
Sec. 1802. Separate basis for certification.
Sec. 1803. Determinations by Secretary of Labor.
Sec. 1804. Monitoring and reporting relating to service sector.

SUBPART B—INDUSTRY NOTIFICATIONS FOLLOWING CERTAIN AFFIRMATIVE DETERMINATIONS

Sec. 1811. Notifications following certain affirmative determinations.
Sec. 1812. Notification to Secretary of Commerce.

SUBPART C—PROGRAM BENEFITS

Sec. 1821. Qualifying Requirements for Workers.
Sec. 1822. Weekly amounts.
Sec. 1823. Limitations on trade readjustment allowances; allowances for extended training and breaks in training.
Sec. 1824. Special rules for calculation of eligibility period.
Sec. 1825. Application of State laws and regulations on good cause for waiver of time limits or late filing of claims.
Sec. 1826. Employment and case management services.
Sec. 1827. Administrative expenses and employment and case management services.
Sec. 1828. Training funding.
Sec. 1829. Prerequisite education; approved training programs.
Sec. 1830. Pre-layoff and part-time training.
Sec. 1831. On-the-job training.
Sec. 1832. Eligibility for unemployment insurance and program benefits while in training.
Sec. 1833. Job search and relocation allowances.

SUBPART D—REEMPLOYMENT TRADE ADJUSTMENT ASSISTANCE PROGRAM

Sec. 1841. Reemployment trade adjustment assistance program.

SUBPART E—OTHER MATTERS

Sec. 1851. Office of Trade Adjustment Assistance.
Sec. 1852. Accountability of State agencies; collection and publication of program data; agreements with States.
Sec. 1853. Verification of eligibility for program benefits.
Sec. 1854. Collection of data and reports; information to workers.
Sec. 1855. Fraud and recovery of overpayments.
Sec. 1856. Sense of Congress on application of trade adjustment assistance.
Sec. 1857. Consultations in promulgation of regulations.
Sec. 1858. Technical corrections.

PART II—TRADE ADJUSTMENT ASSISTANCE FOR FIRMS

Sec. 1861. Expansion to service sector firms.
Sec. 1862. Modification of requirements for certification.
Sec. 1863. Basis for determinations.
Sec. 1864. Oversight and administration; authorization of appropriations.
Sec. 1865. Increased penalties for false statements.
Sec. 1866. Annual report on trade adjustment assistance for firms.
Sec. 1867. Technical corrections.

PART III—TRADE ADJUSTMENT ASSISTANCE FOR COMMUNITIES

Sec. 1871. Purpose.
Sec. 1872. Trade adjustment assistance for communities.
Sec. 1873. Conforming amendments.

PART IV—TRADE ADJUSTMENT ASSISTANCE FOR FARMERS

Sec. 1881. Definitions.
Sec. 1882. Eligibility.
Sec. 1883. Benefits.
Sec. 1884. Report.

Sec. 1885. Fraud and recovery of overpayments.
Sec. 1886. Determination of increases of imports for certain fishermen.
Sec. 1887. Extension of trade adjustment assistance for farmers.

PART V—GENERAL PROVISIONS

Sec. 1891. Effective date.
Sec. 1892. Extension of trade adjustment assistance programs.
Sec. 1893. Termination; related provisions.
Sec. 1894. Government Accountability Office report.
Sec. 1895. Emergency designation.

PART VI—HEALTH COVERAGE IMPROVEMENT

Sec. 1899. Short title.
Sec. 1899A. Improvement of the affordability of the credit.
Sec. 1899B. Payment for monthly premiums paid prior to commencement of advance payments of credit.
Sec. 1899C. TAA recipients not enrolled in training programs eligible for credit.
Sec. 1899D. TAA pre-certification period rule for purposes of determining whether there is a 63-day lapse in creditable coverage.
Sec. 1899E. Continued qualification of family members after certain events.
Sec. 1899F. Extension of COBRA benefits for certain TAA-eligible individuals and PBGC recipients.
Sec. 1899G. Addition of coverage through voluntary employees' beneficiary associations.
Sec. 1899H. Notice requirements.
Sec. 1899I. Survey and report on enhanced health coverage tax credit program.
Sec. 1899J. Authorization of appropriations.
Sec. 1899K. Extension of national emergency grants.
Sec. 1899L. GAO study and report.

Subtitle A—Tax Relief for Individuals and Families

PART I—GENERAL TAX RELIEF

SEC. 1001. MAKING WORK PAY CREDIT.

(a) IN GENERAL.—Subpart C of part IV of subchapter A of chapter 1 is amended by inserting after section 36 the following new section:

"SEC. 36A. MAKING WORK PAY CREDIT.

"(a) ALLOWANCE OF CREDIT.—In the case of an eligible individual, there shall be allowed as a credit against

1 the tax imposed by this subtitle for the taxable year an
2 amount equal to the lesser of—

3   "(1) 6.2 percent of earned income of the tax-
4   payer, or

5   "(2) $400 ($800 in the case of a joint return).

6 "(b) LIMITATION BASED ON MODIFIED ADJUSTED
7 GROSS INCOME.—

8   "(1) IN GENERAL.—The amount allowable as a
9   credit under subsection (a) (determined without re-
10   gard to this paragraph and subsection (c)) for the
11   taxable year shall be reduced (but not below zero) by
12   2 percent of so much of the taxpayer's modified ad-
13   justed gross income as exceeds $75,000 ($150,000
14   in the case of a joint return).

15   "(2) MODIFIED ADJUSTED GROSS INCOME.—
16   For purposes of subparagraph (A), the term 'modi-
17   fied adjusted gross income' means the adjusted
18   gross income of the taxpayer for the taxable year in-
19   creased by any amount excluded from gross income
20   under section 911, 931, or 933.

21 "(c) REDUCTION FOR CERTAIN OTHER PAY-
22 MENTS.—The credit allowed under subsection (a) for any
23 taxable year shall be reduced by the amount of any pay-
24 ments received by the taxpayer during such taxable year
25 under section 2201, and any credit allowed to the taxpayer

1 under section 2202, of the American Recovery and Rein-

2 vestment Tax Act of 2009.

3   "(d) DEFINITIONS AND SPECIAL RULES.—For pur-

4 poses of this section—

5   "(1) ELIGIBLE INDIVIDUAL.—

6   "(A) IN GENERAL.—The term 'eligible in-

7   dividual' means any individual other than—

8   "(i) any nonresident alien individual,

9   "(ii) any individual with respect to

10   whom a deduction under section 151 is al-

11   lowable to another taxpayer for a taxable

12   year beginning in the calendar year in

13   which the individual's taxable year begins,

14   and

15   "(iii) an estate or trust.

16   "(B) IDENTIFICATION NUMBER REQUIRE-

17   MENT.—Such term shall not include any indi-

18   vidual who does not include on the return of tax

19   for the taxable year—

20   "(i) such individual's social security

21   account number, and

22   "(ii) in the case of a joint return, the

23   social security account number of one of

24   the taxpayers on such return.

1   For purposes of the preceding sentence, the so-

2   cial security account number shall not include a

3   TIN issued by the Internal Revenue Service.

4   "(2) EARNED INCOME.—The term 'earned in-

5   come' has the meaning given such term by section

6   32(c)(2), except that such term shall not include net

7   earnings from self-employment which are not taken

8   into account in computing taxable income. For pur-

9   poses of the preceding sentence, any amount ex-

10   cluded from gross income by reason of section 112

11   shall be treated as earned income which is taken

12   into account in computing taxable income for the

13   taxable year.

14   "(e) TERMINATION.—This section shall not apply to

15 taxable years beginning after December 31, 2010.".

16   (b) TREATMENT OF POSSESSIONS.—

17   (1) PAYMENTS TO POSSESSIONS.—

18   (A) MIRROR CODE POSSESSION.—The Sec-

19   retary of the Treasury shall pay to each posses-

20   sion of the United States with a mirror code

21   tax system amounts equal to the loss to that

22   possession by reason of the amendments made

23   by this section with respect to taxable years be-

24   ginning in 2009 and 2010. Such amounts shall

25   be determined by the Secretary of the Treasury

1   based on information provided by the govern-

2   ment of the respective possession.

3   (B) OTHER POSSESSIONS.—The Secretary

4   of the Treasury shall pay to each possession of

5   the United States which does not have a mirror

6   code tax system amounts estimated by the Sec-

7   retary of the Treasury as being equal to the ag-

8   gregate benefits that would have been provided

9   to residents of such possession by reason of the

10   amendments made by this section for taxable

11   years beginning in 2009 and 2010 if a mirror

12   code tax system had been in effect in such pos-

13   session. The preceding sentence shall not apply

14   with respect to any possession of the United

15   States unless such possession has a plan, which

16   has been approved by the Secretary of the

17   Treasury, under which such possession will

18   promptly distribute such payments to the resi-

19   dents of such possession.

20   (2) COORDINATION WITH CREDIT ALLOWED

21   AGAINST UNITED STATES INCOME TAXES.—No cred-

22   it shall be allowed against United States income

23   taxes for any taxable year under section 36A of the

24   Internal Revenue Code of 1986 (as added by this

25   section) to any person—

1   (A) to whom a credit is allowed against

2   taxes imposed by the possession by reason of

3   the amendments made by this section for such

4   taxable year, or

5   (B) who is eligible for a payment under a

6   plan described in paragraph (1)(B) with respect

7   to such taxable year.

8   (3) DEFINITIONS AND SPECIAL RULES.—

9   (A) POSSESSION OF THE UNITED

10   STATES.—For purposes of this subsection, the

11   term "possession of the United States" includes

12   the Commonwealth of Puerto Rico and the

13   Commonwealth of the Northern Mariana Is-

14   lands.

15   (B) MIRROR CODE TAX SYSTEM.—For pur-

16   poses of this subsection, the term "mirror code

17   tax system" means, with respect to any posses-

18   sion of the United States, the income tax sys-

19   tem of such possession if the income tax liabil-

20   ity of the residents of such possession under

21   such system is determined by reference to the

22   income tax laws of the United States as if such

23   possession were the United States.

24   (C) TREATMENT OF PAYMENTS.—For pur-

25   poses of section 1324(b)(2) of title 31, United

1   States Code, the payments under this sub-

2   section shall be treated in the same manner as

3   a refund due from the credit allowed under sec-

4   tion 36A of the Internal Revenue Code of 1986

5   (as added by this section).

6   (c) REFUNDS DISREGARDED IN THE ADMINISTRA-

7 TION OF FEDERAL PROGRAMS AND FEDERALLY AS-

8 SISTED PROGRAMS.—Any credit or refund allowed or

9 made to any individual by reason of section 36A of the

10 Internal Revenue Code of 1986 (as added by this section)

11 or by reason of subsection (b) of this section shall not be

12 taken into account as income and shall not be taken into

13 account as resources for the month of receipt and the fol-

14 lowing 2 months, for purposes of determining the eligi-

15 bility of such individual or any other individual for benefits

16 or assistance, or the amount or extent of benefits or assist-

17 ance, under any Federal program or under any State or

18 local program financed in whole or in part with Federal

19 funds.

20   (d) AUTHORITY RELATING TO CLERICAL ERRORS.—

21 Section 6213(g)(2) is amended by striking "and" at the

22 end of subparagraph (L)(ii), by striking the period at the

23 end of subparagraph (M) and inserting ", and", and by

24 adding at the end the following new subparagraph:

1   "(N) an omission of the reduction required

2   under section 36A(c) with respect to the credit

3   allowed under section 36A or an omission of the

4   correct social security account number required

5   under section 36A(d)(1)(B).".

6   (e) CONFORMING AMENDMENTS.—

7   (1) Section 6211(b)(4)(A) is amended by insert-

8 ing "36A," after "36,".

9   (2) Section 1324(b)(2) of title 31, United

10 States Code, is amended by inserting "36A," after

11 "36,".

12   (3) The table of sections for subpart C of part

13 IV of subchapter A of chapter 1 is amended by in-

14 serting after the item relating to section 36 the fol-

15 lowing new item:

"Sec. 36A. Making work pay credit.".

16   (f) EFFECTIVE DATE.—This section, and the amend-

17 ments made by this section, shall apply to taxable years

18 beginning after December 31, 2008.

19 **SEC. 1002. TEMPORARY INCREASE IN EARNED INCOME TAX**

20   **CREDIT.**

21   (a) IN GENERAL.—Subsection (b) of section 32 is

22 amended by adding at the end the following new para-

23 graph:

1   "(3) SPECIAL RULES FOR 2009 AND 2010.—In

2 the case of any taxable year beginning in 2009 or

3 2010—

4   "(A) INCREASED CREDIT PERCENTAGE

5   FOR 3 OR MORE QUALIFYING CHILDREN.—In

6   the case of a taxpayer with 3 or more qualifying

7   children, the credit percentage is 45 percent.

8   "(B) REDUCTION OF MARRIAGE PEN-

9   ALTY.—

10   "(i) IN GENERAL.—The dollar amount

11   in effect under paragraph (2)(B) shall be

12             $5,000.

13   "(ii) INFLATION ADJUSTMENT.—In

14   the case of any taxable year beginning in

15   2010, the $5,000 amount in clause (i)

16   shall be increased by an amount equal to—

17   "(I) such dollar amount, multi-

18   plied by

19   "(II) the cost of living adjust-

20   ment determined under section 1(f)(3)

21   for the calendar year in which the tax-

22   able year begins determined by sub-

23   stituting 'calendar year 2008' for 'cal-

24   endar year 1992' in subparagraph (B)

25   thereof.

1   "(iii) ROUNDING.—Subparagraph (A)

2   of subsection (j)(2) shall apply after taking

3   into account any increase under clause

4   (ii).".

5   (b) EFFECTIVE DATE.—The amendments made by

6 this section shall apply to taxable years beginning after

7 December 31, 2008.

8 SEC. 1003. TEMPORARY INCREASE OF REFUNDABLE POR-

9   TION OF CHILD CREDIT.

10   (a) IN GENERAL.—Paragraph (4) of section 24(d) is

11 amended to read as follows:

12   "(4) SPECIAL RULE FOR 2009 AND 2010.—Not-

13   withstanding paragraph (3), in the case of any tax-

14   able year beginning in 2009 or 2010, the dollar

15   amount in effect for such taxable year under para-

16   graph (1)(B)(i) shall be $3,000.".

17   (b) EFFECTIVE DATE.—The amendments made by

18 this section shall apply to taxable years beginning after

19 December 31, 2008.

20 SEC. 1004. AMERICAN OPPORTUNITY TAX CREDIT.

21   (a) IN GENERAL.—Section 25A (relating to Hope

22 scholarship credit) is amended by redesignating subsection

23 (i) as subsection (j) and by inserting after subsection (h)

24 the following new subsection:

1   "(i) AMERICAN OPPORTUNITY TAX CREDIT.—In the

2 case of any taxable year beginning in 2009 or 2010—

3   "(1) INCREASE IN CREDIT.—The Hope Scholar-

4   ship Credit shall be an amount equal to the sum

5   of—

6   "(A) 100 percent of so much of the quali-

7   fied tuition and related expenses paid by the

8   taxpayer during the taxable year (for education

9   furnished to the eligible student during any

10   academic period beginning in such taxable year)

11   as does not exceed $2,000, plus

12   "(B) 25 percent of such expenses so paid

13   as exceeds $2,000 but does not exceed $4,000.

14   "(2) CREDIT ALLOWED FOR FIRST 4 YEARS OF

15   POST-SECONDARY EDUCATION.—Subparagraphs (A)

16   and (C) of subsection (b)(2) shall be applied by sub-

17   stituting '4' for '2'.

18   "(3) QUALIFIED TUITION AND RELATED EX-

19   PENSES TO INCLUDE REQUIRED COURSE MATE-

20   RIALS.—Subsection (f)(1)(A) shall be applied by

21   substituting 'tuition, fees, and course materials' for

22   'tuition and fees'.

23   "(4) INCREASE IN AGI LIMITS FOR HOPE

24   SCHOLARSHIP CREDIT.—In lieu of applying sub-

25   section (d) with respect to the Hope Scholarship

1 Credit, such credit (determined without regard to

2 this paragraph) shall be reduced (but not below

3 zero) by the amount which bears the same ratio to

4 such credit (as so determined) as—

5   "(A) the excess of—

6   "(i) the taxpayer's modified adjusted

7   gross income (as defined in subsection

8   (d)(3)) for such taxable year, over

9   "(ii) $80,000 ($160,000 in the case of

10   a joint return), bears to

11   "(B) $10,000 ($20,000 in the case of a

12   joint return).

13   "(5) CREDIT ALLOWED AGAINST ALTERNATIVE

14 MINIMUM TAX.—In the case of a taxable year to

15 which section 26(a)(2) does not apply, so much of

16 the credit allowed under subsection (a) as is attrib-

17 utable to the Hope Scholarship Credit shall not ex-

18 ceed the excess of—

19   "(A) the sum of the regular tax liability

20   (as defined in section 26(b)) plus the tax im-

21   posed by section 55, over

22   "(B) the sum of the credits allowable

23   under this subpart (other than this subsection

24   and sections 23, 25D, and 30D) and section 27

25   for the taxable year.

1   Any reference in this section or section 24, 25, 26,

2   25B, 904, or 1400C to a credit allowable under this

3   subsection shall be treated as a reference to so much

4   of the credit allowable under subsection (a) as is at-

5   tributable to the Hope Scholarship Credit.

6   "(6) PORTION OF CREDIT MADE REFUND-

7   ABLE.—40 percent of so much of the credit allowed

8   under subsection (a) as is attributable to the Hope

9   Scholarship Credit (determined after application of

10   paragraph (4) and without regard to this paragraph

11   and section 26(a)(2) or paragraph (5), as the case

12   may be) shall be treated as a credit allowable under

13   subpart C (and not allowed under subsection (a)).

14   The preceding sentence shall not apply to any tax-

15   payer for any taxable year if such taxpayer is a child

16   to whom subsection (g) of section 1 applies for such

17   taxable year.

18   "(7) COORDINATION WITH MIDWESTERN DIS-

19   ASTER AREA BENEFITS.—In the case of a taxpayer

20   with respect to whom section 702(a)(1)(B) of the

21   Heartland Disaster Tax Relief Act of 2008 applies

22   for any taxable year, such taxpayer may elect to

23   waive the application of this subsection to such tax-

24   payer for such taxable year.".

25   (b) CONFORMING AMENDMENTS.—

(1) Section 24(b)(3)(B) is amended by inserting "25A(i)," after "23,".

(2) Section 25(e)(1)(C)(ii) is amended by inserting "25A(i)," after "24,".

(3) Section 26(a)(1) is amended by inserting "25A(i)," after "24,".

(4) Section 25B(g)(2) is amended by inserting "25A(i)," after "23,".

(5) Section 904(i) is amended by inserting "25A(i)," after "24,".

(6) Section 1400C(d)(2) is amended by inserting "25A(i)," after "24,".

(7) Section 6211(b)(4)(A) is amended by inserting "25A by reason of subsection (i)(6) thereof," after "24(d),".

(8) Section 1324(b)(2) of title 31, United States Code, is amended by inserting "25A," before "35".

(c) TREATMENT OF POSSESSIONS.—

(1) PAYMENTS TO POSSESSIONS.—

(A) MIRROR CODE POSSESSION.—The Secretary of the Treasury shall pay to each possession of the United States with a mirror code tax system amounts equal to the loss to that possession by reason of the application of sec-

1   tion 25A(i)(6) of the Internal Revenue Code of

2   1986 (as added by this section) with respect to

3   taxable years beginning in 2009 and 2010.

4   Such amounts shall be determined by the Sec-

5   retary of the Treasury based on information

6   provided by the government of the respective

7   possession.

8   (B) OTHER POSSESSIONS.—The Secretary

9   of the Treasury shall pay to each possession of

10   the United States which does not have a mirror

11   code tax system amounts estimated by the Sec-

12   retary of the Treasury as being equal to the ag-

13   gregate benefits that would have been provided

14   to residents of such possession by reason of the

15   application of section 25A(i)(6) of such Code

16   (as so added) for taxable years beginning in

17   2009 and 2010 if a mirror code tax system had

18   been in effect in such possession. The preceding

19   sentence shall not apply with respect to any

20   possession of the United States unless such pos-

21   session has a plan, which has been approved by

22   the Secretary of the Treasury, under which

23   such possession will promptly distribute such

24   payments to the residents of such possession.

1   (2) COORDINATION WITH CREDIT ALLOWED

2 AGAINST UNITED STATES INCOME TAXES.—Section

3 25A(i)(6) of such Code (as added by this section)

4 shall not apply to a bona fide resident of any posses-

5 sion of the United States.

6   (3) DEFINITIONS AND SPECIAL RULES.—

7   (A) POSSESSION OF THE UNITED

8   STATES.—For purposes of this subsection, the

9   term "possession of the United States" includes

10   the Commonwealth of Puerto Rico and the

11   Commonwealth of the Northern Mariana Is-

12   lands.

13   (B) MIRROR CODE TAX SYSTEM.—For pur-

14   poses of this subsection, the term "mirror code

15   tax system" means, with respect to any posses-

16   sion of the United States, the income tax sys-

17   tem of such possession if the income tax liabil-

18   ity of the residents of such possession under

19   such system is determined by reference to the

20   income tax laws of the United States as if such

21   possession were the United States.

22   (C) TREATMENT OF PAYMENTS.—For pur-

23   poses of section 1324(b)(2) of title 31, United

24   States Code, the payments under this sub-

25   section shall be treated in the same manner as

1   a refund due from the credit allowed under sec-

2   tion 25A of the Internal Revenue Code of 1986

3   by reason of subsection (i)(6) of such section

4   (as added by this section).

5   (d) EFFECTIVE DATE.—The amendments made by

6 this section shall apply to taxable years beginning after

7 December 31, 2008.

8   (e) APPLICATION OF EGTRRA SUNSET.—The

9 amendment made by subsection (b)(1) shall be subject to

10 title IX of the Economic Growth and Tax Relief Reconcili-

11 ation Act of 2001 in the same manner as the provision

12 of such Act to which such amendment relates.

13   (f) TREASURY STUDIES REGARDING EDUCATION IN-

14 CENTIVES.—

15   (1) STUDY REGARDING COORDINATION WITH

16   NON-TAX STUDENT FINANCIAL ASSISTANCE.—The

17   Secretary of the Treasury and the Secretary of Edu-

18   cation, or their delegates, shall—

19   (A) study how to coordinate the credit al-

20   lowed under section 25A of the Internal Rev-

21   enue Code of 1986 with the Federal Pell Grant

22   program under section 401 of the Higher Edu-

23   cation Act of 1965 to maximize their effective-

24   ness at promoting college affordability, and

1   (B) examine ways to expedite the delivery

2   of the tax credit.

3   (2) STUDY REGARDING INCLUSION OF COMMU-

4   NITY SERVICE REQUIREMENTS.—The Secretary of

5   the Treasury and the Secretary of Education, or

6   their delegates, shall study the feasibility of requir-

7   ing including community service as a condition of

8   taking their tuition and related expenses into ac-

9   count under section 25A of the Internal Revenue

10   Code of 1986.

11   (3) REPORT.—Not later than 1 year after the

12   date of the enactment of this Act, the Secretary of

13   the Treasury, or the Secretary's delegate, shall re-

14   port to Congress on the results of the studies con-

15   ducted under this paragraph.

16 **SEC. 1005. COMPUTER TECHNOLOGY AND EQUIPMENT AL-**

17   **LOWED AS A QUALIFIED HIGHER EDUCATION**

18   **EXPENSE FOR SECTION 529 ACCOUNTS IN**

19   **2009 AND 2010.**

20   (a) IN GENERAL.—Section 529(e)(3)(A) is amended

21 by striking "and" at the end of clause (i), by striking the

22 period at the end of clause (ii), and by adding at the end

23 the following:

24   "(iii) expenses paid or incurred in

25   2009 or 2010 for the purchase of any com-

puter technology or equipment (as defined
in section 170(e)(6)(F)(i)) or Internet access and related services, if such technology, equipment, or services are to be
used by the beneficiary and the beneficiary's family during any of the years the
beneficiary is enrolled at an eligible educational institution.

Clause (iii) shall not include expenses for computer software designed for sports, games, or
hobbies unless the software is predominantly
educational in nature.".

(b) EFFECTIVE DATE.—The amendments made by
this section shall apply to expenses paid or incurred after
December 31, 2008.

SEC. 1006. EXTENSION OF AND INCREASE IN FIRST-TIME
HOMEBUYER CREDIT; WAIVER OF REQUIRE-
MENT TO REPAY.

(a) EXTENSION.—

(1) IN GENERAL.—Section 36(h) is amended by
striking "July 1, 2009" and inserting "December 1,
2009".

(2) CONFORMING AMENDMENT.—Section 36(g)
is amended by striking "July 1, 2009" and inserting
"December 1, 2009".

1   (b) INCREASE.—

2   (1) IN GENERAL.—Section 36(b) is amended by

3 striking "$7,500" each place it appears and insert-

4 ing "$8,000".

5   (2) CONFORMING AMENDMENT.—Section

6 36(b)(1)(B) is amended by striking "$3,750" and

7 inserting "$4,000".

8   (c) WAIVER OF RECAPTURE.—

9   (1) IN GENERAL.—Paragraph (4) of section

10 36(f) is amended by adding at the end the following

11 new subparagraph:

12   "(D) WAIVER OF RECAPTURE FOR PUR-

13   CHASES IN 2009.—In the case of any credit al-

14   lowed with respect to the purchase of a prin-

15   cipal residence after December 31, 2008, and

16   before December 1, 2009—

17   "(i) paragraph (1) shall not apply,

18   and

19   "(ii) paragraph (2) shall apply only if

20   the disposition or cessation described in

21   paragraph (2) with respect to such resi-

22   dence occurs during the 36-month period

23   beginning on the date of the purchase of

24   such residence by the taxpayer.".

1   (2) CONFORMING AMENDMENT.—Subsection (g)

2 of section 36 is amended by striking "subsection

3 (c)" and inserting "subsections (c) and (f)(4)(D)".

4   (d) COORDINATION WITH FIRST-TIME HOMEBUYER

5 CREDIT FOR DISTRICT OF COLUMBIA.—

6   (1) IN GENERAL.—Subsection (e) of section

7 1400C is amended by adding at the end the fol-

8 lowing new paragraph:

9   "(4) COORDINATION WITH NATIONAL FIRST-

10 TIME HOMEBUYERS CREDIT.—No credit shall be al-

11 lowed under this section to any taxpayer with re-

12 spect to the purchase of a residence after December

13 31, 2008, and before December 1, 2009, if a credit

14 under section 36 is allowable to such taxpayer (or

15 the taxpayer's spouse) with respect to such pur-

16 chase.".

17   (2) CONFORMING AMENDMENT.—Section 36(d)

18 is amended by striking paragraph (1).

19   (e) REMOVAL OF PROHIBITION ON FINANCING BY

20 MORTGAGE REVENUE BONDS.—Section 36(d), as amend-

21 ed by subsection (c)(2), is amended by striking paragraph

22 (2) and by redesignating paragraphs (3) and (4) as para-

23 graphs (1) and (2), respectively.

1   (f) EFFECTIVE DATE.—The amendments made by

2 this section shall apply to residences purchased after De-

3 cember 31, 2008.

4 **SEC. 1007. SUSPENSION OF TAX ON PORTION OF UNEM-**

5   **PLOYMENT COMPENSATION.**

6   (a) IN GENERAL.—Section 85 of the Internal Rev-

7 enue Code of 1986 (relating to unemployment compensa-

8 tion) is amended by adding at the end the following new

9 subsection:

10   "(c) SPECIAL RULE FOR 2009.—In the case of any

11 taxable year beginning in 2009, gross income shall not in-

12 clude so much of the unemployment compensation received

13 by an individual as does not exceed $2,400.".

14   (b) EFFECTIVE DATE.—The amendment made by

15 this section shall apply to taxable years beginning after

16 December 31, 2008.

17 **SEC. 1008. ADDITIONAL DEDUCTION FOR STATE SALES TAX**

18   **AND EXCISE TAX ON THE PURCHASE OF CER-**

19   **TAIN MOTOR VEHICLES.**

20   (a) IN GENERAL.—Subsection (a) of section 164 is

21 amended by inserting after paragraph (5) the following

22 new paragraph:

23   "(6) Qualified motor vehicle taxes.".

1   (b) QUALIFIED MOTOR VEHICLE TAXES.—Sub-
2 section (b) of section 164 is amended by adding at the
3 end the following new paragraph:

4   "(6) QUALIFIED MOTOR VEHICLE TAXES.—

5   "(A) IN GENERAL.—For purposes of this
6   section, the term 'qualified motor vehicle taxes'
7   means any State or local sales or excise tax im-
8   posed on the purchase of a qualified motor vehi-
9   cle.

10   "(B) LIMITATION BASED ON VEHICLE
11   PRICE.—The amount of any State or local sales
12   or excise tax imposed on the purchase of a
13   qualified motor vehicle taken into account
14   under subparagraph (A) shall not exceed the
15   portion of such tax attributable to so much of
16   the purchase price as does not exceed $49,500.

17   "(C) INCOME LIMITATION.—The amount
18   otherwise taken into account under subpara-
19   graph (A) (after the application of subpara-
20   graph (B)) for any taxable year shall be re-
21   duced (but not below zero) by the amount
22   which bears the same ratio to the amount which
23   is so treated as—

24   "(i) the excess (if any) of—

1   "(I) the taxpayer's modified ad-

2   justed gross income for such taxable

3   year, over

4   "(II) $125,000 ($250,000 in the

5   case of a joint return), bears to

6   "(ii) $10,000.

7 For purposes of the preceding sentence, the

8 term 'modified adjusted gross income' means

9 the adjusted gross income of the taxpayer for

10 the taxable year (determined without regard to

11 sections 911, 931, and 933).

12   "(D) QUALIFIED MOTOR VEHICLE.—For

13 purposes of this paragraph—

14   "(i) IN GENERAL.—The term 'quali-

15   fied motor vehicle' means—

16   "(I) a passenger automobile or

17   light truck which is treated as a

18   motor vehicle for purposes of title II

19   of the Clean Air Act, the gross vehicle

20   weight rating of which is not more

21   than 8,500 pounds, and the original

22   use of which commences with the tax-

23   payer,

24   "(II) a motorcycle the gross vehi-

25   cle weight rating of which is not more

1   than 8,500 pounds and the original

2   use of which commences with the tax-

3   payer, and

4   "(III) a motor home the original

5   use of which commences with the tax-

6   payer.

7   "(ii) OTHER TERMS.—The terms 'mo-

8   torcycle' and 'motor home' have the mean-

9   ings given such terms under section 571.3

10   of title 49, Code of Federal Regulations

11   (as in effect on the date of the enactment

12   of this paragraph).

13   "(E) QUALIFIED MOTOR VEHICLE TAXES

14   NOT INCLUDED IN COST OF ACQUIRED PROP-

15   ERTY.—The last sentence of subsection (a)

16   shall not apply to any qualified motor vehicle

17   taxes.

18   "(F) COORDINATION WITH GENERAL

19   SALES TAX.—This paragraph shall not apply in

20   the case of a taxpayer who makes an election

21   under paragraph (5) for the taxable year.

22   "(G) TERMINATION.—This paragraph

23   shall not apply to purchases after December 31,

24   2009.".

25 (c) DEDUCTION ALLOWED TO NONITEMIZERS.—

1   (1) IN GENERAL.—Paragraph (1) of section

2   63(c) is amended by striking "and" at the end of

3   subparagraph (C), by striking the period at the end

4   of subparagraph (D) and inserting ", and", and by

5   adding at the end the following new subparagraph:

6   "(E) the motor vehicle sales tax deduc-

7   tion.".

8   (2) DEFINITION.—Section 63(c) is amended by

9   adding at the end the following new paragraph:

10   "(9) MOTOR VEHICLE SALES TAX DEDUC-

11   TION.—For purposes of paragraph (1), the term

12   'motor vehicle sales tax deduction' means the

13   amount allowable as a deduction under section

14   164(a)(6). Such term shall not include any amount

15   taken into account under section 62(a).".

16   (d) TREATMENT OF DEDUCTION UNDER ALTER-

17   NATIVE MINIMUM TAX.—The last sentence of section

18   56(b)(1)(E) is amended by striking "section 63(c)(1)(D)"

19   and inserting "subparagraphs (D) and (E) of section

20   63(c)(1)".

21   (e) EFFECTIVE DATE.—The amendments made by

22   this section shall apply to purchases on or after the date

23   of the enactment of this Act in taxable years ending after

24   such date.

1 **PART II—ALTERNATIVE MINIMUM TAX RELIEF**

2 **SEC. 1011. EXTENSION OF ALTERNATIVE MINIMUM TAX RE-**

3   **LIEF FOR NONREFUNDABLE PERSONAL**

4   **CREDITS.**

5   (a) IN GENERAL.—Paragraph (2) of section 26(a)

6 (relating to special rule for taxable years 2000 through

7 2008) is amended—

8   (1) by striking "or 2008" and inserting "2008,

9   or 2009", and

10   (2) by striking "**2008**" in the heading thereof

11   and inserting "**2009**".

12   (b) EFFECTIVE DATE.—The amendments made by

13 this section shall apply to taxable years beginning after

14 December 31, 2008.

15 **SEC. 1012. EXTENSION OF INCREASED ALTERNATIVE MIN-**

16   **IMUM TAX EXEMPTION AMOUNT.**

17   (a) IN GENERAL.—Paragraph (1) of section 55(d)

18 (relating to exemption amount) is amended—

19   (1) by striking "($69,950 in the case of taxable

20   years beginning in 2008)" in subparagraph (A) and

21   inserting "($70,950 in the case of taxable years be-

22   ginning in 2009)", and

23   (2) by striking "($46,200 in the case of taxable

24   years beginning in 2008)" in subparagraph (B) and

25   inserting "($46,700 in the case of taxable years be-

26   ginning in 2009)".

1   (b) EFFECTIVE DATE.—The amendments made by
2 this section shall apply to taxable years beginning after
3 December 31, 2008.

Subtitle B—Energy Incentives

PART I—RENEWABLE ENERGY INCENTIVES

SEC. 1101. EXTENSION OF CREDIT FOR ELECTRICITY PRODUCED FROM CERTAIN RENEWABLE RESOURCES.

9   (a) IN GENERAL.—Subsection (d) of section 45 is
10 amended—

11   (1) by striking "2010" in paragraph (1) and in-
12   serting "2013",

13   (2) by striking "2011" each place it appears in
14   paragraphs (2), (3), (4), (6), (7) and (9) and insert-
15   ing "2014", and

16   (3) by striking "2012" in paragraph (11)(B)
17   and inserting "2014".

18   (b) TECHNICAL AMENDMENT.—Paragraph (5) of
19 section 45(d) is amended by striking "and before" and
20 all that follows and inserting " and before October 3,
21 2008.".

22   (c) EFFECTIVE DATE.—

23   (1) IN GENERAL.—The amendments made by
24   subsection (a) shall apply to property placed in serv-
25   ice after the date of the enactment of this Act.

1   (2) TECHNICAL AMENDMENT.—The amendment

2   made by subsection (b) shall take effect as if in-

3   cluded in section 102 of the Energy Improvement

4   and Extension Act of 2008.

5 **SEC. 1102. ELECTION OF INVESTMENT CREDIT IN LIEU OF**

6   **PRODUCTION CREDIT.**

7   (a) IN GENERAL.—Subsection (a) of section 48 is

8 amended by adding at the end the following new para-

9 graph:

10   "(5) ELECTION TO TREAT QUALIFIED FACILI-

11   TIES AS ENERGY PROPERTY.—

12   "(A) IN GENERAL.—In the case of any

13   qualified property which is part of a qualified

14   investment credit facility—

15   "(i) such property shall be treated as

16   energy property for purposes of this sec-

17   tion, and

18   "(ii) the energy percentage with re-

19   spect to such property shall be 30 percent.

20   "(B) DENIAL OF PRODUCTION CREDIT.—

21   No credit shall be allowed under section 45 for

22   any taxable year with respect to any qualified

23   investment credit facility.

24   "(C) QUALIFIED INVESTMENT CREDIT FA-

25   CILITY.—For purposes of this paragraph, the

1   term 'qualified investment credit facility' means

2   any of the following facilities if no credit has

3   been allowed under section 45 with respect to

4   such facility and the taxpayer makes an irrev-

5   ocable election to have this paragraph apply to

6   such facility:

7   "(i) WIND FACILITIES.—Any qualified

8   facility (within the meaning of section 45)

9   described in paragraph (1) of section 45(d)

10   if such facility is placed in service in 2009,

11   2010, 2011, or 2012.

12   "(ii) OTHER FACILITIES.—Any quali-

13   fied facility (within the meaning of section

14   45) described in paragraph (2), (3), (4),

15   (6), (7), (9), or (11) of section 45(d) if

16   such facility is placed in service in 2009,

17   2010, 2011, 2012, or 2013.

18   "(D) QUALIFIED PROPERTY.—For pur-

19   poses of this paragraph, the term 'qualified

20   property' means property—

21   "(i) which is—

22   "(I) tangible personal property,

23   or

24   "(II) other tangible property (not

25   including a building or its structural

1   components), but only if such prop-
2   erty is used as an integral part of the
3   qualified investment credit facility,
4   and

5   "(ii) with respect to which deprecia-
6   tion (or amortization in lieu of deprecia-
7   tion) is allowable.".

8   (b) EFFECTIVE DATE.—The amendments made by
9 this section shall apply to facilities placed in service after
10 December 31, 2008.

11 **SEC. 1103. REPEAL OF CERTAIN LIMITATIONS ON CREDIT**
12   **FOR RENEWABLE ENERGY PROPERTY.**

13   (a) REPEAL OF LIMITATION ON CREDIT FOR QUALI-
14 FIED SMALL WIND ENERGY PROPERTY.—Paragraph (4)
15 of section 48(c) is amended by striking subparagraph (B)
16 and by redesignating subparagraphs (C) and (D) as sub-
17 paragraphs (B) and (C).

18   (b) REPEAL OF LIMITATION ON PROPERTY FI-
19 NANCED BY SUBSIDIZED ENERGY FINANCING.—

20   (1) IN GENERAL.—Section 48(a)(4) is amended
21   by adding at the end the following new subpara-
22   graph:

23   "(D) TERMINATION.—This paragraph
24   shall not apply to periods after December 31,
25   2008, under rules similar to the rules of section

1   48(m) (as in effect on the day before the date

2   of the enactment of the Revenue Reconciliation

3   Act of 1990).''.

4   (2) CONFORMING AMENDMENTS.—

5   (A) Section 25C(e)(1) is amended by strik-

6   ing "(8), and (9)" and inserting "and (8)".

7   (B) Section 25D(e) is amended by striking

8   paragraph (9).

9   (C) Section 48A(b)(2) is amended by in-

10   serting "(without regard to subparagraph (D)

11   thereof)" after "section 48(a)(4)".

12   (D) Section 48B(b)(2) is amended by in-

13   serting "(without regard to subparagraph (D)

14   thereof)" after "section 48(a)(4)".

15   (c) EFFECTIVE DATE.—

16   (1) IN GENERAL.—Except as provided in para-

17   graph (2), the amendment made by this section shall

18   apply to periods after December 31, 2008, under

19   rules similar to the rules of section 48(m) of the In-

20   ternal Revenue Code of 1986 (as in effect on the day

21   before the date of the enactment of the Revenue

22   Reconciliation Act of 1990).

23   (2) CONFORMING AMENDMENTS.—The amend-

24   ments made by subparagraphs (A) and (B) of sub-

1 section (b)(2) shall apply to taxable years beginning

2 after December 31, 2008.

3 **SEC. 1104. COORDINATION WITH RENEWABLE ENERGY**

4 **GRANTS.**

5 Section 48 is amended by adding at the end the fol-

6 lowing new subsection:

7 "(d) COORDINATION WITH DEPARTMENT OF TREAS-

8 URY GRANTS.—In the case of any property with respect

9 to which the Secretary makes a grant under section 1603

10 of the American Recovery and Reinvestment Tax Act of

11 2009—

12 "(1) DENIAL OF PRODUCTION AND INVEST-

13 MENT CREDITS.—No credit shall be determined

14 under this section or section 45 with respect to such

15 property for the taxable year in which such grant is

16 made or any subsequent taxable year.

17 "(2) RECAPTURE OF CREDITS FOR PROGRESS

18 EXPENDITURES MADE BEFORE GRANT.—If a credit

19 was determined under this section with respect to

20 such property for any taxable year ending before

21 such grant is made—

22 "(A) the tax imposed under subtitle A on

23 the taxpayer for the taxable year in which such

24 grant is made shall be increased by so much of

25 such credit as was allowed under section 38,

1   "(B) the general business carryforwards

2   under section 39 shall be adjusted so as to re-

3   capture the portion of such credit which was

4   not so allowed, and

5   "(C) the amount of such grant shall be de-

6   termined without regard to any reduction in the

7   basis of such property by reason of such credit.

8   "(3) TREATMENT OF GRANTS.—Any such grant

9   shall—

10   "(A) not be includible in the gross income

11   of the taxpayer, but

12   "(B) shall be taken into account in deter-

13   mining the basis of the property to which such

14   grant relates, except that the basis of such

15   property shall be reduced under section 50(c) in

16   the same manner as a credit allowed under sub-

17   section (a).".

18 **PART II—INCREASED ALLOCATIONS OF NEW**

19   **CLEAN RENEWABLE ENERGY BONDS AND**

20   **QUALIFIED ENERGY CONSERVATION BONDS**

21 **SEC. 1111. INCREASED LIMITATION ON ISSUANCE OF NEW**

22   **CLEAN RENEWABLE ENERGY BONDS.**

23   Subsection (c) of section 54C is amended by adding

24 at the end the following new paragraph:

1   "(4) ADDITIONAL LIMITATION.—The national

2   new clean renewable energy bond limitation shall be

3   increased by $1,600,000,000. Such increase shall be

4   allocated by the Secretary consistent with the rules

5   of paragraphs (2) and (3).".

6   **SEC. 1112. INCREASED LIMITATION ON ISSUANCE OF**

7   **QUALIFIED ENERGY CONSERVATION BONDS.**

8   (a) IN GENERAL.—Section 54D(d) is amended by

9   striking "$800,000,000" and inserting "$3,200,000,000".

10   (b) CLARIFICATION WITH RESPECT TO GREEN COM-

11   MUNITY PROGRAMS.—

12   (1) IN GENERAL.—Clause (ii) of section

13   54D(f)(1)(A) is amended by inserting "(including

14   the use of loans, grants, or other repayment mecha-

15   nisms to implement such programs)" after "green

16   community programs".

17   (2) SPECIAL RULES FOR BONDS FOR IMPLE-

18   MENTING GREEN COMMUNITY PROGRAMS.—Sub-

19   section (e) of section 54D is amended by adding at

20   the end the following new paragraph:

21   "(4) SPECIAL RULES FOR BONDS TO IMPLE-

22   MENT GREEN COMMUNITY PROGRAMS.—In the case

23   of any bond issued for the purpose of providing

24   loans, grants, or other repayment mechanisms for

25   capital expenditures to implement green community

1   programs, such bond shall not be treated as a pri-

2   vate activity bond for purposes of paragraph (3).".

3 **PART III—ENERGY CONSERVATION INCENTIVES**

4 **SEC. 1121. EXTENSION AND MODIFICATION OF CREDIT FOR**

5   **NONBUSINESS ENERGY PROPERTY.**

6   (a) IN GENERAL.—Section 25C is amended by strik-

7 ing subsections (a) and (b) and inserting the following new

8 subsections:

9   "(a) ALLOWANCE OF CREDIT.—In the case of an in-

10 dividual, there shall be allowed as a credit against the tax

11 imposed by this chapter for the taxable year an amount

12 equal to 30 percent of the sum of—

13   "(1) the amount paid or incurred by the tax-

14   payer during such taxable year for qualified energy

15   efficiency improvements, and

16   "(2) the amount of the residential energy prop-

17   erty expenditures paid or incurred by the taxpayer

18   during such taxable year.

19   "(b) LIMITATION.—The aggregate amount of the

20 credits allowed under this section for taxable years begin-

21 ning in 2009 and 2010 with respect to any taxpayer shall

22 not exceed $1,500.".

23   (b) MODIFICATIONS OF STANDARDS FOR ENERGY-

24 EFFICIENT BUILDING PROPERTY.—

(1) ELECTRIC HEAT PUMPS.—Subparagraph (B) of section 25C(d)(3) is amended to read as follows:

> "(B) an electric heat pump which achieves the highest efficiency tier established by the Consortium for Energy Efficiency, as in effect on January 1, 2009.".

(2) CENTRAL AIR CONDITIONERS.—Subparagraph (C) of section 25C(d)(3) is amended by striking "2006" and inserting "2009".

(3) WATER HEATERS.—Subparagraph (D) of section 25C(d)(3) is amended to read as follows:

> "(D) a natural gas, propane, or oil water heater which has either an energy factor of at least 0.82 or a thermal efficiency of at least 90 percent.".

(4) WOOD STOVES.—Subparagraph (E) of section 25C(d)(3) is amended by inserting ", as measured using a lower heating value" after "75 percent".

(c) MODIFICATIONS OF STANDARDS FOR OIL FURNACES AND HOT WATER BOILERS.—

(1) IN GENERAL.—Paragraph (4) of section 25C(d) is amended to read as follows:

1   "(4) QUALIFIED NATURAL GAS, PROPANE, AND

2 OIL FURNACES AND HOT WATER BOILERS.—

3   "(A) QUALIFIED NATURAL GAS FUR-

4   NACE.—The term 'qualified natural gas fur-

5   nace' means any natural gas furnace which

6   achieves an annual fuel utilization efficiency

7   rate of not less than 95.

8   "(B) QUALIFIED NATURAL GAS HOT

9   WATER BOILER.—The term 'qualified natural

10   gas hot water boiler' means any natural gas hot

11   water boiler which achieves an annual fuel utili-

12   zation efficiency rate of not less than 90.

13   "(C) QUALIFIED PROPANE FURNACE.—

14   The term 'qualified propane furnace' means any

15   propane furnace which achieves an annual fuel

16   utilization efficiency rate of not less than 95.

17   "(D) QUALIFIED PROPANE HOT WATER

18   BOILER.—The term 'qualified propane hot

19   water boiler' means any propane hot water boil-

20   er which achieves an annual fuel utilization effi-

21   ciency rate of not less than 90.

22   "(E) QUALIFIED OIL FURNACES.—The

23   term 'qualified oil furnace' means any oil fur-

24   nace which achieves an annual fuel utilization

25   efficiency rate of not less than 90.

1   "(F) QUALIFIED OIL HOT WATER BOIL-

2   ER.—The term 'qualified oil hot water boiler'

3   means any oil hot water boiler which achieves

4   an annual fuel utilization efficiency rate of not

5   less than 90.".

6   (2) CONFORMING AMENDMENT.—Clause (ii) of

7   section 25C(d)(2)(A) is amended to read as follows:

8   "(ii) any qualified natural gas fur-

9   nace, qualified propane furnace, qualified

10   oil furnace, qualified natural gas hot water

11   boiler, qualified propane hot water boiler,

12   or qualified oil hot water boiler, or".

13   (d) MODIFICATIONS OF STANDARDS FOR QUALIFIED

14 ENERGY EFFICIENCY IMPROVEMENTS.—

15   (1) QUALIFICATIONS FOR EXTERIOR WINDOWS,

16   DOORS, AND SKYLIGHTS.—Subsection (c) of section

17   25C is amended by adding at the end the following

18   new paragraph:

19   "(4) QUALIFICATIONS FOR EXTERIOR WIN-

20   DOWS, DOORS, AND SKYLIGHTS.—Such term shall

21   not include any component described in subpara-

22   graph (B) or (C) of paragraph (2) unless such com-

23   ponent is equal to or below a U factor of 0.30 and

24   SHGC of 0.30.".

1   (2) ADDITIONAL QUALIFICATION FOR INSULA-
2   TION.—Subparagraph (A) of section 25C(c)(2) is
3   amended by inserting "and meets the prescriptive
4   criteria for such material or system established by
5   the 2009 International Energy Conservation Code,
6   as such Code (including supplements) is in effect on
7   the date of the enactment of the American Recovery
8   and Reinvestment Tax Act of 2009" after "such
9   dwelling unit".

10   (e) EXTENSION.—Section 25C(g)(2) is amended by
11 striking "December 31, 2009" and inserting "December
12 31, 2010".

13   (f) EFFECTIVE DATES.—

14   (1) IN GENERAL.—Except as provided in para-
15   graph (2), the amendments made by this section
16   shall apply to taxable years beginning after Decem-
17   ber 31, 2008.

18   (2) EFFICIENCY STANDARDS.—The amend-
19   ments made by paragraphs (1), (2), and (3) of sub-
20   section (b) and subsections (c) and (d) shall apply
21   to property placed in service after the date of the en-
22   actment of this Act.

SEC. 1122. MODIFICATION OF CREDIT FOR RESIDENTIAL ENERGY EFFICIENT PROPERTY.

(a) REMOVAL OF CREDIT LIMITATION FOR PROPERTY PLACED IN SERVICE.—

(1) IN GENERAL.—Paragraph (1) of section 25D(b) is amended to read as follows:

"(1) MAXIMUM CREDIT FOR FUEL CELLS.—In the case of any qualified fuel cell property expenditure, the credit allowed under subsection (a) (determined without regard to subsection (c)) for any taxable year shall not exceed $500 with respect to each half kilowatt of capacity of the qualified fuel cell property (as defined in section 48(c)(1)) to which such expenditure relates.".

(2) CONFORMING AMENDMENT.—Paragraph (4) of section 25D(e) is amended—

(A) by striking all that precedes subparagraph (B) and inserting the following:

"(4) FUEL CELL EXPENDITURE LIMITATIONS IN CASE OF JOINT OCCUPANCY.—In the case of any dwelling unit with respect to which qualified fuel cell property expenditures are made and which is jointly occupied and used during any calendar year as a residence by two or more individuals, the following rules shall apply:

1   "(A) MAXIMUM EXPENDITURES FOR FUEL

2   CELLS.—The maximum amount of such ex-

3   penditures which may be taken into account

4   under subsection (a) by all such individuals

5   with respect to such dwelling unit during such

6   calendar year shall be $1,667 in the case of

7   each half kilowatt of capacity of qualified fuel

8   cell property (as defined in section 48(c)(1))

9   with respect to which such expenditures re-

10   late.", and

11   (B) by striking subparagraph (C).

12   (b) EFFECTIVE DATE.—The amendments made by

13 this section shall apply to taxable years beginning after

14 December 31, 2008.

15 **SEC. 1123. TEMPORARY INCREASE IN CREDIT FOR ALTER-**

16   **NATIVE FUEL VEHICLE REFUELING PROP-**

17   **ERTY.**

18   (a) IN GENERAL.—Section 30C(e) is amended by

19 adding at the end the following new paragraph:

20   "(6) SPECIAL RULE FOR PROPERTY PLACED IN

21   SERVICE DURING 2009 AND 2010.—In the case of

22   property placed in service in taxable years beginning

23   after December 31, 2008, and before January 1,

24   2011—

1   "(A) in the case of any such property

2   which does not relate to hydrogen—

3   "(i) subsection (a) shall be applied by

4   substituting '50 percent' for '30 percent',

5   "(ii) subsection (b)(1) shall be applied

6   by substituting '$50,000' for '$30,000',

7   and

8   "(iii) subsection (b)(2) shall be ap-

9   plied by substituting '$2,000' for '$1,000',

10   and

11   "(B) in the case of any such property

12   which relates to hydrogen, subsection (b)(1)

13   shall be applied by substituting '$200,000' for

14   '$30,000'.".

15   (b) EFFECTIVE DATE.—The amendment made by

16 this section shall apply to taxable years beginning after

17 December 31, 2008.

18   **PART IV—MODIFICATION OF CREDIT FOR**

19   **CARBON DIOXIDE SEQUESTRATION**

20 **SEC. 1131. APPLICATION OF MONITORING REQUIREMENTS**

21   **TO CARBON DIOXIDE USED AS A TERTIARY**

22   **INJECTANT.**

23   (a) IN GENERAL.—Section 45Q(a)(2) is amended by

24 striking "and" at the end of subparagraph (A), by striking

25 the period at the end of subparagraph (B) and inserting

1 ", and", and by adding at the end the following new sub-
2 paragraph:

3   "(C) disposed of by the taxpayer in secure
4   geological storage.".

5 (b) CONFORMING AMENDMENTS.—

6   (1) Section 45Q(d)(2) is amended—

7   (A) by striking "subsection (a)(1)(B)" and
8   inserting "paragraph (1)(B) or (2)(C) of sub-
9   section (a)",

10   (B) by striking "and unminable coal
11   seems" and inserting ", oil and gas reservoirs,
12   and unminable coal seams", and

13   (C) by inserting "the Secretary of Energy,
14   and the Secretary of the Interior," after "Envi-
15   ronmental Protection Agency".

16   (2) Section 45Q(a)(1)(B) is amended by insert-
17   ing "and not used by the taxpayer as described in
18   paragraph (2)(B)" after "storage".

19   (3) Section 45Q(e) is amended by striking
20   "captured and disposed of or used as a tertiary
21   injectant" and inserting "taken into account in ac-
22   cordance with subsection (a)".

23 (c) EFFECTIVE DATE.—The amendments made by
24 this section shall apply to carbon dioxide captured after
25 the date of the enactment of this Act.

PART V—PLUG-IN ELECTRIC DRIVE MOTOR VEHICLES

SEC. 1141. CREDIT FOR NEW QUALIFIED PLUG-IN ELECTRIC DRIVE MOTOR VEHICLES.

(a) IN GENERAL.—Section 30D is amended to read as follows:

"SEC. 30D. NEW QUALIFIED PLUG-IN ELECTRIC DRIVE MOTOR VEHICLES.

"(a) ALLOWANCE OF CREDIT.—There shall be allowed as a credit against the tax imposed by this chapter for the taxable year an amount equal to the sum of the credit amounts determined under subsection (b) with respect to each new qualified plug-in electric drive motor vehicle placed in service by the taxpayer during the taxable year.

"(b) PER VEHICLE DOLLAR LIMITATION.—

"(1) IN GENERAL.—The amount determined under this subsection with respect to any new qualified plug-in electric drive motor vehicle is the sum of the amounts determined under paragraphs (2) and (3) with respect to such vehicle.

"(2) BASE AMOUNT.—The amount determined under this paragraph is $2,500.

"(3) BATTERY CAPACITY.—In the case of a vehicle which draws propulsion energy from a battery with not less than 5 kilowatt hours of capacity, the

1 amount determined under this paragraph is $417,

2 plus $417 for each kilowatt hour of capacity in ex-

3 cess of 5 kilowatt hours. The amount determined

4 under this paragraph shall not exceed $5,000.

5 "(c) APPLICATION WITH OTHER CREDITS.—

6 "(1) BUSINESS CREDIT TREATED AS PART OF

7 GENERAL BUSINESS CREDIT.—So much of the credit

8 which would be allowed under subsection (a) for any

9 taxable year (determined without regard to this sub-

10 section) that is attributable to property of a char-

11 acter subject to an allowance for depreciation shall

12 be treated as a credit listed in section 38(b) for such

13 taxable year (and not allowed under subsection (a)).

14 "(2) PERSONAL CREDIT.—

15 "(A) IN GENERAL.—For purposes of this

16 title, the credit allowed under subsection (a) for

17 any taxable year (determined after application

18 of paragraph (1)) shall be treated as a credit

19 allowable under subpart A for such taxable

20 year.

21 "(B) LIMITATION BASED ON AMOUNT OF

22 TAX.—In the case of a taxable year to which

23 section 26(a)(2) does not apply, the credit al-

24 lowed under subsection (a) for any taxable year

1   (determined after application of paragraph (1))

2   shall not exceed the excess of—

3   "(i) the sum of the regular tax liabil-

4   ity (as defined in section 26(b)) plus the

5   tax imposed by section 55, over

6   "(ii) the sum of the credits allowable

7   under subpart A (other than this section

8   and sections 23 and 25D) and section 27

9   for the taxable year.

10   "(d) NEW QUALIFIED PLUG-IN ELECTRIC DRIVE

11 MOTOR VEHICLE.—For purposes of this section—

12   "(1) IN GENERAL.—The term 'new qualified

13 plug-in electric drive motor vehicle' means a motor

14 vehicle—

15   "(A) the original use of which commences

16 with the taxpayer,

17   "(B) which is acquired for use or lease by

18 the taxpayer and not for resale,

19   "(C) which is made by a manufacturer,

20   "(D) which is treated as a motor vehicle

21 for purposes of title II of the Clean Air Act,

22   "(E) which has a gross vehicle weight rat-

23 ing of less than 14,000 pounds, and

1   "(F) which is propelled to a significant ex-

2   tent by an electric motor which draws electricity

3   from a battery which—

4   "(i) has a capacity of not less than 4

5   kilowatt hours, and

6   "(ii) is capable of being recharged

7   from an external source of electricity.

8   "(2) MOTOR VEHICLE.—The term 'motor vehi-

9   cle' means any vehicle which is manufactured pri-

10   marily for use on public streets, roads, and highways

11   (not including a vehicle operated exclusively on a rail

12   or rails) and which has at least 4 wheels.

13   "(3) MANUFACTURER.—The term 'manufac-

14   turer' has the meaning given such term in regula-

15   tions prescribed by the Administrator of the Envi-

16   ronmental Protection Agency for purposes of the ad-

17   ministration of title II of the Clean Air Act (42

18   U.S.C. 7521 et seq.).

19   "(4) BATTERY CAPACITY.—The term 'capacity'

20   means, with respect to any battery, the quantity of

21   electricity which the battery is capable of storing, ex-

22   pressed in kilowatt hours, as measured from a 100

23   percent state of charge to a 0 percent state of

24   charge.

1   "(e) LIMITATION ON NUMBER OF NEW QUALIFIED

2 PLUG-IN ELECTRIC DRIVE MOTOR VEHICLES ELIGIBLE

3 FOR CREDIT.—

4   "(1) IN GENERAL.—In the case of a new quali-

5   fied plug-in electric drive motor vehicle sold during

6   the phaseout period, only the applicable percentage

7   of the credit otherwise allowable under subsection

8   (a) shall be allowed.

9   "(2) PHASEOUT PERIOD.—For purposes of this

10   subsection, the phaseout period is the period begin-

11   ning with the second calendar quarter following the

12   calendar quarter which includes the first date on

13   which the number of new qualified plug-in electric

14   drive motor vehicles manufactured by the manufac-

15   turer of the vehicle referred to in paragraph (1) sold

16   for use in the United States after December 31,

17   2009, is at least 200,000.

18   "(3) APPLICABLE PERCENTAGE.—For purposes

19   of paragraph (1), the applicable percentage is—

20   "(A) 50 percent for the first 2 calendar

21   quarters of the phaseout period,

22   "(B) 25 percent for the 3d and 4th cal-

23   endar quarters of the phaseout period, and

24   "(C) 0 percent for each calendar quarter

25   thereafter.

1   "(4) CONTROLLED GROUPS.—Rules similar to
2 the rules of section 30B(f)(4) shall apply for pur-
3 poses of this subsection.

4 "(f) SPECIAL RULES.—

5   "(1) BASIS REDUCTION.—For purposes of this
6 subtitle, the basis of any property for which a credit
7 is allowable under subsection (a) shall be reduced by
8 the amount of such credit so allowed.

9   "(2) NO DOUBLE BENEFIT.—The amount of
10 any deduction or other credit allowable under this
11 chapter for a new qualified plug-in electric drive
12 motor vehicle shall be reduced by the amount of
13 credit allowed under subsection (a) for such vehicle.

14   "(3) PROPERTY USED BY TAX-EXEMPT ENTI-
15 TY.—In the case of a vehicle the use of which is de-
16 scribed in paragraph (3) or (4) of section 50(b) and
17 which is not subject to a lease, the person who sold
18 such vehicle to the person or entity using such vehi-
19 cle shall be treated as the taxpayer that placed such
20 vehicle in service, but only if such person clearly dis-
21 closes to such person or entity in a document the
22 amount of any credit allowable under subsection (a)
23 with respect to such vehicle (determined without re-
24 gard to subsection (c)).

1   "(4) PROPERTY USED OUTSIDE UNITED STATES

2 NOT QUALIFIED.—No credit shall be allowable under

3 subsection (a) with respect to any property referred

4 to in section 50(b)(1).

5   "(5) RECAPTURE.—The Secretary shall, by reg-

6 ulations, provide for recapturing the benefit of any

7 credit allowable under subsection (a) with respect to

8 any property which ceases to be property eligible for

9 such credit.

10   "(6) ELECTION NOT TO TAKE CREDIT.—No

11 credit shall be allowed under subsection (a) for any

12 vehicle if the taxpayer elects to not have this section

13 apply to such vehicle.

14   "(7) INTERACTION WITH AIR QUALITY AND

15 MOTOR VEHICLE SAFETY STANDARDS.—A motor ve-

16 hicle shall not be considered eligible for a credit

17 under this section unless such vehicle is in compli-

18 ance with—

19   "(A) the applicable provisions of the Clean

20   Air Act for the applicable make and model year

21   of the vehicle (or applicable air quality provi-

22   sions of State law in the case of a State which

23   has adopted such provision under a waiver

24   under section 209(b) of the Clean Air Act), and

1   "(B) the motor vehicle safety provisions of

2   sections 30101 through 30169 of title 49,

3   United States Code.".

4   (b) CONFORMING AMENDMENTS.—

5   (1) Section 30B(d)(3)(D) is amended by strik-

6   ing "subsection (d) thereof" and inserting "sub-

7   section (c) thereof".

8   (2) Section 38(b)(35) is amended by striking

9   "30D(d)(1)" and inserting "30D(c)(1)".

10   (3) Section 1016(a)(25) is amended by striking

11   "section 30D(e)(4)" and inserting "section

12   30D(f)(1)".

13   (4) Section 6501(m) is amended by striking

14   "section 30D(e)(9)" and inserting "section

15   30D(e)(4)".

16   (c) EFFECTIVE DATE.—The amendments made by

17 this section shall apply to vehicles acquired after Decem-

18 ber 31, 2009.

19 **SEC. 1142. CREDIT FOR CERTAIN PLUG-IN ELECTRIC VEHI-**

20   **CLES.**

21   (a) IN GENERAL.—Section 30 is amended to read as

22 follows:

23 **"SEC. 30. CERTAIN PLUG-IN ELECTRIC VEHICLES.**

24   "(a) ALLOWANCE OF CREDIT.—There shall be al-

25 lowed as a credit against the tax imposed by this chapter

1 for the taxable year an amount equal to 10 percent of the

2 cost of any qualified plug-in electric vehicle placed in serv-

3 ice by the taxpayer during the taxable year.

4 "(b) PER VEHICLE DOLLAR LIMITATION.—The

5 amount of the credit allowed under subsection (a) with

6 respect to any vehicle shall not exceed $2,500.

7 "(c) APPLICATION WITH OTHER CREDITS.—

8 "(1) BUSINESS CREDIT TREATED AS PART OF

9 GENERAL BUSINESS CREDIT.—So much of the credit

10 which would be allowed under subsection (a) for any

11 taxable year (determined without regard to this sub-

12 section) that is attributable to property of a char-

13 acter subject to an allowance for depreciation shall

14 be treated as a credit listed in section 38(b) for such

15 taxable year (and not allowed under subsection (a)).

16 "(2) PERSONAL CREDIT.—

17 "(A) IN GENERAL.—For purposes of this

18 title, the credit allowed under subsection (a) for

19 any taxable year (determined after application

20 of paragraph (1)) shall be treated as a credit

21 allowable under subpart A for such taxable

22 year.

23 "(B) LIMITATION BASED ON AMOUNT OF

24 TAX.—In the case of a taxable year to which

25 section 26(a)(2) does not apply, the credit al-

1 lowed under subsection (a) for any taxable year

2 (determined after application of paragraph (1))

3 shall not exceed the excess of—

4   "(i) the sum of the regular tax liabil-

5   ity (as defined in section 26(b)) plus the

6   tax imposed by section 55, over

7   "(ii) the sum of the credits allowable

8   under subpart A (other than this section

9   and sections 23, 25D, and 30D) and sec-

10   tion 27 for the taxable year.

11 "(d) QUALIFIED PLUG-IN ELECTRIC VEHICLE.—For

12 purposes of this section—

13   "(1) IN GENERAL.—The term 'qualified plug-in

14 electric vehicle' means a specified vehicle—

15   "(A) the original use of which commences

16 with the taxpayer,

17   "(B) which is acquired for use or lease by

18 the taxpayer and not for resale,

19   "(C) which is made by a manufacturer,

20   "(D) which is manufactured primarily for

21 use on public streets, roads, and highways,

22   "(E) which has a gross vehicle weight rat-

23 ing of less than 14,000 pounds, and

1   "(F) which is propelled to a significant ex-

2   tent by an electric motor which draws electricity

3   from a battery which—

4   "(i) has a capacity of not less than 4

5   kilowatt hours (2.5 kilowatt hours in the

6   case of a vehicle with 2 or 3 wheels), and

7   "(ii) is capable of being recharged

8   from an external source of electricity.

9   "(2) SPECIFIED VEHICLE.—The term 'specified

10 vehicle' means any vehicle which—

11   "(A) is a low speed vehicle within the

12   meaning of section 571.3 of title 49, Code of

13   Federal Regulations (as in effect on the date of

14   the enactment of the American Recovery and

15   Reinvestment Tax Act of 2009), or

16   "(B) has 2 or 3 wheels.

17   "(3) MANUFACTURER.—The term 'manufac-

18 turer' has the meaning given such term in regula-

19 tions prescribed by the Administrator of the Envi-

20 ronmental Protection Agency for purposes of the ad-

21 ministration of title II of the Clean Air Act (42

22 U.S.C. 7521 et seq.).

23   "(4) BATTERY CAPACITY.—The term 'capacity'

24 means, with respect to any battery, the quantity of

25 electricity which the battery is capable of storing, ex-

1   pressed in kilowatt hours, as measured from a 100

2   percent state of charge to a 0 percent state of

3   charge.

4   "(e) SPECIAL RULES.—

5   "(1) BASIS REDUCTION.—For purposes of this

6   subtitle, the basis of any property for which a credit

7   is allowable under subsection (a) shall be reduced by

8   the amount of such credit so allowed.

9   "(2) NO DOUBLE BENEFIT.—The amount of

10   any deduction or other credit allowable under this

11   chapter for a new qualified plug-in electric drive

12   motor vehicle shall be reduced by the amount of

13   credit allowable under subsection (a) for such vehi-

14   cle.

15   "(3) PROPERTY USED BY TAX-EXEMPT ENTI-

16   TY.—In the case of a vehicle the use of which is de-

17   scribed in paragraph (3) or (4) of section 50(b) and

18   which is not subject to a lease, the person who sold

19   such vehicle to the person or entity using such vehi-

20   cle shall be treated as the taxpayer that placed such

21   vehicle in service, but only if such person clearly dis-

22   closes to such person or entity in a document the

23   amount of any credit allowable under subsection (a)

24   with respect to such vehicle (determined without re-

25   gard to subsection (c)).

1   "(4) PROPERTY USED OUTSIDE UNITED STATES

2   NOT QUALIFIED.—No credit shall be allowable under

3   subsection (a) with respect to any property referred

4   to in section 50(b)(1).

5   "(5) RECAPTURE.—The Secretary shall, by reg-

6   ulations, provide for recapturing the benefit of any

7   credit allowable under subsection (a) with respect to

8   any property which ceases to be property eligible for

9   such credit.

10   "(6) ELECTION NOT TO TAKE CREDIT.—No

11   credit shall be allowed under subsection (a) for any

12   vehicle if the taxpayer elects to not have this section

13   apply to such vehicle.

14   "(f) TERMINATION.—This section shall not apply to

15 any vehicle acquired after December 31, 2011.".

16   (b) CONFORMING AMENDMENTS.—

17   (1)(A) Section 24(b)(3)(B) is amended by in-

18   serting "30," after "25D,".

19   (B) Section 25(e)(1)(C)(ii) is amended by in-

20   serting "30," after "25D,".

21   (C) Section 25B(g)(2) is amended by inserting

22   "30," after "25D,".

23   (D) Section 26(a)(1) is amended by inserting

24   "30," after "25D,".

1   (E) Section 904(i) is amended by striking "and

2 25B" and inserting "25B, 30, and 30D".

3   (F) Section 1400C(d)(2) is amended by striking

4 "and 25D" and inserting "25D, and 30".

5   (2) Paragraph (1) of section 30B(h) is amend-

6 ed to read as follows:

7   "(1) MOTOR VEHICLE.—The term 'motor vehi-

8 cle' means any vehicle which is manufactured pri-

9 marily for use on public streets, roads, and highways

10 (not including a vehicle operated exclusively on a rail

11 or rails) and which has at least 4 wheels.".

12   (3) Section 30C(d)(2)(A) is amended by strik-

13 ing ", 30,".

14   (4)(A) Section 53(d)(1)(B) is amended by strik-

15 ing clause (iii) and redesignating clause (iv) as

16 clause (iii).

17   (B) Subclause (II) of section 53(d)(1)(B)(iii),

18 as so redesignated, is amended by striking "in-

19 creased in the manner provided in clause (iii)".

20   (5) Section 55(c)(3) is amended by striking

21 "30(b)(3),".

22   (6) Section 1016(a)(25) is amended by striking

23 "section 30(d)(1)" and inserting "section 30(e)(1)".

24   (7) Section 6501(m) is amended by striking

25 "section 30(d)(4)" and inserting "section 30(e)(6)".

1   (8) The item in the table of sections for subpart

2   B of part IV of subchapter A of chapter 1 is amend-

3   ed to read as follows:

"Sec. 30. Certain plug-in electric vehicles.".

4   (c) EFFECTIVE DATE.—The amendments made by

5 this section shall apply to vehicles acquired after the date

6 of the enactment of this Act.

7   (d) TRANSITIONAL RULE.—In the case of a vehicle

8 acquired after the date of the enactment of this Act and

9 before January 1, 2010, no credit shall be allowed under

10 section 30 of the Internal Revenue Code of 1986, as added

11 by this section, if credit is allowable under section 30D

12 of such Code with respect to such vehicle.

13   (e) APPLICATION OF EGTRRA SUNSET.—The

14 amendment made by subsection (b)(1)(A) shall be subject

15 to title IX of the Economic Growth and Tax Relief Rec-

16 onciliation Act of 2001 in the same manner as the provi-

17 sion of such Act to which such amendment relates.

18 **SEC. 1143. CONVERSION KITS.**

19   (a) IN GENERAL.—Section 30B (relating to alter-

20 native motor vehicle credit) is amended by redesignating

21 subsections (i) and (j) as subsections (j) and (k), respec-

22 tively, and by inserting after subsection (h) the following

23 new subsection:

24   "(i) PLUG-IN CONVERSION CREDIT.—

1   "(1) IN GENERAL.—For purposes of subsection
2   (a), the plug-in conversion credit determined under
3   this subsection with respect to any motor vehicle
4   which is converted to a qualified plug-in electric
5   drive motor vehicle is 10 percent of so much of the
6   cost of the converting such vehicle as does not ex-
7   ceed $40,000.

8   "(2) QUALIFIED PLUG-IN ELECTRIC DRIVE
9   MOTOR VEHICLE.—For purposes of this subsection,
10   the term 'qualified plug-in electric drive motor vehi-
11   cle' means any new qualified plug-in electric drive
12   motor vehicle (as defined in section 30D, determined
13   without regard to whether such vehicle is made by
14   a manufacturer or whether the original use of such
15   vehicle commences with the taxpayer).

16   "(3) CREDIT ALLOWED IN ADDITION TO OTHER
17   CREDITS.—The credit allowed under this subsection
18   shall be allowed with respect to a motor vehicle not-
19   withstanding whether a credit has been allowed with
20   respect to such motor vehicle under this section
21   (other than this subsection) in any preceding taxable
22   year.

23   "(4) TERMINATION.—This subsection shall not
24   apply to conversions made after December 31,
25   2011.".

1   (b) CREDIT TREATED AS PART OF ALTERNATIVE

2 MOTOR VEHICLE CREDIT.—Section 30B(a) is amended

3 by striking "and" at the end of paragraph (3), by striking

4 the period at the end of paragraph (4) and inserting ",

5 and", and by adding at the end the following new para-

6 graph:

7   "(5) the plug-in conversion credit determined

8   under subsection (i).".

9   (c) NO RECAPTURE FOR VEHICLES CONVERTED TO

10 QUALIFIED PLUG-IN ELECTRIC DRIVE MOTOR VEHI-

11 CLES.—Paragraph (8) of section 30B(h) is amended by

12 adding at the end the following: ", except that no benefit

13 shall be recaptured if such property ceases to be eligible

14 for such credit by reason of conversion to a qualified plug-

15 in electric drive motor vehicle.".

16   (d) EFFECTIVE DATE.—The amendments made by

17 this section shall apply to property placed in service after

18 the date of the enactment of this Act.

19 **SEC. 1144. TREATMENT OF ALTERNATIVE MOTOR VEHICLE**

20   **CREDIT AS A PERSONAL CREDIT ALLOWED**

21   **AGAINST AMT.**

22   (a) IN GENERAL.—Paragraph (2) of section 30B(g)

23 is amended to read as follows:

24   "(2) PERSONAL CREDIT.—

1   "(A) IN GENERAL.—For purposes of this

2   title, the credit allowed under subsection (a) for

3   any taxable year (determined after application

4   of paragraph (1)) shall be treated as a credit

5   allowable under subpart A for such taxable

6   year.

7   "(B) LIMITATION BASED ON AMOUNT OF

8   TAX.—In the case of a taxable year to which

9   section 26(a)(2) does not apply, the credit al-

10   lowed under subsection (a) for any taxable year

11   (determined after application of paragraph (1))

12   shall not exceed the excess of—

13   "(i) the sum of the regular tax liabil-

14   ity (as defined in section 26(b)) plus the

15   tax imposed by section 55, over

16   "(ii) the sum of the credits allowable

17   under subpart A (other than this section

18   and sections 23, 25D, 30, and 30D) and

19   section 27 for the taxable year.".

20 (b) CONFORMING AMENDMENTS.—

21   (1)(A) Section 24(b)(3)(B), as amended by this

22 Act, is amended by inserting "30B," after "30,".

23   (B) Section 25(e)(1)(C)(ii), as amended by this

24 Act, is amended by inserting "30B," after "30,".

1   (C) Section 25B(g)(2), as amended by this Act,

2 is amended by inserting "30B," after "30,".

3   (D) Section 26(a)(1), as amended by this Act,

4 is amended by inserting "30B," after "30,".

5   (E) Section 904(i), as amended by this Act, is

6 amended by inserting "30B," after "30".

7   (F) Section 1400C(d)(2), as amended by this

8 Act, is amended by striking "and 30" and inserting

9 "30, and 30B".

10   (2) Section 30C(d)(2)(A), as amended by this

11 Act, is amended by striking "sections 27 and 30B"

12 and inserting "section 27".

13   (3) Section 55(c)(3) is amended by striking

14 "30B(g)(2),".

15 (c) EFFECTIVE DATE.—The amendments made by

16 this section shall apply to taxable years beginning after

17 December 31, 2008.

18 (d) APPLICATION OF EGTRRA SUNSET.—The

19 amendment made by subsection (b)(1)(A) shall be subject

20 to title IX of the Economic Growth and Tax Relief Rec-

21 onciliation Act of 2001 in the same manner as the provi-

22 sion of such Act to which such amendment relates.

1 **PART VI—PARITY FOR TRANSPORTATION**

2 **FRINGE BENEFITS**

3 **SEC. 1151. INCREASED EXCLUSION AMOUNT FOR COM-**

4 **MUTER TRANSIT BENEFITS AND TRANSIT**

5 **PASSES.**

6   (a) IN GENERAL.—Paragraph (2) of section 132(f)

7 is amended by adding at the end the following flush sen-

8 tence:

9   "In the case of any month beginning on or after the

10   date of the enactment of this sentence and before

11   January 1, 2011, subparagraph (A) shall be applied

12   as if the dollar amount therein were the same as the

13   dollar amount in effect for such month under sub-

14   paragraph (B).".

15   (b) EFFECTIVE DATE.—The amendment made by

16 this section shall apply to months beginning on or after

17 the date of the enactment of this section.

18 # Subtitle C—Tax Incentives for

19 # Business

20 **PART I—TEMPORARY INVESTMENT INCENTIVES**

21 **SEC. 1201. SPECIAL ALLOWANCE FOR CERTAIN PROPERTY**

22 **ACQUIRED DURING 2009.**

23   (a) EXTENSION OF SPECIAL ALLOWANCE.—

24   (1) IN GENERAL.—Paragraph (2) of section

25   168(k) is amended—

1   (A) by striking "January 1, 2010" and in-

2 serting "January 1, 2011", and

3   (B) by striking "January 1, 2009" each

4 place it appears and inserting "January 1,

5 2010".

6 (2) CONFORMING AMENDMENTS.—

7   (A) The heading for subsection (k) of sec-

8 tion 168 is amended by striking "JANUARY 1,

9 2009" and inserting "JANUARY 1, 2010".

10   (B) The heading for clause (ii) of section

11 168(k)(2)(B) is amended by striking "PRE-JAN-

12 UARY 1, 2009" and inserting "PRE-JANUARY 1,

13 2010".

14   (C) Subparagraph (B) of section 168(l)(5)

15 is amended by striking "January 1, 2009" and

16 inserting "January 1, 2010".

17   (D) Subparagraph (C) of section 168(n)(2)

18 is amended by striking "January 1, 2009" and

19 inserting "January 1, 2010".

20   (E) Subparagraph (B) of section

21 1400N(d)(3) is amended by striking "January

22 1, 2009" and inserting "January 1, 2010".

23 (3) TECHNICAL AMENDMENTS.—

24   (A) Subparagraph (D) of section 168(k)(4)

25 is amended—

1   (i) by striking "and" at the end of

2   clause (i),

3   (ii) by redesignating clause (ii) as

4   clause (iii), and

5   (iii) by inserting after clause (i) the

6   following new clause:

7   "(ii) 'April 1, 2008' shall be sub-

8   stituted for 'January 1, 2008' in subpara-

9   graph (A)(iii)(I) thereof, and".

10   (B) Subparagraph (A) of section

11   6211(b)(4) is amended by inserting

12   "168(k)(4)," after "53(e),".

13   (b) EXTENSION OF ELECTION TO ACCELERATE THE

14 AMT AND RESEARCH CREDITS IN LIEU OF BONUS DE-

15 PRECIATION.—

16   (1) IN GENERAL.—Section 168(k)(4) (relating

17   to election to accelerate the AMT and research cred-

18   its in lieu of bonus depreciation) is amended—

19   (A) by striking "2009" and inserting

20   "2010"in subparagraph (D)(iii) (as redesig-

21   nated by subsection (a)(3)), and

22   (B) by adding at the end the following new

23   subparagraph:

24   "(H) SPECIAL RULES FOR EXTENSION

25   PROPERTY.—

1   "(i) TAXPAYERS PREVIOUSLY ELECT-

2   ING ACCELERATION.—In the case of a tax-

3   payer who made the election under sub-

4   paragraph (A) for its first taxable year

5   ending after March 31, 2008—

6   "(I) the taxpayer may elect not

7   to have this paragraph apply to exten-

8   sion property, but

9   "(II) if the taxpayer does not

10   make the election under subclause (I),

11   in applying this paragraph to the tax-

12   payer a separate bonus depreciation

13   amount, maximum amount, and max-

14   imum increase amount shall be com-

15   puted and applied to eligible qualified

16   property which is extension property

17   and to eligible qualified property

18   which is not extension property.

19   "(ii) TAXPAYERS NOT PREVIOUSLY

20   ELECTING ACCELERATION.—In the case of

21   a taxpayer who did not make the election

22   under subparagraph (A) for its first tax-

23   able year ending after March 31, 2008—

24   "(I) the taxpayer may elect to

25   have this paragraph apply to its first

1   taxable year ending after December

2   31, 2008, and each subsequent tax-

3   able year, and

4   "(II) if the taxpayer makes the

5   election under subclause (I), this

6   paragraph shall only apply to eligible

7   qualified property which is extension

8   property.

9   "(iii) EXTENSION PROPERTY.—For

10   purposes of this subparagraph, the term

11   'extension property' means property which

12   is eligible qualified property solely by rea-

13   son of the extension of the application of

14   the special allowance under paragraph (1)

15   pursuant to the amendments made by sec-

16   tion 1201(a) of the American Recovery and

17   Reinvestment Tax Act of 2009 (and the

18   application of such extension to this para-

19   graph pursuant to the amendment made

20   by section 1201(b)(1) of such Act).".

21   (2) TECHNICAL AMENDMENT.—Section

22   6211(b)(4)(A) is amended by inserting "168(k)(4),"

23   after "53(e),".

24   (c) EFFECTIVE DATES.—

1   (1) IN GENERAL.—Except as provided in para-
2   graph (2), the amendments made by this section
3   shall apply to property placed in service after De-
4   cember 31, 2008, in taxable years ending after such
5   date.

6   (2) TECHNICAL AMENDMENTS.—The amend-
7   ments made by subsections (a)(3) and (b)(2) shall
8   apply to taxable years ending after March 31, 2008.

9 SEC. 1202. TEMPORARY INCREASE IN LIMITATIONS ON EX-
10   PENSING OF CERTAIN DEPRECIABLE BUSI-
11   NESS ASSETS.

12   (a) IN GENERAL.—Paragraph (7) of section 179(b)
13 is amended—

14   (1) by striking "2008" and inserting "2008, or
15   2009", and

16   (2) by striking "2008" in the heading thereof
17   and inserting "2008, AND 2009".

18   (b) EFFECTIVE DATE.—The amendments made by
19 this section shall apply to taxable years beginning after
20 December 31, 2008.

21   PART II—SMALL BUSINESS PROVISIONS

22 SEC. 1211. 5-YEAR CARRYBACK OF OPERATING LOSSES OF
23   SMALL BUSINESSES.

24   (a) IN GENERAL.—Subparagraph (H) of section
25 172(b)(1) is amended to read as follows:

1   "(H) CARRYBACK FOR 2008 NET OPER-

2 ATING LOSSES OF SMALL BUSINESSES.—

3   "(i) IN GENERAL.—If an eligible small

4 business elects the application of this sub-

5 paragraph with respect to an applicable

6 2008 net operating loss—

7   "(I) subparagraph (A)(i) shall be

8 applied by substituting any whole

9 number elected by the taxpayer which

10 is more than 2 and less than 6 for '2',

11   "(II) subparagraph (E)(ii) shall

12 be applied by substituting the whole

13 number which is one less than the

14 whole number substituted under sub-

15 clause (I) for '2', and

16   "(III) subparagraph (F) shall not

17 apply.

18   "(ii) APPLICABLE 2008 NET OPER-

19 ATING LOSS.—For purposes of this sub-

20 paragraph, the term 'applicable 2008 net

21 operating loss' means—

22   "(I) the taxpayer's net operating

23 loss for any taxable year ending in

24 2008, or

1   "(II) if the taxpayer elects to

2   have this subclause apply in lieu of

3   subclause (I), the taxpayer's net oper-

4   ating loss for any taxable year begin-

5   ning in 2008.

6   "(iii) ELECTION.—Any election under

7   this subparagraph shall be made in such

8   manner as may be prescribed by the Sec-

9   retary, and shall be made by the due date

10   (including extension of time) for filing the

11   taxpayer's return for the taxable year of

12   the net operating loss. Any such election,

13   once made, shall be irrevocable. Any elec-

14   tion under this subparagraph may be made

15   only with respect to 1 taxable year.

16   "(iv) ELIGIBLE SMALL BUSINESS.—

17   For purposes of this subparagraph, the

18   term 'eligible small business' has the

19   meaning given such term by subparagraph

20   (F)(iii), except that in applying such sub-

21   paragraph, section 448(c) shall be applied

22   by   substituting   '$15,000,000'   for

23   '$5,000,000' each place it appears.".

1   (b) CONFORMING AMENDMENT.—Section 172 is
2 amended by striking subsection (k) and by redesignating
3 subsection (l) as subsection (k).

4   (c) ANTI-ABUSE RULES.—The Secretary of Treasury
5 or the Secretary's designee shall prescribe such rules as
6 are necessary to prevent the abuse of the purposes of the
7 amendments made by this section, including anti-stuffing
8 rules, anti-churning rules (including rules relating to sale-
9 leasebacks), and rules similar to the rules under section
10 1091 of the Internal Revenue Code of 1986 relating to
11 losses from wash sales.

12   (d) EFFECTIVE DATE.—

13   (1) IN GENERAL.—Except as otherwise pro-
14   vided in this subsection, the amendments made by
15   this section shall apply to net operating losses aris-
16   ing in taxable years ending after December 31,
17   2007.

18   (2) TRANSITIONAL RULE.—In the case of a net
19   operating loss for a taxable year ending before the
20   date of the enactment of this Act—

21   (A) any election made under section
22   172(b)(3) of the Internal Revenue Code of
23   1986 with respect to such loss may (notwith-
24   standing such section) be revoked before the ap-
25   plicable date,

1   (B) any election made under section

2   172(b)(1)(H) of such Code with respect to such

3   loss shall (notwithstanding such section) be

4   treated as timely made if made before the appli-

5   cable date, and

6   (C) any application under section 6411(a)

7   of such Code with respect to such loss shall be

8   treated as timely filed if filed before the appli-

9   cable date.

10 For purposes of this paragraph, the term "applica-

11 ble date" means the date which is 60 days after the

12 date of the enactment of this Act.

13 **SEC. 1212. DECREASED REQUIRED ESTIMATED TAX PAY-**

14   **MENTS IN 2009 FOR CERTAIN SMALL BUSI-**

15   **NESSES.**

16 Paragraph (1) of section 6654(d) is amended by add-

17 ing at the end the following new subparagraph:

18   "(D) SPECIAL RULE FOR 2009.—

19   "(i) IN GENERAL.—Notwithstanding

20   subparagraph (C), in the case of any tax-

21   able year beginning in 2009, clause (ii) of

22   subparagraph (B) shall be applied to any

23   qualified individual by substituting '90 per-

24   cent' for '100 percent'.

"(ii) QUALIFIED INDIVIDUAL.—For purposes of this subparagraph, the term 'qualified individual' means any individual if—

"(I) the adjusted gross income shown on the return of such individual for the preceding taxable year is less than $500,000, and

"(II) such individual certifies that more than 50 percent of the gross income shown on the return of such individual for the preceding taxable year was income from a small business.

A certification under subclause (II) shall be in such form and manner and filed at such time as the Secretary may by regulations prescribe.

"(iii) INCOME FROM A SMALL BUSINESS.—For purposes of clause (ii), income from a small business means, with respect to any individual, income from a trade or business the average number of employees of which was less than 500 employees for

1   the calendar year ending with or within the

2   preceding taxable year of the individual.

3   "(iv) SEPARATE RETURNS.—In the

4   case of a married individual (within the

5   meaning of section 7703) who files a sepa-

6   rate return for the taxable year for which

7   the amount of the installment is being de-

8   termined, clause (ii)(I) shall be applied by

9   substituting '$250,000' for '$500,000'.

10   "(v) ESTATES AND TRUSTS.—In the

11   case of an estate or trust, adjusted gross

12   income shall be determined as provided in

13   section 67(e).".

14 **PART III—INCENTIVES FOR NEW JOBS**

15 **SEC. 1221. INCENTIVES TO HIRE UNEMPLOYED VETERANS**

16   **AND DISCONNECTED YOUTH.**

17   (a) IN GENERAL.—Subsection (d) of section 51 is

18 amended by adding at the end the following new para-

19 graph:

20   "(14) CREDIT ALLOWED FOR UNEMPLOYED

21   VETERANS AND DISCONNECTED YOUTH HIRED IN

22   2009 OR 2010.—

23   "(A) IN GENERAL.—Any unemployed vet-

24   eran or disconnected youth who begins work for

25   the employer during 2009 or 2010 shall be

1 treated as a member of a targeted group for
2 purposes of this subpart.

3   "(B) DEFINITIONS.—For purposes of this
4 paragraph—

5   "(i) UNEMPLOYED VETERAN.—The
6   term 'unemployed veteran' means any vet-
7   eran (as defined in paragraph (3)(B), de-
8   termined without regard to clause (ii)
9   thereof) who is certified by the designated
10   local agency as—

11   "(I) having been discharged or
12   released from active duty in the
13   Armed Forces at any time during the
14   5-year period ending on the hiring
15   date, and

16   "(II) being in receipt of unem-
17   ployment compensation under State or
18   Federal law for not less than 4 weeks
19   during the 1-year period ending on
20   the hiring date.

21   "(ii) DISCONNECTED YOUTH.—The
22   term 'disconnected youth' means any indi-
23   vidual who is certified by the designated
24   local agency—

1   "(I) as having attained age 16

2   but not age 25 on the hiring date,

3   "(II) as not regularly attending

4   any secondary, technical, or post-sec-

5   ondary school during the 6-month pe-

6   riod preceding the hiring date,

7   "(III) as not regularly employed

8   during such 6-month period, and

9   "(IV) as not readily employable

10   by reason of lacking a sufficient num-

11   ber of basic skills.".

12   (b) EFFECTIVE DATE.—The amendments made by

13 this section shall apply to individuals who begin work for

14 the employer after December 31, 2008.

PART IV—RULES RELATING TO DEBT INSTRUMENTS

SEC. 1231. DEFERRAL AND RATABLE INCLUSION OF INCOME ARISING FROM BUSINESS INDEBTEDNESS DISCHARGED BY THE REACQUISITION OF A DEBT INSTRUMENT.

21   (a) IN GENERAL.—Section 108 (relating to income

22 from discharge of indebtedness) is amended by adding at

23 the end the following new subsection:

24   "(i) DEFERRAL AND RATABLE INCLUSION OF IN-

25 COME ARISING FROM BUSINESS INDEBTEDNESS DIS-

1 CHARGED BY THE REACQUISITION OF A DEBT INSTRU-
2 MENT.—

3   "(1) IN GENERAL.—At the election of the tax-
4   payer, income from the discharge of indebtedness in
5   connection with the reacquisition after December 31,
6   2008, and before January 1, 2011, of an applicable
7   debt instrument shall be includible in gross income
8   ratably over the 5-taxable-year period beginning
9   with—

10   "(A) in the case of a reacquisition occur-
11   ring in 2009, the fifth taxable year following
12   the taxable year in which the reacquisition oc-
13   curs, and

14   "(B) in the case of a reacquisition occur-
15   ring in 2010, the fourth taxable year following
16   the taxable year in which the reacquisition oc-
17   curs.

18   "(2) DEFERRAL OF DEDUCTION FOR ORIGINAL
19   ISSUE DISCOUNT IN DEBT FOR DEBT EXCHANGES.—

20   "(A) IN GENERAL.—If, as part of a reac-
21   quisition to which paragraph (1) applies, any
22   debt instrument is issued for the applicable
23   debt instrument being reacquired (or is treated
24   as so issued under subsection (e)(4) and the
25   regulations thereunder) and there is any origi-

1   nal issue discount determined under subpart A

2   of part V of subchapter P of this chapter with

3   respect to the debt instrument so issued—

4   "(i) except as provided in clause (ii),

5   no deduction otherwise allowable under

6   this chapter shall be allowed to the issuer

7   of such debt instrument with respect to the

8   portion of such original issue discount

9   which—

10   "(I) accrues before the 1st tax-

11   able year in the 5-taxable-year period

12   in which income from the discharge of

13   indebtedness attributable to the reac-

14   quisition of the debt instrument is in-

15   cludible under paragraph (1), and

16   "(II) does not exceed the income

17   from the discharge of indebtedness

18   with respect to the debt instrument

19   being reacquired, and

20   "(ii) the aggregate amount of deduc-

21   tions disallowed under clause (i) shall be

22   allowed as a deduction ratably over the 5-

23   taxable-year period described in clause

24   (i)(I).

1   If the amount of the original issue discount ac-

2   cruing before such 1st taxable year exceeds the

3   income from the discharge of indebtedness with

4   respect to the applicable debt instrument being

5   reacquired, the deductions shall be disallowed in

6   the order in which the original issue discount is

7   accrued.

8   "(B) DEEMED DEBT FOR DEBT EX-

9   CHANGES.—For purposes of subparagraph (A),

10   if any debt instrument is issued by an issuer

11   and the proceeds of such debt instrument are

12   used directly or indirectly by the issuer to reac-

13   quire an applicable debt instrument of the

14   issuer, the debt instrument so issued shall be

15   treated as issued for the debt instrument being

16   reacquired. If only a portion of the proceeds

17   from a debt instrument are so used, the rules

18   of subparagraph (A) shall apply to the portion

19   of any original issue discount on the newly

20   issued debt instrument which is equal to the

21   portion of the proceeds from such instrument

22   used to reacquire the outstanding instrument.

23   "(3) APPLICABLE DEBT INSTRUMENT.—For

24   purposes of this subsection—

"(A) APPLICABLE DEBT INSTRUMENT.—
The term 'applicable debt instrument' means
any debt instrument which was issued by—

"(i) a C corporation, or

"(ii) any other person in connection
with the conduct of a trade or business by
such person.

"(B) DEBT INSTRUMENT.—The term 'debt
instrument' means a bond, debenture, note, certificate, or any other instrument or contractual
arrangement constituting indebtedness (within
the meaning of section 1275(a)(1)).

"(4) REACQUISITION.—For purposes of this
subsection—

"(A) IN GENERAL.—The term 'reacquisition' means, with respect to any applicable debt
instrument, any acquisition of the debt instrument by—

"(i) the debtor which issued (or is
otherwise the obligor under) the debt instrument, or

"(ii) a related person to such debtor.

"(B) ACQUISITION.—The term 'acquisition' shall, with respect to any applicable debt
instrument, include an acquisition of the debt

1   instrument for cash, the exchange of the debt

2   instrument for another debt instrument (includ-

3   ing an exchange resulting from a modification

4   of the debt instrument), the exchange of the

5   debt instrument for corporate stock or a part-

6   nership interest, and the contribution of the

7   debt instrument to capital. Such term shall also

8   include the complete forgiveness of the indebt-

9   edness by the holder of the debt instrument.

10   "(5) OTHER DEFINITIONS AND RULES.—For

11   purposes of this subsection—

12   "(A) RELATED PERSON.—The determina-

13   tion of whether a person is related to another

14   person shall be made in the same manner as

15   under subsection (e)(4).

16   "(B) ELECTION.—

17   "(i) IN GENERAL.—An election under

18   this subsection with respect to any applica-

19   ble debt instrument shall be made by in-

20   cluding with the return of tax imposed by

21   chapter 1 for the taxable year in which the

22   reacquisition of the debt instrument occurs

23   a statement which—

24   "(I) clearly identifies such instru-

25   ment, and

1   "(II) includes the amount of in-

2   come to which paragraph (1) applies

3   and such other information as the

4   Secretary may prescribe.

5   "(ii) ELECTION IRREVOCABLE.—Such

6   election, once made, is irrevocable.

7   "(iii) PASS-THRU ENTITIES.—In the

8   case of a partnership, S corporation, or

9   other pass-thru entity, the election under

10   this subsection shall be made by the part-

11   nership, the S corporation, or other entity

12   involved.

13   "(C) COORDINATION WITH OTHER EXCLU-

14   SIONS.—If a taxpayer elects to have this sub-

15   section apply to an applicable debt instrument,

16   subparagraphs (A), (B), (C), and (D) of sub-

17   section (a)(1) shall not apply to the income

18   from the discharge of such indebtedness for the

19   taxable year of the election or any subsequent

20   taxable year.

21   "(D) ACCELERATION OF DEFERRED

22   ITEMS.—

23   "(i) IN GENERAL.—In the case of the

24   death of the taxpayer, the liquidation or

25   sale of substantially all the assets of the

1 taxpayer (including in a title 11 or similar

2 case), the cessation of business by the tax-

3 payer, or similar circumstances, any item

4 of income or deduction which is deferred

5 under this subsection (and has not pre-

6 viously been taken into account) shall be

7 taken into account in the taxable year in

8 which such event occurs (or in the case of

9 a title 11 or similar case, the day before

10 the petition is filed).

11 "(ii) SPECIAL RULE FOR PASS-THRU

12 ENTITIES.—The rule of clause (i) shall

13 also apply in the case of the sale or ex-

14 change or redemption of an interest in a

15 partnership, S corporation, or other pass-

16 thru entity by a partner, shareholder, or

17 other person holding an ownership interest

18 in such entity.

19 "(6) SPECIAL RULE FOR PARTNERSHIPS.—In

20 the case of a partnership, any income deferred under

21 this subsection shall be allocated to the partners in

22 the partnership immediately before the discharge in

23 the manner such amounts would have been included

24 in the distributive shares of such partners under sec-

25 tion 704 if such income were recognized at such

1   time. Any decrease in a partner's share of partner-

2   ship liabilities as a result of such discharge shall not

3   be taken into account for purposes of section 752 at

4   the time of the discharge to the extent it would

5   cause the partner to recognize gain under section

6   731. Any decrease in partnership liabilities deferred

7   under the preceding sentence shall be taken into ac-

8   count by such partner at the same time, and to the

9   extent remaining in the same amount, as income de-

10   ferred under this subsection is recognized.

11   "(7) SECRETARIAL AUTHORITY.—The Secretary

12   may prescribe such regulations, rules, or other guid-

13   ance as may be necessary or appropriate for pur-

14   poses of applying this subsection, including—

15   "(A) extending the application of the rules

16   of paragraph (5)(D) to other circumstances

17   where appropriate,

18   "(B) requiring reporting of the election

19   (and such other information as the Secretary

20   may require) on returns of tax for subsequent

21   taxable years, and

22   "(C) rules for the application of this sub-

23   section to partnerships, S corporations, and

24   other pass-thru entities, including for the allo-

25   cation of deferred deductions.".

1   (b) EFFECTIVE DATE.—The amendments made by
2 this section shall apply to discharges in taxable years end-
3 ing after December 31, 2008.

4 SEC. 1232. MODIFICATIONS OF RULES FOR ORIGINAL ISSUE

5   DISCOUNT ON CERTAIN HIGH YIELD OBLIGA-

6   TIONS.

7   (a) SUSPENSION OF SPECIAL RULES.—Section
8 163(e)(5) (relating to special rules for original issue dis-
9 count on certain high yield obligations) is amended by re-
10 designating subparagraph (F) as subparagraph (G) and
11 by inserting after subparagraph (E) the following new
12 subparagraph:

13   "(F) SUSPENSION OF APPLICATION OF
14   PARAGRAPH.—

15   "(i) TEMPORARY SUSPENSION.—This
16   paragraph shall not apply to any applicable
17   high yield discount obligation issued during
18   the period beginning on September 1,
19   2008, and ending on December 31, 2009,
20   in exchange (including an exchange result-
21   ing from a modification of the debt instru-
22   ment) for an obligation which is not an ap-
23   plicable high yield discount obligation and
24   the issuer (or obligor) of which is the same
25   as the issuer (or obligor) of such applicable

1   high yield discount obligation. The pre-

2   ceding sentence shall not apply to any obli-

3   gation the interest on which is interest de-

4   scribed in section 871(h)(4) (without re-

5   gard to subparagraph (D) thereof) or to

6   any obligation issued to a related person

7   (within the meaning of section 108(e)(4)).

8   "(ii) SUCCESSIVE APPLICATION.—Any

9   obligation to which clause (i) applies shall

10   not be treated as an applicable high yield

11   discount obligation for purposes of apply-

12   ing this subparagraph to any other obliga-

13   tion issued in exchange for such obligation.

14   "(iii) SECRETARIAL AUTHORITY TO

15   SUSPEND APPLICATION.—The Secretary

16   may apply this paragraph with respect to

17   debt instruments issued in periods fol-

18   lowing the period described in clause (i) if

19   the Secretary determines that such appli-

20   cation is appropriate in light of distressed

21   conditions in the debt capital markets.".

22   (b) INTEREST RATE USED IN DETERMINING HIGH

23 YIELD OBLIGATIONS.—The last sentence of section

24 163(i)(1) is amended—

25   (1) by inserting "(i)" after "regulation", and

1   (2) by inserting ", or (ii) permit, on a tem-

2   porary basis, a rate to be used with respect to any

3   debt instrument which is higher than the applicable

4   Federal rate if the Secretary determines that such

5   rate is appropriate in light of distressed conditions

6   in the debt capital markets" before the period at the

7   end.

8   (c) EFFECTIVE DATE.—

9   (1) SUSPENSION.—The amendments made by

10   subsection (a) shall apply to obligations issued after

11   August 31, 2008, in taxable years ending after such

12   date.

13   (2) INTEREST RATE AUTHORITY.—The amend-

14   ments made by subsection (b) shall apply to obliga-

15   tions issued after December 31, 2009, in taxable

16   years ending after such date.

17   **PART V—QUALIFIED SMALL BUSINESS STOCK**

18   **SEC. 1241. SPECIAL RULES APPLICABLE TO QUALIFIED**

19   **SMALL BUSINESS STOCK FOR 2009 AND 2010.**

20   (a) IN GENERAL.—Section 1202(a) is amended by

21 adding at the end the following new paragraph:

22   "(3) SPECIAL RULES FOR 2009 AND 2010.—In

23   the case of qualified small business stock acquired

24   after the date of the enactment of this paragraph

25   and before January 1, 2011—

1   "(A) paragraph (1) shall be applied by

2   substituting '75 percent' for '50 percent', and

3   "(B) paragraph (2) shall not apply.".

4 (b) EFFECTIVE DATE.—The amendment made by

5 this section shall apply to stock acquired after the date

6 of the enactment of this Act.

7   **PART VI—S CORPORATIONS**

8 **SEC. 1251. TEMPORARY REDUCTION IN RECOGNITION PE-**

9   **RIOD FOR BUILT-IN GAINS TAX.**

10 (a) IN GENERAL.—Paragraph (7) of section 1374(d)

11 (relating to definitions and special rules) is amended to

12 read as follows:

13   "(7) RECOGNITION PERIOD.—

14   "(A) IN GENERAL.—The term 'recognition

15   period' means the 10-year period beginning

16   with the 1st day of the 1st taxable year for

17   which the corporation was an S corporation.

18   "(B) SPECIAL RULE FOR 2009 AND 2010.—

19   In the case of any taxable year beginning in

20   2009 or 2010, no tax shall be imposed on the

21   net recognized built-in gain of an S corporation

22   if the 7th taxable year in the recognition period

23   preceded such taxable year. The preceding sen-

24   tence shall be applied separately with respect to

25   any asset to which paragraph (8) applies.

1   "(C) SPECIAL RULE FOR DISTRIBUTIONS

2   TO SHAREHOLDERS.—For purposes of applying

3   this section to any amount includible in income

4   by reason of distributions to shareholders pur-

5   suant to section 593(e)—

6   "(i) subparagraph (A) shall be applied

7   without regard to the phrase '10-year', and

8   "(ii) subparagraph (B) shall not

9   apply.".

10   (b) EFFECTIVE DATE.—The amendment made by

11 this section shall apply to taxable years beginning after

12 December 31, 2008.

PART VII—RULES RELATING TO OWNERSHIP CHANGES

SEC. 1261. CLARIFICATION OF REGULATIONS RELATED TO LIMITATIONS ON CERTAIN BUILT-IN LOSSES FOLLOWING AN OWNERSHIP CHANGE.

18   (a) FINDINGS.—Congress finds as follows:

19   (1) The delegation of authority to the Secretary

20   of the Treasury under section 382(m) of the Inter-

21   nal Revenue Code of 1986 does not authorize the

22   Secretary to provide exemptions or special rules that

23   are restricted to particular industries or classes of

24   taxpayers.

1 (2) Internal Revenue Service Notice 2008–83 is

2 inconsistent with the congressional intent in enact-

3 ing such section 382(m).

4 (3) The legal authority to prescribe Internal

5 Revenue Service Notice 2008–83 is doubtful.

6 (4) However, as taxpayers should generally be

7 able to rely on guidance issued by the Secretary of

8 the Treasury legislation is necessary to clarify the

9 force and effect of Internal Revenue Service Notice

10 2008–83 and restore the proper application under

11 the Internal Revenue Code of 1986 of the limitation

12 on built-in losses following an ownership change of

13 a bank.

14 (b) DETERMINATION OF FORCE AND EFFECT OF IN-

15 TERNAL REVENUE SERVICE NOTICE 2008–83 EXEMPT-

16 ING BANKS FROM LIMITATION ON CERTAIN BUILT–IN

17 LOSSES FOLLOWING OWNERSHIP CHANGE.—

18 (1) IN GENERAL.—Internal Revenue Service

19 Notice 2008–83—

20 (A) shall be deemed to have the force and

21 effect of law with respect to any ownership

22 change (as defined in section 382(g) of the In-

23 ternal Revenue Code of 1986) occurring on or

24 before January 16, 2009, and

1   (B) shall have no force or effect with re-

2   spect to any ownership change after such date.

3   (2) BINDING CONTRACTS.—Notwithstanding

4 paragraph (1), Internal Revenue Service Notice

5 2008–83 shall have the force and effect of law with

6 respect to any ownership change (as so defined)

7 which occurs after January 16, 2009, if such

8 change—

9   (A) is pursuant to a written binding con-

10   tract entered into on or before such date, or

11   (B) is pursuant to a written agreement en-

12   tered into on or before such date and such

13   agreement was described on or before such date

14   in a public announcement or in a filing with the

15   Securities and Exchange Commission required

16   by reason of such ownership change.

17 **SEC. 1262. TREATMENT OF CERTAIN OWNERSHIP CHANGES**

18   **FOR PURPOSES OF LIMITATIONS ON NET OP-**

19   **ERATING LOSS CARRYFORWARDS AND CER-**

20   **TAIN BUILT-IN LOSSES.**

21   (a) IN GENERAL.—Section 382 is amended by adding

22 at the end the following new subsection:

23   "(n) SPECIAL RULE FOR CERTAIN OWNERSHIP

24 CHANGES.—

1   "(1) IN GENERAL.—The limitation contained in

2   subsection (a) shall not apply in the case of an own-

3   ership change which is pursuant to a restructuring

4   plan of a taxpayer which—

5   "(A) is required under a loan agreement or

6   a commitment for a line of credit entered into

7   with the Department of the Treasury under the

8   Emergency Economic Stabilization Act of 2008,

9   and

10   "(B) is intended to result in a rationaliza-

11   tion of the costs, capitalization, and capacity

12   with respect to the manufacturing workforce of,

13   and suppliers to, the taxpayer and its subsidi-

14   aries.

15   "(2) SUBSEQUENT ACQUISITIONS.—Paragraph

16   (1) shall not apply in the case of any subsequent

17   ownership change unless such ownership change is

18   described in such paragraph.

19   "(3) LIMITATION BASED ON CONTROL IN COR-

20   PORATION.—

21   "(A) IN GENERAL.—Paragraph (1) shall

22   not apply in the case of any ownership change

23   if, immediately after such ownership change,

24   any person (other than a voluntary employees'

25   beneficiary association under section 501(c)(9))

1 owns stock of the new loss corporation pos-
2 sessing 50 percent or more of the total com-
3 bined voting power of all classes of stock enti-
4 tled to vote, or of the total value of the stock
5 of such corporation.

6 "(B) TREATMENT OF RELATED PER-
7 SONS.—

8 "(i) IN GENERAL.—Related persons
9 shall be treated as a single person for pur-
10 poses of this paragraph.

11 "(ii) RELATED PERSONS.—For pur-
12 poses of clause (i), a person shall be treat-
13 ed as related to another person if—

14 "(I) such person bears a relation-
15 ship to such other person described in
16 section 267(b) or 707(b), or

17 "(II) such persons are members
18 of a group of persons acting in con-
19 cert.".

20 (b) EFFECTIVE DATE.—The amendment made by
21 this section shall apply to ownership changes after the
22 date of the enactment of this Act.

Subtitle D—Manufacturing Recovery Provisions

SEC. 1301. TEMPORARY EXPANSION OF AVAILABILITY OF INDUSTRIAL DEVELOPMENT BONDS TO FACILITIES MANUFACTURING INTANGIBLE PROPERTY.

(a) IN GENERAL.—Subparagraph (C) of section 144(a)(12) is amended—

(1) by striking "For purposes of this paragraph, the term" and inserting "For purposes of this paragraph—

"(i) IN GENERAL.—The term", and

(2) by striking the last sentence and inserting the following new clauses:

"(ii) CERTAIN FACILITIES INCLUDED.—Such term includes facilities which are directly related and ancillary to a manufacturing facility (determined without regard to this clause) if—

"(I) such facilities are located on the same site as the manufacturing facility, and

"(II) not more than 25 percent of the net proceeds of the issue are used to provide such facilities.

1   "(iii) SPECIAL RULES FOR BONDS

2   ISSUED IN 2009 AND 2010.—In the case of

3   any issue made after the date of enactment

4   of this clause and before January 1, 2011,

5   clause (ii) shall not apply and the net pro-

6   ceeds from a bond shall be considered to

7   be used to provide a manufacturing facility

8   if such proceeds are used to provide—

9   "(I) a facility which is used in

10   the creation or production of intan-

11   gible property which is described in

12   section 197(d)(1)(C)(iii), or

13   "(II) a facility which is function-

14   ally related and subordinate to a man-

15   ufacturing facility (determined with-

16   out regard to this subclause) if such

17   facility is located on the same site as

18   the manufacturing facility.".

19   (b) EFFECTIVE DATE.—The amendments made by

20 this section shall apply to obligations issued after the date

21 of the enactment of this Act.

22 **SEC. 1302. CREDIT FOR INVESTMENT IN ADVANCED EN-**

23   **ERGY FACILITIES.**

24   (a) IN GENERAL.—Section 46 (relating to amount of

25 credit) is amended by striking "and" at the end of para-

1 graph (3), by striking the period at the end of paragraph

2 (4), and by adding at the end the following new para-

3 graph:

4   "(5) the qualifying advanced energy project

5   credit.".

6   (b) AMOUNT OF CREDIT.—Subpart E of part IV of

7 subchapter A of chapter 1 (relating to rules for computing

8 investment credit) is amended by inserting after section

9 48B the following new section:

10 **"SEC. 48C. QUALIFYING ADVANCED ENERGY PROJECT**

11   **CREDIT.**

12   "(a) IN GENERAL.—For purposes of section 46, the

13 qualifying advanced energy project credit for any taxable

14 year is an amount equal to 30 percent of the qualified

15 investment for such taxable year with respect to any quali-

16 fying advanced energy project of the taxpayer.

17   "(b) QUALIFIED INVESTMENT.—

18   "(1) IN GENERAL.—For purposes of subsection

19   (a), the qualified investment for any taxable year is

20   the basis of eligible property placed in service by the

21   taxpayer during such taxable year which is part of

22   a qualifying advanced energy project.

23   "(2) CERTAIN QUALIFIED PROGRESS EXPENDI-

24   TURES RULES MADE APPLICABLE.—Rules similar to

25   the rules of subsections (c)(4) and (d) of section 46

1   (as in effect on the day before the enactment of the

2   Revenue Reconciliation Act of 1990) shall apply for

3   purposes of this section.

4   "(3) LIMITATION.—The amount which is treat-

5   ed for all taxable years with respect to any quali-

6   fying advanced energy project shall not exceed the

7   amount designated by the Secretary as eligible for

8   the credit under this section.

9   "(c) DEFINITIONS.—

10   "(1) QUALIFYING ADVANCED ENERGY

11   PROJECT.—

12   "(A) IN GENERAL.—The term 'qualifying

13   advanced energy project' means a project—

14   "(i) which re-equips, expands, or es-

15   tablishes a manufacturing facility for the

16   production of—

17   "(I) property designed to be used

18   to produce energy from the sun, wind,

19   geothermal deposits (within the mean-

20   ing of section 613(e)(2)), or other re-

21   newable resources,

22   "(II) fuel cells, microturbines, or

23   an energy storage system for use with

24   electric or hybrid-electric motor vehi-

25   cles,

1   "(III) electric grids to support

2   the transmission of intermittent

3   sources of renewable energy, including

4   storage of such energy,

5   "(IV) property designed to cap-

6   ture and sequester carbon dioxide

7   emissions,

8   "(V) property designed to refine

9   or blend renewable fuels or to produce

10   energy conservation technologies (in-

11   cluding energy-conserving lighting

12   technologies and smart grid tech-

13   nologies),

14   "(VI) new qualified plug-in elec-

15   tric drive motor vehicles (as defined

16   by section 30D), qualified plug-in

17   electric vehicles (as defined by section

18   30(d)), or components which are de-

19   signed specifically for use with such

20   vehicles, including electric motors,

21   generators, and power control units,

22   or

23   "(VII) other advanced energy

24   property designed to reduce green-

1   house gas emissions as may be deter-

2   mined by the Secretary, and

3   "(ii) any portion of the qualified in-

4   vestment of which is certified by the Sec-

5   retary under subsection (d) as eligible for

6   a credit under this section.

7   "(B) EXCEPTION.—Such term shall not in-

8   clude any portion of a project for the produc-

9   tion of any property which is used in the refin-

10   ing or blending of any transportation fuel

11   (other than renewable fuels).

12   "(2) ELIGIBLE PROPERTY.—The term 'eligible

13   property' means any property—

14   "(A) which is necessary for the production

15   of property described in paragraph (1)(A)(i),

16   "(B) which is—

17   "(i) tangible personal property, or

18   "(ii) other tangible property (not in-

19   cluding a building or its structural compo-

20   nents), but only if such property is used as

21   an integral part of the qualified investment

22   credit facility, and

23   "(C) with respect to which depreciation (or

24   amortization in lieu of depreciation) is allow-

25   able.

1   "(d) QUALIFYING ADVANCED ENERGY PROJECT

2 PROGRAM.—

3   "(1) ESTABLISHMENT.—

4   "(A) IN GENERAL.—Not later than 180

5   days after the date of enactment of this section,

6   the Secretary, in consultation with the Sec-

7   retary of Energy, shall establish a qualifying

8   advanced energy project program to consider

9   and award certifications for qualified invest-

10   ments eligible for credits under this section to

11   qualifying advanced energy project sponsors.

12   "(B) LIMITATION.—The total amount of

13   credits that may be allocated under the pro-

14   gram shall not exceed $2,300,000,000.

15   "(2) CERTIFICATION.—

16   "(A) APPLICATION PERIOD.—Each appli-

17   cant for certification under this paragraph shall

18   submit an application containing such informa-

19   tion as the Secretary may require during the 2-

20   year period beginning on the date the Secretary

21   establishes the program under paragraph (1).

22   "(B) TIME TO MEET CRITERIA FOR CER-

23   TIFICATION.—Each applicant for certification

24   shall have 1 year from the date of acceptance

25   by the Secretary of the application during

which to provide to the Secretary evidence that
the requirements of the certification have been
met.

"(C) PERIOD OF ISSUANCE.—An applicant
which receives a certification shall have 3 years
from the date of issuance of the certification in
order to place the project in service and if such
project is not placed in service by that time period, then the certification shall no longer be
valid.

"(3) SELECTION CRITERIA.—In determining
which qualifying advanced energy projects to certify
under this section, the Secretary—

"(A) shall take into consideration only
those projects where there is a reasonable expectation of commercial viability, and

"(B) shall take into consideration which
projects—

"(i) will provide the greatest domestic
job creation (both direct and indirect) during the credit period,

"(ii) will provide the greatest net impact in avoiding or reducing air pollutants
or anthropogenic emissions of greenhouse
gases,

"(iii) have the greatest potential for technological innovation and commercial deployment,

"(iv) have the lowest levelized cost of generated or stored energy, or of measured reduction in energy consumption or greenhouse gas emission (based on costs of the full supply chain), and

"(v) have the shortest project time from certification to completion.

"(4) REVIEW AND REDISTRIBUTION.—

"(A) REVIEW.—Not later than 4 years after the date of enactment of this section, the Secretary shall review the credits allocated under this section as of such date.

"(B) REDISTRIBUTION.—The Secretary may reallocate credits awarded under this section if the Secretary determines that—

"(i) there is an insufficient quantity of qualifying applications for certification pending at the time of the review, or

"(ii) any certification made pursuant to paragraph (2) has been revoked pursuant to paragraph (2)(B) because the project subject to the certification has been

1   delayed as a result of third party opposi-

2   tion or litigation to the proposed project.

3   "(C) REALLOCATION.—If the Secretary de-

4   termines that credits under this section are

5   available for reallocation pursuant to the re-

6   quirements set forth in paragraph (2), the Sec-

7   retary is authorized to conduct an additional

8   program for applications for certification.

9   "(5) DISCLOSURE OF ALLOCATIONS.—The Sec-

10   retary shall, upon making a certification under this

11   subsection, publicly disclose the identity of the appli-

12   cant and the amount of the credit with respect to

13   such applicant.

14   "(e) DENIAL OF DOUBLE BENEFIT.—A credit shall

15   not be allowed under this section for any qualified invest-

16   ment for which a credit is allowed under section 48, 48A,

17   or 48B.".

18   (c) CONFORMING AMENDMENTS.—

19   (1) Section 49(a)(1)(C) is amended by striking

20   "and" at the end of clause (iii), by striking the pe-

21   riod at the end of clause (iv) and inserting ", and",

22   and by adding after clause (iv) the following new

23   clause:

1   "(v) the basis of any property which

2   is part of a qualifying advanced energy

3   project under section 48C.".

4   (2) The table of sections for subpart E of part

5 IV of subchapter A of chapter 1 is amended by in-

6 serting after the item relating to section 48B the fol-

7 lowing new item:

"48C. Qualifying advanced energy project credit.".

8   (d) EFFECTIVE DATE.—The amendments made by

9 this section shall apply to periods after the date of the

10 enactment of this Act, under rules similar to the rules of

11 section 48(m) of the Internal Revenue Code of 1986 (as

12 in effect on the day before the date of the enactment of

13 the Revenue Reconciliation Act of 1990).

Subtitle E—Economic Recovery Tools

16 **SEC. 1401. RECOVERY ZONE BONDS.**

17   (a) IN GENERAL.—Subchapter Y of chapter 1 is

18 amended by adding at the end the following new part:

19   **"PART III—RECOVERY ZONE BONDS**

"Sec. 1400U–1. Allocation of recovery zone bonds.
"Sec. 1400U–2. Recovery zone economic development bonds.
"Sec. 1400U–3. Recovery zone facility bonds.

20 **"SEC. 1400U–1. ALLOCATION OF RECOVERY ZONE BONDS.**

21   "(a) ALLOCATIONS.—

22   "(1) IN GENERAL.—

"(A) GENERAL ALLOCATION.—The Secretary shall allocate the national recovery zone economic development bond limitation and the national recovery zone facility bond limitation among the States in the proportion that each such State's 2008 State employment decline bears to the aggregate of the 2008 State employment declines for all of the States.

"(B) MINIMUM ALLOCATION.—The Secretary shall adjust the allocations under subparagraph (A) for any calendar year for each State to the extent necessary to ensure that no State receives less than 0.9 percent of the national recovery zone economic development bond limitation and 0.9 percent of the national recovery zone facility bond limitation.

"(2) 2008 STATE EMPLOYMENT DECLINE.—For purposes of this subsection, the term '2008 State employment decline' means, with respect to any State, the excess (if any) of—

"(A) the number of individuals employed in such State determined for December 2007, over

"(B) the number of individuals employed in such State determined for December 2008.

"(3) ALLOCATIONS BY STATES.—

"(A) IN GENERAL.—Each State with respect to which an allocation is made under paragraph (1) shall reallocate such allocation among the counties and large municipalities in such State in the proportion to each such county's or municipality's 2008 employment decline bears to the aggregate of the 2008 employment declines for all the counties and municipalities in such State. A county or municipality may waive any portion of an allocation made under this subparagraph.

"(B) LARGE MUNICIPALITIES.—For purposes of subparagraph (A), the term 'large municipality' means a municipality with a population of more than 100,000.

"(C) DETERMINATION OF LOCAL EMPLOYMENT DECLINES.—For purposes of this paragraph, the employment decline of any municipality or county shall be determined in the same manner as determining the State employment decline under paragraph (2), except that in the case of a municipality any portion of which is in a county, such portion shall be

1   treated as part of such municipality and not

2   part of such county.

3   "(4) NATIONAL LIMITATIONS.—

4   "(A) RECOVERY ZONE ECONOMIC DEVEL-

5   OPMENT BONDS.—There is a national recovery

6   zone economic development bond limitation of

7               $10,000,000,000.

8   "(B) RECOVERY ZONE FACILITY BONDS.—

9   There is a national recovery zone facility bond

10   limitation of $15,000,000,000.

11   "(b) RECOVERY ZONE.—For purposes of this part,

12 the term 'recovery zone' means—

13   "(1) any area designated by the issuer as hav-

14   ing significant poverty, unemployment, rate of home

15   foreclosures, or general distress,

16   "(2) any area designated by the issuer as eco-

17   nomically distressed by reason of the closure or re-

18   alignment of a military installation pursuant to the

19   Defense Base Closure and Realignment Act of 1990,

20   and

21   "(3) any area for which a designation as an em-

22   powerment zone or renewal community is in effect.

1 **"SEC. 1400U–2. RECOVERY ZONE ECONOMIC DEVELOPMENT**

2   **BONDS.**

3   "(a) IN GENERAL.—In the case of a recovery zone

4 economic development bond—

5   "(1) such bond shall be treated as a qualified

6   bond for purposes of section 6431, and

7   "(2) subsection (b) of such section shall be ap-

8   plied by substituting '45 percent' for '35 percent'.

9   "(b) RECOVERY ZONE ECONOMIC DEVELOPMENT

10 BOND.—

11   "(1) IN GENERAL.—For purposes of this sec-

12   tion, the term 'recovery zone economic development

13   bond' means any build America bond (as defined in

14   section 54AA(d)) issued before January 1, 2011, as

15   part of issue if—

16   "(A) 100 percent of the excess of—

17   "(i) the available project proceeds (as

18   defined in section 54A) of such issue, over

19   "(ii) the amounts in a reasonably re-

20   quired reserve (within the meaning of sec-

21   tion 150(a)(3)) with respect to such issue,

22   are to be used for one or more qualified eco-

23   nomic development purposes, and

24   "(B) the issuer designates such bond for

25   purposes of this section.

"(2) LIMITATION ON AMOUNT OF BONDS DESIGNATED.—The maximum aggregate face amount of bonds which may be designated by any issuer under paragraph (1) shall not exceed the amount of the recovery zone economic development bond limitation allocated to such issuer under section 1400U–1.

"(c) QUALIFIED ECONOMIC DEVELOPMENT PURPOSE.—For purposes of this section, the term 'qualified economic development purpose' means expenditures for purposes of promoting development or other economic activity in a recovery zone, including—

"(1) capital expenditures paid or incurred with respect to property located in such zone,

"(2) expenditures for public infrastructure and construction of public facilities, and

"(3) expenditures for job training and educational programs.

"SEC. 1400U–3. RECOVERY ZONE FACILITY BONDS.

"(a) IN GENERAL.—For purposes of part IV of subchapter B (relating to tax exemption requirements for State and local bonds), the term 'exempt facility bond' includes any recovery zone facility bond.

"(b) RECOVERY ZONE FACILITY BOND.—

1   "(1) IN GENERAL.—For purposes of this sec-

2   tion, the term 'recovery zone facility bond' means

3   any bond issued as part of an issue if—

4   "(A) 95 percent or more of the net pro-

5   ceeds (as defined in section 150(a)(3)) of such

6   issue are to be used for recovery zone property,

7   "(B) such bond is issued before January 1,

8   2011, and

9   "(C) the issuer designates such bond for

10   purposes of this section.

11   "(2) LIMITATION ON AMOUNT OF BONDS DES-

12   IGNATED.—The maximum aggregate face amount of

13   bonds which may be designated by any issuer under

14   paragraph (1) shall not exceed the amount of recov-

15   ery zone facility bond limitation allocated to such

16   issuer under section 1400U–1.

17   "(c) RECOVERY ZONE PROPERTY.—For purposes of

18 this section—

19   "(1) IN GENERAL.—The term 'recovery zone

20   property' means any property to which section 168

21   applies (or would apply but for section 179) if—

22   "(A) such property was constructed, recon-

23   structed, renovated, or acquired by purchase (as

24   defined in section 179(d)(2)) by the taxpayer

after the date on which the designation of the
recovery zone took effect,

"(B) the original use of which in the recovery zone commences with the taxpayer, and

"(C) substantially all of the use of which is in the recovery zone and is in the active conduct of a qualified business by the taxpayer in such zone.

"(2) QUALIFIED BUSINESS.—The term 'qualified business' means any trade or business except that—

"(A) the rental to others of real property located in a recovery zone shall be treated as a qualified business only if the property is not residential rental property (as defined in section 168(e)(2)), and

"(B) such term shall not include any trade or business consisting of the operation of any facility described in section 144(c)(6)(B).

"(3) SPECIAL RULES FOR SUBSTANTIAL RENOVATIONS AND SALE-LEASEBACK.—Rules similar to the rules of subsections (a)(2) and (b) of section 1397D shall apply for purposes of this subsection.

"(d) NONAPPLICATION OF CERTAIN RULES.—Sections 146 (relating to volume cap) and 147(d) (relating

1 to acquisition of existing property not permitted) shall not
2 apply to any recovery zone facility bond.".

3   (b) CLERICAL AMENDMENT.—The table of parts for
4 subchapter Y of chapter 1 of such Code is amended by
5 adding at the end the following new item:

"PART III. RECOVERY ZONE BONDS.".

6   (c) EFFECTIVE DATE.—The amendments made by
7 this section shall apply to obligations issued after the date
8 of the enactment of this Act.

9 **SEC. 1402. TRIBAL ECONOMIC DEVELOPMENT BONDS.**

10   (a) IN GENERAL.—Section 7871 is amended by add-
11 ing at the end the following new subsection:

12   "(f) TRIBAL ECONOMIC DEVELOPMENT BONDS.—

13   "(1) ALLOCATION OF LIMITATION.—

14   "(A) IN GENERAL.—The Secretary shall
15   allocate the national tribal economic develop-
16   ment bond limitation among the Indian tribal
17   governments in such manner as the Secretary,
18   in consultation with the Secretary of the Inte-
19   rior, determines appropriate.

20   "(B) NATIONAL LIMITATION.—There is a
21   national tribal economic development bond limi-
22   tation of $2,000,000,000.

23   "(2) BONDS TREATED AS EXEMPT FROM
24   TAX.—In the case of a tribal economic development
25   bond—

"(A) notwithstanding subsection (c), such bond shall be treated for purposes of this title in the same manner as if such bond were issued by a State,

"(B) the Indian tribal government issuing such bond and any instrumentality of such Indian tribal government shall be treated as a State for purposes of section 141, and

"(C) section 146 shall not apply.

"(3) TRIBAL ECONOMIC DEVELOPMENT BOND.—

"(A) IN GENERAL.—For purposes of this section, the term 'tribal economic development bond' means any bond issued by an Indian tribal government—

"(i) the interest on which would be exempt from tax under section 103 if issued by a State or local government, and

"(ii) which is designated by the Indian tribal government as a tribal economic development bond for purposes of this subsection.

"(B) EXCEPTIONS.—Such term shall not include any bond issued as part of an issue if

1   any portion of the proceeds of such issue are

2   used to finance—

3   "(i) any portion of a building in which

4   class II or class III gaming (as defined in

5   section 4 of the Indian Gaming Regulatory

6   Act) is conducted or housed or any other

7   property actually used in the conduct of

8   such gaming, or

9   "(ii) any facility located outside the

10   Indian reservation (as defined in section

11   168(j)(6)).

12   "(C) LIMITATION ON AMOUNT OF BONDS

13   DESIGNATED.—The maximum aggregate face

14   amount of bonds which may be designated by

15   any Indian tribal government under subpara-

16   graph (A) shall not exceed the amount of na-

17   tional tribal economic development bond limita-

18   tion allocated to such government under para-

19   graph (1).".

20   (b) STUDY.—The Secretary of the Treasury, or the

21 Secretary's delegate, shall conduct a study of the effects

22 of the amendment made by subsection (a). Not later than

23 1 year after the date of the enactment of this Act, the

24 Secretary of the Treasury, or the Secretary's delegate,

25 shall report to Congress on the results of the study con-

1 ducted under this paragraph, including the Secretary's

2 recommendations regarding such amendment.

3   (c) EFFECTIVE DATE.—The amendment made by

4 subsection (a) shall apply to obligations issued after the

5 date of the enactment of this Act.

6 **SEC. 1403. INCREASE IN NEW MARKETS TAX CREDIT.**

7   (a) IN GENERAL.—Section 45D(f)(1) is amended—

8   (1) by striking "and" at the end of subpara-

9   graph (C),

10   (2) by striking ", 2007, 2008, and 2009." in

11   subparagraph (D), and inserting "and 2007,", and

12   (3) by adding at the end the following new sub-

13   paragraphs:

14   "(E) $5,000,000,000 for 2008, and

15   "(F) $5,000,000,000 for 2009.".

16   (b) SPECIAL RULE FOR ALLOCATION OF INCREASED

17 2008 LIMITATION.—The amount of the increase in the

18 new markets tax credit limitation for calendar year 2008

19 by reason of the amendments made by subsection (a) shall

20 be allocated in accordance with section 45D(f)(2) of the

21 Internal Revenue Code of 1986 to qualified community de-

22 velopment entities (as defined in section 45D(c) of such

23 Code) which—

24   (1) submitted an allocation application with re-

25   spect to calendar year 2008, and

1   (2)(A) did not receive an allocation for such cal-

2 endar year, or

3   (B) received an allocation for such calendar

4 year in an amount less than the amount requested

5 in the allocation application.

6 **SEC. 1404. COORDINATION OF LOW-INCOME HOUSING**

7   **CREDIT AND LOW-INCOME HOUSING GRANTS.**

8   Subsection (i) of section 42 is amended by adding at

9 the end the following new paragraph:

10   "(9) COORDINATION WITH LOW-INCOME HOUS-

11 ING GRANTS.—

12   "(A) REDUCTION IN STATE HOUSING

13   CREDIT CEILING FOR LOW-INCOME HOUSING

14   GRANTS RECEIVED IN 2009.—For purposes of

15   this section, the amounts described in clauses

16   (i) through (iv) of subsection (h)(3)(C) with re-

17   spect to any State for 2009 shall each be re-

18   duced by so much of such amount as is taken

19   into account in determining the amount of any

20   grant to such State under section 1602 of the

21   American Recovery and Reinvestment Tax Act

22   of 2009.

23   "(B) SPECIAL RULE FOR BASIS.—Basis of

24   a qualified low-income building shall not be re-

1 duced by the amount of any grant described in

2 subparagraph (A).".

Subtitle F—Infrastructure
Financing Tools

PART I—IMPROVED MARKETABILITY FOR TAX-
EXEMPT BONDS

SEC. 1501. DE MINIMIS SAFE HARBOR EXCEPTION FOR TAX-
EXEMPT INTEREST EXPENSE OF FINANCIAL
INSTITUTIONS.

10 (a) IN GENERAL.—Subsection (b) of section 265 is

11 amended by adding at the end the following new para-

12 graph:

13 "(7) DE MINIMIS EXCEPTION FOR BONDS

14 ISSUED DURING 2009 OR 2010.—

15 "(A) IN GENERAL.—In applying paragraph

16 (2)(A), there shall not be taken into account

17 tax-exempt obligations issued during 2009 or

18 2010.

19 "(B) LIMITATION.—The amount of tax-ex-

20 empt obligations not taken into account by rea-

21 son of subparagraph (A) shall not exceed 2 per-

22 cent of the amount determined under para-

23 graph (2)(B).

24 "(C) REFUNDINGS.—For purposes of this

25 paragraph, a refunding bond (whether a current

1   or advance refunding) shall be treated as issued

2   on the date of the issuance of the refunded

3   bond (or in the case of a series of refundings,

4   the original bond).''.

5   (b) TREATMENT AS FINANCIAL INSTITUTION PREF-

6 ERENCE ITEM.—Clause (iv) of section 291(e)(1)(B) is

7 amended by adding at the end the following: ''That por-

8 tion of any obligation not taken into account under para-

9 graph (2)(A) of section 265(b) by reason of paragraph (7)

10 of such section shall be treated for purposes of this section

11 as having been acquired on August 7, 1986.''.

12   (c) EFFECTIVE DATE.—The amendments made by

13 this section shall apply to obligations issued after Decem-

14 ber 31, 2008.

15 **SEC. 1502. MODIFICATION OF SMALL ISSUER EXCEPTION**

16   **TO TAX-EXEMPT INTEREST EXPENSE ALLOCA-**

17   **TION RULES FOR FINANCIAL INSTITUTIONS.**

18   (a) IN GENERAL.—Paragraph (3) of section 265(b)

19 (relating to exception for certain tax-exempt obligations)

20 is amended by adding at the end the following new sub-

21 paragraph:

22   ''(G) SPECIAL RULES FOR OBLIGATIONS

23   ISSUED DURING 2009 AND 2010.—

24   ''(i) INCREASE IN LIMITATION.—In

25   the case of obligations issued during 2009

or 2010, subparagraphs (C)(i), (D)(i), and (D)(iii)(II) shall each be applied by substituting '$30,000,000' for '$10,000,000'.

"(ii) QUALIFIED 501(C)(3) BONDS TREATED AS ISSUED BY EXEMPT ORGANIZATION.—In the case of a qualified 501(c)(3) bond (as defined in section 145) issued during 2009 or 2010, this paragraph shall be applied by treating the 501(c)(3) organization for whose benefit such bond was issued as the issuer.

"(iii) SPECIAL RULE FOR QUALIFIED FINANCINGS.—In the case of a qualified financing issue issued during 2009 or 2010—

"(I) subparagraph (F) shall not apply, and

"(II) any obligation issued as a part of such issue shall be treated as a qualified tax-exempt obligation if the requirements of this paragraph are met with respect to each qualified portion of the issue (determined by treating each qualified portion as a separate issue which is issued by the

1   qualified borrower with respect to

2   which such portion relates).

3   "(iv) QUALIFIED FINANCING ISSUE.—

4   For purposes of this subparagraph, the

5   term 'qualified financing issue' means any

6   composite, pooled, or other conduit financ-

7   ing issue the proceeds of which are used

8   directly or indirectly to make or finance

9   loans to 1 or more ultimate borrowers each

10   of whom is a qualified borrower.

11   "(v) QUALIFIED PORTION.—For pur-

12   poses of this subparagraph, the term

13   'qualified portion' means that portion of

14   the proceeds which are used with respect

15   to each qualified borrower under the issue.

16   "(vi) QUALIFIED BORROWER.—For

17   purposes of this subparagraph, the term

18   'qualified borrower' means a borrower

19   which is a State or political subdivision

20   thereof or an organization described in sec-

21   tion 501(c)(3) and exempt from taxation

22   under section 501(a).".

23   (b) EFFECTIVE DATE.—The amendment made by

24 this section shall apply to obligations issued after Decem-

25 ber 31, 2008.

1 **SEC. 1503. TEMPORARY MODIFICATION OF ALTERNATIVE**

2 **MINIMUM TAX LIMITATIONS ON TAX-EXEMPT**

3 **BONDS.**

4   (a) INTEREST ON PRIVATE ACTIVITY BONDS ISSUED

5 DURING 2009 AND 2010 NOT TREATED AS TAX PREF-

6 ERENCE ITEM.—Subparagraph (C) of section 57(a)(5) is

7 amended by adding at the end a new clause:

8   "(vi) EXCEPTION FOR BONDS ISSUED

9   IN 2009 AND 2010.—

10   "(I) IN GENERAL.—For purposes

11   of clause (i), the term 'private activity

12   bond' shall not include any bond

13   issued after December 31, 2008, and

14   before January 1, 2011.

15   "(II) TREATMENT OF REFUND-

16   ING BONDS.—For purposes of sub-

17   clause (I), a refunding bond (whether

18   a current or advance refunding) shall

19   be treated as issued on the date of the

20   issuance of the refunded bond (or in

21   the case of a series of refundings, the

22   original bond).

23   "(III) EXCEPTION FOR CERTAIN

24   REFUNDING BONDS.—Subclause (II)

25   shall not apply to any refunding bond

26   which is issued to refund any bond

1 which was issued after December 31,

2 2003, and before January 1, 2009.''.

3 (b) NO ADJUSTMENT TO ADJUSTED CURRENT

4 EARNINGS FOR INTEREST ON TAX-EXEMPT BONDS

5 ISSUED DURING 2009 AND 2010.—Subparagraph (B) of

6 section 56(g)(4) is amended by adding at the end the fol-

7 lowing new clause:

8 ''(iv) TAX EXEMPT INTEREST ON

9 BONDS ISSUED IN 2009 AND 2010.—

10 ''(I) IN GENERAL.—Clause (i)

11 shall not apply in the case of any in-

12 terest on a bond issued after Decem-

13 ber 31, 2008, and before January 1,

14 2011.

15 ''(II) TREATMENT OF REFUND-

16 ING BONDS.—For purposes of sub-

17 clause (I), a refunding bond (whether

18 a current or advance refunding) shall

19 be treated as issued on the date of the

20 issuance of the refunded bond (or in

21 the case of a series of refundings, the

22 original bond).

23 ''(III) EXCEPTION FOR CERTAIN

24 REFUNDING BONDS.—Subclause (II)

25 shall not apply to any refunding bond

1   which is issued to refund any bond

2   which was issued after December 31,

3   2003, and before January 1, 2009.''.

4   (c) EFFECTIVE DATE.—The amendments made by

5 this section shall apply to obligations issued after Decem-

6 ber 31, 2008.

7 **SEC. 1504. MODIFICATION TO HIGH SPEED INTERCITY RAIL**

8   **FACILITY BONDS.**

9   (a) IN GENERAL.—Paragraph (1) of section 142(i)

10 is amended by striking "operate at speeds in excess of"

11 and inserting "be capable of attaining a maximum speed

12 in excess of".

13   (b) EFFECTIVE DATE.—The amendment made by

14 this section shall apply to obligations issued after the date

15 of the enactment of this Act.

16 **PART II—DELAY IN APPLICATION OF WITH-**

17   **HOLDING TAX ON GOVERNMENT CONTRAC-**

18   **TORS**

19 **SEC. 1511. DELAY IN APPLICATION OF WITHHOLDING TAX**

20   **ON GOVERNMENT CONTRACTORS.**

21   Subsection (b) of section 511 of the Tax Increase

22 Prevention and Reconciliation Act of 2005 is amended by

23 striking "December 31, 2010" and inserting "December

24 31, 2011".

1 **PART III—TAX CREDIT BONDS FOR SCHOOLS**

2 SEC. 1521. QUALIFIED SCHOOL CONSTRUCTION BONDS.

3   (a) IN GENERAL.—Subpart I of part IV of sub-

4 chapter A of chapter 1 is amended by adding at the end

5 the following new section:

6 "SEC. 54F. QUALIFIED SCHOOL CONSTRUCTION BONDS.

7   "(a) QUALIFIED SCHOOL CONSTRUCTION BOND.—

8 For purposes of this subchapter, the term 'qualified school

9 construction bond' means any bond issued as part of an

10 issue if—

11   "(1) 100 percent of the available project pro-

12   ceeds of such issue are to be used for the construc-

13   tion, rehabilitation, or repair of a public school facil-

14   ity or for the acquisition of land on which such a fa-

15   cility is to be constructed with part of the proceeds

16   of such issue,

17   "(2) the bond is issued by a State or local gov-

18   ernment within the jurisdiction of which such school

19   is located, and

20   "(3) the issuer designates such bond for pur-

21   poses of this section.

22   "(b) LIMITATION ON AMOUNT OF BONDS DES-

23 IGNATED.—The maximum aggregate face amount of

24 bonds issued during any calendar year which may be des-

25 ignated under subsection (a) by any issuer shall not exceed

1 the limitation amount allocated under subsection (d) for

2 such calendar year to such issuer.

3   "(c) NATIONAL LIMITATION ON AMOUNT OF BONDS

4 DESIGNATED.—There is a national qualified school con-

5 struction bond limitation for each calendar year. Such lim-

6 itation is—

7   "(1) $11,000,000,000 for 2009,

8   "(2) $11,000,000,000 for 2010, and

9   "(3) except as provided in subsection (e), zero

10   after 2010.

11   "(d) ALLOCATION OF LIMITATION.—

12   "(1) ALLOCATION AMONG STATES.—Except as

13   provided in paragraph (2)(C), the limitation applica-

14   ble under subsection (c) for any calendar year shall

15   be allocated by the Secretary among the States in

16   proportion to the respective amounts each such

17   State is eligible to receive under section 1124 of the

18   Elementary and Secondary Education Act of 1965

19   (20 U.S.C. 6333) for the most recent fiscal year

20   ending before such calendar year. The limitation

21   amount allocated to a State under the preceding

22   sentence shall be allocated by the State to issuers

23   within such State.

24   "(2) 40 PERCENT OF LIMITATION ALLOCATED

25   AMONG LARGEST SCHOOL DISTRICTS.—

1   "(A) IN GENERAL.—40 percent of the limi-

2   tation applicable under subsection (c) for any

3   calendar year shall be allocated under subpara-

4   graph (B) by the Secretary among local edu-

5   cational agencies which are large local edu-

6   cational agencies for such year.

7   "(B)   ALLOCATION   FORMULA.—The

8   amount to be allocated under subparagraph (A)

9   for any calendar year shall be allocated among

10   large local educational agencies in proportion to

11   the respective amounts each such agency re-

12   ceived under section 1124 of the Elementary

13   and Secondary Education Act of 1965 (20

14   U.S.C. 6333) for the most recent fiscal year

15   ending before such calendar year.

16   "(C)   REDUCTION   IN   STATE   ALLOCA-

17   TION.—The allocation to any State under para-

18   graph (1) shall be reduced by the aggregate

19   amount of the allocations under this paragraph

20   to large local educational agencies within such

21   State.

22   "(D) ALLOCATION OF UNUSED LIMITATION

23   TO STATE.—The amount allocated under this

24   paragraph to a large local educational agency

25   for any calendar year may be reallocated by

1 such agency to the State in which such agency

2 is located for such calendar year. Any amount

3 reallocated to a State under the preceding sen-

4 tence may be allocated as provided in para-

5 graph (1).

6 "(E) LARGE LOCAL EDUCATIONAL AGEN-

7 CY.—For purposes of this paragraph, the term

8 'large local educational agency' means, with re-

9 spect to a calendar year, any local educational

10 agency if such agency is—

11 "(i) among the 100 local educational

12 agencies with the largest numbers of chil-

13 dren aged 5 through 17 from families liv-

14 ing below the poverty level, as determined

15 by the Secretary using the most recent

16 data available from the Department of

17 Commerce that are satisfactory to the Sec-

18 retary, or

19 "(ii) 1 of not more than 25 local edu-

20 cational agencies (other than those de-

21 scribed in clause (i)) that the Secretary of

22 Education determines (based on the most

23 recent data available satisfactory to the

24 Secretary) are in particular need of assist-

25 ance, based on a low level of resources for

1   school construction, a high level of enroll-

2   ment growth, or such other factors as the

3   Secretary deems appropriate.

4   "(3) ALLOCATIONS TO CERTAIN POSSES-

5 SIONS.—The amount to be allocated under para-

6 graph (1) to any possession of the United States

7 other than Puerto Rico shall be the amount which

8 would have been allocated if all allocations under

9 paragraph (1) were made on the basis of respective

10 populations of individuals below the poverty line (as

11 defined by the Office of Management and Budget).

12 In making other allocations, the amount to be allo-

13 cated under paragraph (1) shall be reduced by the

14 aggregate amount allocated under this paragraph to

15 possessions of the United States.

16   "(4) ALLOCATIONS FOR INDIAN SCHOOLS.—In

17 addition to the amounts otherwise allocated under

18 this subsection, $200,000,000 for calendar year

19 2009, and $200,000,000 for calendar year 2010,

20 shall be allocated by the Secretary of the Interior for

21 purposes of the construction, rehabilitation, and re-

22 pair of schools funded by the Bureau of Indian Af-

23 fairs. In the case of amounts allocated under the

24 preceding sentence, Indian tribal governments (as

1   defined in section 7701(a)(40)) shall be treated as

2   qualified issuers for purposes of this subchapter.

3   "(e) CARRYOVER OF UNUSED LIMITATION.—If for

4 any calendar year—

5   "(1) the amount allocated under subsection (d)

6   to any State, exceeds

7   "(2) the amount of bonds issued during such

8   year which are designated under subsection (a) pur-

9   suant to such allocation,

10 the limitation amount under such subsection for such

11 State for the following calendar year shall be increased

12 by the amount of such excess. A similar rule shall apply

13 to the amounts allocated under subsection (d)(4).".

14   (b) CONFORMING AMENDMENTS.—

15   (1) Paragraph (1) of section 54A(d) is amended

16   by striking "or" at the end of subparagraph (C), by

17   inserting "or" at the end of subparagraph (D), and

18   by inserting after subparagraph (D) the following

19   new subparagraph:

20   "(E) a qualified school construction

21   bond,".

22   (2) Subparagraph (C) of section 54A(d)(2) is

23   amended by striking "and" at the end of clause (iii),

24   by striking the period at the end of clause (iv) and

1 inserting ", and", and by adding at the end the fol-

2 lowing new clause:

3   "(v) in the case of a qualified school

4   construction bond, a purpose specified in

5   section 54F(a)(1).".

6   (3) The table of sections for subpart I of part

7 IV of subchapter A of chapter 1 is amended by add-

8 ing at the end the following new item:

"Sec. 54F. Qualified school construction bonds.".

9   (c) EFFECTIVE DATE.—The amendments made by

10 this section shall apply to obligations issued after the date

11 of the enactment of this Act.

12 SEC. 1522. EXTENSION AND EXPANSION OF QUALIFIED

13   ZONE ACADEMY BONDS.

14   (a) IN GENERAL.—Section 54E(c)(1) is amended by

15 striking "and 2009" and inserting "and $1,400,000,000

16 for 2009 and 2010".

17   (b) EFFECTIVE DATE.—The amendment made by

18 this section shall apply to obligations issued after Decem-

19 ber 31, 2008.

20   **PART IV—BUILD AMERICA BONDS**

21 SEC. 1531. BUILD AMERICA BONDS.

22   (a) IN GENERAL.—Part IV of subchapter A of chap-

23 ter 1 is amended by adding at the end the following new

24 subpart:

1 **"Subpart J—Build America Bonds**

"Sec. 54AA. Build America bonds.

2 **"SEC. 54AA. BUILD AMERICA BONDS.**

3   "(a) IN GENERAL.—If a taxpayer holds a build

4 America bond on one or more interest payment dates of

5 the bond during any taxable year, there shall be allowed

6 as a credit against the tax imposed by this chapter for

7 the taxable year an amount equal to the sum of the credits

8 determined under subsection (b) with respect to such

9 dates.

10   "(b) AMOUNT OF CREDIT.—The amount of the credit

11 determined under this subsection with respect to any in-

12 terest payment date for a build America bond is 35 per-

13 cent of the amount of interest payable by the issuer with

14 respect to such date .

15   "(c) LIMITATION BASED ON AMOUNT OF TAX.—

16   "(1) IN GENERAL.—The credit allowed under

17   subsection (a) for any taxable year shall not exceed

18   the excess of—

19   "(A) the sum of the regular tax liability

20   (as defined in section 26(b)) plus the tax im-

21   posed by section 55, over

22   "(B) the sum of the credits allowable

23   under this part (other than subpart C and this

24   subpart).

1   "(2) CARRYOVER OF UNUSED CREDIT.—If the

2 credit allowable under subsection (a) exceeds the

3 limitation imposed by paragraph (1) for such taxable

4 year, such excess shall be carried to the succeeding

5 taxable year and added to the credit allowable under

6 subsection (a) for such taxable year (determined be-

7 fore the application of paragraph (1) for such suc-

8 ceeding taxable year).

9   "(d) BUILD AMERICA BOND.—

10   "(1) IN GENERAL.—For purposes of this sec-

11 tion, the term 'build America bond' means any obli-

12 gation (other than a private activity bond) if—

13   "(A) the interest on such obligation would

14 (but for this section) be excludable from gross

15 income under section 103,

16   "(B) such obligation is issued before Janu-

17 ary 1, 2011, and

18   "(C) the issuer makes an irrevocable elec-

19 tion to have this section apply.

20   "(2) APPLICABLE RULES.—For purposes of ap-

21 plying paragraph (1)—

22   "(A) for purposes of section 149(b), a

23 build America bond shall not be treated as fed-

24 erally guaranteed by reason of the credit al-

25 lowed under subsection (a) or section 6431,

1   "(B) for purposes of section 148, the yield

2   on a build America bond shall be determined

3   without regard to the credit allowed under sub-

4   section (a), and

5   "(C) a bond shall not be treated as a build

6   America bond if the issue price has more than

7   a de minimis amount (determined under rules

8   similar to the rules of section 1273(a)(3)) of

9   premium over the stated principal amount of

10   the bond.

11   "(e) INTEREST PAYMENT DATE.—For purposes of

12 this section, the term 'interest payment date' means any

13 date on which the holder of record of the build America

14 bond is entitled to a payment of interest under such bond.

15   "(f) SPECIAL RULES.—

16   "(1) INTEREST ON BUILD AMERICA BONDS IN-

17   CLUDIBLE IN GROSS INCOME FOR FEDERAL INCOME

18   TAX PURPOSES.—For purposes of this title, interest

19   on any build America bond shall be includible in

20   gross income.

21   "(2) APPLICATION OF CERTAIN RULES.—Rules

22   similar to the rules of subsections (f), (g), (h), and

23   (i) of section 54A shall apply for purposes of the

24   credit allowed under subsection (a).

1   "(g) SPECIAL RULE FOR QUALIFIED BONDS ISSUED

2 BEFORE 2011.—In the case of a qualified bond issued be-

3 fore January 1, 2011—

4   "(1) ISSUER ALLOWED REFUNDABLE CRED-

5   IT.—In lieu of any credit allowed under this section

6   with respect to such bond, the issuer of such bond

7   shall be allowed a credit as provided in section 6431.

8   "(2) QUALIFIED BOND.—For purposes of this

9   subsection, the term 'qualified bond' means any

10   build America bond issued as part of an issue if—

11   "(A) 100 percent of the excess of—

12   "(i) the available project proceeds (as

13   defined in section 54A) of such issue, over

14   "(ii) the amounts in a reasonably re-

15   quired reserve (within the meaning of sec-

16   tion 150(a)(3)) with respect to such issue,

17   are to be used for capital expenditures, and

18   "(B) the issuer makes an irrevocable elec-

19   tion to have this subsection apply.

20   "(h) REGULATIONS.—The Secretary may prescribe

21 such regulations and other guidance as may be necessary

22 or appropriate to carry out this section and section

23 6431.".

1   (b) CREDIT FOR QUALIFIED BONDS ISSUED BEFORE

2 2011.—Subchapter B of chapter 65 is amended by adding

3 at the end the following new section:

4 **"SEC. 6431. CREDIT FOR QUALIFIED BONDS ALLOWED TO**

5   **ISSUER.**

6   "(a) IN GENERAL.—In the case of a qualified bond

7 issued before January 1, 2011, the issuer of such bond

8 shall be allowed a credit with respect to each interest pay-

9 ment under such bond which shall be payable by the Sec-

10 retary as provided in subsection (b).

11   "(b) PAYMENT OF CREDIT.—The Secretary shall pay

12 (contemporaneously with each interest payment date

13 under such bond) to the issuer of such bond (or to any

14 person who makes such interest payments on behalf of the

15 issuer) 35 percent of the interest payable under such bond

16 on such date.

17   "(c) APPLICATION OF ARBITRAGE RULES.—For pur-

18 poses of section 148, the yield on a qualified bond shall

19 be reduced by the credit allowed under this section.

20   "(d) INTEREST PAYMENT DATE.—For purposes of

21 this subsection, the term 'interest payment date' means

22 each date on which interest is payable by the issuer under

23 the terms of the bond.

142

1   "(e) QUALIFIED BOND.—For purposes of this sub-
2 section, the term 'qualified bond' has the meaning given
3 such term in section 54AA(g).".

4   (c) CONFORMING AMENDMENTS.—

5   (1) Section 1324(b)(2) of title 31, United
6   States Code, is amended by striking "or 6428" and
7   inserting "6428, or 6431,".

8   (2) Section 54A(c)(1)(B) is amended by strik-
9   ing "subpart C" and inserting "subparts C and J".

10   (3) Sections 54(c)(2), 1397E(c)(2), and
11   1400N(l)(3)(B) are each amended by striking "and
12   I" and inserting ", I, and J".

13   (4) Section 6211(b)(4)(A) is amended by strik-
14   ing "and 6428" and inserting "6428, and 6431".

15   (5) Section 6401(b)(1) is amended by striking
16   "and I" and inserting "I, and J".

17   (6) The table of subparts for part IV of sub-
18   chapter A of chapter 1 is amended by adding at the
19   end the following new item:

"SUBPART J. BUILD AMERICA BONDS.".

20   (7) The table of section for subchapter B of
21   chapter 65 is amended by adding at the end the fol-
22   lowing new item:

"Sec. 6431. Credit for qualified bonds allowed to issuer.".

23   (d) TRANSITIONAL COORDINATION WITH STATE
24 LAW.—Except as otherwise provided by a State after the

1 date of the enactment of this Act, the interest on any build

2 America bond (as defined in section 54AA of the Internal

3 Revenue Code of 1986, as added by this section) and the

4 amount of any credit determined under such section with

5 respect to such bond shall be treated for purposes of the

6 income tax laws of such State as being exempt from Fed-

7 eral income tax.

8   (e) EFFECTIVE DATE.—The amendments made by

9 this section shall apply to obligations issued after the date

10 of the enactment of this Act.

11 **PART V—REGULATED INVESTMENT COMPANIES**

12   **ALLOWED TO PASS-THRU TAX CREDIT BOND**

13   **CREDITS**

14 **SEC. 1541. REGULATED INVESTMENT COMPANIES AL-**

15   **LOWED TO PASS-THRU TAX CREDIT BOND**

16   **CREDITS.**

17   (a) IN GENERAL.—Part I of subchapter M of chapter

18 1 is amended by inserting after section 853 the following

19 new section:

20 **"SEC. 853A. CREDITS FROM TAX CREDIT BONDS ALLOWED**

21   **TO SHAREHOLDERS.**

22   "(a) GENERAL RULE.—A regulated investment

23 company—

1   "(1) which holds (directly or indirectly) one or

2   more tax credit bonds on one or more applicable

3   dates during the taxable year, and

4   "(2) which meets the requirements of section

5   852(a) for the taxable year,

6 may elect the application of this section with respect to

7 credits allowable to the investment company during such

8 taxable year with respect to such bonds.

9   "(b) EFFECT OF ELECTION.—If the election provided

10 in subsection (a) is in effect for any taxable year—

11   "(1) the regulated investment company shall

12   not be allowed any credits to which subsection (a)

13   applies for such taxable year,

14   "(2) the regulated investment company shall—

15   "(A) include in gross income (as interest)

16   for such taxable year an amount equal to the

17   amount that such investment company would

18   have included in gross income with respect to

19   such credits if this section did not apply, and

20   "(B) increase the amount of the dividends

21   paid deduction for such taxable year by the

22   amount of such income, and

23   "(3) each shareholder of such investment com-

24   pany shall—

1   "(A) include in gross income an amount

2   equal to such shareholder's proportionate share

3   of the interest income attributable to such cred-

4   its, and

5   "(B) be allowed the shareholder's propor-

6   tionate share of such credits against the tax im-

7   posed by this chapter.

8   "(c) NOTICE TO SHAREHOLDERS.—For purposes of

9   subsection (b)(3), the shareholder's proportionate share

10   of—

11   "(1) credits described in subsection (a), and

12   "(2) gross income in respect of such credits,

13   shall not exceed the amounts so designated by the regu-

14   lated investment company in a written notice mailed to

15   its shareholders not later than 60 days after the close of

16   its taxable year.

17   "(d) MANNER OF MAKING ELECTION AND NOTI-

18   FYING SHAREHOLDERS.—The election provided in sub-

19   section (a) and the notice to shareholders required by sub-

20   section (c) shall be made in such manner as the Secretary

21   may prescribe.

22   "(e) DEFINITIONS AND SPECIAL RULES.—

23   "(1) DEFINITIONS.—For purposes of this

24   subsection—

1   "(A) TAX CREDIT BOND.—The term 'tax

2   credit bond' means—

3   "(i) a qualified tax credit bond (as de-

4   fined in section 54A(d)),

5   "(ii) a build America bond (as defined

6   in section 54AA(d)), and

7   "(iii) any bond for which a credit is

8   allowable under subpart H of part IV of

9   subchapter A of this chapter.

10   "(B) APPLICABLE DATE.—The term 'ap-

11   plicable date' means—

12   "(i) in the case of a qualified tax

13   credit bond or a bond described in sub-

14   paragraph (A)(iii), any credit allowance

15   date (as defined in section 54A(e)(1)), and

16   "(ii) in the case of a build America

17   bond (as defined in section 54AA(d)), any

18   interest payment date (as defined in sec-

19   tion 54AA(e)).

20   "(2) STRIPPED TAX CREDIT BONDS.—If the

21   ownership of a tax credit bond is separated from the

22   credit with respect to such bond, subsection (a) shall

23   be applied by reference to the instruments evidenc-

24   ing the entitlement to the credit rather than the tax

25   credit bond.

1   "(f) REGULATIONS, ETC.—The Secretary shall pre-

2 scribe such regulations or other guidance as may be nec-

3 essary or appropriate to carry out the purposes of this

4 section, including methods for determining a shareholder's

5 proportionate share of credits.".

6   (b) CONFORMING AMENDMENTS.—

7   (1) Section 54(l) is amended by striking para-

8   graph (4) and by redesignating paragraphs (5) and

9   (6) as paragraphs (4) and (5), respectively.

10   (2) Section 54A(h) is amended to read as fol-

11   lows:

12   "(h) BONDS HELD BY REAL ESTATE INVESTMENT

13 TRUSTS.—If any qualified tax credit bond is held by a

14 real estate investment trust, the credit determined under

15 subsection (a) shall be allowed to beneficiaries of such

16 trust (and any gross income included under subsection (f)

17 with respect to such credit shall be distributed to such

18 beneficiaries) under procedures prescribed by the Sec-

19 retary.".

20   (3) The table of sections for part I of sub-

21   chapter M of chapter 1 is amended by inserting

22   after the item relating to section 853 the following

23   new item:

"Sec. 853A. Credits from tax credit bonds allowed to shareholders.".

1   (c) EFFECTIVE DATE.—The amendments made by
2 this section shall apply to taxable years ending after the
3 date of the enactment of this Act.

Subtitle G—Other Provisions

5 **SEC. 1601. APPLICATION OF CERTAIN LABOR STANDARDS**
6   **TO PROJECTS FINANCED WITH CERTAIN TAX-**
7   **FAVORED BONDS.**

8   Subchapter IV of chapter 31 of the title 40, United
9 States Code, shall apply to projects financed with the pro-
10 ceeds of—

11   (1) any new clean renewable energy bond (as
12   defined in section 54C of the Internal Revenue Code
13   of 1986) issued after the date of the enactment of
14   this Act,

15   (2) any qualified energy conservation bond (as
16   defined in section 54D of the Internal Revenue Code
17   of 1986) issued after the date of the enactment of
18   this Act,

19   (3) any qualified zone academy bond (as de-
20   fined in section 54E of the Internal Revenue Code
21   of 1986) issued after the date of the enactment of
22   this Act,

23   (4) any qualified school construction bond (as
24   defined in section 54F of the Internal Revenue Code
25   of 1986), and

1   (5) any recovery zone economic development

2   bond (as defined in section 1400U–2 of the Internal

3   Revenue Code of 1986).

4 SEC. 1602. GRANTS TO STATES FOR LOW-INCOME HOUSING

5   PROJECTS IN LIEU OF LOW-INCOME HOUS-

6   ING CREDIT ALLOCATIONS FOR 2009.

7   (a) IN GENERAL.—The Secretary of the Treasury

8 shall make a grant to the housing credit agency of each

9 State in an amount equal to such State's low-income hous-

10 ing grant election amount.

11   (b) LOW-INCOME HOUSING GRANT ELECTION

12 AMOUNT.—For purposes of this section, the term "low-

13 income housing grant election amount" means, with re-

14 spect to any State, such amount as the State may elect

15 which does not exceed 85 percent of the product of—

16   (1) the sum of—

17   (A) 100 percent of the State housing credit

18   ceiling for 2009 which is attributable to

19   amounts described in clauses (i) and (iii) of sec-

20   tion 42(h)(3)(C) of the Internal Revenue Code

21   of 1986, and

22   (B) 40 percent of the State housing credit

23   ceiling for 2009 which is attributable to

24   amounts described in clauses (ii) and (iv) of

25   such section, multiplied by

1   (2) 10.

2   (c) SUBAWARDS FOR LOW-INCOME BUILDINGS.—

3   (1) IN GENERAL.—A State housing credit agen-

4   cy receiving a grant under this section shall use such

5   grant to make subawards to finance the construction

6   or acquisition and rehabilitation of qualified low-in-

7   come buildings. A subaward under this section may

8   be made to finance a qualified low-income building

9   with or without an allocation under section 42 of the

10   Internal Revenue Code of 1986, except that a State

11   housing credit agency may make subawards to fi-

12   nance qualified low-income buildings without an allo-

13   cation only if it makes a determination that such use

14   will increase the total funds available to the State to

15   build and rehabilitate affordable housing. In com-

16   plying with such determination requirement, a State

17   housing credit agency shall establish a process in

18   which applicants that are allocated credits are re-

19   quired to demonstrate good faith efforts to obtain

20   investment commitments for such credits before the

21   agency makes such subawards.

22   (2) SUBAWARDS SUBJECT TO SAME REQUIRE-

23   MENTS AS LOW-INCOME HOUSING CREDIT ALLOCA-

24   TIONS.—Any such subaward with respect to any

25   qualified low-income building shall be made in the

1   same manner and shall be subject to the same limi-

2   tations (including rent, income, and use restrictions

3   on such building) as an allocation of housing credit

4   dollar amount allocated by such State housing credit

5   agency under section 42 of the Internal Revenue

6   Code of 1986, except that such subawards shall not

7   be limited by, or otherwise affect (except as provided

8   in subsection (h)(3)(J) of such section), the State

9   housing credit ceiling applicable to such agency.

10   (3) COMPLIANCE AND ASSET MANAGEMENT.—

11   The State housing credit agency shall perform asset

12   management functions to ensure compliance with

13   section 42 of the Internal Revenue Code of 1986

14   and the long-term viability of buildings funded by

15   any subaward under this section. The State housing

16   credit agency may collect reasonable fees from a

17   subaward recipient to cover expenses associated with

18   the performance of its duties under this paragraph.

19   The State housing credit agency may retain an

20   agent or other private contractor to satisfy the re-

21   quirements of this paragraph.

22   (4) RECAPTURE.—The State housing credit

23   agency shall impose conditions or restrictions, in-

24   cluding a requirement providing for recapture, on

25   any subaward under this section so as to assure that

1   the building with respect to which such subaward is

2   made remains a qualified low-income building during

3   the compliance period. Any such recapture shall be

4   payable to the Secretary of the Treasury for deposit

5   in the general fund of the Treasury and may be en-

6   forced by means of liens or such other methods as

7   the Secretary of the Treasury determines appro-

8   priate.

9   (d) RETURN OF UNUSED GRANT FUNDS.—Any grant

10 funds not used to make subawards under this section be-

11 fore January 1, 2011, shall be returned to the Secretary

12 of the Treasury on such date. Any subawards returned

13 to the State housing credit agency on or after such date

14 shall be promptly returned to the Secretary of the Treas-

15 ury. Any amounts returned to the Secretary of the Treas-

16 ury under this subsection shall be deposited in the general

17 fund of the Treasury.

18   (e) DEFINITIONS.—Any term used in this section

19 which is also used in section 42 of the Internal Revenue

20 Code of 1986 shall have the same meaning for purposes

21 of this section as when used in such section 42. Any ref-

22 erence in this section to the Secretary of the Treasury

23 shall be treated as including the Secretary's delegate.

1   (f) APPROPRIATIONS.—There is hereby appropriated
2 to the Secretary of the Treasury such sums as may be
3 necessary to carry out this section.

4 **SEC. 1603. GRANTS FOR SPECIFIED ENERGY PROPERTY IN**
5 **LIEU OF TAX CREDITS.**

6   (a) IN GENERAL.—Upon application, the Secretary
7 of the Treasury shall, subject to the requirements of this
8 section, provide a grant to each person who places in serv-
9 ice specified energy property to reimburse such person for
10 a portion of the expense of such property as provided in
11 subsection (b). No grant shall be made under this section
12 with respect to any property unless such property—

13   (1) is placed in service during 2009 or 2010, or

14   (2) is placed in service after 2010 and before
15   the credit termination date with respect to such
16   property, but only if the construction of such prop-
17   erty began during 2009 or 2010.

18   (b) GRANT AMOUNT.—

19   (1) IN GENERAL.—The amount of the grant
20   under subsection (a) with respect to any specified
21   energy property shall be the applicable percentage of
22   the basis of such property.

23   (2) APPLICABLE PERCENTAGE.—For purposes
24   of paragraph (1), the term "applicable percentage"
25   means—

(A) 30 percent in the case of any property described in paragraphs (1) through (4) of subsection (d), and

(B) 10 percent in the case of any other property.

(3) DOLLAR LIMITATIONS.—In the case of property described in paragraph (2), (6), or (7) of subsection (d), the amount of any grant under this section with respect to such property shall not exceed the limitation described in section 48(c)(1)(B), 48(c)(2)(B), or 48(c)(3)(B) of the Internal Revenue Code of 1986, respectively, with respect to such property.

(c) TIME FOR PAYMENT OF GRANT.—The Secretary of the Treasury shall make payment of any grant under subsection (a) during the 60-day period beginning on the later of—

(1) the date of the application for such grant, or

(2) the date the specified energy property for which the grant is being made is placed in service.

(d) SPECIFIED ENERGY PROPERTY.—For purposes of this section, the term "specified energy property" means any of the following:

1   (1) QUALIFIED FACILITIES.—Any qualified
2   property (as defined in section 48(a)(5)(D) of the
3   Internal Revenue Code of 1986) which is part of a
4   qualified facility (within the meaning of section 45
5   of such Code) described in paragraph (1), (2), (3),
6   (4), (6), (7), (9), or (11) of section 45(d) of such
7   Code.

8   (2) QUALIFIED FUEL CELL PROPERTY.—Any
9   qualified fuel cell property (as defined in section
10   48(c)(1) of such Code).

11   (3) SOLAR PROPERTY.—Any property described
12   in clause (i) or (ii) of section 48(a)(3)(A) of such
13   Code.

14   (4) QUALIFIED SMALL WIND ENERGY PROP-
15   ERTY.—Any qualified small wind energy property
16   (as defined in section 48(c)(4) of such Code).

17   (5) GEOTHERMAL PROPERTY.—Any property
18   described in clause (iii) of section 48(a)(3)(A) of
19   such Code.

20   (6) QUALIFIED MICROTURBINE PROPERTY.—
21   Any qualified microturbine property (as defined in
22   section 48(c)(2) of such Code).

23   (7) COMBINED HEAT AND POWER SYSTEM
24   PROPERTY.—Any combined heat and power system

1 property (as defined in section 48(c)(3) of such

2 Code).

3   (8) GEOTHERMAL HEAT PUMP PROPERTY.—

4   Any property described in clause (vii) of section

5   48(a)(3)(A) of such Code.

6 Such term shall not include any property unless deprecia-

7 tion (or amortization in lieu of depreciation) is allowable

8 with respect to such property.

9   (e) CREDIT TERMINATION DATE.—For purposes of

10 this section, the term "credit termination date" means—

11   (1) in the case of any specified energy property

12   which is part of a facility described in paragraph (1)

13   of section 45(d) of the Internal Revenue Code of

14   1986, January 1, 2013,

15   (2) in the case of any specified energy property

16   which is part of a facility described in paragraph

17   (2), (3), (4), (6), (7), (9), or (11) of section 45(d)

18   of such Code, January 1, 2014, and

19   (3) in the case of any specified energy property

20   described in section 48 of such Code, January 1,

21   2017.

22 In the case of any property which is described in para-

23 graph (3) and also in another paragraph of this sub-

24 section, paragraph (3) shall apply with respect to such

25 property.

1   (f) APPLICATION OF CERTAIN RULES.—In making

2 grants under this section, the Secretary of the Treasury

3 shall apply rules similar to the rules of section 50 of the

4 Internal Revenue Code of 1986. In applying such rules,

5 if the property is disposed of, or otherwise ceases to be

6 specified energy property, the Secretary of the Treasury

7 shall provide for the recapture of the appropriate percent-

8 age of the grant amount in such manner as the Secretary

9 of the Treasury determines appropriate.

10   (g) EXCEPTION FOR CERTAIN NON-TAXPAYERS.—

11 The Secretary of the Treasury shall not make any grant

12 under this section to—

13   (1) any Federal, State, or local government (or

14   any political subdivision, agency, or instrumentality

15   thereof),

16   (2) any organization described in section 501(c)

17   of the Internal Revenue Code of 1986 and exempt

18   from tax under section 501(a) of such Code,

19   (3) any entity referred to in paragraph (4) of

20   section 54(j) of such Code, or

21   (4) any partnership or other pass-thru entity

22   any partner (or other holder of an equity or profits

23   interest) of which is described in paragraph (1), (2)

24   or (3).

1   (h) DEFINITIONS.—Terms used in this section which
2 are also used in section 45 or 48 of the Internal Revenue
3 Code of 1986 shall have the same meaning for purposes
4 of this section as when used in such section 45 or 48.
5 Any reference in this section to the Secretary of the Treas-
6 ury shall be treated as including the Secretary's delegate.

7   (i) APPROPRIATIONS.—There is hereby appropriated
8 to the Secretary of the Treasury such sums as may be
9 necessary to carry out this section.

10   (j) TERMINATION.—The Secretary of the Treasury
11 shall not make any grant to any person under this section
12 unless the application of such person for such grant is re-
13 ceived before October 1, 2011.

14 **SEC. 1604. INCREASE IN PUBLIC DEBT LIMIT.**

15   Subsection (b) of section 3101 of title 31, United
16 States Code, is amended by striking out the dollar limita-
17 tion contained in such subsection and inserting
18 "$12,104,000,000,000".

Subtitle H—Prohibition on Collection of Certain Payments Made Under the Continued Dumping and Subsidy Offset Act of 2000

SEC. 1701. PROHIBITION ON COLLECTION OF CERTAIN PAYMENTS MADE UNDER THE CONTINUED DUMPING AND SUBSIDY OFFSET ACT OF 2000.

(a) IN GENERAL.—Notwithstanding any other provision of law, neither the Secretary of Homeland Security nor any other person may—

    (1) require repayment of, or attempt in any other way to recoup, any payments described in subsection (b); or

    (2) offset any past, current, or future distributions of antidumping or countervailing duties assessed with respect to imports from countries that are not parties to the North American Free Trade Agreement in an attempt to recoup any payments described in subsection (b).

(b) PAYMENTS DESCRIBED.—Payments described in this subsection are payments of antidumping or countervailing duties made pursuant to the Continued Dumping and Subsidy Offset Act of 2000 (section 754 of the Tariff Act of 1930 (19 U.S.C. 1675c; repealed by subtitle F of

1 title VII of the Deficit Reduction Act of 2005 (Public Law

2 109–171; 120 Stat. 154))) that were—

3   (1) assessed and paid on imports of goods from

4   countries that are parties to the North American

5   Free Trade Agreement; and

6   (2) distributed on or after January 1, 2001,

7   and before January 1, 2006.

8   (c) PAYMENT OF FUNDS COLLECTED OR WITH-

9 HELD.—Not later than the date that is 60 days after the

10 date of the enactment of this Act, the Secretary of Home-

11 land Security shall—

12   (1) refund any repayments, or any other

13   recoupment, of payments described in subsection (b);

14   and

15   (2) fully distribute any antidumping or counter-

16   vailing duties that the U.S. Customs and Border

17   Protection is withholding as an offset as described in

18   subsection (a)(2).

19   (d) LIMITATION.—Nothing in this section shall be

20 construed to prevent the Secretary of Homeland Security,

21 or any other person, from requiring repayment of, or at-

22 tempting to otherwise recoup, any payments described in

23 subsection (b) as a result of—

24   (1) a finding of false statements or other mis-

25   conduct by a recipient of such a payment; or

1   (2) the reliquidation of an entry with respect to

2 which such a payment was made.

Subtitle I—Trade Adjustment Assistance

SEC. 1800. SHORT TITLE.

6   This subtitle may be cited as the "Trade and

7 Globalization Adjustment Assistance Act of 2009".

PART I—TRADE ADJUSTMENT ASSISTANCE FOR WORKERS

Subpart A—Trade Adjustment Assistance for Service Sector Workers

SEC. 1801. EXTENSION OF TRADE ADJUSTMENT ASSIST-ANCE TO SERVICE SECTOR AND PUBLIC AGENCY WORKERS; SHIFTS IN PRODUCTION.

15   (a) DEFINITIONS.—Section 247 of the Trade Act of

16 1974 (19 U.S.C. 2319) is amended—

17   (1) in paragraph (1)—

18   (A) by striking "or appropriate subdivision

19   of a firm"; and

20   (B) by striking "or subdivision";

21   (2) in paragraph (2), by striking "employ-

22 ment—" and all that follows and inserting "employ-

23 ment, has been totally or partially separated from

24 such employment.";

1   (3) by inserting after paragraph (2) the fol-

2 lowing:

3   "(3) Subject to section 222(d)(5), the term

4 'firm' means—

5   "(A) a firm, including an agricultural firm,

6   service sector firm, or public agency; or

7   "(B) an appropriate subdivision thereof.";

8   (4) by inserting after paragraph (6) the fol-

9 lowing:

10   "(7) The term 'public agency' means a depart-

11 ment or agency of a State or local government or of

12 the Federal Government, or a subdivision thereof.";

13   (5) in paragraph (11), by striking ", or in a

14 subdivision of which,"; and

15   (6) by adding at the end the following:

16   "(18) The term 'service sector firm' means a

17 firm engaged in the business of supplying services.".

18 (b) GROUP ELIGIBILITY REQUIREMENTS.—Section

19 222 of the Trade Act of 1974 (19 U.S.C. 2272) is

20 amended—

21   (1) in subsection (a)(2)—

22   (A) by amending subparagraph (A)(ii) to

23   read as follows:

1   "(ii)(I) imports of articles or services like or di-

2 rectly competitive with articles produced or services

3 supplied by such firm have increased;

4   "(II) imports of articles like or directly competi-

5 tive with articles—

6   "(aa) into which one or more component

7   parts produced by such firm are directly incor-

8   porated, or

9   "(bb) which are produced directly using

10   services supplied by such firm,

11 have increased; or

12   "(III) imports of articles directly incorporating

13 one or more component parts produced outside the

14 United States that are like or directly competitive

15 with imports of articles incorporating one or more

16 component parts produced by such firm have in-

17 creased; and"; and

18   (B) by amending subparagraph (B) to read

19   as follows:

20   "(B)(i)(I) there has been a shift by such work-

21 ers' firm to a foreign country in the production of

22 articles or the supply of services like or directly com-

23 petitive with articles which are produced or services

24 which are supplied by such firm; or

1   "(II) such workers' firm has acquired from a

2   foreign country articles or services that are like or

3   directly competitive with articles which are produced

4   or services which are supplied by such firm; and

5   "(ii) the shift described in clause (i)(I) or the

6   acquisition of articles or services described in clause

7   (i)(II) contributed importantly to such workers' sep-

8   aration or threat of separation.";

9   (2) by redesignating subsections (b) and (c) as

10   subsections (c) and (d), respectively; and

11   (3) by inserting after subsection (a) the fol-

12   lowing:

13 "(b) ADVERSELY AFFECTED WORKERS IN PUBLIC

14 AGENCIES.—A group of workers in a public agency shall

15 be certified by the Secretary as eligible to apply for adjust-

16 ment assistance under this chapter pursuant to a petition

17 filed under section 221 if the Secretary determines that—

18   "(1) a significant number or proportion of the

19   workers in the public agency have become totally or

20   partially separated, or are threatened to become to-

21   tally or partially separated;

22   "(2) the public agency has acquired from a for-

23   eign country services like or directly competitive with

24   services which are supplied by such agency; and

1   "(3) the acquisition of services described in

2   paragraph (2) contributed importantly to such work-

3   ers' separation or threat of separation.".

4   (c) BASIS FOR SECRETARY'S DETERMINATIONS.—

5 Section 222 of the Trade Act of 1974 (19 U.S.C. 2272),

6 as amended, is further amended by adding at the end the

7 following:

8   "(e) BASIS FOR SECRETARY'S DETERMINATIONS.—

9   "(1) IN GENERAL.—The Secretary shall, in de-

10   termining whether to certify a group of workers

11   under section 223, obtain from the workers' firm, or

12   a customer of the workers' firm, information the

13   Secretary determines to be necessary to make the

14   certification, through questionnaires and in such

15   other manner as the Secretary determines appro-

16   priate.

17   "(2) ADDITIONAL INFORMATION.—The Sec-

18   retary may seek additional information to determine

19   whether to certify a group of workers under sub-

20   section (a), (b), or (c)—

21   "(A) by contacting—

22   "(i) officials or employees of the work-

23   ers' firm;

24   "(ii) officials of customers of the

25   workers' firm;

166

1   "(iii) officials of certified or recog-

2   nized unions or other duly authorized rep-

3   resentatives of the group of workers; or

4   "(iv) one-stop operators or one-stop

5   partners (as defined in section 101 of the

6   Workforce Investment Act of 1998 (29

7   U.S.C. 2801)); or

8   "(B) by using other available sources of in-

9   formation.

10   "(3) VERIFICATION OF INFORMATION.—

11   "(A) CERTIFICATION.—The Secretary shall

12   require a firm or customer to certify—

13   "(i) all information obtained under

14   paragraph (1) from the firm or customer

15   (as the case may be) through question-

16   naires; and

17   "(ii) all other information obtained

18   under paragraph (1) from the firm or cus-

19   tomer (as the case may be) on which the

20   Secretary relies in making a determination

21   under section 223, unless the Secretary

22   has a reasonable basis for determining that

23   such information is accurate and complete

24   without being certified.

1   "(B) USE OF SUBPOENAS.—The Secretary

2   shall require the workers' firm or a customer of

3   the workers' firm to provide information re-

4   quested by the Secretary under paragraph (1)

5   by subpoena pursuant to section 249 if the firm

6   or customer (as the case may be) fails to pro-

7   vide the information within 20 days after the

8   date of the Secretary's request, unless the firm

9   or customer (as the case may be) demonstrates

10   to the satisfaction of the Secretary that the

11   firm or customer (as the case may be) will pro-

12   vide the information within a reasonable period

13   of time.

14   "(C) PROTECTION OF CONFIDENTIAL IN-

15   FORMATION.—The Secretary may not release

16   information obtained under paragraph (1) that

17   the Secretary considers to be confidential busi-

18   ness information unless the firm or customer

19   (as the case may be) submitting the confidential

20   business information had notice, at the time of

21   submission, that the information would be re-

22   leased by the Secretary, or the firm or customer

23   (as the case may be) subsequently consents to

24   the release of the information. Nothing in this

25   subparagraph shall be construed to prohibit the

1   Secretary from providing such confidential busi-

2   ness information to a court in camera or to an-

3   other party under a protective order issued by

4   a court.".

5   (d) PENALTIES.—Section 244 of the Trade Act of

6 1974 (19 U.S.C. 2316) is amended to read as follows:

7 **"SEC. 244. PENALTIES.**

8   "Any person who—

9   "(1) makes a false statement of a material fact

10   knowing it to be false, or knowingly fails to disclose

11   a material fact, for the purpose of obtaining or in-

12   creasing for that person or for any other person any

13   payment authorized to be furnished under this chap-

14   ter or pursuant to an agreement under section 239,

15   or

16   "(2) makes a false statement of a material fact

17   knowing it to be false, or knowingly fails to disclose

18   a material fact, when providing information to the

19   Secretary during an investigation of a petition under

20   section 221,

21 shall be imprisoned for not more than one year, or fined

22 under title 18, United States Code, or both.".

23   (e) CONFORMING AMENDMENTS.—

24   (1) Section 221(a) of the Trade Act of 1974

25   (19 U.S.C. 2271(a)) is amended—

(A) in paragraph (1)—

(i) in the matter preceding subpara-graph (A)—

(I) by striking "Secretary" and inserting "Secretary of Labor"; and

(II) by striking "or subdivision" and inserting "(as defined in section 247)"; and

(ii) in subparagraph (A), by striking "(including workers in an agricultural firm or subdivision of any agricultural firm)";

(B) in paragraph (2)(A), by striking "rapid response assistance" and inserting "rapid response activities"; and

(C) in paragraph (3), by inserting "and on the website of the Department of Labor" after "Federal Register".

(2) Section 222 of the Trade Act of 1974 (19 U.S.C. 2272), as amended, is further amended—

(A) by striking "(including workers in any agricultural firm or subdivision of an agricul-tural firm)" each place it appears;

(B) in subsection (a)—

1   (i) in paragraph (1), by striking ", or

2   an appropriate subdivision of the firm,";

3   and

4   (ii) in paragraph (2), by striking "or

5   subdivision" each place it appears;

6   (C) in subsection (c) (as redesignated)—

7   (i) in paragraph (2)—

8   (I) by striking "(or subdivision)"

9   each place it appears;

10   (II) by inserting "or service"

11   after "the article"; and

12   (III) by striking "(c) (3)" and in-

13   serting "(d) (3)"; and

14   (ii) in paragraph (3), by striking "(or

15   subdivision)" each place it appears; and

16   (D) in subsection (d) (as redesignated)—

17   (i) by striking "For purposes" and in-

18   serting "DEFINITIONS.—For purposes";

19   (ii) in paragraph (2), by striking ", or

20   appropriate subdivision of a firm," each

21   place it appears;

22   (iii) by amending paragraph (3) to

23   read as follows:

24   "(3) DOWNSTREAM PRODUCER.—

1   "(A) IN GENERAL.—The term 'down-

2   stream producer' means a firm that performs

3   additional, value-added production processes or

4   services directly for another firm for articles or

5   services with respect to which a group of work-

6   ers in such other firm has been certified under

7   subsection (a).

8   "(B) VALUE-ADDED PRODUCTION PROC-

9   ESSES OR SERVICES.—For purposes of subpara-

10   graph (A), value-added production processes or

11   services include final assembly, finishing, test-

12   ing, packaging, or maintenance or transpor-

13   tation services.";

14   (iv) in paragraph (4)—

15   (I) by striking "(or subdivision)";

16   and

17   (II) by inserting ", or services,

18   used in the production of articles or in

19   the supply of services, as the case may

20   be," after "for articles"; and

21   (v) by adding at the end the following:

22   "(5) REFERENCE TO FIRM.—For purposes of

23   subsection (a), the term 'firm' does not include a

24   public agency.".

1   (3) Section 231(a)(2) of the Trade Act of 1974

2   (19 U.S.C. 2291(a)(2)) is amended—

3   (A) in the matter preceding subparagraph

4   (A), by striking "or subdivision of a firm"; and

5   (B) in subparagraph (C), by striking "or

6   subdivision".

7 **SEC. 1802. SEPARATE BASIS FOR CERTIFICATION.**

8   Section 222 of the Trade Act of 1974 (19 U.S.C.

9 2272), as amended, is further amended by adding at the

10 end the following:

11   "(f) FIRMS IDENTIFIED BY THE INTERNATIONAL

12 TRADE COMMISSION.—Notwithstanding any other provi-

13 sion of this chapter, a group of workers covered by a peti-

14 tion filed under section 221 shall be certified under sub-

15 section (a) as eligible to apply for adjustment assistance

16 under this chapter if—

17   "(1) the workers' firm is publicly identified by

18   name by the International Trade Commission as a

19   member of a domestic industry in an investigation

20   resulting in—

21   "(A) an affirmative determination of seri-

22   ous injury or threat thereof under section

23   202(b)(1);

1   "(B) an affirmative determination of mar-
2   ket disruption or threat thereof under section
3   421(b)(1); or

4   "(C) an affirmative final determination of
5   material injury or threat thereof under section
6   705(b)(1)(A) or 735(b)(1)(A) of the Tariff Act
7   of 1930 (19 U.S.C. 1671d(b)(1)(A) and
8   1673d(b)(1)(A));

9   "(2) the petition is filed during the one-year pe-
10   riod beginning on the date on which—

11   "(A) a summary of the report submitted to
12   the President by the International Trade Com-
13   mission under section 202(f)(1) with respect to
14   the affirmative determination described in para-
15   graph (1)(A) is published in the Federal Reg-
16   ister under section 202(f)(3); or

17   "(B) notice of an affirmative determination
18   described in subparagraph (B) or (C) of para-
19   graph (1) is published in the Federal Register;
20   and

21   "(3) the workers have become totally or par-
22   tially separated from the workers' firm within—

23   "(A) the one-year period described in para-
24   graph (2); or

174

1   "(B) notwithstanding section 223(b), the

2   one-year period preceding the one-year period

3   described in paragraph (2).".

SEC. 1803. DETERMINATIONS BY SECRETARY OF LABOR.

5   Section 223 of the Trade Act of 1974 (19 U.S.C.

6 2273) is amended—

7   (1) in subsection (b), by striking "or appro-

8   priate subdivision of the firm before his application"

9   and all that follows and inserting "before the work-

10   er's application under section 231 occurred more

11   than one year before the date of the petition on

12   which such certification was granted.";

13   (2) in subsection (c), by striking "together with

14   his reasons" and inserting "and on the website of

15   the Department of Labor, together with the Sec-

16   retary's reasons";

17   (3) in subsection (d)—

18   (A) by striking "or subdivision of the

19   firm" and all that follows through "he shall"

20   and inserting ", that total or partial separations

21   from such firm are no longer attributable to the

22   conditions specified in section 222, the Sec-

23   retary shall"; and

24   (B) by striking "together with his reasons"

25   and inserting "and on the website of the De-

1   partment of Labor, together with the Sec-

2   retary's reasons''; and

3   (4) by adding at the end the following:

4   "(e) STANDARDS FOR INVESTIGATIONS AND DETER-

5 MINATIONS.—

6   "(1) IN GENERAL.—The Secretary shall estab-

7   lish standards, including data requirements, for in-

8   vestigations of petitions filed under section 221 and

9   criteria for making determinations under subsection

10   (a).

11   "(2) CONSULTATIONS.—Not less than 90 days

12   before issuing a final rule with respect to the stand-

13   ards required under paragraph (1), the Secretary

14   shall consult with the Committee on Finance of the

15   Senate and the Committee on Ways and Means of

16   the House of Representatives with respect to such

17   rule.''.

18 **SEC. 1804. MONITORING AND REPORTING RELATING TO**

19   **SERVICE SECTOR.**

20   (a) IN GENERAL.—Section 282 of the Trade Act of

21 1974 (19 U.S.C. 2393) is amended—

22   (1) in the heading, by striking "**SYSTEM**" and

23   inserting "**AND DATA COLLECTION**";

24   (2) in the first sentence—

(A) by striking "The Secretary" and inserting "(a) MONITORING PROGRAMS.—The Secretary";

(B) by inserting "and services" after "imports of articles";

(C) by inserting "and domestic supply of services" after "domestic production";

(D) by inserting "or supplying services" after "producing articles"; and

(E) by inserting ", or supply of services," after "changes in production"; and

(3) by adding at the end the following:

"(b) COLLECTION OF DATA AND REPORTS ON SERVICE SECTOR.—

"(1) SECRETARY OF LABOR.—Not later than 90 days after the date of the enactment of this subsection, the Secretary of Labor shall implement a system to collect data on adversely affected workers employed in the service sector that includes the number of workers by State and industry, and by the cause of the dislocation of each worker, as identified in the certification.

"(2) SECRETARY OF COMMERCE.—Not later than 1 year after such date of enactment, the Secretary of Commerce shall, in consultation with the

1   Secretary of Labor, conduct a study and submit to

2   the Committee on Finance of the Senate and the

3   Committee on Ways and Means of the House of

4   Representatives a report on ways to improve the

5   timeliness and coverage of data on trade in services,

6   including methods to identify increased imports due

7   to the relocation of United States firms to foreign

8   countries, and increased imports due to United

9   States firms acquiring services from firms in foreign

10   countries.''.

11   (b) CLERICAL AMENDMENT.—The table of contents

12 of the Trade Act of 1974 is amended by striking the item

13 relating to section 282 and inserting the following:

"Sec. 282. Trade monitoring and data collection.".

14   (c) EFFECTIVE DATE.—The amendments made by

15 this section shall take effect on the date of the enactment

16 of this Act.

17 **Subpart B—Industry Notifications Following Certain**

18 **Affirmative Determinations**

19 **SEC. 1811. NOTIFICATIONS FOLLOWING CERTAIN AFFIRMA-**

20   **TIVE DETERMINATIONS.**

21   (a) IN GENERAL.—Section 224 of the Trade Act of

22 1974 (19 U.S.C. 2274) is amended—

23   (1) by amending the heading to read as follows:

1 **"SEC. 224. STUDY AND NOTIFICATIONS REGARDING CER-**

2   **TAIN AFFIRMATIVE DETERMINATIONS; IN-**

3   **DUSTRY NOTIFICATION OF ASSISTANCE.";**

4   (2) in subsection (a), by striking "Whenever"

5 and inserting "STUDY OF DOMESTIC INDUSTRY.—

6 Whenever";

7   (3) in subsection (b)—

8   (A) by striking "The report" and inserting

9   "REPORT BY THE SECRETARY.—The report";

10   and

11   (B) by inserting "and on the website of the

12   Department of Labor" after "Federal Reg-

13   ister"; and

14   (4) by adding at the end the following:

15   "(c) NOTIFICATIONS FOLLOWING AFFIRMATIVE

16 GLOBAL SAFEGUARD DETERMINATIONS.—Upon making

17 an affirmative determination under section 202(b)(1), the

18 Commission shall promptly notify the Secretary of Labor

19 and the Secretary of Commerce and, in the case of a deter-

20 mination with respect to an agricultural commodity, the

21 Secretary of Agriculture, of the determination.

22   "(d) NOTIFICATIONS FOLLOWING AFFIRMATIVE BI-

23 LATERAL OR PLURILATERAL SAFEGUARD DETERMINA-

24 TIONS.—

25   "(1) NOTIFICATIONS OF DETERMINATIONS OF

26   MARKET DISRUPTION.—Upon making an affirmative

1 determination under section 421(b)(1), the Commis-
2 sion shall promptly notify the Secretary of Labor
3 and the Secretary of Commerce and, in the case of
4 a determination with respect to an agricultural com-
5 modity, the Secretary of Agriculture, of the deter-
6 mination.

7 "(2) NOTIFICATIONS REGARDING TRADE
8 AGREEMENT SAFEGUARDS.—Upon making an af-
9 firmative determination in a proceeding initiated
10 under an applicable safeguard provision (other than
11 a provision described in paragraph (3)) that is en-
12 acted to implement a trade agreement to which the
13 United States is a party, the Commission shall
14 promptly notify the Secretary of Labor and the Sec-
15 retary of Commerce and, in the case of a determina-
16 tion with respect to an agricultural commodity, the
17 Secretary of Agriculture, of the determination.

18 "(3) NOTIFICATIONS REGARDING TEXTILE AND
19 APPAREL SAFEGUARDS.—Upon making an affirma-
20 tive determination in a proceeding initiated under
21 any safeguard provision relating to textile and ap-
22 parel articles that is enacted to implement a trade
23 agreement to which the United States is a party, the
24 President shall promptly notify the Secretary of

1 Labor and the Secretary of Commerce of the deter-

2 mination.

3 "(e) NOTIFICATIONS FOLLOWING CERTAIN AFFIRM-

4 ATIVE DETERMINATIONS UNDER TITLE VII OF THE TAR-

5 IFF ACT OF 1930.—Upon making an affirmative deter-

6 mination under section 705(b)(1)(A) or 735(b)(1)(A) of

7 the Tariff Act of 1930 (19 U.S.C. 1671d(b)(1)(A) and

8 1673d(b)(1)(A)), the Commission shall promptly notify

9 the Secretary of Labor and the Secretary of Commerce

10 and, in the case of a determination with respect to an agri-

11 cultural commodity, the Secretary of Agriculture, of the

12 determination.

13 "(f) INDUSTRY NOTIFICATION OF ASSISTANCE.—

14 Upon receiving a notification of a determination under

15 subsection (c), (d), or (e) with respect to a domestic

16 industry—

17 "(1) the Secretary of Labor shall—

18 "(A) notify the representatives of the do-

19 mestic industry affected by the determination,

20 firms publicly identified by name during the

21 course of the proceeding relating to the deter-

22 mination, and any certified or recognized union

23 or, to the extent practicable, other duly author-

24 ized representative of workers employed by such

25 representatives of the domestic industry, of—

1   "(i) the allowances, training, employ-
2   ment services, and other benefits available
3   under this chapter;
4   "(ii) the manner in which to file a pe-
5   tition and apply for such benefits; and
6   "(iii) the availability of assistance in
7   filing such petitions;
8   "(B) notify the Governor of each State in
9 which one or more firms in the industry de-
10 scribed in subparagraph (A) are located of the
11 Commission's determination and the identity of
12 the firms; and
13   "(C) upon request, provide any assistance
14 that is necessary to file a petition under section
15 221;
16 "(2) the Secretary of Commerce shall—
17   "(A) notify the representatives of the do-
18 mestic industry affected by the determination
19 and any firms publicly identified by name dur-
20 ing the course of the proceeding relating to the
21 determination of—
22   "(i) the benefits available under chap-
23   ter 3;
24   "(ii) the manner in which to file a pe-
25   tition and apply for such benefits; and

"(iii) the availability of assistance in filing such petitions; and

"(B) upon request, provide any assistance that is necessary to file a petition under section 251; and

"(3) in the case of an affirmative determination based upon imports of an agricultural commodity, the Secretary of Agriculture shall—

"(A) notify representatives of the domestic industry affected by the determination and any agricultural commodity producers publicly identified by name during the course of the proceeding relating to the determination of—

"(i) the benefits available under chapter 6;

"(ii) the manner in which to file a petition and apply for such benefits; and

"(iii) the availability of assistance in filing such petitions; and

"(B) upon request, provide any assistance that is necessary to file a petition under section 292.

"(g) REPRESENTATIVES OF THE DOMESTIC INDUS-TRY.—For purposes of subsection (f), the term 'represent-

1 atives of the domestic industry' means the persons that

2 petitioned for relief in connection with—

3   "(1) a proceeding under section 202 or 421 of

4   this Act;

5   "(2) a proceeding under section 702(b) or

6   732(b) of the Tariff Act of 1930 (19 U.S.C.

7   1671d(b) and 1673d(b)); or

8   "(3) any safeguard investigation described in

9   subsection (d)(2) or (d)(3).".

10   (b) CLERICAL AMENDMENT.—The table of contents

11 of the Trade Act of 1974 is amended by striking the item

12 relating to section 224 and inserting the following:

> "Sec. 224. Study and notifications regarding certain affirmative determina-
> tions; industry notification of assistance.".

13 **SEC. 1812. NOTIFICATION TO SECRETARY OF COMMERCE.**

14   Section 225 of the Trade Act of 1974 (19 U.S.C.

15 2275) is amended by adding at the end the following:

16   "(c) Upon issuing a certification under section 223,

17 the Secretary shall notify the Secretary of Commerce of

18 the identity of each firm covered by the certification.".

19   **Subpart C—Program Benefits**

20 **SEC. 1821. QUALIFYING REQUIREMENTS FOR WORKERS.**

21   (a) IN GENERAL.—Section 231(a)(5)(A)(ii) of the

22 Trade Act of 1974 (19 U.S.C. 2291 (a)(5)(A)(ii)) is

23 amended—

1   (1) by striking subclauses (I) and (II) and in-

2 serting the following:

3   "(I) in the case of a worker whose

4   most recent total separation from adversely

5   affected employment that meets the re-

6   quirements of paragraphs (1) and (2) oc-

7   curs after the date on which the Secretary

8   issues a certification covering the worker,

9   the last day of the 26th week after such

10   total separation,

11   "(II) in the case of a worker whose

12   most recent total separation from adversely

13   affected employment that meets the re-

14   quirements of paragraphs (1) and (2) oc-

15   curs before the date on which the Sec-

16   retary issues a certification covering the

17   worker, the last day of the 26th week after

18   the date of such certification,";

19 (2) in subclause (III)—

20   (A) by striking "later of the dates specified

21 in subclause (I) or (II)" and inserting "date

22 specified in subclause (I) or (II), as the case

23 may be"; and

24   (B) by striking "or" at the end;

1   (3) by redesignating subclause (IV) as sub-

2 clause (V); and

3   (4) by inserting after subclause (III) the fol-

4 lowing:

5   "(IV) in the case of a worker who

6   fails to enroll by the date required by sub-

7   clause (I), (II), or (III), as the case may

8   be, due to the failure to provide the worker

9   with timely information regarding the date

10   specified in such subclause, the last day of

11   a period determined by the Secretary, or".

12 (b) WAIVERS OF TRAINING REQUIREMENTS.—Sec-

13 tion 231(c) of the Trade Act of 1974 (19 U.S.C. 2291(c))

14 is amended—

15   (1) in paragraph (1)(B)—

16   (A) by striking "The worker possesses"

17   and inserting the following:

18   "(i) IN GENERAL.—The worker pos-

19   sesses"; and

20   (B) by adding at the end the following:

21   "(ii) MARKETABLE SKILLS DE-

22   FINED.—For purposes of clause (i), the

23   term 'marketable skills' may include the

24   possession of a postgraduate degree from

25   an institution of higher education (as de-

1   fined in section 102 of the Higher Edu-

2   cation Act of 1965 (20 U.S.C. 1002)) or

3   an equivalent institution, or the possession

4   of an equivalent postgraduate certification

5   in a specialized field.'';

6   (2) in paragraph (2)(A), by striking "A waiver"

7 and inserting "Except as provided in paragraph

8 (3)(B), a waiver"; and

9   (3) in paragraph (3)—

10   (A) in subparagraph (A), by striking "Pur-

11   suant to an agreement under section 239, the

12   Secretary may authorize a" and inserting "An

13   agreement under section 239 shall authorize a";

14   (B) by redesignating subparagraph (B) as

15   subparagraph (C); and

16   (C) by inserting after subparagraph (A)

17   the following:

18   "(B) REVIEW OF WAIVERS.—An agree-

19   ment under section 239 shall require a cooper-

20   ating State to review each waiver issued by the

21   State under subparagraph (A), (B), (D), (E),

22   or (F) of paragraph (1)—

23   "(i) 3 months after the date on which

24   the State issues the waiver; and

25   "(ii) on a monthly basis thereafter.".

(c) Conforming Amendments.—

(1) Section 231 of the Trade Act of 1974 (19 U.S.C. 2291), as amended, is further amended—

(A) in subsection (a), in the matter preceding paragraph (1), by striking "more than 60 days" and all that follows through "section 221" and inserting "on or after the date of such certification"; and

(B) in subsection (b)—

(i) by striking paragraph (2); and

(ii) in paragraph (1)—

(I) by striking "(1)";

(II) by redesignating subparagraphs (A) and (B) as paragraphs (1) and (2), respectively;

(III) by redesignating clauses (i) and (ii) as subparagraphs (A) and (B), respectively; and

(IV) by redesignating subclauses (I) and (II) as clauses (i) and (ii), respectively.

(2) Section 233 of the Trade Act of 1974 (19 U.S.C. 2293) is amended—

(A) by striking subsection (b); and

1   (B) by redesignating subsections (c)

2   through (g) as subsections (b) through (f), re-

3   spectively.

4 **SEC. 1822. WEEKLY AMOUNTS.**

5   Section 232 of the Trade Act of 1974 (19 U.S.C.

6 2292) is amended—

7   (1) in subsection (a)—

8   (A) by striking "subsections (b) and (c)"

9   and inserting "subsections (b), (c), and (d)";

10   (B) by striking "total unemployment" the

11   first place it appears and inserting "unemploy-

12   ment"; and

13   (C) in paragraph (2), by inserting before

14   the period the following: ", except that in the

15   case of an adversely affected worker who is par-

16   ticipating in training under this chapter, such

17   income shall not include earnings from work for

18   such week that are equal to or less than the

19   most recent weekly benefit amount of the unem-

20   ployment insurance payable to the worker for a

21   week of total unemployment preceding the

22   worker's first exhaustion of unemployment in-

23   surance (as determined for purposes of section

24   231(a)(3)(B))"; and

25   (2) by adding at the end the following:

1   "(d) ELECTION OF TRADE READJUSTMENT ALLOW-

2 ANCE   OR   UNEMPLOYMENT   INSURANCE.—Notwith-

3 standing section 231(a)(3)(B), an adversely affected work-

4 er may elect to receive a trade readjustment allowance in-

5 stead of unemployment insurance during any week with

6 respect to which the worker—

7   "(1) is entitled to receive unemployment insur-

8   ance as a result of the establishment by the worker

9   of a new benefit year under State law, based in

10   whole or in part upon part-time or short-term em-

11   ployment in which the worker engaged after the

12   worker's most recent total separation from adversely

13   affected employment; and

14   "(2) is otherwise entitled to a trade readjust-

15   ment allowance.".

16 **SEC. 1823. LIMITATIONS ON TRADE READJUSTMENT AL-**

17   **LOWANCES; ALLOWANCES FOR EXTENDED**

18   **TRAINING AND BREAKS IN TRAINING.**

19   Section 233(a) of the Trade Act of 1974 (19 U.S.C.

20 2293(a)) is amended—

21   (1) in paragraph (2), by inserting "under para-

22   graph (1)" after "trade readjustment allowance";

23   and

24   (2) in paragraph (3)—

1   (A) in the matter preceding subparagraph

2 (A)—

3   (i) by striking "training approved for

4 him" and inserting "a training program

5 approved for the worker";

6   (ii) by striking "52 additional weeks"

7 and inserting "78 additional weeks"; and

8   (iii) by striking "52-week" and insert-

9 ing "91-week"; and

10   (B) in the matter following subparagraph

11 (B), by striking "52-week" and inserting "91-

12 week".

13 **SEC. 1824. SPECIAL RULES FOR CALCULATION OF ELIGI-**

14   **BILITY PERIOD.**

15 Section 233 of the Trade Act of 1974 (19 U.S.C.

16 2293), as amended, is further amended by adding at the

17 end the following:

18 "(g) SPECIAL RULE FOR CALCULATING SEPARA-

19 TION.—Notwithstanding any other provision of this chap-

20 ter, any period during which a judicial or administrative

21 appeal is pending with respect to the denial by the Sec-

22 retary of a petition under section 223 shall not be counted

23 for purposes of calculating the period of separation under

24 subsection (a)(2).

1   "(h) SPECIAL RULE FOR JUSTIFIABLE CAUSE.—If
2 the Secretary determines that there is justifiable cause,
3 the Secretary may extend the period during which trade
4 readjustment allowances are payable to an adversely af-
5 fected worker under paragraphs (2) and (3) of subsection
6 (a) (but not the maximum amounts of such allowances
7 that are payable under this section).

8   "(i) SPECIAL RULE WITH RESPECT TO MILITARY
9 SERVICE.—

10   "(1) IN GENERAL.—Notwithstanding any other
11   provision of this chapter, the Secretary may waive
12   any requirement of this chapter that the Secretary
13   determines is necessary to ensure that an adversely
14   affected worker who is a member of a reserve com-
15   ponent of the Armed Forces and serves a period of
16   duty described in paragraph (2) is eligible to receive
17   a trade readjustment allowance, training, and other
18   benefits under this chapter in the same manner and
19   to the same extent as if the worker had not served
20   the period of duty.

21   "(2) PERIOD OF DUTY DESCRIBED.—An ad-
22   versely affected worker serves a period of duty de-
23   scribed in this paragraph if, before completing train-
24   ing under section 236, the worker—

1   "(A) serves on active duty for a period of

2   more than 30 days under a call or order to ac-

3   tive duty of more than 30 days; or

4   "(B) in the case of a member of the Army

5   National Guard of the United States or Air Na-

6   tional Guard of the United States, performs

7   full-time National Guard duty under section

8   502(f) of title 32, United States Code, for 30

9   consecutive days or more when authorized by

10   the President or the Secretary of Defense for

11   the purpose of responding to a national emer-

12   gency declared by the President and supported

13   by Federal funds.".

14 **SEC. 1825. APPLICATION OF STATE LAWS AND REGULA-**

15 **TIONS ON GOOD CAUSE FOR WAIVER OF TIME**

16 **LIMITS OR LATE FILING OF CLAIMS.**

17   Section 234 of the Trade Act of 1974 (19 U.S.C.

18 2294) is amended—

19   (1) by striking "Except where inconsistent" and

20   inserting "(a) IN GENERAL.—Except where incon-

21   sistent"; and

22   (2) by adding at the end the following:

23   "(b) SPECIAL RULE WITH RESPECT TO STATE LAWS

24 AND REGULATIONS ON GOOD CAUSE FOR WAIVER OF

25 TIME LIMITS OR LATE FILING OF CLAIMS.—Any law,

1 regulation, policy, or practice of a cooperating State that

2 allows for a waiver for good cause of any time limitation

3 relating to the administration of the State unemployment

4 insurance law shall, in the administration of the program

5 under this chapter by the State, apply to any time limita-

6 tion with respect to an application for a trade readjust-

7 ment allowance or enrollment in training under this chap-

8 ter.''.

9 **SEC. 1826. EMPLOYMENT AND CASE MANAGEMENT SERV-**

10   **ICES.**

11   (a) IN GENERAL.—Section 235 of the Trade Act of

12 1974 (19 U.S.C. 2295) is amended to read as follows:

13 **''SEC. 235. EMPLOYMENT AND CASE MANAGEMENT SERV-**

14   **ICES.**

15   ''The Secretary shall make available, directly or

16 through agreements with States under section 239, to ad-

17 versely affected workers and adversely affected incumbent

18 workers covered by a certification under subchapter A of

19 this chapter the following employment and case manage-

20 ment services:

21   ''(1) Comprehensive and specialized assessment

22   of skill levels and service needs, including through—

23   ''(A) diagnostic testing and use of other

24   assessment tools; and

1   "(B) in-depth interviewing and evaluation

2   to identify employment barriers and appropriate

3   employment goals.

4   "(2) Development of an individual employment

5 plan to identify employment goals and objectives,

6 and appropriate training to achieve those goals and

7 objectives.

8   "(3) Information on training available in local

9 and regional areas, information on individual coun-

10 seling to determine which training is suitable train-

11 ing, and information on how to apply for such train-

12 ing.

13   "(4) Information on how to apply for financial

14 aid, including referring workers to educational op-

15 portunity centers described in section 402F of the

16 Higher Education Act of 1965 (20 U.S.C. 1070a–

17 16), where applicable, and notifying workers that the

18 workers may request financial aid administrators at

19 institutions of higher education (as defined in sec-

20 tion 102 of such Act (20 U.S.C. 1002)) to use the

21 administrators' discretion under section 479A of

22 such Act (20 U.S.C. 1087tt) to use current year in-

23 come data, rather than preceding year income data,

24 for determining the amount of need of the workers

1   for Federal financial assistance under title IV of

2   such Act (20 U.S.C. 1070 et seq.).

3   "(5) Short-term prevocational services, includ-

4   ing development of learning skills, communications

5   skills, interviewing skills, punctuality, personal main-

6   tenance skills, and professional conduct to prepare

7   individuals for employment or training.

8   "(6) Individual career counseling, including job

9   search and placement counseling, during the period

10   in which the individual is receiving a trade adjust-

11   ment allowance or training under this chapter, and

12   after receiving such training for purposes of job

13   placement.

14   "(7) Provision of employment statistics infor-

15   mation, including the provision of accurate informa-

16   tion relating to local, regional, and national labor

17   market areas, including—

18   "(A) job vacancy listings in such labor

19   market areas;

20   "(B) information on jobs skills necessary

21   to obtain jobs identified in job vacancy listings

22   described in subparagraph (A);

23   "(C) information relating to local occupa-

24   tions that are in demand and earnings potential

25   of such occupations; and

1   "(D) skills requirements for local occupa-

2   tions described in subparagraph (C).

3   "(8) Information relating to the availability of

4   supportive services, including services relating to

5   child care, transportation, dependent care, housing

6   assistance, and need-related payments that are nec-

7   essary to enable an individual to participate in train-

8   ing.".

9   (b) CLERICAL AMENDMENT.—The table of contents

10 of the Trade Act of 1974 is amended by striking the item

11 relating to section 235 and inserting the following:

"235. Employment and case management services.".

12 **SEC. 1827. ADMINISTRATIVE EXPENSES AND EMPLOYMENT**

13   **AND CASE MANAGEMENT SERVICES.**

14   (a) IN GENERAL.—Part II of subchapter B of chap-

15 ter 2 of title II of the Trade Act of 1974 (19 U.S.C. 2295

16 et seq.) is amended by inserting after section 235 the fol-

17 lowing:

18 **"SEC. 235A. FUNDING FOR ADMINISTRATIVE EXPENSES**

19   **AND EMPLOYMENT AND CASE MANAGEMENT**

20   **SERVICES.**

21   "(a) FUNDING FOR ADMINISTRATIVE EXPENSES AND

22 EMPLOYMENT AND CASE MANAGEMENT SERVICES.—

23   "(1) IN GENERAL.—In addition to any funds

24   made available to a State to carry out section 236

25   for a fiscal year, the State shall receive for the fiscal

1   year a payment in an amount that is equal to 15

2   percent of the amount of such funds.

3   "(2) USE OF FUNDS.—A State that receives a

4   payment under paragraph (1) shall—

5   "(A) use not more than ⅔ of such pay-

6   ment for the administration of the trade adjust-

7   ment assistance for workers program under this

8   chapter, including for—

9   "(i) processing waivers of training re-

10   quirements under section 231;

11   "(ii) collecting, validating, and report-

12   ing data required under this chapter; and

13   "(iii) providing reemployment trade

14   adjustment assistance under section 246;

15   and

16   "(B) use not less than ⅓ of such payment

17   for employment and case management services

18   under section 235.

19   "(b) ADDITIONAL FUNDING FOR EMPLOYMENT AND

20 CASE MANAGEMENT SERVICES.—

21   "(1) IN GENERAL.—In addition to any funds

22   made available to a State to carry out section 236

23   and the payment under subsection (a)(1) for a fiscal

24   year, the Secretary shall provide to the State for the

25   fiscal year a payment in the amount of $350,000.

1   "(2) USE OF FUNDS.—A State that receives a

2   payment under paragraph (1) shall use such pay-

3   ment for the purpose of providing employment and

4   case management services under section 235.

5   "(3) VOLUNTARY RETURN OF FUNDS.—A State

6   that receives a payment under paragraph (1) may

7   decline or otherwise return such payment to the Sec-

8   retary.".

9   (b) CLERICAL AMENDMENT.—The table of contents

10 of the Trade Act of 1974 is amended by inserting after

11 the item relating to section 235 the following:

> "Sec. 235A. Funding for administrative expenses and employment and case management services.".

12   (c) EFFECTIVE DATE.—The amendments made by

13 this section shall take effect on the date of the enactment

14 of this Act.

15 **SEC. 1828. TRAINING FUNDING.**

16   (a) IN GENERAL.—Section 236(a)(2) of the Trade

17 Act of 1974 (19 U.S.C. 2296(a)(2)) is amended to read

18 as follows:

19   "(2)(A) The total amount of payments that may be

20 made under paragraph (1) shall not exceed—

21   "(i) for each of the fiscal years 2009 and 2010,

22     $575,000,000; and

23   "(ii) for the period beginning October 1, 2010,

24   and ending December 31, 2010, $143,750,000.

1   "(B)(i) The Secretary shall, as soon as practicable

2 after the beginning of each fiscal year, make an initial dis-

3 tribution of the funds made available to carry out this sec-

4 tion, in accordance with the requirements of subparagraph

5 (C).

6   "(ii) The Secretary shall ensure that not less than

7 90 percent of the funds made available to carry out this

8 section for a fiscal year are distributed to the States by

9 not later than July 15 of that fiscal year.

10   "(C)(i) In making the initial distribution of funds

11 pursuant to subparagraph (B)(i) for a fiscal year, the Sec-

12 retary shall hold in reserve 35 percent of the funds made

13 available to carry out this section for that fiscal year for

14 additional distributions during the remainder of the fiscal

15 year.

16   "(ii) Subject to clause (iii), in determining how to ap-

17 portion the initial distribution of funds pursuant to sub-

18 paragraph (B)(i) in a fiscal year, the Secretary shall take

19 into account, with respect to each State—

20   "(I) the trend in the number of workers covered

21   by certifications of eligibility under this chapter dur-

22   ing the most recent 4 consecutive calendar quarters

23   for which data are available;

24   "(II) the trend in the number of workers par-

25   ticipating in training under this section during the

1   most recent 4 consecutive calendar quarters for

2   which data are available;

3   "(III) the number of workers estimated to be

4   participating in training under this section during

5   the fiscal year;

6   "(IV) the amount of funding estimated to be

7   necessary to provide training approved under this

8   section to such workers during the fiscal year; and

9   "(V) such other factors as the Secretary con-

10   siders appropriate relating to the provision of train-

11   ing under this section.

12   "(iii) In no case may the amount of the initial dis-

13   tribution to a State pursuant to subparagraph (B)(i) in

14   a fiscal year be less than 25 percent of the initial distribu-

15   tion to the State in the preceding fiscal year.

16   "(D) The Secretary shall establish procedures for the

17   distribution of the funds that remain available for the fis-

18   cal year after the initial distribution required under sub-

19   paragraph (B)(i). Such procedures may include the dis-

20   tribution of funds pursuant to requests submitted by

21   States in need of such funds.

22   "(E) If, during a fiscal year, the Secretary estimates

23   that the amount of funds necessary to pay the costs of

24   training approved under this section will exceed the dollar

25   amount limitation specified in subparagraph (A), the Sec-

1 retary shall decide how the amount of funds made avail-
2 able to carry out this section that have not been distrib-
3 uted at the time of the estimate will be apportioned among
4 the States for the remainder of the fiscal year.".

5   (b) DETERMINATIONS REGARDING TRAINING.—Sec-
6 tion 236(a)(9) of the Trade Act of 1974 (19 U.S.C.
7 2296(a)(9)) is amended—

8   (1) by striking "The Secretary" and inserting
9   "(A) Subject to subparagraph (B), the Secretary";
10   and

11   (2) by adding at the end the following:

12   "(B)(i) In determining under paragraph (1)(E)
13 whether a worker is qualified to undertake and complete
14 training, the Secretary may approve training for a period
15 longer than the worker's period of eligibility for trade re-
16 adjustment allowances under part I if the worker dem-
17 onstrates a financial ability to complete the training after
18 the expiration of the worker's period of eligibility for such
19 trade readjustment allowances.

20   "(ii) In determining the reasonable cost of training
21 under paragraph (1)(F) with respect to a worker, the Sec-
22 retary may consider whether other public or private funds
23 are reasonably available to the worker, except that the
24 Secretary may not require a worker to obtain such funds

1 as a condition of approval of training under paragraph

2 (1).".

3   (c) REGULATIONS.—Section 236 of the Trade Act of

4 1974 (19 U.S.C. 2296) is amended by adding at the end

5 the following:

6   "(g) REGULATIONS WITH RESPECT TO APPORTION-

7 MENT OF TRAINING FUNDS TO STATES.—

8   "(1) IN GENERAL.—Not later than 1 year after

9   the date of the enactment of this subsection, the

10   Secretary shall issue such regulations as may be nec-

11   essary to carry out the provisions of subsection

12   (a)(2).

13   "(2) CONSULTATIONS.—The Secretary shall

14   consult with the Committee on Finance of the Sen-

15   ate and the Committee on Ways and Means of the

16   House of Representatives not less than 90 days be-

17   fore issuing any regulation pursuant to paragraph

18   (1).".

19   (d) EFFECTIVE DATE.—This section and the amend-

20 ments made by this section shall take effect upon the expi-

21 ration of the 90-day period beginning on the date of the

22 enactment of this Act, except that—

23   (1) subparagraph (A) of section 236(a)(2) of

24   the Trade Act of 1974, as amended by subsection

1   (a) of this section, shall take effect on the date of

2   the enactment of this Act; and

3   (2) subparagraphs (B), (C), and (D) of such

4   section 236(a)(2) shall take effect on October 1,

5   2009.

6 **SEC. 1829. PREREQUISITE EDUCATION; APPROVED TRAIN-**

7   **ING PROGRAMS.**

8   (a) IN GENERAL.—Section 236(a)(5) of the Trade

9 Act of 1974 (19 U.S.C. 2296(a)(5)) is amended—

10   (1) in subparagraph (A)—

11   (A) by striking "and" at the end of clause

12   (i);

13   (B) by adding "and" at the end of clause

14   (ii); and

15   (C) by inserting after clause (ii) the fol-

16   lowing:

17   "(iii) apprenticeship programs registered

18   under the Act of August 16, 1937 (commonly

19   known as the 'National Apprenticeship Act'; 50

20   Stat. 664, chapter 663; 29 U.S.C. 50 et seq.),";

21   (2) by redesignating subparagraphs (E) and

22   (F) as subparagraphs (F) and (G), respectively;

23   (3) by inserting after subparagraph (D) the fol-

24   lowing:

1   "(E) any program of prerequisite education or

2 coursework required to enroll in training that may

3 be approved under this section,";

4   (4) in subparagraph (F)(ii), as redesignated by

5 paragraph (2), by striking "and" at the end;

6   (5) in subparagraph (G), as redesignated by

7 paragraph (2), by striking the period at the end and

8 inserting ", and"; and

9   (6) by adding at the end the following:

10   "(H) any training program or coursework at an

11 accredited institution of higher education (described

12 in section 102 of the Higher Education Act of 1965

13 (20 U.S.C. 1002)), including a training program or

14 coursework for the purpose of—

15   "(i) obtaining a degree or certification; or

16   "(ii) completing a degree or certification

17 that the worker had previously begun at an ac-

18 credited institution of higher education.

19 The Secretary may not limit approval of a training pro-

20 gram under paragraph (1) to a program provided pursu-

21 ant to title I of the Workforce Investment Act of 1998

22 (29 U.S.C. 2801 et seq.).".

23   (b) CONFORMING AMENDMENTS.—Section 233 of the

24 Trade Act of 1974 (19 U.S.C. 2293) is amended—

1   (1) in subsection (a)(2), by inserting "pre-
2 requisite education or" after "requires a program
3 of"; and

4   (2) in subsection (f) (as redesignated by section
5 1821(c) of this subtitle), by inserting "prerequisite
6 education or" after "includes a program of".

7   (c) TECHNICAL CORRECTIONS.—Section 236 of the
8 Trade Act of 1974 (19 U.S.C. 2296) is amended—

9   (1) in subsection (a)—

10   (A) in paragraph (1), in the flush text, by
11 striking "his behalf" and inserting "the work-
12 er's behalf"; and

13   (B) in paragraph (3), by striking "this
14 paragraph (1)" and inserting "paragraph (1)";
15 and

16   (2) in subsection (b)(2), by striking ", and"
17 and inserting a period.

18 **SEC. 1830. PRE-LAYOFF AND PART-TIME TRAINING.**

19   (a) PRE-LAYOFF TRAINING.—

20   (1) IN GENERAL.—Section 236(a) of the Trade
21 Act of 1974 (19 U.S.C. 2296(a)) is amended—

22   (A) in paragraph (1), by inserting after
23 "determines" the following: ", with respect to
24 an adversely affected worker or an adversely af-
25 fected incumbent worker,";

1   (B) in paragraph (4)—

2   (i) in subparagraphs (A) and (B), by

3   inserting "or an adversely affected incum-

4   bent worker" after "an adversely affected

5   worker" each place it appears; and

6   (ii) in subparagraph (C), by inserting

7   "or adversely affected incumbent worker"

8   after "adversely affected worker" each

9   place it appears;

10   (C) in paragraph (5), in the matter pre-

11   ceding subparagraph (A), by striking "The

12   training programs" and inserting "Except as

13   provided in paragraph (10), the training pro-

14   grams";

15   (D) in paragraph (6)(B), by inserting "or

16   adversely affected incumbent worker" after

17   "adversely affected worker";

18   (E) in paragraph (7)(B), by inserting "or

19   adversely affected incumbent worker" after

20   "adversely affected worker"; and

21   (F) by inserting after paragraph (9) the

22   following:

23   "(10) In the case of an adversely affected incumbent

24 worker, the Secretary may not approve—

1   "(A) on-the-job training under paragraph

2   (5)(A)(i); or

3   "(B) customized training under paragraph

4   (5)(A)(ii), unless such training is for a position

5   other than the worker's adversely affected employ-

6   ment.

7   "(11) If the Secretary determines that an adversely

8 affected incumbent worker for whom the Secretary ap-

9 proved training under this section is no longer threatened

10 with a total or partial separation, the Secretary shall ter-

11 minate the approval of such training.".

12   (2) DEFINITIONS.—Section 247 of the Trade

13   Act of 1974 (19 U.S.C. 2319), as amended, is fur-

14   ther amended by adding at the end the following:

15   "(19) The term 'adversely affected incumbent

16   worker' means a worker who—

17   "(A) is a member of a group of workers

18   who have been certified as eligible to apply for

19   adjustment assistance under subchapter A;

20   "(B) has not been totally or partially sepa-

21   rated from adversely affected employment; and

22   "(C) the Secretary determines, on an indi-

23   vidual basis, is threatened with total or partial

24   separation.".

1   (b) PART-TIME TRAINING.—Section 236 of the

2 Trade Act of 1974 (19 U.S.C. 2296), as amended, is fur-

3 ther amended by adding at the end the following:

4   "(h) PART-TIME TRAINING.—

5   "(1) IN GENERAL.—The Secretary may approve

6   full-time or part-time training for a worker under

7   subsection (a).

8   "(2) LIMITATION.—Notwithstanding paragraph

9   (1), a worker participating in part-time training ap-

10   proved under subsection (a) may not receive a trade

11   readjustment allowance under section 231.".

12 **SEC. 1831. ON-THE-JOB TRAINING.**

13   (a) IN GENERAL.—Section 236(c) of the Trade Act

14 of 1974 (19 U.S.C. 2296(c)) is amended—

15   (1) by redesignating paragraphs (1) through

16   (10) as subparagraphs (A) through (J) and moving

17   such subparagraphs 2 ems to the right;

18   (2) by striking "(c) The Secretary shall" and

19   all that follows through "such costs," and inserting

20   the following:

21   "(c) ON-THE-JOB TRAINING REQUIREMENTS.—

22   "(1) IN GENERAL.—The Secretary may approve

23   on-the-job training for any adversely affected worker

24   if—

1   "(A) the worker meets the requirements

2   for training to be approved under subsection

3   (a)(1);

4   "(B) the Secretary determines that on-the-

5   job training—

6   "(i) can reasonably be expected to

7   lead to suitable employment with the em-

8   ployer offering the on-the-job training;

9   "(ii) is compatible with the skills of

10   the worker;

11   "(iii) includes a curriculum through

12   which the worker will gain the knowledge

13   or skills to become proficient in the job for

14   which the worker is being trained; and

15   "(iv) can be measured by benchmarks

16   that indicate that the worker is gaining

17   such knowledge or skills; and

18   "(C) the State determines that the on-the-

19   job training program meets the requirements of

20   clauses (iii) and (iv) of subparagraph (B).

21   "(2) MONTHLY PAYMENTS.—The Secretary

22   shall pay the costs of on-the-job training approved

23   under paragraph (1) in monthly installments.

24   "(3) CONTRACTS FOR ON-THE-JOB TRAINING.—

"(A) IN GENERAL.—The Secretary shall ensure, in entering into a contract with an employer to provide on-the-job training to a worker under this subsection, that the skill requirements of the job for which the worker is being trained, the academic and occupational skill level of the worker, and the work experience of the worker are taken into consideration.

"(B) TERM OF CONTRACT.—Training under any such contract shall be limited to the period of time required for the worker receiving on-the-job training to become proficient in the job for which the worker is being trained, but may not exceed 104 weeks in any case.

"(4) EXCLUSION OF CERTAIN EMPLOYERS.—The Secretary shall not enter into a contract for on-the-job training with an employer that exhibits a pattern of failing to provide workers receiving on-the-job training from the employer with—

"(A) continued, long-term employment as regular employees; and

"(B) wages, benefits, and working conditions that are equivalent to the wages, benefits, and working conditions provided to regular employees who have worked a similar period of

1   time and are doing the same type of work as

2   workers receiving on-the-job training from the

3   employer.

4   "(5) LABOR STANDARDS.—The Secretary may

5 pay the costs of on-the-job training,"; and

6   (3) in paragraph (5), as redesignated—

7   (A) in subparagraph (I), as redesignated

8   by paragraph (1) of this section, by striking

9   "paragraphs (1), (2), (3), (4), (5), and (6)"

10   and inserting "subparagraphs (A), (B), (C),

11   (D), (E), and (F)"; and

12   (B) in subparagraph (J), as redesignated

13   by paragraph (1) of this section, by striking

14   "paragraph (8)" and inserting "subparagraph

15   (H)".

16 (b) REPEAL OF PREFERENCE FOR TRAINING ON THE

17 JOB.—Section 236(a)(1) of the Trade Act of 1974 (19

18 U.S.C. 2296(a)(1)) is amended by striking the last sen-

19 tence.

20 **SEC. 1832. ELIGIBILITY FOR UNEMPLOYMENT INSURANCE**

21   **AND PROGRAM BENEFITS WHILE IN TRAIN-**

22   **ING.**

23 Section 236(d) of the Trade Act of 1974 (19 U.S.C.

24 2296(d)) is amended to read as follows:

1   "(d) ELIGIBILITY.—An adversely affected worker

2 may not be determined to be ineligible or disqualified for

3 unemployment insurance or program benefits under this

4 subchapter—

5   "(1) because the worker—

6   "(A) is enrolled in training approved under

7   subsection (a);

8   "(B) left work—

9   "(i) that was not suitable employment

10   in order to enroll in such training; or

11   "(ii) that the worker engaged in on a

12   temporary basis during a break in such

13   training or a delay in the commencement

14   of such training; or

15   "(C) left on-the-job training not later than

16   30 days after commencing such training be-

17   cause the training did not meet the require-

18   ments of subsection (c)(1)(B); or

19   "(2) because of the application to any such

20 week in training of the provisions of State law or

21 Federal unemployment insurance law relating to

22 availability for work, active search for work, or re-

23 fusal to accept work.".

SEC. 1833. JOB SEARCH AND RELOCATION ALLOWANCES.

(a) JOB SEARCH ALLOWANCES.—Section 237 of the Trade Act of 1974 (19 U.S.C. 2297) is amended—

(1) in subsection (a)(2)(C)(ii), by striking ", unless the worker received a waiver under section 231(c)"; and

(2) in subsection (b)—

(A) in paragraph (1), by striking "90 percent of the cost of" and inserting "all"; and

(B) in paragraph (2), by striking "$1,250" and inserting "$1,500".

(b) RELOCATION ALLOWANCES.—Section 238 of the Trade Act of 1974 (19 U.S.C. 2298) is amended—

(1) in subsection (a)(2)(E)(ii), by striking ", unless the worker received a waiver under section 231(c)"; and

(2) in subsection (b)—

(A) in paragraph (1), by striking "90 percent of the" and inserting "all"; and

(B) in paragraph (2), by striking "$1,250" and inserting "$1,500".

1   **Subpart D—Reemployment Trade Adjustment**

2   **Assistance Program**

3 SEC. 1841. REEMPLOYMENT TRADE ADJUSTMENT ASSIST-

4   ANCE PROGRAM.

5   (a) IN GENERAL.—Section 246 of the Trade Act of

6 1974 (19 U.S.C. 2318) is amended—

7   (1) by amending the heading to read as follows:

8 "SEC. 246. REEMPLOYMENT TRADE ADJUSTMENT ASSIST-

9   ANCE PROGRAM.";

10   (2) in subsection (a)—

11   (A) in paragraph (1)—

12   (i) by striking "Not later than" and

13   all that follows through "2002, the Sec-

14   retary" and inserting "The Secretary";

15   and

16   (ii) by striking "an alternative trade

17   adjustment assistance program for older

18   workers" and inserting "a reemployment

19   trade adjustment assistance program";

20   (B) in paragraph (2)—

21   (i) in subparagraph (A)—

22   (I) in the matter preceding clause

23   (i), by striking "for a period not to

24   exceed 2 years" and inserting "for the

25   eligibility period under subparagraph

1   (A) or (B) of paragraph (4) (as the

2   case may be)"; and

3   (II) by striking clauses (i) and

4   (ii) and inserting the following:

5   "(i) the wages received by the worker

6   at the time of separation; and

7   "(ii) the wages received by the worker

8   from reemployment.";

9   (ii) in subparagraph (B)—

10   (I) by striking "for a period not

11   to exceed 2 years" and inserting "for

12   the eligibility period under subpara-

13   graph (A) or (B) of paragraph (4) (as

14   the case may be)"; and

15   (II) by striking ", as added by

16   section 201 of the Trade Act of

17   2002"; and

18   (iii) by adding at the end the fol-

19   lowing:

20   "(C) TRAINING AND OTHER SERVICES.—A

21 worker described in paragraph (3)(B) partici-

22 pating in the program established under para-

23 graph (1) is eligible to receive training approved

24 under section 236 and employment and case

25 management services under section 235."; and

1   (C) by striking paragraphs (3) through (5)

2 and inserting the following:

3 "(3) ELIGIBILITY.—

4   "(A) IN GENERAL.—A group of workers

5 certified under subchapter A as eligible for ad-

6 justment assistance under subchapter A is eligi-

7 ble for benefits described in paragraph (2)

8 under the program established under paragraph

9 (1).

10   "(B) INDIVIDUAL ELIGIBILITY.—A worker

11 in a group of workers described in subpara-

12 graph (A) may elect to receive benefits de-

13 scribed in paragraph (2) under the program es-

14 tablished under paragraph (1) if the worker—

15   "(i) is at least 50 years of age;

16   "(ii) earns not more than $55,000

17   each year in wages from reemployment;

18   "(iii)(I) is employed on a full-time

19   basis as defined by the law of the State in

20   which the worker is employed and is not

21   enrolled in a training program approved

22   under section 236; or

23   "(II) is employed at least 20 hours

24   per week and is enrolled in a training pro-

25   gram approved under section 236; and

1   "(iv) is not employed at the firm from

2   which the worker was separated.

3   "(4) ELIGIBILITY PERIOD FOR PAYMENTS.—

4   "(A) WORKER WHO HAS NOT RECEIVED

5   TRADE READJUSTMENT ALLOWANCE.—In the

6   case of a worker described in paragraph (3)(B)

7   who has not received a trade readjustment al-

8   lowance under part I of subchapter B pursuant

9   to the certification described in paragraph

10   (3)(A), the worker may receive benefits de-

11   scribed in paragraph (2) for a period not to ex-

12   ceed 2 years beginning on the earlier of—

13   "(i) the date on which the worker ex-

14   hausts all rights to unemployment insur-

15   ance based on the separation of the worker

16   from the adversely affected employment

17   that is the basis of the certification; or

18   "(ii) the date on which the worker ob-

19   tains reemployment described in paragraph

20   (3)(B).

21   "(B) WORKER WHO HAS RECEIVED TRADE

22   READJUSTMENT ALLOWANCE.—In the case of a

23   worker described in paragraph (3)(B) who has

24   received a trade readjustment allowance under

25   part I of subchapter B pursuant to the certifi-

1 cation described in paragraph (3)(A), the work-

2 er may receive benefits described in paragraph

3 (2) for a period of 104 weeks beginning on the

4 date on which the worker obtains reemployment

5 described in paragraph (3)(B), reduced by the

6 total number of weeks for which the worker re-

7 ceived such trade readjustment allowance.

8 "(5) TOTAL AMOUNT OF PAYMENTS.—

9 "(A) IN GENERAL.—The payments de-

10 scribed in paragraph (2)(A) made to a worker

11 may not exceed—

12 "(i) $12,000 per worker during the

13 eligibility period under paragraph (4)(A);

14 or

15 "(ii) the amount described in subpara-

16 graph (B) per worker during the eligibility

17 period under paragraph (4)(B).

18 "(B) AMOUNT DESCRIBED.—The amount

19 described in this subparagraph is the amount

20 equal to the product of—

21 "(i) $12,000, and

22 "(ii) the ratio of—

23 "(I) the total number of weeks in

24 the eligibility period under paragraph

25 (4)(B) with respect to the worker, to

"(II) 104 weeks.

"(6) CALCULATION OF AMOUNT OF PAYMENTS FOR CERTAIN WORKERS.—

"(A) IN GENERAL.—In the case of a worker described in paragraph (3)(B)(iii)(II), paragraph (2)(A) shall be applied by substituting the percentage described in subparagraph (B) for '50 percent'.

"(B) PERCENTAGE DESCRIBED.—The percentage described in this subparagraph is the percentage—

"(i) equal to ½ of the ratio of—

"(I) the number of weekly hours of employment of the worker referred to in paragraph (3)(B)(iii)(II), to

"(II) the number of weekly hours of employment of the worker at the time of separation, but

"(ii) in no case more than 50 percent.

"(7) LIMITATION ON OTHER BENEFITS.—A worker described in paragraph (3)(B) may not receive a trade readjustment allowance under part I of subchapter B pursuant to the certification described in paragraph (3)(A) during any week for which the

1 worker receives a payment described in paragraph

2 (2)(A).''; and

3   (3) in subsection (b)(2), by striking "subsection

4 (a)(3)(B)'' and inserting "subsection (a)(3)''.

5   (b) EXTENSION OF PROGRAM.—Section 246(b)(1) of

6 the Trade Act of 1974 (19 U.S.C. 2318(b)(1)) is amended

7 by striking "the date that is 5 years" and all that follows

8 through the end period and inserting "December 31,

9 2010.''.

10   (c) CLERICAL AMENDMENT.—The table of contents

11 of the Trade Act of 1974 is amended by striking the item

12 relating to section 246 and inserting the following:

"Sec. 246. Reemployment trade adjustment assistance program.".

13   **Subpart E—Other Matters**

14 **SEC. 1851. OFFICE OF TRADE ADJUSTMENT ASSISTANCE.**

15   (a) IN GENERAL.—Subchapter C of chapter 2 of title

16 II of the Trade Act of 1974 (19 U.S.C. 2311 et seq.) is

17 amended by adding at the end the following:

18 **"SEC. 249A. OFFICE OF TRADE ADJUSTMENT ASSISTANCE.**

19   "(a) ESTABLISHMENT.—There is established in the

20 Department of Labor an office to be known as the Office

21 of Trade Adjustment Assistance (in this section referred

22 to as the 'Office').

23   "(b) HEAD OF OFFICE.—The head of the Office shall

24 be an administrator, who shall report directly to the Dep-

25 uty Assistant Secretary for Employment and Training.

"(c) PRINCIPAL FUNCTIONS.—The principal functions of the administrator of the Office shall be—

"(1) to oversee and implement the administration of trade adjustment assistance program under
this chapter; and

"(2) to carry out functions delegated to the
Secretary of Labor under this chapter, including—

"(A) making determinations under section
223;

"(B) providing information under section
225 about trade adjustment assistance to workers and assisting such workers to prepare petitions or applications for program benefits;

"(C) providing assistance to employers of
groups of workers that have filed petitions
under section 221 in submitting information required by the Secretary relating to the petitions;

"(D) ensuring workers covered by a certification of eligibility under subchapter A receive
the employment and case management services
described in section 235;

"(E) ensuring that States fully comply
with agreements entered into under section
239;

1   "(F) advocating for workers applying for

2   benefits available under this chapter;

3   "(G) establishing and overseeing a hotline

4   that workers, employers, and other entities may

5   call to obtain information regarding eligibility

6   criteria, procedural requirements, and benefits

7   available under this chapter; and

8   "(H) carrying out such other duties with

9   respect to this chapter as the Secretary speci-

10   fies for purposes of this section.

11   "(d) ADMINISTRATION.—

12   "(1) DESIGNATION.—The administrator shall

13   designate an employee of the Department of Labor

14   with appropriate experience and expertise to carry

15   out the duties described in paragraph (2).

16   "(2) DUTIES.—The employee designated under

17   paragraph (1) shall—

18   "(A) receive complaints and requests for

19   assistance related to the trade adjustment as-

20   sistance program under this chapter;

21   "(B) resolve such complaints and requests

22   for assistance, in coordination with other em-

23   ployees of the Office;

1   "(C) compile basic information concerning

2   such complaints and requests for assistance;

3   and

4   "(D) carry out such other duties with re-

5   spect to this chapter as the Secretary specifies

6   for purposes of this section.".

7   (b) CLERICAL AMENDMENT.—The table of contents

8 of the Trade Act of 1974 is amended by inserting after

9 the item relating to section 249 the following:

"Sec. 249A. Office of Trade Adjustment Assistance.".

10 **SEC. 1852. ACCOUNTABILITY OF STATE AGENCIES; COLLEC-**

11   **TION AND PUBLICATION OF PROGRAM DATA;**

12   **AGREEMENTS WITH STATES.**

13   (a) IN GENERAL.—Section 239(a) of the Trade Act

14 of 1974 (19 U.S.C. 2311(a)) is amended—

15   (1) by amending clause (2) to read as follows:

16   "(2) in accordance with subsection (f), shall make

17   available to adversely affected workers and adversely

18   affected incumbent workers covered by a certifi-

19   cation under subchapter A the employment and case

20   management services described in section 235,"; and

21   (2) by striking "will" each place it appears and

22   inserting "shall".

23   (b) FORM AND MANNER OF DATA.—Section 239 of

24 the Trade Act of 1974 (19 U.S.C. 2311) is amended—

1   (1) by redesignating subsections (c) through (g)

2   as subsections (d) through (h), respectively; and

3   (2) by inserting after subsection (b) the fol-

4   lowing:

5   "(c) FORM AND MANNER OF DATA.—Each agree-

6   ment under this subchapter shall—

7   "(1) provide the Secretary with the authority to

8   collect any data the Secretary determines necessary

9   to meet the requirements of this chapter; and

10   "(2) specify the form and manner in which any

11 such data requested by the Secretary shall be re-

12 ported.".

13 (c) STATE ACTIVITIES.—Section 239(g) of the Trade

14 Act of 1974 (as redesignated) is amended—

15   (1) in paragraph (3), by striking "and" at the

16 end;

17   (2) by amending paragraph (4) to read as fol-

18 lows:

19   "(4) perform outreach to, intake of, and ori-

20 entation for adversely affected workers and adversely

21 affected incumbent workers covered by a certifi-

22 cation under subchapter A with respect to assistance

23 and benefits available under this chapter, and"; and

24   (3) by adding at the end the following:

1   "(5) make employment and case management

2   services described in section 235 available to ad-

3   versely affected workers and adversely affected in-

4   cumbent workers covered by a certification under

5   subchapter A and, if funds provided to carry out this

6   chapter are insufficient to make such services avail-

7   able, make arrangements to make such services

8   available through other Federal programs.".

9   (d) REPORTING REQUIREMENT.—Section 239(h) of

10 the Trade Act of 1974 (as redesignated) is amended by

11 striking "1998." and inserting "1998 (29 U.S.C. 2822(b))

12 and a description of the State's rapid response activities

13 under section 221(a)(2)(A).".

14   (e) CONTROL MEASURES.—Section 239 of the Trade

15 Act of 1974 (19 U.S.C. 2311), as amended, is further

16 amended by adding at the end the following:

17   "(i) CONTROL MEASURES.—

18   "(1) IN GENERAL.—The Secretary shall require

19   each cooperating State and cooperating State agency

20   to implement effective control measures and to effec-

21   tively oversee the operation and administration of

22   the trade adjustment assistance program under this

23   chapter, including by means of monitoring the oper-

24   ation of control measures to improve the accuracy

1 and timeliness of the data being collected and re-

2 ported.

3   "(2) DEFINITION.—For purposes of paragraph

4 (1), the term 'control measures' means measures

5 that—

6   "(A) are internal to a system used by a

7 State to collect data; and

8   "(B) are designed to ensure the accuracy

9 and verifiability of such data.

10 "(j) DATA REPORTING.—

11   "(1) IN GENERAL.—Any agreement entered

12 into under this section shall require the cooperating

13 State or cooperating State agency to report to the

14 Secretary on a quarterly basis comprehensive per-

15 formance accountability data, to consist of—

16   "(A) the core indicators of performance de-

17 scribed in paragraph (2)(A);

18   "(B) the additional indicators of perform-

19 ance described in paragraph (2)(B), if any; and

20   "(C) a description of efforts made to im-

21 prove outcomes for workers under the trade ad-

22 justment assistance program.

23   "(2) CORE INDICATORS DESCRIBED.—

24   "(A) IN GENERAL.—The core indicators of

25 performance described in this paragraph are—

1   "(i) the percentage of workers receiv-

2   ing benefits under this chapter who are

3   employed during the second calendar quar-

4   ter following the calendar quarter in which

5   the workers cease receiving such benefits;

6   "(ii) the percentage of such workers

7   who are employed in each of the third and

8   fourth calendar quarters following the cal-

9   endar quarter in which the workers cease

10   receiving such benefits; and

11   "(iii) the earnings of such workers in

12   each of the third and fourth calendar quar-

13   ters following the calendar quarter in

14   which the workers cease receiving such

15   benefits.

16   "(B) ADDITIONAL INDICATORS.—The Sec-

17   retary and a cooperating State or cooperating

18   State agency may agree upon additional indica-

19   tors of performance for the trade adjustment

20   assistance program under this chapter, as ap-

21   propriate.

22   "(3) STANDARDS WITH RESPECT TO RELI-

23   ABILITY OF DATA.—In preparing the quarterly re-

24   port required by paragraph (1), each cooperating

25   State or cooperating State agency shall establish

1   procedures that are consistent with guidelines to be

2   issued by the Secretary to ensure that the data re-

3   ported are valid and reliable.".

4 **SEC. 1853. VERIFICATION OF ELIGIBILITY FOR PROGRAM**

5   **BENEFITS.**

6   Section 239 of the Trade Act of 1974 (19 U.S.C.

7 2311), as amended, is further amended by adding at the

8 end the following:

9   "(k) VERIFICATION OF ELIGIBILITY FOR PROGRAM

10 BENEFITS.—

11   "(1) IN GENERAL.—An agreement under this

12   subchapter shall provide that the State shall periodi-

13   cally redetermine that a worker receiving benefits

14   under this subchapter who is not a citizen or na-

15   tional of the United States remains in a satisfactory

16   immigration status. Once satisfactory immigration

17   status has been initially verified through the immi-

18   gration status verification system described in sec-

19   tion 1137(d) of the Social Security Act (42 U.S.C.

20   1320b-7(d)) for purposes of establishing a worker's

21   eligibility for unemployment compensation, the State

22   shall reverify the worker's immigration status if the

23   documentation provided during initial verification

24   will expire during the period in which that worker is

25   potentially eligible to receive benefits under this sub-

1   chapter. The State shall conduct such redetermina-

2   tion in a timely manner, utilizing the immigration

3   status verification system described in section

4   1137(d) of the Social Security Act (42 U.S.C.

5   1320b-7(d)).

6   "(2) PROCEDURES.—The Secretary shall estab-

7   lish procedures to ensure the uniform application by

8   the States of the requirements of this subsection.".

9 **SEC. 1854. COLLECTION OF DATA AND REPORTS; INFORMA-**

10   **TION TO WORKERS.**

11   (a) IN GENERAL.—Subchapter C of chapter 2 of title

12 II of the Trade Act of 1974 (19 U.S.C. 2311 et seq.),

13 as amended, is further amended by adding at the end the

14 following:

15 **"SEC. 249B. COLLECTION AND PUBLICATION OF DATA AND**

16   **REPORTS; INFORMATION TO WORKERS.**

17   "(a) IN GENERAL.—Not later than 180 days after

18 the date of the enactment of this section, the Secretary

19 shall implement a system to collect and report the data

20 described in subsection (b), as well as any other informa-

21 tion that the Secretary considers appropriate to effectively

22 carry out this chapter.

23   "(b) DATA TO BE INCLUDED.—The system required

24 under subsection (a) shall include collection of and report-

25 ing on the following data for each fiscal year:

"(1) DATA ON PETITIONS FILED, CERTIFIED, AND DENIED.—

"(A) The number of petitions filed, certified, and denied under this chapter.

"(B) The number of workers covered by petitions filed, certified, and denied.

"(C) The number of petitions, classified by—

"(i) the basis for certification, including increased imports, shifts in production, and other bases of eligibility; and

"(ii) congressional district of the United States.

"(D) The average time for processing such petitions.

"(2) DATA ON BENEFITS RECEIVED.—

"(A) The number of workers receiving benefits under this chapter.

"(B) The number of workers receiving each type of benefit, including training, trade readjustment allowances, employment and case management services, and relocation and job search allowances, and, to the extent feasible, credits for health insurance costs under section 35 of the Internal Revenue Code of 1986.

1   "(C) The average time during which such

2   workers receive each such type of benefit.

3   "(3) DATA ON TRAINING.—

4   "(A) The number of workers enrolled in

5   training approved under section 236, classified

6   by major types of training, including classroom

7   training, training through distance learning, on-

8   the-job training, and customized training.

9   "(B) The number of workers enrolled in

10   full-time training and part-time training.

11   "(C) The average duration of training.

12   "(D) The number of training waivers

13   granted under section 231(c), classified by type

14   of waiver.

15   "(E) The number of workers who complete

16   training and the duration of such training.

17   "(F) The number of workers who do not

18   complete training.

19   "(4) DATA ON OUTCOMES.—

20   "(A) A summary of the quarterly reports

21   required under section 239(j).

22   "(B) The sectors in which workers are em-

23   ployed after receiving benefits under this chap-

24   ter.

1   "(5) DATA ON RAPID RESPONSE ACTIVITIES.—

2   Whether rapid response activities were provided with

3   respect to each petition filed under section 221.

4   "(c) CLASSIFICATION OF DATA.—To the extent pos-

5 sible, in collecting and reporting the data described in sub-

6 section (b), the Secretary shall classify the data by indus-

7 try, State, and national totals.

8   "(d) REPORT.—Not later than December 15 of each

9 year, the Secretary shall submit to the Committee on Fi-

10 nance of the Senate and the Committee on Ways and

11 Means of the House of Representatives a report that

12 includes—

13   "(1) a summary of the information collected

14   under this section for the preceding fiscal year;

15   "(2) information on the distribution of funds to

16   each State pursuant to section 236(a)(2); and

17   "(3) any recommendations of the Secretary

18   with respect to changes in eligibility requirements,

19   benefits, or training funding under this chapter

20   based on the data collected under this section.

21   "(e) AVAILABILITY OF DATA.—

22   "(1) IN GENERAL.—The Secretary shall make

23   available to the public, by publishing on the website

24   of the Department of Labor and by other means, as

25   appropriate—

1   "(A) the report required under subsection

2   (d);

3   "(B) the data collected under this section,

4   in a searchable format; and

5   "(C) a list of cooperating States and co-

6   operating State agencies that failed to submit

7   the data required by this section to the Sec-

8   retary in a timely manner.

9   "(2) UPDATES.—The Secretary shall update

10 the data under paragraph (1) on a quarterly basis.".

11   (b) CLERICAL AMENDMENT.—The table of contents

12 of the Trade Act of 1974 is amended by inserting after

13 the item relating to section 249A the following:

> "Sec. 249B. Collection and publication of data and reports; information to workers.".

14   (c) EFFECTIVE DATE.—The amendments made by

15 this section shall take effect on the date of the enactment

16 of this Act.

17 **SEC. 1855. FRAUD AND RECOVERY OF OVERPAYMENTS.**

18   Section 243(a)(1) of the Trade Act of 1974 (19

19 U.S.C. 2315(a)(1)) is amended—

20   (1) in the matter preceding subparagraph (A)—

21   (A) by striking "may waive" and inserting

22   "shall waive"; and

23   (B) by striking ", in accordance with

24   guidelines prescribed by the Secretary,"; and

1   (2) in subparagraph (B), by striking "would be

2   contrary to equity and good conscience" and insert-

3   ing "would cause a financial hardship for the indi-

4   vidual (or the individual's household, if applicable)

5   when taking into consideration the income and re-

6   sources reasonably available to the individual (or

7   household) and other ordinary living expenses of the

8   individual (or household)".

9 **SEC. 1856. SENSE OF CONGRESS ON APPLICATION OF**

10   **TRADE ADJUSTMENT ASSISTANCE.**

11   (a) IN GENERAL.—Chapter 5 of title II of the Trade

12 Act of 1974 (19 U.S.C. 2391 et seq.) is amended by add-

13 ing at the end the following:

14 **"SEC. 288. SENSE OF CONGRESS.**

15   "It is the sense of Congress that the Secretaries of

16 Labor, Commerce, and Agriculture should apply the provi-

17 sions of chapter 2 (relating to adjustment assistance for

18 workers), chapter 3 (relating to adjustment assistance for

19 firms), chapter 4 (relating to adjustment assistance for

20 communities), and chapter 6 (relating to adjustment as-

21 sistance for farmers), respectively, with the utmost regard

22 for the interests of workers, firms, communities, and farm-

23 ers petitioning for benefits under such chapters.".

1   (b) CLERICAL AMENDMENT.—The table of contents

2 of the Trade Act of 1974 is amended by inserting after

3 the item relating to section 287 the following:

"Sec. 288. Sense of Congress.".

4 SEC. 1857. CONSULTATIONS IN PROMULGATION OF REGU-

5   LATIONS.

6   Section 248 of the Trade Act of 1974 (19 U.S.C.

7 2320) is amended—

8   (1) by striking "The Secretary shall" and in-

9   serting the following:

10   "(a) IN GENERAL.—The Secretary shall"; and

11   (2) by adding at the end the following:

12   "(b) CONSULTATIONS.—Not later than 90 days be-

13 fore issuing a regulation under subsection (a), the Sec-

14 retary shall consult with the Committee on Finance of the

15 Senate and the Committee on Ways and Means of the

16 House of Representatives with respect to the regulation.".

17 SEC. 1858. TECHNICAL CORRECTIONS.

18   (a) DETERMINATIONS BY SECRETARY OF LABOR.—

19 Section 223(c) of the Trade Act of 1974 (19 U.S.C.

20 2273(c)) is amended by striking "his determination" and

21 inserting "a determination".

22   (b) QUALIFYING REQUIREMENTS FOR WORKERS.—

23 Section 231(a) of the Trade Act of 1974 (19 U.S.C.

24 2291(a)) is amended—

25   (1) in paragraph (1)—

1   (A) in the matter preceding subparagraph

2   (A), by striking "his application" and inserting

3   "the worker's application"; and

4   (B) in subparagraph (A), by striking "he

5   is covered" and inserting "the worker is cov-

6   ered";

7   (2) in paragraph (2)—

8   (A) in subparagraph (A), by striking the

9   period and inserting a comma; and

10   (B) in subparagraph (D), by striking "5

11   U.S.C. 8521(a)(1)" and inserting "section

12   8521(a)(1) of title 5, United States Code"; and

13   (3) in paragraph (3)—

14   (A) by striking "he" each place it appears

15   and inserting "the worker"; and

16   (B) in subparagraph (C), by striking

17   "him" and inserting "the worker".

18   (c) SUBPOENA POWER.—Section 249 of the Trade

19 Act of 1974 (19 U.S.C. 2321) is amended—

20   (1) in the section heading, by striking "**SUB-**

21   **PENA**" and inserting "**SUBPOENA**";

22   (2) by striking "subpena" and inserting "sub-

23   poena" each place it appears; and

24   (3) in subsection (a), by striking "him" and in-

25   serting "the Secretary".

1   (d) CLERICAL AMENDMENT.—The table of contents

2 of the Trade Act of 1974 is amended by striking the item

3 relating to section 249 and inserting the following:

"Sec. 249. Subpoena power.".

4 PART II—TRADE ADJUSTMENT ASSISTANCE FOR

5 FIRMS

6 SEC. 1861. EXPANSION TO SERVICE SECTOR FIRMS.

7   (a) IN GENERAL.—Section 251 of the Trade Act of

8 1974 (19 U.S.C. 2341) is amended by inserting "or serv-

9 ice sector firm" after "agricultural firm" each place it ap-

10 pears.

11   (b) DEFINITION OF SERVICE SECTOR FIRM.—Sec-

12 tion 261 of the Trade Act of 1974 (19 U.S.C. 2351) is

13 amended—

14   (1) by striking "chapter," and inserting "chap-

15   ter:";

16   (2) by striking "the term 'firm'" and inserting

17   the following:

18   "(1) FIRM.—The term 'firm'"; and

19   (3) by adding at the end the following:

20   "(2) SERVICE SECTOR FIRM.—The term 'service

21   sector firm' means a firm engaged in the business

22   of supplying services.".

23   (c) CONFORMING AMENDMENTS.—

24   (1) Section 251(c)(1)(C) of the Trade Act of

25   1974 (19 U.S.C. 2341(c)(1)(C)) is amended—

1   (A) by inserting "or services" after "arti-

2 cles" the first place it appears; and

3   (B) by inserting "or services which are

4 supplied" after "produced".

5   (2) Section 251(c)(2)(B)(ii) of such Act is

6 amended to read as follows:

7   "(ii) Any firm that engages in exploration or

8 drilling for oil or natural gas, or otherwise produces

9 oil or natural gas, shall be considered to be pro-

10 ducing articles directly competitive with imports of

11 oil and with imports of natural gas.".

12 **SEC. 1862. MODIFICATION OF REQUIREMENTS FOR CER-**

13   **TIFICATION.**

14 Section 251(c)(1)(B) of the Trade Act of 1974 (19

15 U.S.C. 2341(c)(1)(B)) is amended to read as follows:

16   "(B) that—

17   "(i) sales or production, or both, of the

18   firm have decreased absolutely,

19   "(ii) sales or production, or both, of an ar-

20   ticle or service that accounted for not less than

21   25 percent of the total sales or production of

22   the firm during the 12-month period preceding

23   the most recent 12-month period for which date

24   are available have decreased absolutely,

1   "(iii) sales or production, or both, of the

2   firm during the most recent 12-month period

3   for which data are available have decreased

4   compared to—

5   "(I) the average annual sales or pro-

6   duction for the firm during the 24-month

7   period preceding that 12-month period, or

8   "(II) the average annual sales or pro-

9   duction for the firm during the 36-month

10   period preceding that 12-month period,

11   and

12   "(iv) sales or production, or both, of an ar-

13   ticle or service that accounted for not less than

14   25 percent of the total sales or production of

15   the firm during the most recent 12-month pe-

16   riod for which data are available have decreased

17   compared to—

18   "(I) the average annual sales or pro-

19   duction for the article or service during the

20   24-month period preceding that 12-month

21   period, or

22   "(II) the average annual sales or pro-

23   duction for the article or service during the

24   36-month period preceding that 12-month

25   period, and".

SEC. 1863. BASIS FOR DETERMINATIONS.

Section 251 of the Trade Act of 1974 (19 U.S.C. 2341), as amended, is further amended by adding at the end the following:

"(e) BASIS FOR SECRETARY'S DETERMINATIONS.— For purposes of subsection (c)(1)(C), the Secretary may determine that there are increased imports of like or directly competitive articles or services, if customers accounting for a significant percentage of the decrease in the sales or production of the firm certify to the Secretary that such customers have increased their imports of such articles or services from a foreign country, either absolutely or relative to their acquisition of such articles or services from suppliers located in the United States.

"(f) NOTIFICATION TO FIRMS OF AVAILABILITY OF BENEFITS.—Upon receiving notice from the Secretary of Labor under section 225 of the identity of a firm that is covered by a certification issued under section 223, the Secretary of Commerce shall notify the firm of the availability of adjustment assistance under this chapter.".

SEC. 1864. OVERSIGHT AND ADMINISTRATION; AUTHORIZATION OF APPROPRIATIONS.

(a) IN GENERAL.—Chapter 3 of title II of the Trade Act of 1974 (19 U.S.C. 2341 et seq.) is amended—

(1) by striking sections 254, 255, 256, and 257;

1   (2) by redesignating sections 258, 259, 260,

2 261, 262, 264, and 265, as sections 256, 257, 258,

3 259, 260, 261, and 262, respectively; and

4   (3) by inserting after section 253 the following:

5 **"SEC. 254. OVERSIGHT AND ADMINISTRATION.**

6   "(a) IN GENERAL.—The Secretary shall, to such ex-

7 tent and in such amounts as are provided in appropria-

8 tions Acts, provide grants to intermediary organizations

9 (referred to in section 253(b)(1)) throughout the United

10 States pursuant to agreements with such intermediary or-

11 ganizations. Each such agreement shall require the inter-

12 mediary organization to provide benefits to firms certified

13 under section 251. The Secretary shall, to the maximum

14 extent practicable, provide by October 1, 2010, that con-

15 tracts entered into with intermediary organizations be for

16 a 12-month period and that all such contracts have the

17 same beginning date and the same ending date.

18   "(b) DISTRIBUTION OF FUNDS.—

19   "(1) IN GENERAL.—Not later than 90 days

20   after the date of the enactment of this subsection,

21   the Secretary shall develop a methodology for the

22   distribution of funds among the intermediary organi-

23   zations described in subsection (a).

24   "(2) PROMPT INITIAL DISTRIBUTION.—The

25   methodology described in paragraph (1) shall ensure

1   the prompt initial distribution of funds and establish

2   additional criteria governing the apportionment and

3   distribution of the remainder of such funds among

4   the intermediary organizations.

5   "(3) CRITERIA.—The methodology described in

6   paragraph (1) shall include criteria based on the

7   data in the annual report on the trade adjustment

8   assistance for firms program described in section

9   1866 of the Trade and Globalization Adjustment As-

10   sistance Act of 2009.

11   "(c) REQUIREMENTS FOR CONTRACTS.—An agree-

12   ment with an intermediary organization described in sub-

13   section (a) shall require the intermediary organization to

14   contract for the supply of services to carry out grants

15   under this chapter in accordance with terms and condi-

16   tions that are consistent with guidelines established by the

17   Secretary.

18   "(d) CONSULTATIONS.—

19   "(1) CONSULTATIONS REGARDING METHOD-

20   OLOGY.—The Secretary shall consult with the Com-

21   mittee on Finance of the Senate and the Committee

22   on Ways and Means of the House of

23   Representatives—

1   "(A) not less than 30 days before final-

2   izing the methodology described in subsection

3   (b); and

4   "(B) not less than 60 days before adopting

5   any changes to such methodology.

6   "(2) CONSULTATIONS REGARDING GUIDE-

7   LINES.—The Secretary shall consult with the Com-

8   mittee on Finance of the Senate and the Committee

9   on Ways and Means of the House of Representatives

10   not less than 60 days before finalizing the guidelines

11   described in subsection (c) or adopting any subse-

12   quent changes to such guidelines.

13   **"SEC. 255. AUTHORIZATION OF APPROPRIATIONS.**

14   "(a) IN GENERAL.—There are authorized to be ap-

15 propriated to the Secretary $50,000,000 for each of the

16 fiscal years 2009 through 2010, and $12,501,000 for the

17 period beginning October 1, 2010, and ending December

18 31, 2010, to carry out the provisions of this chapter.

19 Amounts appropriated pursuant to this subsection shall—

20   "(1) be available to provide adjustment assist-

21   ance to firms that file a petition for such assistance

22   pursuant to this chapter on or before December 31,

23   2010; and

24   "(2) otherwise remain available until expended.

1   "(b) PERSONNEL.—Of the amounts appropriated

2 pursuant to this section for each fiscal year, $350,000

3 shall be available for full-time positions in the Department

4 of Commerce to administer the provisions of this chapter.

5 Of such funds the Secretary shall make available to the

6 Economic Development Administration such sums as may

7 be necessary to establish the position of Director of Ad-

8 justment Assistance for Firms and such other full-time po-

9 sitions as may be appropriate to administer the provisions

10 of this chapter.".

11   (b) RESIDUAL AUTHORITY.—The Secretary of Com-

12 merce shall have the authority to modify, terminate, re-

13 solve, liquidate, or take any other action with respect to

14 a loan, guarantee, contract, or any other financial assist-

15 ance that was extended under section 254, 255, 256, or

16 257 of the Trade Act of 1974 (19 U.S.C. 2344, 2345,

17 2346, and 2347), as in effect on the day before the effec-

18 tive date set forth in section 1891.

19   (c) CONFORMING AMENDMENTS.—

20   (1) Section 256 of the Trade Act of 1974, as

21   redesignated by subsection (a) of this section, is

22   amended by striking subsection (d).

23   (2) Section 258 of the Trade Act of 1974, as

24   redesignated by subsection (a) of this section, is

25   amended—

1   (A) in the first sentence, by striking "and

2 financial"; and

3   (B) in the last sentence—

4   (i) by striking "sections 253 and 254"

5 and inserting "section 253"; and

6   (ii) by striking "title 28 of the United

7 States Code" and inserting "title 28,

8 United States Code".

9 (d) CLERICAL AMENDMENTS.—The table of contents

10 of the Trade Act of 1974 is amended by striking the items

11 relating to sections 254, 255, 256, 257, 258, 259, 260,

12 261, 262, 264, and 265, and inserting the following:

"Sec. 254. Oversight and administration.
"Sec. 255. Authorization of appropriations.
"Sec. 256. Protective provisions.
"Sec. 257. Penalties.
"Sec. 258. Civil actions.
"Sec. 259. Definitions.
"Sec. 260. Regulations.
"Sec. 261. Study by Secretary of Commerce when International Trade Commission begins investigation; action where there is affirmative finding.
"Sec. 262. Assistance to industries.".

13 (e) EFFECTIVE DATE.—This section and the amend-

14 ments made by this section shall take effect upon the expi-

15 ration of the 90-day period beginning on the date of the

16 enactment of this Act, except that subsections (b) and (d)

17 of section 254 of the Trade Act of 1974 (as added by sub-

18 section (a) of this section) shall take effect on such date

19 of enactment.

1 **SEC. 1865. INCREASED PENALTIES FOR FALSE STATE-**
2 **MENTS.**

3   Section 257 of the Trade Act of 1974, as redesig-
4 nated by section 1864(a), is amended to read as follows:

5 **"SEC. 257. PENALTIES.**

6   "Any person who—

7   "(1) makes a false statement of a material fact
8   knowing it to be false, or knowingly fails to disclose
9   a material fact, or willfully overvalues any security,
10   for the purpose of influencing in any way a deter-
11   mination under this chapter, or for the purpose of
12   obtaining money, property, or anything of value
13   under this chapter, or

14   "(2) makes a false statement of a material fact
15   knowing it to be false, or knowingly fails to disclose
16   a material fact, when providing information to the
17   Secretary during an investigation of a petition under
18   this chapter,

19 shall be imprisoned for not more than 2 years, or fined
20 under title 18, United States Code, or both.".

21 **SEC. 1866. ANNUAL REPORT ON TRADE ADJUSTMENT AS-**
22 **SISTANCE FOR FIRMS.**

23   (a) IN GENERAL.—Not later than December 15,
24 2009, and each year thereafter, the Secretary of Com-
25 merce shall prepare a report containing data regarding the
26 trade adjustment assistance for firms program provided

1 for in chapter 3 of title II of the Trade Act of 1974 (19

2 U.S.C. 2341 et seq.) for the preceding fiscal year. The

3 data shall include the following:

4   (1) The number of firms that inquired about

5   the program.

6   (2) The number of petitions filed under section

7   251.

8   (3) The number of petitions certified and de-

9   nied.

10   (4) The average time for processing petitions.

11   (5) The number of petitions filed and firms cer-

12   tified for each congressional district of the United

13   States.

14   (6) The number of firms that received assist-

15   ance in preparing their petitions.

16   (7) The number of firms that received assist-

17   ance developing business recovery plans.

18   (8) The number of business recovery plans ap-

19   proved and denied by the Secretary of Commerce.

20   (9) Sales, employment, and productivity at each

21   firm participating in the program at the time of cer-

22   tification.

23   (10) Sales, employment, and productivity at

24   each firm upon completion of the program and each

25   year for the 2-year period following completion.

1   (11) The financial assistance received by each

2 firm participating in the program.

3   (12) The financial contribution made by each

4 firm participating in the program.

5   (13) The types of technical assistance included

6 in the business recovery plans of firms participating

7 in the program.

8   (14) The number of firms leaving the program

9 before completing the project or projects in their

10 business recovery plans and the reason the project

11 was not completed.

12 (b) CLASSIFICATION OF DATA.—To the extent pos-

13 sible, in collecting and reporting the data described in sub-

14 section (a), the Secretary shall classify the data by inter-

15 mediary organization, State, and national totals.

16 (c) REPORT TO CONGRESS; PUBLICATION.—The Sec-

17 retary of Commerce shall—

18   (1) submit the report described in subsection

19 (a) to the Committee on Finance of the Senate and

20 the Committee on Ways and Means of the House of

21 Representatives; and

22   (2) publish the report in the Federal Register

23 and on the website of the Department of Commerce.

24 (d) PROTECTION OF CONFIDENTIAL INFORMA-

25 TION.—The Secretary of Commerce may not release infor-

1 mation described in subsection (a) that the Secretary con-
2 siders to be confidential business information unless the
3 person submitting the confidential business information
4 had notice, at the time of submission, that such informa-
5 tion would be released by the Secretary, or such person
6 subsequently consents to the release of the information.
7 Nothing in this subsection shall be construed to prohibit
8 the Secretary from providing such confidential business in-
9 formation to a court in camera or to another party under
10 a protective order issued by a court.

11 **SEC. 1867. TECHNICAL CORRECTIONS.**

12   (a) IN GENERAL.—Section 251 of the Trade Act of
13 1974 (19 U.S.C. 2341), as amended, is further
14 amended—

15   (1) in subsection (a), by striking "he has" and
16   inserting "the Secretary has"; and

17   (2) in subsection (d), by striking "60 days" and
18   inserting "40 days".

19   (b) TECHNICAL ASSISTANCE.—Section 253(a)(3) of
20 the Trade Act of 1974 (19 U.S.C. 2343(a)(3)) is amended
21 by striking "of a certified firm" and inserting "to a cer-
22 tified firm".

1 **PART III—TRADE ADJUSTMENT ASSISTANCE FOR**

2 **COMMUNITIES**

3 SEC. 1871. PURPOSE.

4   The purpose of the amendments made by this part

5 is to assist communities impacted by trade with economic

6 adjustment through the coordination of Federal, State,

7 and local resources, the creation of community-based de-

8 velopment strategies, and the development and provision

9 of programs that meet the training needs of workers cov-

10 ered by certifications under section 223.

11 SEC. 1872. TRADE ADJUSTMENT ASSISTANCE FOR COMMU-

12   NITIES.

13   (a) IN GENERAL.—Chapter 4 of title II of the Trade

14 Act of 1974 (19 U.S.C. 2371 et seq.) is amended to read

15 as follows:

16 **"CHAPTER 4—TRADE ADJUSTMENT**

17 **ASSISTANCE FOR COMMUNITIES**

18 **"Subchapter A—Trade Adjustment Assistance**

19 **for Communities**

20 "SEC. 271. DEFINITIONS.

21   "In this subchapter:

22   "(1) AGRICULTURAL COMMODITY PRODUCER.—

23   The term 'agricultural commodity producer' has the

24   meaning given that term in section 291.

25   "(2) COMMUNITY.—The term 'community'

26   means a city, county, or other political subdivision of

1   a State or a consortium of political subdivisions of

2   a State.

3   "(3) COMMUNITY IMPACTED BY TRADE.—The

4   term 'community impacted by trade' means a com-

5   munity described in section 273(b)(2).

6   "(4) ELIGIBLE COMMUNITY.—The term 'eligible

7   community' means a community that the Secretary

8   has determined under section 273(b)(1) is eligible to

9   apply for assistance under this subchapter.

10   "(5) SECRETARY.—The term 'Secretary' means

11   the Secretary of Commerce.

12   **"SEC. 272. ESTABLISHMENT OF TRADE ADJUSTMENT AS-**

13   **SISTANCE FOR COMMUNITIES PROGRAM.**

14   "Not later than August 1, 2009, the Secretary shall

15 establish a trade adjustment assistance for communities

16 program at the Department of Commerce under which the

17 Secretary shall—

18   "(1) provide technical assistance under section

19   274 to communities impacted by trade to facilitate

20   the economic adjustment of those communities; and

21   "(2) award grants to communities impacted by

22   trade to carry out strategic plans developed under

23   section 276.

24   **"SEC. 273. ELIGIBILITY; NOTIFICATION.**

25   "(a) PETITION.—

1   "(1) IN GENERAL.—A community may submit

2 a petition to the Secretary for an affirmative deter-

3 mination under subsection (b)(1) that the commu-

4 nity is eligible to apply for assistance under this sub-

5 chapter if—

6   "(A) on or after August 1, 2009, one or

7   more certifications described in subsection

8   (b)(3) are made with respect to the community;

9   and

10   "(B) the community submits the petition

11   not later than 180 days after the date of the

12   most recent certification.

13   "(2) SPECIAL RULE WITH RESPECT TO CER-

14 TAIN COMMUNITIES.—In the case of a community

15 with respect to which one or more certifications de-

16 scribed in subsection (b)(3) were made on or after

17 January 1, 2007, and before August 1, 2009, the

18 community may submit not later than February 1,

19 2010, a petition to the Secretary for an affirmative

20 determination under subsection (b)(1).

21 "(b) AFFIRMATIVE DETERMINATION.—

22   "(1) IN GENERAL.—The Secretary shall make

23 an affirmative determination that a community is el-

24 igible to apply for assistance under this subchapter

1   if the Secretary determines that the community is a

2   community impacted by trade.

3   "(2) COMMUNITY IMPACTED BY TRADE.—A

4   community is a community impacted by trade if—

5   "(A) one or more certifications described

6   in paragraph (3) are made with respect to the

7   community; and

8   "(B) the Secretary determines that the

9   community is significantly affected by the

10   threat to, or the loss of, jobs associated with

11   any such certification.

12   "(3) CERTIFICATION DESCRIBED.—A certifi-

13   cation described in this paragraph is a

14   certification—

15   "(A) by the Secretary of Labor that a

16   group of workers in the community is eligible to

17   apply for assistance under section 223;

18   "(B) by the Secretary of Commerce that a

19   firm located in the community is eligible to

20   apply for adjustment assistance under section

21   251; or

22   "(C) by the Secretary of Agriculture that

23   a group of agricultural commodity producers in

24   the community is eligible to apply for adjust-

25   ment assistance under section 293.

1   "(c) NOTIFICATIONS.—

2   "(1) NOTIFICATION TO THE GOVERNOR.—The

3 Governor of a State shall be notified promptly—

4   "(A) by the Secretary of Labor, upon mak-

5   ing a determination that a group of workers in

6   the State is eligible for assistance under section

7   223;

8   "(B) by the Secretary of Commerce, upon

9   making a determination that a firm in the

10   State is eligible for assistance under section

11   251; and

12   "(C) by the Secretary of Agriculture, upon

13   making a determination that a group of agricul-

14   tural commodity producers in the State is eligi-

15   ble for assistance under section 293.

16   "(2) NOTIFICATION TO COMMUNITY.—Upon

17 making an affirmative determination under sub-

18 section (b)(1) that a community is eligible to apply

19 for assistance under this subchapter, the Secretary

20 shall promptly notify the community and the Gov-

21 ernor of the State in which the community is

22 located—

23   "(A) of the affirmative determination;

24   "(B) of the applicable provisions of this

25   subchapter; and

1   "(C) of the means for obtaining assistance

2   under this subchapter and other appropriate

3   economic assistance that may be available to

4   the community.

5 **"SEC. 274. TECHNICAL ASSISTANCE.**

6   "(a) IN GENERAL.—The Secretary shall provide com-

7 prehensive technical assistance to an eligible community

8 to assist the community to—

9   "(1) diversify and strengthen the economy in

10   the community;

11   "(2) identify significant impediments to eco-

12   nomic development that result from the impact of

13   trade on the community; and

14   "(3) develop a strategic plan under section 276

15   to address economic adjustment and workforce dis-

16   location in the community, including unemployment

17   among agricultural commodity producers.

18   "(b) COORDINATION OF FEDERAL RESPONSE.—The

19 Secretary shall coordinate the Federal response to an eligi-

20 ble community by—

21   "(1) identifying Federal, State, and local re-

22   sources that are available to assist the community in

23   responding to economic distress; and

24   "(2) assisting the community in accessing avail-

25   able Federal assistance and ensuring that such as-

1   sistance is provided in a targeted, integrated man-

2   ner.

3   "(c) INTERAGENCY COMMUNITY ASSISTANCE WORK-

4   ING GROUP.—

5   "(1) IN GENERAL.—The Secretary shall estab-

6   lish an interagency Community Assistance Working

7   Group, to be chaired by the Secretary or the Sec-

8   retary's designee, which shall assist the Secretary

9   with the coordination of the Federal response pursu-

10 ant to subsection (b).

11   "(2) MEMBERSHIP.—The Working Group shall

12 consist of representatives of any Federal department

13 or agency with responsibility for providing economic

14 adjustment assistance, including the Department of

15 Agriculture, the Department of Defense, the Depart-

16 ment of Education, the Department of Labor, the

17 Department of Housing and Urban Development,

18 the Department of Health and Human Services, the

19 Small Business Administration, the Department of

20 the Treasury, and any other Federal, State, or re-

21 gional public department or agency the Secretary de-

22 termines to be appropriate.

23 **"SEC. 275. GRANTS FOR ELIGIBLE COMMUNITIES.**

24   "(a) IN GENERAL.—The Secretary may award a

25 grant under this section to an eligible community to assist

1 the community in carrying out any project or program

2 that is included in a strategic plan developed by the com-

3 munity under section 276.

4   "(b) APPLICATION.—

5   "(1) IN GENERAL.—An eligible community

6   seeking to receive a grant under this section shall

7   submit a grant application to the Secretary that

8   contains—

9   "(A) the strategic plan developed by the

10   community under section 276(a)(1)(A) and ap-

11   proved by the Secretary under section

12   276(a)(1)(B); and

13   "(B) a description of the project or pro-

14   gram included in the strategic plan with respect

15   to which the community seeks the grant.

16   "(2) COORDINATION AMONG GRANT PRO-

17 GRAMS.—If an entity in an eligible community is

18   seeking or plans to seek a Community College and

19   Career Training Grant under section 278 or a Sec-

20   tor Partnership Grant under section 279A while the

21   eligible community is seeking a grant under this sec-

22   tion, the eligible community shall include in the

23   grant application a description of how the eligible

24   community will integrate any projects or programs

25   carried out using a grant under this section with any

1   projects or programs that may be carried out using

2   such other grants.

3   "(c) LIMITATION.—An eligible community may not

4 be awarded more than $5,000,000 under this section.

5   "(d) COST-SHARING.—

6   "(1) FEDERAL SHARE.—The Federal share of a

7   project or program for which a grant is awarded

8   under this section may not exceed 95 percent of the

9   cost of such project or program.

10   "(2) COMMUNITY SHARE.—The Secretary shall

11   require, as a condition of awarding a grant to an eli-

12   gible community under this section, that the eligible

13   community contribute not less than an amount equal

14   to 5 percent of the amount of the grant toward the

15   cost of the project or program for which the grant

16   is awarded.

17   "(e) GRANTS TO SMALL- AND MEDIUM-SIZED COM-

18 MUNITIES.—The Secretary shall give priority to grant ap-

19 plications submitted under this section by eligible commu-

20 nities that are small- and medium-sized communities.

21   "(f) ANNUAL REPORT.—Not later than December 15

22 in each of the calendar years 2009 through 2011, the Sec-

23 retary shall submit to the Committee on Finance of the

24 Senate and the Committee on Ways and Means of the

25 House of Representatives a report—

1   "(1) describing each grant awarded under this
2 section during the preceding fiscal year; and

3   "(2) assessing the impact on the eligible com-
4 munity of each such grant awarded in a fiscal year
5 before the fiscal year referred to in paragraph (1).

6 **"SEC. 276. STRATEGIC PLANS.**

7 "(a) IN GENERAL.—

8   "(1) DEVELOPMENT.—An eligible community
9 that intends to apply for a grant under section 275
10 shall—

11   "(A) develop a strategic plan for the com-
12   munity's economic adjustment to the impact of
13   trade; and

14   "(B) submit the plan to the Secretary for
15   evaluation and approval.

16   "(2) INVOLVEMENT OF PRIVATE AND PUBLIC
17 ENTITIES.—

18   "(A) IN GENERAL.—To the extent prac-
19   ticable, an eligible community shall consult with
20   entities described in subparagraph (B) in devel-
21   oping a strategic plan under paragraph (1).

22   "(B) ENTITIES DESCRIBED.—Entities de-
23   scribed in this subparagraph are public and pri-
24   vate entities within the eligible community,
25   including—

1   "(i) local, county, or State govern-

2   ment agencies serving the community;

3   "(ii) firms, including small- and me-

4   dium-sized firms, within the community;

5   "(iii) local workforce investment

6   boards established under section 117 of the

7   Workforce Investment Act of 1998 (29

8   U.S.C. 2832);

9   "(iv) labor organizations, including

10   State labor federations and labor-manage-

11   ment initiatives, representing workers in

12   the community; and

13   "(v) educational institutions, local

14   educational agencies, or other training pro-

15   viders serving the community.

16 "(b) CONTENTS.—The strategic plan shall, at a min-

17 imum, contain the following:

18   "(1) A description and analysis of the capacity

19 of the eligible community to achieve economic ad-

20 justment to the impact of trade.

21   "(2) An analysis of the economic development

22 challenges and opportunities facing the community

23 as well as the strengths and weaknesses of the econ-

24 omy of the community.

1   "(3) An assessment of the commitment of the

2 eligible community to the strategic plan over the

3 long term and the participation and input of mem-

4 bers of the community affected by economic disloca-

5 tion.

6   "(4) A description of the role and the participa-

7 tion of the entities described in subsection (a)(2)(B)

8 in developing the strategic plan.

9   "(5) A description of the projects to be under-

10 taken by the eligible community under the strategic

11 plan.

12   "(6) A description of how the strategic plan

13 and the projects to be undertaken by the eligible

14 community will facilitate the community's economic

15 adjustment.

16   "(7) A description of the educational and train-

17 ing programs available to workers in the eligible

18 community and the future employment needs of the

19 community.

20   "(8) An assessment of the cost of implementing

21 the strategic plan, the timing of funding required by

22 the eligible community to implement the strategic

23 plan, and the method of financing to be used to im-

24 plement the strategic plan.

"(9) A strategy for continuing the economic adjustment of the eligible community after the completion of the projects described in paragraph (5).

"(c) GRANTS TO DEVELOP STRATEGIC PLANS.—

"(1) IN GENERAL.—The Secretary, upon receipt of an application from an eligible community, may award a grant to the community to assist the community in developing a strategic plan under subsection (a)(1). A grant awarded under this paragraph shall not exceed 75 percent of the cost of developing the strategic plan.

"(2) FUNDS TO BE USED.—Of the funds appropriated pursuant to section 277(c), the Secretary may make available not more than $25,000,000 for each of the fiscal years 2009 and 2010, and $6,250,000 for the period beginning October 1, 2010, and ending December 31, 2010, to provide grants to eligible communities under paragraph (1).

"SEC. 277. GENERAL PROVISIONS.

"(a) REGULATIONS.—

"(1) IN GENERAL.—The Secretary shall prescribe such regulations as are necessary to carry out the provisions of this subchapter, including—

1   "(A) establishing specific guidelines for the

2   submission and evaluation of strategic plans

3   under section 276;

4   "(B) establishing specific guidelines for the

5   submission and evaluation of grant applications

6   under section 275; and

7   "(C) administering the grant programs es-

8   tablished under sections 275 and 276.

9   "(2) CONSULTATIONS.—The Secretary shall

10   consult with the Committee on Finance of the Sen-

11   ate and the Committee on Ways and Means of the

12   House of Representatives not less than 90 days

13   prior to promulgating any final rule or regulation

14   pursuant to paragraph (1).

15   "(b) PERSONNEL.—The Secretary shall designate

16 such staff as may be necessary to carry out the respon-

17 sibilities described in this subchapter.

18   "(c) AUTHORIZATION OF APPROPRIATIONS.—

19   "(1) IN GENERAL.—There are authorized to be

20   appropriated to the Secretary $150,000,000 for each

21   of the fiscal years 2009 and 2010, and $37,500,000

22   for the period beginning October 1, 2010, and end-

23   ing December 31, 2010, to carry out this sub-

24   chapter.

1   "(2) AVAILABILITY.—Amounts appropriated

2 pursuant to this subchapter—

3   "(A) shall be available to provide adjust-

4 ment assistance to communities that have been

5 approved for assistance pursuant to this chap-

6 ter on or before December 31, 2010; and

7   "(B) shall otherwise remain available until

8 expended.

9   "(3) SUPPLEMENT NOT SUPPLANT.—Funds ap-

10 propriated pursuant to this subchapter shall be used

11 to supplement and not supplant other Federal,

12 State, and local public funds expended to provide

13 economic development assistance for communities.

"Subchapter B—Community College and Career Training Grant Program

16 **"SEC. 278. COMMUNITY COLLEGE AND CAREER TRAINING**

17   **GRANT PROGRAM.**

18   "(a) GRANTS AUTHORIZED.—

19   "(1) IN GENERAL.—Beginning August 1, 2009,

20 the Secretary may award Community College and

21 Career Training Grants to eligible institutions for

22 the purpose of developing, offering, or improving

23 educational or career training programs for workers

24 eligible for training under section 236.

1 "(2) LIMITATIONS.—An eligible institution may

2 not be awarded—

3   "(A) more than one grant under this sec-

4 tion; or

5   "(B) a grant under this section in excess

6 of $1,000,000.

7 "(b) DEFINITIONS.—In this section:

8 "(1) ELIGIBLE INSTITUTION.—The term 'eligi-

9 ble institution' means an institution of higher edu-

10 cation (as defined in section 102 of the Higher Edu-

11 cation Act of 1965 (20 U.S.C. 1002)), but only with

12 respect to a program offered by the institution that

13 can be completed in not more than 2 years.

14 "(2) SECRETARY.—The term 'Secretary' means

15 the Secretary of Labor.

16 "(c) GRANT PROPOSALS.—

17 "(1) IN GENERAL.—An eligible institution seek-

18 ing to receive a grant under this section shall submit

19 a grant proposal to the Secretary at such time, in

20 such manner, and containing such information as

21 the Secretary may require.

22 "(2) GUIDELINES.—Not later than June 1,

23 2009, the Secretary shall—

24   "(A) promulgate guidelines for the submis-

25 sion of grant proposals under this section; and

1   "(B) publish and maintain such guidelines

2   on the website of the Department of Labor.

3   "(3) ASSISTANCE.—The Secretary shall offer

4   assistance in preparing a grant proposal to any eligi-

5   ble institution that requests such assistance.

6   "(4) GENERAL REQUIREMENTS FOR GRANT

7   PROPOSALS.—

8   "(A) IN GENERAL.—A grant proposal sub-

9   mitted to the Secretary under this section shall

10   include a detailed description of—

11   "(i) the specific project for which the

12   grant proposal is submitted, including the

13   manner in which the grant will be used to

14   develop, offer, or improve an educational

15   or career training program that is suited

16   to workers eligible for training under sec-

17   tion 236;

18   "(ii) the extent to which the project

19   for which the grant proposal is submitted

20   will meet the educational or career training

21   needs of workers in the community served

22   by the eligible institution who are eligible

23   for training under section 236;

24   "(iii) the extent to which the project

25   for which the grant proposal is submitted

1   fits within any overall strategic plan devel-

2   oped by an eligible community under sec-

3   tion 276;

4   "(iv) the extent to which the project

5   for which the grant proposal is submitted

6   relates to any project funded by a Sector

7   Partnership Grant awarded under section

8   279A; and

9   "(v) any previous experience of the el-

10   igible institution in providing educational

11   or career training programs to workers eli-

12   gible for training under section 236.

13   "(B) ABSENCE OF EXPERIENCE.—The ab-

14   sence of any previous experience in providing

15   educational or career training programs de-

16   scribed in subparagraph (A)(v) shall not auto-

17   matically disqualify an eligible institution from

18   receiving a grant under this section.

19   "(5) COMMUNITY OUTREACH REQUIRED.—In

20   order to be considered by the Secretary, a grant pro-

21   posal submitted by an eligible institution under this

22   section shall—

23   "(A) demonstrate that the eligible

24   institution—

1   "(i) reached out to employers, and

2   other entities described in section

3   276(a)(2)(B) to identify—

4   "(I) any shortcomings in existing

5   educational and career training oppor-

6   tunities available to workers in the

7   community; and

8   "(II) any future employment op-

9   portunities within the community and

10   the educational and career training

11   skills required for workers to meet the

12   future employment demand;

13   "(ii) reached out to other similarly sit-

14   uated institutions in an effort to benefit

15   from any best practices that may be shared

16   with respect to providing educational or ca-

17   reer training programs to workers eligible

18   for training under section 236; and

19   "(iii) reached out to any eligible part-

20   nership in the community that has sought

21   or received a Sector Partnership Grant

22   under section 279A to enhance the effec-

23   tiveness of each grant and avoid duplica-

24   tion of efforts; and

25   "(B) include a detailed description of—

"(i) the extent and outcome of the outreach conducted under subparagraph (A);

"(ii) the extent to which the project for which the grant proposal is submitted will contribute to meeting any short-comings identified under subparagraph (A)(i)(I) or any educational or career training needs identified under subparagraph (A)(i)(II); and

"(iii) the extent to which employers, including small- and medium-sized firms within the community, have demonstrated a commitment to employing workers who would benefit from the project for which the grant proposal is submitted.

"(d) CRITERIA FOR AWARD OF GRANTS.—

"(1) IN GENERAL.—Subject to the appropriation of funds, the Secretary shall award a grant under this section based on—

"(A) a determination of the merits of the grant proposal submitted by the eligible institution to develop, offer, or improve educational or career training programs to be made available

1 to workers eligible for training under section

2 236;

3   "(B) an evaluation of the likely employ-

4   ment opportunities available to workers who

5   complete an educational or career training pro-

6   gram that the eligible institution proposes to

7   develop, offer, or improve; and

8   "(C) an evaluation of prior demand for

9   training programs by workers eligible for train-

10   ing under section 236 in the community served

11   by the eligible institution, as well as the avail-

12   ability and capacity of existing training pro-

13   grams to meet future demand for training pro-

14   grams.

15 "(2) PRIORITY FOR CERTAIN COMMUNITIES.—

16 In awarding grants under this section, the Secretary

17 shall give priority to an eligible institution that

18 serves a community that the Secretary of Commerce

19 has determined under section 273 is eligible to apply

20 for assistance under subchapter A within the 5-year

21 period preceding the date on which the grant pro-

22 posal is submitted to the Secretary under this sec-

23 tion.

24 "(3) MATCHING REQUIREMENTS.—A grant

25 awarded under this section may not be used to sat-

1   isfy any private matching requirement under any

2   other provision of law.

3   "(e) ANNUAL REPORT.—Not later than December 15

4 in each of the calendar years 2009 through 2011, the Sec-

5 retary shall submit to the Committee on Finance of the

6 Senate and the Committee on Ways and Means of the

7 House of Representatives a report—

8   "(1) describing each grant awarded under this

9   section during the preceding fiscal year; and

10   "(2) assessing the impact of each award of a

11   grant under this section in a fiscal year preceding

12   the fiscal year referred to in paragraph (1) on work-

13   ers receiving training under section 236.

14 **"SEC. 279. AUTHORIZATION OF APPROPRIATIONS.**

15   "(a) AUTHORIZATION OF APPROPRIATIONS.—There

16 are authorized to be appropriated to the Secretary of

17 Labor $40,000,000 for each of the fiscal years 2009 and

18 2010, and $10,000,000 for the period beginning October

19 1, 2010, and ending December 31, 2010, to fund the Com-

20 munity College and Career Training Grant Program.

21 Funds appropriated pursuant to this section shall remain

22 available until expended.

23   "(b) SUPPLEMENT NOT SUPPLANT.—Funds appro-

24 priated pursuant to this section shall be used to supple-

25 ment and not supplant other Federal, State, and local

1 public funds expended to support community college and

2 career training programs.

3 "Subchapter C—Industry or Sector Partner-

4   ship Grant Program for Communities Im-

5   pacted by Trade

6 "SEC. 279A. INDUSTRY OR SECTOR PARTNERSHIP GRANT

7   PROGRAM FOR COMMUNITIES IMPACTED BY

8   TRADE.

9   "(a) PURPOSE.—The purpose of this subchapter is

10 to facilitate efforts by industry or sector partnerships to

11 strengthen and revitalize industries and create employ-

12 ment opportunities for workers in communities impacted

13 by trade.

14   "(b) DEFINITIONS.—In this subchapter:

15   "(1) COMMUNITY IMPACTED BY TRADE.—The

16   term 'community impacted by trade' has the mean-

17   ing given that term in section 271.

18   "(2) DISLOCATED WORKER.—The term 'dis-

19   located worker' means a worker who has been totally

20   or partially separated, or is threatened with total or

21   partial separation, from employment in an industry

22   or sector in a community impacted by trade.

23   "(3) ELIGIBLE PARTNERSHIP.—The term 'eligi-

24   ble partnership' means a voluntary partnership com-

25   posed of public and private persons, firms, or other

1   entities within a community impacted by trade, that

2   shall include representatives of—

3   "(A) an industry or sector within the com-

4   munity, including an industry association;

5   "(B) local, county, or State government;

6   "(C) multiple firms in the industry or sec-

7   tor, including small- and medium-sized firms,

8   within the community;

9   "(D) local workforce investment boards es-

10   tablished under section 117 of the Workforce

11   Investment Act of 1998 (29 U.S.C. 2832);

12   "(E) labor organizations, including State

13   labor federations and labor-management initia-

14   tives, representing workers in the community;

15   and

16   "(F) educational institutions, local edu-

17   cational agencies, or other training providers

18   serving the community.

19   "(4) LEAD ENTITY.—The term 'lead entity'

20   means—

21   "(A) an entity designated by the eligible

22   partnership to be responsible for submitting a

23   grant proposal under subsection (e) and serving

24   as the eligible partnership's fiscal agent in ex-

1   pending any Sector Partnership Grant awarded

2   under this section; or

3   "(B) a State agency designated by the

4   Governor of the State to carry out the respon-

5   sibilities described in subparagraph (A).

6   "(5) SECRETARY.—The term 'Secretary' means

7   the Secretary of Labor.

8   "(6) TARGETED INDUSTRY OR SECTOR.—The

9   term 'targeted industry or sector' means the indus-

10   try or sector represented by an eligible partnership.

11   "(c) SECTOR PARTNERSHIP GRANTS AUTHOR-

12   IZED.—Beginning on August 1, 2009, and subject to the

13   appropriation of funds, the Secretary shall award Sector

14   Partnership Grants to eligible partnerships to assist the

15   eligible partnerships in carrying out projects, over periods

16   of not more than 3 years, to strengthen and revitalize in-

17   dustries and sectors and create employment opportunities

18   for dislocated workers.

19   "(d) USE OF SECTOR PARTNERSHIP GRANTS.—An

20   eligible partnership may use a Sector Partnership Grant

21   to carry out any project that the Secretary determines will

22   further the purpose of this subchapter, which may

23   include—

24   "(1) identifying the skill needs of the targeted

25   industry or sector and any gaps in the available sup-

1 ply of skilled workers in the community impacted by
2 trade, and developing strategies for filling the gaps,
3 including by—

4   "(A) developing systems to better link
5   firms in the targeted industry or sector to avail-
6   able skilled workers;

7   "(B) helping firms in the targeted industry
8   or sector to obtain access to new sources of
9   qualified job applicants;

10   "(C) retraining dislocated and incumbent
11   workers; or

12   "(D) facilitating the training of new skilled
13   workers by aligning the instruction provided by
14   local suppliers of education and training serv-
15   ices with the needs of the targeted industry or
16   sector;

17   "(2) analyzing the skills and education levels of
18 dislocated and incumbent workers and developing
19 training to address skill gaps that prevent such
20 workers from obtaining jobs in the targeted industry
21 or sector;

22   "(3) helping firms, especially small- and me-
23 dium-sized firms, in the targeted industry or sector
24 increase their productivity and the productivity of
25 their workers;

1   ''(4) helping such firms retain incumbent work-
2   ers;

3   ''(5) developing learning consortia of small- and
4   medium-sized firms in the targeted industry or sec-
5   tor with similar training needs to enable the firms
6   to combine their purchases of training services, and
7   thereby lower their training costs;

8   ''(6) providing information and outreach activi-
9   ties to firms in the targeted industry or sector re-
10   garding the activities of the eligible partnership and
11   other local service suppliers that could assist the
12   firms in meeting needs for skilled workers;

13   ''(7) seeking, applying, and disseminating best
14   practices learned from similarly situated commu-
15   nities impacted by trade in the development and im-
16   plementation of economic growth and revitalization
17   strategies; and

18   ''(8) identifying additional public and private
19   resources to support the activities described in this
20   subsection, which may include the option to apply
21   for a community grant under section 275 or a Com-
22   munity College and Career Training Grant under
23   section 278 (subject to meeting any additional re-
24   quirements of those sections).

25   ''(e) GRANT PROPOSALS.—

1   "(1) IN GENERAL.—The lead entity of an eligi-
2   ble partnership seeking to receive a Sector Partner-
3   ship Grant under this section shall submit a grant
4   proposal to the Secretary at such time, in such man-
5   ner, and containing such information as the Sec-
6   retary may require.

7   "(2) GENERAL REQUIREMENTS OF GRANT PRO-
8   POSALS.—A grant proposal submitted under para-
9   graph (1) shall, at a minimum—

10   "(A) identify the members of the eligible
11   partnership;

12   "(B) identify the targeted industry or sec-
13   tor for which the eligible partnership intends to
14   carry out projects using the Sector Partnership
15   Grant;

16   "(C) describe the goals that the eligible
17   partnership intends to achieve to promote the
18   targeted industry or sector;

19   "(D) describe the projects that the eligible
20   partnership will undertake to achieve such
21   goals;

22   "(E) demonstrate that the eligible partner-
23   ship has the organizational capacity to carry
24   out the projects described in subparagraph (D);

25   "(F) explain—

1   "(i) whether—

2   "(I) the community impacted by

3   trade has sought or received a com-

4   munity grant under section 275;

5   "(II) an eligible institution in the

6   community has sought or received a

7   Community College and Career Train-

8   ing Grant under section 278; or

9   "(III) any other entity in the

10   community has received funds pursu-

11   ant to any other federally funded

12   training project; and

13   "(ii) how the eligible partnership will

14   coordinate its use of a Sector Partnership

15   Grant with the use of such other grants or

16   funds in order to enhance the effectiveness

17   of each grant and any such funds and

18   avoid duplication of efforts; and

19   "(G) include performance measures, devel-

20   oped based on the performance measures issued

21   by the Secretary under subsection (g)(2), and a

22   timeline for measuring progress toward achiev-

23   ing the goals described in subparagraph (C).

24   "(f) AWARD OF GRANTS.—

1   "(1) IN GENERAL.—Upon application by the
2   lead entity of an eligible partnership, the Secretary
3   may award a Sector Partnership Grant to the eligi-
4   ble partnership to assist the partnership in carrying
5   out any of the projects in the grant proposal that
6   the Secretary determines will further the purposes of
7   this subchapter.

8   "(2) LIMITATIONS.—An eligible partnership
9   may not be awarded—

10   "(A) more than one Sector Partnership
11   Grant; or

12   "(B) a total grant award under this sub-
13   chapter in excess of—

14   "(i) except as provided in clause (ii),
15          $2,500,000; or

16   "(ii) in the case of an eligible partner-
17   ship located within a community impacted
18   by trade that is not served by an institu-
19   tion receiving a Community College and
20   Career Training Grant under section 278,
21          $3,000,000.

22 "(g) ADMINISTRATION BY THE SECRETARY.—

23   "(1) TECHNICAL ASSISTANCE AND OVER-
24 SIGHT.—

1   "(A) IN GENERAL.—The Secretary shall
2   provide technical assistance to, and oversight
3   of, the lead entity of an eligible partnership in
4   applying for and administering Sector Partner-
5   ship Grants awarded under this section.

6   "(B) TECHNICAL ASSISTANCE.—Technical
7   assistance provided under subparagraph (A)
8   shall include providing conferences and such
9   other methods of collecting and disseminating
10   information on best practices developed by eligi-
11   ble partnerships as the Secretary determines
12   appropriate.

13   "(C) GRANTS OR CONTRACTS FOR TECH-
14   NICAL ASSISTANCE.—The Secretary may award
15   a grant or contract to one or more national or
16   State organizations to provide technical assist-
17   ance to foster the planning, formation, and im-
18   plementation of eligible partnerships.

19   "(2) PERFORMANCE MEASURES.—The Sec-
20   retary shall issue a range of performance measures,
21   with quantifiable benchmarks, and methodologies
22   that eligible partnerships may use to measure
23   progress toward the goals described in subsection
24   (e). In developing such measures, the Secretary shall
25   consider the benefits of the eligible partnership and

1   its activities for workers, firms, industries, and com-

2   munities.

3   "(h) REPORTS.—

4   "(1) PROGRESS REPORT.—Not later than 1

5   year after receiving a Sector Partnership Grant, and

6   3 years thereafter, the lead entity shall submit to

7   the Secretary, on behalf of the eligible partnership,

8   a report containing—

9   "(A) a detailed description of the progress

10   made toward achieving the goals described in

11   subsection (e)(2)(C), using the performance

12   measures required under subsection (e)(2)(G);

13   "(B) a detailed evaluation of the impact of

14   the grant award on workers and employers in

15   the community impacted by trade; and

16   "(C) a detailed description of all expendi-

17   tures of funds awarded to the eligible partner-

18   ship under the Sector Partnership Grant ap-

19   proved by the Secretary under this subchapter.

20   "(2) ANNUAL REPORT.—Not later than Decem-

21   ber 15 in each of the calendar years 2009 through

22   2011, the Secretary shall submit to the Committee

23   on Finance of the Senate and the Committee on

24   Ways and Means of the House of Representatives a

25   report—

1   "(A) describing each Sector Partnership

2   Grant awarded to an eligible partnership during

3   the preceding fiscal year; and

4   "(B) assessing the impact of each Sector

5   Partnership Grant awarded in a fiscal year pre-

6   ceding the fiscal year referred to in subpara-

7   graph (A) on workers and employers in commu-

8   nities impacted by trade.

9 **"SEC. 279B. AUTHORIZATION OF APPROPRIATIONS.**

10   "(a) IN GENERAL.—There are authorized to be ap-

11 propriated to the Secretary of Labor $40,000,000 for each

12 of the fiscal years 2009 and 2010, and $10,000,000 for

13 the period beginning October 1, 2010, and ending Decem-

14 ber 31, 2010, to carry out the Sector Partnership Grant

15 program under section 279A. Funds appropriated pursu-

16 ant to this section shall remain available until expended.

17   "(b) SUPPLEMENT NOT SUPPLANT.—Funds appro-

18 priated pursuant to this section shall be used to supple-

19 ment and not supplant other Federal, State, and local

20 public funds expended to support the economic develop-

21 ment of local communities.

22   "(c) ADMINISTRATIVE COSTS.—The Secretary may

23 retain not more than 5 percent of the funds appropriated

24 pursuant to this section for each fiscal year to administer

1 the Sector Partnership Grant program under section

2 279A.

"Subchapter D—General Provisions

"SEC. 279C. RULE OF CONSTRUCTION.

5   "Nothing in this chapter prevents a worker from re-

6 ceiving trade adjustment assistance under chapter 2 of

7 this title at the same time the worker is receiving assist-

8 ance in any manner from—

9   "(1) a community receiving a community grant

10   under subchapter A;

11   "(2) an eligible institution receiving a Commu-

12   nity College and Career Training Grant under sub-

13   chapter B; or

14   "(3) an eligible partnership receiving a Sector

15   Partnership Grant under subchapter C.".

SEC. 1873. CONFORMING AMENDMENTS.

17   (a) TABLE OF CONTENTS.—The table of contents of

18 the Trade Act of 1974 is amended by striking the items

19 relating to chapter 4 of title II and inserting the following:

"CHAPTER 4—TRADE ADJUSTMENT ASSISTANCE FOR COMMUNITIES

"Subchapter A—Trade Adjustment Assistance for Communities

"Sec. 271. Definitions.
"Sec. 272. Establishment of trade adjustment assistance for communities program.
"Sec. 273. Eligibility; notification.
"Sec. 274. Technical assistance.
"Sec. 275. Grants for eligible communities.
"Sec. 276. Strategic plans.
"Sec. 277. General provisions.

"Subchapter B—Community College and Career Training Grant Program

"Sec. 278. Community college and career training grant program.
"Sec. 279. Authorization of appropriations.

"Subchapter C—Industry or Sector Partnership Grant Program for
Communities Impacted by Trade

"Sec. 279A. Industry or sector partnership grant program for communities impacted by trade.
"Sec. 279B. Authorization of appropriations.

"Subchapter D—General Provisions

"Sec. 279C. Rule of construction."

1   (b) JUDICIAL REVIEW.—

2   (1) Section 284(a) of the Trade Act of 1974

3   (19 U.S.C. 2395(a)) is amended—

4   (A) by inserting "or 296" after "section

5   293";

6   (B) by striking "or any other interested

7   domestic party" and inserting "or authorized

8   representative of a community"; and

9   (C) by striking "section 271" and inserting

10   "section 273".

11   (2) Section 1581(d) of title 28, United States

12   Code, is amended—

13   (A) in paragraph (2), by striking "; and"

14   and inserting a semicolon;

15   (B) in paragraph (3)—

16   (i) by striking "271" and inserting

17   "273"; and

18   (ii) by striking the period and insert-

19   ing "; and"; and

20   (C) by adding at the end the following:

1   "(4) any final determination of the Secretary of

2   Agriculture under section 293 or 296 of the Trade

3   Act of 1974 (19 U.S.C. 2401b) with respect to the

4   eligibility of a group of agricultural commodity pro-

5   ducers for adjustment assistance under such Act.".

6 PART IV—TRADE ADJUSTMENT ASSISTANCE FOR

7 FARMERS

8 SEC. 1881. DEFINITIONS.

9   Section 291 of the Trade Act of 1974 (19 U.S.C.

10 2401) is amended—

11   (1) by amending paragraph (1) to read as fol-

12   lows:

13   "(1) AGRICULTURAL COMMODITY.—The term

14   'agricultural commodity' includes—

15   "(A) any agricultural commodity (includ-

16   ing livestock) in its raw or natural state;

17   "(B) any class of goods within an agricul-

18   tural commodity; and

19   "(C) in the case of an agricultural com-

20   modity producer described in paragraph (2)(B),

21   wild-caught aquatic species.";

22   (2) by amending paragraph (2) to read as fol-

23   lows:

1   "(2) AGRICULTURAL COMMODITY PRODUCER.—

2 The   term   'agricultural   commodity   producer'

3 means—

4   "(A) a person that shares in the risk of

5   producing an agricultural commodity and that

6   is entitled to a share of the commodity for mar-

7   keting, including an operator, a sharecropper,

8   or a person that owns or rents the land on

9   which the commodity is produced; or

10   "(B) a person that reports gain or loss

11   from the trade or business of fishing on the

12   person's annual Federal income tax return for

13   the taxable year that most closely corresponds

14   to the marketing year with respect to which a

15   petition is filed under section 292."; and

16   (3) by adding at the end the following:

17   "(7) MARKETING YEAR.—The term 'marketing

18 year' means—

19   "(A) a marketing year designated by the

20   Secretary with respect to an agricultural com-

21   modity; or

22   "(B) in the case of an agricultural com-

23   modity with respect to which the Secretary does

24   not designate a marketing year, a calendar

25   year.".

1 **SEC. 1882. ELIGIBILITY.**

2   (a) IN GENERAL.—Section 292 of the Trade Act of

3 1974 (19 U.S.C. 2401a) is amended by striking sub-

4 sections (c) through (e) and inserting the following:

5   "(c) GROUP ELIGIBILITY REQUIREMENTS.—The

6 Secretary shall certify a group of agricultural commodity

7 producers as eligible to apply for adjustment assistance

8 under this chapter if the Secretary determines that—

9   "(1)(A) the national average price of the agri-

10   cultural commodity produced by the group during

11   the most recent marketing year for which data are

12   available is less than 85 percent of the average of

13   the national average price for the commodity in the

14   3 marketing years preceding such marketing year;

15   "(B) the quantity of production of the agricul-

16   tural commodity produced by the group during such

17   marketing year is less than 85 percent of the aver-

18   age of the quantity of production of the commodity

19   produced by the group in the 3 marketing years pre-

20   ceding such marketing year;

21   "(C) the value of production of the agricultural

22   commodity produced by the group during such mar-

23   keting year is less than 85 percent of the average

24   value of production of the commodity produced by

25   the group in the 3 marketing years preceding such

26   marketing year; or

1   "(D) the cash receipts for the agricultural com-

2 modity produced by the group during such mar-

3 keting year are less than 85 percent of the average

4 of the cash receipts for the commodity produced by

5 the group in the 3 marketing years preceding such

6 marketing year;

7   "(2) the volume of imports of articles like or di-

8 rectly competitive with the agricultural commodity

9 produced by the group in the marketing year with

10 respect to which the group files the petition in-

11 creased compared to the average volume of such im-

12 ports during the 3 marketing years preceding such

13 marketing year; and

14   "(3) the increase in such imports contributed

15 importantly to the decrease in the national average

16 price, quantity of production, or value of production

17 of, or cash receipts for, the agricultural commodity,

18 as described in paragraph (1).

19 "(d) ELIGIBILITY OF CERTAIN OTHER PRO-

20 DUCERS.—An agricultural commodity producer or group

21 of producers that resides outside of the State or region

22 identified in the petition filed under subsection (a) may

23 file a request to become a party to that petition not later

24 than 15 days after the date the notice is published in the

1 Federal Register under subsection (a) with respect to that
2 petition.

3 "(e) TREATMENT OF CLASSES OF GOODS WITHIN A
4 COMMODITY.—In any case in which there are separate
5 classes of goods within an agricultural commodity, the
6 Secretary shall treat each class as a separate commodity
7 in determining under subsection (c)—

8 "(1) group eligibility;

9 "(2) the national average price, quantity of pro-
10 duction, or value of production, or cash receipts; and

11 "(3) the volume of imports.".

12 (b) CONFORMING AMENDMENTS.—Section 293 of the
13 Trade Act of 1974 (19 U.S.C. 2401b) is amended—

14 (1) in subsection (a), by striking "section 292
15 (c) or (d), as the case may be," and inserting "sec-
16 tion 292(c)"; and

17 (2) in subsection (c), by striking "decline in
18 price for" and inserting "decrease in the national
19 average price, quantity of production, or value of
20 production of, or cash receipts for,".

21 **SEC. 1883. BENEFITS.**

22 (a) IN GENERAL.—Section 296 of the Trade Act of
23 1974 (19 U.S.C. 2401e) is amended to read as follows:

1 **"SEC. 296. QUALIFYING REQUIREMENTS AND BENEFITS**

2 **FOR AGRICULTURAL COMMODITY PRO-**

3 **DUCERS.**

4 "(a) IN GENERAL.—

5 "(1) REQUIREMENTS.—

6 "(A) IN GENERAL.—Benefits under this

7 chapter shall be available to an agricultural

8 commodity producer covered by a certification

9 under this chapter who files an application for

10 such benefits not later than 90 days after the

11 date on which the Secretary makes a deter-

12 mination and issues a certification of eligibility

13 under section 293, if the producer submits to

14 the Secretary sufficient information to establish

15 that—

16 "(i) the producer produced the agri-

17 cultural commodity covered by the applica-

18 tion filed under this subsection in the mar-

19 keting year with respect to which the peti-

20 tion is filed and in at least 1 of the 3 mar-

21 keting years preceding that marketing

22 year;

23 "(ii)(I) the quantity of the agricul-

24 tural commodity that was produced by the

25 producer in the marketing year with re-

26 spect to which the petition is filed has de-

1   creased compared to the most recent mar-

2   keting year preceding that marketing year

3   for which data are available; or

4   "(II)(aa) the price received for the ag-

5   ricultural commodity by the producer dur-

6   ing the marketing year with respect to

7   which the petition is filed has decreased

8   compared to the average price for the com-

9   modity received by the producer in the 3

10   marketing years preceding that marketing

11   year; or

12   "(bb) the county level price main-

13   tained by the Secretary for the agricultural

14   commodity on the date on which the peti-

15   tion is filed has decreased compared to the

16   average county level price for the com-

17   modity in the 3 marketing years preceding

18   the date on which the petition is filed; and

19   "(iii) the producer is not receiving—

20   "(I) cash benefits under chapter

21   2 or 3; or

22   "(II) benefits based on the pro-

23   duction of an agricultural commodity

24   covered by another petition filed

25   under this chapter.

"(B) SPECIAL RULE WITH RESPECT TO CROPS NOT GROWN EVERY YEAR.—For purposes of subparagraph (A)(ii)(II)(aa), if a petition is filed with respect to an agricultural commodity that is not produced by the producer every year, an agricultural commodity producer producing that commodity may establish the average price received for the commodity by the producer in the 3 marketing years preceding the year with respect to which the petition is filed by using average price data for the 3 most recent marketing years in which the producer produced the commodity and for which data are available.

"(2) LIMITATIONS BASED ON ADJUSTED GROSS INCOME.—

"(A) IN GENERAL.—Notwithstanding any other provision of this chapter, an agricultural commodity producer shall not be eligible for assistance under this chapter in any year in which the average adjusted gross income (as defined in section 1001D(a) of the Food Security Act of 1985 (7 U.S.C. 1308–3a(a))) of the producer exceeds the level set forth in subparagraph (A) or (B) of section 1001D(b)(1) of the Food Se-

1 curity Act of 1985 (7 U.S.C. 1308–3a(b)(1)),

2 whichever is applicable.

3 "(B) DEMONSTRATION OF COMPLIANCE.—

4 An agricultural commodity producer shall pro-

5 vide to the Secretary such information as the

6 Secretary determines necessary to demonstrate

7 that the producer is in compliance with the lim-

8 itation under subparagraph (A).

9 "(C) COUNTER-CYCLICAL AND ACRE PAY-

10 MENTS.—The total amount of payments made

11 to an agricultural commodity producer under

12 this chapter during any crop year may not ex-

13 ceed the limitations on payments set forth in

14 subsections (b)(2), (b)(3), (c)(2), and (c)(3) of

15 section 1001 of the Food Security Act of 1985

16 (7 U.S.C. 1308).

17 "(b) TECHNICAL ASSISTANCE.—

18 "(1) INITIAL TECHNICAL ASSISTANCE.—

19 "(A) IN GENERAL.—An agricultural com-

20 modity producer that files an application and

21 meets the requirements under subsection (a)(1)

22 shall be entitled to receive initial technical as-

23 sistance designed to improve the competitive-

24 ness of the production and marketing of the ag-

25 ricultural commodity with respect to which the

1   producer was certified under this chapter. Such

2   assistance shall include information regarding—

3   "(i) improving the yield and mar-

4   keting of that agricultural commodity; and

5   "(ii) the feasibility and desirability of

6   substituting one or more alternative agri-

7   cultural commodities for that agricultural

8   commodity.

9   "(B) TRANSPORTATION AND SUBSISTENCE

10   EXPENSES.—

11   "(i) IN GENERAL.—The Secretary

12   may authorize supplemental assistance

13   necessary to defray reasonable transpor-

14   tation and subsistence expenses incurred

15   by an agricultural commodity producer in

16   connection with initial technical assistance

17   under subparagraph (A) if such assistance

18   is provided at facilities that are not within

19   normal commuting distance of the regular

20   place of residence of the producer.

21   "(ii) EXCEPTIONS.—The Secretary

22   may not authorize payments to an agricul-

23   tural commodity producer under clause

24   (i)—

1   "(I) for subsistence expenses that

2   exceed the lesser of—

3   "(aa) the actual per diem

4   expenses for subsistence incurred

5   by the producer; or

6   "(bb) the prevailing per

7   diem allowance rate authorized

8   under Federal travel regulations;

9   or

10   "(II) for travel expenses that ex-

11   ceed the prevailing mileage rate au-

12   thorized under the Federal travel reg-

13   ulations.

14   "(2) INTENSIVE TECHNICAL ASSISTANCE.—A

15 producer that has completed initial technical assist-

16 ance under paragraph (1) shall be eligible to partici-

17 pate in intensive technical assistance. Such assist-

18 ance shall consist of—

19   "(A) a series of courses to further assist

20   the producer in improving the competitiveness

21   of the producer in producing—

22   "(i) the agricultural commodity with

23   respect to which the producer was certified

24   under this chapter; or

1   "(ii) another agricultural commodity;

2   and

3   "(B) assistance in developing an initial

4   business plan based on the courses completed

5   under subparagraph (A).

6   "(3) INITIAL BUSINESS PLAN.—

7   "(A) APPROVAL BY SECRETARY.—The Sec-

8   retary shall approve an initial business plan de-

9   veloped under paragraph (2)(B) if the plan—

10   "(i) reflects the skills gained by the

11   producer through the courses described in

12   paragraph (2)(A); and

13   "(ii) demonstrates how the producer

14   will apply those skills to the circumstances

15   of the producer.

16   "(B) FINANCIAL ASSISTANCE FOR IMPLE-

17   MENTING INITIAL BUSINESS PLAN.—Upon ap-

18   proval of the producer's initial business plan by

19   the Secretary under subparagraph (A), a pro-

20   ducer shall be entitled to an amount not to ex-

21   ceed $4,000 to—

22   "(i) implement the initial business

23   plan; or

24   "(ii) develop a long-term business ad-

25   justment plan under paragraph (4).

"(4) LONG-TERM BUSINESS ADJUSTMENT
PLAN.—

"(A) IN GENERAL.—A producer that has
completed intensive technical assistance under
paragraph (2) and whose initial business plan
has been approved under paragraph (3)(A)
shall be eligible for, in addition to the amount
under subparagraph (C), assistance in developing a long-term business adjustment plan.

"(B) APPROVAL OF LONG-TERM BUSINESS
ADJUSTMENT PLANS.—The Secretary shall approve a long-term business adjustment plan developed under subparagraph (A) if the Secretary determines that the plan—

"(i) includes steps reasonably calculated to materially contribute to the economic adjustment of the producer to
changing market conditions;

"(ii) takes into consideration the interests of the workers employed by the producer; and

"(iii) demonstrates that the producer
will have sufficient resources to implement
the business plan.

1   "(C) PLAN IMPLEMENTATION.—Upon ap-
2   proval of the producer's long-term business ad-
3   justment plan under subparagraph (B), a pro-
4   ducer shall be entitled to an amount not to ex-
5   ceed $8,000 to implement the long-term busi-
6   ness adjustment plan.

7   "(c) MAXIMUM AMOUNT OF ASSISTANCE.—An agri-
8 cultural commodity producer may receive not more than
9 $12,000 under paragraphs (3) and (4) of subsection (b)
10 in the 36-month period following certification under sec-
11 tion 293.

12   "(d) LIMITATIONS ON OTHER ASSISTANCE.—An ag-
13 ricultural commodity producer that receives benefits under
14 this chapter (other than initial technical assistance under
15 subsection (b)(1)) shall not be eligible for cash benefits
16 under chapter 2 or 3.".

17   (b) CLERICAL AMENDMENT.—The table of contents
18 of the Trade Act of 1974 is amended by striking the item
19 relating to section 296 and inserting the following:

"Sec. 296. Qualifying requirements and benefits for agricultural commodity producers.".

20 **SEC. 1884. REPORT.**

21   Section 293 of the Trade Act of 1974 (19 U.S.C.
22 2401b) is amended by adding at the end the following:

23   "(d) REPORT BY THE SECRETARY.—Not later than
24 January 30, 2010, and annually thereafter, the Secretary

1 of Agriculture shall submit to the Committee on Finance
2 of the Senate and the Committee on Ways and Means of
3 the House of Representatives a report containing the fol-
4 lowing information with respect to adjustment assistance
5 provided under this chapter during the preceding fiscal
6 year:

7   "(1) A list of the agricultural commodities cov-
8   ered by a certification under this chapter.

9   "(2) The States or regions in which such com-
10   modities are produced and the aggregate amount of
11   such commodities produced in each such State or re-
12   gion.

13   "(3) The total number of agricultural com-
14   modity producers, by congressional district, receiving
15   benefits under this chapter.

16   "(4) The total number of agricultural com-
17   modity producers, by congressional district, receiving
18   technical assistance under this chapter.".

19 **SEC. 1885. FRAUD AND RECOVERY OF OVERPAYMENTS.**

20   Section 297(a)(1) of the Trade Act of 1974 (19
21 U.S.C. 2401f(a)(1)) is amended by inserting "or has ex-
22 pended funds received under this chapter for a purpose
23 that was not approved by the Secretary," after "entitled,".

SEC. 1886. DETERMINATION OF INCREASES OF IMPORTS FOR CERTAIN FISHERMEN.

For purposes of chapters 2 and 6 of title II of the Trade Act of 1974 (19 U.S.C. 2251 et seq.), in the case of an agricultural commodity producer that—

      (1) is a fisherman or aquaculture producer, and

      (2) is otherwise eligible for adjustment assistance under chapter 2 or 6, as the case may be,

the increase in imports of articles like or directly competitive with the agricultural commodity produced by such producer may be based on imports of wild-caught seafood, farm-raised seafood, or both.

SEC. 1887. EXTENSION OF TRADE ADJUSTMENT ASSISTANCE FOR FARMERS.

Section 298(a) of the Trade Act of 1974 (19 U.S.C. 2401g(a)) is amended by striking "fiscal years 2003 through 2007" and all that follows through the end period and inserting "fiscal years 2009 and 2010, and $22,500,000 for the period beginning October 1, 2010, and ending December 31, 2010, to carry out the purposes of this chapter, including administrative costs, and salaries and expenses of employees of the Department of Agriculture.".

PART V—GENERAL PROVISIONS

1

2 **SEC. 1891. EFFECTIVE DATE.**

3 (a) IN GENERAL.—Except as otherwise provided in

4 this subtitle, and subsection (b) of this section, this sub-

5 title and the amendments made by this subtitle—

6 (1) shall take effect upon the expiration of the

7 90-day period beginning on the date of the enact-

8 ment of this Act; and

9 (2) shall apply to—

10 (A) petitions for certification filed under

11 chapter 2, 3, or 6 of title II of the Trade Act

12 of 1974 on or after the effective date described

13 in paragraph (1); and

14 (B) petitions for assistance and proposals

15 for grants filed under chapter 4 of title II of

16 the Trade Act of 1974 on or after such effective

17 date.

18 (b) CERTIFICATIONS MADE BEFORE EFFECTIVE

19 DATE.—Notwithstanding subsection (a)—

20 (1) a worker shall continue to receive (or be eli-

21 gible to receive) trade adjustment assistance and

22 other benefits under subchapter B of chapter 2 of

23 title II of the Trade Act of 1974, as in effect on the

24 day before the effective date described in subsection

25 (a)(1), for any week for which the worker meets the

26 eligibility requirements of such chapter 2 as in effect

on the day before such effective date, if the
worker—

    (A) is certified as eligible for trade adjust-
ment assistance benefits under such chapter 2
pursuant to a petition filed under section 221
of the Trade Act of 1974 on or before such effective date; and

    (B) would otherwise be eligible to receive
trade adjustment assistance benefits under such
chapter as in effect on the day before such effective date;

(2) a worker shall continue to receive (or be eligible to receive) benefits under section 246(a)(2) of
the Trade Act of 1974, as in effect on the day before the effective date described in subsection (a)(1),
for such period for which the worker meets the eligibility requirements of section 246 of that Act as in
effect on the day before such effective date, if the
worker—

    (A) is certified as eligible for benefits
under such section 246 pursuant to a petition
filed under section 221 of the Trade Act of
1974 on or before such effective date; and

(B) would otherwise be eligible to receive benefits under such section 246(a)(2) as in effect on the day before such effective date; and

(3) a firm shall continue to receive (or be eligible to receive) adjustment assistance under chapter 3 of title II of the Trade Act of 1974, as in effect on the day before the effective date described in subsection (a)(1), for such period for which the firm meets the eligibility requirements of such chapter 3 as in effect on the day before such effective date, if the firm—

(A) is certified as eligible for benefits under such chapter 3 pursuant to a petition filed under section 251 of the Trade Act of 1974 on or before such effective date; and

(B) would otherwise be eligible to receive benefits under such chapter 3 as in effect on the day before such effective date.

SEC. 1892. EXTENSION OF TRADE ADJUSTMENT ASSIST-ANCE PROGRAMS.

(a) FOR WORKERS.—Section 245(a) of the Trade Act of 1974 (19 U.S.C. 2317(a)) is amended by striking "December 31, 2007" and inserting "December 31, 2010".

(b) TERMINATION.—Section 285 of the Trade Act of 1974 (19 U.S.C. 2271 note prec.) is amended—

1   (1) in subsection (a), by striking "December

2   31, 2007" each place it appears and inserting "De-

3   cember 31, 2010"; and

4   (2) by amending subsection (b) to read as fol-

5   lows:

6   "(b) OTHER ASSISTANCE.—

7   "(1) ASSISTANCE FOR FIRMS.—

8   "(A) IN GENERAL.—Except as provided in

9   subparagraph (B), technical assistance and

10   grants may not be provided under chapter 3

11   after December 31, 2010.

12   "(B) EXCEPTION.—Notwithstanding sub-

13   paragraph (A), any technical assistance or

14   grant approved under chapter 3 on or before

15   December 31, 2010, may be provided—

16   "(i) to the extent funds are available

17   pursuant to such chapter for such purpose;

18   and

19   "(ii) to the extent the recipient of the

20   technical assistance or grant is otherwise

21   eligible to receive such technical assistance

22   or grant, as the case may be.

23   "(2) FARMERS.—

24   "(A) IN GENERAL.—Except as provided in

25   subparagraph (B), technical assistance and fi-

1 nancial assistance may not be provided under

2 chapter 6 after December 31, 2010.

3 "(B) EXCEPTION.—Notwithstanding sub-

4 paragraph (A), any technical or financial assist-

5 ance approved under chapter 6 on or before De-

6 cember 31, 2010, may be provided—

7 "(i) to the extent funds are available

8 pursuant to such chapter for such purpose;

9 and

10 "(ii) to the extent the recipient of the

11 technical or financial assistance is other-

12 wise eligible to receive such technical or fi-

13 nancial assistance, as the case may be.

14 "(3) ASSISTANCE FOR COMMUNITIES.—

15 "(A) IN GENERAL.—Except as provided in

16 subparagraph (B), technical assistance and

17 grants may not be provided under chapter 4

18 after December 31, 2010.

19 "(B) EXCEPTION.—Notwithstanding sub-

20 paragraph (A), any technical assistance or

21 grant approved under chapter 4 on or before

22 December 31, 2010, may be provided—

23 "(i) to the extent funds are available

24 pursuant to such chapter for such purpose;

25 and

1   "(ii) to the extent the recipient of the

2   technical assistance or grant is otherwise

3   eligible to receive such technical assistance

4   or grant, as the case may be.".

5 **SEC. 1893. TERMINATION; RELATED PROVISIONS.**

6   (a) SUNSET.—

7   (1) IN GENERAL.—Subject to paragraph (2),

8 the amendments made by this subtitle to chapters 2,

9 3, 4, 5, and 6 of title II of the Trade Act of 1974

10 (19 U.S.C. 2271 et seq.) shall not apply on or after

11 January 1, 2011.

12   (2) EXCEPTION.—The amendments made by

13 this subtitle to section 285 of the Trade Act of 1974

14 shall continue to apply on and after January 1,

15 2011, with respect to—

16   (A) workers certified as eligible for trade

17   adjustment assistance benefits under chapter 2

18   of title II of that Act pursuant to petitions filed

19   under section 221 of that Act before January 1,

20   2011;

21   (B) firms certified as eligible for technical

22   assistance or grants under chapter 3 of title II

23   of that Act pursuant to petitions filed under

24   section 251 of that Act before January 1, 2011;

1   (C) recipients approved for technical as-

2   sistance or grants under chapter 4 of title II of

3   that Act pursuant to petitions for assistance or

4   proposals for grants (as the case may be) filed

5   pursuant to such chapter before January 1,

6   2011; and

7   (D) agricultural commodity producers cer-

8   tified as eligible for technical or financial assist-

9   ance under chapter 6 of title II of that Act pur-

10   suant to petitions filed under section 292 of

11   that Act before January 1, 2011.

12   (b) APPLICATION OF PRIOR LAW.—Chapters 2, 3, 4,

13 5, and 6 of title II of the Trade Act of 1974 (19 U.S.C.

14 2271 et seq.) shall be applied and administered beginning

15 January 1, 2011, as if the amendments made by this sub-

16 title (other than part VI) had never been enacted, except

17 that in applying and administering such chapters—

18   (1) section 245 of that Act shall be applied and

19   administered by substituting "2011" for "2007";

20   (2) section 246(b) of that Act shall be applied

21   and administered by substituting "December 31,

22   2011" for "the date that is 5 years" and all that fol-

23   lows through "State";

24   (3) section 256(b) of that Act shall be applied

25   and administered by substituting "the 1-year period

1   beginning January 1, 2011" for "each of fiscal years

2   2003 through 2007, and $4,000,000 for the 3-

3   month period beginning October 1, 2007";

4   (4) section 298(a) of that Act shall be applied

5   and administered by substituting "the 1-year period

6   beginning January 1, 2011" for "each of the fiscal

7   years" and all that follows through "October 1,

8   2007"; and

9   (5) subject to subsection (a)(2), section 285 of

10   that Act shall be applied and administered—

11   (A) in subsection (a), by substituting

12   "2011" for "2007" each place it appears; and

13   (B) by applying and administering sub-

14   section (b) as if it read as follows:

15   "(b) OTHER ASSISTANCE.—

16   "(1) ASSISTANCE FOR FIRMS.—

17   "(A) IN GENERAL.—Except as provided in

18   subparagraph (B), assistance may not be pro-

19   vided under chapter 3 after December 31,

20   2011.

21   "(B) EXCEPTION.—Notwithstanding sub-

22   paragraph (A), any assistance approved under

23   chapter 3 on or before December 31, 2011, may

24   be provided—

1   "(i) to the extent funds are available

2   pursuant to such chapter for such purpose;

3   and

4   "(ii) to the extent the recipient of the

5   assistance is otherwise eligible to receive

6   such assistance.

7   "(2) FARMERS.—

8   "(A) IN GENERAL.—Except as provided in

9   subparagraph (B), assistance may not be pro-

10   vided under chapter 6 after December 31,

11   2011.

12   "(B) EXCEPTION.—Notwithstanding sub-

13   paragraph (A), any assistance approved under

14   chapter 6 on or before December 31, 2011, may

15   be provided—

16   "(i) to the extent funds are available

17   pursuant to such chapter for such purpose;

18   and

19   "(ii) to the extent the recipient of the

20   assistance is otherwise eligible to receive

21   such assistance.".

22 **SEC. 1894. GOVERNMENT ACCOUNTABILITY OFFICE RE-**

23   **PORT.**

24   Not later than September 30, 2012, the Comptroller

25 General of the United States shall prepare and submit to

1 the Committee on Finance of the Senate and the Com-

2 mittee on Ways and Means of the House of Representa-

3 tives a comprehensive report on the operation and effec-

4 tiveness of the amendments made by this subtitle to chap-

5 ters 2, 3, 4, and 6 of the Trade Act of 1974.

6 **SEC. 1895. EMERGENCY DESIGNATION.**

7 Amounts appropriated pursuant to this subtitle are

8 designated as an emergency requirement and necessary to

9 meet emergency needs pursuant to section 204(a) of S.

10 Con. Res. 21 (110th Congress) and section 301(b)(2) of

11 S. Con. Res. 70 (110th Congress), the concurrent resolu-

12 tions on the budget for fiscal years 2008 and 2009.

13 **PART VI—HEALTH COVERAGE IMPROVEMENT**

14 **SEC. 1899. SHORT TITLE.**

15 This part may be cited as the "TAA Health Coverage

16 Improvement Act of 2009".

17 **SEC. 1899A. IMPROVEMENT OF THE AFFORDABILITY OF**

18 **THE CREDIT.**

19 (a) IMPROVEMENT OF AFFORDABILITY.—

20 (1) IN GENERAL.—Section 35(a) of the Internal

21 Revenue Code of 1986 (relating to credit for health

22 insurance costs of eligible individuals) is amended by

23 inserting "(80 percent in the case of eligible cov-

24 erage months beginning before January 1, 2011)"

25 after "65 percent".

1   (2) CONFORMING AMENDMENT.—Section

2   7527(b) of such Code (relating to advance payment

3   of credit for health insurance costs of eligible indi-

4   viduals) is amended by inserting "(80 percent in the

5   case of eligible coverage months beginning before

6   January 1, 2011)" after "65 percent".

7   (b) EFFECTIVE DATE.—The amendments made by

8 this section shall apply to coverage months beginning on

9 or after the first day of the first month beginning 60 days

10 after the date of the enactment of this Act.

11 **SEC. 1899B. PAYMENT FOR MONTHLY PREMIUMS PAID**

12   **PRIOR TO COMMENCEMENT OF ADVANCE**

13   **PAYMENTS OF CREDIT.**

14   (a) PAYMENT FOR PREMIUMS DUE PRIOR TO COM-

15 MENCEMENT OF ADVANCE PAYMENTS OF CREDIT.—Sec-

16 tion 7527 of the Internal Revenue Code of 1986 (relating

17 to advance payment of credit for health insurance costs

18 of eligible individuals) is amended by adding at the end

19 the following new subsection:

20   "(e) PAYMENT FOR PREMIUMS DUE PRIOR TO COM-

21 MENCEMENT OF ADVANCE PAYMENTS.—In the case of eli-

22 gible coverage months beginning before January 1,

23 2011—

24   "(1) IN GENERAL.—The program established

25   under subsection (a) shall provide that the Secretary

1   shall make 1 or more retroactive payments on behalf

2   of a certified individual in an aggregate amount

3   equal to 80 percent of the premiums for coverage of

4   the taxpayer and qualifying family members under

5   qualified health insurance for eligible coverage

6   months (as defined in section 35(b)) occurring prior

7   to the first month for which an advance payment is

8   made on behalf of such individual under subsection

9   (a).

10   "(2) REDUCTION OF PAYMENT FOR AMOUNTS

11   RECEIVED UNDER NATIONAL EMERGENCY

12   GRANTS.—The amount of any payment determined

13   under paragraph (1) shall be reduced by the amount

14   of any payment made to the taxpayer for the pur-

15   chase of qualified health insurance under a national

16   emergency grant pursuant to section 173(f) of the

17   Workforce Investment Act of 1998 for a taxable

18   year including the eligible coverage months described

19   in paragraph (1).".

20   (b) EFFECTIVE DATE.—The amendments made by

21 this section shall apply to coverage months beginning after

22 December 31, 2008.

23   (c) TRANSITIONAL RULE.—The Secretary of the

24 Treasury shall not be required to make any payments

25 under section 7527(e) of the Internal Revenue Code of

1 1986, as added by this section, until after the date that
2 is 6 months after the date of the enactment of this Act.

3 **SEC. 1899C. TAA RECIPIENTS NOT ENROLLED IN TRAINING**
4 **PROGRAMS ELIGIBLE FOR CREDIT.**

5 (a) IN GENERAL.—Paragraph (2) of section 35(c) of
6 the Internal Revenue Code of 1986 (defining eligible TAA
7 recipient) is amended to read as follows:

8 "(2) ELIGIBLE TAA RECIPIENT.—

9 "(A) IN GENERAL.—Except as provided in
10 subparagraph (B), the term 'eligible TAA re-
11 cipient' means, with respect to any month, any
12 individual who is receiving for any day of such
13 month a trade readjustment allowance under
14 chapter 2 of title II of the Trade Act of 1974
15 or who would be eligible to receive such allow-
16 ance if section 231 of such Act were applied
17 without regard to subsection (a)(3)(B) of such
18 section. An individual shall continue to be treat-
19 ed as an eligible TAA recipient during the first
20 month that such individual would otherwise
21 cease to be an eligible TAA recipient by reason
22 of the preceding sentence.

23 "(B) SPECIAL RULE.—In the case of any
24 eligible coverage month beginning after the date
25 of the enactment of this paragraph and before

1   January 1, 2011, the term 'eligible TAA recipi-

2   ent' means, with respect to any month, any in-

3   dividual who—

4   "(i) is receiving for any day of such

5   month a trade readjustment allowance

6   under chapter 2 of title II of the Trade

7   Act of 1974,

8   "(ii) would be eligible to receive such

9   allowance except that such individual is in

10   a break in training provided under a train-

11   ing program approved under section 236 of

12   such Act that exceeds the period specified

13   in section 233(e) of such Act, but is within

14   the period for receiving such allowances

15   provided under section 233(a) of such Act,

16   or

17   "(iii) is receiving unemployment com-

18   pensation (as defined in section 85(b)) for

19   any day of such month and who would be

20   eligible to receive such allowance for such

21   month if section 231 of such Act were ap-

22   plied without regard to subsections

23   (a)(3)(B) and (a)(5) thereof.

24   An individual shall continue to be treated as an

25   eligible TAA recipient during the first month

1   that such individual would otherwise cease to be

2   an eligible TAA recipient by reason of the pre-

3   ceding sentence.".

4   (b) EFFECTIVE DATE.—The amendment made by

5 this section shall apply to coverage months beginning after

6 the date of the enactment of this Act.

7 SEC. 1899D. TAA PRE-CERTIFICATION PERIOD RULE FOR

8   PURPOSES OF DETERMINING WHETHER

9   THERE IS A 63-DAY LAPSE IN CREDITABLE

10   COVERAGE.

11   (a) IRC AMENDMENT.—Section 9801(c)(2) of the In-

12 ternal Revenue Code of 1986 (relating to not counting pe-

13 riods before significant breaks in creditable coverage) is

14 amended by adding at the end the following new subpara-

15 graph:

16   "(D) TAA-ELIGIBLE INDIVIDUALS.—In the

17   case of plan years beginning before January 1,

18   2011—

19   "(i) TAA PRE-CERTIFICATION PERIOD

20   RULE.—In the case of a TAA-eligible indi-

21   vidual, the period beginning on the date

22   the individual has a TAA-related loss of

23   coverage and ending on the date which is

24   7 days after the date of the issuance by

25   the Secretary (or by any person or entity

1   designated by the Secretary) of a qualified

2   health insurance costs credit eligibility cer-

3   tificate for such individual for purposes of

4   section 7527 shall not be taken into ac-

5   count in determining the continuous period

6   under subparagraph (A).

7   "(ii) DEFINITIONS.—The terms 'TAA-

8   eligible individual' and 'TAA-related loss of

9   coverage' have the meanings given such

10   terms in section 4980B(f)(5)(C)(iv).".

11 (b) ERISA AMENDMENT.—Section 701(c)(2) of the

12 Employee Retirement Income Security Act of 1974 (29

13 U.S.C. 1181(c)(2)) is amended by adding at the end the

14 following new subparagraph:

15   "(C) TAA-ELIGIBLE INDIVIDUALS.—In the

16   case of plan years beginning before January 1,

17   2011—

18   "(i) TAA PRE-CERTIFICATION PERIOD

19   RULE.—In the case of a TAA-eligible indi-

20   vidual, the period beginning on the date

21   the individual has a TAA-related loss of

22   coverage and ending on the date that is 7

23   days after the date of the issuance by the

24   Secretary (or by any person or entity des-

25   ignated by the Secretary) of a qualified

1   health insurance costs credit eligibility cer-

2   tificate for such individual for purposes of

3   section 7527 of the Internal Revenue Code

4   of 1986 shall not be taken into account in

5   determining the continuous period under

6   subparagraph (A).

7   "(ii) DEFINITIONS.—The terms 'TAA-

8   eligible individual' and 'TAA-related loss of

9   coverage' have the meanings given such

10   terms in section 605(b)(4).".

11   (c) PHSA AMENDMENT.—Section 2701(c)(2) of the

12 Public Health Service Act (42 U.S.C. 300gg(c)(2)) is

13 amended by adding at the end the following new subpara-

14 graph:

15   "(C) TAA-ELIGIBLE INDIVIDUALS.—In the

16   case of plan years beginning before January 1,

17   2011—

18   "(i) TAA PRE-CERTIFICATION PERIOD

19   RULE.—In the case of a TAA-eligible indi-

20   vidual, the period beginning on the date

21   the individual has a TAA-related loss of

22   coverage and ending on the date that is 7

23   days after the date of the issuance by the

24   Secretary (or by any person or entity des-

25   ignated by the Secretary) of a qualified

1   health insurance costs credit eligibility cer-

2   tificate for such individual for purposes of

3   section 7527 of the Internal Revenue Code

4   of 1986 shall not be taken into account in

5   determining the continuous period under

6   subparagraph (A).

7   "(ii) DEFINITIONS.—The terms 'TAA-

8   eligible individual' and 'TAA-related loss of

9   coverage' have the meanings given such

10   terms in section 2205(b)(4).".

11   (d) EFFECTIVE DATE.—The amendments made by

12 this section shall apply to plan years beginning after the

13 date of the enactment of this Act.

14 **SEC. 1899E. CONTINUED QUALIFICATION OF FAMILY MEM-**

15   **BERS AFTER CERTAIN EVENTS.**

16   (a) IN GENERAL.—Subsection (g) of section 35 of

17 such Code is amended by redesignating paragraph (9) as

18 paragraph (10) and inserting after paragraph (8) the fol-

19 lowing new paragraph:

20   "(9) CONTINUED QUALIFICATION OF FAMILY

21   MEMBERS AFTER CERTAIN EVENTS.—In the case of

22   eligible coverage months beginning before January

23   1, 2011—

24   "(A) MEDICARE ELIGIBILITY.—In the case

25   of any month which would be an eligible cov-

1   erage month with respect to an eligible indi-

2   vidual but for subsection (f)(2)(A), such month

3   shall be treated as an eligible coverage month

4   with respect to such eligible individual solely for

5   purposes of determining the amount of the

6   credit under this section with respect to any

7   qualifying family members of such individual

8   (and any advance payment of such credit under

9   section 7527). This subparagraph shall only

10   apply with respect to the first 24 months after

11   such eligible individual is first entitled to the

12   benefits described in subsection (f)(2)(A).

13   "(B) DIVORCE.—In the case of the final-

14   ization of a divorce between an eligible indi-

15   vidual and such individual's spouse, such spouse

16   shall be treated as an eligible individual for pur-

17   poses of this section and section 7527 for a pe-

18   riod of 24 months beginning with the date of

19   such finalization, except that the only qualifying

20   family members who may be taken into account

21   with respect to such spouse are those individ-

22   uals who were qualifying family members imme-

23   diately before such finalization.

24   "(C) DEATH.—In the case of the death of

25   an eligible individual—

1   "(i) any spouse of such individual (de-

2   termined at the time of such death) shall

3   be treated as an eligible individual for pur-

4   poses of this section and section 7527 for

5   a period of 24 months beginning with the

6   date of such death, except that the only

7   qualifying family members who may be

8   taken into account with respect to such

9   spouse are those individuals who were

10   qualifying family members immediately be-

11   fore such death, and

12   "(ii) any individual who was a quali-

13   fying family member of the decedent imme-

14   diately before such death (or, in the case

15   of an individual to whom paragraph (4)

16   applies, the taxpayer to whom the deduc-

17   tion under section 151 is allowable) shall

18   be treated as an eligible individual for pur-

19   poses of this section and section 7527 for

20   a period of 24 months beginning with the

21   date of such death, except that in deter-

22   mining the amount of such credit only

23   such qualifying family member may be

24   taken into account.".

1   (b) CONFORMING AMENDMENT.—Section 173(f) of
2 the Workforce Investment Act of 1998 (29 U.S.C.
3 2918(f)) is amended by adding at the end the following:
4   "(8) CONTINUED QUALIFICATION OF FAMILY
5   MEMBERS AFTER CERTAIN EVENTS.—In the case of
6   eligible coverage months beginning before January
7   1, 2011—
8   "(A) MEDICARE ELIGIBILITY.—In the case
9   of any month which would be an eligible cov-
10   erage month with respect to an eligible indi-
11   vidual but for paragraph (7)(B)(i), such month
12   shall be treated as an eligible coverage month
13   with respect to such eligible individual solely for
14   purposes of determining the eligibility of quali-
15   fying family members of such individual under
16   this subsection. This subparagraph shall only
17   apply with respect to the first 24 months after
18   such eligible individual is first entitled to the
19   benefits described in paragraph (7)(B)(i).
20   "(B) DIVORCE.—In the case of the final-
21   ization of a divorce between an eligible indi-
22   vidual and such individual's spouse, such spouse
23   shall be treated as an eligible individual for pur-
24   poses of this subsection for a period of 24
25   months beginning with the date of such final-

1   ization, except that the only qualifying family
2   members who may be taken into account with
3   respect to such spouse are those individuals who
4   were qualifying family members immediately be-
5   fore such finalization.
6   "(C) DEATH.—In the case of the death of
7   an eligible individual—
8   "(i) any spouse of such individual (de-
9   termined at the time of such death) shall
10   be treated as an eligible individual for pur-
11   poses of this subsection for a period of 24
12   months beginning with the date of such
13   death, except that the only qualifying fam-
14   ily members who may be taken into ac-
15   count with respect to such spouse are those
16   individuals who were qualifying family
17   members immediately before such death,
18   and
19   "(ii) any individual who was a quali-
20   fying family member of the decedent imme-
21   diately before such death shall be treated
22   as an eligible individual for purposes this
23   subsection for a period of 24 months be-
24   ginning with the date of such death, except
25   that no qualifying family members may be

1   taken into account with respect to such in-

2   dividual.".

3   (c) EFFECTIVE DATE.—The amendments made by

4 this section shall apply to months beginning after Decem-

5 ber 31, 2009.

6 **SEC. 1899F. EXTENSION OF COBRA BENEFITS FOR CERTAIN**

7   **TAA-ELIGIBLE INDIVIDUALS AND PBGC RE-**

8   **CIPIENTS.**

9   (a) ERISA AMENDMENTS.—Section 602(2)(A) of the

10 Employee Retirement Income Security Act of 1974 (29

11 U.S.C. 1162(2)(A)) is amended—

12   (1) by moving clause (v) to after clause (iv) and

13   before the flush left sentence beginning with "In the

14   case of a qualified beneficiary";

15   (2) by striking "In the case of a qualified bene-

16   ficiary" and inserting the following:

17   "(vi) SPECIAL RULE FOR DIS-

18   ABILITY.—In the case of a qualified bene-

19   ficiary"; and

20   (3) by redesignating clauses (v) and (vi), as

21   amended by paragraphs (1) and (2), as clauses (vii)

22   and (viii), respectively, and by inserting after clause

23   (iv) the following new clauses:

24   "(v) SPECIAL RULE FOR PBGC RECIPI-

25   ENTS.—In the case of a qualifying event

1   described in section 603(2) with respect to

2   a covered employee who (as of such quali-

3   fying event) has a nonforfeitable right to a

4   benefit any portion of which is to be paid

5   by the Pension Benefit Guaranty Corpora-

6   tion under title IV, notwithstanding clause

7   (i) or (ii), the date of the death of the cov-

8   ered employee, or in the case of the sur-

9   viving spouse or dependent children of the

10   covered employee, 24 months after the

11   date of the death of the covered employee.

12   The preceding sentence shall not require

13   any period of coverage to extend beyond

14   December 31, 2010.

15   "(vi) SPECIAL RULE FOR TAA-ELIGI-

16   BLE INDIVIDUALS.—In the case of a quali-

17   fying event described in section 603(2)

18   with respect to a covered employee who is

19   (as of the date that the period of coverage

20   would, but for this clause or clause (vii),

21   otherwise terminate under clause (i) or

22   (ii)) a TAA-eligible individual (as defined

23   in section 605(b)(4)(B)), the period of cov-

24   erage shall not terminate by reason of

25   clause (i) or (ii), as the case may be, be-

1   fore the later of the date specified in such

2   clause or the date on which such individual

3   ceases to be such a TAA-eligible individual.

4   The preceding sentence shall not require

5   any period of coverage to extend beyond

6   December 31, 2010.''.

7 (b) IRC AMENDMENTS.—Clause (i) of section

8 4980B(f)(2)(B) of the Internal Revenue Code of 1986 is

9 amended—

10   (1) by striking "In the case of a qualified bene-

11 ficiary" and inserting the following:

12   "(VI) SPECIAL RULE FOR DIS-

13   ABILITY.—In the case of a qualified

14   beneficiary", and

15   (2) by redesignating subclauses (V) and (VI),

16 as amended by paragraph (1), as subclauses (VII)

17 and (VIII), respectively, and by inserting after

18 clause (IV) the following new subclauses:

19   "(V) SPECIAL RULE FOR PBGC

20   RECIPIENTS.—In the case of a quali-

21   fying event described in paragraph

22   (3)(B) with respect to a covered em-

23   ployee who (as of such qualifying

24   event) has a nonforfeitable right to a

25   benefit any portion of which is to be

1 paid by the Pension Benefit Guaranty

2 Corporation under title IV of the Em-

3 ployee Retirement Income Security

4 Act of 1974, notwithstanding sub-

5 clause (I) or (II), the date of the

6 death of the covered employee, or in

7 the case of the surviving spouse or de-

8 pendent children of the covered em-

9 ployee, 24 months after the date of

10 the death of the covered employee.

11 The preceding sentence shall not re-

12 quire any period of coverage to extend

13 beyond December 31, 2010.

14 "(VI) SPECIAL RULE FOR TAA-

15 ELIGIBLE INDIVIDUALS.—In the case

16 of a qualifying event described in

17 paragraph (3)(B) with respect to a

18 covered employee who is (as of the

19 date that the period of coverage

20 would, but for this subclause or sub-

21 clause (VII), otherwise terminate

22 under subclause (I) or (II)) a TAA-el-

23 igible individual (as defined in para-

24 graph (5)(C)(iv)(II)), the period of

25 coverage shall not terminate by reason

of subclause (I) or (II), as the case
may be, before the later of the date
specified in such subclause or the date
on which such individual ceases to be
such a TAA-eligible individual. The
preceding sentence shall not require
any period of coverage to extend beyond December 31, 2010.".

(c) PHSA AMENDMENTS.—Section 2202(2)(A) of
the Public Health Service Act (42 U.S.C. 300bb-2(2)(A))
is amended—

(1) by striking "In the case of a qualified beneficiary" and inserting the following:

"(v) SPECIAL RULE FOR DIS-
ABILITY.—In the case of a qualified beneficiary"; and

(2) by redesignating clauses (iv) and (v), as
amended by paragraph (1), as clauses (v) and (vi),
respectively, and by inserting after clause (iii) the
following new clause:

"(iv) SPECIAL RULE FOR TAA-ELIGI-
BLE INDIVIDUALS.—In the case of a qualifying event described in section 2203(2)
with respect to a covered employee who is
(as of the date that the period of coverage

would, but for this clause or clause (v),
otherwise terminate under clause (i) or
(ii)) a TAA-eligible individual (as defined
in section 2205(b)(4)(B)), the period of
coverage shall not terminate by reason of
clause (i) or (ii), as the case may be, before the later of the date specified in such
clause or the date on which such individual
ceases to be such a TAA-eligible individual.
The preceding sentence shall not require
any period of coverage to extend beyond
December 31, 2010.''.

(d) EFFECTIVE DATE.—The amendments made by
this section shall apply to periods of coverage which would
(without regard to the amendments made by this section)
end on or after the date of the enactment of this Act.

SEC. 1899G. ADDITION OF COVERAGE THROUGH VOL-
UNTARY EMPLOYEES' BENEFICIARY ASSOCIA-
TIONS.

(a) IN GENERAL.—Paragraph (1) of section 35(e) of
the Internal Revenue Code of 1986 is amended by adding
at the end the following new subparagraph:

"(K) In the case of eligible coverage
months beginning before January 1, 2011, coverage under an employee benefit plan funded by

1   a voluntary employees' beneficiary association

2   (as defined in section 501(c)(9)) established

3   pursuant to an order of a bankruptcy court, or

4   by agreement with an authorized representative,

5   as provided in section 1114 of title 11, United

6   States Code.''.

7   (b) EFFECTIVE DATE.—The amendments made by

8 this section shall apply to coverage months beginning after

9 the date of the enactment of this Act.

10 **SEC. 1899H. NOTICE REQUIREMENTS.**

11   (a) IN GENERAL.—Subsection (d) of section 7527 of

12 the Internal Revenue Code of 1986 (relating to qualified

13 health insurance costs credit eligibility certificate) is

14 amended to read as follows:

15   ''(d) QUALIFIED HEALTH INSURANCE COSTS ELIGI-

16 BILITY CERTIFICATE.—

17   ''(1) IN GENERAL.—For purposes of this sec-

18   tion, the term 'qualified health insurance costs eligi-

19   bility certificate' means any written statement that

20   an individual is an eligible individual (as defined in

21   section 35(c)) if such statement provides such infor-

22   mation as the Secretary may require for purposes of

23   this section and—

24   ''(A) in the case of an eligible TAA recipi-

25   ent (as defined in section 35(c)(2)) or an eligi-

330

ble alternative TAA recipient (as defined in section 35(c)(3)), is certified by the Secretary of
Labor (or by any other person or entity designated by the Secretary), or

"(B) in the case of an eligible PBGC pension recipient (as defined in section 35(c)(4)), is
certified by the Pension Benefit Guaranty Corporation (or by any other person or entity designated by the Secretary).

"(2) INCLUSION OF CERTAIN INFORMATION.—
In the case of any statement described in paragraph
(1) which is issued before January 1, 2011, such
statement shall not be treated as a qualified health
insurance costs credit eligibility certificate unless
such statement includes—

"(A) the name, address, and telephone
number of the State office or offices responsible
for providing the individual with assistance with
enrollment in qualified health insurance (as defined in section 35(e)),

"(B) a list of the coverage options that are
treated as qualified health insurance (as so defined) by the State in which the individual resides, and

1   "(C) in the case of a TAA-eligible indi-

2   vidual (as defined in section

3   4980B(f)(5)(C)(iv)(II)), a statement informing

4   the individual that the individual has 63 days

5   from the date that is 7 days after the date of

6   the issuance of such certificate to enroll in such

7   insurance without a lapse in creditable coverage

8   (as defined in section 9801(c)).".

9   (b) EFFECTIVE DATE.—The amendment made by

10 this section shall apply to certificates issued after the date

11 that is 6 months after the date of the enactment of this

12 Act.

13 **SEC. 1899I. SURVEY AND REPORT ON ENHANCED HEALTH**

14   **COVERAGE TAX CREDIT PROGRAM.**

15   (a) SURVEY.—

16   (1) IN GENERAL.—The Secretary of the Treas-

17   ury shall conduct a biennial survey of eligible indi-

18   viduals (as defined in section 35(c) of the Internal

19   Revenue Code of 1986) relating to the health cov-

20   erage tax credit under section 35 of the Internal

21   Revenue Code of 1986 (hereinafter in this section

22   referred to as the "health coverage tax credit").

23   (2) INFORMATION OBTAINED.—The survey con-

24   ducted under subsection (a) shall obtain the fol-

25   lowing information:

1   (A) HCTC PARTICIPANTS.—In the case of
2   eligible individuals receiving the health coverage
3   tax credit (including individuals participating in
4   the health coverage tax credit program under
5   section 7527 of such Code, hereinafter in this
6   section referred to as the "HCTC program")—

7   (i) demographic information of such
8   individuals, including income and edu-
9   cation levels,

10   (ii) satisfaction of such individuals
11   with the enrollment process in the HCTC
12   program,

13   (iii) satisfaction of such individuals
14   with available health coverage options
15   under the credit, including level of pre-
16   miums, benefits, deductibles, cost-sharing
17   requirements, and the adequacy of provider
18   networks, and

19   (iv) any other information that the
20   Secretary determines is appropriate.

21   (B) NON-HCTC PARTICIPANTS.—In the
22   case of eligible individuals not receiving the
23   health coverage tax credit—

        (i) demographic information of each individual, including income and education levels,

        (ii) whether the individual was aware of the health coverage tax credit or the HCTC program,

        (iii) the reasons the individual has not enrolled in the HCTC program, including whether such reasons include the burden of the process of enrollment and the affordability of coverage,

        (iv) whether the individual has health insurance coverage, and, if so, the source of such coverage, and

        (v) any other information that the Secretary determines is appropriate.

(3) REPORT.—Not later than December 31 of each year in which a survey is conducted under paragraph (1) (beginning in 2010), the Secretary of the Treasury shall report to the Committee on Finance and the Committee on Health, Education, Labor, and Pensions of the Senate and the Committee on Ways and Means, the Committee on Education and Labor, and the Committee on Energy and Commerce of the House of Representatives the

1   findings of the most recent survey conducted under

2   paragraph (1).

3   (b) REPORT.—Not later than October 1 of each year

4   (beginning in 2010), the Secretary of the Treasury (after

5   consultation with the Secretary of Health and Human

6   Services, and, in the case of the information required

7   under paragraph (7), the Secretary of Labor) shall report

8   to the Committee on Finance and the Committee on

9   Health, Education, Labor, and Pensions of the Senate and

10 the Committee on Ways and Means, the Committee on

11 Education and Labor, and the Committee on Energy and

12 Commerce of the House of Representatives the following

13 information with respect to the most recent taxable year

14 ending before such date:

15   (1) In each State and nationally—

16   (A) the total number of eligible individuals

17   (as defined in section 35(c) of the Internal Rev-

18   enue Code of 1986) and the number of eligible

19   individuals receiving the health coverage tax

20   credit,

21   (B) the total number of such eligible indi-

22   viduals who receive an advance payment of the

23   health coverage tax credit through the HCTC

24   program,

1   (C) the average length of the time period
2   of the participation of eligible individuals in the
3   HCTC program, and

4   (D) the total number of participating eligi-
5   ble individuals in the HCTC program who are
6   enrolled in each category of coverage as de-
7   scribed in section 35(e)(1) of such Code,
8   with respect to each category of eligible individuals
9   described in section 35(c)(1) of such Code.

10   (2) In each State and nationally, an analysis
11 of—

12   (A) the range of monthly health insurance
13 premiums, for self-only coverage and for family
14 coverage, for individuals receiving the health
15 coverage tax credit, and

16   (B) the average and median monthly
17 health insurance premiums, for self-only cov-
18 erage and for family coverage, for individuals
19 receiving the health coverage tax credit,
20 with respect to each category of coverage as de-
21 scribed in section 35(e)(1) of such Code.

22   (3) In each State and nationally, an analysis of
23 the following information with respect to the health
24 insurance coverage of individuals receiving the
25 health coverage tax credit who are enrolled in cov-

erage described in subparagraphs (B) through (H)
of section 35(e)(1) of such Code:

    (A) Deductible amounts.

    (B) Other out-of-pocket cost-sharing
amounts.

    (C) A description of any annual or lifetime
limits on coverage or any other significant limits on coverage services, or benefits.

The information required under this paragraph shall be reported with respect to each category of coverage described in such subparagraphs.

    (4) In each State and nationally, the gender and average age of eligible individuals (as defined in section 35(c) of such Code) who receive the health coverage tax credit, in each category of coverage described in section 35(e)(1) of such Code, with respect to each category of eligible individuals described in such section.

    (5) The steps taken by the Secretary of the Treasury to increase the participation rates in the HCTC program among eligible individuals, including outreach and enrollment activities.

    (6) The cost of administering the HCTC program by function, including the cost of subcontractors, and recommendations on ways to reduce ad-

1   ministrative costs, including recommended statutory

2   changes.

3   (7) The number of States applying for and re-

4   ceiving national emergency grants under section

5   173(f) of the Workforce Investment Act of 1998 (29

6   U.S.C. 2918(f)), the activities funded by such grants

7   on a State-by-State basis, and the time necessary for

8   application approval of such grants.

9 **SEC. 1899J. AUTHORIZATION OF APPROPRIATIONS.**

10   There is authorized to be appropriated $80,000,000

11 for the period of fiscal years 2009 through 2010 to imple-

12 ment the amendments made by, and the provisions of, sec-

13 tions 1899 through 1899I of this part.

14 **SEC. 1899K. EXTENSION OF NATIONAL EMERGENCY**

15   **GRANTS.**

16   (a) IN GENERAL.—Section 173(f) of the Workforce

17 Investment Act of 1998 (29 U.S.C. 2918(f)), as amended

18 by this Act, is amended—

19   (1) by striking paragraph (1) and inserting the

20   following new paragraph:

21   "(1) USE OF FUNDS.—

22   "(A) HEALTH INSURANCE COVERAGE FOR

23   ELIGIBLE INDIVIDUALS IN ORDER TO OBTAIN

24   QUALIFIED HEALTH INSURANCE THAT HAS

25   GUARANTEED ISSUE AND OTHER CONSUMER

1   PROTECTIONS.—Funds made available to a

2   State or entity under paragraph (4)(A) of sub-

3   section (a) may be used to provide an eligible

4   individual described in paragraph (4)(C) and

5   such individual's qualifying family members

6   with health insurance coverage for the 3-month

7   period that immediately precedes the first eligi-

8   ble coverage month (as defined in section 35(b)

9   of the Internal Revenue Code of 1986) in which

10   such eligible individual and such individual's

11   qualifying family members are covered by quali-

12   fied health insurance that meets the require-

13   ments described in clauses (i) through (v) of

14   section 35(e)(2)(A) of the Internal Revenue

15   Code of 1986 (or such longer minimum period

16   as is necessary in order for such eligible indi-

17   vidual and such individual's qualifying family

18   members to be covered by qualified health in-

19   surance that meets such requirements).

20   "(B) ADDITIONAL USES.—Funds made

21   available to a State or entity under paragraph

22   (4)(A) of subsection (a) may be used by the

23   State or entity for the following:

24   "(i) HEALTH INSURANCE COV-

25   ERAGE.—To assist an eligible individual

and such individual's qualifying family
members with enrolling in health insurance
coverage and qualified health insurance or
paying premiums for such coverage or insurance.

"(ii) ADMINISTRATIVE EXPENSES AND
START-UP EXPENSES TO ESTABLISH
GROUP HEALTH PLAN COVERAGE OPTIONS
FOR QUALIFIED HEALTH INSURANCE.—To
pay the administrative expenses related to
the enrollment of eligible individuals and
such individuals' qualifying family members in health insurance coverage and
qualified health insurance, including—

"(I) eligibility verification activities;

"(II) the notification of eligible
individuals of available health insurance and qualified health insurance
options;

"(III) processing qualified health
insurance costs credit eligibility certificates provided for under section
7527 of the Internal Revenue Code of
1986;

1   "(IV) providing assistance to eli-

2   gible individuals in enrolling in health

3   insurance coverage and qualified

4   health insurance;

5   "(V) the development or installa-

6   tion of necessary data management

7   systems; and

8   "(VI) any other expenses deter-

9   mined appropriate by the Secretary,

10   including start-up costs and on going

11   administrative expenses, in order for

12   the State to treat the coverage de-

13   scribed in subparagraphs (C) through

14   (H) of section 35(e)(1) of the Internal

15   Revenue Code of 1986 as qualified

16   health insurance under that section.

17   "(iii) OUTREACH.—To pay for out-

18   reach to eligible individuals to inform such

19   individuals of available health insurance

20   and qualified health insurance options, in-

21   cluding outreach consisting of notice to eli-

22   gible individuals of such options made

23   available after the date of enactment of

24   this clause and direct assistance to help

25   potentially eligible individuals and such in-

1   dividual's qualifying family members qual-

2   ify and remain eligible for the credit estab-

3   lished under section 35 of the Internal

4   Revenue Code of 1986 and advance pay-

5   ment of such credit under section 7527 of

6   such Code.

7   "(iv) BRIDGE FUNDING.—To assist

8   potentially eligible individuals to purchase

9   qualified health insurance coverage prior to

10   issuance of a qualified health insurance

11   costs credit eligibility certificate under sec-

12   tion 7527 of the Internal Revenue Code of

13   1986 and commencement of advance pay-

14   ment, and receipt of expedited payment,

15   under subsections (a) and (e), respectively,

16   of that section.

17   "(C) RULE OF CONSTRUCTION.—The in-

18   clusion of a permitted use under this paragraph

19   shall not be construed as prohibiting a similar

20   use of funds permitted under subsection (g).";

21   and

22   (2) by striking paragraph (2) and inserting the

23 following new paragraph:

24   "(2) QUALIFIED HEALTH INSURANCE.—For

25 purposes of this subsection and subsection (g), the

1   term 'qualified health insurance' has the meaning

2   given that term in section 35(e) of the Internal Rev-

3   enue Code of 1986.''.

4   (b) FUNDING.—Section 174(c)(1) of the Workforce

5 Investment Act of 1998 (29 U.S.C. 2919(c)(1)) is

6 amended—

7   (1) in the paragraph heading, by striking "AU-

8   THORIZATION AND APPROPRIATION FOR FISCAL

9   YEAR 2002" and inserting "APPROPRIATIONS"; and

10   (2) by striking subparagraph (A) and inserting

11   the following new subparagraph:

12   "(A) to carry out subsection (a)(4)(A) of

13   section 173—

14   "(i) $10,000,000 for fiscal year 2002;

15   and

16   "(ii) $150,000,000 for the period of

17   fiscal years 2009 through 2010; and".

18 **SEC. 1899L. GAO STUDY AND REPORT.**

19   (a) STUDY.—The Comptroller General of the United

20 States shall conduct a study regarding the health insur-

21 ance tax credit allowed under section 35 of the Internal

22 Revenue Code of 1986.

23   (b) REPORT.—Not later than March 1, 2010, the

24 Comptroller General shall submit a report to Congress re-

1 garding the results of the study conducted under sub-

2 section (a). Such report shall include an analysis of—

3   (1) the administrative costs—

4   (A) of the Federal Government with re-

5   spect to such credit and the advance payment

6   of such credit under section 7527 of such Code,

7   and

8   (B) of providers of qualified health insur-

9   ance with respect to providing such insurance

10   to eligible individuals and their qualifying fam-

11   ily members,

12   (2) the health status and relative risk status of

13 eligible individuals and qualifying family members

14 covered under such insurance,

15   (3) participation in such credit and the advance

16 payment of such credit by eligible individuals and

17 their qualifying family members, including the rea-

18 sons why such individuals did or did not participate

19 and the effect of the amendments made by this part

20 on such participation, and

21   (4) the extent to which eligible individuals and

22 their qualifying family members—

23   (A) obtained health insurance other than

24   qualifying health insurance, or

1   (B) went without health insurance cov-

2   erage.

3   (c) ACCESS TO RECORDS.—For purposes of con-

4 ducting the study required under this section, the Comp-

5 troller General and any of his duly authorized representa-

6 tives shall have access to, and the right to examine and

7 copy, all documents, records, and other recorded

8 information—

9   (1) within the possession or control of providers

10   of qualified health insurance, and

11   (2) determined by the Comptroller General (or

12   any such representative) to be relevant to the study.

13 The Comptroller General shall not disclose the identity of

14 any provider of qualified health insurance or any eligible

15 individual in making any information obtained under this

16 section available to the public.

17   (d) DEFINITIONS.—Any term which is defined in sec-

18 tion 35 of the Internal Revenue Code of 1986 shall have

19 the same meaning when used in this section.

1 TITLE II—ASSISTANCE FOR UN-
2 EMPLOYED WORKERS AND
3 STRUGGLING FAMILIES

4 SEC. 2000. SHORT TITLE; TABLE OF CONTENTS OF TITLE.

5   (a) SHORT TITLE.—This title may be cited as the

6 "Assistance for Unemployed Workers and Struggling

7 Families Act".

8   (b) TABLE OF CONTENTS OF TITLE.—The table of

9 contents of this title is as follows:

TITLE II—ASSISTANCE FOR UNEMPLOYED WORKERS AND
STRUGGLING FAMILIES

Sec. 2000. Short title; table of contents of title.

Subtitle A—Unemployment Insurance

Sec. 2001. Extension of emergency unemployment compensation program.
Sec. 2002. Increase in unemployment compensation benefits.
Sec. 2003. Special transfers for unemployment compensation modernization.
Sec. 2004. Temporary assistance for states with advances.
Sec. 2005. Full Federal funding of extended unemployment compensation for a limited period.
Sec. 2006. Temporary increase in extended unemployment benefits under the Railroad Unemployment Insurance Act.

Subtitle B—Assistance for Vulnerable Individuals

Sec. 2101. Emergency fund for TANF program.
Sec. 2102. Extension of TANF supplemental grants.
Sec. 2103. Clarification of authority of States to use TANF funds carried over from prior years to provide TANF benefits and services.
Sec. 2104. Temporary resumption of prior child support law.

Subtitle C—Economic Recovery Payments to Certain Individuals

Sec. 2201. Economic recovery payment to recipients of social security, supplemental security income, railroad retirement benefits, and veterans disability compensation or pension benefits.
Sec. 2202. Special credit for certain government retirees.

Subtitle A—Unemployment Insurance

SEC. 2001. EXTENSION OF EMERGENCY UNEMPLOYMENT COMPENSATION PROGRAM.

(a) IN GENERAL.—Section 4007 of the Supplemental Appropriations Act, 2008 (Public Law 110–252; 26 U.S.C. 3304 note), as amended by section 4 of the Unemployment Compensation Extension Act of 2008 (Public Law 110–449; 122 Stat. 5015), is amended—

(1) by striking "March 31, 2009" each place it appears and inserting "December 31, 2009";

(2) in the heading for subsection (b)(2), by striking "MARCH 31, 2009" and inserting "DECEMBER 31, 2009"; and

(3) in subsection (b)(3), by striking "August 27, 2009" and inserting "May 31, 2010".

(b) FINANCING PROVISIONS.—Section 4004 of such Act is amended by adding at the end the following:

"(e) TRANSFER OF FUNDS.—Notwithstanding any other provision of law, the Secretary of the Treasury shall transfer from the general fund of the Treasury (from funds not otherwise appropriated)—

"(1) to the extended unemployment compensation account (as established by section 905 of the Social Security Act) such sums as the Secretary of

1   Labor estimates to be necessary to make payments

2   to States under this title by reason of the amend-

3   ments made by section 2001(a) of the Assistance for

4   Unemployed Workers and Struggling Families Act;

5   and

6   "(2) to the employment security administration

7   account (as established by section 901 of the Social

8   Security Act) such sums as the Secretary of Labor

9   estimates to be necessary for purposes of assisting

10   States in meeting administrative costs by reason of

11   the amendments referred to in paragraph (1).

12 There are appropriated from the general fund of the

13 Treasury, without fiscal year limitation, the sums referred

14 to in the preceding sentence and such sums shall not be

15 required to be repaid.".

16 **SEC. 2002. INCREASE IN UNEMPLOYMENT COMPENSATION**

17   **BENEFITS.**

18   (a) FEDERAL-STATE AGREEMENTS.—Any State

19 which desires to do so may enter into and participate in

20 an agreement under this section with the Secretary of

21 Labor (hereinafter in this section referred to as the "Sec-

22 retary"). Any State which is a party to an agreement

23 under this section may, upon providing 30 days' written

24 notice to the Secretary, terminate such agreement.

25   (b) PROVISIONS OF AGREEMENT.—

1   (1) ADDITIONAL COMPENSATION.—Any agree-

2   ment under this section shall provide that the State

3   agency of the State will make payments of regular

4   compensation to individuals in amounts and to the

5   extent that they would be determined if the State

6   law of the State were applied, with respect to any

7   week for which the individual is (disregarding this

8   section) otherwise entitled under the State law to re-

9   ceive regular compensation, as if such State law had

10   been modified in a manner such that the amount of

11   regular compensation (including dependents' allow-

12   ances) payable for any week shall be equal to the

13   amount determined under the State law (before the

14   application of this paragraph) plus an additional

15   $25.

16   (2) ALLOWABLE METHODS OF PAYMENT.—Any

17   additional compensation provided for in accordance

18   with paragraph (1) shall be payable either—

19   (A) as an amount which is paid at the

20   same time and in the same manner as any reg-

21   ular compensation otherwise payable for the

22   week involved; or

23   (B) at the option of the State, by pay-

24   ments which are made separately from, but on

1   the same weekly basis as, any regular com-

2   pensation otherwise payable.

3   (c) NONREDUCTION RULE.—An agreement under

4 this section shall not apply (or shall cease to apply) with

5 respect to a State upon a determination by the Secretary

6 that the method governing the computation of regular

7 compensation under the State law of that State has been

8 modified in a manner such that—

9   (1) the average weekly benefit amount of reg-

10   ular compensation which will be payable during the

11   period of the agreement (determined disregarding

12   any additional amounts attributable to the modifica-

13   tion described in subsection (b)(1)) will be less than

14   (2) the average weekly benefit amount of reg-

15   ular compensation which would otherwise have been

16   payable during such period under the State law, as

17   in effect on December 31, 2008.

18   (d) PAYMENTS TO STATES.—

19   (1) IN GENERAL.—

20   (A) FULL REIMBURSEMENT.—There shall

21   be paid to each State which has entered into an

22   agreement under this section an amount equal

23   to 100 percent of—

24   (i) the total amount of additional

25   compensation (as described in subsection

(b)(1)) paid to individuals by the State pursuant to such agreement; and

(ii) any additional administrative expenses incurred by the State by reason of such agreement (as determined by the Secretary).

(B) TERMS OF PAYMENTS.—Sums payable to any State by reason of such State's having an agreement under this section shall be payable, either in advance or by way of reimbursement (as determined by the Secretary), in such amounts as the Secretary estimates the State will be entitled to receive under this section for each calendar month, reduced or increased, as the case may be, by any amount by which the Secretary finds that his estimates for any prior calendar month were greater or less than the amounts which should have been paid to the State. Such estimates may be made on the basis of such statistical, sampling, or other method as may be agreed upon by the Secretary and the State agency of the State involved.

(2) CERTIFICATIONS.—The Secretary shall from time to time certify to the Secretary of the

1 Treasury for payment to each State the sums pay-
2 able to such State under this section.

3   (3) APPROPRIATION.—There are appropriated
4 from the general fund of the Treasury, without fiscal
5 year limitation, such sums as may be necessary for
6 purposes of this subsection.

7 (e) APPLICABILITY.—

8   (1) IN GENERAL.—An agreement entered into
9 under this section shall apply to weeks of
10 unemployment—

11   (A) beginning after the date on which such
12   agreement is entered into; and

13   (B) ending before January 1, 2010.

14   (2) TRANSITION RULE FOR INDIVIDUALS RE-
15 MAINING ENTITLED TO REGULAR COMPENSATION AS
16 OF JANUARY 1, 2010.—In the case of any individual
17 who, as of the date specified in paragraph (1)(B),
18 has not yet exhausted all rights to regular com-
19 pensation under the State law of a State with re-
20 spect to a benefit year that began before such date,
21 additional compensation (as described in subsection
22 (b)(1)) shall continue to be payable to such indi-
23 vidual for any week beginning on or after such date
24 for which the individual is otherwise eligible for reg-
25 ular compensation with respect to such benefit year.

1   (3) TERMINATION.—Notwithstanding any other

2   provision of this subsection, no additional compensa-

3   tion (as described in subsection (b)(1)) shall be pay-

4   able for any week beginning after June 30, 2010.

5   (f) FRAUD AND OVERPAYMENTS.—The provisions of

6 section 4005 of the Supplemental Appropriations Act,

7 2008 (Public Law 110–252; 122 Stat. 2356) shall apply

8 with respect to additional compensation (as described in

9 subsection (b)(1)) to the same extent and in the same

10 manner as in the case of emergency unemployment com-

11 pensation.

12   (g) APPLICATION TO OTHER UNEMPLOYMENT BENE-

13 FITS.—

14   (1) IN GENERAL.—Each agreement under this

15   section shall include provisions to provide that the

16   purposes of the preceding provisions of this section

17   shall be applied with respect to unemployment bene-

18   fits described in subsection (i)(3) to the same extent

19   and in the same manner as if those benefits were

20   regular compensation.

21   (2) ELIGIBILITY AND TERMINATION RULES.—

22   Additional compensation (as described in subsection

23   (b)(1))—

24   (A) shall not be payable, pursuant to this

25   subsection, with respect to any unemployment

1   benefits described in subsection (i)(3) for any

2   week beginning on or after the date specified in

3   subsection (e)(1)(B), except in the case of an

4   individual who was eligible to receive additional

5   compensation (as so described) in connection

6   with any regular compensation or any unem-

7   ployment benefits described in subsection (i)(3)

8   for any period of unemployment ending before

9   such date; and

10   (B) shall in no event be payable for any

11   week beginning after the date specified in sub-

12   section (e)(3).

13   (h) DISREGARD OF ADDITIONAL COMPENSATION FOR

14 PURPOSES OF MEDICAID AND SCHIP.—The monthly

15 equivalent of any additional compensation paid under this

16 section shall be disregarded in considering the amount of

17 income of an individual for any purposes under title XIX

18 and title XXI of the Social Security Act.

19   (i) DEFINITIONS.—For purposes of this section—

20   (1) the terms "compensation", "regular com-

21   pensation", "benefit year", "State", "State agency",

22   "State law", and "week" have the respective mean-

23   ings given such terms under section 205 of the Fed-

24   eral-State Extended Unemployment Compensation

25   Act of 1970 (26 U.S.C. 3304 note);

(2) the term "emergency unemployment compensation" means emergency unemployment compensation under title IV of the Supplemental Appropriations Act, 2008 (Public Law 110–252; 122 Stat. 2353); and

(3) any reference to unemployment benefits described in this paragraph shall be considered to refer to—

(A) extended compensation (as defined by section 205 of the Federal-State Extended Unemployment Compensation Act of 1970); and

(B) unemployment compensation (as defined by section 85(b) of the Internal Revenue Code of 1986) provided under any program administered by a State under an agreement with the Secretary.

SEC. 2003. SPECIAL TRANSFERS FOR UNEMPLOYMENT COMPENSATION MODERNIZATION.

(a) IN GENERAL.—Section 903 of the Social Security Act (42 U.S.C. 1103) is amended by adding at the end the following:

"Special Transfers in Fiscal Years 2009, 2010, and 2011 for Modernization

"(f)(1)(A) In addition to any other amounts, the Secretary of Labor shall provide for the making of unemploy-

1 ment compensation modernization incentive payments
2 (hereinafter 'incentive payments') to the accounts of the
3 States in the Unemployment Trust Fund, by transfer from
4 amounts reserved for that purpose in the Federal unem-
5 ployment account, in accordance with succeeding provi-
6 sions of this subsection.

7 "(B) The maximum incentive payment allowable
8 under this subsection with respect to any State shall, as
9 determined by the Secretary of Labor, be equal to the
10 amount obtained by multiplying $7,000,000,000 by the
11 same ratio as would apply under subsection (a)(2)(B) for
12 purposes of determining such State's share of any excess
13 amount (as described in subsection (a)(1)) that would
14 have been subject to transfer to State accounts, as of Oc-
15 tober 1, 2008, under the provisions of subsection (a).

16 "(C) Of the maximum incentive payment determined
17 under subparagraph (B) with respect to a State—

18   "(i) one-third shall be transferred to the ac-
19   count of such State upon a certification under para-
20   graph (4)(B) that the State law of such State meets
21   the requirements of paragraph (2); and

22   "(ii) the remainder shall be transferred to the
23   account of such State upon a certification under
24   paragraph (4)(B) that the State law of such State
25   meets the requirements of paragraph (3).

1   "(2) The State law of a State meets the requirements

2 of this paragraph if such State law—

3   "(A) uses a base period that includes the most

4   recently completed calendar quarter before the start

5   of the benefit year for purposes of determining eligi-

6   bility for unemployment compensation; or

7   "(B) provides that, in the case of an individual

8   who would not otherwise be eligible for unemploy-

9   ment compensation under the State law because of

10   the use of a base period that does not include the

11   most recently completed calendar quarter before the

12   start of the benefit year, eligibility shall be deter-

13   mined using a base period that includes such cal-

14   endar quarter.

15   "(3) The State law of a State meets the requirements

16 of this paragraph if such State law includes provisions to

17 carry out at least 2 of the following subparagraphs:

18   "(A) An individual shall not be denied regular

19   unemployment compensation under any State law

20   provisions relating to availability for work, active

21   search for work, or refusal to accept work, solely be-

22   cause such individual is seeking only part-time work

23   (as defined by the Secretary of Labor), except that

24   the State law provisions carrying out this subpara-

25   graph may exclude an individual if a majority of the

1 weeks of work in such individual's base period do
2 not include part-time work (as so defined).

3   "(B) An individual shall not be disqualified
4 from regular unemployment compensation for sepa-
5 rating from employment if that separation is for any
6 compelling family reason. For purposes of this sub-
7 paragraph, the term 'compelling family reason'
8 means the following:

9   "(i) Domestic violence, verified by such
10 reasonable and confidential documentation as
11 the State law may require, which causes the in-
12 dividual reasonably to believe that such individ-
13 ual's continued employment would jeopardize
14 the safety of the individual or of any member
15 of the individual's immediate family (as defined
16 by the Secretary of Labor).

17   "(ii) The illness or disability of a member
18 of the individual's immediate family (as those
19 terms are defined by the Secretary of Labor).

20   "(iii) The need for the individual to accom-
21 pany such individual's spouse—

22   "(I) to a place from which it is im-
23 practical for such individual to commute;
24 and

1   "(II) due to a change in location of

2   the spouse's employment.

3   "(C)(i) Weekly unemployment compensation is

4 payable under this subparagraph to any individual

5 who is unemployed (as determined under the State

6 unemployment compensation law), has exhausted all

7 rights to regular unemployment compensation under

8 the State law, and is enrolled and making satisfac-

9 tory progress in a State-approved training program

10 or in a job training program authorized under the

11 Workforce Investment Act of 1998, except that such

12 compensation is not required to be paid to an indi-

13 vidual who is receiving similar stipends or other

14 training allowances for non-training costs.

15   "(ii) Each State-approved training program or

16 job training program referred to in clause (i) shall

17 prepare individuals who have been separated from a

18 declining occupation, or who have been involuntarily

19 and indefinitely separated from employment as a re-

20 sult of a permanent reduction of operations at the

21 individual's place of employment, for entry into a

22 high-demand occupation.

23   "(iii) The amount of unemployment compensa-

24 tion payable under this subparagraph to an indi-

1 vidual for a week of unemployment shall be equal

2 to—

3   "(I) the individual's average weekly benefit

4   amount (including dependents' allowances) for

5   the most recent benefit year, less

6   "(II) any deductible income, as determined

7   under State law.

8 The total amount of unemployment compensation

9 payable under this subparagraph to any individual

10 shall be equal to at least 26 times the individual's

11 average weekly benefit amount (including depend-

12 ents' allowances) for the most recent benefit year.

13   "(D) Dependents' allowances are provided, in

14 the case of any individual who is entitled to receive

15 regular unemployment compensation and who has

16 any dependents (as defined by State law), in an

17 amount equal to at least $15 per dependent per

18 week, subject to any aggregate limitation on such al-

19 lowances which the State law may establish (but

20 which aggregate limitation on the total allowance for

21 dependents paid to an individual may not be less

22 than $50 for each week of unemployment or 50 per-

23 cent of the individual's weekly benefit amount for

24 the benefit year, whichever is less), except that a

25 State law may provide for a reasonable reduction in

1   the amount of any such allowance for a week of less

2   than total unemployment.

3   "(4)(A) Any State seeking an incentive payment

4 under this subsection shall submit an application therefor

5 at such time, in such manner, and complete with such in-

6 formation as the Secretary of Labor may within 60 days

7 after the date of the enactment of this subsection prescribe

8 (whether by regulation or otherwise), including informa-

9 tion relating to compliance with the requirements of para-

10 graph (2) or (3), as well as how the State intends to use

11 the incentive payment to improve or strengthen the State's

12 unemployment compensation program. The Secretary of

13 Labor shall, within 30 days after receiving a complete ap-

14 plication, notify the State agency of the State of the Sec-

15 retary's findings with respect to the requirements of para-

16 graph (2) or (3) (or both).

17   "(B)(i) If the Secretary of Labor finds that the State

18 law provisions (disregarding any State law provisions

19 which are not then currently in effect as permanent law

20 or which are subject to discontinuation) meet the require-

21 ments of paragraph (2) or (3), as the case may be, the

22 Secretary of Labor shall thereupon make a certification

23 to that effect to the Secretary of the Treasury, together

24 with a certification as to the amount of the incentive pay-

25 ment to be transferred to the State account pursuant to

1 that finding. The Secretary of the Treasury shall make
2 the appropriate transfer within 7 days after receiving such
3 certification.

4   "(ii) For purposes of clause (i), State law provisions
5 which are to take effect within 12 months after the date
6 of their certification under this subparagraph shall be con-
7 sidered to be in effect as of the date of such certification.

8   "(C)(i) No certification of compliance with the re-
9 quirements of paragraph (2) or (3) may be made with re-
10 spect to any State whose State law is not otherwise eligible
11 for certification under section 303 or approvable under
12 section 3304 of the Federal Unemployment Tax Act.

13   "(ii) No certification of compliance with the require-
14 ments of paragraph (3) may be made with respect to any
15 State whose State law is not in compliance with the re-
16 quirements of paragraph (2).

17   "(iii) No application under subparagraph (A) may be
18 considered if submitted before the date of the enactment
19 of this subsection or after the latest date necessary (as
20 specified by the Secretary of Labor) to ensure that all in-
21 centive payments under this subsection are made before
22 October 1, 2011.

23   "(5)(A) Except as provided in subparagraph (B), any
24 amount transferred to the account of a State under this
25 subsection may be used by such State only in the payment

1 of cash benefits to individuals with respect to their unem-
2 ployment (including for dependents' allowances and for
3 unemployment compensation under paragraph (3)(C)), ex-
4 clusive of expenses of administration.

5   "(B) A State may, subject to the same conditions as
6 set forth in subsection (c)(2) (excluding subparagraph (B)
7 thereof, and deeming the reference to 'subsections (a) and
8 (b)' in subparagraph (D) thereof to include this sub-
9 section), use any amount transferred to the account of
10 such State under this subsection for the administration
11 of its unemployment compensation law and public employ-
12 ment offices.

13   "(6) Out of any money in the Federal unemployment
14 account not otherwise appropriated, the Secretary of the
15 Treasury shall reserve $7,000,000,000 for incentive pay-
16 ments under this subsection. Any amount so reserved shall
17 not be taken into account for purposes of any determina-
18 tion under section 902, 910, or 1203 of the amount in
19 the Federal unemployment account as of any given time.
20 Any amount so reserved for which the Secretary of the
21 Treasury has not received a certification under paragraph
22 (4)(B) by the deadline described in paragraph (4)(C)(iii)
23 shall, upon the close of fiscal year 2011, become unre-
24 stricted as to use as part of the Federal unemployment
25 account.

1   "(7) For purposes of this subsection, the terms 'ben-
2 efit year', 'base period', and 'week' have the respective
3 meanings given such terms under section 205 of the Fed-
4 eral-State Extended Unemployment Compensation Act of
5 1970 (26 U.S.C. 3304 note).

6 "Special Transfer in Fiscal Year 2009 for Administration

7   "(g)(1) In addition to any other amounts, the Sec-
8 retary of the Treasury shall transfer from the employment
9 security administration account to the account of each
10 State in the Unemployment Trust Fund, within 30 days
11 after the date of the enactment of this subsection, the
12 amount determined with respect to such State under para-
13 graph (2).

14   "(2) The amount to be transferred under this sub-
15 section to a State account shall (as determined by the Sec-
16 retary of Labor and certified by such Secretary to the Sec-
17 retary of the Treasury) be equal to the amount obtained
18 by multiplying $500,000,000 by the same ratio as deter-
19 mined under subsection (f)(1)(B) with respect to such
20 State.

21   "(3) Any amount transferred to the account of a
22 State as a result of the enactment of this subsection may
23 be used by the State agency of such State only in the pay-
24 ment of expenses incurred by it for—

1   "(A) the administration of the provisions of its

2   State law carrying out the purposes of subsection

3   (f)(2) or any subparagraph of subsection (f)(3);

4   "(B) improved outreach to individuals who

5   might be eligible for regular unemployment com-

6   pensation by virtue of any provisions of the State

7   law which are described in subparagraph (A);

8   "(C) the improvement of unemployment benefit

9   and unemployment tax operations, including re-

10   sponding to increased demand for unemployment

11   compensation; and

12   "(D) staff-assisted reemployment services for

13   unemployment compensation claimants.".

14   (b) REGULATIONS.—The Secretary of Labor may

15 prescribe any regulations, operating instructions, or other

16 guidance necessary to carry out the amendment made by

17 subsection (a).

18 **SEC. 2004. TEMPORARY ASSISTANCE FOR STATES WITH AD-**

19   **VANCES.**

20   Section 1202(b) of the Social Security Act (42 U.S.C.

21 1322(b)) is amended by adding at the end the following

22 new paragraph:

23   "(10)(A) With respect to the period beginning on the

24 date of enactment of this paragraph and ending on De-

25 cember 31, 2010—

1   "(i) any interest payment otherwise due from a

2   State under this subsection during such period shall

3   be deemed to have been made by the State; and

4   "(ii) no interest shall accrue during such period

5   on any advance or advances made under section

6   1201 to a State.

7   "(B) The provisions of subparagraph (A) shall have

8 no effect on the requirement for interest payments under

9 this subsection after the period described in such subpara-

10 graph or on the accrual of interest under this subsection

11 after such period.".

12 **SEC. 2005. FULL FEDERAL FUNDING OF EXTENDED UNEM-**

13   **PLOYMENT COMPENSATION FOR A LIMITED**

14   **PERIOD.**

15   (a) IN GENERAL.—In the case of sharable extended

16 compensation and sharable regular compensation paid for

17 weeks of unemployment beginning after the date of the

18 enactment of this section and before January 1, 2010, sec-

19 tion 204(a)(1) of the Federal-State Extended Unemploy-

20 ment Compensation Act of 1970 (26 U.S.C. 3304 note)

21 shall be applied by substituting "100 percent of" for "one-

22 half of".

23   (b) SPECIAL RULE.—At the option of a State, for

24 any weeks of unemployment beginning after the date of

25 the enactment of this section and before January 1, 2010,

1 an individual's eligibility period (as described in section

2 203(c) of the Federal-State Extended Unemployment

3 Compensation Act of 1970) shall, for purposes of any de-

4 termination of eligibility for extended compensation under

5 the State law of such State, be considered to include any

6 week which begins—

7   (1) after the date as of which such individual

8   exhausts all rights to emergency unemployment com-

9   pensation; and

10   (2) during an extended benefit period that

11   began on or before the date described in paragraph

12   (1).

13   (c) LIMITED EXTENSION.—In the case of an indi-

14 vidual who receives extended compensation with respect to

15 1 or more weeks of unemployment beginning after the date

16 of the enactment of this Act and before January 1, 2010,

17 the provisions of subsections (a) and (b) shall, at the op-

18 tion of a State, be applied by substituting "ending before

19 June 1, 2010" for "before January 1, 2010".

20   (d) EXTENSION OF TEMPORARY FEDERAL MATCH-

21 ING FOR THE FIRST WEEK OF EXTENDED BENEFITS FOR

22 STATES WITH NO WAITING WEEK.—

23   (1) IN GENERAL.—Section 5 of the Unemploy-

24   ment Compensation Extension Act of 2008 (Public

1   Law 110–449) is amended by striking "December 8,

2   2009" and inserting "May 30, 2010".

3   (2) EFFECTIVE DATE.—The amendment made

4   by paragraph (1) shall take effect as if included in

5   the enactment of the Unemployment Compensation

6   Extension Act of 2008 (Public Law 110–449).

7   (e) DEFINITIONS.—For purposes of this section—

8   (1) the terms "sharable extended compensa-

9   tion" and "sharable regular compensation" have the

10   respective meanings given such terms under section

11   204 of the Federal-State Extended Unemployment

12   Compensation Act of 1970;

13   (2) the terms "extended compensation",

14   "State", "State law", and "week" have the respec-

15   tive meanings given such terms under section 205 of

16   the Federal-State Extended Unemployment Com-

17   pensation Act of 1970;

18   (3) the term "emergency unemployment com-

19   pensation" means benefits payable to individuals

20   under title IV of the Supplemental Appropriations

21   Act, 2008 with respect to their unemployment; and

22   (4) the term "extended benefit period" means

23   an extended benefit period as determined in accord-

24   ance with applicable provisions of the Federal-State

1 Extended Unemployment Compensation Act of

2 1970.

3 (f) REGULATIONS.—The Secretary of Labor may pre-

4 scribe any operating instructions or regulations necessary

5 to carry out this section.

6 **SEC. 2006. TEMPORARY INCREASE IN EXTENDED UNEM-**

7 **PLOYMENT BENEFITS UNDER THE RAILROAD**

8 **UNEMPLOYMENT INSURANCE ACT.**

9 (a) IN GENERAL.—Section 2(c)(2) of the Railroad

10 Unemployment Insurance Act (45 U.S.C. 352(c)(2)) is

11 amended by adding at the end the following:

12 "(D) TEMPORARY INCREASE IN EXTENDED

13 UNEMPLOYMENT BENEFITS.—

14 "(i) EMPLOYEES WITH 10 OR MORE

15 YEARS OF SERVICE.—Subject to clause

16 (iii), in the case of an employee who has

17 10 or more years of service (as so defined),

18 with respect to extended unemployment

19 benefits—

20 "(I) subparagraph (A) shall be

21 applied by substituting '130 days of

22 unemployment' for '65 days of unem-

23 ployment'; and

24 "(II) subparagraph (B) shall be

25 applied by inserting '(or, in the case

1   of unemployment benefits, 13 con-

2   secutive 14-day periods)' after '7 con-

3   secutive 14-day periods'.

4   "(ii) EMPLOYEES WITH LESS THAN 10

5   YEARS OF SERVICE.—Subject to clause

6   (iii), in the case of an employee who has

7   less than 10 years of service (as so de-

8   fined), with respect to extended unemploy-

9   ment benefits, this paragraph shall apply

10   to such an employee in the same manner

11   as this paragraph would apply to an em-

12   ployee described in clause (i) if such clause

13   had not been enacted.

14   "(iii) APPLICATION.—The provisions

15   of clauses (i) and (ii) shall apply to an em-

16   ployee who received normal benefits for

17   days of unemployment under this Act dur-

18   ing the period beginning July 1, 2008, and

19   ending on June 30, 2009, except that no

20   extended benefit period under this para-

21   graph shall begin after December 31,

22   2009. Notwithstanding the preceding sen-

23   tence, no benefits shall be payable under

24   this subparagraph and clauses (i) and (ii)

25   shall no longer be applicable upon the ex-

1 haustion of the funds appropriated under

2 clause (iv) for payment of benefits under

3 this subparagraph.

4 "(iv) APPROPRIATION.—Out of any

5 funds in the Treasury not otherwise appro-

6 priated, there are appropriated

7 $20,000,000 to cover the cost of additional

8 extended unemployment benefits provided

9 under this subparagraph, to remain avail-

10 able until expended.".

11 (b) FUNDING FOR ADMINISTRATION.—Out of any

12 funds in the Treasury not otherwise appropriated, there

13 are appropriated to the Railroad Retirement Board

14 $80,000 to cover the administrative expenses associated

15 with the payment of additional extended unemployment

16 benefits under section 2(c)(2)(D) of the Railroad Unem-

17 ployment Insurance Act, as added by subsection (a), to

18 remain available until expended.

19 # Subtitle B—Assistance for

20 # Vulnerable Individuals

21 **SEC. 2101. EMERGENCY FUND FOR TANF PROGRAM.**

22 (a) TEMPORARY FUND.—

23 (1) IN GENERAL.—Section 403 of the Social

24 Security Act (42 U.S.C. 603) is amended by adding

25 at the end the following:

1   "(c) EMERGENCY FUND.—

2   "(1) ESTABLISHMENT.—There is established in

3 the Treasury of the United States a fund which

4 shall be known as the 'Emergency Contingency

5 Fund for State Temporary Assistance for Needy

6 Families Programs' (in this subsection referred to as

7 the 'Emergency Fund').

8   "(2) DEPOSITS INTO FUND.—

9   "(A) IN GENERAL.—Out of any money in

10   the Treasury of the United States not otherwise

11   appropriated, there are appropriated for fiscal

12   year 2009, \$5,000,000,000 for payment to the

13   Emergency Fund.

14   "(B) AVAILABILITY AND USE OF FUNDS.—

15   The amounts appropriated to the Emergency

16   Fund under subparagraph (A) shall remain

17   available through fiscal year 2010 and shall be

18   used to make grants to States in each of fiscal

19   years 2009 and 2010 in accordance with the re-

20   quirements of paragraph (3).

21   "(C) LIMITATION.—In no case may the

22   Secretary make a grant from the Emergency

23   Fund for a fiscal year after fiscal year 2010.

24   "(3) GRANTS.—

372

1   "(A) GRANT RELATED TO CASELOAD IN-
2   CREASES.—

3   "(i) IN GENERAL.—For each calendar
4   quarter in fiscal year 2009 or 2010, the
5   Secretary shall make a grant from the
6   Emergency Fund to each State that—

7   "(I) requests a grant under this
8   subparagraph for the quarter; and

9   "(II) meets the requirement of
10   clause (ii) for the quarter.

11   "(ii) CASELOAD INCREASE REQUIRE-
12   MENT.—A State meets the requirement of
13   this clause for a quarter if the average
14   monthly assistance caseload of the State
15   for the quarter exceeds the average month-
16   ly assistance caseload of the State for the
17   corresponding quarter in the emergency
18   fund base year of the State.

19   "(iii) AMOUNT OF GRANT.—Subject to
20   paragraph (5), the amount of the grant to
21   be made to a State under this subpara-
22   graph for a quarter shall be an amount
23   equal to 80 percent of the amount (if any)
24   by which the total expenditures of the
25   State for basic assistance (as defined by

373

the Secretary) in the quarter, whether
under the State program funded under this
part or as qualified State expenditures, exceeds the total expenditures of the State
for such assistance for the corresponding
quarter in the emergency fund base year of
the State.

"(B) GRANT RELATED TO INCREASED EX-
PENDITURES FOR NON-RECURRENT SHORT
TERM BENEFITS.—

"(i) IN GENERAL.—For each calendar
quarter in fiscal year 2009 or 2010, the
Secretary shall make a grant from the
Emergency Fund to each State that—

"(I) requests a grant under this
subparagraph for the quarter; and

"(II) meets the requirement of
clause (ii) for the quarter.

"(ii) NON-RECURRENT SHORT TERM
EXPENDITURE REQUIREMENT.—A State
meets the requirement of this clause for a
quarter if the total expenditures of the
State for non-recurrent short term benefits
in the quarter, whether under the State
program funded under this part or as

1   qualified State expenditures, exceeds the

2   total expenditures of the State for non-re-

3   current short term benefits in the cor-

4   responding quarter in the emergency fund

5   base year of the State.

6   "(iii) AMOUNT OF GRANT.—Subject to

7   paragraph (5), the amount of the grant to

8   be made to a State under this subpara-

9   graph for a quarter shall be an amount

10   equal to 80 percent of the excess described

11   in clause (ii).

12   "(C) GRANT RELATED TO INCREASED EX-

13   PENDITURES FOR SUBSIDIZED EMPLOYMENT.—

14   "(i) IN GENERAL.—For each calendar

15   quarter in fiscal year 2009 or 2010, the

16   Secretary shall make a grant from the

17   Emergency Fund to each State that—

18   "(I) requests a grant under this

19   subparagraph for the quarter; and

20   "(II) meets the requirement of

21   clause (ii) for the quarter.

22   "(ii) SUBSIDIZED EMPLOYMENT EX-

23   PENDITURE REQUIREMENT.—A State

24   meets the requirement of this clause for a

25   quarter if the total expenditures of the

1   State for subsidized employment in the

2   quarter, whether under the State program

3   funded under this part or as qualified

4   State expenditures, exceeds the total such

5   expenditures of the State in the cor-

6   responding quarter in the emergency fund

7   base year of the State.

8   "(iii) AMOUNT OF GRANT.—Subject to

9   paragraph (5), the amount of the grant to

10   be made to a State under this subpara-

11   graph for a quarter shall be an amount

12   equal to 80 percent of the excess described

13   in clause (ii).

14   "(4) AUTHORITY TO MAKE NECESSARY ADJUST-

15 MENTS TO DATA AND COLLECT NEEDED DATA.—In

16 determining the size of the caseload of a State and

17 the expenditures of a State for basic assistance, non-

18 recurrent short-term benefits, and subsidized em-

19 ployment, during any period for which the State re-

20 quests funds under this subsection, and during the

21 emergency fund base year of the State, the Sec-

22 retary may make appropriate adjustments to the

23 data, on a State-by-State basis, to ensure that the

24 data are comparable with respect to the groups of

25 families served and the types of aid provided. The

1   Secretary may develop a mechanism for collecting

2   expenditure data, including procedures which allow

3   States to make reasonable estimates, and may set

4   deadlines for making revisions to the data.

5   "(5) LIMITATION.—The total amount payable

6   to a single State under subsection (b) and this sub-

7   section for fiscal years 2009 and 2010 combined

8   shall not exceed 50 percent of the annual State fam-

9   ily assistance grant.

10   "(6) LIMITATIONS ON USE OF FUNDS.—A State

11   to which an amount is paid under this subsection

12   may use the amount only as authorized by section

13   404.

14   "(7) TIMING OF IMPLEMENTATION.—The Sec-

15   retary shall implement this subsection as quickly as

16   reasonably possible, pursuant to appropriate guid-

17   ance to States.

18   "(8) APPLICATION TO INDIAN TRIBES.—This

19   subsection shall apply to an Indian tribe with an ap-

20   proved tribal family assistance plan under section

21   412 in the same manner as this subsection applies

22   to a State.

23   "(9) DEFINITIONS.—In this subsection:

24   "(A) AVERAGE MONTHLY ASSISTANCE

25   CASELOAD DEFINED.—The term 'average

monthly assistance caseload' means, with respect to a State and a quarter, the number of
families receiving assistance during the quarter
under the State program funded under this
part or as qualified State expenditures, subject
to adjustment under paragraph (4).

"(B) EMERGENCY FUND BASE YEAR.—

"(i) IN GENERAL.—The term 'emergency fund base year' means, with respect
to a State and a category described in
clause (ii), whichever of fiscal year 2007 or
2008 is the fiscal year in which the
amount described by the category with respect to the State is the lesser.

"(ii) CATEGORIES DESCRIBED.—The
categories described in this clause are the
following:

"(I) The average monthly assistance caseload of the State.

"(II) The total expenditures of
the State for non-recurrent short term
benefits, whether under the State program funded under this part or as
qualified State expenditures.

1   "(III) The total expenditures of

2   the State for subsidized employment,

3   whether under the State program

4   funded under this part or as qualified

5   State expenditures.

6   "(C) QUALIFIED STATE EXPENDITURES.—

7   The term 'qualified State expenditures' has the

8   meaning given the term in section 409(a)(7).".

9   (2) REPEAL.—Effective October 1, 2010, sub-

10   section (c) of section 403 of the Social Security Act

11   (42 U.S.C. 603) (as added by paragraph (1)) is re-

12   pealed, except that paragraph (9) of such subsection

13   shall remain in effect until October 1, 2011, but

14   only with respect to section 407(b)(3)(A)(i) of such

15   Act.

16   (b) TEMPORARY MODIFICATION OF CASELOAD RE-

17 DUCTION CREDIT.—Section 407(b)(3)(A)(i) of such Act

18 (42 U.S.C. 607(b)(3)(A)(i)) is amended by inserting "(or

19 if the immediately preceding fiscal year is fiscal year 2008,

20 2009, or 2010, then, at State option, during the emer-

21 gency fund base year of the State with respect to the aver-

22 age monthly assistance caseload of the State (within the

23 meaning of section 403(c)(9)), except that, if a State

24 elects such option for fiscal year 2008, the emergency fund

1 base year of the State with respect to such caseload shall
2 be fiscal year 2007))'' before "under the State".

3   (c) DISREGARD FROM LIMITATION ON TOTAL PAY-
4 MENTS TO TERRITORIES.—Section 1108(a)(2) of the So-
5 cial Security Act (42 U.S.C. 1308(a)(2)) is amended by
6 inserting "403(c)(3)," after "403(a)(5),".

7   (d) SUNSET OF OTHER TEMPORARY PROVISIONS.—

8   (1) DISREGARD FROM LIMITATION ON TOTAL
9 PAYMENTS TO TERRITORIES.—Effective October 1,
10 2010, section 1108(a)(2) of the Social Security Act
11 (42 U.S.C. 1308(a)(2)) is amended by striking
12 "403(c)(3)," (as added by subsection (c)).

13   (2) CASELOAD REDUCTION CREDIT.—Effective
14 October 1, 2011, section 407(b)(3)(A)(i) of such Act
15 (42 U.S.C. 607(b)(3)(A)(i)) is amended by striking
16 "(or if the immediately preceding fiscal year is fiscal
17 year 2008, 2009, or 2010, then, at State option,
18 during the emergency fund base year of the State
19 with respect to the average monthly assistance case-
20 load of the State (within the meaning of section
21 403(c)(9)), except that, if a State elects such option
22 for fiscal year 2008, the emergency fund base year
23 of the State with respect to such caseload shall be
24 fiscal year 2007))'' (as added by subsection (b)).

SEC. 2102. EXTENSION OF TANF SUPPLEMENTAL GRANTS.

(a) EXTENSION THROUGH FISCAL YEAR 2010.—Section 7101(a) of the Deficit Reduction Act of 2005 (Public Law 109–171; 120 Stat. 135), as amended by section 301(a) of the Medicare Improvements for Patients and Providers Act of 2008 (Public Law 110–275), is amended by striking "fiscal year 2009" and inserting "fiscal year 2010".

(b) CONFORMING AMENDMENT.—Section 403(a)(3)(H)(ii) of the Social Security Act (42 U.S.C. 603(a)(3)(H)(ii)) is amended to read as follows:

"(ii) subparagraph (G) shall be applied as if 'fiscal year 2010' were substituted for 'fiscal year 2001'; and".

SEC. 2103. CLARIFICATION OF AUTHORITY OF STATES TO USE TANF FUNDS CARRIED OVER FROM PRIOR YEARS TO PROVIDE TANF BENEFITS AND SERVICES.

Section 404(e) of the Social Security Act (42 U.S.C. 604(e)) is amended to read as follows:

"(e) AUTHORITY TO CARRY OVER CERTAIN AMOUNTS FOR BENEFITS OR SERVICES OR FOR FUTURE CONTINGENCIES.—A State or tribe may use a grant made to the State or tribe under this part for any fiscal year to provide, without fiscal year limitation, any benefit or

1 service that may be provided under the State or tribal pro-

2 gram funded under this part.".

3 **SEC. 2104. TEMPORARY RESUMPTION OF PRIOR CHILD**

4   **SUPPORT LAW.**

5   During the period that begins on October 1, 2008,

6 and ends on September 30, 2010, section 455(a)(1) of the

7 Social Security Act (42 U.S.C. 655(a)(1)) shall be applied

8 and administered as if the phrase "from amounts paid to

9 the State under section 458 or" does not appear in such

10 section.

11 **Subtitle C—Economic Recovery**

12 **Payments to Certain Individuals**

13 **SEC. 2201. ECONOMIC RECOVERY PAYMENT TO RECIPIENTS**

14   **OF SOCIAL SECURITY, SUPPLEMENTAL SECU-**

15   **RITY INCOME, RAILROAD RETIREMENT BENE-**

16   **FITS, AND VETERANS DISABILITY COMPENSA-**

17   **TION OR PENSION BENEFITS.**

18   (a) AUTHORITY TO MAKE PAYMENTS.—

19   (1) ELIGIBILITY.—

20   (A) IN GENERAL.—Subject to paragraph

21   (5)(B), the Secretary of the Treasury shall dis-

22   burse a $250 payment to each individual who,

23   for any month during the 3-month period end-

24   ing with the month which ends prior to the

25   month that includes the date of the enactment

1 of this Act, is entitled to a benefit payment de-

2 scribed in clause (i), (ii), or (iii) of subpara-

3 graph (B) or is eligible for a SSI cash benefit

4 described in subparagraph (C).

5 (B) BENEFIT PAYMENT DESCRIBED.—For

6 purposes of subparagraph (A):

7 (i) TITLE II BENEFIT.—A benefit pay-

8 ment described in this clause is a monthly

9 insurance benefit payable (without regard

10 to sections 202(j)(1) and 223(b) of the So-

11 cial Security Act (42 U.S.C. 402(j)(1),

12 423(b)) under—

13 (I) section 202(a) of such Act

14 (42 U.S.C. 402(a));

15 (II) section 202(b) of such Act

16 (42 U.S.C. 402(b));

17 (III) section 202(c) of such Act

18 (42 U.S.C. 402(c));

19 (IV) section 202(d)(1)(B)(ii) of

20 such Act (42 U.S.C.

21 402(d)(1)(B)(ii));

22 (V) section 202(e) of such Act

23 (42 U.S.C. 402(e));

24 (VI) section 202(f) of such Act

25 (42 U.S.C. 402(f));

(VII) section 202(g) of such Act (42 U.S.C. 402(g));

(VIII) section 202(h) of such Act (42 U.S.C. 402(h));

(IX) section 223(a) of such Act (42 U.S.C. 423(a));

(X) section 227 of such Act (42 U.S.C. 427); or

(XI) section 228 of such Act (42 U.S.C. 428).

(ii) RAILROAD RETIREMENT BEN-EFIT.—A benefit payment described in this clause is a monthly annuity or pension payment payable (without regard to section 5(a)(ii) of the Railroad Retirement Act of 1974 (45 U.S.C. 231d(a)(ii))) under—

(I) section 2(a)(1) of such Act (45 U.S.C. 231a(a)(1));

(II) section 2(c) of such Act (45 U.S.C. 231a(c));

(III) section 2(d)(1)(i) of such Act (45 U.S.C. 231a(d)(1)(i));

(IV) section 2(d)(1)(ii) of such Act (45 U.S.C. 231a(d)(1)(ii));

1   (V) section 2(d)(1)(iii)(C) of such

2   Act to an adult disabled child (45

3   U.S.C. 231a(d)(1)(iii)(C));

4   (VI) section 2(d)(1)(iv) of such

5   Act (45 U.S.C. 231a(d)(1)(iv));

6   (VII) section 2(d)(1)(v) of such

7   Act (45 U.S.C. 231a(d)(1)(v)); or

8   (VIII) section 7(b)(2) of such Act

9   (45 U.S.C. 231f(b)(2)) with respect to

10   any of the benefit payments described

11   in clause (i) of this subparagraph.

12   (iii) VETERANS BENEFIT.—A benefit

13   payment described in this clause is a com-

14   pensation or pension payment payable

15   under—

16   (I) section 1110, 1117, 1121,

17   1131, 1141, or 1151 of title 38,

18   United States Code;

19   (II) section 1310, 1312, 1313,

20   1315, 1316, or 1318 of title 38,

21   United States Code;

22   (III) section 1513, 1521, 1533,

23   1536, 1537, 1541, 1542, or 1562 of

24   title 38, United States Code; or

1   (IV) section 1805, 1815, or 1821

2   of title 38, United States Code,

3   to a veteran, surviving spouse, child, or

4   parent as described in paragraph (2), (3),

5   (4)(A)(ii), or (5) of section 101, title 38,

6   United States Code, who received that ben-

7   efit during any month within the 3 month

8   period ending with the month which ends

9   prior to the month that includes the date

10   of the enactment of this Act.

11   (C) SSI CASH BENEFIT DESCRIBED.—A

12 SSI cash benefit described in this subparagraph

13 is a cash benefit payable under section 1611

14 (other than under subsection (e)(1)(B) of such

15 section) or 1619(a) of the Social Security Act

16 (42 U.S.C. 1382, 1382h).

17   (2) REQUIREMENT.—A payment shall be made

18 under paragraph (1) only to individuals who reside

19 in 1 of the 50 States, the District of Columbia,

20 Puerto Rico, Guam, the United States Virgin Is-

21 lands, American Samoa, or the Northern Mariana

22 Islands. For purposes of the preceding sentence, the

23 determination of the individual's residence shall be

24 based on the current address of record under a pro-

25 gram specified in paragraph (1).

1   (3) NO DOUBLE PAYMENTS.—An individual

2 shall be paid only 1 payment under this section, re-

3 gardless of whether the individual is entitled to, or

4 eligible for, more than 1 benefit or cash payment de-

5 scribed in paragraph (1).

6   (4) LIMITATION.—A payment under this section

7 shall not be made—

8   (A) in the case of an individual entitled to

9   a benefit specified in paragraph (1)(B)(i) or

10   paragraph (1)(B)(ii)(VIII) if, for the most re-

11   cent month of such individual's entitlement in

12   the 3-month period described in paragraph (1),

13   such individual's benefit under such paragraph

14   was not payable by reason of subsection (x) or

15   (y) of section 202 the Social Security Act (42

16   U.S.C. 402) or section 1129A of such Act (42

17   U.S.C. 1320a-8a);

18   (B) in the case of an individual entitled to

19   a benefit specified in paragraph (1)(B)(iii) if,

20   for the most recent month of such individual's

21   entitlement in the 3 month period described in

22   paragraph (1), such individual's benefit under

23   such paragraph was not payable, or was re-

24   duced, by reason of section 1505, 5313, or

25   5313B of title 38, United States Code;

1   (C) in the case of an individual entitled to

2   a benefit specified in paragraph (1)(C) if, for

3   such most recent month, such individual's ben-

4   efit under such paragraph was not payable by

5   reason of subsection (e)(1)(A) or (e)(4) of sec-

6   tion 1611 (42 U.S.C. 1382) or section 1129A

7   of such Act (42 U.S.C. 1320a-8a); or

8   (D) in the case of any individual whose

9   date of death occurs before the date on which

10   the individual is certified under subsection (b)

11   to receive a payment under this section.

12   (5) TIMING AND MANNER OF PAYMENTS.—

13   (A) IN GENERAL.—The Secretary of the

14   Treasury shall commence disbursing payments

15   under this section at the earliest practicable

16   date but in no event later than 120 days after

17   the date of enactment of this Act. The Sec-

18   retary of the Treasury may disburse any pay-

19   ment electronically to an individual in such

20   manner as if such payment was a benefit pay-

21   ment or cash benefit to such individual under

22   the applicable program described in subpara-

23   graph (B) or (C) of paragraph (1).

24   (B) DEADLINE.—No payments shall be

25   disbursed under this section after December 31,

1   2010, regardless of any determinations of enti-

2   tlement to, or eligibility for, such payments

3   made after such date.

4   (b) IDENTIFICATION OF RECIPIENTS.—The Commis-

5 sioner of Social Security, the Railroad Retirement Board,

6 and the Secretary of Veterans Affairs shall certify the in-

7 dividuals entitled to receive payments under this section

8 and provide the Secretary of the Treasury with the infor-

9 mation needed to disburse such payments. A certification

10 of an individual shall be unaffected by any subsequent de-

11 termination or redetermination of the individual's entitle-

12 ment to, or eligibility for, a benefit specified in subpara-

13 graph (B) or (C) of subsection (a)(1).

14   (c) TREATMENT OF PAYMENTS.—

15   (1) PAYMENT TO BE DISREGARDED FOR PUR-

16   POSES OF ALL FEDERAL AND FEDERALLY ASSISTED

17   PROGRAMS.—A payment under subsection (a) shall

18   not be regarded as income and shall not be regarded

19   as a resource for the month of receipt and the fol-

20   lowing 9 months, for purposes of determining the

21   eligibility of the recipient (or the recipient's spouse

22   or family) for benefits or assistance, or the amount

23   or extent of benefits or assistance, under any Fed-

24   eral program or under any State or local program fi-

25   nanced in whole or in part with Federal funds.

1   (2) PAYMENT NOT CONSIDERED INCOME FOR

2   PURPOSES OF TAXATION.—A payment under sub-

3   section (a) shall not be considered as gross income

4   for purposes of the Internal Revenue Code of 1986.

5   (3) PAYMENTS PROTECTED FROM ASSIGN-

6   MENT.—The provisions of sections 207 and

7   1631(d)(1) of the Social Security Act (42 U.S.C.

8   407, 1383(d)(1)), section 14(a) of the Railroad Re-

9   tirement Act of 1974 (45 U.S.C. 231m(a)), and sec-

10   tion 5301 of title 38, United States Code, shall

11   apply to any payment made under subsection (a) as

12   if such payment was a benefit payment or cash ben-

13   efit to such individual under the applicable program

14   described in subparagraph (B) or (C) of subsection

15   (a)(1).

16   (4) PAYMENTS SUBJECT TO OFFSET.—Notwith-

17   standing paragraph (3), for purposes of section

18   3716 of title 31, United States Code, any payment

19   made under this section shall not be considered a

20   benefit payment or cash benefit made under the ap-

21   plicable program described in subparagraph (B) or

22   (C) of subsection (a)(1) and all amounts paid shall

23   be subject to offset to collect delinquent debts.

24   (d) PAYMENT TO REPRESENTATIVE PAYEES AND FI-

25 DUCIARIES.—

1   (1) IN GENERAL.—In any case in which an in-
2 dividual who is entitled to a payment under sub-
3 section (a) and whose benefit payment or cash ben-
4 efit described in paragraph (1) of that subsection is
5 paid to a representative payee or fiduciary, the pay-
6 ment under subsection (a) shall be made to the indi-
7 vidual's representative payee or fiduciary and the en-
8 tire payment shall be used only for the benefit of the
9 individual who is entitled to the payment.

10   (2) APPLICABILITY.—

11   (A) PAYMENT ON THE BASIS OF A TITLE
12   II OR SSI BENEFIT.—Section 1129(a)(3) of the
13   Social Security Act (42 U.S.C. 1320a–8(a)(3))
14   shall apply to any payment made on the basis
15   of an entitlement to a benefit specified in para-
16   graph (1)(B)(i) or (1)(C) of subsection (a) in
17   the same manner as such section applies to a
18   payment under title II or XVI of such Act.

19   (B) PAYMENT ON THE BASIS OF A RAIL-
20   ROAD RETIREMENT BENEFIT.—Section 13 of
21   the Railroad Retirement Act (45 U.S.C. 231l)
22   shall apply to any payment made on the basis
23   of an entitlement to a benefit specified in para-
24   graph (1)(B)(ii) of subsection (a) in the same

1 manner as such section applies to a payment
2 under such Act.

3   (C) PAYMENT ON THE BASIS OF A VET-
4 ERANS BENEFIT.—Sections 5502, 6106, and
5 6108 of title 38, United States Code, shall
6 apply to any payment made on the basis of an
7 entitlement to a benefit specified in paragraph
8 (1)(B)(iii) of subsection (a) in the same manner
9 as those sections apply to a payment under that
10 title.

11 (e) APPROPRIATION.—Out of any sums in the Treas-
12 ury of the United States not otherwise appropriated, the
13 following sums are appropriated for the period of fiscal
14 years 2009 through 2011, to remain available until ex-
15 pended, to carry out this section:

16   (1) For the Secretary of the Treasury,
17 $131,000,000 for administrative costs incurred in
18 carrying out this section, section 2202, section 36A
19 of the Internal Revenue Code of 1986 (as added by
20 this Act), and other provisions of this Act or the
21 amendments made by this Act relating to the Inter-
22 nal Revenue Code of 1986.

23   (2) For the Commissioner of Social Security—
24   (A) such sums as may be necessary for
25 payments to individuals certified by the Com-

1 missioner of Social Security as entitled to re-

2 ceive a payment under this section; and

3   (B) $90,000,000 for the Social Security

4 Administration's Limitation on Administrative

5 Expenses for costs incurred in carrying out this

6 section.

7 (3) For the Railroad Retirement Board—

8   (A) such sums as may be necessary for

9 payments to individuals certified by the Rail-

10 road Retirement Board as entitled to receive a

11 payment under this section; and

12   (B) $1,400,000 to the Railroad Retirement

13 Board's Limitation on Administration for ad-

14 ministrative costs incurred in carrying out this

15 section.

16 (4)(A) For the Secretary of Veterans Affairs—

17   (i) such sums as may be necessary for

18 the Compensation and Pensions account,

19 for payments to individuals certified by the

20 Secretary of Veterans Affairs as entitled to

21 receive a payment under this section; and

22   (ii) $100,000 for the Information Sys-

23 tems Technology account and $7,100,000

24 for the General Operating Expenses ac-

1   count for administrative costs incurred in

2   carrying out this section.

3   (B) The Department of Veterans Affairs Com-

4   pensation and Pensions account shall hereinafter be

5   available for payments authorized under subsection

6   (a)(1)(A) to individuals entitled to a benefit payment

7   described in subsection (a)(1)(B)(iii).

8 **SEC. 2202. SPECIAL CREDIT FOR CERTAIN GOVERNMENT**

9   **RETIREES.**

10   (a) IN GENERAL.—In the case of an eligible indi-

11 vidual, there shall be allowed as a credit against the tax

12 imposed by subtitle A of the Internal Revenue Code of

13 1986 for the first taxable year beginning in 2009 an

14 amount equal $250 ($500 in the case of a joint return

15 where both spouses are eligible individuals).

16   (b) ELIGIBLE INDIVIDUAL.—For purposes of this

17 section—

18   (1) IN GENERAL.—The term "eligible indi-

19   vidual" means any individual—

20   (A) who receives during the first taxable

21   year beginning in 2009 any amount as a pen-

22   sion or annuity for service performed in the em-

23   ploy of the United States or any State, or any

24   instrumentality thereof, which is not considered

1 employment for purposes of chapter 21 of the

2 Internal Revenue Code of 1986, and

3 (B) who does not receive a payment under

4 section 2201 during such taxable year.

5 (2) IDENTIFICATION NUMBER REQUIREMENT.—

6 Such term shall not include any individual who does

7 not include on the return of tax for the taxable

8 year—

9 (A) such individual's social security ac-

10 count number, and

11 (B) in the case of a joint return, the social

12 security account number of one of the taxpayers

13 on such return.

14 For purposes of the preceding sentence, the social

15 security account number shall not include a TIN (as

16 defined in section 7701(a)(41) of the Internal Rev-

17 enue Code of 1986) issued by the Internal Revenue

18 Service. Any omission of a correct social security ac-

19 count number required under this subparagraph

20 shall be treated as a mathematical or clerical error

21 for purposes of applying section 6213(g)(2) of such

22 Code to such omission.

23 (c) TREATMENT OF CREDIT.—

24 (1) REFUNDABLE CREDIT.—

1   (A) IN GENERAL.—The credit allowed by

2   subsection (a) shall be treated as allowed by

3   subpart C of part IV of subchapter A of chap-

4   ter 1 of the Internal Revenue Code of 1986.

5   (B) APPROPRIATIONS.—For purposes of

6   section 1324(b)(2) of title 31, United States

7   Code, the credit allowed by subsection (a) shall

8   be treated in the same manner a refund from

9   the credit allowed under section 36A of the In-

10   ternal Revenue Code of 1986 (as added by this

11   Act).

12   (2) DEFICIENCY RULES.—For purposes of sec-

13   tion 6211(b)(4)(A) of the Internal Revenue Code of

14   1986, the credit allowable by subsection (a) shall be

15   treated in the same manner as the credit allowable

16   under section 36A of the Internal Revenue Code of

17   1986 (as added by this Act).

18   (d) REFUNDS DISREGARDED IN THE ADMINISTRA-

19 TION OF FEDERAL PROGRAMS AND FEDERALLY AS-

20 SISTED PROGRAMS.—Any credit or refund allowed or

21 made to any individual by reason of this section shall not

22 be taken into account as income and shall not be taken

23 into account as resources for the month of receipt and the

24 following 2 months, for purposes of determining the eligi-

25 bility of such individual or any other individual for benefits

1 or assistance, or the amount or extent of benefits or assist-

2 ance, under any Federal program or under any State or

3 local program financed in whole or in part with Federal

4 funds.

5 # TITLE III—PREMIUM ASSIST-
6 # ANCE FOR COBRA BENEFITS

7 **SEC. 3000. TABLE OF CONTENTS.**

8 The table of contents of this title is as follows:

TITLE III—PREMIUM ASSISTANCE FOR COBRA BENEFITS

Sec. 3000. Table of contents.
Sec. 3001. Premium assistance for COBRA benefits.

9 **SEC. 3001. PREMIUM ASSISTANCE FOR COBRA BENEFITS.**

10 (a) PREMIUM ASSISTANCE FOR COBRA CONTINU-

11 ATION COVERAGE FOR INDIVIDUALS AND THEIR FAMI-

12 LIES.—

13 (1) PROVISION OF PREMIUM ASSISTANCE.—

14 (A) REDUCTION OF PREMIUMS PAY-

15 ABLE.—In the case of any premium for a pe-

16 riod of coverage beginning on or after the date

17 of the enactment of this Act for COBRA con-

18 tinuation coverage with respect to any assist-

19 ance eligible individual, such individual shall be

20 treated for purposes of any COBRA continu-

21 ation provision as having paid the amount of

22 such premium if such individual pays (or a per-

23 son other than such individual's employer pays

1   on behalf of such individual) 35 percent of the

2   amount of such premium (as determined with-

3   out regard to this subsection).

4   (B) PLAN ENROLLMENT OPTION.—

5   (i) IN GENERAL.—Notwithstanding

6   the COBRA continuation provisions, an as-

7   sistance eligible individual may, not later

8   than 90 days after the date of notice of the

9   plan enrollment option described in this

10   subparagraph, elect to enroll in coverage

11   under a plan offered by the employer in-

12   volved, or the employee organization in-

13   volved (including, for this purpose, a joint

14   board of trustees of a multiemployer trust

15   affiliated with one or more multiemployer

16   plans), that is different than coverage

17   under the plan in which such individual

18   was enrolled at the time the qualifying

19   event occurred, and such coverage shall be

20   treated as COBRA continuation coverage

21   for purposes of the applicable COBRA con-

22   tinuation coverage provision.

23   (ii) REQUIREMENTS.—An assistance

24   eligible individual may elect to enroll in

1 different coverage as described in clause (i)

2 only if—

3   (I) the employer involved has

4 made a determination that such em-

5 ployer will permit assistance eligible

6 individuals to enroll in different cov-

7 erage as provided for this subpara-

8 graph;

9   (II) the premium for such dif-

10 ferent coverage does not exceed the

11 premium for coverage in which the in-

12 dividual was enrolled at the time the

13 qualifying event occurred;

14   (III) the different coverage in

15 which the individual elects to enroll is

16 coverage that is also offered to the ac-

17 tive employees of the employer at the

18 time at which such election is made;

19 and

20   (IV) the different coverage is

21 not—

22   (aa) coverage that provides

23   only dental, vision, counseling, or

24   referral services (or a combina-

25   tion of such services);

1   (bb) a flexible spending ar-

2   rangement (as defined in section

3   106(c)(2) of the Internal Rev-

4   enue Code of 1986); or

5   (cc) coverage that provides

6   coverage for services or treat-

7   ments furnished in an on-site

8   medical facility maintained by

9   the employer and that consists

10   primarily of first-aid services,

11   prevention and wellness care, or

12   similar care (or a combination of

13   such care).

14   (C) PREMIUM REIMBURSEMENT.—For pro-

15 visions providing the balance of such premium,

16 see section 6432 of the Internal Revenue Code

17 of 1986, as added by paragraph (12).

18   (2) LIMITATION OF PERIOD OF PREMIUM AS-

19 SISTANCE.—

20   (A) IN GENERAL.—Paragraph (1)(A) shall

21 not apply with respect to any assistance eligible

22 individual for months of coverage beginning on

23 or after the earlier of—

24   (i) the first date that such individual

25   is eligible for coverage under any other

1   group health plan (other than coverage

2   consisting of only dental, vision, coun-

3   seling, or referral services (or a combina-

4   tion thereof), coverage under a flexible

5   spending arrangement (as defined in sec-

6   tion 106(c)(2) of the Internal Revenue

7   Code of 1986), or coverage of treatment

8   that is furnished in an on-site medical fa-

9   cility maintained by the employer and that

10   consists primarily of first-aid services, pre-

11   vention and wellness care, or similar care

12   (or a combination thereof)) or is eligible

13   for benefits under title XVIII of the Social

14   Security Act, or

15   (ii) the earliest of—

16   (I) the date which is 9 months

17   after the first day of the first month

18   that paragraph (1)(A) applies with re-

19   spect to such individual,

20   (II) the date following the expira-

21   tion of the maximum period of con-

22   tinuation coverage required under the

23   applicable COBRA continuation cov-

24   erage provision, or

1   (III) the date following the expi-
2   ration of the period of continuation
3   coverage allowed under paragraph
4   (4)(B)(ii).

5   (B) TIMING OF ELIGIBILITY FOR ADDI-
6   TIONAL COVERAGE.—For purposes of subpara-
7   graph (A)(i), an individual shall not be treated
8   as eligible for coverage under a group health
9   plan before the first date on which such indi-
10   vidual could be covered under such plan.

11   (C) NOTIFICATION REQUIREMENT.—An
12   assistance eligible individual shall notify in writ-
13   ing the group health plan with respect to which
14   paragraph (1)(A) applies if such paragraph
15   ceases to apply by reason of subparagraph
16   (A)(i). Such notice shall be provided to the
17   group health plan in such time and manner as
18   may be specified by the Secretary of Labor.

19   (3) ASSISTANCE ELIGIBLE INDIVIDUAL.—For
20   purposes of this section, the term "assistance eligible
21   individual" means any qualified beneficiary if—

22   (A) at any time during the period that be-
23   gins with September 1, 2008, and ends with
24   December 31, 2009, such qualified beneficiary
25   is eligible for COBRA continuation coverage,

1   (B) such qualified beneficiary elects such

2   coverage, and

3   (C) the qualifying event with respect to the

4   COBRA continuation coverage consists of the

5   involuntary termination of the covered employ-

6   ee's employment and occurred during such pe-

7   riod.

8   (4) EXTENSION OF ELECTION PERIOD AND EF-

9 FECT ON COVERAGE.—

10   (A) IN GENERAL.—For purposes of apply-

11   ing section 605(a) of the Employee Retirement

12   Income   Security   Act   of   1974,   section

13   4980B(f)(5)(A) of the Internal Revenue Code

14   of 1986, section 2205(a) of the Public Health

15   Service Act, and section 8905a(c)(2) of title 5,

16   United States Code, in the case of an individual

17   who does not have an election of COBRA con-

18   tinuation coverage in effect on the date of the

19   enactment of this Act but who would be an as-

20   sistance eligible individual if such election were

21   so in effect, such individual may elect the

22   COBRA   continuation   coverage   under   the

23   COBRA continuation coverage provisions con-

24   taining such sections during the period begin-

25   ning on the date of the enactment of this Act

1   and ending 60 days after the date on which the

2   notification required under paragraph (7)(C) is

3   provided to such individual.

4   (B) COMMENCEMENT OF COVERAGE; NO

5   REACH-BACK.—Any COBRA continuation cov-

6   erage elected by a qualified beneficiary during

7   an extended election period under subparagraph

8   (A)—

9   (i) shall commence with the first pe-

10   riod of coverage beginning on or after the

11   date of the enactment of this Act, and

12   (ii) shall not extend beyond the period

13   of COBRA continuation coverage that

14   would have been required under the appli-

15   cable COBRA continuation coverage provi-

16   sion if the coverage had been elected as re-

17   quired under such provision.

18   (C) PREEXISTING CONDITIONS.—With re-

19   spect to a qualified beneficiary who elects

20   COBRA continuation coverage pursuant to sub-

21   paragraph (A), the period—

22   (i) beginning on the date of the quali-

23   fying event, and

24   (ii) ending with the beginning of the

25   period described in subparagraph (B)(i),

1   shall be disregarded for purposes of deter-

2   mining the 63-day periods referred to in section

3   701(c)(2) of the Employee Retirement Income

4   Security Act of 1974, section 9801(c)(2) of the

5   Internal Revenue Code of 1986, and section

6   2701(c)(2) of the Public Health Service Act.

7   (5) EXPEDITED REVIEW OF DENIALS OF PRE-

8   MIUM ASSISTANCE.—In any case in which an indi-

9   vidual requests treatment as an assistance eligible

10   individual and is denied such treatment by the group

11   health plan, the Secretary of Labor (or the Sec-

12   retary of Health and Human Services in connection

13   with COBRA continuation coverage which is pro-

14   vided other than pursuant to part 6 of subtitle B of

15   title I of the Employee Retirement Income Security

16   Act of 1974), in consultation with the Secretary of

17   the Treasury, shall provide for expedited review of

18   such denial. An individual shall be entitled to such

19   review upon application to such Secretary in such

20   form and manner as shall be provided by such Sec-

21   retary. Such Secretary shall make a determination

22   regarding such individual's eligibility within 15 busi-

23   ness days after receipt of such individual's applica-

24   tion for review under this paragraph. Either Sec-

25   retary's determination upon review of the denial

1 shall be de novo and shall be the final determination

2 of such Secretary. A reviewing court shall grant def-

3 erence to such Secretary's determination. The provi-

4 sions of this paragraph, paragraphs (1) through (4),

5 and paragraph (7) shall be treated as provisions of

6 title I of the Employee Retirement Income Security

7 Act of 1974 for purposes of part 5 of subtitle B of

8 such title.

9   (6) DISREGARD OF SUBSIDIES FOR PURPOSES

10 OF FEDERAL AND STATE PROGRAMS.—Notwith-

11 standing any other provision of law, any premium

12 reduction with respect to an assistance eligible indi-

13 vidual under this subsection shall not be considered

14 income or resources in determining eligibility for, or

15 the amount of assistance or benefits provided under,

16 any other public benefit provided under Federal law

17 or the law of any State or political subdivision there-

18 of.

19   (7) NOTICES TO INDIVIDUALS.—

20   (A) GENERAL NOTICE.—

21   (i) IN GENERAL.—In the case of no-

22   tices provided under section 606(a)(4) of

23   the Employee Retirement Income Security

24   Act of 1974 (29 U.S.C. 1166(4)), section

25   4980B(f)(6)(D) of the Internal Revenue

1   Code of 1986, section 2206(4) of the Pub-

2   lic Health Service Act (42 U.S.C. 300bb-

3   6(4)), or section 8905a(f)(2)(A) of title 5,

4   United States Code, with respect to indi-

5   viduals who, during the period described in

6   paragraph (3)(A), become entitled to elect

7   COBRA continuation coverage, the re-

8   quirements of such sections shall not be

9   treated as met unless such notices include

10   an additional notification to the recipient

11   of—

12   (I) the availability of premium

13   reduction with respect to such cov-

14   erage under this subsection, and

15   (II) the option to enroll in dif-

16   ferent coverage if the employer per-

17   mits assistance eligible individuals to

18   elect enrollment in different coverage

19   (as described in paragraph (1)(B)).

20   (ii) ALTERNATIVE NOTICE.—In the

21   case of COBRA continuation coverage to

22   which the notice provision under such sec-

23   tions does not apply, the Secretary of

24   Labor, in consultation with the Secretary

25   of the Treasury and the Secretary of

1   Health and Human Services, shall, in con-

2   sultation with administrators of the group

3   health plans (or other entities) that provide

4   or administer the COBRA continuation

5   coverage involved, provide rules requiring

6   the provision of such notice.

7   (iii) FORM.—The requirement of the

8   additional notification under this subpara-

9   graph may be met by amendment of exist-

10   ing notice forms or by inclusion of a sepa-

11   rate document with the notice otherwise

12   required.

13   (B) SPECIFIC REQUIREMENTS.—Each ad-

14   ditional notification under subparagraph (A)

15   shall include—

16   (i) the forms necessary for estab-

17   lishing eligibility for premium reduction

18   under this subsection,

19   (ii) the name, address, and telephone

20   number necessary to contact the plan ad-

21   ministrator and any other person main-

22   taining relevant information in connection

23   with such premium reduction,

1   (iii) a description of the extended elec-

2   tion period provided for in paragraph

3   (4)(A),

4   (iv) a description of the obligation of

5   the qualified beneficiary under paragraph

6   (2)(C) to notify the plan providing continu-

7   ation coverage of eligibility for subsequent

8   coverage under another group health plan

9   or eligibility for benefits under title XVIII

10   of the Social Security Act and the penalty

11   provided under section 6720C of the Inter-

12   nal Revenue Code of 1986 for failure to so

13   notify the plan,

14   (v) a description, displayed in a

15   prominent manner, of the qualified bene-

16   ficiary's right to a reduced premium and

17   any conditions on entitlement to the re-

18   duced premium, and

19   (vi) a description of the option of the

20   qualified beneficiary to enroll in different

21   coverage if the employer permits such ben-

22   eficiary to elect to enroll in such different

23   coverage under paragraph (1)(B).

24   (C) NOTICE IN CONNECTION WITH EX-

25   TENDED ELECTION PERIODS.—In the case of

1   any assistance eligible individual (or any indi-

2   vidual described in paragraph (4)(A)) who be-

3   came entitled to elect COBRA continuation cov-

4   erage before the date of the enactment of this

5   Act, the administrator of the group health plan

6   (or other entity) involved shall provide (within

7   60 days after the date of enactment of this Act)

8   for the additional notification required to be

9   provided under subparagraph (A) and failure to

10   provide such notice shall be treated as a failure

11   to meet the notice requirements under the ap-

12   plicable COBRA continuation provision.

13   (D) MODEL NOTICES.—Not later than 30

14   days after the date of enactment of this Act—

15   (i) the Secretary of the Labor, in con-

16   sultation with the Secretary of the Treas-

17   ury and the Secretary of Health and

18   Human Services, shall prescribe models for

19   the additional notification required under

20   this paragraph (other than the additional

21   notification described in clause (ii)), and

22   (ii) in the case of any additional noti-

23   fication provided pursuant to subpara-

24   graph (A) under section 8905a(f)(2)(A) of

25   title 5, United States Code, the Office of

1   Personnel Management shall prescribe a

2   model for such additional notification.

3   (8) REGULATIONS.—The Secretary of the

4 Treasury may prescribe such regulations or other

5 guidance as may be necessary or appropriate to

6 carry out the provisions of this subsection, including

7 the prevention of fraud and abuse under this sub-

8 section, except that the Secretary of Labor and the

9 Secretary of Health and Human Services may pre-

10 scribe such regulations (including interim final regu-

11 lations) or other guidance as may be necessary or

12 appropriate to carry out the provisions of para-

13 graphs (5), (7), and (9).

14   (9) OUTREACH.—The Secretary of Labor, in

15 consultation with the Secretary of the Treasury and

16 the Secretary of Health and Human Services, shall

17 provide outreach consisting of public education and

18 enrollment assistance relating to premium reduction

19 provided under this subsection. Such outreach shall

20 target employers, group health plan administrators,

21 public assistance programs, States, insurers, and

22 other entities as determined appropriate by such

23 Secretaries. Such outreach shall include an initial

24 focus on those individuals electing continuation cov-

25 erage who are referred to in paragraph (7)(C). In-

1 formation on such premium reduction, including en-

2 rollment, shall also be made available on websites of

3 the Departments of Labor, Treasury, and Health

4 and Human Services.

5 (10) DEFINITIONS.—For purposes of this

6 section—

7 (A) ADMINISTRATOR.—The term "admin-

8 istrator" has the meaning given such term in

9 section 3(16)(A) of the Employee Retirement

10 Income Security Act of 1974.

11 (B) COBRA CONTINUATION COVERAGE.—

12 The term "COBRA continuation coverage"

13 means continuation coverage provided pursuant

14 to part 6 of subtitle B of title I of the Em-

15 ployee Retirement Income Security Act of 1974

16 (other than under section 609), title XXII of

17 the Public Health Service Act, section 4980B of

18 the Internal Revenue Code of 1986 (other than

19 subsection (f)(1) of such section insofar as it

20 relates to pediatric vaccines), or section 8905a

21 of title 5, United States Code, or under a State

22 program that provides comparable continuation

23 coverage. Such term does not include coverage

24 under a health flexible spending arrangement

25 under a cafeteria plan within the meaning of

1 section 125 of the Internal Revenue Code of

2 1986.

3   (C) COBRA CONTINUATION PROVISION.—

4 The term "COBRA continuation provision"

5 means the provisions of law described in sub-

6 paragraph (B).

7   (D) COVERED EMPLOYEE.—The term

8 "covered employee" has the meaning given such

9 term in section 607(2) of the Employee Retire-

10 ment Income Security Act of 1974.

11   (E) QUALIFIED BENEFICIARY.—The term

12 "qualified beneficiary" has the meaning given

13 such term in section 607(3) of the Employee

14 Retirement Income Security Act of 1974.

15   (F) GROUP HEALTH PLAN.—The term

16 "group health plan" has the meaning given

17 such term in section 607(1) of the Employee

18 Retirement Income Security Act of 1974.

19   (G) STATE.—The term "State" includes

20 the District of Columbia, the Commonwealth of

21 Puerto Rico, the Virgin Islands, Guam, Amer-

22 ican Samoa, and the Commonwealth of the

23 Northern Mariana Islands.

24   (H) PERIOD OF COVERAGE.—Any ref-

25 erence in this subsection to a period of coverage

1   shall be treated as a reference to a monthly or
2   shorter period of coverage with respect to which
3   premiums are charged with respect to such cov-
4   erage.

5   (11) REPORTS.—

6   (A) INTERIM REPORT.—The Secretary of
7   the Treasury shall submit an interim report to
8   the Committee on Education and Labor, the
9   Committee on Ways and Means, and the Com-
10   mittee on Energy and Commerce of the House
11   of Representatives and the Committee on
12   Health, Education, Labor, and Pensions and
13   the Committee on Finance of the Senate re-
14   garding the premium reduction provided under
15   this subsection that includes—

16   (i) the number of individuals provided
17   such assistance as of the date of the re-
18   port; and

19   (ii) the total amount of expenditures
20   incurred (with administrative expenditures
21   noted separately) in connection with such
22   assistance as of the date of the report.

23   (B) FINAL REPORT.—As soon as prac-
24   ticable after the last period of COBRA continu-
25   ation coverage for which premium reduction is

1   provided under this section, the Secretary of the

2   Treasury shall submit a final report to each

3   Committee referred to in subparagraph (A) that

4   includes—

5   (i) the number of individuals provided

6   premium reduction under this section;

7   (ii) the average dollar amount

8   (monthly and annually) of premium reduc-

9   tions provided to such individuals; and

10   (iii) the total amount of expenditures

11   incurred (with administrative expenditures

12   noted separately) in connection with pre-

13   mium reduction under this section.

14   (12) COBRA PREMIUM ASSISTANCE.—

15   (A) IN GENERAL.—Subchapter B of chap-

16   ter 65 of the Internal Revenue Code of 1986,

17   as amended by this Act, is amended by adding

18   at the end the following new section:

19 **"SEC. 6432. COBRA PREMIUM ASSISTANCE.**

20   "(a) IN GENERAL.—The person to whom premiums

21 are payable under COBRA continuation coverage shall be

22 reimbursed as provided in subsection (c) for the amount

23 of premiums not paid by assistance eligible individuals by

24 reason of section 3002(a) of the Health Insurance Assist-

25 ance for the Unemployed Act of 2009.

1   "(b) PERSON ENTITLED TO REIMBURSEMENT.—For

2 purposes of subsection (a), except as otherwise provided

3 by the Secretary, the person to whom premiums are pay-

4 able under COBRA continuation coverage shall be treated

5 as being—

6   "(1) in the case of any group health plan which

7   is a multiemployer plan (as defined in section 3(37)

8   of the Employee Retirement Income Security Act of

9   1974), the plan,

10   "(2) in the case of any group health plan not

11   described in paragraph (1)—

12   "(A) which is subject to the COBRA con-

13   tinuation provisions contained in—

14   "(i) the Internal Revenue Code of

15   1986,

16   "(ii) the Employee Retirement Income

17   Security Act of 1974,

18   "(iii) the Public Health Service Act,

19   or

20   "(iv) title 5, United States Code, or

21   "(B) under which some or all of the cov-

22   erage is not provided by insurance,

23   the employer maintaining the plan, and

1   "(3) in the case of any group health plan not

2   described in paragraph (1) or (2), the insurer pro-

3   viding the coverage under the group health plan.

4   "(c) METHOD OF REIMBURSEMENT.—Except as oth-

5 erwise provided by the Secretary—

6   "(1) TREATMENT AS PAYMENT OF PAYROLL

7   TAXES.—Each person entitled to reimbursement

8   under subsection (a) (and filing a claim for such re-

9   imbursement at such time and in such manner as

10   the Secretary may require) shall be treated for pur-

11   poses of this title and section 1324(b)(2) of title 31,

12   United States Code, as having paid to the Secretary,

13   on the date that the assistance eligible individual's

14   premium payment is received, payroll taxes in an

15   amount equal to the portion of such reimbursement

16   which relates to such premium. To the extent that

17   the amount treated as paid under the preceding sen-

18   tence exceeds the amount of such person's liability

19   for such taxes, the Secretary shall credit or refund

20   such excess in the same manner as if it were an

21   overpayment of such taxes.

22   "(2) OVERSTATEMENTS.—Any overstatement of

23   the reimbursement to which a person is entitled

24   under this section (and any amount paid by the Sec-

25   retary as a result of such overstatement) shall be

1   treated as an underpayment of payroll taxes by such

2   person and may be assessed and collected by the

3   Secretary in the same manner as payroll taxes.

4   "(3) REIMBURSEMENT CONTINGENT ON PAY-

5   MENT OF REMAINING PREMIUM.—No reimbursement

6   may be made under this section to a person with re-

7   spect to any assistance eligible individual until after

8   the reduced premium required under section

9   3002(a)(1)(A) of such Act with respect to such indi-

10   vidual has been received.

11   "(d) DEFINITIONS.—For purposes of this section—

12   "(1) PAYROLL TAXES.—The term 'payroll

13   taxes' means—

14   "(A) amounts required to be deducted and

15   withheld for the payroll period under section

16   3402 (relating to wage withholding),

17   "(B) amounts required to be deducted for

18   the payroll period under section 3102 (relating

19   to FICA employee taxes), and

20   "(C) amounts of the taxes imposed for the

21   payroll period under section 3111 (relating to

22   FICA employer taxes).

23   "(2) PERSON.—The term 'person' includes any

24   governmental entity.

1   "(e) REPORTING.—Each person entitled to reim-

2 bursement under subsection (a) for any period shall sub-

3 mit such reports (at such time and in such manner) as

4 the Secretary may require, including—

5   "(1) an attestation of involuntary termination

6   of employment for each covered employee on the

7   basis of whose termination entitlement to reimburse-

8   ment is claimed under subsection (a),

9   "(2) a report of the amount of payroll taxes off-

10   set under subsection (a) for the reporting period and

11   the estimated offsets of such taxes for the subse-

12   quent reporting period in connection with reimburse-

13   ments under subsection (a), and

14   "(3) a report containing the TINs of all covered

15   employees, the amount of subsidy reimbursed with

16   respect to each covered employee and qualified bene-

17   ficiaries, and a designation with respect to each cov-

18   ered employee as to whether the subsidy reimburse-

19   ment is for coverage of 1 individual or 2 or more in-

20   dividuals.

21   "(f) REGULATIONS.—The Secretary shall issue such

22 regulations or other guidance as may be necessary or ap-

23 propriate to carry out this section, including—

24   "(1) the requirement to report information or

25   the establishment of other methods for verifying the

1   correct amounts of reimbursements under this sec-

2   tion, and

3   "(2) the application of this section to group

4   health plans that are multiemployer plans (as de-

5   fined in section 3(37) of the Employee Retirement

6   Income Security Act of 1974).".

7   (B) SOCIAL SECURITY TRUST FUNDS HELD

8   HARMLESS.—In determining any amount trans-

9   ferred or appropriated to any fund under the

10   Social Security Act, section 6432 of the Inter-

11   nal Revenue Code of 1986 shall not be taken

12   into account.

13   (C) CLERICAL AMENDMENT.—The table of

14   sections for subchapter B of chapter 65 of the

15   Internal Revenue Code of 1986 is amended by

16   adding at the end the following new item:

"Sec. 6432. COBRA premium assistance.".

17   (D) EFFECTIVE DATE.—The amendments

18   made by this paragraph shall apply to pre-

19   miums to which subsection (a)(1)(A) applies.

20   (E) SPECIAL RULE.—

21   (i) IN GENERAL.—In the case of an

22   assistance eligible individual who pays,

23   with respect to the first period of COBRA

24   continuation coverage to which subsection

25   (a)(1)(A) applies or the immediately subse-

quent period, the full premium amount for
such coverage, the person to whom such
payment is payable shall—

    (I) make a reimbursement pay-
ment to such individual for the
amount of such premium paid in excess of the amount required to be paid
under subsection (a)(1)(A); or

    (II) provide credit to the indi-
vidual for such amount in a manner
that reduces one or more subsequent
premium payments that the individual
is required to pay under such subsection for the coverage involved.

    (ii) REIMBURSING EMPLOYER.—A
person to which clause (i) applies shall be
reimbursed as provided for in section 6432
of the Internal Revenue Code of 1986 for
any payment made, or credit provided, to
the employee under such clause.

    (iii) PAYMENT OR CREDITS.—Unless
it is reasonable to believe that the credit
for the excess payment in clause (i)(II) will
be used by the assistance eligible individual
within 180 days of the date on which the

person receives from the individual the payment of the full premium amount, a person to which clause (i) applies shall make the payment required under such clause to the individual within 60 days of such payment of the full premium amount. If, as of any day within the 180-day period, it is no longer reasonable to believe that the credit will be used during that period, payment equal to the remainder of the credit outstanding shall be made to the individual within 60 days of such day.

(13) PENALTY FOR FAILURE TO NOTIFY HEALTH PLAN OF CESSATION OF ELIGIBILITY FOR PREMIUM ASSISTANCE.—

(A) IN GENERAL.—Part I of subchapter B of chapter 68 of the Internal Revenue Code of 1986 is amended by adding at the end the following new section:

"SEC. 6720C. PENALTY FOR FAILURE TO NOTIFY HEALTH PLAN OF CESSATION OF ELIGIBILITY FOR COBRA PREMIUM ASSISTANCE.

"(a) IN GENERAL.—Any person required to notify a group health plan under section 3002(a)(2)(C)) of the Health Insurance Assistance for the Unemployed Act of

1 2009 who fails to make such a notification at such time

2 and in such manner as the Secretary of Labor may require

3 shall pay a penalty of 110 percent of the premium reduc-

4 tion provided under such section after termination of eligi-

5 bility under such subsection.

6   "(b) REASONABLE CAUSE EXCEPTION.—No penalty

7 shall be imposed under subsection (a) with respect to any

8 failure if it is shown that such failure is due to reasonable

9 cause and not to willful neglect.".

10   (B) CLERICAL AMENDMENT.—The table of

11   sections of part I of subchapter B of chapter 68

12   of such Code is amended by adding at the end

13   the following new item:

"Sec. 6720C. Penalty for failure to notify health plan of cessation of eligibility for COBRA premium assistance.".

14   (C) EFFECTIVE DATE.—The amendments

15   made by this paragraph shall apply to failures

16   occurring after the date of the enactment of

17   this Act.

18   (14) COORDINATION WITH HCTC.—

19   (A) IN GENERAL.—Subsection (g) of sec-

20   tion 35 of the Internal Revenue Code of 1986

21   is amended by redesignating paragraph (9) as

22   paragraph (10) and inserting after paragraph

23   (8) the following new paragraph:

1   "(9) COBRA PREMIUM ASSISTANCE.—In the

2   case of an assistance eligible individual who receives

3   premium reduction for COBRA continuation cov-

4   erage under section 3002(a) of the Health Insurance

5   Assistance for the Unemployed Act of 2009 for any

6   month during the taxable year, such individual shall

7   not be treated as an eligible individual, a certified

8   individual, or a qualifying family member for pur-

9   poses of this section or section 7527 with respect to

10   such month.".

11   (B) EFFECTIVE DATE.—The amendment

12   made by subparagraph (A) shall apply to tax-

13   able years ending after the date of the enact-

14   ment of this Act.

15   (15) EXCLUSION OF COBRA PREMIUM ASSIST-

16   ANCE FROM GROSS INCOME.—

17   (A) IN GENERAL.—Part III of subchapter

18   B of chapter 1 of the Internal Revenue Code of

19   1986 is amended by inserting after section

20   139B the following new section:

21 **"SEC. 139C. COBRA PREMIUM ASSISTANCE.**

22   "In the case of an assistance eligible individual (as

23 defined in section 3002 of the Health Insurance Assist-

24 ance for the Unemployed Act of 2009), gross income does

1 not include any premium reduction provided under sub-
2 section (a) of such section.".

3   (B) CLERICAL AMENDMENT.—The table of
4   sections for part III of subchapter B of chapter
5   1 of such Code is amended by inserting after
6   the item relating to section 139B the following
7   new item:

"Sec. 139C. COBRA premium assistance.".

8   (C) EFFECTIVE DATE.—The amendments
9   made by this paragraph shall apply to taxable
10   years ending after the date of the enactment of
11   this Act.

12   (b) ELIMINATION OF PREMIUM SUBSIDY FOR HIGH-
13 INCOME INDIVIDUALS.—

14   (1) RECAPTURE OF SUBSIDY FOR HIGH-INCOME
15   INDIVIDUALS.—If—

16   (A) premium assistance is provided under
17   this section with respect to any COBRA con-
18   tinuation coverage which covers the taxpayer,
19   the taxpayer's spouse, or any dependent (within
20   the meaning of section 152 of the Internal Rev-
21   enue Code of 1986, determined without regard
22   to subsections (b)(1), (b)(2), and (d)(1)(B)
23   thereof) of the taxpayer during any portion of
24   the taxable year, and

1   (B) the taxpayer's modified adjusted gross

2   income for such taxable year exceeds $125,000

3   ($250,000 in the case of a joint return),

4 then the tax imposed by chapter 1 of such Code with

5 respect to the taxpayer for such taxable year shall

6 be increased by the amount of such assistance.

7   (2) PHASE-IN OF RECAPTURE.—

8   (A) IN GENERAL.—In the case of a tax-

9   payer whose modified adjusted gross income for

10   the taxable year does not exceed $145,000

11   ($290,000 in the case of a joint return), the in-

12   crease in the tax imposed under paragraph (1)

13   shall not exceed the phase-in percentage of such

14   increase (determined without regard to this

15   paragraph).

16   (B) PHASE-IN PERCENTAGE.—For pur-

17   poses of this subsection, the term "phase-in

18   percentage" means the ratio (expressed as a

19   percentage) obtained by dividing—

20   (i) the excess of described in subpara-

21   graph (B) of paragraph (1), by

22   (ii) $20,000 ($40,000 in the case of a

23   joint return).

24   (3) OPTION FOR HIGH-INCOME INDIVIDUALS TO

25 WAIVE ASSISTANCE AND AVOID RECAPTURE.—Not-

1   withstanding subsection (a)(3), an individual shall

2   not be treated as an assistance eligible individual for

3   purposes of this section and section 6432 of the In-

4   ternal Revenue Code of 1986 if such individual—

5   (A) makes a permanent election (at such

6   time and in such form and manner as the Sec-

7   retary of the Treasury may prescribe) to waive

8   the right to the premium assistance provided

9   under this section, and

10   (B) notifies the entity to whom premiums

11   are reimbursed under section 6432(a) of such

12   Code of such election.

13   (4) MODIFIED ADJUSTED GROSS INCOME.—For

14   purposes of this subsection, the term "modified ad-

15   justed gross income" means the adjusted gross in-

16   come (as defined in section 62 of the Internal Rev-

17   enue Code of 1986) of the taxpayer for the taxable

18   year increased by any amount excluded from gross

19   income under section 911, 931, or 933 of such Code.

20   (5) CREDITS NOT ALLOWED AGAINST TAX,

21   ETC.—For purposes determining regular tax liability

22   under section 26(b) of such Code, the increase in tax

23   under this subsection shall not be treated as a tax

24   imposed under chapter 1 of such Code.

1   (6) REGULATIONS.—The Secretary of the
2   Treasury shall issue such regulations or other guid-
3   ance as are necessary or appropriate to carry out
4   this subsection, including requirements that the enti-
5   ty to whom premiums are reimbursed under section
6   6432(a) of the Internal Revenue Code of 1986 re-
7   port to the Secretary, and to each assistance eligible
8   individual, the amount of premium assistance pro-
9   vided under subsection (a) with respect to each such
10 individual.

11   (7) EFFECTIVE DATE.—The provisions of this
12 subsection shall apply to taxable years ending after
13 the date of the enactment of this Act.

TITLE IV—MEDICARE AND MEDICAID HEALTH INFORMATION TECHNOLOGY; MISCELLANEOUS MEDICARE PROVISIONS

SEC. 4001. TABLE OF CONTENTS OF TITLE.

20   The table of contents of this title is as follows:

TITLE IV—MEDICARE AND MEDICAID HEALTH INFORMATION TECHNOLOGY; MISCELLANEOUS MEDICARE PROVISIONS

Sec. 4001. Table of contents of title.

Subtitle A—Medicare Incentives

Sec. 4101. Incentives for eligible professionals.
Sec. 4102. Incentives for hospitals.
Sec. 4103. Treatment of payments and savings; implementation funding.
Sec. 4104. Studies and reports on health information technology.

Subtitle B—Medicaid Incentives

Sec. 4201. Medicaid provider HIT adoption and operation payments; implementation funding.

Subtitle C—Miscellaneous Medicare Provisions

Sec. 4301. Moratoria on certain Medicare regulations.
Sec. 4302. Long-term care hospital technical corrections.

Subtitle A—Medicare Incentives

SEC. 4101. INCENTIVES FOR ELIGIBLE PROFESSIONALS.

(a) INCENTIVE PAYMENTS.—Section 1848 of the Social Security Act (42 U.S.C. 1395w–4) is amended by adding at the end the following new subsection:

"(o) INCENTIVES FOR ADOPTION AND MEANINGFUL USE OF CERTIFIED EHR TECHNOLOGY.—

"(1) INCENTIVE PAYMENTS.—

"(A) IN GENERAL.—

"(i) IN GENERAL.—Subject to the succeeding subparagraphs of this paragraph, with respect to covered professional services furnished by an eligible professional during a payment year (as defined in subparagraph (E)), if the eligible professional is a meaningful EHR user (as determined under paragraph (2)) for the EHR reporting period with respect to such year, in addition to the amount otherwise paid under this part, there also shall be paid to the eligible professional (or to an employer or facility in the cases described in clause

1   (A) of section 1842(b)(6)), from the Fed-

2   eral Supplementary Medical Insurance

3   Trust Fund established under section 1841

4   an amount equal to 75 percent of the Sec-

5   retary's estimate (based on claims sub-

6   mitted not later than 2 months after the

7   end of the payment year) of the allowed

8   charges under this part for all such cov-

9   ered professional services furnished by the

10   eligible professional during such year.

11   "(ii) NO INCENTIVE PAYMENTS WITH

12   RESPECT TO YEARS AFTER 2016.—No in-

13   centive payments may be made under this

14   subsection with respect to a year after

15   2016.

16   "(B) LIMITATIONS ON AMOUNTS OF IN-

17   CENTIVE PAYMENTS.—

18   "(i) IN GENERAL.—In no case shall

19   the amount of the incentive payment pro-

20   vided under this paragraph for an eligible

21   professional for a payment year exceed the

22   applicable amount specified under this sub-

23   paragraph with respect to such eligible

24   professional and such year.

1   "(ii) AMOUNT.—Subject to clauses

2 (iii) through (v), the applicable amount

3 specified in this subparagraph for an eligi-

4 ble professional is as follows:

5   "(I) For the first payment year

6   for such professional, $15,000 (or, if

7   the first payment year for such eligi-

8   ble professional is 2011 or 2012,

9    $18,000).

10   "(II) For the second payment

11   year for such professional, $12,000.

12   "(III) For the third payment

13   year for such professional, $8,000.

14   "(IV) For the fourth payment

15   year for such professional, $4,000.

16   "(V) For the fifth payment year

17   for such professional, $2,000.

18   "(VI) For any succeeding pay-

19   ment year for such professional, $0.

20   "(iii) PHASE DOWN FOR ELIGIBLE

21 PROFESSIONALS FIRST ADOPTING EHR

22 AFTER 2013.—If the first payment year for

23 an eligible professional is after 2013, then

24 the amount specified in this subparagraph

25 for a payment year for such professional is

the same as the amount specified in clause (ii) for such payment year for an eligible professional whose first payment year is 2013.

"(iv) INCREASE FOR CERTAIN ELIGI-BLE PROFESSIONALS.—In the case of an eligible professional who predominantly furnishes services under this part in an area that is designated by the Secretary (under section 332(a)(1)(A) of the Public Health Service Act) as a health professional shortage area, the amount that would otherwise apply for a payment year for such professional under subclauses (I) through (V) of clause (ii) shall be increased by 10 percent. In implementing the preceding sentence, the Secretary may, as determined appropriate, apply provisions of subsections (m) and (u) of section 1833 in a similar manner as such provisions apply under such subsection.

"(v) NO INCENTIVE PAYMENT IF FIRST ADOPTING AFTER 2014.—If the first payment year for an eligible professional is after 2014 then the applicable amount

432

1 specified in this subparagraph for such

2 professional for such year and any subse-

3 quent year shall be $0.

4 "(C) NON-APPLICATION TO HOSPITAL-

5 BASED ELIGIBLE PROFESSIONALS.—

6 "(i) IN GENERAL.—No incentive pay-

7 ment may be made under this paragraph

8 in the case of a hospital-based eligible pro-

9 fessional.

10 "(ii) HOSPITAL-BASED ELIGIBLE PRO-

11 FESSIONAL.—For purposes of clause (i),

12 the term 'hospital-based eligible profes-

13 sional' means, with respect to covered pro-

14 fessional services furnished by an eligible

15 professional during the EHR reporting pe-

16 riod for a payment year, an eligible profes-

17 sional, such as a pathologist, anesthesiol-

18 ogist, or emergency physician, who fur-

19 nishes substantially all of such services in

20 a hospital setting (whether inpatient or

21 outpatient) and through the use of the fa-

22 cilities and equipment, including qualified

23 electronic health records, of the hospital.

24 The determination of whether an eligible

25 professional is a hospital-based eligible pro-

fessional shall be made on the basis of the
site of service (as defined by the Secretary)
and without regard to any employment or
billing arrangement between the eligible
professional and any other provider.

"(D) PAYMENT.—

"(i) FORM OF PAYMENT.—The payment under this paragraph may be in the
form of a single consolidated payment or
in the form of such periodic installments
as the Secretary may specify.

"(ii) COORDINATION OF APPLICATION
OF LIMITATION FOR PROFESSIONALS IN
DIFFERENT PRACTICES.—In the case of an
eligible professional furnishing covered professional services in more than one practice
(as specified by the Secretary), the Secretary shall establish rules to coordinate
the incentive payments, including the application of the limitation on amounts of
such incentive payments under this paragraph, among such practices.

"(iii) COORDINATION WITH MED-
ICAID.—The Secretary shall seek, to the
maximum extent practicable, to avoid du-

1　plicative requirements from Federal and

2　State governments to demonstrate mean-

3　ingful use of certified EHR technology

4　under this title and title XIX. The Sec-

5　retary may also adjust the reporting peri-

6　ods under such title and such subsections

7　in order to carry out this clause.

8　"(E) PAYMENT YEAR DEFINED.—

9　　"(i) IN GENERAL.—For purposes of

10　this subsection, the term 'payment year'

11　means a year beginning with 2011.

12　　"(ii) FIRST, SECOND, ETC. PAYMENT

13　YEAR.—The term 'first payment year'

14　means, with respect to covered professional

15　services furnished by an eligible profes-

16　sional, the first year for which an incentive

17　payment is made for such services under

18　this subsection. The terms 'second pay-

19　ment year', 'third payment year', 'fourth

20　payment year', and 'fifth payment year'

21　mean, with respect to covered professional

22　services furnished by such eligible profes-

23　sional, each successive year immediately

24　following the first payment year for such

25　professional.

"(2) MEANINGFUL EHR USER.—

"(A) IN GENERAL.—For purposes of paragraph (1), an eligible professional shall be treated as a meaningful EHR user for an EHR reporting period for a payment year (or, for purposes of subsection (a)(7), for an EHR reporting period under such subsection for a year) if each of the following requirements is met:

"(i) MEANINGFUL USE OF CERTIFIED EHR TECHNOLOGY.—The eligible professional demonstrates to the satisfaction of the Secretary, in accordance with subparagraph (C)(i), that during such period the professional is using certified EHR technology in a meaningful manner, which shall include the use of electronic prescribing as determined to be appropriate by the Secretary.

"(ii) INFORMATION EXCHANGE.—The eligible professional demonstrates to the satisfaction of the Secretary, in accordance with subparagraph (C)(i), that during such period such certified EHR technology is connected in a manner that provides, in

1   accordance with law and standards appli-

2   cable to the exchange of information, for

3   the electronic exchange of health informa-

4   tion to improve the quality of health care,

5   such as promoting care coordination.

6   "(iii) REPORTING ON MEASURES

7   USING EHR.—Subject to subparagraph

8   (B)(ii) and using such certified EHR tech-

9   nology, the eligible professional submits in-

10   formation for such period, in a form and

11   manner specified by the Secretary, on such

12   clinical quality measures and such other

13   measures as selected by the Secretary

14   under subparagraph (B)(i).

15 The Secretary may provide for the use of alter-

16 native means for meeting the requirements of

17 clauses (i), (ii), and (iii) in the case of an eligi-

18 ble professional furnishing covered professional

19 services in a group practice (as defined by the

20 Secretary). The Secretary shall seek to improve

21 the use of electronic health records and health

22 care quality over time by requiring more strin-

23 gent measures of meaningful use selected under

24 this paragraph.

25   "(B) REPORTING ON MEASURES.—

1   "(i) SELECTION.—The Secretary shall

2   select measures for purposes of subpara-

3   graph (A)(iii) but only consistent with the

4   following:

5   "(I) The Secretary shall provide

6   preference to clinical quality measures

7   that have been endorsed by the entity

8   with a contract with the Secretary

9   under section 1890(a).

10   "(II) Prior to any measure being

11   selected under this subparagraph, the

12   Secretary shall publish in the Federal

13   Register such measure and provide for

14   a period of public comment on such

15   measure.

16   "(ii) LIMITATION.—The Secretary

17   may not require the electronic reporting of

18   information on clinical quality measures

19   under subparagraph (A)(iii) unless the

20   Secretary has the capacity to accept the in-

21   formation electronically, which may be on

22   a pilot basis.

23   "(iii) COORDINATION OF REPORTING

24   OF INFORMATION.—In selecting such

25   measures, and in establishing the form and

1 manner for reporting measures under sub-

2 paragraph (A)(iii), the Secretary shall seek

3 to avoid redundant or duplicative reporting

4 otherwise required, including reporting

5 under subsection (k)(2)(C).

6   "(C) DEMONSTRATION OF MEANINGFUL

7 USE OF CERTIFIED EHR TECHNOLOGY AND IN-

8 FORMATION EXCHANGE.—

9   "(i) IN GENERAL.—A professional

10 may satisfy the demonstration requirement

11 of clauses (i) and (ii) of subparagraph (A)

12 through means specified by the Secretary,

13 which may include—

14   "(I) an attestation;

15   "(II) the submission of claims

16 with appropriate coding (such as a

17 code indicating that a patient encoun-

18 ter was documented using certified

19 EHR technology);

20   "(III) a survey response;

21   "(IV) reporting under subpara-

22 graph (A)(iii); and

23   "(V) other means specified by the

24 Secretary.

1   "(ii) USE OF PART D DATA.—Not-

2   withstanding sections 1860D–15(d)(2)(B)

3   and 1860D–15(f)(2), the Secretary may

4   use data regarding drug claims submitted

5   for purposes of section 1860D–15 that are

6   necessary for purposes of subparagraph

7   (A).

8   "(3) APPLICATION.—

9   "(A) PHYSICIAN REPORTING SYSTEM

10   RULES.—Paragraphs (5), (6), and (8) of sub-

11   section (k) shall apply for purposes of this sub-

12   section in the same manner as they apply for

13   purposes of such subsection.

14   "(B) COORDINATION WITH OTHER PAY-

15   MENTS.—The provisions of this subsection shall

16   not be taken into account in applying the provi-

17   sions of subsection (m) of this section and of

18   section 1833(m) and any payment under such

19   provisions shall not be taken into account in

20   computing allowable charges under this sub-

21   section.

22   "(C) LIMITATIONS ON REVIEW.—There

23   shall be no administrative or judicial review

24   under section 1869, section 1878, or otherwise,

25   of—

1   "(i) the methodology and standards
2   for determining payment amounts under
3   this subsection and payment adjustments
4   under subsection (a)(7)(A), including the
5   limitation under paragraph (1)(B) and co-
6   ordination under clauses (ii) and (iii) of
7   paragraph (1)(D);

8   "(ii) the methodology and standards
9   for determining a meaningful EHR user
10   under paragraph (2), including selection of
11   measures under paragraph (2)(B), speci-
12   fication of the means of demonstrating
13   meaningful EHR use under paragraph
14   (2)(C), and the hardship exception under
15   subsection (a)(7)(B);

16   "(iii) the methodology and standards
17   for determining a hospital-based eligible
18   professional under paragraph (1)(C); and

19   "(iv) the specification of reporting pe-
20   riods under paragraph (5) and the selec-
21   tion of the form of payment under para-
22   graph (1)(D)(i).

23   "(D) POSTING ON WEBSITE.—The Sec-
24   retary shall post on the Internet website of the
25   Centers for Medicare & Medicaid Services, in an

1   easily understandable format, a list of the

2   names, business addresses, and business phone

3   numbers of the eligible professionals who are

4   meaningful EHR users and, as determined ap-

5   propriate by the Secretary, of group practices

6   receiving incentive payments under paragraph

7   (1).

8   "(4) CERTIFIED EHR TECHNOLOGY DEFINED.—

9 For purposes of this section, the term 'certified

10 EHR technology' means a qualified electronic health

11 record (as defined in section 3000(13) of the Public

12 Health Service Act) that is certified pursuant to sec-

13 tion 3001(c)(5) of such Act as meeting standards

14 adopted under section 3004 of such Act that are ap-

15 plicable to the type of record involved (as determined

16 by the Secretary, such as an ambulatory electronic

17 health record for office-based physicians or an inpa-

18 tient hospital electronic health record for hospitals).

19   "(5) DEFINITIONS.—For purposes of this sub-

20 section:

21   "(A) COVERED PROFESSIONAL SERV-

22   ICES.—The term 'covered professional services'

23   has the meaning given such term in subsection

24   (k)(3).

1   "(B) EHR REPORTING PERIOD.—The

2   term 'EHR reporting period' means, with re-

3   spect to a payment year, any period (or peri-

4   ods) as specified by the Secretary.

5   "(C) ELIGIBLE PROFESSIONAL.—The term

6   'eligible professional' means a physician, as de-

7   fined in section 1861(r).".

8   (b) INCENTIVE PAYMENT ADJUSTMENT.—Section

9 1848(a) of the Social Security Act (42 U.S.C. 1395w–

10 4(a)) is amended by adding at the end the following new

11 paragraph:

12   "(7) INCENTIVES FOR MEANINGFUL USE OF

13 CERTIFIED EHR TECHNOLOGY.—

14   "(A) ADJUSTMENT.—

15   "(i) IN GENERAL.—Subject to sub-

16   paragraphs (B) and (D), with respect to

17   covered professional services furnished by

18   an eligible professional during 2015 or any

19   subsequent payment year, if the eligible

20   professional is not a meaningful EHR user

21   (as determined under subsection (o)(2)) for

22   an EHR reporting period for the year, the

23   fee schedule amount for such services fur-

24   nished by such professional during the year

25   (including the fee schedule amount for pur-

1   poses of determining a payment based on

2   such amount) shall be equal to the applica-

3   ble percent of the fee schedule amount that

4   would otherwise apply to such services

5   under this subsection (determined after ap-

6   plication of paragraph (3) but without re-

7   gard to this paragraph).

8   "(ii) APPLICABLE PERCENT.—Subject

9   to clause (iii), for purposes of clause (i),

10   the term 'applicable percent' means—

11   "(I) for 2015, 99 percent (or, in

12   the case of an eligible professional

13   who was subject to the application of

14   the payment adjustment under section

15   1848(a)(5) for 2014, 98 percent);

16   "(II) for 2016, 98 percent; and

17   "(III) for 2017 and each subse-

18   quent year, 97 percent.

19   "(iii) AUTHORITY TO DECREASE AP-

20   PLICABLE PERCENTAGE FOR 2018 AND

21   SUBSEQUENT YEARS.—For 2018 and each

22   subsequent year, if the Secretary finds that

23   the proportion of eligible professionals who

24   are meaningful EHR users (as determined

25   under subsection (o)(2)) is less than 75

1   percent, the applicable percent shall be de-
2   creased by 1 percentage point from the ap-
3   plicable percent in the preceding year, but
4   in no case shall the applicable percent be
5   less than 95 percent.

6   "(B) SIGNIFICANT HARDSHIP EXCEP-
7   TION.—The Secretary may, on a case-by-case
8   basis, exempt an eligible professional from the
9   application of the payment adjustment under
10   subparagraph (A) if the Secretary determines,
11   subject to annual renewal, that compliance with
12   the requirement for being a meaningful EHR
13   user would result in a significant hardship, such
14   as in the case of an eligible professional who
15   practices in a rural area without sufficient
16   Internet access. In no case may an eligible pro-
17   fessional be granted an exemption under this
18   subparagraph for more than 5 years.

19   "(C) APPLICATION OF PHYSICIAN REPORT-
20   ING SYSTEM RULES.—Paragraphs (5), (6), and
21   (8) of subsection (k) shall apply for purposes of
22   this paragraph in the same manner as they
23   apply for purposes of such subsection.

24   "(D) NON-APPLICATION TO HOSPITAL-
25   BASED ELIGIBLE PROFESSIONALS.—No pay-

1 ment adjustment may be made under subpara-

2 graph (A) in the case of hospital-based eligible

3 professionals (as defined in subsection

4 (o)(1)(C)(ii)).

5 "(E) DEFINITIONS.—For purposes of this

6 paragraph:

7 "(i) COVERED PROFESSIONAL SERV-

8 ICES.—The term 'covered professional

9 services' has the meaning given such term

10 in subsection (k)(3).

11 "(ii) EHR REPORTING PERIOD.—The

12 term 'EHR reporting period' means, with

13 respect to a year, a period (or periods)

14 specified by the Secretary.

15 "(iii) ELIGIBLE PROFESSIONAL.—The

16 term 'eligible professional' means a physi-

17 cian, as defined in section 1861(r).".

18 (c) APPLICATION TO CERTAIN MA-AFFILIATED ELI-

19 GIBLE PROFESSIONALS.—Section 1853 of the Social Secu-

20 rity Act (42 U.S.C. 1395w–23) is amended by adding at

21 the end the following new subsection:

22 "(l) APPLICATION OF ELIGIBLE PROFESSIONAL IN-

23 CENTIVES FOR CERTAIN MA ORGANIZATIONS FOR ADOP-

24 TION AND MEANINGFUL USE OF CERTIFIED EHR TECH-

25 NOLOGY.—

1   "(1) IN GENERAL.—Subject to paragraphs (3)

2   and (4), in the case of a qualifying MA organization,

3   the provisions of sections 1848(o) and 1848(a)(7)

4   shall apply with respect to eligible professionals de-

5   scribed in paragraph (2) of the organization who the

6   organization attests under paragraph (6) to be

7   meaningful EHR users in a similar manner as they

8   apply to eligible professionals under such sections.

9   Incentive payments under paragraph (3) shall be

10   made to and payment adjustments under paragraph

11   (4) shall apply to such qualifying organizations.

12   "(2) ELIGIBLE PROFESSIONAL DESCRIBED.—

13   With respect to a qualifying MA organization, an eli-

14   gible professional described in this paragraph is an

15   eligible professional (as defined for purposes of sec-

16   tion 1848(o)) who—

17   "(A)(i) is employed by the organization; or

18   "(ii)(I) is employed by, or is a partner of,

19   an entity that through contract with the organi-

20   zation furnishes at least 80 percent of the enti-

21   ty's Medicare patient care services to enrollees

22   of such organization; and

23   "(II) furnishes at least 80 percent of the

24   professional services of the eligible professional

1   covered under this title to enrollees of the orga-

2   nization; and

3   "(B) furnishes, on average, at least 20

4   hours per week of patient care services.

5   "(3) ELIGIBLE PROFESSIONAL INCENTIVE PAY-

6   MENTS.—

7   "(A) IN GENERAL.—In applying section

8   1848(o) under paragraph (1), instead of the ad-

9   ditional payment amount under section

10   1848(o)(1)(A) and subject to subparagraph

11   (B), the Secretary may substitute an amount

12   determined by the Secretary to the extent fea-

13   sible and practical to be similar to the esti-

14   mated amount in the aggregate that would be

15   payable if payment for services furnished by

16   such professionals was payable under part B in-

17   stead of this part.

18   "(B) AVOIDING DUPLICATION OF PAY-

19   MENTS.—

20   "(i) IN GENERAL.—In the case of an

21   eligible professional described in paragraph

22   (2)—

23   "(I) that is eligible for the max-

24   imum incentive payment under section

25   1848(o)(1)(A) for the same payment

1   period, the payment incentive shall be

2   made only under such section and not

3   under this subsection; and

4   "(II) that is eligible for less than

5   such maximum incentive payment for

6   the same payment period, the pay-

7   ment incentive shall be made only

8   under this subsection and not under

9   section 1848(o)(1)(A).

10   "(ii) METHODS.—In the case of an el-

11   igible professional described in paragraph

12   (2) who is eligible for an incentive payment

13   under section 1848(o)(1)(A) but is not de-

14   scribed in clause (i) for the same payment

15   period, the Secretary shall develop a

16   process—

17   "(I) to ensure that duplicate pay-

18   ments are not made with respect to

19   an eligible professional both under

20   this subsection and under section

21   1848(o)(1)(A); and

22   "(II) to collect data from Medi-

23   care Advantage organizations to en-

24   sure against such duplicate payments.

1   "(C) FIXED SCHEDULE FOR APPLICATION

2   OF LIMITATION ON INCENTIVE PAYMENTS FOR

3   ALL ELIGIBLE PROFESSIONALS.—In applying

4   section 1848(o)(1)(B)(ii) under subparagraph

5   (A), in accordance with rules specified by the

6   Secretary, a qualifying MA organization shall

7   specify a year (not earlier than 2011) that shall

8   be treated as the first payment year for all eli-

9   gible professionals with respect to such organi-

10   zation.

11   "(4) PAYMENT ADJUSTMENT.—

12   "(A) IN GENERAL.—In applying section

13   1848(a)(7) under paragraph (1), instead of the

14   payment adjustment being an applicable per-

15   cent of the fee schedule amount for a year

16   under such section, subject to subparagraph

17   (D), the payment adjustment under paragraph

18   (1) shall be equal to the percent specified in

19   subparagraph (B) for such year of the payment

20   amount otherwise provided under this section

21   for such year.

22   "(B) SPECIFIED PERCENT.—The percent

23   specified under this subparagraph for a year is

24   100 percent minus a number of percentage

25   points equal to the product of—

1   "(i) the number of percentage points

2   by which the applicable percent (under sec-

3   tion 1848(a)(7)(A)(ii)) for the year is less

4   than 100 percent; and

5   "(ii) the Medicare physician expendi-

6   ture proportion specified in subparagraph

7   (C) for the year.

8   "(C) MEDICARE PHYSICIAN EXPENDITURE

9   PROPORTION.—The Medicare physician expend-

10   iture proportion under this subparagraph for a

11   year is the Secretary's estimate of the propor-

12   tion, of the expenditures under parts A and B

13   that are not attributable to this part, that are

14   attributable to expenditures for physicians'

15   services.

16   "(D) APPLICATION OF PAYMENT ADJUST-

17   MENT.—In the case that a qualifying MA orga-

18   nization attests that not all eligible profes-

19   sionals of the organization are meaningful EHR

20   users with respect to a year, the Secretary shall

21   apply the payment adjustment under this para-

22   graph based on the proportion of all such eligi-

23   ble professionals of the organization that are

24   not meaningful EHR users for such year.

"(5) QUALIFYING MA ORGANIZATION DE-
FINED.—In this subsection and subsection (m), the
term 'qualifying MA organization' means a Medicare
Advantage organization that is organized as a health
maintenance organization (as defined in section
2791(b)(3) of the Public Health Service Act).

"(6) MEANINGFUL EHR USER ATTESTATION.—
For purposes of this subsection and subsection (m),
a qualifying MA organization shall submit an attestation, in a form and manner specified by the Secretary which may include the submission of such attestation as part of submission of the initial bid
under section 1854(a)(1)(A)(iv), identifying—

"(A) whether each eligible professional described in paragraph (2), with respect to such
organization is a meaningful EHR user (as defined in section 1848(o)(2)) for a year specified
by the Secretary; and

"(B) whether each eligible hospital described in subsection (m)(1), with respect to
such organization, is a meaningful EHR user
(as defined in section 1886(n)(3)) for an applicable period specified by the Secretary.

"(7) POSTING ON WEBSITE.—The Secretary
shall post on the Internet website of the Centers for

1   Medicare & Medicaid Services, in an easily under-

2   standable format, a list of the names, business ad-

3   dresses, and business phone numbers of—

4   "(A) each qualifying MA organization re-

5   ceiving an incentive payment under this sub-

6   section for eligible professionals of the organiza-

7   tion; and

8   "(B) the eligible professionals of such or-

9   ganization for which such incentive payment is

10   based.

11   "(8) LIMITATION ON REVIEW.—There shall be

12   no administrative or judicial review under section

13   1869, section 1878, or otherwise, of—

14   "(A) the methodology and standards for

15   determining payment amounts and payment ad-

16   justments under this subsection, including

17   avoiding duplication of payments under para-

18   graph (3)(B) and the specification of rules for

19   the fixed schedule for application of limitation

20   on incentive payments for all eligible profes-

21   sionals under paragraph (3)(C);

22   "(B) the methodology and standards for

23   determining eligible professionals under para-

24   graph (2); and

1   "(C) the methodology and standards for

2   determining a meaningful EHR user under sec-

3   tion 1848(o)(2), including specification of the

4   means of demonstrating meaningful EHR use

5   under section 1848(o)(3)(C) and selection of

6   measures under section 1848(o)(3)(B).".

7   (d) STUDY AND REPORT RELATING TO MA ORGANI-

8 ZATIONS.—

9   (1) STUDY.—The Secretary of Health and

10   Human Services shall conduct a study on the extent

11   to which and manner in which payment incentives

12   and adjustments (such as under sections 1848(o)

13   and 1848(a)(7) of the Social Security Act) could be

14   made available to professionals, as defined in

15   1861(r), who are not eligible for HIT incentive pay-

16   ments under section 1848(o) and receive payments

17   for Medicare patient services nearly-exclusively

18   through contractual arrangements with one or more

19   Medicare Advantage organizations, or an inter-

20   mediary organization or organizations with contracts

21   with Medicare Advantage organizations. Such study

22   shall assess approaches for measuring meaningful

23   use of qualified EHR technology among such profes-

24   sionals and mechanisms for delivering incentives and

25   adjustments to those professionals, including

1 through incentive payments and adjustments

2 through Medicare Advantage organizations or inter-

3 mediary organizations.

4   (2) REPORT.—Not later than 120 days after

5 the date of the enactment of this Act, the Secretary

6 of Health and Human Services shall submit to Con-

7 gress a report on the findings and the conclusions of

8 the study conducted under paragraph (1), together

9 with recommendations for such legislation and ad-

10 ministrative action as the Secretary determines ap-

11 propriate.

12   (e) CONFORMING AMENDMENTS.—Section 1853 of

13 the Social Security Act (42 U.S.C. 1395w–23) is

14 amended—

15   (1) in subsection (a)(1)(A), by striking "and

16 (i)" and inserting "(i), and (l)";

17   (2) in subsection (c)—

18   (A) in paragraph (1)(D)(i), by striking

19   "section 1886(h)" and inserting "sections

20   1848(o) and 1886(h)"; and

21   (B) in paragraph (6)(A), by inserting after

22   "under part B," the following: "excluding ex-

23   penditures attributable to subsections (a)(7)

24   and (o) of section 1848,"; and

1   (3) in subsection (f), by inserting "and for pay-

2 ments under subsection (l)" after "with the organi-

3 zation".

4   (f) CONFORMING AMENDMENTS TO E-PRE-

5 SCRIBING.—

6   (1) Section 1848(a)(5)(A) of the Social Security

7 Act (42 U.S.C. 1395w–4(a)(5)(A)) is amended—

8   (A) in clause (i), by striking "or any sub-

9   sequent year" and inserting ", 2013 or 2014";

10   and

11   (B) in clause (ii), by striking "and each

12   subsequent year".

13   (2) Section 1848(m)(2) of such Act (42 U.S.C.

14 1395w–4(m)(2)) is amended—

15   (A) in subparagraph (A), by striking "For

16   2009" and inserting "Subject to subparagraph

17   (D), for 2009"; and

18   (B) by adding at the end the following new

19   subparagraph:

20   "(D) LIMITATION WITH RESPECT TO EHR

21   INCENTIVE PAYMENTS.—The provisions of this

22   paragraph shall not apply to an eligible profes-

23   sional (or, in the case of a group practice under

24   paragraph (3)(C), to the group practice) if, for

25   the EHR reporting period the eligible profes-

1   sional (or group practice) receives an incentive

2   payment under subsection (o)(1)(A) with re-

3   spect to a certified EHR technology (as defined

4   in subsection (o)(4)) that has the capability of

5   electronic prescribing.''.

6 **SEC. 4102. INCENTIVES FOR HOSPITALS.**

7 (a) INCENTIVE PAYMENT.—

8   (1) IN GENERAL.—Section 1886 of the Social

9 Security Act (42 U.S.C. 1395ww) is amended by

10 adding at the end the following new subsection:

11 ''(n) INCENTIVES FOR ADOPTION AND MEANINGFUL

12 USE OF CERTIFIED EHR TECHNOLOGY.—

13   ''(1) IN GENERAL.—Subject to the succeeding

14 provisions of this subsection, with respect to inpa-

15 tient hospital services furnished by an eligible hos-

16 pital during a payment year (as defined in para-

17 graph (2)(G)), if the eligible hospital is a meaningful

18 EHR user (as determined under paragraph (3)) for

19 the EHR reporting period with respect to such year,

20 in addition to the amount otherwise paid under this

21 section, there also shall be paid to the eligible hos-

22 pital, from the Federal Hospital Insurance Trust

23 Fund established under section 1817, an amount

24 equal to the applicable amount specified in para-

25 graph (2)(A) for the hospital for such payment year.

1   "(2) PAYMENT AMOUNT.—

2   "(A) IN GENERAL.—Subject to the suc-

3   ceeding subparagraphs of this paragraph, the

4   applicable amount specified in this subpara-

5   graph for an eligible hospital for a payment

6   year is equal to the product of the following:

7   "(i) INITIAL AMOUNT.—The sum of—

8   "(I) the base amount specified in

9   subparagraph (B); plus

10   "(II)   the   discharge   related

11   amount specified in subparagraph (C)

12   for a 12-month period selected by the

13   Secretary with respect to such pay-

14   ment year.

15   "(ii) MEDICARE SHARE.—The Medi-

16   care share as specified in subparagraph

17   (D) for the eligible hospital for a period se-

18   lected by the Secretary with respect to

19   such payment year.

20   "(iii)   TRANSITION   FACTOR.—The

21   transition factor specified in subparagraph

22   (E) for the eligible hospital for the pay-

23   ment year.

24   "(B) BASE AMOUNT.—The base amount

25   specified in this subparagraph is $2,000,000.

1   "(C) DISCHARGE RELATED AMOUNT.—The

2 discharge related amount specified in this sub-

3 paragraph for a 12-month period selected by

4 the Secretary shall be determined as the sum of

5 the amount, estimated based upon total dis-

6 charges for the eligible hospital (regardless of

7 any source of payment) for the period, for each

8 discharge up to the 23,000th discharge as fol-

9 lows:

10   "(i) For the first through 1,149th dis-

11   charge, $0.

12   "(ii) For the 1,150th through the

13   23,000th discharge, $200.

14   "(iii) For any discharge greater than

15   the 23,000th, $0.

16   "(D) MEDICARE SHARE.—The Medicare

17 share specified under this subparagraph for an

18 eligible hospital for a period selected by the

19 Secretary for a payment year is equal to the

20 fraction—

21   "(i) the numerator of which is the

22   sum (for such period and with respect to

23   the eligible hospital) of—

24   "(I) the estimated number of in-

25   patient-bed-days (as established by

1 the Secretary) which are attributable

2 to individuals with respect to whom

3 payment may be made under part A;

4 and

5   "(II) the estimated number of in-

6 patient-bed-days (as so established)

7 which are attributable to individuals

8 who are enrolled with a Medicare Ad-

9 vantage organization under part C;

10 and

11   "(ii) the denominator of which is the

12 product of—

13   "(I) the estimated total number

14 of inpatient-bed-days with respect to

15 the eligible hospital during such pe-

16 riod; and

17   "(II) the estimated total amount

18 of the eligible hospital's charges dur-

19 ing such period, not including any

20 charges that are attributable to char-

21 ity care (as such term is used for pur-

22 poses of hospital cost reporting under

23 this title), divided by the estimated

24 total amount of the hospital's charges

25 during such period.

1   Insofar as the Secretary determines that data

2   are not available on charity care necessary to

3   calculate the portion of the formula specified in

4   clause (ii)(II), the Secretary shall use data on

5   uncompensated care and may adjust such data

6   so as to be an appropriate proxy for charity

7   care including a downward adjustment to elimi-

8   nate bad debt data from uncompensated care

9   data. In the absence of the data necessary, with

10   respect to a hospital, for the Secretary to com-

11   pute the amount described in clause (ii)(II), the

12   amount under such clause shall be deemed to

13   be 1. In the absence of data, with respect to a

14   hospital, necessary to compute the amount de-

15   scribed in clause (i)(II), the amount under such

16   clause shall be deemed to be 0.

17   "(E) TRANSITION FACTOR SPECIFIED.—

18   "(i) IN GENERAL.—Subject to clause

19   (ii), the transition factor specified in this

20   subparagraph for an eligible hospital for a

21   payment year is as follows:

22   "(I) For the first payment year

23   for such hospital, 1.

24   "(II) For the second payment

25   year for such hospital, ¾.

1   "(III) For the third payment

2   year for such hospital, ½.

3   "(IV) For the fourth payment

4   year for such hospital, ¼.

5   "(V) For any succeeding pay-

6   ment year for such hospital, 0.

7   "(ii) PHASE DOWN FOR ELIGIBLE

8   HOSPITALS FIRST ADOPTING EHR AFTER

9   2013.—If the first payment year for an eli-

10   gible hospital is after 2013, then the tran-

11   sition factor specified in this subparagraph

12   for a payment year for such hospital is the

13   same as the amount specified in clause (i)

14   for such payment year for an eligible hos-

15   pital for which the first payment year is

16   2013. If the first payment year for an eli-

17   gible hospital is after 2015 then the transi-

18   tion factor specified in this subparagraph

19   for such hospital and for such year and

20   any subsequent year shall be 0.

21   "(F) FORM OF PAYMENT.—The payment

22 under this subsection for a payment year may

23 be in the form of a single consolidated payment

24 or in the form of such periodic installments as

25 the Secretary may specify.

1   "(G) PAYMENT YEAR DEFINED.—

2   "(i) IN GENERAL.—For purposes of

3   this subsection, the term 'payment year'

4   means a fiscal year beginning with fiscal

5   year 2011.

6   "(ii) FIRST, SECOND, ETC. PAYMENT

7   YEAR.—The term 'first payment year'

8   means, with respect to inpatient hospital

9   services furnished by an eligible hospital,

10   the first fiscal year for which an incentive

11   payment is made for such services under

12   this subsection. The terms 'second pay-

13   ment year', 'third payment year', and

14   'fourth payment year' mean, with respect

15   to an eligible hospital, each successive year

16   immediately following the first payment

17   year for that hospital.

18   "(3) MEANINGFUL EHR USER.—

19   "(A) IN GENERAL.—For purposes of para-

20   graph (1), an eligible hospital shall be treated

21   as a meaningful EHR user for an EHR report-

22   ing period for a payment year (or, for purposes

23   of subsection (b)(3)(B)(ix), for an EHR report-

24   ing period under such subsection for a fiscal

year) if each of the following requirements are
met:

"(i) MEANINGFUL USE OF CERTIFIED
EHR TECHNOLOGY.—The eligible hospital
demonstrates to the satisfaction of the Secretary, in accordance with subparagraph
(C)(i), that during such period the hospital
is using certified EHR technology in a
meaningful manner.

"(ii) INFORMATION EXCHANGE.—The
eligible hospital demonstrates to the satisfaction of the Secretary, in accordance
with subparagraph (C)(i), that during such
period such certified EHR technology is
connected in a manner that provides, in
accordance with law and standards applicable to the exchange of information, for
the electronic exchange of health information to improve the quality of health care,
such as promoting care coordination.

"(iii) REPORTING ON MEASURES
USING EHR.—Subject to subparagraph
(B)(ii) and using such certified EHR technology, the eligible hospital submits information for such period, in a form and

1   manner specified by the Secretary, on such

2   clinical quality measures and such other

3   measures as selected by the Secretary

4   under subparagraph (B)(i).

5 The Secretary shall seek to improve the use of

6 electronic health records and health care quality

7 over time by requiring more stringent measures

8 of meaningful use selected under this para-

9 graph.

10   "(B) REPORTING ON MEASURES.—

11   "(i) SELECTION.—The Secretary shall

12   select measures for purposes of subpara-

13   graph (A)(iii) but only consistent with the

14   following:

15   "(I) The Secretary shall provide

16   preference to clinical quality measures

17   that have been selected for purposes

18   of applying subsection (b)(3)(B)(viii)

19   or that have been endorsed by the en-

20   tity with a contract with the Secretary

21   under section 1890(a).

22   "(II) Prior to any measure (other

23   than a clinical quality measure that

24   has been selected for purposes of ap-

25   plying subsection (b)(3)(B)(viii))

being selected under this subparagraph, the Secretary shall publish in
the Federal Register such measure
and provide for a period of public
comment on such measure.

"(ii) LIMITATIONS.—The Secretary
may not require the electronic reporting of
information on clinical quality measures
under subparagraph (A)(iii) unless the
Secretary has the capacity to accept the information electronically, which may be on
a pilot basis.

"(iii) COORDINATION OF REPORTING
OF INFORMATION.—In selecting such
measures, and in establishing the form and
manner for reporting measures under subparagraph (A)(iii), the Secretary shall seek
to avoid redundant or duplicative reporting
with reporting otherwise required, including reporting under subsection
(b)(3)(B)(viii).

"(C) DEMONSTRATION OF MEANINGFUL
USE OF CERTIFIED EHR TECHNOLOGY AND IN-
FORMATION EXCHANGE.—

1   "(i) IN GENERAL.—An eligible hos-

2   pital may satisfy the demonstration re-

3   quirement of clauses (i) and (ii) of sub-

4   paragraph (A) through means specified by

5   the Secretary, which may include—

6   "(I) an attestation;

7   "(II) the submission of claims

8   with appropriate coding (such as a

9   code indicating that inpatient care

10   was documented using certified EHR

11   technology);

12   "(III) a survey response;

13   "(IV) reporting under subpara-

14   graph (A)(iii); and

15   "(V) other means specified by the

16   Secretary.

17   "(ii) USE OF PART D DATA.—Not-

18   withstanding sections 1860D–15(d)(2)(B)

19   and 1860D–15(f)(2), the Secretary may

20   use data regarding drug claims submitted

21   for purposes of section 1860D–15 that are

22   necessary for purposes of subparagraph

23   (A).

24   "(4) APPLICATION.—

1   "(A) LIMITATIONS ON REVIEW.—There

2   shall be no administrative or judicial review

3   under section 1869, section 1878, or otherwise,

4   of—

5   "(i) the methodology and standards

6   for determining payment amounts under

7   this subsection and payment adjustments

8   under subsection (b)(3)(B)(ix), including

9   selection of periods under paragraph (2)

10   for determining, and making estimates or

11   using proxies of, discharges under para-

12   graph (2)(C) and inpatient-bed-days, hos-

13   pital charges, charity charges, and Medi-

14   care share under paragraph (2)(D);

15   "(ii) the methodology and standards

16   for determining a meaningful EHR user

17   under paragraph (3), including selection of

18   measures under paragraph (3)(B), speci-

19   fication of the means of demonstrating

20   meaningful EHR use under paragraph

21   (3)(C), and the hardship exception under

22   subsection (b)(3)(B)(ix)(II); and

23   "(iii) the specification of EHR report-

24   ing periods under paragraph (6)(B) and

1   the selection of the form of payment under

2   paragraph (2)(F).

3   "(B) POSTING ON WEBSITE.—The Sec-

4   retary shall post on the Internet website of the

5   Centers for Medicare & Medicaid Services, in an

6   easily understandable format, a list of the

7   names of the eligible hospitals that are mean-

8   ingful EHR users under this subsection or sub-

9   section (b)(3)(B)(ix) (and a list of the names of

10   critical access hospitals to which paragraph (3)

11   or (4) of section 1814(l) applies), and other rel-

12   evant data as determined appropriate by the

13   Secretary. The Secretary shall ensure that an

14   eligible hospital (or critical access hospital) has

15   the opportunity to review the other relevant

16   data that are to be made public with respect to

17   the hospital (or critical access hospital) prior to

18   such data being made public.

19   "(5) CERTIFIED EHR TECHNOLOGY DEFINED.—

20   The term 'certified EHR technology' has the mean-

21   ing given such term in section 1848(o)(4).

22   "(6) DEFINITIONS.—For purposes of this sub-

23   section:

24   "(A) EHR REPORTING PERIOD.—The term

25   'EHR reporting period' means, with respect to

1   a payment year, any period (or periods) as

2   specified by the Secretary.

3   "(B) ELIGIBLE HOSPITAL.—The term 'eli-

4   gible hospital' means a subsection (d) hos-

5   pital.".

6   (2) CRITICAL ACCESS HOSPITALS.—Section

7   1814(l) of the Social Security Act (42 U.S.C.

8   1395f(l)) is amended—

9   (A) in paragraph (1), by striking "para-

10   graph (2)" and inserting "the subsequent para-

11   graphs of this subsection"; and

12   (B) by adding at the end the following new

13   paragraph:

14   "(3)(A) The following rules shall apply in deter-

15 mining payment and reasonable costs under paragraph (1)

16 for costs described in subparagraph (C) for a critical ac-

17 cess hospital that would be a meaningful EHR user (as

18 would be determined under paragraph (3) of section

19 1886(n)) for an EHR reporting period for a cost reporting

20 period beginning during a payment year if such critical

21 access hospital was treated as an eligible hospital under

22 such section:

23   "(i) The Secretary shall compute reasonable

24   costs by expensing such costs in a single payment

25   year and not depreciating such costs over a period

1 of years (and shall include as costs with respect to

2 cost reporting periods beginning during a payment

3 year costs from previous cost reporting periods to

4 the extent they have not been fully depreciated as of

5 the period involved).

6 "(ii) There shall be substituted for the Medi-

7 care share that would otherwise be applied under

8 paragraph (1) a percent (not to exceed 100 percent)

9 equal to the sum of—

10 "(I) the Medicare share (as would be speci-

11 fied under paragraph (2)(D) of section

12 1886(n)) for such critical access hospital if such

13 critical access hospital was treated as an eligible

14 hospital under such section; and

15 "(II) 20 percentage points.

16 "(B) The payment under this paragraph with respect

17 to a critical access hospital shall be paid through a prompt

18 interim payment (subject to reconciliation) after submis-

19 sion and review of such information (as specified by the

20 Secretary) necessary to make such payment, including in-

21 formation necessary to apply this paragraph. In no case

22 may payment under this paragraph be made with respect

23 to a cost reporting period beginning during a payment

24 year after 2015 and in no case may a critical access hos-

1 pital receive payment under this paragraph with respect

2 to more than 4 consecutive payment years.

3   "(C) The costs described in this subparagraph are

4 costs for the purchase of certified EHR technology to

5 which purchase depreciation (excluding interest) would

6 apply if payment was made under paragraph (1) and not

7 under this paragraph.

8   "(D) For purposes of this paragraph, paragraph (4),

9 and paragraph (5), the terms 'certified EHR technology',

10 'eligible hospital', 'EHR reporting period', and 'payment

11 year' have the meanings given such terms in sections

12 1886(n).".

13   (b) INCENTIVE MARKET BASKET ADJUSTMENT.—

14   (1) IN GENERAL.—Section 1886(b)(3)(B) of

15   the Social Security Act (42 U.S.C.

16   1395ww(b)(3)(B)) is amended—

17   (A) in clause (viii)(I), by inserting "(or,

18   beginning with fiscal year 2015, by one-quar-

19   ter)" after "2.0 percentage points"; and

20   (B) by adding at the end the following new

21   clause:

22   "(ix)(I) For purposes of clause (i) for fiscal year

23 2015 and each subsequent fiscal year, in the case of an

24 eligible hospital (as defined in subsection (n)(6)(A)) that

25 is not a meaningful EHR user (as defined in subsection

1 (n)(3)) for an EHR reporting period for such fiscal year,

2 three-quarters of the applicable percentage increase other-

3 wise applicable under clause (i) for such fiscal year shall

4 be reduced by 33⅓ percent for fiscal year 2015, 66⅔ per-

5 cent for fiscal year 2016, and 100 percent for fiscal year

6 2017 and each subsequent fiscal year. Such reduction

7 shall apply only with respect to the fiscal year involved

8 and the Secretary shall not take into account such reduc-

9 tion in computing the applicable percentage increase under

10 clause (i) for a subsequent fiscal year.

11   "(II) The Secretary may, on a case-by-case basis, ex-

12 empt a subsection (d) hospital from the application of sub-

13 clause (I) with respect to a fiscal year if the Secretary

14 determines, subject to annual renewal, that requiring such

15 hospital to be a meaningful EHR user during such fiscal

16 year would result in a significant hardship, such as in the

17 case of a hospital in a rural area without sufficient Inter-

18 net access. In no case may a hospital be granted an ex-

19 emption under this subclause for more than 5 years.

20   "(III) For fiscal year 2015 and each subsequent fis-

21 cal year, a State in which hospitals are paid for services

22 under section 1814(b)(3) shall adjust the payments to

23 each subsection (d) hospital in the State that is not a

24 meaningful EHR user (as defined in subsection (n)(3))

25 in a manner that is designed to result in an aggregate

1 reduction in payments to hospitals in the State that is
2 equivalent to the aggregate reduction that would have oc-
3 curred if payments had been reduced to each subsection
4 (d) hospital in the State in a manner comparable to the
5 reduction under the previous provisions of this clause. The
6 State shall report to the Secretary the methodology it will
7 use to make the payment adjustment under the previous
8 sentence.

9 "(IV) For purposes of this clause, the term 'EHR
10 reporting period' means, with respect to a fiscal year, any
11 period (or periods) as specified by the Secretary.".

12   (2) CRITICAL ACCESS HOSPITALS.—Section
13   1814(l) of the Social Security Act (42 U.S.C.
14   1395f(l)), as amended by subsection (a)(2), is fur-
15   ther amended by adding at the end the following
16   new paragraphs:

17 "(4)(A) Subject to subparagraph (C), for cost report-
18 ing periods beginning in fiscal year 2015 or a subsequent
19 fiscal year, in the case of a critical access hospital that
20 is not a meaningful EHR user (as would be determined
21 under paragraph (3) of section 1886(n) if such critical ac-
22 cess hospital was treated as an eligible hospital under such
23 section) for an EHR reporting period with respect to such
24 fiscal year, paragraph (1) shall be applied by substituting

1 the applicable percent under subparagraph (B) for the

2 percent described in such paragraph (1).

3   "(B) The percent described in this subparagraph is—

4   "(i) for fiscal year 2015, 100.66 percent;

5   "(ii) for fiscal year 2016, 100.33 percent; and

6   "(iii) for fiscal year 2017 and each subsequent

7 fiscal year, 100 percent.

8   "(C) The provisions of subclause (II) of section

9 1886(b)(3)(B)(ix) shall apply with respect to subpara-

10 graph (A) for a critical access hospital with respect to a

11 cost reporting period beginning in a fiscal year in the same

12 manner as such subclause applies with respect to sub-

13 clause (I) of such section for a subsection (d) hospital with

14 respect to such fiscal year.

15   "(5) There shall be no administrative or judicial re-

16 view under section 1869, section 1878, or otherwise, of—

17   "(A) the methodology and standards for deter-

18 mining the amount of payment and reasonable cost

19 under paragraph (3) and payment adjustments

20 under paragraph (4), including selection of periods

21 under section 1886(n)(2) for determining, and mak-

22 ing estimates or using proxies of, inpatient-bed-days,

23 hospital charges, charity charges, and Medicare

24 share under subparagraph (D) of section

25 1886(n)(2);

1   "(B) the methodology and standards for deter-

2 mining a meaningful EHR user under section

3 1886(n)(3) as would apply if the hospital was treat-

4 ed as an eligible hospital under section 1886(n), and

5 the hardship exception under paragraph (4)(C);

6   "(C) the specification of EHR reporting periods

7 under section 1886(n)(6)(B) as applied under para-

8 graphs (3) and (4); and

9   "(D) the identification of costs for purposes of

10 paragraph (3)(C).".

11   (c) APPLICATION TO CERTAIN MA-AFFILIATED ELI-

12 GIBLE HOSPITALS.—Section 1853 of the Social Security

13 Act (42 U.S.C. 1395w–23), as amended by section

14 4101(c), is further amended by adding at the end the fol-

15 lowing new subsection:

16   "(m) APPLICATION OF ELIGIBLE HOSPITAL INCEN-

17 TIVES FOR CERTAIN MA ORGANIZATIONS FOR ADOPTION

18 AND MEANINGFUL USE OF CERTIFIED EHR TECH-

19 NOLOGY.—

20   "(1) APPLICATION.—Subject to paragraphs (3)

21 and (4), in the case of a qualifying MA organization,

22 the provisions of sections 1886(n) and

23 1886(b)(3)(B)(ix) shall apply with respect to eligible

24 hospitals described in paragraph (2) of the organiza-

25 tion which the organization attests under subsection

1   (l)(6) to be meaningful EHR users in a similar man-
2   ner as they apply to eligible hospitals under such
3   sections. Incentive payments under paragraph (3)
4   shall be made to and payment adjustments under
5   paragraph (4) shall apply to such qualifying organi-
6   zations.

7   "(2) ELIGIBLE HOSPITAL DESCRIBED.—With
8   respect to a qualifying MA organization, an eligible
9   hospital described in this paragraph is an eligible
10   hospital (as defined in section 1886(n)(6)(A)) that is
11   under common corporate governance with such orga-
12   nization and serves individuals enrolled under an
13   MA plan offered by such organization.

14   "(3) ELIGIBLE HOSPITAL INCENTIVE PAY-
15   MENTS.—

16   "(A) IN GENERAL.—In applying section
17   1886(n)(2) under paragraph (1), instead of the
18   additional payment amount under section
19   1886(n)(2), there shall be substituted an
20   amount determined by the Secretary to be simi-
21   lar to the estimated amount in the aggregate
22   that would be payable if payment for services
23   furnished by such hospitals was payable under
24   part A instead of this part. In implementing the
25   previous sentence, the Secretary—

1   "(i) shall, insofar as data to deter-
2   mine the discharge related amount under
3   section 1886(n)(2)(C) for an eligible hos-
4   pital are not available to the Secretary, use
5   such alternative data and methodology to
6   estimate such discharge related amount as
7   the Secretary determines appropriate; and
8   "(ii) shall, insofar as data to deter-
9   mine the medicare share described in sec-
10   tion 1886(n)(2)(D) for an eligible hospital
11   are not available to the Secretary, use such
12   alternative data and methodology to esti-
13   mate such share, which data and method-
14   ology may include use of the inpatient-bed-
15   days (or discharges) with respect to an eli-
16   gible hospital during the appropriate pe-
17   riod which are attributable to both individ-
18   uals for whom payment may be made
19   under part A or individuals enrolled in an
20   MA plan under a Medicare Advantage or-
21   ganization under this part as a proportion
22   of the estimated total number of patient-
23   bed-days (or discharges) with respect to
24   such hospital during such period.

"(B) AVOIDING DUPLICATION OF PAY-
MENTS.—

"(i) IN GENERAL.—In the case of a
hospital that for a payment year is an eligible hospital described in paragraph (2)
and for which at least one-third of their
discharges (or bed-days) of Medicare patients for the year are covered under part
A, payment for the payment year shall be
made only under section 1886(n) and not
under this subsection.

"(ii) METHODS.—In the case of a
hospital that is an eligible hospital described in paragraph (2) and also is eligible for an incentive payment under section
1886(n) but is not described in clause (i)
for the same payment period, the Secretary
shall develop a process—

"(I) to ensure that duplicate payments are not made with respect to
an eligible hospital both under this
subsection and under section 1886(n);
and

1   "(II) to collect data from Medi-
2   care Advantage organizations to en-
3   sure against such duplicate payments.
4   "(4) PAYMENT ADJUSTMENT.—

5   "(A) Subject to paragraph (3), in the case
6   of a qualifying MA organization (as defined in
7   section 1853(l)(5)), if, according to the attesta-
8   tion of the organization submitted under sub-
9   section (l)(6) for an applicable period, one or
10   more eligible hospitals (as defined in section
11   1886(n)(6)(A)) that are under common cor-
12   porate governance with such organization and
13   that serve individuals enrolled under a plan of-
14   fered by such organization are not meaningful
15   EHR users (as defined in section 1886(n)(3))
16   with respect to a period, the payment amount
17   payable under this section for such organization
18   for such period shall be the percent specified in
19   subparagraph (B) for such period of the pay-
20   ment amount otherwise provided under this sec-
21   tion for such period.

22   "(B) SPECIFIED PERCENT.—The percent
23   specified under this subparagraph for a year is
24   100 percent minus a number of percentage
25   points equal to the product of—

"(i) the number of the percentage point reduction effected under section 1886(b)(3)(B)(ix)(I) for the period; and

"(ii) the Medicare hospital expenditure proportion specified in subparagraph (C) for the year.

"(C) MEDICARE HOSPITAL EXPENDITURE PROPORTION.—The Medicare hospital expenditure proportion under this subparagraph for a year is the Secretary's estimate of the proportion, of the expenditures under parts A and B that are not attributable to this part, that are attributable to expenditures for inpatient hospital services.

"(D) APPLICATION OF PAYMENT ADJUSTMENT.—In the case that a qualifying MA organization attests that not all eligible hospitals are meaningful EHR users with respect to an applicable period, the Secretary shall apply the payment adjustment under this paragraph based on a methodology specified by the Secretary, taking into account the proportion of such eligible hospitals, or discharges from such hospitals, that are not meaningful EHR users for such period.

1   "(5) POSTING ON WEBSITE.—The Secretary

2 shall post on the Internet website of the Centers for

3 Medicare & Medicaid Services, in an easily under-

4 standable format—

5   "(A) a list of the names, business address-

6   es, and business phone numbers of each quali-

7   fying MA organization receiving an incentive

8   payment under this subsection for eligible hos-

9   pitals described in paragraph (2); and

10   "(B) a list of the names of the eligible hos-

11   pitals for which such incentive payment is

12   based.

13   "(6) LIMITATIONS ON REVIEW.—There shall be

14 no administrative or judicial review under section

15 1869, section 1878, or otherwise, of—

16   "(A) the methodology and standards for

17   determining payment amounts and payment ad-

18   justments under this subsection, including

19   avoiding duplication of payments under para-

20   graph (3)(B);

21   "(B) the methodology and standards for

22   determining eligible hospitals under paragraph

23   (2); and

24   "(C) the methodology and standards for

25   determining a meaningful EHR user under sec-

1   tion 1886(n)(3), including specification of the

2   means of demonstrating meaningful EHR use

3   under subparagraph (C) of such section and se-

4   lection of measures under subparagraph (B) of

5   such section.".

6 (d) CONFORMING AMENDMENTS.—

7   (1) Section 1814(b) of the Social Security Act

8   (42 U.S.C. 1395f(b)) is amended—

9   (A) in paragraph (3), in the matter pre-

10   ceding subparagraph (A), by inserting ", sub-

11   ject to section 1886(d)(3)(B)(ix)(III)," after

12   "then"; and

13   (B) by adding at the end the following:

14   "For purposes of applying paragraph (3), there

15   shall be taken into account incentive payments,

16   and payment adjustments under subsection

17   (b)(3)(B)(ix) or (n) of section 1886.".

18   (2) Section 1851(i)(1) of the Social Security

19 Act (42 U.S.C. 1395w–21(i)(1)) is amended by

20 striking "and 1886(h)(3)(D)" and inserting

21 "1886(h)(3)(D), and 1853(m)".

22   (3) Section 1853 of the Social Security Act (42

23 U.S.C. 1395w–23), as amended by section 4101(d),

24 is amended—

25   (A) in subsection (c)—

1   (i) in paragraph (1)(D)(i), by striking

2   "1848(o)" and inserting ", 1848(o), and

3   1886(n)"; and

4   (ii) in paragraph (6)(A), by inserting

5   "and subsections (b)(3)(B)(ix) and (n) of

6   section 1886" after "section 1848"; and

7   (B) in subsection (f), by inserting "and

8   subsection (m)" after "under subsection (l)".

SEC. 4103. TREATMENT OF PAYMENTS AND SAVINGS; IM-PLEMENTATION FUNDING.

(a) PREMIUM HOLD HARMLESS.—

    (1) IN GENERAL.—Section 1839(a)(1) of the Social Security Act (42 U.S.C. 1395r(a)(1)) is amended by adding at the end the following: "In applying this paragraph there shall not be taken into account additional payments under section 1848(o) and section 1853(l)(3) and the Government contribution under section 1844(a)(3).".

    (2) PAYMENT.—Section 1844(a) of such Act (42 U.S.C. 1395w(a)) is amended—

        (A) in paragraph (2), by striking the period at the end and inserting "; plus"; and

        (B) by adding at the end the following new paragraph:

1   "(3) a Government contribution equal to the

2   amount of payment incentives payable under sec-

3   tions 1848(o) and 1853(l)(3).".

4   (b) MEDICARE IMPROVEMENT FUND.—Section 1898

5 of the Social Security Act (42 U.S.C. 1395iii), as added

6 by section 7002(a) of the Supplemental Appropriations

7 Act, 2008 (Public Law 110–252) and as amended by sec-

8 tion 188(a)(2) of the Medicare Improvements for Patients

9 and Providers Act of 2008 (Public Law 110–275; 122

10 Stat. 2589) and by section 6 of the QI Program Supple-

11 mental Funding Act of 2008, is amended—

12   (1) in subsection (a)—

13   (A) by inserting "medicare" before "fee-

14   for-service"; and

15   (B) by inserting before the period at the

16   end the following: "including, but not limited

17   to, an increase in the conversion factor under

18   section 1848(d) to address, in whole or in part,

19   any projected shortfall in the conversion factor

20   for 2014 relative to the conversion factor for

21   2008 and adjustments to payments for items

22   and services furnished by providers of services

23   and suppliers under such original medicare fee-

24   for-service program"; and

25   (2) in subsection (b)—

1   (A) in paragraph (1), by striking "during

2   fiscal year 2014," and all that follows and in-

3   serting the following: "during—

4   "(A) fiscal year 2014, $22,290,000,000;

5   and

6   "(B) fiscal year 2020 and each subsequent

7   fiscal year, the Secretary's estimate, as of July

8   1 of the fiscal year, of the aggregate reduction

9   in expenditures under this title during the pre-

10   ceding fiscal year directly resulting from the re-

11   duction in payment amounts under sections

12   1848(a)(7), 1853(l)(4), 1853(m)(4), and

13   1886(b)(3)(B)(ix)."; and

14   (B) by adding at the end the following new

15   paragraph:

16   "(4) No EFFECT ON PAYMENTS IN SUBSE-

17   QUENT YEARS.—In the case that expenditures from

18   the Fund are applied to, or otherwise affect, a pay-

19   ment rate for an item or service under this title for

20   a year, the payment rate for such item or service

21   shall be computed for a subsequent year as if such

22   application or effect had never occurred.".

23   (c) IMPLEMENTATION FUNDING.—In addition to

24 funds otherwise available, out of any funds in the Treas-

25 ury not otherwise appropriated, there are appropriated to

1 the Secretary of Health and Human Services for the Cen-

2 ter for Medicare & Medicaid Services Program Manage-

3 ment Account, $100,000,000 for each of fiscal years 2009

4 through 2015 and $45,000,000 for fiscal year 2016, which

5 shall be available for purposes of carrying out the provi-

6 sions of (and amendments made by) this subtitle.

7 Amounts appropriated under this subsection for a fiscal

8 year shall be available until expended.

9 **SEC. 4104. STUDIES AND REPORTS ON HEALTH INFORMA-**

10 **TION TECHNOLOGY.**

11 (a) STUDY AND REPORT ON APPLICATION OF EHR

12 PAYMENT INCENTIVES FOR PROVIDERS NOT RECEIVING

13 OTHER INCENTIVE PAYMENTS.—

14 (1) STUDY.—

15 (A) IN GENERAL.—The Secretary of

16 Health and Human Services shall conduct a

17 study to determine the extent to which and

18 manner in which payment incentives (such as

19 under title XVIII or XIX of the Social Security

20 Act) and other funding for purposes of imple-

21 menting and using certified EHR technology

22 (as defined in section 1848(o)(4) of the Social

23 Security Act, as added by section 4101(a))

24 should be made available to health care pro-

25 viders who are receiving minimal or no payment

1   incentives or other funding under this Act,

2   under title XIII of division A, under title XVIII

3   or XIX of such Act, or otherwise, for such pur-

4   poses.

5   (B) DETAILS OF STUDY.—Such study shall

6   include an examination of—

7   (i) the adoption rates of certified

8   EHR technology by such health care pro-

9   viders;

10   (ii) the clinical utility of such tech-

11   nology by such health care providers;

12   (iii) whether the services furnished by

13   such health care providers are appropriate

14   for or would benefit from the use of such

15   technology;

16   (iv) the extent to which such health

17   care providers work in settings that might

18   otherwise receive an incentive payment or

19   other funding under this Act, under title

20   XIII of division A, under title XVIII or

21   XIX of the Social Security Act, or other-

22   wise;

23   (v) the potential costs and the poten-

24   tial benefits of making payment incentives

1   and other funding available to such health

2   care providers; and

3   (vi) any other issues the Secretary

4   deems to be appropriate.

5   (2) REPORT.—Not later than June 30, 2010,

6   the Secretary shall submit to Congress a report on

7   the findings and conclusions of the study conducted

8   under paragraph (1).

9   (b) STUDY AND REPORT ON AVAILABILITY OF OPEN

10 SOURCE HEALTH INFORMATION TECHNOLOGY SYS-

11 TEMS.—

12   (1) STUDY.—

13   (A) IN GENERAL.—The Secretary of

14   Health and Human Services shall, in consulta-

15   tion with the Under Secretary for Health of the

16   Veterans Health Administration, the Director

17   of the Indian Health Service, the Secretary of

18   Defense, the Director of the Agency for

19   Healthcare Research and Quality, the Adminis-

20   trator of the Health Resources and Services Ad-

21   ministration, and the Chairman of the Federal

22   Communications Commission, conduct a study

23   on—

24   (i) the current availability of open

25   source health information technology sys-

1   tems to Federal safety net providers (in-

2   cluding small, rural providers);

3   (ii) the total cost of ownership of such

4   systems in comparison to the cost of pro-

5   prietary commercial products available;

6   (iii) the ability of such systems to re-

7   spond to the needs of, and be applied to,

8   various populations (including children and

9   disabled individuals); and

10   (iv) the capacity of such systems to

11   facilitate interoperability.

12   (B) CONSIDERATIONS.—In conducting the

13   study under subparagraph (A), the Secretary of

14   Health and Human Services shall take into ac-

15   count the circumstances of smaller health care

16   providers, health care providers located in rural

17   or other medically underserved areas, and safe-

18   ty net providers that deliver a significant level

19   of health care to uninsured individuals, Med-

20   icaid beneficiaries, SCHIP beneficiaries, and

21   other vulnerable individuals.

22   (2) REPORT.—Not later than October 1, 2010,

23   the Secretary of Health and Human Services shall

24   submit to Congress a report on the findings and the

25   conclusions of the study conducted under paragraph

1   (1), together with recommendations for such legisla-

2   tion and administrative action as the Secretary de-

3   termines appropriate.

4   Subtitle B—Medicaid Incentives

5   **SEC. 4201. MEDICAID PROVIDER HIT ADOPTION AND OPER-**

6   **ATION PAYMENTS; IMPLEMENTATION FUND-**

7   **ING.**

8   (a) IN GENERAL.—Section 1903 of the Social Secu-

9   rity Act (42 U.S.C. 1396b) is amended—

10   (1) in subsection (a)(3)—

11   (A) by striking "and" at the end of sub-

12   paragraph (D);

13   (B) by striking "plus" at the end of sub-

14   paragraph (E) and inserting "and"; and

15   (C) by adding at the end the following new

16   subparagraph:

17   "(F)(i) 100 percent of so much of the

18   sums expended during such quarter as are at-

19   tributable to payments to Medicaid providers

20   described in subsection (t)(1) to encourage the

21   adoption and use of certified EHR technology;

22   and

23   "(ii) 90 percent of so much of the sums ex-

24   pended during such quarter as are attributable

25   to payments for reasonable administrative ex-

1   penses related to the administration of pay-

2   ments described in clause (i) if the State meets

3   the condition described in subsection (t)(9);

4   plus"; and

5   (2) by inserting after subsection (s) the fol-

6   lowing new subsection:

7   "(t)(1) For purposes of subsection (a)(3)(F), the pay-

8 ments described in this paragraph to encourage the adop-

9 tion and use of certified EHR technology are payments

10 made by the State in accordance with this subsection —

11   "(A) to Medicaid providers described in para-

12   graph (2)(A) not in excess of 85 percent of net aver-

13   age allowable costs (as defined in paragraph (3)(E))

14   for certified EHR technology (and support services

15   including maintenance and training that is for, or is

16   necessary for the adoption and operation of, such

17   technology) with respect to such providers; and

18   "(B) to Medicaid providers described in para-

19   graph (2)(B) not in excess of the maximum amount

20   permitted under paragraph (5) for the provider in-

21   volved.

22   "(2) In this subsection and subsection (a)(3)(F), the

23 term 'Medicaid provider' means—

24   "(A) an eligible professional (as defined in

25   paragraph (3)(B))—

1   "(i) who is not hospital-based and has at

2   least 30 percent of the professional's patient

3   volume (as estimated in accordance with a

4   methodology established by the Secretary) at-

5   tributable to individuals who are receiving med-

6   ical assistance under this title;

7   "(ii) who is not described in clause (i), who

8   is a pediatrician, who is not hospital-based, and

9   who has at least 20 percent of the profes-

10   sional's patient volume (as estimated in accord-

11   ance with a methodology established by the Sec-

12   retary) attributable to individuals who are re-

13   ceiving medical assistance under this title; and

14   "(iii) who practices predominantly in a

15   Federally qualified health center or rural health

16   clinic and has at least 30 percent of the profes-

17   sional's patient volume (as estimated in accord-

18   ance with a methodology established by the Sec-

19   retary) attributable to needy individuals (as de-

20   fined in paragraph (3)(F)); and

21   "(B)(i) a children's hospital, or

22   "(ii) an acute-care hospital that is not described

23   in clause (i) and that has at least 10 percent of the

24   hospital's patient volume (as estimated in accord-

25   ance with a methodology established by the Sec-

1   retary) attributable to individuals who are receiving

2   medical assistance under this title.

3 An eligible professional shall not qualify as a Medicaid

4 provider under this subsection unless any right to payment

5 under sections 1848(o) and 1853(l) with respect to the

6 eligible professional has been waived in a manner specified

7 by the Secretary. For purposes of calculating patient vol-

8 ume under subparagraph (A)(iii), insofar as it is related

9 to uncompensated care, the Secretary may require the ad-

10 justment of such uncompensated care data so that it

11 would be an appropriate proxy for charity care, including

12 a downward adjustment to eliminate bad debt data from

13 uncompensated care. In applying subparagraphs (A) and

14 (B)(ii), the methodology established by the Secretary for

15 patient volume shall include individuals enrolled in a Med-

16 icaid managed care plan (under section 1903(m) or sec-

17 tion 1932).

18   "(3) In this subsection and subsection (a)(3)(F):

19   "(A) The term 'certified EHR technology'

20   means a qualified electronic health record (as de-

21   fined in 3000(13) of the Public Health Service Act)

22   that is certified pursuant to section 3001(c)(5) of

23   such Act as meeting standards adopted under sec-

24   tion 3004 of such Act that are applicable to the type

25   of record involved (as determined by the Secretary,

1   such as an ambulatory electronic health record for

2   office-based physicians or an inpatient hospital elec-

3   tronic health record for hospitals).

4   "(B) The term 'eligible professional' means a—

5   "(i) physician;

6   "(ii) dentist;

7   "(iii) certified nurse mid-wife;

8   "(iv) nurse practitioner; and

9   "(v) physician assistant insofar as the as-

10   sistant is practicing in a rural health clinic that

11   is led by a physician assistant or is practicing

12   in a Federally qualified health center that is so

13   led.

14   "(C) The term 'average allowable costs' means,

15   with respect to certified EHR technology of Med-

16   icaid providers described in paragraph (2)(A) for—

17   "(i) the first year of payment with respect

18   to such a provider, the average costs for the

19   purchase and initial implementation or upgrade

20   of such technology (and support services includ-

21   ing training that is for, or is necessary for the

22   adoption and initial operation of, such tech-

23   nology) for such providers, as determined by

24   the Secretary based upon studies conducted

25   under paragraph (4)(C); and

1   "(ii) a subsequent year of payment with

2   respect to such a provider, the average costs

3   not described in clause (i) relating to the oper-

4   ation, maintenance, and use of such technology

5   for such providers, as determined by the Sec-

6   retary based upon studies conducted under

7   paragraph (4)(C).

8   "(D) The term 'hospital-based' means, with re-

9   spect to an eligible professional, a professional (such

10   as a pathologist, anesthesiologist, or emergency phy-

11   sician) who furnishes substantially all of the individ-

12   ual's professional services in a hospital setting

13   (whether inpatient or outpatient) and through the

14   use of the facilities and equipment, including quali-

15   fied electronic health records, of the hospital. The

16   determination of whether an eligible professional is

17   a hospital-based eligible professional shall be made

18   on the basis of the site of service (as defined by the

19   Secretary) and without regard to any employment or

20   billing arrangement between the eligible professional

21   and any other provider.

22   "(E) The term 'net average allowable costs'

23   means, with respect to a Medicaid provider described

24   in paragraph (2)(A), average allowable costs reduced

25   by any payment that is made to such Medicaid pro-

1   vider from any other source (other than under this

2   subsection or by a State or local government) that

3   is directly attributable to payment for certified EHR

4   technology or support services described in subpara-

5   graph (C).

6   "(F) The term 'needy individual' means, with

7   respect to a Medicaid provider, an individual—

8   "(i) who is receiving assistance under this

9   title;

10   "(ii) who is receiving assistance under title

11   XXI;

12   "(iii) who is furnished uncompensated care

13   by the provider; or

14   "(iv) for whom charges are reduced by the

15   provider on a sliding scale basis based on an in-

16   dividual's ability to pay.

17   "(4)(A) With respect to a Medicaid provider de-

18 scribed in paragraph (2)(A), subject to subparagraph (B),

19 in no case shall—

20   "(i) the net average allowable costs under

21   this subsection for the first year of payment

22   (which may not be later than 2016), which is

23   intended to cover the costs described in para-

24   graph (3)(C)(i), exceed $25,000 (or such lesser

1   amount as the Secretary determines based on

2   studies conducted under subparagraph (C));

3   "(ii) the net average allowable costs under

4   this subsection for a subsequent year of pay-

5   ment, which is intended to cover costs described

6   in paragraph (3)(C)(ii), exceed \$10,000; and

7   "(iii) payments be made for costs described

8   in clause (ii) after 2021 or over a period of

9   longer than 5 years.

10   "(B) In the case of Medicaid provider described in

11 paragraph (2)(A)(ii), the dollar amounts specified in sub-

12 paragraph (A) shall be ⅔ of the dollar amounts otherwise

13 specified.

14   "(C) For the purposes of determining average allow-

15 able costs under this subsection, the Secretary shall study

16 the average costs to Medicaid providers described in para-

17 graph (2)(A) of purchase and initial implementation and

18 upgrade of certified EHR technology described in para-

19 graph (3)(C)(i) and the average costs to such providers

20 of operations, maintenance, and use of such technology de-

21 scribed in paragraph (3)(C)(ii). In determining such costs

22 for such providers, the Secretary may utilize studies of

23 such amounts submitted by States.

1   "(5)(A) In no case shall the payments described in

2 paragraph (1)(B) with respect to a Medicaid provider de-

3 scribed in paragraph (2)(B) exceed—

4   "(i) in the aggregate the product of—

5   "(I) the overall hospital EHR amount

6   for the provider computed under subpara-

7   graph (B); and

8   "(II) the Medicaid share for such pro-

9   vider computed under subparagraph (C);

10   "(ii) in any year 50 percent of the product de-

11   scribed in clause (i); and

12   "(iii) in any 2-year period 90 percent of such

13   product.

14   "(B) For purposes of this paragraph, the overall hos-

15 pital EHR amount, with respect to a Medicaid provider,

16 is the sum of the applicable amounts specified in section

17 1886(n)(2)(A) for such provider for the first 4 payment

18 years (as estimated by the Secretary) determined as if the

19 Medicare share specified in clause (ii) of such section were

20 1. The Secretary shall establish, in consultation with the

21 State, the overall hospital EHR amount for each such

22 Medicaid provider eligible for payments under paragraph

23 (1)(B). For purposes of this subparagraph in computing

24 the amounts under section 1886(n)(2)(C) for payment

25 years after the first payment year, the Secretary shall as-

1 sume that in subsequent payment years discharges in-
2 crease at the average annual rate of growth of the most
3 recent 3 years for which discharge data are available per
4 year.

5   "(C) The Medicaid share computed under this sub-
6 paragraph, for a Medicaid provider for a period specified
7 by the Secretary, shall be calculated in the same manner
8 as the Medicare share under section 1886(n)(2)(D) for
9 such a hospital and period, except that there shall be sub-
10 stituted for the numerator under clause (i) of such section
11 the amount that is equal to the number of inpatient-bed-
12 days (as established by the Secretary) which are attrib-
13 utable to individuals who are receiving medical assistance
14 under this title and who are not described in section
15 1886(n)(2)(D)(i). In computing inpatient-bed-days under
16 the previous sentence, the Secretary shall take into ac-
17 count inpatient-bed-days attributable to inpatient-bed-
18 days that are paid for individuals enrolled in a Medicaid
19 managed care plan (under section 1903(m) or section
20 1932).

21   "(D) In no case may the payments described in para-
22 graph (1)(B) with respect to a Medicaid provider de-
23 scribed in paragraph (2)(B) be paid—

1   "(i) for any year beginning after 2016 unless

2   the provider has been provided payment under para-

3   graph (1)(B) for the previous year; and

4   "(ii) over a period of more than 6 years of pay-

5   ment.

6   "(6) Payments described in paragraph (1) are not in

7 accordance with this subsection unless the following re-

8 quirements are met:

9   "(A)(i) The State provides assurances satisfac-

10   tory to the Secretary that amounts received under

11   subsection (a)(3)(F) with respect to payments to a

12   Medicaid provider are paid, subject to clause (ii), di-

13   rectly to such provider (or to an employer or facility

14   to which such provider has assigned payments) with-

15   out any deduction or rebate.

16   "(ii) Amounts described in clause (i) may also

17   be paid to an entity promoting the adoption of cer-

18   tified EHR technology, as designated by the State,

19   if participation in such a payment arrangement is

20   voluntary for the eligible professional involved and if

21   such entity does not retain more than 5 percent of

22   such payments for costs not related to certified

23   EHR technology (and support services including

24   maintenance and training) that is for, or is nec-

25   essary for the operation of, such technology.

1   "(B) A Medicaid provider described in para-

2 graph (2)(A) is responsible for payment of the re-

3 maining 15 percent of the net average allowable

4 cost.

5   "(C)(i) Subject to clause (ii), with respect to

6 payments to a Medicaid provider—

7   "(I) for the first year of payment to the

8   Medicaid provider under this subsection, the

9   Medicaid provider demonstrates that it is en-

10   gaged in efforts to adopt, implement, or up-

11   grade certified EHR technology; and

12   "(II) for a year of payment, other than the

13   first year of payment to the Medicaid provider

14   under this subsection, the Medicaid provider

15   demonstrates meaningful use of certified EHR

16   technology through a means that is approved by

17   the State and acceptable to the Secretary, and

18   that may be based upon the methodologies ap-

19   plied under section 1848(o) or 1886(n).

20   "(ii) In the case of a Medicaid provider who has

21 completed adopting, implementing, or upgrading

22 such technology prior to the first year of payment to

23 the Medicaid provider under this subsection, clause

24 (i)(I) shall not apply and clause (i)(II) shall apply

25 to each year of payment to the Medicaid provider

1 under this subsection, including the first year of

2 payment.

3   "(D) To the extent specified by the Secretary,

4 the certified EHR technology is compatible with

5 State or Federal administrative management sys-

6 tems.

7 For purposes of subparagraph (B), a Medicaid provider

8 described in paragraph (2)(A) may accept payments for

9 the costs described in such subparagraph from a State or

10 local government. For purposes of subparagraph (C), in

11 establishing the means described in such subparagraph,

12 which may include clinical quality reporting to the State,

13 the State shall ensure that populations with unique needs,

14 such as children, are appropriately addressed.

15   "(7) With respect to Medicaid providers described in

16 paragraph (2)(A), the Secretary shall ensure coordination

17 of payment with respect to such providers under sections

18 1848(o) and 1853(l) and under this subsection to assure

19 no duplication of funding. Such coordination shall include,

20 to the extent practicable, a data matching process between

21 State Medicaid agencies and the Centers for Medicare &

22 Medicaid Services using national provider identifiers. For

23 such purposes, the Secretary may require the submission

24 of such data relating to payments to such Medicaid pro-

25 viders as the Secretary may specify.

1   "(8) In carrying out paragraph (6)(C), the State and

2 Secretary shall seek, to the maximum extent practicable,

3 to avoid duplicative requirements from Federal and State

4 governments to demonstrate meaningful use of certified

5 EHR technology under this title and title XVIII. In doing

6 so, the Secretary may deem satisfaction of requirements

7 for such meaningful use for a payment year under title

8 XVIII to be sufficient to qualify as meaningful use under

9 this subsection. The Secretary may also specify the report-

10 ing periods under this subsection in order to carry out this

11 paragraph.

12   "(9) In order to be provided Federal financial partici-

13 pation under subsection (a)(3)(F)(ii), a State must dem-

14 onstrate to the satisfaction of the Secretary, that the

15 State—

16   "(A) is using the funds provided for the pur-

17   poses of administering payments under this sub-

18   section, including tracking of meaningful use by

19   Medicaid providers;

20   "(B) is conducting adequate oversight of the

21   program under this subsection, including routine

22   tracking of meaningful use attestations and report-

23   ing mechanisms; and

24   "(C) is pursuing initiatives to encourage the

25   adoption of certified EHR technology to promote

1   health care quality and the exchange of health care

2   information under this title, subject to applicable

3   laws and regulations governing such exchange.

4   "(10) The Secretary shall periodically submit reports

5 to the Committee on Energy and Commerce of the House

6 of Representatives and the Committee on Finance of the

7 Senate on status, progress, and oversight of payments de-

8 scribed in paragraph (1), including steps taken to carry

9 out paragraph (7). Such reports shall also describe the

10 extent of adoption of certified EHR technology among

11 Medicaid providers resulting from the provisions of this

12 subsection and any improvements in health outcomes, clin-

13 ical quality, or efficiency resulting from such adoption.".

14   (b) IMPLEMENTATION FUNDING.—In addition to

15 funds otherwise available, out of any funds in the Treas-

16 ury not otherwise appropriated, there are appropriated to

17 the Secretary of Health and Human Services for the Cen-

18 ters for Medicare & Medicaid Services Program Manage-

19 ment Account, $40,000,000 for each of fiscal years 2009

20 through 2015 and $20,000,000 for fiscal year 2016, which

21 shall be available for purposes of carrying out the provi-

22 sions of (and the amendments made by) this section.

23 Amounts appropriated under this subsection for a fiscal

24 year shall be available until expended.

Subtitle C—Miscellaneous Medicare Provisions

SEC. 4301. MORATORIA ON CERTAIN MEDICARE REGULATIONS.

(a) DELAY IN PHASE OUT OF MEDICARE HOSPICE BUDGET NEUTRALITY ADJUSTMENT FACTOR DURING FISCAL YEAR 2009.—Notwithstanding any other provision of law, including the final rule published on August 8, 2008, 73 Federal Register 46464 et seq., relating to Medicare Program; Hospice Wage Index for Fiscal Year 2009, the Secretary of Health and Human Services shall not phase out or eliminate the budget neutrality adjustment factor in the Medicare hospice wage index before October 1, 2009, and the Secretary shall recompute and apply the final Medicare hospice wage index for fiscal year 2009 as if there had been no reduction in the budget neutrality adjustment factor.

(b) NON-APPLICATION OF PHASED-OUT INDIRECT MEDICAL EDUCATION (IME) ADJUSTMENT FACTOR FOR FISCAL YEAR 2009.—

(1) IN GENERAL.—Section 412.322 of title 42, Code of Federal Regulations, shall be applied without regard to paragraph (c) of such section, and the Secretary of Health and Human Services shall recompute payments for discharges occurring on or

1 after October 1, 2008, as if such paragraph had

2 never been in effect.

3   (2) No EFFECT ON SUBSEQUENT YEARS.—

4 Nothing in paragraph (1) shall be construed as hav-

5 ing any effect on the application of paragraph (d) of

6 section 412.322 of title 42, Code of Federal Regula-

7 tions.

8   (c) FUNDING FOR IMPLEMENTATION.—In addition to

9 funds otherwise available, for purposes of implementing

10 the provisions of subsections (a) and (b), including costs

11 incurred in reprocessing claims in carrying out such provi-

12 sions, the Secretary of Health and Human Services shall

13 provide for the transfer from the Federal Hospital Insur-

14 ance Trust Fund established under section 1817 of the

15 Social Security Act (42 U.S.C. 1395i) to the Centers for

16 Medicare & Medicaid Services Program Management Ac-

17 count of $2,000,000 for fiscal year 2009.

18 **SEC. 4302. LONG-TERM CARE HOSPITAL TECHNICAL COR-**

19   **RECTIONS.**

20   (a) PAYMENT.—Subsection (c) of section 114 of the

21 Medicare, Medicaid, and SCHIP Extension Act of 2007

22 (Public Law 110–173) is amended—

23   (1) in paragraph (1)—

24   (A) by amending the heading to read as

25   follows: "DELAY IN APPLICATION OF 25 PER-

1   CENT PATIENT THRESHOLD PAYMENT ADJUST-

2   MENT'';

3   (B) by striking ''the date of the enactment

4   of this Act'' and inserting ''July 1, 2007,''; and

5   (C) in subparagraph (A), by inserting ''or

6   to a long-term care hospital, or satellite facility,

7   that as of December 29, 2007, was co-located

8   with an entity that is a provider-based, off-cam-

9   pus location of a subsection (d) hospital which

10   did not provide services payable under section

11   1886(d) of the Social Security Act at the off-

12   campus location'' after ''freestanding long-term

13   care hospitals''; and

14   (2) in paragraph (2)—

15   (A) in subparagraph (B)(ii), by inserting

16   ''or that is described in section 412.22(h)(3)(i)

17   of such title'' before the period; and

18   (B) in subparagraph (C), by striking ''the

19   date of the enactment of this Act'' and insert-

20   ing ''October 1, 2007 (or July 1, 2007, in the

21   case of a satellite facility described in section

22   412.22(h)(3)(i) of title 42, Code of Federal

23   Regulations)''.

24   (b) MORATORIUM.—Subsection (d)(3)(A) of such sec-

25   tion is amended by striking ''if the hospital or facility''

1 and inserting "if the hospital or facility obtained a certifi-
2 cate of need for an increase in beds that is in a State
3 for which such certificate of need is required and that was
4 issued on or after April 1, 2005, and before December
5 29, 2007, or if the hospital or facility".

6   (c) EFFECTIVE DATE.—The amendments made by
7 this section shall be effective and apply as if included in
8 the enactment of the Medicare, Medicaid, and SCHIP Ex-
9 tension Act of 2007 (Public Law 110–173).

10 TITLE V—STATE FISCAL RELIEF

11 **SEC. 5000. PURPOSES; TABLE OF CONTENTS.**

12   (a) PURPOSES.—The purposes of this title are as fol-
13 lows:

14   (1) To provide fiscal relief to States in a period
15   of economic downturn.

16   (2) To protect and maintain State Medicaid
17   programs during a period of economic downturn, in-
18   cluding by helping to avert cuts to provider payment
19   rates and benefits or services, and to prevent con-
20   strictions of income eligibility requirements for such
21   programs, but not to promote increases in such re-
22   quirements.

23   (b) TABLE OF CONTENTS.—The table of contents for
24 this title is as follows:

TITLE V—STATE FISCAL RELIEF

Sec. 5000. Purposes; table of contents.

Sec. 5001. Temporary increase of Medicaid FMAP.
Sec. 5002. Temporary increase in DSH allotments during recession.
Sec. 5003. Extension of moratoria on certain Medicaid final regulations.
Sec. 5004. Extension of transitional medical assistance (TMA).
Sec. 5005. Extension of the qualifying individual (QI) program.
Sec. 5006. Protections for Indians under Medicaid and CHIP.
Sec. 5007. Funding for oversight and implementation.
Sec. 5008. GAO study and report regarding State needs during periods of national economic downturn.

SEC. 5001. TEMPORARY INCREASE OF MEDICAID FMAP.

(a) PERMITTING MAINTENANCE OF FMAP.—Subject to subsections (e), (f), and (g), if the FMAP determined without regard to this section for a State for—

(1) fiscal year 2009 is less than the FMAP as so determined for fiscal year 2008, the FMAP for the State for fiscal year 2008 shall be substituted for the State's FMAP for fiscal year 2009, before the application of this section;

(2) fiscal year 2010 is less than the FMAP as so determined for fiscal year 2008 or fiscal year 2009 (after the application of paragraph (1)), the greater of such FMAP for the State for fiscal year 2008 or fiscal year 2009 shall be substituted for the State's FMAP for fiscal year 2010, before the application of this section; and

(3) fiscal year 2011 is less than the FMAP as so determined for fiscal year 2008, fiscal year 2009 (after the application of paragraph (1)), or fiscal year 2010 (after the application of paragraph (2)), the greatest of such FMAP for the State for fiscal

1   year 2008, fiscal year 2009, or fiscal year 2010 shall

2   be substituted for the State's FMAP for fiscal year

3   2011, before the application of this section, but only

4   for the first calendar quarter in fiscal year 2011.

5   (b) GENERAL 6.2 PERCENTAGE POINT INCREASE.—

6   (1) IN GENERAL.—Subject to subsections (e),

7   (f), and (g) and paragraph (2), for each State for

8   calendar quarters during the recession adjustment

9   period (as defined in subsection (h)(3)), the FMAP

10   (after the application of subsection (a)) shall be in-

11   creased (without regard to any limitation otherwise

12   specified in section 1905(b) of the Social Security

13   Act (42 U.S.C. 1396d(b))) by 6.2 percentage points.

14   (2) SPECIAL ELECTION FOR TERRITORIES.—In

15   the case of a State that is not one of the 50 States

16   or the District of Columbia, paragraph (1) shall only

17   apply if the State makes a one-time election, in a

18   form and manner specified by the Secretary and for

19   the entire recession adjustment period, to apply the

20   increase in FMAP under paragraph (1) and a 15

21   percent increase under subsection (d) instead of ap-

22   plying a 30 percent increase under subsection (d).

23   (c) ADDITIONAL RELIEF BASED ON INCREASE IN

24 UNEMPLOYMENT.—

(1) IN GENERAL.—Subject to subsections (e), (f), and (g), if a State is a qualifying State under paragraph (2) for a calendar quarter occurring during the recession adjustment period, the FMAP for the State shall be further increased by the number of percentage points equal to the product of—

(A) the State percentage applicable for the State under section 1905(b) of the Social Security Act (42 U.S.C. 1396d(b)) after the application of subsection (a) and after the application of ½ of the increase under subsection (b); and

(B) the applicable percent determined in paragraph (3) for the calendar quarter (or, if greater, for a previous such calendar quarter).

(2) QUALIFYING CRITERIA.—

(A) IN GENERAL.—For purposes of paragraph (1), a State qualifies for additional relief under this subsection for a calendar quarter occurring during the recession adjustment period if the State is 1 of the 50 States or the District of Columbia and the State satisfies any of the following criteria for the quarter:

(i) The State unemployment increase percentage (as defined in paragraph (4))

1   for the quarter is at least 1.5 percentage

2   points but less than 2.5 percentage points.

3   (ii) The State unemployment increase

4   percentage for the quarter is at least 2.5

5   percentage points but less than 3.5 per-

6   centage points.

7   (iii) The State unemployment increase

8   percentage for the quarter is at least 3.5

9   percentage points.

10   (B) MAINTENANCE OF STATUS.—If a

11   State qualifies for additional relief under this

12   subsection for a calendar quarter, it shall be

13   deemed to have qualified for such relief for each

14   subsequent calendar quarter ending before July

15   1, 2010.

16   (3) APPLICABLE PERCENT.—

17   (A) IN GENERAL.—For purposes of para-

18   graph (1), subject to subparagraph (B), the ap-

19   plicable percent is—

20   (i) 5.5 percent, if the State satisfies

21   the criteria described in paragraph

22   (2)(A)(i) for the calendar quarter;

23   (ii) 8.5 percent if the State satisfies

24   the criteria described in paragraph

25   (2)(A)(ii) for the calendar quarter; and

(iii) 11.5 percent if the State satisfies the criteria described in paragraph (2)(A)(iii) for the calendar quarter.

(B) MAINTENANCE OF HIGHER APPLICABLE PERCENT.—

(i) HOLD HARMLESS PERIOD.—If the percent applied to a State under subparagraph (A) for any calendar quarter in the recession adjustment period beginning on or after January 1, 2009, and ending before July 1, 2010, (determined without regard to this subparagraph) is less than the percent applied for the preceding quarter (as so determined), the higher applicable percent shall continue in effect for each subsequent calendar quarter ending before July 1, 2010.

(ii) NOTICE OF LOWER APPLICABLE PERCENT.—The Secretary shall notify a State at least 60 days prior to applying any lower applicable percent to the State under this paragraph.

(4) COMPUTATION OF STATE UNEMPLOYMENT INCREASE PERCENTAGE.—

1   (A) IN GENERAL.—In this subsection, the

2   "State unemployment increase percentage" for

3   a State for a calendar quarter is equal to the

4   number of percentage points (if any) by

5   which—

6   (i) the average monthly unemployment

7   rate for the State for months in the most

8   recent previous 3-consecutive-month period

9   for which data are available, subject to

10   subparagraph (C); exceeds

11   (ii) the lowest average monthly unem-

12   ployment rate for the State for any 3-con-

13   secutive-month period preceding the period

14   described in clause (i) and beginning on or

15   after January 1, 2006.

16   (B) AVERAGE MONTHLY UNEMPLOYMENT

17   RATE DEFINED.—In this paragraph, the term

18   "average monthly unemployment rate" means

19   the average of the monthly number unemployed,

20   divided by the average of the monthly civilian

21   labor force, seasonally adjusted, as determined

22   based on the most recent monthly publications

23   of the Bureau of Labor Statistics of the De-

24   partment of Labor.

25   (C) SPECIAL RULE.—With respect to—

1   (i) the first 2 calendar quarters of the

2   recession adjustment period, the most re-

3   cent previous 3-consecutive-month period

4   described in subparagraph (A)(i) shall be

5   the 3-consecutive-month period beginning

6   with October 2008; and

7   (ii) the last 2 calendar quarters of the

8   recession adjustment period, the most re-

9   cent previous 3-consecutive-month period

10   described in such subparagraph shall be

11   the 3-consecutive-month period beginning

12   with December 2009, or, if it results in a

13   higher applicable percent under paragraph

14   (3), the 3-consecutive-month period begin-

15   ning with January 2010.

16   (d) INCREASE IN CAP ON MEDICAID PAYMENTS TO

17 TERRITORIES.—Subject to subsections (f) and (g), with

18 respect to entire fiscal years occurring during the reces-

19 sion adjustment period and with respect to fiscal years

20 only a portion of which occurs during such period (and

21 in proportion to the portion of the fiscal year that occurs

22 during such period), the amounts otherwise determined for

23 Puerto Rico, the Virgin Islands, Guam, the Northern Mar-

24 iana Islands, and American Samoa under subsections (f)

25 and (g) of section 1108 of the Social Security Act (42

1   6 U.S.C. 1308) shall each be increased by 30 percent (or,

2   in the case of an election under subsection (b)(2), 15 per-

3   cent). In the case of such an election by a territory, sub-

4   section (a)(1) of such section shall be applied without re-

5   gard to any increase in payment made to the territory

6   under part E of title IV of such Act that is attributable

7   to the increase in FMAP effected under subsection (b) for

8   the territory.

9   (e) SCOPE OF APPLICATION.—The increases in the

10 FMAP for a State under this section shall apply for pur-

11 poses of title XIX of the Social Security Act and shall

12 not apply with respect to—

13   (1) disproportionate share hospital payments

14   described in section 1923 of such Act (42 U.S.C.

15   1396r–4);

16   (2) payments under title IV of such Act (42

17   U.S.C. 601 et seq.) (except that the increases under

18   subsections (a) and (b) shall apply to payments

19   under part E of title IV of such Act (42 U.S.C. 670

20   et seq.) and, for purposes of the application of this

21   section to the District of Columbia, payments under

22   such part shall be deemed to be made on the basis

23   of the FMAP applied with respect to such District

24   for purposes of title XIX and as increased under

25   subsection (b));

1   (3) payments under title XXI of such Act (42

2   U.S.C. 1397aa et seq.);

3   (4) any payments under title XIX of such Act

4   that are based on the enhanced FMAP described in

5   section 2105(b) of such Act (42 U.S.C. 1397ee(b));

6   or

7   (5) any payments under title XIX of such Act

8   that are attributable to expenditures for medical as-

9   sistance provided to individuals made eligible under

10   a State plan under title XIX of the Social Security

11   Act (including under any waiver under such title or

12   under section 1115 of such Act (42 U.S.C. 1315))

13   because of income standards (expressed as a per-

14   centage of the poverty line) for eligibility for medical

15   assistance that are higher than the income stand-

16   ards (as so expressed) for such eligibility as in effect

17   on July 1, 2008, (including as such standards were

18   proposed to be in effect under a State law enacted

19   but not effective as of such date or a State plan

20   amendment or waiver request under title XIX of

21   such Act that was pending approval on such date).

22   (f) STATE INELIGIBILITY; LIMITATION; SPECIAL

23 RULES.—

24   (1) MAINTENANCE OF ELIGIBILITY REQUIRE-

25   MENTS.—

1   (A) IN GENERAL.—Subject to subpara-

2   graphs (B) and (C), a State is not eligible for

3   an increase in its FMAP under subsection (a),

4   (b), or (c), or an increase in a cap amount

5   under subsection (d), if eligibility standards,

6   methodologies, or procedures under its State

7   plan under title XIX of the Social Security Act

8   (including any waiver under such title or under

9   section 1115 of such Act (42 U.S.C. 1315)) are

10   more restrictive than the eligibility standards,

11   methodologies, or procedures, respectively,

12   under such plan (or waiver) as in effect on July

13   1, 2008.

14   (B) STATE REINSTATEMENT OF ELIGI-

15   BILITY PERMITTED.—Subject to subparagraph

16   (C), a State that has restricted eligibility stand-

17   ards, methodologies, or procedures under its

18   State plan under title XIX of the Social Secu-

19   rity Act (including any waiver under such title

20   or under section 1115 of such Act (42 U.S.C.

21   1315)) after July 1, 2008, is no longer ineli-

22   gible under subparagraph (A) beginning with

23   the first calendar quarter in which the State

24   has reinstated eligibility standards, methodolo-

25   gies, or procedures that are no more restrictive

than the eligibility standards, methodologies, or procedures, respectively, under such plan (or waiver) as in effect on July 1, 2008.

(C) SPECIAL RULES.—A State shall not be ineligible under subparagraph (A)—

(i) for the calendar quarters before July 1, 2009, on the basis of a restriction that was applied after July 1, 2008, and before the date of the enactment of this Act, if the State prior to July 1, 2009, has reinstated eligibility standards, methodologies, or procedures that are no more restrictive than the eligibility standards, methodologies, or procedures, respectively, under such plan (or waiver) as in effect on July 1, 2008; or

(ii) on the basis of a restriction that was directed to be made under State law as in effect on July 1, 2008, and would have been in effect as of such date, but for a delay in the effective date of a waiver under section 1115 of such Act with respect to such restriction.

(2) COMPLIANCE WITH PROMPT PAY REQUIRE-MENTS.—

1   (A) APPLICATION TO PRACTITIONERS.—

2   (i) IN GENERAL.—Subject to the suc-

3   ceeding provisions of this subparagraph, no

4   State shall be eligible for an increased

5   FMAP rate as provided under this section

6   for any claim received by a State from a

7   practitioner subject to the terms of section

8   1902(a)(37)(A) of the Social Security Act

9   (42 U.S.C. 1396a(a)(37)(A)) for such days

10   during any period in which that State has

11   failed to pay claims in accordance with

12   such section as applied under title XIX of

13   such Act.

14   (ii) REPORTING REQUIREMENT.—

15   Each State shall report to the Secretary,

16   on a quarterly basis, its compliance with

17   the requirements of clause (i) as such re-

18   quirements pertain to claims made for cov-

19   ered services during each month of the

20   preceding quarter.

21   (iii) WAIVER AUTHORITY.—The Sec-

22   retary may waive the application of clause

23   (i) to a State, or the reporting requirement

24   imposed under clause (ii), during any pe-

25   riod in which there are exigent cir-

1 cumstances, including natural disasters,
2 that prevent the timely processing of
3 claims or the submission of such a report.

4   (iv) APPLICATION TO CLAIMS.—
5 Clauses (i) and (ii) shall only apply to
6 claims made for covered services after the
7 date of enactment of this Act.

8 (B) APPLICATION TO NURSING FACILITIES
9 AND HOSPITALS.—

10   (i) IN GENERAL.—Subject to clause
11 (ii), the provisions of subparagraph (A)
12 shall apply with respect to a nursing facil-
13 ity or hospital, insofar as it is paid under
14 title XIX of the Social Security Act on the
15 basis of submission of claims, in the same
16 or similar manner (but within the same
17 timeframe) as such provisions apply to
18 practitioners described in such subpara-
19 graph.

20   (ii) GRACE PERIOD.—Notwithstanding
21 clause (i), no period of ineligibility shall be
22 imposed against a State prior to June 1,
23 2009, on the basis of the State failing to
24 pay a claim in accordance with such
25 clause.

522

1   (3) STATE'S APPLICATION TOWARD RAINY DAY

2 FUND.—A State is not eligible for an increase in its

3 FMAP under subsection (b) or (c), or an increase in

4 a cap amount under subsection (d), if any amounts

5 attributable (directly or indirectly) to such increase

6 are deposited or credited into any reserve or rainy

7 day fund of the State.

8   (4) NO WAIVER AUTHORITY.—Except as pro-

9 vided in paragraph (2)(A)(iii), the Secretary may

10 not waive the application of this subsection or sub-

11 section (g) under section 1115 of the Social Security

12 Act or otherwise.

13   (5) LIMITATION OF FMAP TO 100 PERCENT.—In

14 no case shall an increase in FMAP under this sec-

15 tion result in an FMAP that exceeds 100 percent.

16   (6) TREATMENT OF CERTAIN EXPENDI-

17 TURES.—With respect to expenditures described in

18 section 2105(a)(1)(B) of the Social Security Act (42

19 U.S.C. 1397ee(a)(1)(B)), as in effect before April 1,

20 2009, that are made during the period beginning on

21 October 1, 2008, and ending on March 31, 2009,

22 any additional Federal funds that are paid to a

23 State as a result of this section that are attributable

24 to such expenditures shall not be counted against

1   any allotment under section 2104 of such Act (42

2   U.S.C. 1397dd).

3   (g) REQUIREMENTS.—

4   (1) STATE REPORTS.—Each State that is paid

5   additional Federal funds as a result of this section

6   shall, not later than September 30, 2011, submit a

7   report to the Secretary, in such form and such man-

8   ner as the Secretary shall determine, regarding how

9   the additional Federal funds were expended.

10   (2) ADDITIONAL REQUIREMENT FOR CERTAIN

11   STATES.—In the case of a State that requires polit-

12   ical subdivisions within the State to contribute to-

13   ward the non-Federal share of expenditures under

14   the State Medicaid plan required under section

15   1902(a)(2) of the Social Security Act (42 U.S.C.

16   1396a(a)(2)), the State is not eligible for an in-

17   crease in its FMAP under subsection (b) or (c), or

18   an increase in a cap amount under subsection (d),

19   if it requires that such political subdivisions pay for

20   quarters during the recession adjustment period a

21   greater percentage of the non-Federal share of such

22   expenditures, or a greater percentage of the non-

23   Federal share of payments under section 1923, than

24   the respective percentage that would have been re-

1   quired by the State under such plan on September

2   30, 2008, prior to application of this section.

3   (h) DEFINITIONS.—In this section, except as other-

4 wise provided:

5   (1) FMAP.—The term "FMAP" means the

6   Federal medical assistance percentage, as defined in

7   section 1905(b) of the Social Security Act (42

8   U.S.C. 1396d(b)), as determined without regard to

9   this section except as otherwise specified.

10   (2) POVERTY LINE.—The term "poverty line"

11   has the meaning given such term in section 673(2)

12   of the Community Services Block Grant Act (42

13   U.S.C. 9902(2)), including any revision required by

14   such section.

15   (3) RECESSION ADJUSTMENT PERIOD.—The

16   term "recession adjustment period" means the pe-

17   riod beginning on October 1, 2008, and ending on

18   December 31, 2010.

19   (4) SECRETARY.—The term "Secretary" means

20   the Secretary of Health and Human Services.

21   (5) STATE.—The term "State" has the mean-

22   ing given such term in section 1101(a)(1) of the So-

23   cial Security Act (42 U.S.C. 1301(a)(1)) for pur-

24   poses of title XIX of the Social Security Act (42

25   U.S.C. 1396 et seq.).

1 (i) SUNSET.—This section shall not apply to items
2 and services furnished after the end of the recession ad-
3 justment period.

4 (j) LIMITATION ON FMAP CHANGE.—The increase
5 in FMAP effected under section 614 of the Children's
6 Health Insurance Program Reauthorization Act of 2009
7 shall not apply in the computation of the enhanced FMAP
8 under title XXI or XIX of the Social Security Act for any
9 period (notwithstanding subsection (i)).

10 **SEC. 5002. TEMPORARY INCREASE IN DSH ALLOTMENTS**
11 **DURING RECESSION.**

12 Section 1923(f)(3) of the Social Security Act (42
13 U.S.C. 1396r–4(f)(3)) is amended—

14 (1) in subparagraph (A), by striking "para-
15 graph (6)" and inserting "paragraph (6) and sub-
16 paragraph (E)"; and

17 (2) by adding at the end the following new sub-
18 paragraph:

19 "(E) TEMPORARY INCREASE IN ALLOT-
20 MENTS DURING RECESSION.—

21 "(i) IN GENERAL.—Subject to clause
22 (ii), the DSH allotment for any State—

23 "(I) for fiscal year 2009 is equal
24 to 102.5 percent of the DSH allot-
25 ment that would be determined under

1   this paragraph for the State for fiscal

2   year 2009 without application of this

3   subparagraph, notwithstanding sub-

4   paragraphs (B) and (C);

5   "(II) for fiscal year 2010 is equal

6   to 102.5 percent of the DSH allot-

7   ment for the State for fiscal year

8   2009, as determined under subclause

9   (I); and

10   "(III) for each succeeding fiscal

11   year is equal to the DSH allotment

12   for the State under this paragraph de-

13   termined without applying subclauses

14   (I) and (II).

15   "(ii) APPLICATION.—Clause (i) shall

16   not apply to a State for a year in the case

17   that the DSH allotment for such State for

18   such year under this paragraph determined

19   without applying clause (i) would grow

20   higher than the DSH allotment specified

21   under clause (i) for the State for such

22   year.".

1 **SEC. 5003. EXTENSION OF MORATORIA ON CERTAIN MED-**

2 **ICAID FINAL REGULATIONS.**

3   (a) FINAL REGULATIONS RELATING TO OPTIONAL

4 CASE MANAGEMENT SERVICES AND ALLOWABLE PRO-

5 VIDER TAXES.—Section 7001(a)(3)(A) of the Supple-

6 mental Appropriations Act, 2008 (Public Law 110–252)

7 is amended by striking "April 1, 2009" and inserting

8 "July 1, 2009".

9   (b) FINAL REGULATION RELATING TO SCHOOL-

10 BASED ADMINISTRATION AND SCHOOL-BASED TRANS-

11 PORTATION.—Section 206 of the Medicare, Medicaid, and

12 SCHIP Extension Act of 2007 (Public Law 110–173), as

13 amended by section 7001(a)(2) of the Supplemental Ap-

14 propriations Act, 2008 (Public Law 110–252), is amended

15 by inserting "(July 1, 2009, in the case of the final regula-

16 tion relating to school-based administration and school-

17 based transportation)" after "April 1, 2009,".

18   (c) FINAL REGULATION RELATING TO OUTPATIENT

19 HOSPITAL FACILITY SERVICES.—Notwithstanding any

20 other provision of law, with respect to expenditures for

21 services furnished during the period beginning on Decem-

22 ber 8, 2008, and ending on June 30, 2009, the Secretary

23 of Health and Human Services shall not take any action

24 (through promulgation of regulation, issuance of regu-

25 latory guidance, use of Federal payment audit procedures,

26 or other administrative action, policy, or practice, includ-

1 ing a Medical Assistance Manual transmittal or letter to
2 State Medicaid directors) to implement the final regula-
3 tion relating to clarification of the definition of outpatient
4 hospital facility services under the Medicaid program pub-
5 lished on November 7, 2008 (73 Federal Register 66187).

6   (d) SENSE OF CONGRESS.—It is the sense of Con-
7 gress that the Secretary of Health and Human Services
8 should not promulgate as final regulations any of the fol-
9 lowing proposed Medicaid regulations:

10   (1) COST LIMITS FOR CERTAIN PROVIDERS.—
11   The proposed regulation published on January 18,
12   2007, (72 Federal Register 2236) (and the pur-
13   ported final regulation published on May 29, 2007
14   (72 Federal Register 29748) and determined by the
15   United States District Court for the District of Co-
16   lumbia to have been "improperly promulgated", *Ala-*
17   *meda County Medical Center, et al., v. Leavitt, et al.,*
18   Civil Action No. 08-0422, Mem. at 4 (D.D.C. May
19   23, 2008)).

20   (2) PAYMENTS FOR GRADUATE MEDICAL EDU-
21   CATION.—The proposed regulation published on May
22   23, 2007 (72 Federal Register 28930).

23   (3) REHABILITATIVE SERVICES.—The proposed
24   regulation published on August 13, 2007 (72 Fed-
25   eral Register 45201).

SEC. 5004. EXTENSION OF TRANSITIONAL MEDICAL ASSIST-ANCE (TMA).

(a) 18-MONTH EXTENSION.—

(1) IN GENERAL.—Sections 1902(e)(1)(B) and 1925(f) of the Social Security Act (42 U.S.C. 1396a(e)(1)(B), 1396r–6(f)) are each amended by striking "September 30, 2003" and inserting "December 31, 2010".

(2) EFFECTIVE DATE.—The amendments made by this subsection shall take effect on July 1, 2009.

(b) STATE OPTION OF INITIAL 12-MONTH ELIGIBILITY.—Section 1925 of the Social Security Act (42 U.S.C. 1396r–6) is amended—

(1) in subsection (a)(1), by inserting "but subject to paragraph (5)" after "Notwithstanding any other provision of this title";

(2) by adding at the end of subsection (a) the following:

"(5) OPTION OF 12-MONTH INITIAL ELIGIBILITY PERIOD.—A State may elect to treat any reference in this subsection to a 6-month period (or 6 months) as a reference to a 12-month period (or 12 months). In the case of such an election, subsection (b) shall not apply."; and

1   (3) in subsection (b)(1), by inserting "but sub-

2   ject to subsection (a)(5)" after "Notwithstanding

3   any other provision of this title".

4   (c) REMOVAL OF REQUIREMENT FOR PREVIOUS RE-

5 CEIPT OF MEDICAL ASSISTANCE.—Section 1925(a)(1) of

6 such Act (42 U.S.C. 1396r–6(a)(1)), as amended by sub-

7 section (b)(1), is further amended—

8   (1) by inserting "subparagraph (B) and" before

9   "paragraph (5)";

10   (2) by redesignating the matter after "RE-

11   QUIREMENT.—" as a subparagraph (A) with the

12   heading "IN GENERAL.—" and with the same inden-

13   tation as subparagraph (B) (as added by paragraph

14   (3)); and

15   (3) by adding at the end the following:

16   "(B) STATE OPTION TO WAIVE REQUIRE-

17   MENT FOR 3 MONTHS BEFORE RECEIPT OF

18   MEDICAL ASSISTANCE.—A State may, at its op-

19   tion, elect also to apply subparagraph (A) in

20   the case of a family that was receiving such aid

21   for fewer than three months or that had applied

22   for and was eligible for such aid for fewer than

23   3 months during the 6 immediately preceding

24   months described in such subparagraph.".

1   (d) CMS REPORT ON ENROLLMENT AND PARTICIPA-

2 TION RATES UNDER TMA.—Section 1925 of such Act (42

3 U.S.C. 1396r–6), as amended by this section, is further

4 amended by adding at the end the following new sub-

5 section:

6   "(g) COLLECTION AND REPORTING OF PARTICIPA-

7 TION INFORMATION.—

8   "(1) COLLECTION OF INFORMATION FROM

9   STATES.—Each State shall collect and submit to the

10   Secretary (and make publicly available), in a format

11   specified by the Secretary, information on average

12   monthly enrollment and average monthly participa-

13   tion rates for adults and children under this section

14   and of the number and percentage of children who

15   become ineligible for medical assistance under this

16   section whose medical assistance is continued under

17   another eligibility category or who are enrolled under

18   the State's child health plan under title XXI. Such

19   information shall be submitted at the same time and

20   frequency in which other enrollment information

21   under this title is submitted to the Secretary.

22   "(2) ANNUAL REPORTS TO CONGRESS.—Using

23   the information submitted under paragraph (1), the

24   Secretary shall submit to Congress annual reports

1   concerning enrollment and participation rates de-

2   scribed in such paragraph.".

3   (e) EFFECTIVE DATE.—The amendments made by

4 subsections (b) through (d) shall take effect on July 1,

5 2009.

6 **SEC. 5005. EXTENSION OF THE QUALIFYING INDIVIDUAL**

7   **(QI) PROGRAM.**

8   (a) EXTENSION.—Section 1902(a)(10)(E)(iv) of the

9 Social Security Act (42 U.S.C. 1396a(a)(10)(E)(iv)) is

10 amended by striking "December 2009" and inserting "De-

11 cember 2010".

12   (b) EXTENDING TOTAL AMOUNT AVAILABLE FOR

13 ALLOCATION.—Section 1933(g) of such Act (42 U.S.C.

14 1396u–3(g)) is amended—

15   (1) in paragraph (2)—

16   (A) by striking "and" at the end of sub-

17   paragraph (K);

18   (B) in subparagraph (L), by striking the

19   period at the end and inserting a semicolon;

20   and

21   (C) by adding at the end the following new

22   subparagraphs:

23   "(M) for the period that begins on Janu-

24   ary 1, 2010, and ends on September 30, 2010,

1   the total allocation amount is $412,500,000;

2   and

3   "(N) for the period that begins on October

4   1, 2010, and ends on December 31, 2010, the

5   total allocation amount is $150,000,000."; and

6   (2) in paragraph (3), in the matter preceding

7   subparagraph (A), by striking "or (L)" and insert-

8   ing "(L), or (N)".

SEC. 5006. PROTECTIONS FOR INDIANS UNDER MEDICAID AND CHIP.

11   (a) PREMIUMS AND COST SHARING PROTECTION

12 UNDER MEDICAID.—

13   (1) IN GENERAL.—Section 1916 of the Social

14   Security Act (42 U.S.C. 1396o) is amended—

15   (A) in subsection (a), in the matter pre-

16   ceding paragraph (1), by striking "and (i)" and

17   inserting ", (i), and (j)"; and

18   (B) by adding at the end the following new

19   subsection:

20   "(j) NO PREMIUMS OR COST SHARING FOR INDIANS

21 FURNISHED ITEMS OR SERVICES DIRECTLY BY INDIAN

22 HEALTH PROGRAMS OR THROUGH REFERRAL UNDER

23 CONTRACT HEALTH SERVICES.—

1   "(1) NO COST SHARING FOR ITEMS OR SERV-

2 ICES FURNISHED TO INDIANS THROUGH INDIAN

3 HEALTH PROGRAMS.—

4   "(A) IN GENERAL.—No enrollment fee,

5 premium, or similar charge, and no deduction,

6 copayment, cost sharing, or similar charge shall

7 be imposed against an Indian who is furnished

8 an item or service directly by the Indian Health

9 Service, an Indian Tribe, Tribal Organization,

10 or Urban Indian Organization or through refer-

11 ral under contract health services for which

12 payment may be made under this title.

13   "(B) NO REDUCTION IN AMOUNT OF PAY-

14 MENT TO INDIAN HEALTH PROVIDERS.—Pay-

15 ment due under this title to the Indian Health

16 Service, an Indian Tribe, Tribal Organization,

17 or Urban Indian Organization, or a health care

18 provider through referral under contract health

19 services for the furnishing of an item or service

20 to an Indian who is eligible for assistance under

21 such title, may not be reduced by the amount

22 of any enrollment fee, premium, or similar

23 charge, or any deduction, copayment, cost shar-

24 ing, or similar charge that would be due from

1   the Indian but for the operation of subpara-

2   graph (A).

3   "(2) RULE OF CONSTRUCTION.—Nothing in

4 this subsection shall be construed as restricting the

5 application of any other limitations on the imposi-

6 tion of premiums or cost sharing that may apply to

7 an individual receiving medical assistance under this

8 title who is an Indian.".

9   (2) CONFORMING AMENDMENT.—Section

10 1916A(b)(3) of such Act (42 U.S.C. 1396o–1(b)(3))

11 is amended—

12   (A) in subparagraph (A), by adding at the

13   end the following new clause:

14   "(vii) An Indian who is furnished an

15   item or service directly by the Indian

16   Health Service, an Indian Tribe, Tribal

17   Organization or Urban Indian Organiza-

18   tion or through referral under contract

19   health services."; and

20   (B) in subparagraph (B), by adding at the

21   end the following new clause:

22   "(x) Items and services furnished to

23   an Indian directly by the Indian Health

24   Service, an Indian Tribe, Tribal Organiza-

25   tion or Urban Indian Organization or

1   through referral under contract health

2   services.".

3   (b) TREATMENT OF CERTAIN PROPERTY FROM RE-

4 SOURCES FOR MEDICAID AND CHIP ELIGIBILITY.—

5   (1) MEDICAID.—Section 1902 of the Social Se-

6   curity Act (42 U.S.C. 1396a), as amended by sec-

7   tions 203(c) and 211(a)(1)(A)(ii) of the Children's

8   Health Insurance Program Reauthorization Act of

9   2009 (Public Law 111–3), is amended by adding at

10   the end the following new subsection:

11   "(ff) Notwithstanding any other requirement of this

12 title or any other provision of Federal or State law, a State

13 shall disregard the following property from resources for

14 purposes of determining the eligibility of an individual who

15 is an Indian for medical assistance under this title:

16   "(1) Property, including real property and im-

17   provements, that is held in trust, subject to Federal

18   restrictions, or otherwise under the supervision of

19   the Secretary of the Interior, located on a reserva-

20   tion, including any federally recognized Indian

21   Tribe's reservation, pueblo, or colony, including

22   former reservations in Oklahoma, Alaska Native re-

23   gions established by the Alaska Native Claims Set-

24   tlement Act, and Indian allotments on or near a res-

1 ervation as designated and approved by the Bureau

2 of Indian Affairs of the Department of the Interior.

3 "(2) For any federally recognized Tribe not de-

4 scribed in paragraph (1), property located within the

5 most recent boundaries of a prior Federal reserva-

6 tion.

7 "(3) Ownership interests in rents, leases, royal-

8 ties, or usage rights related to natural resources (in-

9 cluding extraction of natural resources or harvesting

10 of timber, other plants and plant products, animals,

11 fish, and shellfish) resulting from the exercise of fed-

12 erally protected rights.

13 "(4) Ownership interests in or usage rights to

14 items not covered by paragraphs (1) through (3)

15 that have unique religious, spiritual, traditional, or

16 cultural significance or rights that support subsist-

17 ence or a traditional lifestyle according to applicable

18 tribal law or custom.".

19 (2) APPLICATION TO CHIP.—Section 2107(e)(1)

20 of such Act (42 U.S.C. 1397gg(e)(1)), as amended

21 by sections 203(a)(2), 203(d)(2), 214(b), 501(d)(2),

22 and 503(a)(1) of the Children's Health Insurance

23 Program Reauthorization Act of 2009 (Public Law

24 111–3), is amended—

1   (A) by redesignating subparagraphs (C)

2   through (I), as subparagraphs (D) through (J),

3   respectively; and

4   (B) by inserting after subparagraph (B),

5   the following new subparagraph:

6   "(C) Section 1902(ff) (relating to dis-

7   regard of certain property for purposes of mak-

8   ing eligibility determinations).".

9   (c) CONTINUATION OF CURRENT LAW PROTECTIONS

10 OF CERTAIN INDIAN PROPERTY FROM MEDICAID ESTATE

11 RECOVERY.—Section 1917(b)(3) of the Social Security

12 Act (42 U.S.C. 1396p(b)(3)) is amended—

13   (1) by inserting "(A)" after "(3)"; and

14   (2) by adding at the end the following new sub-

15   paragraph:

16   "(B) The standards specified by the Sec-

17   retary under subparagraph (A) shall require

18   that the procedures established by the State

19   agency under subparagraph (A) exempt income,

20   resources, and property that are exempt from

21   the application of this subsection as of April 1,

22   2003, under manual instructions issued to carry

23   out this subsection (as in effect on such date)

24   because of the Federal responsibility for Indian

25   Tribes and Alaska Native Villages. Nothing in

1   this subparagraph shall be construed as pre-

2   venting the Secretary from providing additional

3   estate recovery exemptions under this title for

4   Indians.''.

5 (d) RULES APPLICABLE UNDER MEDICAID AND

6 CHIP TO MANAGED CARE ENTITIES WITH RESPECT TO

7 INDIAN ENROLLEES AND INDIAN HEALTH CARE PRO-

8 VIDERS AND INDIAN MANAGED CARE ENTITIES.—

9   (1) IN GENERAL.—Section 1932 of the Social

10   Security Act (42 U.S.C. 1396u–2) is amended by

11   adding at the end the following new subsection:

12 ''(h) SPECIAL RULES WITH RESPECT TO INDIAN EN-

13 ROLLEES, INDIAN HEALTH CARE PROVIDERS, AND IN-

14 DIAN MANAGED CARE ENTITIES.—

15   ''(1) ENROLLEE OPTION TO SELECT AN INDIAN

16   HEALTH CARE PROVIDER AS PRIMARY CARE PRO-

17   VIDER.—In the case of a non-Indian Medicaid man-

18   aged care entity that—

19   ''(A) has an Indian enrolled with the enti-

20   ty; and

21   ''(B) has an Indian health care provider

22   that is participating as a primary care provider

23   within the network of the entity,

24   insofar as the Indian is otherwise eligible to receive

25   services from such Indian health care provider and

1   the Indian health care provider has the capacity to

2   provide primary care services to such Indian, the

3   contract with the entity under section 1903(m) or

4   under section 1905(t)(3) shall require, as a condi-

5   tion of receiving payment under such contract, that

6   the Indian shall be allowed to choose such Indian

7   health care provider as the Indian's primary care

8   provider under the entity.

9   "(2) ASSURANCE OF PAYMENT TO INDIAN

10   HEALTH CARE PROVIDERS FOR PROVISION OF COV-

11   ERED SERVICES.—Each contract with a managed

12   care entity under section 1903(m) or under section

13   1905(t)(3) shall require any such entity, as a condi-

14   tion of receiving payment under such contract, to

15   satisfy the following requirements:

16   "(A) DEMONSTRATION OF ACCESS TO IN-

17   DIAN HEALTH CARE PROVIDERS AND APPLICA-

18   TION OF ALTERNATIVE PAYMENT ARRANGE-

19   MENTS.—Subject to subparagraph (C), to—

20   "(i) demonstrate that the number of

21   Indian health care providers that are par-

22   ticipating providers with respect to such

23   entity are sufficient to ensure timely access

24   to covered Medicaid managed care services

1   for those Indian enrollees who are eligible

2   to receive services from such providers; and

3   "(ii) agree to pay Indian health care

4   providers, whether such providers are par-

5   ticipating or nonparticipating providers

6   with respect to the entity, for covered Med-

7   icaid managed care services provided to

8   those Indian enrollees who are eligible to

9   receive services from such providers at a

10   rate equal to the rate negotiated between

11   such entity and the provider involved or, if

12   such a rate has not been negotiated, at a

13   rate that is not less than the level and

14   amount of payment which the entity would

15   make for the services if the services were

16   furnished by a participating provider which

17   is not an Indian health care provider.

18   The Secretary shall establish procedures for ap-

19   plying the requirements of clause (i) in States

20   where there are no or few Indian health pro-

21   viders.

22   "(B) PROMPT PAYMENT.—To agree to

23   make prompt payment (consistent with rule for

24   prompt payment of providers under section

25   1932(f)) to Indian health care providers that

1   are participating providers with respect to such

2   entity or, in the case of an entity to which sub-

3   paragraph (A)(ii) or (C) applies, that the entity

4   is required to pay in accordance with that sub-

5   paragraph.

6   "(C) APPLICATION OF SPECIAL PAYMENT

7   REQUIREMENTS FOR FEDERALLY-QUALIFIED

8   HEALTH CENTERS AND FOR SERVICES PRO-

9   VIDED BY CERTAIN INDIAN HEALTH CARE PRO-

10   VIDERS.—

11   "(i) FEDERALLY-QUALIFIED HEALTH

12   CENTERS.—

13   "(I) MANAGED CARE ENTITY

14   PAYMENT REQUIREMENT.—To agree

15   to pay any Indian health care provider

16   that is a federally-qualified health

17   center under this title but not a par-

18   ticipating provider with respect to the

19   entity, for the provision of covered

20   Medicaid managed care services by

21   such provider to an Indian enrollee of

22   the entity at a rate equal to the

23   amount of payment that the entity

24   would pay a federally-qualified health

25   center that is a participating provider

1   with respect to the entity but is not

2   an Indian health care provider for

3   such services.

4   "(II) CONTINUED APPLICATION

5   OF STATE REQUIREMENT TO MAKE

6   SUPPLEMENTAL PAYMENT.—Nothing

7   in subclause (I) or subparagraph (A)

8   or (B) shall be construed as waiving

9   the application of section 1902(bb)(5)

10   regarding the State plan requirement

11   to make any supplemental payment

12   due under such section to a federally-

13   qualified health center for services

14   furnished by such center to an en-

15   rollee of a managed care entity (re-

16   gardless of whether the federally-

17   qualified health center is or is not a

18   participating provider with the entity).

19   "(ii) PAYMENT RATE FOR SERVICES

20   PROVIDED BY CERTAIN INDIAN HEALTH

21   CARE PROVIDERS.—If the amount paid by

22   a managed care entity to an Indian health

23   care provider that is not a federally-quali-

24   fied health center for services provided by

25   the provider to an Indian enrollee with the

1   managed care entity is less than the rate

2   that applies to the provision of such serv-

3   ices by the provider under the State plan,

4   the plan shall provide for payment to the

5   Indian health care provider, whether the

6   provider is a participating or nonpartici-

7   pating provider with respect to the entity,

8   of the difference between such applicable

9   rate and the amount paid by the managed

10   care entity to the provider for such serv-

11   ices.

12   "(D) CONSTRUCTION.—Nothing in this

13 paragraph shall be construed as waiving the ap-

14 plication of section 1902(a)(30)(A) (relating to

15 application of standards to assure that pay-

16 ments are consistent with efficiency, economy,

17 and quality of care).

18 "(3) SPECIAL RULE FOR ENROLLMENT FOR IN-

19 DIAN MANAGED CARE ENTITIES.—Regarding the ap-

20 plication of a Medicaid managed care program to In-

21 dian Medicaid managed care entities, an Indian

22 Medicaid managed care entity may restrict enroll-

23 ment under such program to Indians in the same

24 manner as Indian Health Programs may restrict the

25 delivery of services to Indians.

1   "(4) DEFINITIONS.—For purposes of this sub-

2 section:

3   "(A) INDIAN HEALTH CARE PROVIDER.—

4   The term 'Indian health care provider' means

5   an Indian Health Program or an Urban Indian

6   Organization.

7   "(B) INDIAN MEDICAID MANAGED CARE

8   ENTITY.—The term 'Indian Medicaid managed

9   care entity' means a managed care entity that

10   is controlled (within the meaning of the last

11   sentence of section 1903(m)(1)(C)) by the In-

12   dian Health Service, a Tribe, Tribal Organiza-

13   tion, or Urban Indian Organization, or a con-

14   sortium, which may be composed of 1 or more

15   Tribes, Tribal Organizations, or Urban Indian

16   Organizations, and which also may include the

17   Service.

18   "(C) NON-INDIAN MEDICAID MANAGED

19   CARE ENTITY.—The term 'non-Indian Medicaid

20   managed care entity' means a managed care en-

21   tity that is not an Indian Medicaid managed

22   care entity.

23   "(D) COVERED MEDICAID MANAGED CARE

24   SERVICES.—The term 'covered Medicaid man-

25   aged care services' means, with respect to an

1   individual enrolled with a managed care entity,

2   items and services for which benefits are avail-

3   able with respect to the individual under the

4   contract between the entity and the State in-

5   volved.

6   "(E) MEDICAID MANAGED CARE PRO-

7   GRAM.—The term 'Medicaid managed care pro-

8   gram' means a program under sections

9   1903(m), 1905(t), and 1932 and includes a

10   managed care program operating under a waiv-

11   er under section 1915(b) or 1115 or other-

12   wise.".

13   (2) APPLICATION TO CHIP.—Section 2107(e)(1)

14 of such Act (42 U.S.C. 1397gg(1)), as amended by

15 subsection (b)(2), is amended—

16   (A) by redesignating subparagraph (J) as

17   subparagraph (K); and

18   (B) by inserting after subparagraph (I) the

19   following new subparagraph:

20   "(J) Subsections (a)(2)(C) and (h) of sec-

21   tion 1932.".

22   (e) CONSULTATION ON MEDICAID, CHIP, AND OTHER

23 HEALTH CARE PROGRAMS FUNDED UNDER THE SOCIAL

24 SECURITY ACT INVOLVING INDIAN HEALTH PROGRAMS

25 AND URBAN INDIAN ORGANIZATIONS.—

1   (1) CONSULTATION WITH TRIBAL TECHNICAL

2   ADVISORY GROUP (TTAG).—The Secretary of Health

3   and Human Services shall maintain within the Cen-

4   ters for Medicaid & Medicare Services (CMS) a

5   Tribal Technical Advisory Group (TTAG), which

6   was first established in accordance with require-

7   ments of the charter dated September 30, 2003, and

8   the Secretary of Health and Human Services shall

9   include in such Group a representative of a national

10   urban Indian health organization and a representa-

11   tive of the Indian Health Service. The inclusion of

12   a representative of a national urban Indian health

13   organization in such Group shall not affect the non-

14   application of the Federal Advisory Committee Act

15   (5 U.S.C. App.) to such Group.

16   (2) SOLICITATION OF ADVICE UNDER MEDICAID

17   AND CHIP.—

18   (A) MEDICAID STATE PLAN AMEND-

19   MENT.—Section 1902(a) of the Social Security

20   Act (42 U.S.C. 1396a(a)), as amended by sec-

21   tion 501(d)(1) of the Children's Health Insur-

22   ance Program Reauthorization Act of 2009

23   (Public Law 111–3), (42 U.S.C. 1396a(a)) is

24   amended—

548

1   (i) in paragraph (71), by striking

2   "and" at the end;

3   (ii) in paragraph (72), by striking the

4   period at the end and inserting "; and";

5   and

6   (iii) by inserting after paragraph (72),

7   the following new paragraph:

8   "(73) in the case of any State in which 1 or

9 more Indian Health Programs or Urban Indian Or-

10 ganizations furnishes health care services, provide

11 for a process under which the State seeks advice on

12 a regular, ongoing basis from designees of such In-

13 dian Health Programs and Urban Indian Organiza-

14 tions on matters relating to the application of this

15 title that are likely to have a direct effect on such

16 Indian Health Programs and Urban Indian Organi-

17 zations and that—

18   "(A) shall include solicitation of advice

19   prior to submission of any plan amendments,

20   waiver requests, and proposals for demonstra-

21   tion projects likely to have a direct effect on In-

22   dians, Indian Health Programs, or Urban In-

23   dian Organizations; and

24   "(B) may include appointment of an advi-

25   sory committee and of a designee of such In-

1   dian Health Programs and Urban Indian Orga-

2   nizations to the medical care advisory com-

3   mittee advising the State on its State plan

4   under this title.''.

5   (B) APPLICATION TO CHIP.—Section

6   2107(e)(1) of such Act (42 U.S.C. 1397gg(1)),

7   as amended by subsections (b)(2) and (d) (2),

8   is amended—

9   (i) by redesignating subparagraphs

10   (B), (C), (D), (E), (F), (G), (H), (I), (J),

11   and (K) as subparagraphs (D), (F), (B),

12   (E), (G), (I), (H), (J), (K), and (L), re-

13   spectively;

14   (ii) by moving such subparagraphs so

15   as to appear in alphabetical order; and

16   (iii) by inserting after subparagraph

17   (B) (as so redesiganted and moved) the

18   following new subparagraph:

19   ''(C) Section 1902(a)(73) (relating to re-

20   quiring certain States to seek advice from des-

21   ignees of Indian Health Programs and Urban

22   Indian Organizations).''.

23   (3) RULE OF CONSTRUCTION.—Nothing in the

24   amendments made by this subsection shall be con-

25   strued as superseding existing advisory committees,

1   working groups, guidance, or other advisory proce-

2   dures established by the Secretary of Health and

3   Human Services or by any State with respect to the

4   provision of health care to Indians.

5   (f) EFFECTIVE DATE.—The amendments made by

6   this section shall take effect on July 1, 2009.

7   **SEC. 5007. FUNDING FOR OVERSIGHT AND IMPLEMENTA-**

8   **TION.**

9   (a) OVERSIGHT.—For purposes of ensuring the prop-

10   er expenditure of Federal funds under title XIX of the

11   Social Security Act (42 U.S.C. 1396 et seq.), there is ap-

12   propriated to the Office of the Inspector General of the

13   Department of Health and Human Services, out of any

14   money in the Treasury not otherwise appropriated and

15   without further appropriation, $31,250,000 for fiscal year

16   2009, which shall remain available for expenditure until

17   September 30, 2011, and shall be in addition to any other

18   amounts appropriated or made available to such Office for

19   such purposes.

20   (b) IMPLEMENTATION OF INCREASED FMAP.—For

21   purposes of carrying out section 5001, there is appro-

22   priated to the Secretary of Health and Human Services,

23   out of any money in the Treasury not otherwise appro-

24   priated and without further appropriation, $5,000,000 for

25   fiscal year 2009, which shall remain available for expendi-

1 ture until September 30, 2011, and shall be in addition
2 to any other amounts appropriated or made available to
3 such Secretary for such purposes.

4 **SEC. 5008. GAO STUDY AND REPORT REGARDING STATE**
5   **NEEDS DURING PERIODS OF NATIONAL ECO-**
6   **NOMIC DOWNTURN.**

7   (a) IN GENERAL.—The Comptroller General of the
8 United States shall study the period of national economic
9 downturn in effect on the date of enactment of this Act,
10 as well as previous periods of national economic downturn
11 since 1974, for the purpose of developing recommenda-
12 tions for addressing the needs of States during such peri-
13 ods. As part of such analysis, the Comptroller General
14 shall study the past and projected effects of temporary in-
15 creases in the Federal medical assistance percentage
16 under the Medicaid program with respect to such periods.

17   (b) REPORT.—Not later than April 1, 2011, the
18 Comptroller General of the United States shall submit a
19 report to the appropriate committees of Congress on the
20 results of the study conducted under paragraph (1). Such
21 report shall include the following:

22   (1) Such recommendations as the Comptroller
23   General determines appropriate for modifying the
24   national economic downturn assistance formula for
25   temporary adjustment of the Federal medical assist-

1   ance percentage under Medicaid (also referred to as

2   a "countercyclical FMAP") described in GAO report

3   number GAO–07–97 to improve the effectiveness of

4   the application of such percentage in addressing the

5   needs of States during periods of national economic

6   downturn, including recommendations for—

7   (A) improvements to the factors that would

8   begin and end the application of such percent-

9   age;

10   (B) how the determination of the amount

11   of such percentage could be adjusted to address

12   State and regional economic variations during

13   such periods; and

14   (C) how the determination of the amount

15   of such percentage could be adjusted to be more

16   responsive to actual Medicaid costs incurred by

17   States during such periods.

18   (2) An analysis of the impact on States during

19   such periods of—

20   (A) declines in private health benefits cov-

21   erage;

22   (B) declines in State revenues; and

23   (C) caseload maintenance and growth

24   under Medicaid, the Children's Health Insur-

25   ance Program, or any other publicly-funded

1   programs to provide health benefits coverage

2   for State residents.

3   (3) Identification of, and recommendations for

4   addressing, the effects on States of any other spe-

5   cific economic indicators that the Comptroller Gen-

6   eral determines appropriate.

7 TITLE VI—BROADBAND TECH-
8 NOLOGY OPPORTUNITIES
9 PROGRAM

10 SEC. 6000. TABLE OF CONTENTS.

11   The table of contents of this title is as follows:

TITLE VI—BROADBAND TECHNOLOGY OPPORTUNITIES PROGRAM

Sec. 6000. Table of contents.
Sec. 6001. Broadband Technology Opportunities Program.

12 SEC. 6001. BROADBAND TECHNOLOGY OPPORTUNITIES

13   PROGRAM.

14   (a) The Assistant Secretary of Commerce for Com-

15 munications and Information (Assistant Secretary), in

16 consultation with the Federal Communications Commis-

17 sion (Commission), shall establish a national broadband

18 service development and expansion program in conjunction

19 with the technology opportunities program, which shall be

20 referred to as the Broadband Technology Opportunities

21 Program. The Assistant Secretary shall ensure that the

22 program complements and enhances and does not conflict

23 with other Federal broadband initiatives and programs.

1   (b) The purposes of the program are to—

2   (1) provide access to broadband service to con-

3 sumers residing in unserved areas of the United

4 States;

5   (2) provide improved access to broadband serv-

6 ice to consumers residing in underserved areas of

7 the United States;

8   (3) provide broadband education, awareness,

9 training, access, equipment, and support to—

10   (A) schools, libraries, medical and

11 healthcare providers, community colleges and

12 other institutions of higher education, and other

13 community support organizations and entities

14 to facilitate greater use of broadband service by

15 or through these organizations;

16   (B) organizations and agencies that pro-

17 vide outreach, access, equipment, and support

18 services to facilitate greater use of broadband

19 service by low-income, unemployed, aged, and

20 otherwise vulnerable populations; and

21   (C) job-creating strategic facilities located

22 within a State-designated economic zone, Eco-

23 nomic Development District designated by the

24 Department of Commerce, Renewal Community

25 or Empowerment Zone designated by the De-

1   partment of Housing and Urban Development,

2   or Enterprise Community designated by the De-

3   partment of Agriculture;

4   (4) improve access to, and use of, broadband

5 service by public safety agencies; and

6   (5) stimulate the demand for broadband, eco-

7 nomic growth, and job creation.

8   (c) The Assistant Secretary may consult a State, the

9 District of Columbia, or territory or possession of the

10 United States with respect to—

11   (1) the identification of areas described in sub-

12   section (b)(1) or (2) located in that State; and

13   (2) the allocation of grant funds within that

14   State for projects in or affecting the State.

15   (d) The Assistant Secretary shall—

16   (1) establish and implement the grant program

17   as expeditiously as practicable;

18   (2) ensure that all awards are made before the

19   end of fiscal year 2010;

20   (3) seek such assurances as may be necessary

21   or appropriate from grantees under the program

22   that they will substantially complete projects sup-

23   ported by the program in accordance with project

24   timelines, not to exceed 2 years following an award;

25   and

1   (4) report on the status of the program to the

2   Committees on Appropriations of the House of Rep-

3   resentatives and the Senate, the Committee on En-

4   ergy and Commerce of the House of Representa-

5   tives, and the Committee on Commerce, Science, and

6   Transportation of the Senate, every 90 days.

7   (e) To be eligible for a grant under the program, an

8 applicant shall—

9   (1)(A) be a State or political subdivision there-

10   of, the District of Columbia, a territory or posses-

11   sion of the United States, an Indian tribe (as de-

12   fined in section 4 of the Indian Self-Determination

13   and Education Assistance Act (25 U.S.C. 450(b)) or

14   native Hawaiian organization;

15   (B) a nonprofit—

16   (i) foundation,

17   (ii) corporation,

18   (iii) institution, or

19   (iv) association; or

20   (C) any other entity, including a

21   broadband service or infrastructure provider,

22   that the Assistant Secretary finds by rule to be

23   in the public interest. In establishing such rule,

24   the Assistant Secretary shall to the extent prac-

1   ticable promote the purposes of this section in

2   a technologically neutral manner;

3   (2) submit an application, at such time, in such

4   form, and containing such information as the Assist-

5   ant Secretary may require;

6   (3) provide a detailed explanation of how any

7   amount received under the program will be used to

8   carry out the purposes of this section in an efficient

9   and expeditious manner, including a showing that

10   the project would not have been implemented during

11   the grant period without Federal grant assistance;

12   (4) demonstrate, to the satisfaction of the As-

13   sistant Secretary, that it is capable of carrying out

14   the project or function to which the application re-

15   lates in a competent manner in compliance with all

16   applicable Federal, State, and local laws;

17   (5) demonstrate, to the satisfaction of the As-

18   sistant Secretary, that it will appropriate (if the ap-

19   plicant is a State or local government agency) or

20   otherwise unconditionally obligate, from non-Federal

21   sources, funds required to meet the requirements of

22   subsection (f);

23   (6) disclose to the Assistant Secretary the

24   source and amount of other Federal or State fund-

25   ing sources from which the applicant receives, or has

1   applied for, funding for activities or projects to

2   which the application relates; and

3   (7) provide such assurances and procedures as

4   the Assistant Secretary may require to ensure that

5   grant funds are used and accounted for in an appro-

6   priate manner.

7   (f) The Federal share of any project may not exceed

8 80 percent, except that the Assistant Secretary may in-

9 crease the Federal share of a project above 80 percent

10 if—

11   (1) the applicant petitions the Assistant Sec-

12 retary for a waiver; and

13   (2) the Assistant Secretary determines that the

14 petition demonstrates financial need.

15 (g) The Assistant Secretary may make competitive

16 grants under the program to—

17   (1) acquire equipment, instrumentation, net-

18 working capability, hardware and software, digital

19 network technology, and infrastructure for

20 broadband services;

21   (2) construct and deploy broadband service re-

22 lated infrastructure;

23   (3) ensure access to broadband service by com-

24 munity anchor institutions;

559

1   (4) facilitate access to broadband service by
2   low-income, unemployed, aged, and otherwise vulner-
3   able populations in order to provide educational and
4   employment opportunities to members of such popu-
5   lations;

6   (5) construct and deploy broadband facilities
7   that improve public safety broadband communica-
8   tions services; and

9   (6) undertake such other projects and activities
10   as the Assistant Secretary finds to be consistent
11   with the purposes for which the program is estab-
12   lished.

13   (h) The Assistant Secretary, in awarding grants
14   under this section, shall, to the extent practical—

15   (1) award not less than 1 grant in each State;
16   (2) consider whether an application to deploy
17   infrastructure in an area—

18   (A) will, if approved, increase the afford-
19   ability of, and subscribership to, service to the
20   greatest population of users in the area;

21   (B) will, if approved, provide the greatest
22   broadband speed possible to the greatest popu-
23   lation of users in the area;

24   (C) will, if approved, enhance service for
25   health care delivery, education, or children to

1 the greatest population of users in the area;

2 and

3 (D) will, if approved, not result in unjust

4 enrichment as a result of support for non-recur-

5 ring costs through another Federal program for

6 service in the area; and

7 (3) consider whether the applicant is a socially

8 and economically disadvantaged small business con-

9 cern as defined under section 8(a) of the Small

10 Business Act (15 U.S.C. 637).

11 (i) The Assistant Secretary—

12 (1) shall require any entity receiving a grant

13 pursuant to this section to report quarterly, in a for-

14 mat specified by the Assistant Secretary, on such

15 entity's use of the assistance and progress fulfilling

16 the objectives for which such funds were granted,

17 and the Assistant Secretary shall make these reports

18 available to the public;

19 (2) may establish additional reporting and in-

20 formation requirements for any recipient of any as-

21 sistance made available pursuant to this section;

22 (3) shall establish appropriate mechanisms to

23 ensure appropriate use and compliance with all

24 terms of any use of funds made available pursuant

25 to this section;

1   (4) may, in addition to other authority under

2   applicable law, deobligate awards to grantees that

3   demonstrate an insufficient level of performance, or

4   wasteful or fraudulent spending, as defined in ad-

5   vance by the Assistant Secretary, and award these

6   funds competitively to new or existing applicants

7   consistent with this section; and

8   (5) shall create and maintain a fully searchable

9   database, accessible on the Internet at no cost to the

10   public, that contains at least a list of each entity

11   that has applied for a grant under this section, a de-

12   scription of each application, the status of each such

13   application, the name of each entity receiving funds

14   made available pursuant to this section, the purpose

15   for which such entity is receiving such funds, each

16   quarterly report submitted by the entity pursuant to

17   this section, and such other information sufficient to

18   allow the public to understand and monitor grants

19   awarded under the program.

20   (j) Concurrent with the issuance of the Request for

21 Proposal for grant applications pursuant to this section,

22 the Assistant Secretary shall, in coordination with the

23 Commission, publish the non-discrimination and network

24 interconnection obligations that shall be contractual condi-

25 tions of grants awarded under this section, including, at

1 a minimum, adherence to the principles contained in the

2 Commission's broadband policy statement (FCC 05-15,

3 adopted August 5, 2005).

4   (k)(1) Not later than 1 year after the date of enact-

5 ment of this section, the Commission shall submit to the

6 Committee on Energy and Commerce of the House of

7 Representatives and the Committee on Commerce,

8 Science, and Transportation of the Senate, a report con-

9 taining a national broadband plan.

10   (2) The national broadband plan required by

11   this section shall seek to ensure that all people of

12   the United States have access to broadband capa-

13   bility and shall establish benchmarks for meeting

14   that goal. The plan shall also include—

15   (A) an analysis of the most effective and

16   efficient mechanisms for ensuring broadband

17   access by all people of the United States;

18   (B) a detailed strategy for achieving af-

19   fordability of such service and maximum utiliza-

20   tion of broadband infrastructure and service by

21   the public;

22   (C) an evaluation of the status of deploy-

23   ment of broadband service, including progress

24   of projects supported by the grants made pur-

25   suant to this section; and

1   (D) a plan for use of broadband infrastruc-
2   ture and services in advancing consumer wel-
3   fare, civic participation, public safety and home-
4   land security, community development, health
5   care delivery, energy independence and effi-
6   ciency, education, worker training, private sec-
7   tor investment, entrepreneurial activity, job cre-
8   ation and economic growth, and other national
9   purposes.

10   (3) In developing the plan, the Commission
11   shall have access to data provided to other Govern-
12   ment agencies under the Broadband Data Improve-
13   ment Act (47 U.S.C. 1301 note).

14   (l) The Assistant Secretary shall develop and main-
15   tain a comprehensive nationwide inventory map of existing
16   broadband service capability and availability in the United
17   States that depicts the geographic extent to which
18   broadband service capability is deployed and available
19   from a commercial provider or public provider throughout
20   each State. Not later than 2 years after the date of the
21   enactment of this Act, the Assistant Secretary shall make
22   the broadband inventory map developed and maintained
23   pursuant to this section accessible by the public on a
24   World Wide Web site of the National Telecommunications

1 and Information Administration in a form that is inter-

2 active and searchable.

3   (m) The Assistant Secretary shall have the authority

4 to prescribe such rules as are necessary to carry out the

5 purposes of this section.

6 # TITLE VII—LIMITS ON
7 # EXECUTIVE COMPENSATION

8 **SEC. 7000. TABLE OF CONTENTS.**

9   The table of contents of this title is as follows:

TITLE VII—LIMITS ON EXECUTIVE COMPENSATION

Sec. 7000. Table of contents.
Sec. 7001. Executive compensation and corporate governance.
Sec. 7002. Applicability with respect to loan modifications.

10 **SEC. 7001. EXECUTIVE COMPENSATION AND CORPORATE**

11   **GOVERNANCE.**

12   Section 111 of the Emergency Economic Stabilization

13 Act of 2008 (12 U.S.C. 5221) is amended to read as fol-

14 lows:

15 **"SEC. 111. EXECUTIVE COMPENSATION AND CORPORATE**

16   **GOVERNANCE.**

17   "(a) DEFINITIONS.—For purposes of this section, the

18 following definitions shall apply:

19   "(1) SENIOR EXECUTIVE OFFICER.—The term

20   'senior executive officer' means an individual who is

21   1 of the top 5 most highly paid executives of a pub-

22   lic company, whose compensation is required to be

23   disclosed pursuant to the Securities Exchange Act of

1 1934, and any regulations issued thereunder, and

2 non-public company counterparts.

3   "(2) GOLDEN PARACHUTE PAYMENT.—The

4 term 'golden parachute payment' means any pay-

5 ment to a senior executive officer for departure from

6 a company for any reason, except for payments for

7 services performed or benefits accrued.

8   "(3) TARP RECIPIENT.—The term 'TARP re-

9 cipient' means any entity that has received or will

10 receive financial assistance under the financial as-

11 sistance provided under the TARP.

12   "(4) COMMISSION.—The term 'Commission'

13 means the Securities and Exchange Commission.

14   "(5) PERIOD IN WHICH OBLIGATION IS OUT-

15 STANDING; RULE OF CONSTRUCTION.—For purposes

16 of this section, the period in which any obligation

17 arising from financial assistance provided under the

18 TARP remains outstanding does not include any pe-

19 riod during which the Federal Government only

20 holds warrants to purchase common stock of the

21 TARP recipient.

22 "(b) EXECUTIVE COMPENSATION AND CORPORATE

23 GOVERNANCE.—

24   "(1) ESTABLISHMENT OF STANDARDS.—During

25 the period in which any obligation arising from fi-

1 nancial assistance provided under the TARP re-

2 mains outstanding, each TARP recipient shall be

3 subject to—

4   "(A) the standards established by the Sec-

5   retary under this section; and

6   "(B) the provisions of section 162(m)(5) of

7   the Internal Revenue Code of 1986, as applica-

8   ble.

9   "(2) STANDARDS REQUIRED.—The Secretary

10 shall require each TARP recipient to meet appro-

11 priate standards for executive compensation and cor-

12 porate governance.

13   "(3) SPECIFIC REQUIREMENTS.—The standards

14 established under paragraph (2) shall include the

15 following:

16   "(A) Limits on compensation that exclude

17   incentives for senior executive officers of the

18   TARP recipient to take unnecessary and exces-

19   sive risks that threaten the value of such recipi-

20   ent during the period in which any obligation

21   arising from financial assistance provided under

22   the TARP remains outstanding.

23   "(B) A provision for the recovery by such

24   TARP recipient of any bonus, retention award,

25   or incentive compensation paid to a senior exec-

utive officer and any of the next 20 most highly-compensated employees of the TARP recipient based on statements of earnings, revenues,
gains, or other criteria that are later found to
be materially inaccurate.

"(C) A prohibition on such TARP recipient
making any golden parachute payment to a senior executive officer or any of the next 5 most
highly-compensated employees of the TARP recipient during the period in which any obligation arising from financial assistance provided
under the TARP remains outstanding.

"(D)(i) A prohibition on such TARP recipient paying or accruing any bonus, retention
award, or incentive compensation during the period in which any obligation arising from financial assistance provided under the TARP remains outstanding, except that any prohibition
developed under this paragraph shall not apply
to the payment of long-term restricted stock by
such TARP recipient, provided that such long-
term restricted stock—

"(I) does not fully vest during the period in which any obligation arising from

1   financial assistance provided to that TARP

2   recipient remains outstanding;

3   "(II) has a value in an amount that

4   is not greater than ⅓ of the total amount

5   of annual compensation of the employee re-

6   ceiving the stock; and

7   "(III) is subject to such other terms

8   and conditions as the Secretary may deter-

9   mine is in the public interest.

10   "(ii) The prohibition required under clause

11 (i) shall apply as follows:

12   "(I) For any financial institution that

13   received   financial   assistance   provided

14   under   the   TARP   equal   to   less   than

15       $25,000,000, the prohibition shall apply

16   only to the most highly compensated em-

17   ployee of the financial institution.

18   "(II) For any financial institution

19   that received financial assistance provided

20   under   the   TARP   equal   to   at   least

21       $25,000,000, but less than $250,000,000,

22   the prohibition shall apply to at least the

23   5 most highly-compensated employees of

24   the financial institution, or such higher

25   number as the Secretary may determine is

1   in the public interest with respect to any

2   TARP recipient.

3   "(III) For any financial institution

4   that received financial assistance provided

5   under the TARP equal to at

6   least\$250,000,000, but less than

7   \$500,000,000, the prohibition shall apply

8   to the senior executive officers and at least

9   the 10 next most highly-compensated em-

10   ployees, or such higher number as the Sec-

11   retary may determine is in the public inter-

12   est with respect to any TARP recipient.

13   "(IV) For any financial institution

14   that received financial assistance provided

15   under the TARP equal to \$500,000,000 or

16   more, the prohibition shall apply to the

17   senior executive officers and at least the 20

18   next most highly-compensated employees,

19   or such higher number as the Secretary

20   may determine is in the public interest

21   with respect to any TARP recipient.

22   "(iii) The prohibition required under clause

23   (i) shall not be construed to prohibit any bonus

24   payment required to be paid pursuant to a writ-

25   ten employment contract executed on or before

1   February 11, 2009, as such valid employment

2   contracts are determined by the Secretary or

3   the designee of the Secretary.

4   "(E) A prohibition on any compensation

5   plan that would encourage manipulation of the

6   reported earnings of such TARP recipient to

7   enhance the compensation of any of its employ-

8   ees.

9   "(F) A requirement for the establishment

10 of a Board Compensation Committee that

11 meets the requirements of subsection (c).

12   "(4) CERTIFICATION OF COMPLIANCE.—The

13 chief executive officer and chief financial officer (or

14 the equivalents thereof) of each TARP recipient

15 shall provide a written certification of compliance by

16 the TARP recipient with the requirements of this

17 section—

18   "(A) in the case of a TARP recipient, the

19 securities of which are publicly traded, to the

20 Securities and Exchange Commission, together

21 with annual filings required under the securities

22 laws; and

23   "(B) in the case of a TARP recipient that

24 is not a publicly traded company, to the Sec-

25 retary.

1   ''(c) BOARD COMPENSATION COMMITTEE.—

2   ''(1) ESTABLISHMENT OF BOARD REQUIRED.—

3   Each TARP recipient shall establish a Board Com-

4   pensation Committee, comprised entirely of inde-

5   pendent directors, for the purpose of reviewing em-

6   ployee compensation plans.

7   ''(2) MEETINGS.—The Board Compensation

8   Committee of each TARP recipient shall meet at

9   least semiannually to discuss and evaluate employee

10   compensation plans in light of an assessment of any

11   risk posed to the TARP recipient from such plans.

12   ''(3) COMPLIANCE BY NON-SEC REG-

13   ISTRANTS.—In the case of any TARP recipient, the

14   common or preferred stock of which is not registered

15   pursuant to the Securities Exchange Act of 1934,

16   and that has received $25,000,000 or less of TARP

17   assistance, the duties of the Board Compensation

18   Committee under this subsection shall be carried out

19   by the board of directors of such TARP recipient.

20   ''(d) LIMITATION ON LUXURY EXPENDITURES.—The

21   board of directors of any TARP recipient shall have in

22   place a company-wide policy regarding excessive or luxury

23   expenditures, as identified by the Secretary, which may

24   include excessive expenditures on—

25   ''(1) entertainment or events;

1   "(2) office and facility renovations;

2   "(3) aviation or other transportation services;

3   or

4   "(4) other activities or events that are not rea-

5   sonable expenditures for staff development, reason-

6   able performance incentives, or other similar meas-

7   ures conducted in the normal course of the business

8   operations of the TARP recipient.

9   "(e) SHAREHOLDER APPROVAL OF EXECUTIVE COM-

10 PENSATION.—

11   "(1) ANNUAL SHAREHOLDER APPROVAL OF EX-

12   ECUTIVE COMPENSATION.—Any proxy or consent or

13   authorization for an annual or other meeting of the

14   shareholders of any TARP recipient during the pe-

15   riod in which any obligation arising from financial

16   assistance provided under the TARP remains out-

17   standing shall permit a separate shareholder vote to

18   approve the compensation of executives, as disclosed

19   pursuant to the compensation disclosure rules of the

20   Commission (which disclosure shall include the com-

21   pensation discussion and analysis, the compensation

22   tables, and any related material).

23   "(2) NONBINDING VOTE.—A shareholder vote

24   described in paragraph (1) shall not be binding on

25   the board of directors of a TARP recipient, and may

1   not be construed as overruling a decision by such

2   board, nor to create or imply any additional fidu-

3   ciary duty by such board, nor shall such vote be con-

4   strued to restrict or limit the ability of shareholders

5   to make proposals for inclusion in proxy materials

6   related to executive compensation.

7   "(3) DEADLINE FOR RULEMAKING.—Not later

8   than 1 year after the date of enactment of the

9   American Recovery and Reinvestment Act of 2009,

10   the Commission shall issue any final rules and regu-

11   lations required by this subsection.

12   "(f) REVIEW OF PRIOR PAYMENTS TO EXECU-

13 TIVES.—

14   "(1) IN GENERAL.—The Secretary shall review

15   bonuses, retention awards, and other compensation

16   paid to the senior executive officers and the next 20

17   most highly-compensated employees of each entity

18   receiving TARP assistance before the date of enact-

19   ment of the American Recovery and Reinvestment

20   Act of 2009, to determine whether any such pay-

21   ments were inconsistent with the purposes of this

22   section or the TARP or were otherwise contrary to

23   the public interest.

24   "(2) NEGOTIATIONS FOR REIMBURSEMENT.—If

25   the Secretary makes a determination described in

1   paragraph (1), the Secretary shall seek to negotiate

2   with the TARP recipient and the subject employee

3   for appropriate reimbursements to the Federal Gov-

4   ernment with respect to compensation or bonuses.

5   "(g) No Impediment to Withdrawal by TARP

6 Recipients.—Subject to consultation with the appro-

7 priate Federal banking agency (as that term is defined

8 in section 3 of the Federal Deposit Insurance Act), if any,

9 the Secretary shall permit a TARP recipient to repay any

10 assistance previously provided under the TARP to such

11 financial institution, without regard to whether the finan-

12 cial institution has replaced such funds from any other

13 source or to any waiting period, and when such assistance

14 is repaid, the Secretary shall liquidate warrants associated

15 with such assistance at the current market price.

16   "(h) Regulations.—The Secretary shall promul-

17 gate regulations to implement this section.".

18 **SEC. 7002. APPLICABILITY WITH RESPECT TO LOAN MODI-**

19 **FICATIONS.**

20   Section 109(a) of the Emergency Economic Stabiliza-

21 tion Act of 2008 (12 U.S.C. 5219(a)) is amended—

22   (1) by striking "To the extent" and inserting

23   the following:

24   "(1) In general.—To the extent"; and

25   (2) by adding at the end the following:

1   "(2) WAIVER OF CERTAIN PROVISIONS IN CON-

2   NECTION WITH LOAN MODIFICATIONS.—The Sec-

3   retary shall not be required to apply executive com-

4   pensation restrictions under section 111, or to re-

5   ceive warrants or debt instruments under section

6   113, solely in connection with any loan modification

7   under this section.".

DIVISION B—TAX, UNEMPLOYMENT, HEALTH, STATE FISCAL RELIEF, AND OTHER PROVISIONS

TITLE I—TAX PROVISIONS

A. Tax Relief for Individuals and Families

1. Making Work Pay Credit (sec. 1001 of the House bill, sec. 1001 of the Senate amendment, sec. 1001 of the conference agreement, and new sec. 36A of the Code)

PRESENT LAW

Earned income tax credit

Low- and moderate-income workers may be eligible for the refundable earned income tax credit ("EITC"). Eligibility for the EITC is based on earned income, adjusted gross income, investment income, filing status, and immigration and work status in the United States. The amount of the EITC is based on the presence and number of qualifying children in the worker's family, as well as on adjusted gross income and earned income.

The EITC generally equals a specified percentage of earned income[1] up to a maximum dollar amount. The maximum amount applies over a certain income range and then diminishes to zero over a specified phaseout range. For taxpayers with earned income (or adjusted gross income ("AGI"), if greater) in excess of the beginning of the phaseout range, the maximum EITC amount is reduced by the phaseout rate multiplied by the amount of earned income (or AGI, if greater) in excess of the beginning of the phaseout range. For taxpayers with earned income (or AGI, if greater) in excess of the end of the phaseout range, no credit is allowed.

The EITC is a refundable credit, meaning that if the amount of the credit exceeds the taxpayer's Federal income tax liability, the excess is payable to the taxpayer as a direct transfer payment. Under an advance payment system, eligible taxpayers may elect to receive the credit in their paychecks, rather than waiting to claim a refund on their tax returns filed by April 15 of the following year.

Child credit

An individual may claim a tax credit for each qualifying child under the age of 17. The amount of the credit per child is $1,000 through 2010 and $500 thereafter. A child who is not a citizen, national, or resident of the United States cannot be a qualifying child.

The credit is phased out for individuals with income over certain threshold amounts. Specifically, the otherwise allowable child

---

[1] Earned income is defined as (1) wages, salaries, tips, and other employee compensation, but only if such amounts are includible in gross income, plus (2) the amount of the individual's net self-employment earnings.

tax credit is reduced by $50 for each $1,000 (or fraction thereof) of modified adjusted gross income over $75,000 for single individuals or heads of households, $110,000 for married individuals filing joint returns, and $55,000 for married individuals filing separate returns. For purposes of this limitation, modified adjusted gross income includes certain otherwise excludable income earned by U.S. citizens or residents living abroad or in certain U.S. territories.

The credit is allowable against the regular tax and the alternative minimum tax. To the extent the child credit exceeds the taxpayer's tax liability, the taxpayer is eligible for a refundable credit (the additional child tax credit) equal to 15 percent of earned income in excess of a threshold dollar amount (the "earned income" formula). The threshold dollar amount is $12,550 (for 2009), and is indexed for inflation.

Families with three or more children may determine the additional child tax credit using the "alternative formula," if this results in a larger credit than determined under the earned income formula. Under the alternative formula, the additional child tax credit equals the amount by which the taxpayer's social security taxes exceed the taxpayer's earned income tax credit.

Earned income is defined as the sum of wages, salaries, tips, and other taxable employee compensation plus net self-employment earnings. Unlike the EITC, which also includes the preceding items in its definition of earned income, the additional child tax credit is based only on earned income to the extent it is included in computing taxable income. For example, some ministers' parsonage allowances are considered self-employment income, and thus are considered earned income for purposes of computing the EITC, but the allowances are excluded from gross income for individual income tax purposes, and thus are not considered earned income for purposes of the additional child tax credit.

HOUSE BILL

In general

The provision provides eligible individuals a refundable income tax credit for two years (taxable years beginning in 2009 and 2010).

The credit is the lesser of (1) 6.2 percent of an individual's earned income or (2) $500 ($1,000 in the case of a joint return). For these purposes, the earned income definition is the same as for the earned income tax credit with two modifications. First, earned income for these purposes does not include net earnings from self-employment which are not taken into account in computing taxable income. Second, earned income for these purposes includes combat pay excluded from gross income under section 112.[2]

The credit is phased out at a rate of two percent of the eligible individual's modified adjusted gross income above $75,000 ($150,000 in the case of a joint return). For these purposes an eligible individual's modified adjusted gross income is the eligible individual's adjusted gross income increased by any amount excluded from gross income under sections 911, 931, or 933. An eligible individual means any individual other than: (1) a nonresident alien; (2)

---

[2] Unless otherwise stated, all section references are to the Internal Revenue Code of 1986, as amended (the "Code").

an individual with respect to whom another individual may claim a dependency deduction for a taxable year beginning in a calendar year in which the eligible individual's taxable year begins; and (3) an estate or trust. Each eligible individual must satisfy identical taxpayer identification number requirements to those applicable to the earned income tax credit.

Treatment of the U.S. possessions

Mirror code possessions [3]

The U.S. Treasury will make payments to each mirror code possession in an amount equal to the aggregate amount of the credits allowable by reason of the provision to that possession's residents against its income tax. This amount will be determined by the Treasury Secretary based on information provided by the government of the respective possession. For purposes of these payments, a possession is a mirror code possession if the income tax liability of residents of the possession under that possession's income tax system is determined by reference to the U.S. income tax laws as if the possession were the United States.

Non-mirror code possessions [4]

To each possession that does not have a mirror code tax system, the U.S. Treasury will make two payments (for 2009 and 2010, respectively) in an amount estimated by the Secretary as being equal to the aggregate credits that would have been allowed to residents of that possession if a mirror code tax system had been in effect in that possession. Accordingly, the amount of each payment to a non-mirror Code possession will be an estimate of the aggregate amount of the credits that would be allowed to the possession's residents if the credit provided by the provision to U.S. residents were provided by the possession to its residents. This payment will not be made to any U.S. possession unless that possession has a plan that has been approved by the Secretary under which the possession will promptly distribute the payment to its residents.

General rules

No credit against U.S. income tax is permitted under the provision for any person to whom a credit is allowed against possession income taxes as a result of the provision (for example, under that possession's mirror income tax). Similarly, no credit against U.S. income tax is permitted for any person who is eligible for a payment under a non-mirror code possession's plan for distributing to its residents the payment described above from the U.S. Treasury.

For purposes of the payments to the possessions, the Commonwealth of Puerto Rico and the Commonwealth of the Northern Mariana Islands are considered possessions of the United States.

For purposes of the rule permitting the Treasury Secretary to disburse appropriated amounts for refunds due from certain credit provisions of the Internal Revenue Code of 1986, the payments re-

---

[3] Possessions with mirror code tax systems are the United States Virgin Islands, Guam, and the Commonwealth of the Northern Mariana Islands.

[4] Possessions that do not have mirror code tax systems are Puerto Rico and American Samoa.

quired to be made to possessions under the provision are treated in the same manner as a refund due from the credit allowed under the provision.

Federal programs or Federally-assisted programs

Any credit or refund allowed or made to an individual under this provision (including to any resident of a U.S. possession) is not taken into account as income and shall not be taken into account as resources for the month of receipt and the following two months for purposes of determining eligibility of such individual or any other individual for benefits or assistance, or the amount or extent of benefits or assistance, under any Federal program or under any State or local program financed in whole or in part with Federal funds.

Income tax withholding

Taxpayers' reduced tax liability under the provision shall be expeditiously implemented through revised income tax withholding schedules produced by the Internal Revenue Service. These revised income tax withholding schedules should be designed to reduce taxpayers' income tax withheld for each remaining pay period in the remainder of 2009 by an amount equal to the amount that withholding would have been reduced had the provision been reflected in the income tax withholding schedules for the entire taxable year.

Effective date

The provision applies to taxable years beginning after December 31, 2008.

SENATE AMENDMENT

In general

The Senate is the same as the House bill, except that the credit is phased out at a rate of four percent (rather than two percent) of the eligible individual's modified adjusted gross income above $70,000 ($140,000 in the case of a joint return).

Also, the Senate amendment provides that the otherwise allowable credit allowed under the provision is reduced by the amount of any payment received by the taxpayer pursuant to the provisions of the bill providing economic recovery payments under the Veterans Administration, Railroad Retirement Board, and the Social Security Administration. The provision treats the failure to reduce the credit by the amount of these payments, and the omission of the correct TIN, as clerical errors. This allows the IRS to assess any tax resulting from such failure or omission without the requirement to send the taxpayer a notice of deficiency allowing the taxpayer the right to file a petition with the Tax Court.

Income tax withholding

The Senate amendment also provides for a more accelerated delivery of the credit in 2009 through revised income tax withholding schedules produced by the Department of the Treasury. Under the Senate amendment, these revised income tax withholding schedules would be designed to reduce taxpayers' income tax withheld for the remainder of 2009 in such a manner that the full annual benefit of the provision is reflected in income tax withheld during the remainder of 2009.

CONFERENCE AGREEMENT

In general

The provision provides eligible individuals a refundable income tax credit for two years (taxable years beginning in 2009 and 2010). The credit is the lesser of (1) 6.2 percent of an individual's earned income or (2) $400 ($800 in the case of a joint return). For these purposes, the earned income definition is the same as for the earned income tax credit with two modifications. First, earned income for these purposes does not include net earnings from self-employment which are not taken into account in computing taxable income. Second, earned income for these purposes includes combat pay excluded from gross income under section 112.

The credit is phased out at a rate of two percent of the eligible individual's modified adjusted gross income above $75,000 ($150,000 in the case of a joint return). For these purposes an eligible individual's modified adjusted gross income is the eligible individual's adjusted gross income increased by any amount excluded from gross income under sections 911, 931, or 933. An eligible individual means any individual other than: (1) a nonresident alien; (2) an individual with respect to whom another individual may claim a dependency deduction for a taxable year beginning in a calendar year in which the eligible individual's taxable year begins; and (3) an estate or trust.

Also, the conference agreement provides that the otherwise allowable making work pay credit allowed under the provision is reduced by the amount of any payment received by the taxpayer pursuant to the provisions of the bill providing economic recovery payments under the Veterans Administration, Railroad Retirement Board, and the Social Security Administration and a temporary refundable tax credit for certain government retirees.[5] The conference agreement treats the failure to reduce the making work pay credit by the amount of such payments or credit, and the omission of the correct TIN, as clerical errors. This allows the IRS to assess any tax resulting from such failure or omission without the requirement to send the taxpayer a notice of deficiency allowing the taxpayer the right to file a petition with the Tax Court.

Each tax return on which this credit is claimed must include the social security number of the taxpayer (in the case of a joint return, the social security number of at least one spouse).

Treatment of the U.S. possessions

The conference agreement follows the House bill and the Senate amendment.

---

[5] The credit for certain government employees is available for 2009. The credit is $250 ($500 for a joint return where both spouses are eligible individuals). An eligible individual for these purposes is an individual: (1) who receives an amount as a pension or annuity for service performed in the employ of the United States or any State or any instrumentality thereof, which is not considered employment for purposes of Social Security taxes; and (2) who does not receive an economic recovery payment under the Veterans Administration, Railroad Retirement Board, or the Social Security Administration.

Federal programs or Federally-assisted programs

The conference agreement follows the House bill and the Senate amendment.

Income tax withholding

The conference agreement follows the Senate amendment.

Effective date

The provision applies to taxable years beginning after December 31, 2008.

2. Increase in the earned income tax credit (sec. 1101 of the House bill, sec. 1002 of the Senate amendment, sec. 1002 of the conference agreement, and sec. 32 of the Code)

PRESENT LAW

Overview

Low- and moderate-income workers may be eligible for the refundable earned income tax credit ("EITC"). Eligibility for the EITC is based on earned income, adjusted gross income, investment income, filing status, and immigration and work status in the United States. The amount of the EITC is based on the presence and number of qualifying children in the worker's family, as well as on adjusted gross income and earned income.

The EITC generally equals a specified percentage of earned income[6] up to a maximum dollar amount. The maximum amount applies over a certain income range and then diminishes to zero over a specified phaseout range. For taxpayers with earned income (or adjusted gross income (AGI), if greater) in excess of the beginning of the phaseout range, the maximum EITC amount is reduced by the phaseout rate multiplied by the amount of earned income (or AGI, if greater) in excess of the beginning of the phaseout range. For taxpayers with earned income (or AGI, if greater) in excess of the end of the phaseout range, no credit is allowed.

An individual is not eligible for the EITC if the aggregate amount of disqualified income of the taxpayer for the taxable year exceeds $3,100 (for 2009). This threshold is indexed for inflation. Disqualified income is the sum of: (1) interest (taxable and tax exempt); (2) dividends; (3) net rent and royalty income (if greater than zero); (4) capital gains net income; and (5) net passive income (if greater than zero) that is not self-employment income.

The EITC is a refundable credit, meaning that if the amount of the credit exceeds the taxpayer's Federal income tax liability, the excess is payable to the taxpayer as a direct transfer payment. Under an advance payment system, eligible taxpayers may elect to receive the credit in their paychecks, rather than waiting to claim a refund on their tax returns filed by April 15 of the following year.

---

[6] Earned income is defined as (1) wages, salaries, tips, and other employee compensation, but only if such amounts are includible in gross income, plus (2) the amount of the individual's net self-employment earnings.

Filing status

An unmarried individual may claim the EITC if he or she files as a single filer or as a head of household. Married individuals generally may not claim the EITC unless they file jointly. An exception to the joint return filing requirement applies to certain spouses who are separated. Under this exception, a married taxpayer who is separated from his or her spouse for the last six months of the taxable year shall not be considered as married (and, accordingly, may file a return as head of household and claim the EITC), provided that the taxpayer maintains a household that constitutes the principal place of abode for a dependent child (including a son, stepson, daughter, stepdaughter, adopted child, or a foster child) for over half the taxable year,[7] and pays over half the cost of maintaining the household in which he or she resides with the child during the year.

Presence of qualifying children and amount of the earned income credit

Three separate credit schedules apply: one schedule for taxpayers with no qualifying children, one schedule for taxpayers with no qualifying child, and one schedule for taxpayers with more than one qualifying child.[8]

Taxpayers with no qualifying children may claim a credit if they are over age 24 and below age 65. The credit is 7.65 percent of earnings up to $5,970, resulting in a maximum credit of $457 for 2009. The maximum is available for those with incomes between $5,970 and $7,470 ($10,590 if married filing jointly). The credit begins to phase down at a rate of 7.65 percent of earnings above $7,470 ($10,590 if married filing jointly) resulting in a $0 credit at $13,440 of earnings ($16,560 if married filing jointly).

Taxpayers with one qualifying child may claim a credit in 2009 of 34 percent of their earnings up to $8,950, resulting in a maximum credit of $3,043. The maximum credit is available for those with earnings between $8,950 and $16,420 ($19,540 if married filing jointly). The credit begins to phase down at a rate of 15.98 percent of earnings above $16,420 ($19,540 if married filing jointly). The credit is phased down to $0 at $35,463 of earnings ($38,583 if married filing jointly).

Taxpayers with more than one qualifying child may claim a credit in 2009 of 40 percent of earnings up to $12,570, resulting in a maximum credit of $5,028. The maximum credit is available for those with earnings between $12,570 and $16,420 ($19,540 if married filing jointly). The credit begins to phase down at a rate of 21.06 percent of earnings above $16,420 ($19,540 if married filing jointly). The credit is phased down to $0 at $40,295 of earnings ($43,415 if married filing jointly).

If more than one taxpayer lives with a qualifying child, only one of these taxpayers may claim the child for purposes of the EITC. If multiple eligible taxpayers actually claim the same qualifying child, then a tiebreaker rule determines which taxpayer is entitled to the EITC with respect to the qualifying child. Any eligible

---

[7] A foster child must reside with the taxpayer for the entire taxable year.
[8] All income thresholds are indexed for inflation annually.

taxpayer with at least one qualifying child who does not claim the EITC with respect to qualifying children due to failure to meet certain identification requirements with respect to such children (i.e., providing the name, age and taxpayer identification number of each of such children) may not claim the EITC for taxpayers without qualifying children.

HOUSE BILL

Three or more qualifying children

The provision increases the EITC credit percentage for families with three or more qualifying children to 45 percent for 2009 and 2010. For example, in 2009 taxpayers with three or more qualifying children may claim a credit of 45 percent of earnings up to $12,570, resulting in a maximum credit of $5,656.50.

Provide additional marriage penalty relief through higher threshold phase-out amounts for married couples filing joint returns

The provision increases the threshold phase-out amounts for married couples filing joint returns to $5,000 [9] above the threshold phase-out amounts for singles, surviving spouses, and heads of households for 2009 and 2010. For example, in 2009 the maximum credit of $3,043 for one qualifying child is available for those with earnings between $8,950 and $16,420 ($21,420 if married filing jointly). The credit begins to phase down at a rate of 15.98 percent of earnings above $16,420 ($21,420 if married filing jointly). The credit is phased down to $0 at $35,463 of earnings ($40,463 if married filing jointly).

Effective date

The provision is effective for taxable years beginning after December 31, 2008.

SENATE AMENDMENT

The Senate amendment is the same as the House bill.

CONFERENCE AGREEMENT

The conference agreement follows the House bill and the Senate amendment.

3. Increase of refundable portion of the child credit (sec. 1102 of the House bill, sec. 1003 of the Senate amendment, sec. 1003 of the conference agreement and sec. 24 of the Code)

PRESENT LAW

An individual may claim a tax credit for each qualifying child under the age of 17. The amount of the credit per child is $1,000 through 2010, and $500 thereafter. A child who is not a citizen, national, or resident of the United States cannot be a qualifying child.

The credit is phased out for individuals with income over certain threshold amounts. Specifically, the otherwise allowable child tax credit is reduced by $50 for each $1,000 (or fraction thereof) of

---

[9] The $5,000 is indexed for inflation in the case of taxable years beginning in 2010.

modified adjusted gross income over $75,000 for single individuals or heads of households, $110,000 for married individuals filing joint returns, and $55,000 for married individuals filing separate returns. For purposes of this limitation, modified adjusted gross income includes certain otherwise excludable income earned by U.S. citizens or residents living abroad or in certain U.S. territories.

The credit is allowable against the regular tax and the alternative minimum tax. To the extent the child credit exceeds the taxpayer's tax liability, the taxpayer is eligible for a refundable credit (the additional child tax credit) equal to 15 percent of earned income in excess of a threshold dollar amount (the "earned income" formula). The threshold dollar amount is $12,550 (for 2009), and is indexed for inflation.

Families with three or more children may determine the additional child tax credit using the "alternative formula," if this results in a larger credit than determined under the earned income formula. Under the alternative formula, the additional child tax credit equals the amount by which the taxpayer's social security taxes exceed the taxpayer's earned income tax credit ("EITC").

Earned income is defined as the sum of wages, salaries, tips, and other taxable employee compensation plus net self-employment earnings. Unlike the EITC, which also includes the preceding items in its definition of earned income, the additional child tax credit is based only on earned income to the extent it is included in computing taxable income. For example, some ministers' parsonage allowances are considered self-employment income and thus, are considered earned income for purposes of computing the EITC, but the allowances are excluded from gross income for individual income tax purposes and thus, are not considered earned income for purposes of the additional child tax credit.

Any credit or refund allowed or made to an individual under this provision (including to any resident of a U.S. possession) is not taken into account as income and shall not be taken into account as resources for the month of receipt and the following two months for purposes of determining eligibility of such individual or any other individual for benefits or assistance, or the amount or extent of benefits or assistance, under any Federal program or under any State or local program financed in whole or in part with Federal funds.

HOUSE BILL

The provision modifies the earned income formula for the determination of the refundable child credit to apply to 15 percent of earned income in excess of $0 for taxable years beginning in 2009 and 2010.

Effective date.—The provision is effective for taxable years beginning after December 31, 2008.

SENATE AMENDMENT

The Senate amendment is the same as the House bill except that the refundable child credit is calculated to apply to 15 percent of earned income in excess of $8,100 for taxable years beginning in 2009 and 2010.

CONFERENCE AGREEMENT

The conference agreement follows the House bill and the Senate amendment except that the refundable child credit is calculated to apply to 15 percent of earned income in excess of $3,000 for taxable years beginning in 2009 and 2010.

4. American Opportunity Tax credit (sec. 1201 of the House bill, sec. 1004 of the Senate amendment, sec. 1004 of the conference agreement, and sec. 25A of the Code)

PRESENT LAW

Individual taxpayers are allowed to claim a nonrefundable credit, the Hope credit, against Federal income taxes of up to $1,800 (for 2009) per eligible student per year for qualified tuition and related expenses paid for the first two years of the student's post-secondary education in a degree or certificate program.[10] The Hope credit rate is 100 percent on the first $1,200 of qualified tuition and related expenses, and 50 percent on the next $1,200 of qualified tuition and related expenses; these dollar amounts are indexed for inflation, with the amount rounded down to the next lowest multiple of $100. Thus, for example, a taxpayer who incurs $1,200 of qualified tuition and related expenses for an eligible student is eligible (subject to the adjusted gross income phaseout described below) for a $1,200 Hope credit. If a taxpayer incurs $2,400 of qualified tuition and related expenses for an eligible student, then he or she is eligible for a $1,800 Hope credit.

The Hope credit that a taxpayer may otherwise claim is phased out ratably for taxpayers with modified adjusted gross income between $50,000 and $60,000 ($100,000 and $120,000 for married taxpayers filing a joint return) for 2009. The adjusted gross income phaseout ranges are indexed for inflation, with the amount rounded down to the next lowest multiple of $1,000.

The qualified tuition and related expenses must be incurred on behalf of the taxpayer, the taxpayer's spouse, or a dependent of the taxpayer. The Hope credit is available with respect to an individual student for two taxable years, provided that the student has not completed the first two years of post-secondary education before the beginning of the second taxable year.

The Hope credit is available in the taxable year the expenses are paid, subject to the requirement that the education is furnished to the student during that year or during an academic period beginning during the first three months of the next taxable year. Qualified tuition and related expenses paid with the proceeds of a loan generally are eligible for the Hope credit. The repayment of a loan itself is not a qualified tuition or related expense.

A taxpayer may claim the Hope credit with respect to an eligible student who is not the taxpayer or the taxpayer's spouse (e.g., in cases in which the student is the taxpayer's child) only if the taxpayer claims the student as a dependent for the taxable year for which the credit is claimed. If a student is claimed as a dependent,

---

[10] Sec. 25A. The Hope credit generally may not be claimed against a taxpayer's alternative minimum tax liability. However, the credit may be claimed against a taxpayer's alternative minimum tax liability for taxable years beginning prior to January 1, 2009.

the student is not entitled to claim a Hope credit for that taxable year on the student's own tax return. If a parent (or other taxpayer) claims a student as a dependent, any qualified tuition and related expenses paid by the student are treated as paid by the parent (or other taxpayer) for purposes of determining the amount of qualified tuition and related expenses paid by such parent (or other taxpayer) under the provision. In addition, for each taxable year, a taxpayer may elect either the Hope credit, the Lifetime Learning credit, or an above-the-line deduction for qualified tuition and related expenses with respect to an eligible student.

The Hope credit is available for "qualified tuition and related expenses," which include tuition and fees (excluding nonacademic fees) required to be paid to an eligible educational institution as a condition of enrollment or attendance of an eligible student at the institution. Charges and fees associated with meals, lodging, insurance, transportation, and similar personal, living, or family expenses are not eligible for the credit. The expenses of education involving sports, games, or hobbies are not qualified tuition and related expenses unless this education is part of the student's degree program.

Qualified tuition and related expenses generally include only out-of-pocket expenses. Qualified tuition and related expenses do not include expenses covered by employer-provided educational assistance and scholarships that are not required to be included in the gross income of either the student or the taxpayer claiming the credit. Thus, total qualified tuition and related expenses are reduced by any scholarship or fellowship grants excludable from gross income under section 117 and any other tax-free educational benefits received by the student (or the taxpayer claiming the credit) during the taxable year. The Hope credit is not allowed with respect to any education expense for which a deduction is claimed under section 162 or any other section of the Code.

An eligible student for purposes of the Hope credit is an individual who is enrolled in a degree, certificate, or other program (including a program of study abroad approved for credit by the institution at which such student is enrolled) leading to a recognized educational credential at an eligible educational institution. The student must pursue a course of study on at least a half-time basis. A student is considered to pursue a course of study on at least a half-time basis if the student carries at least one half the normal full-time work load for the course of study the student is pursuing for at least one academic period that begins during the taxable year. To be eligible for the Hope credit, a student must not have been convicted of a Federal or State felony consisting of the possession or distribution of a controlled substance.

Eligible educational institutions generally are accredited postsecondary educational institutions offering credit toward a bachelor's degree, an associate's degree, or another recognized post-secondary credential. Certain proprietary institutions and post-secondary vocational institutions also are eligible educational institutions. To qualify as an eligible educational institution, an institution must be eligible to participate in Department of Education student aid programs.

Effective for taxable years beginning after December 31, 2010, the changes to the Hope credit made by the Economic Growth and Tax Relief Reconciliation Act of 2001 ("EGTRRA") no longer apply. The principal EGTRRA change scheduled to expire is the change that permitted a taxpayer to claim a Hope credit in the same year that he or she claims an exclusion from a Coverdell education savings account. Thus, after 2010, a taxpayer cannot claim a Hope credit in the same year he or she claims an exclusion from a Coverdell education savings account.

HOUSE BILL

The provision modifies the Hope credit for taxable years beginning in 2009 or 2010. The modified credit is referred to as the American Opportunity Tax credit. The allowable modified credit is up to $2,500 per eligible student per year for qualified tuition and related expenses paid for each of the first four years of the student's post-secondary education in a degree or certificate program. The modified credit rate is 100 percent on the first $2,000 of qualified tuition and related expenses, and 25 percent on the next $2,000 of qualified tuition and related expenses. For purposes of the modified credit, the definition of qualified tuition and related expenses is expanded to include course materials.

Under the provision, the modified credit is available with respect to an individual student for four years, provided that the student has not completed the first four years of post-secondary education before the beginning of the fourth taxable year. Thus, the modified credit, in addition to other modifications, extends the application of the Hope credit to two more years of post-secondary education.

The modified credit that a taxpayer may otherwise claim is phased out ratably for taxpayers with modified adjusted gross income between $80,000 and $90,000 ($160,000 and $180,000 for married taxpayers filing a joint return). The modified credit may be claimed against a taxpayer's alternative minimum tax liability.

Forty percent of a taxpayer's otherwise allowable modified credit is refundable. However, no portion of the modified credit is refundable if the taxpayer claiming the credit is a child to whom section 1(g) applies for such taxable year (generally, any child under age 18 or any child under age 24 who is a student providing less than one-half of his or her own support, who has at least one living parent and does not file a joint return).

In addition, the provision requires the Secretary of the Treasury to conduct two studies and submit a report to Congress on the results of those studies within one year after the date of enactment. The first study shall examine how to coordinate the Hope and Lifetime Learning credits with the Pell grant program. The second study shall examine requiring students to perform community service as a condition of taking their tuition and related expenses into account for purposes of the Hope and Lifetime Learning credits.

Effective date.—The provision is effective with respect to taxable years beginning after December 31, 2008.

The Senate amendment is the same as the House bill, except that the Senate amendment provides that only 30 percent of a taxpayer's otherwise allowable modified credit is refundable.

The conference agreement follows the House bill, with the following modifications. Under the conference agreement, bona fide residents of the U.S. possessions (American Samoa, Commonwealth of the Northern Mariana Islands, Commonwealth of Puerto Rico, Guam, Virgin Islands) are not permitted to claim the refundable portion of the American opportunity credit in the United States. Rather, a bona fide resident of a mirror code possession (Commonwealth of the Northern Mariana Islands, Guam, Virgin Islands) may claim the refundable portion of the credit in the possession in which the individual is a resident. Similarly, a bona fide resident of a non-mirror code possession (Commonwealth of Puerto Rico, American Samoa) may claim the refundable portion of the credit in the possession in which the individual is a resident, but only if that possession establishes a plan for permitting the claim under its internal law.

The conference agreement provides that the U.S. Treasury will make payments to the possessions in respect of credits allowable to their residents under their internal laws. Specifically, the U.S. Treasury will make payments to each mirror code possession in an amount equal to the aggregate amount of the refundable portion of the credits allowable by reason of the provision to that possession's residents against its income tax. This amount will be determined by the Treasury Secretary based on information provided by the government of the respective possession. To each possession that does not have a mirror code tax system, the U.S. Treasury will make two payments (for 2009 and 2010, respectively) in an amount estimated by the Secretary as being equal to the aggregate amount of the refundable portion of the credits that would have been allowed to residents of that possession if a mirror code tax system had been in effect in that possession. Accordingly, the amount of each payment to a non-mirror code possession will be an estimate of the aggregate amount of the refundable portion of the credits that would be allowed to the possession's residents if the credit provided by the provision to U.S. residents were provided by the possession to its residents. This payment will not be made to any U.S. possession unless that possession has a plan that has been approved by the Secretary under which the possession will promptly distribute the payment to its residents.

5. Temporarily allow computer technology and equipment as a qualified higher education expense for qualified tuition programs (sec. 1005 of the Senate amendment, sec. 1005 of the conference agreement, and sec. 529 of the Code)

Section 529 provides specified income tax and transfer tax rules for the treatment of accounts and contracts established under qualified tuition programs.[11] A qualified tuition program is a program established and maintained by a State or agency or instrumentality thereof, or by one or more eligible educational institutions, which satisfies certain requirements and under which a person may purchase tuition credits or certificates on behalf of a designated beneficiary that entitle the beneficiary to the waiver or payment of qualified higher education expenses of the beneficiary (a "prepaid tuition program"). In the case of a program established and maintained by a State or agency or instrumentality thereof, a qualified tuition program also includes a program under which a person may make contributions to an account that is established for the purpose of satisfying the qualified higher education expenses of the designated beneficiary of the account, provided it satisfies certain specified requirements (a "savings account program"). Under both types of qualified tuition programs, a contributor establishes an account for the benefit of a particular designated beneficiary to provide for that beneficiary's higher education expenses.

For this purpose, qualified higher education expenses means tuition, fees, books, supplies, and equipment required for the enrollment or attendance of a designated beneficiary at an eligible educational institution, and expenses for special needs services in the case of a special needs beneficiary that are incurred in connection with such enrollment or attendance. Qualified higher education expenses generally also include room and board for students who are enrolled at least half-time.

Contributions to a qualified tuition program must be made in cash. Section 529 does not impose a specific dollar limit on the amount of contributions, account balances, or prepaid tuition benefits relating to a qualified tuition account; however, the program is required to have adequate safeguards to prevent contributions in excess of amounts necessary to provide for the beneficiary's qualified higher education expenses. Contributions generally are treated as a completed gift eligible for the gift tax annual exclusion. Contributions are not tax deductible for Federal income tax purposes, although they may be deductible for State income tax purposes. Amounts in the account accumulate on a tax-free basis (i.e., income on accounts in the plan is not subject to current income tax).

Distributions from a qualified tuition program are excludable from the distributee's gross income to the extent that the total distribution does not exceed the qualified higher education expenses incurred for the beneficiary. If a distribution from a qualified tuition program exceeds the qualified higher education expenses incurred for the beneficiary, the portion of the excess that is treated as earnings generally is subject to income tax and an additional 10-percent tax. Amounts in a qualified tuition program may be rolled over to another qualified tuition program for the same beneficiary or for a member of the family of that beneficiary without income tax consequences.

In general, prepaid tuition contracts and tuition savings accounts established under a qualified tuition program involve prepayments or contributions made by one or more individuals for the

---

[11] For purposes of this description, the term "account" is used interchangeably to refer to a prepaid tuition benefit contract or a tuition savings account established pursuant to a qualified tuition program.

benefit of a designated beneficiary, with decisions with respect to the contract or account to be made by an individual who is not the designated beneficiary. Qualified tuition accounts or contracts generally require the designation of a person (generally referred to as an "account owner") whom the program administrator (oftentimes a third party administrator retained by the State or by the educational institution that established the program) may look to for decisions, recordkeeping, and reporting with respect to the account established for a designated beneficiary. The person or persons who make the contributions to the account need not be the same person who is regarded as the account owner for purposes of administering the account. Under many qualified tuition programs, the account owner generally has control over the account or contract, including the ability to change designated beneficiaries and to withdraw funds at any time and for any purpose. Thus, in practice, qualified tuition accounts or contracts generally involve a contributor, a designated beneficiary, an account owner (who oftentimes is not the contributor or the designated beneficiary), and an administrator of the account or contract.[12]

No provision.

The provision expands the definition of qualified higher education expenses for expenses paid or incurred in 2009 and 2010 to include expenses for certain computer technology and equipment to be used by the designated beneficiary while enrolled at an eligible educational institution.

Effective date.—The provision is effective for expenses paid or incurred after December 31, 2008.

The conference agreement follows the Senate amendment.

6. Modifications to homebuyer credit (sec. 1301 of the House bill, sec. 1006 of the Senate amendment, sec. 1006 of the conference agreement, and sec. 36 of the Code)

A taxpayer who is a first-time homebuyer is allowed a refundable tax credit equal to the lesser of $7,500 ($3,750 for a married individual filing separately) or 10 percent of the purchase price of a principal residence. The credit is allowed for the tax year in which the taxpayer purchases the home unless the taxpayer makes an election as described below. The credit is allowed for qualifying home purchases on or after April 9, 2008 and before July 1, 2009 (without regard to whether there was a binding contract to purchase prior to April 9, 2008).

---

[12] Section 529 refers to contributors and designated beneficiaries, but does not define or otherwise refer to the term account owner, which is a commonly used term among qualified tuition programs.

The credit phases out for individual taxpayers with modified adjusted gross income between $75,000 and $95,000 ($150,000 and $170,000 for joint filers) for the year of purchase.

A taxpayer is considered a first-time homebuyer if such individual had no ownership interest in a principal residence in the United States during the three-year period prior to the purchase of the home to which the credit applies.

No credit is allowed if the D.C. homebuyer credit is allowable for the taxable year the residence is purchased or a prior taxable year. A taxpayer is not permitted to claim the credit if the taxpayer's financing is from tax-exempt mortgage revenue bonds, if the taxpayer is a nonresident alien, or if the taxpayer disposes of the residence (or it ceases to be a principal residence) before the close of a taxable year for which a credit otherwise would be allowable.

The credit is recaptured ratably over fifteen years with no interest charge beginning in the second taxable year after the taxable year in which the home is purchased. For example, if the taxpayer purchases a home in 2008, the credit is allowed on the 2008 tax return, and repayments commence with the 2010 tax return. If the taxpayer sells the home (or the home ceases to be used as the principal residence of the taxpayer or the taxpayer's spouse) prior to complete repayment of the credit, any remaining credit repayment amount is due on the tax return for the year in which the home is sold (or ceases to be used as the principal residence). However, the credit repayment amount may not exceed the amount of gain from the sale of the residence to an unrelated person. For this purpose, gain is determined by reducing the basis of the residence by the amount of the credit to the extent not previously recaptured. No amount is recaptured after the death of a taxpayer. In the case of an involuntary conversion of the home, recapture is not accelerated if a new principal residence is acquired within a two-year period. In the case of a transfer of the residence to a spouse or to a former spouse incident to divorce, the transferee spouse (and not the transferor spouse) will be responsible for any future recapture.

An election is provided to treat a home purchased in the eligible period in 2009 as if purchased on December 31, 2008 for purposes of claiming the credit on the 2008 tax return and for establishing the beginning of the recapture period. Taxpayers may amend their returns for this purpose.

HOUSE BILL

The provision waives the recapture of the credit for qualifying home purchases after December 31, 2008 and before July 1, 2009. This waiver of recapture applies without regard to whether the taxpayer elects to treat the purchase in 2009 as occurring on December 31, 2008. If the taxpayer disposes of the home or the home otherwise ceases to be the principal residence of the taxpayer within 36 months from the date of purchase, the present law rules for recapture of the credit will still apply.

Effective date.—The provision applies to residences purchased after December 31, 2008.

SENATE AMENDMENT

The Senate amendment repeals the existing section 36 for purchases on or after the date of enactment of the American Recovery and Reinvestment Act of 2009.

A taxpayer is allowed a new nonrefundable tax credit equal to the lesser of $15,000 ($7,500 for a married individual filing separately) or 10 percent of the purchase price of a principal residence. The credit is allowed for the tax year in which the taxpayer purchases the home unless the taxpayer makes an election as described below. The credit is allowed for qualifying home purchases after the date of enactment of the American Recovery and Reinvestment Act and on or before the date that is one year after such date of enactment.

The credit is limited to the excess of regular tax liability plus alternative minimum tax liability over the sum of other nonrefundable personal credits.

No credit is allowed for any purchase for which the section 36 first-time homebuyer credit or the D.C. homebuyer credit is allowable. If a credit is allowed under this provision in the case of any individual (and such individual's spouse, if married) with respect to the purchase of any principal residence, no credit is allowed with respect to the purchase of any other principal residence by such individual or a spouse of such individual.

If the taxpayer disposes of the residence (or it ceases to be a principal residence) at any time within 24 months after the date on which the taxpayer purchased the residence, then the credit shall be subject to recapture for the taxable year in which such disposition occurred (or in which the taxpayer failed to occupy the residence as a principal residence). No amount is recaptured after the death of a taxpayer or in the case of a member of the Armed Forces of the United States on active duty who fails to meet the residency requirement pursuant to a military order and incident to a permanent change of station. In the case of an involuntary conversion of the home, recapture is not accelerated if a new principal residence is acquired within a two-year period. In the case of a transfer of the residence to a spouse or to a former spouse incident to divorce, the transferee spouse (and not the transferor spouse) will be responsible for any future recapture.

A further election is provided to treat a home purchased in the eligible period as if purchased on December 31, 2008 for purposes of claiming the credit on the 2008 tax return. Taxpayers may amend their returns for this purpose.

Effective date.—The provision applies to purchases after the date of enactment.

CONFERENCE AGREEMENT

The conference agreement extends the existing homebuyer credit for qualifying home purchases before December 1, 2009. In addition, it increases the maximum credit amount to $8,000 ($4,000 for a married individual filing separately) and waives the recapture of the credit for qualifying home purchases after December 31, 2008 and before December 1, 2009. This waiver of recapture applies without regard to whether the taxpayer elects to treat the purchase in 2009 as occurring on December 31, 2008. If the taxpayer disposes of the home or the home otherwise ceases to be the principal residence of the taxpayer within 36 months from the date of purchase, the present law rules for recapture of the credit will apply.

The conference agreement modifies the coordination with the first-time homebuyer credit for residents of the District of Columbia under section 1400C. No credit under section 1400C shall be allowed to any taxpayer with respect to the purchase of a residence during 2009 if a credit under section 36 is allowable to such taxpayer (or the taxpayer's spouse) with respect to such purchase. Taxpayers thus qualify for the more generous national first-time homebuyer credit rather than the D.C. homebuyer credit for qualifying purchases in 2009. No credit under section 36 is allowed for a taxpayer who claimed the D.C. homebuyer credit in any prior taxable year.

The conference agreement removes the prohibition on claiming the credit if the residence is financed by the proceeds of a mortgage revenue bond, a qualified mortgage issue the interest on which is exempt from tax under section 103.

Effective date.—The provision applies to residences purchased after December 31, 2008.

7. Election to substitute grants to States for low-income housing projects in lieu of low-income housing credit allocation for 2009 (secs. 1302 and 1711 of the House bill, secs. 1404 and 1602 of the conference agreement, and sec. 42 of the Code)

PRESENT LAW

In general

The low-income housing credit may be claimed over a 10-year period by owners of certain residential rental property for the cost of rental housing occupied by tenants having incomes below specified levels.[13] The amount of the credit for any taxable year in the credit period is the applicable percentage of the qualified basis of each qualified low-income building. The qualified basis of any qualified low-income building for any taxable year equals the applicable fraction of the eligible basis of the building.

Volume limits

A low-income housing credit is allowable only if the owner of a qualified building receives a housing credit allocation from the State or local housing credit agency. Generally, the aggregate credit authority provided annually to each State for calendar year 2009 is $2.30 per resident, with a minimum annual cap of $2,665,000 for certain small population States.[14] These amounts are indexed for inflation. Projects that also receive financing with proceeds of tax-exempt bonds issued subject to the private activity bond volume limit do not require an allocation of the low-income housing credit.

---

[13] Sec. 42.
[14] Rev. Proc. 2008–66.

Basic rule for Federal grants

The basis of a qualified building must be reduced by the amount of any federal grant with respect to such building.

HOUSE BILL

Low-income housing grant election amount

The Secretary of the Treasury shall make a grant to the State housing credit agency of each State in an amount equal to the low-income housing grant election amount.

The low-income housing grant election amount for a State is an amount elected by the State subject to certain limits. The maximum low-income housing grant election amount for a State may not exceed 85 percent of the product of ten and the sum of the State's: (1) unused housing credit ceiling for 2008; (2) any returns to the State during 2009 of credit allocations previously made by the State; (3) 40 percent of the State's 2009 credit allocation; and (4) 40 percent of the State's share of the national pool allocated in 2009, if any.

Grants under this provision are not taxable income to recipients.

Subawards to low-income housing credit buildings

A State receiving a grant under this provision is to use these monies to make subawards to finance the construction, or acquisition and rehabilitation of qualified low-income buildings as defined under the low-income housing credit. A subaward may be made to finance a qualified low-income building regardless of whether the building has an allocation of low-income housing credit. However, in the case of qualified low-income buildings without allocations of the low-income housing credit, the State housing credit agency must make a determination that the subaward with respect to such building will increase the total funds available to the State to build and rehabilitate affordable housing. In conjunction with this determination the State housing credit agency must establish a process in which applicants for the subawards must demonstrate good faith efforts to obtain investment commitments before the agency makes such subawards.

Any building receiving grant money from a subaward is required to satisfy the low-income housing credit rules. The State housing credit agency shall perform asset management functions to ensure compliance with the low-income housing credit rules and the long-term viability of buildings financed with these subawards. [15] Failure to satisfy the low-income housing credit rules will result in recapture enforced by means of liens or other methods that the Secretary of the Treasury (or delegate) deems appropriate. Any such recapture will be payable to the Secretary of the Treasury for deposit in the general fund of the Treasury.

Any grant funds not used to make subawards before January 1, 2011 and any grant monies from subawards returned on or after January 1, 2011 must be returned to the Secretary of the Treasury.

---

[15] The State housing credit agency may collect reasonable fees from subaward recipients to cover the expenses of the agency's asset management duties. Alternatively, the State housing credit agency may retain a third party to perform these asset management duties.

Basic rule for Federal grants

The grants received under this provision do not reduce tax basis of a qualified low-income building.

Reduction in low-income housing credit volume limit for 2009

The otherwise applicable low-income housing credit volume limit for any State for 2009 is reduced by the amount taken into account in determining the low-income housing grant election amount.

Appropriations

The provision appropriates to the Secretary of the Treasury such sums as may be necessary to carry out this provision.

Effective date

The provision is effective on the date of enactment.

SENATE AMENDMENT

No provision.

CONFERENCE AGREEMENT

The conference agreement follows the House bill.

8. Election to accelerate the low-income housing credit allocation (sec. 1903 of the Senate amendment)

PRESENT LAW

In general

The low-income housing credit may be claimed over a 10-year period by owners of certain residential rental property for the cost of rental housing occupied by tenants having incomes below specified levels.[16] The amount of the credit for any taxable year in the credit period is the applicable percentage of the qualified basis of each qualified low-income building. The qualified basis of any qualified low-income building for any taxable year equals the applicable fraction of the eligible basis of the building.

Volume limits

A low-income housing credit is allowable only if the owner of a qualified building receives a housing credit allocation from the State or local housing credit agency. Generally, the aggregate credit authority provided annually to each State for calendar year 2009 is $2.30 per resident, with a minimum annual cap of $2,665,000 for certain small population States.[17] These amounts are indexed for inflation. Projects that also receive financing with proceeds of tax-exempt bonds issued subject to the private activity bond volume limit do not require an allocation of the low-income housing credit.

HOUSE BILL

No provision.

---

[16] Sec. 42.
[17] Rev. Proc. 2008–66.

The provision allows a taxpayer election to double the amount of the otherwise allowable low-income housing tax credit with respect to a project for each of the taxpayer's first three taxable years beginning after December 31, 2008. The otherwise allowable low-income housing tax credit over the remaining credit period for the project with respect to a taxpayer making the election will be reduced on a pro rata basis by an amount equal to the acceleration in the first three years.

The election is only available for non-federally subsidized low-income housing projects placed in service after December 31, 2008 which are pursuant to a low-income housing credit allocation from a State housing credit ceiling before 2011 (e.g. an allocation of 2011 credit ceiling makes the project ineligible for the election). Further, the election is limited to low-income housing tax credit initial investments made pursuant to a binding agreement by the taxpayer after December 31, 2008 and before January 1, 2011. For example, a taxpayer could not make this election with respect to initial investments made pursuant to a binding agreement in existence on January 1, 2008 even though the building is not placed-in-service until after December 31, 2008.

The election shall be made in a time and manner prescribed by the Secretary of the Treasury (or his delegate). The election is irrevocable. In the case of a partnership the election can only be made at the partnership level, not by individual partners.

Effective date.—The provision is effective on the date of enactment.

CONFERENCE AGREEMENT

The conference agreement does not follow the Senate amendment.

9. Exclusion from gross income for unemployment compensation benefits (sec. 1007 of the Senate amendment, sec. 1007 of the conference agreement, and sec. 85 of the Code)

PRESENT LAW

An individual must include in gross income any unemployment compensation benefits received under the laws of the United States or any State.

HOUSE BILL

No provision.

SENATE AMENDMENT

The Senate amendment provides that up to $2,400 of unemployment compensation benefits received in 2009 are excluded from gross income by the recipient.

Effective date.—The provision is effective for taxable years beginning after December 31, 2008.

CONFERENCE AGREEMENT

The conference agreement follows the Senate amendment.

10. Deduction for interest on indebtedness for the purchase of qualified motor vehicles (sec. 1008 of the Senate amendment)

In the case of a taxpayer other than a corporation, no deduction is allowed for personal interest paid or accrued during the taxable year. Personal interest is all interest other than (1) interest paid or accrued on indebtedness properly allocable to a trade or business; (2) investment interest; (3) interest which is taken into account in computing income or loss from a passive activity of the taxpayer; (4) qualified home mortgage interest; (5) certain estate tax related interest; and (6) certain interest on educational loans.

No provision.

The Senate amendment provides an above-the-line deduction for qualified motor vehicle interest. Qualified motor vehicle interest means any interest paid or accrued during the taxable year on any indebtedness incurred after November 12, 2008 and before January 1, 2010 to acquire a qualified motor vehicle and secured by such vehicle. It also includes interest on any indebtedness secured by such qualified motor vehicle resulting from the refinancing of otherwise qualified motor vehicle interest. The amount of qualified indebtedness is limited to $49,500 ($24,750 in the case of a married individual filing separately). The deduction is phased out for taxpayers with modified adjusted gross income between $125,000 and $135,000 ($250,000 and $260,000 in the case of a joint return).

If the indebtedness includes the amounts of any State or local sales or excise taxes paid or accrued by the taxpayer in connection with the acquisition of a qualified motor vehicle for which a deduction is allowed under section 164(a)(6) (relating to the deduction of State and local sales or excise taxes on qualified motor vehicles), the aggregate amount of such indebtedness taken into account shall be reduced, but not below zero, by the amount of any such taxes for which such deduction is allowed.

A qualified motor vehicle means a passenger automobile or light truck acquired for use by the taxpayer and not for resale after November 12, 2008 and before January 1, 2010, the original use of which commences with the taxpayer and which has a gross vehicle weight rating of not more than 8,500 pounds.

Any person who is engaged in a trade or business and receives from any individual $600 or more of qualified motor vehicle interest for any calendar year is required to report certain information as the Secretary may prescribe and furnish information to such individual on or before January 31 of the year following the calendar year for which the interest is received.

Effective date.—The provision is effective for taxable years beginning after December 31, 2008.

The conference agreement does not follow the Senate amendment.

11. Deduction for State sales tax and excise tax on the purchase of qualified motor vehicles (sec. 1009 of the Senate amendment, sec. 1008 of the conference agreement, and secs. 63 and 164 of the Code)

PRESENT LAW

In general, a deduction from gross income is allowed for certain taxes for the taxable year within which the taxes are paid or accrued. These include State and local, and foreign, real property taxes; State and local personal property taxes; State, local, and foreign income, war profits, and excess profit taxes; generation skipping transfer taxes; environmental taxes imposed by section 59A; and taxes paid or accrued within the taxable year in carrying on a trade or business or an activity described in section 212 (relating to the expenses for production of income). At the election of the taxpayer for the taxable year, a taxpayer may deduct State and local sales taxes in lieu of State and local income taxes. No deduction is allowed for any general sales tax imposed with respect to an item at a rate other than the general rate of tax, except in the case of a lower rate of tax applicable to items of food, clothing, medical supplies, and motor vehicles. In the case of motor vehicles, if the rate of tax exceeds the general rate, such excess shall be disregarded and the general rate shall be treated as the rate of tax.

HOUSE BILL

No provision.

SENATE AMENDMENT

The Senate amendment provides an above-the-line deduction for qualified motor vehicle taxes. Qualified motor vehicle taxes include any State or local sales or excise tax imposed on the purchase of a qualified motor vehicle. A qualified motor vehicle means a passenger automobile or light truck acquired for use by the taxpayer and not for resale after November 12, 2008 and before January 1, 2010, the original use of which commences with the taxpayer and which has a gross vehicle weight rating of not more than 8,500 pounds.

The deduction is limited to sales tax of up to $49,500.

The deduction is phased out for taxpayers with modified adjusted gross income between $125,000 and $135,000 ($250,000 and $260,000 in the case of a joint return).

Notwithstanding other provisions of present law, qualified motor vehicle taxes are not treated as part of the cost of acquired property or, in the case of a disposition, as a reduction in the amount realized on the disposition.

A taxpayer who makes an election to deduct State and local sales taxes for the taxable year shall not be allowed the above-the-line deduction for qualified motor vehicle taxes.

537

If the indebtedness described in section 163(h)(5)(A) includes the amounts of any State or local sales or excise taxes paid or accrued by the taxpayer in connection with the acquisition of a qualified motor vehicle, the aggregate amount of such indebtedness taken into account shall be reduced, but not below zero, by the amount of any such taxes for which a deduction is allowed.

Effective date.—The provision is effective for taxable years beginning after December 31, 2008.

CONFERENCE AGREEMENT

The conference agreement does not include the House bill or the Senate amendment. The conference agreement provides a deduction for qualified motor vehicle taxes. It expands the definition of taxes allowed as a deduction to include qualified motor vehicle taxes paid or accrued within the taxable year. A taxpayer who itemizes and makes an election to deduct State and local sales taxes for qualified motor vehicles for the taxable year shall not be allowed the increased standard deduction for qualified motor vehicle taxes.

Qualified motor vehicle taxes include any State or local sales or excise tax imposed on the purchase of a qualified motor vehicle. A qualified motor vehicle means a passenger automobile, light truck, or motorcycle which has a gross vehicle weight rating of not more than 8,500 pounds, or a motor home acquired for use by the taxpayer after the date of enactment and before January 1, 2010, the original use of which commences with the taxpayer.

The deduction is limited to the tax on up to $49,500 of the purchase price of a qualified motor vehicle. The deduction is phased out for taxpayers with modified adjusted gross income between $125,000 and $135,000 ($250,000 and $260,000 in the case of a joint return).

Effective date.—The provision is effective for purchases on or after the date of enactment and before January 1, 2010.

12. Extend alternative minimum tax relief for individuals (secs. 1011 and 1012 of the Senate amendment, secs. 1011 and 1012 of the conference agreement, and secs. 26 and 55 of the Code)

PRESENT LAW

Present law imposes an alternative minimum tax ("AMT") on individuals. The AMT is the amount by which the tentative minimum tax exceeds the regular income tax. An individual's tentative minimum tax is the sum of (1) 26 percent of so much of the taxable excess as does not exceed $175,000 ($87,500 in the case of a married individual filing a separate return) and (2) 28 percent of the remaining taxable excess. The taxable excess is so much of the alternative minimum taxable income ("AMTI") as exceeds the exemption amount. The maximum tax rates on net capital gain and dividends used in computing the regular tax are used in computing the tentative minimum tax. AMTI is the individual's taxable income adjusted to take account of specified preferences and adjustments.

The exemption amounts are: (1) $69,950 for taxable years beginning in 2008 and $45,000 in taxable years beginning after 2008 in the case of married individuals filing a joint return and surviving spouses; (2) $46,200 for taxable years beginning in 2008 and $33,750 in taxable years beginning after 2008 in the case of other unmarried individuals; (3) $34,975 for taxable years beginning in 2008 and $22,500 in taxable years beginning after 2008 in the case of married individuals filing separate returns; and (4) $22,500 in the case of an estate or trust. The exemption amount is phased out by an amount equal to 25 percent of the amount by which the individual's AMTI exceeds (1) $150,000 in the case of married individuals filing a joint return and surviving spouses, (2) $112,500 in the case of other unmarried individuals, and (3) $75,000 in the case of married individuals filing separate returns or an estate or a trust. These amounts are not indexed for inflation.

Present law provides for certain nonrefundable personal tax credits (i.e., the dependent care credit, the credit for the elderly and disabled, the adoption credit, the child credit, the credit for interest on certain home mortgages, the Hope Scholarship and Lifetime Learning credits, the credit for savers, the credit for certain nonbusiness energy property, the credit for residential energy efficient property, the credit for plug-in electric drive motor vehicles; and the D.C. first-time homebuyer credit).

For taxable years beginning before 2009, the nonrefundable personal credits are allowed to the extent of the full amount of the individual's regular tax and alternative minimum tax.

For taxable years beginning after 2008, the nonrefundable personal credits (other than the adoption credit, the child credit, the credit for savers, the credit for residential energy efficient property, and the credit for plug-in electric drive motor vehicles) are allowed only to the extent that the individual's regular income tax liability exceeds the individual's tentative minimum tax, determined without regard to the minimum tax foreign tax credit. The adoption credit, the child credit, the credit for savers, the credit for residential energy efficient property, and the credit for plug-in electric drive motor vehicles are allowed to the full extent of the individual's regular tax and alternative minimum tax.[18]

HOUSE BILL

No provision.

SENATE AMENDMENT

The Senate amendment provides that the individual AMT exemption amount for taxable years beginning in 2009 is $70,950, in the case of married individuals filing a joint return and surviving spouses; (2) $46,700 in the case of other unmarried individuals; and (3) $35,475 in the case of married individuals filing separate returns.

For taxable years beginning in 2009, the provision allows an individual to offset the entire regular tax liability and alternative minimum tax liability by the nonrefundable personal credits.

Effective date.—The provision is effective for taxable years beginning in 2009.

---

[18] The rule applicable to the adoption credit and child credit is subject to the EGTRRA sunset.

539

The conference agreement follows the Senate amendment.

B. TAX INCENTIVES FOR BUSINESS

1. Special allowance for certain property acquired during 2009 and extension of election to accelerate AMT and research credits in lieu of bonus depreciation (sec. 1401 of the House bill, sec. 1201 of the Senate amendment, sec. 1201 of the conference agreement, and sec. 168(k) of the Code)

PRESENT LAW

An additional first-year depreciation deduction is allowed equal to 50 percent of the adjusted basis of qualified property placed in service during 2008 (and 2009 for certain longer-lived and transportation property).[19] The additional first-year depreciation deduction is allowed for both regular tax and alternative minimum tax purposes for the taxable year in which the property is placed in service.[20] The basis of the property and the depreciation allowances in the year of purchase and later years are appropriately adjusted to reflect the additional first-year depreciation deduction. In addition, there are no adjustments to the allowable amount of depreciation for purposes of computing a taxpayer's alternative minimum taxable income with respect to property to which the provision applies. The amount of the additional first-year depreciation deduction is not affected by a short taxable year. The taxpayer may elect out of additional first-year depreciation for any class of property for any taxable year.

The interaction of the additional first-year depreciation allowance with the otherwise applicable depreciation allowance may be illustrated as follows. Assume that in 2008, a taxpayer purchases new depreciable property and places it in service.[21] The property's cost is $1,000, and it is five-year property subject to the half-year convention. The amount of additional first-year depreciation allowed is $500. The remaining $500 of the cost of the property is deductible under the rules applicable to 5-year property. Thus, 20 percent, or $100, is also allowed as a depreciation deduction in 2008. The total depreciation deduction with respect to the property for 2008 is $600. The remaining $400 cost of the property is recovered under otherwise applicable rules for computing depreciation.

In order for property to qualify for the additional first-year depreciation deduction it must meet all of the following requirements. First, the property must be (1) property to which MACRS applies with an applicable recovery period of 20 years or less, (2) water utility property (as defined in section 168(e)(5)), (3) computer software other than computer software covered by section 197, or (4)

---

[19] Sec. 168(k). The additional first-year depreciation deduction is subject to the general rules regarding whether an item is deductible under section 162 or instead is subject to capitalization under section 263 or section 263A.

[20] However, the additional first-year depreciation deduction is not allowed for purposes of computing earnings and profits.

[21] Assume that the cost of the property is not eligible for expensing under section 179.

qualified leasehold improvement property (as defined in section 168(k)(3)).[22]

Second, the original use [23] of the property must commence with the taxpayer after December 31, 2007.[24] Third, the taxpayer must purchase the property within the applicable time period. Finally, the property must be placed in service after December 31, 2007, and before January 1, 2009. An extension of the placed in service date of one year (i.e., to January 1, 2010) is provided for certain property with a recovery period of ten years or longer and certain transportation property.[25] Transportation property is defined as tangible personal property used in the trade or business of transporting persons or property.

The applicable time period for acquired property is (1) after December 31, 2007, and before January 1, 2009, but only if no binding written contract for the acquisition is in effect before January 1, 2008, or (2) pursuant to a binding written contract which was entered into after December 31, 2007, and before January 1, 2009.[26] With respect to property that is manufactured, constructed, or produced by the taxpayer for use by the taxpayer, the taxpayer must begin the manufacture, construction, or production of the property after December 31, 2007, and before January 1, 2009. Property that is manufactured, constructed, or produced for the taxpayer by another person under a contract that is entered into prior to the manufacture, construction, or production of the property is considered to be manufactured, constructed, or produced by the taxpayer. For property eligible for the extended placed in service date, a special rule limits the amount of costs eligible for the additional first-year depreciation. With respect to such property, only the portion of the basis that is properly attributable to the costs incurred before January 1, 2009 ("progress expenditures") is eligible for the additional first-year depreciation.[27]

Property does not qualify for the additional first-year depreciation deduction when the user of such property (or a related party) would not have been eligible for the additional first-year depreciation deduction if the user (or a related party) were treated as the

---

[22] A special rule precludes the additional first-year depreciation deduction for any property that is required to be depreciated under the alternative depreciation system of MACRS.

[23] The term "original use" means the first use to which the property is put, whether or not such use corresponds to the use of such property by the taxpayer.

If in the normal course of its business a taxpayer sells fractional interests in property to unrelated third parties, then the original use of such property begins with the first user of each fractional interest (i.e., each fractional owner is considered the original user of its proportionate share of the property).

[24] A special rule applies in the case of certain leased property. In the case of any property that is originally placed in service by a person and that is sold to the taxpayer and leased back to such person by the taxpayer within three months after the date that the property was placed in service, the property would be treated as originally placed in service by the taxpayer not earlier than the date that the property is used under the leaseback.

If property is originally placed in service by a lessor (including by operation of section 168(k)(2)(D)(i)), such property is sold within three months after the date that the property was placed in service, and the user of such property does not change, then the property is treated as originally placed in service by the taxpayer not earlier than the date of such sale.

[25] In order for property to qualify for the extended placed in service date, the property is required to have an estimated production period exceeding one year and a cost exceeding $1 million.

[26] Property does not fail to qualify for the additional first-year depreciation merely because a binding written contract to acquire a component of the property is in effect prior to January 1, 2008.

[27] For purposes of determining the amount of eligible progress expenditures, it is intended that rules similar to sec. 46(d)(3) as in effect prior to the Tax Reform Act of 1986 shall apply.

owner. For example, if a taxpayer sells to a related party property that was under construction prior to January 1, 2008, the property does not qualify for the additional first-year depreciation deduction. Similarly, if a taxpayer sells to a related party property that was subject to a binding written contract prior to January 1, 2008, the property does not qualify for the additional first-year depreciation deduction. As a further example, if a taxpayer (the lessee) sells property in a sale-leaseback arrangement, and the property otherwise would not have qualified for the additional first-year depreciation deduction if it were owned by the taxpayer-lessee, then the lessor is not entitled to the additional first-year depreciation deduction.

The limitation on the amount of depreciation deductions allowed with respect to certain passenger automobiles (sec. 280F) is increased in the first year by $8,000 for automobiles that qualify (and do not elect out of the increased first year deduction). The $8,000 increase is not indexed for inflation.

Corporations otherwise eligible for additional first year depreciation under section 168(k) may elect to claim additional research or minimum tax credits in lieu of claiming depreciation under section 168(k) for "eligible qualified property" placed in service after March 31, 2008 and before December 31, 2008.[28] A corporation making the election forgoes the depreciation deductions allowable under section 168(k) and instead increases the limitation under section 38(c) on the use of research credits or section 53(c) on the use of minimum tax credits.[29] The increases in the allowable credits are treated as refundable for purposes of this provision. The depreciation for qualified property is calculated for both regular tax and AMT purposes using the straight-line method in place of the method that would otherwise be used absent the election under this provision.

The research credit or minimum tax credit limitation is increased by the bonus depreciation amount, which is equal to 20 percent of bonus depreciation[30] for certain eligible qualified property that could be claimed absent an election under this provision. Generally, eligible qualified property included in the calculation is bonus depreciation property that meets the following requirements: (1) the original use of the property must commence with the taxpayer after March 31, 2008; (2) the taxpayer must purchase the property either (a) after March 31, 2008, and before January 1, 2009, but only if no binding written contract for the acquisition is in effect before April 1, 2008,[31] or (b) pursuant to a binding written contract which was entered into after March 31, 2008, and before

---

[28] Sec. 168(k)(4). In the case of an electing corporation that is a partner in a partnership, the corporate partner's distributive share of partnership items is determined as if section 168(k) does not apply to any eligible qualified property and the straight line method is used to calculate depreciation of such property.

[29] Special rules apply to an applicable partnership.

[30] For this purpose, bonus depreciation is the difference between (i) the aggregate amount of depreciation for all eligible qualified property determined if section 168(k)(1) applied using the most accelerated depreciation method (determined without regard to this provision), and shortest life allowable for each property, and (ii) the amount of depreciation that would be determined if section 168(k)(1) did not apply using the same method and life for each property.

[31] In the case of passenger aircraft, the written binding contract limitation does not apply.

January 1, 2009;[32] and (3) the property must be placed in service after March 31, 2008, and before January 1, 2009 (January 1, 2010 for certain longer-lived and transportation property).

The bonus depreciation amount is limited to the lesser of: (1) $30 million, or (2) six percent of the sum of research credit carryforwards from taxable years beginning before January 1, 2006 and minimum tax credits allocable to the adjusted minimum tax imposed for taxable years beginning before January 1, 2006. All corporations treated as a single employer under section 52(a) are treated as one taxpayer for purposes of the limitation, as well as for electing the application of this provision.

HOUSE BILL

The provision extends the additional first-year depreciation deduction for one year, generally through 2009 (through 2010 for certain longer-lived and transportation property).[33]

Effective date.—The provision is effective for property placed in service after December 31, 2008.

SENATE AMENDMENT

The provision extends the additional first-year depreciation deduction for one year, generally through 2009 (through 2010 for certain longer-lived and transportation property).

The provision generally permits corporations to increase the research credit or minimum tax credit limitation by the bonus depreciation amount with respect to certain property placed in service in 2009 (2010 in the case of certain longer-lived and transportation property). The provision applies with respect to extension property, which is defined as property that is eligible qualified property solely because it meets the requirements under the extension of the special allowance for certain property acquired during 2009.

Under the provision, a taxpayer that has made an election to increase the research credit or minimum tax credit limitation for eligible qualified property for its first taxable year ending after March 31, 2008, may choose not to make this election for extension property. Further, the provision allows a taxpayer that has not made an election for eligible qualified property for its first taxable year ending after March 31, 2008, to make the election for extension property for its first taxable year ending after December 31, 2008, and for each subsequent year. In the case of a taxpayer electing to increase the research or minimum tax credit for both eligible qualified property and extension property, a separate bonus depreciation amount, maximum amount, and maximum increase amount is computed and applied to each group of property.[34]

---

[32] Special rules apply to property manufactured, constructed, or produced by the taxpayer for use by the taxpayer.

[33] The provision does not modify the property eligible for the election to accelerate AMT and research credits in lieu of bonus depreciation under section 168(k)(4). However, the provision includes a technical amendment to section 168(k)(4)(D) providing that no written binding contract for the acquisition of eligible qualified property may be in effect before April 1, 2008 (effective for taxable years ending after March 31, 2008).

[34] In computing the maximum amount, the maximum increase amount for extension property is reduced by bonus depreciation amounts for preceding taxable years only with respect to extension property.

Effective date.—The extension of the additional first-year depreciation deduction is generally effective for property placed in service after December 31, 2008.

The extension of the election to accelerate AMT and research credits in lieu of bonus depreciation is effective for taxable years ending after December 31, 2008.

CONFERENCE AGREEMENT

The conference agreement follows the Senate amendment.

2. Temporary increase in limitations on expensing of certain depreciable business assets (sec. 1402 of the House bill, sec. 1202 of the Senate amendment, sec. 1202 of the conference agreement, and sec. 179 of the Code)

PRESENT LAW

In lieu of depreciation, a taxpayer with a sufficiently small amount of annual investment may elect to deduct (or "expense") such costs under section 179. Present law provides that the maximum amount a taxpayer may expense for taxable years beginning in 2008 is $250,000 of the cost of qualifying property placed in service for the taxable year.[35] For taxable years beginning in 2009 and 2010, the limitation is $125,000. In general, qualifying property is defined as depreciable tangible personal property that is purchased for use in the active conduct of a trade or business. Off-the-shelf computer software placed in service in taxable years beginning before 2011 is treated as qualifying property. For taxable years beginning in 2008, the $250,000 amount is reduced (but not below zero) by the amount by which the cost of qualifying property placed in service during the taxable year exceeds $800,000. For taxable years beginning in 2009 and 2010, the $125,000 amount is reduced (but not below zero) by the amount by which the cost of qualifying property placed in service during the taxable year exceeds $500,000. The $125,000 and $500,000 amounts are indexed for inflation in taxable years beginning in 2009 and 2010.

The amount eligible to be expensed for a taxable year may not exceed the taxable income for a taxable year that is derived from the active conduct of a trade or business (determined without regard to this provision). Any amount that is not allowed as a deduction because of the taxable income limitation may be carried forward to succeeding taxable years (subject to similar limitations). No general business credit under section 38 is allowed with respect to any amount for which a deduction is allowed under section 179. An expensing election is made under rules prescribed by the Secretary.[36]

---

[35] Additional section 179 incentives are provided with respect to qualified property meeting applicable requirements that is used by a business in an empowerment zone (sec. 1397A) or a renewal community (sec. 1400J), qualified section 179 Gulf Opportunity Zone property (sec. 1400N(e)), qualified Recovery Assistance property placed in service in the Kansas disaster area (Pub. L. No. 110–234, sec. 15345 (2008)), and qualified disaster assistance property (sec. 179(e)).

[36] Sec. 179(c)(1). Under Treas. Reg. sec. 1.179–5, applicable to property placed in service in taxable years beginning after 2002 and before 2008, a taxpayer is permitted to make or revoke an election under section 179 without the consent of the Commissioner on an amended Federal tax return for that taxable year. This amended return must be filed within the time prescribed by law for filing an amended return for the taxable year. T.D. 9209, July 12, 2005.

For taxable years beginning in 2011 and thereafter (or before 2003), the following rules apply. A taxpayer with a sufficiently small amount of annual investment may elect to deduct up to $25,000 of the cost of qualifying property placed in service for the taxable year. The $25,000 amount is reduced (but not below zero) by the amount by which the cost of qualifying property placed in service during the taxable year exceeds $200,000. The $25,000 and $200,000 amounts are not indexed for inflation. In general, qualifying property is defined as depreciable tangible personal property that is purchased for use in the active conduct of a trade or business (not including off-the-shelf computer software). An expensing election may be revoked only with consent of the Commissioner.[37]

HOUSE BILL

The provision extends the $250,000 and $800,000 amounts to taxable years beginning in 2009.

Effective date.—The provision is effective for taxable years beginning after December 31, 2008.

SENATE AMENDMENT

The Senate amendment is the same as the House bill.

CONFERENCE AGREEMENT

The conference agreement follows the House bill and the Senate amendment.

3. Five-year carryback of operating losses (secs. 1411 and 1412 of the House bill, secs. 1211 and 1212 of the Senate amendment, sec. 1211 of the conference agreement, and sec. 172 of the Code)

PRESENT LAW

Under present law, a net operating loss ("NOL") generally means the amount by which a taxpayer's business deductions exceed its gross income. In general, an NOL may be carried back two years and carried over 20 years to offset taxable income in such years.[38] NOLs offset taxable income in the order of the taxable years to which the NOL may be carried.[39]

The alternative minimum tax rules provide that a taxpayer's NOL deduction cannot reduce the taxpayer's alternative minimum taxable income ("AMTI") by more than 90 percent of the AMTI.

Different rules apply with respect to NOLs arising in certain circumstances. A three-year carryback applies with respect to NOLs (1) arising from casualty or theft losses of individuals, or (2) attributable to Presidentially declared disasters for taxpayers engaged in a farming business or a small business. A five-year carryback applies to NOLs (1) arising from a farming loss (regardless of whether the loss was incurred in a Presidentially declared disaster area), (2) certain amounts related to Hurricane Katrina, Gulf Opportunity Zone, and Midwestern Disaster Area, or (3) quali-

---

[37] Sec. 179(c)(2).
[38] Sec. 172(b)(1)(A).
[39] Sec. 172(b)(2).

fied disaster losses.[40] Special rules also apply to real estate investment trusts (no carryback), specified liability losses (10-year carryback), and excess interest losses (no carryback to any year preceding a corporate equity reduction transaction). Additionally, a special rule applies to certain electric utility companies.

In the case of a life insurance company, present law allows a deduction for the operations loss carryovers and carrybacks to the taxable year, in lieu of the deduction for net operation losses allowed to other corporations.[41] A life insurance company is permitted to treat a loss from operations (as defined under section 810(c)) for any taxable year as an operations loss carryback to each of the three taxable years preceding the loss year and an operations loss carryover to each of the 15 taxable years following the loss year.[42] Special rules apply to new life insurance companies.

HOUSE BILL

The House bill provides an election[43] to increase the present-law carryback period for an applicable 2008 or 2009 NOL from two years to any whole number of years elected by the taxpayer which is more than two and less than six. An applicable NOL is the taxpayer's NOL for any taxable year ending in 2008 or 2009, or if elected by the taxpayer, the NOL for any taxable year beginning in 2008 or 2009. If an election is made to increase the carryback period, the applicable NOL is permanently reduced by 10 percent.

These provisions may be illustrated by the following example. Taxpayer incurs a $100 NOL for its taxable year ended January 31, 2008 and elects to carryback the NOL five years to its taxable year ended January 31, 2003. Under the provision, Taxpayer must first permanently reduce the NOL by 10 percent, or $10, and then may carryback the $90 NOL to its taxable year ended January 31, 2003.

The provision also suspends the 90-percent limitation on the use of any alternative tax NOL deduction attributable to carrybacks of losses from taxable years ending during 2008 or 2009, and carryovers of losses to such taxable years (this rule applies to taxable years beginning in 2008 or 2009 if an election is in place to use such years as applicable NOLs).

For life insurance companies, the provision provides an election to increase the present-law carryback period for an applicable loss from operations from three years to four or five years. An applicable loss from operations is the taxpayer's loss from operations for any taxable year ending in 2008 or 2009, or if elected by the taxpayer, the loss from operations for any taxable year beginning in 2008 or 2009. If an election is made to increase the carryback period, the applicable loss from operations is permanently reduced by 10 percent.

---

[40] Sec. 172(b)(1)(J).
[41] Secs. 810, 805(a)(5).
[42] Sec. 810(b)(1).
[43] For all elections under this provision, the common parent of a group of corporations filing a consolidated return makes the election, which is binding on all such corporations.

The provision does not apply to: (1) any taxpayer if (a) the Federal Government acquires, at any time,[44] an equity interest in the taxpayer pursuant to the Emergency Economic Stabilization Act of 2008, or (b) the Federal Government acquires, at any time, any warrant (or other right) to acquire any equity interest with respect to the taxpayer pursuant to such Act; (2) the Federal National Mortgage Association and the Federal Home Loan Mortgage Corporation; or (3) any taxpayer that in 2008 or 2009[45] is a member of the same affiliated group (as defined in section 1504 without regard to subsection (b) thereof) as a taxpayer to which the provision does not otherwise apply.

Effective date.—The provision is generally effective for net operating losses arising in taxable years ending after December 31, 2007. The modification to the alternative tax NOL deduction applies to taxable years ending after 1997.[46] The modification with respect to operating loss deductions of life insurance companies applies to losses from operations arising in taxable years ending after December 31, 2007.

For an NOL or loss from operations for a taxable year ending before the enactment of the provision, the provision includes the following transition rules: (1) any election to waive the carryback period under either sections 172(b)(3) or 810(b)(3) with respect to such loss may be revoked before the applicable date; (2) any election to increase the carryback period under this provision is treated as timely made if made before the applicable date; and (3) any application for a tentative carryback adjustment under section 6411(a) with respect to such loss is treated as timely filed if filed before the applicable date. For purposes of the transition rules, the applicable date is the date which is 60 days after the date of the enactment of the provision.

SENATE AMENDMENT

The Senate amendment is generally the same as the House bill, except that the Senate amendment does not include the permanent reduction of the NOL for taxpayers electing to increase the carryback period.

Effective date.—The effective date follows the House bill.

CONFERENCE AGREEMENT

The conference agreement provides an eligible small business with an election[47] to increase the present-law carryback period for an applicable 2008 NOL from two years to any whole number of years elected by the taxpayer that is more than two and less than

---

[44] For example, if the Federal government acquires an equity interest in the taxpayer during 2010, or in later years, the taxpayer is not entitled to the extended carryback rules under this provision. If the carryback has previously been claimed, amended filings may be necessary to reflect this disallowance.

[45] For example, a taxpayer with an NOL in 2008 that in 2010 joins an affiliated group with a member in which the Federal Government has an equity interest pursuant to the Emergency Economic Stabilization Act of 2008 may not utilize the extended carryback rules under this provision with regard to the 2008 NOL. The taxpayer is required to amend prior filings to reflect the permitted carryback period.

[46] NOL deductions from as early as taxable years ending after 1997 may be carried forward to 2008 and utilize the provision suspending the 90 percent limitation on alternative tax NOL deductions.

[47] For all elections under this provision, the common parent of a group of corporations filing a consolidated return makes the election, which is binding on all such corporations.

six. An eligible small business is a taxpayer meeting a $15,000,000 gross receipts test.[48] An applicable NOL is the taxpayer's NOL for any taxable year ending in 2008, or if elected by the taxpayer, the NOL for any taxable year beginning in 2008. However, any election under this provision may be made only with respect to one taxable year.

Effective date.—The conference agreement provision is effective for net operating losses arising in taxable years ending after December 31, 2007.

For an NOL for a taxable year ending before the enactment of the provision, the provision includes the following transition rules: (1) any election to waive the carryback period under either section 172(b)(3) with respect to such loss may be revoked before the applicable date; (2) any election to increase the carryback period under this provision is treated as timely made if made before the applicable date; and (3) any application for a tentative carryback adjustment under section 6411(a) with respect to such loss is treated as timely filed if filed before the applicable date. For purposes of the transition rules, the applicable date is the date which is 60 days after the date of the enactment of the provision.

4. Estimated tax payments (sec. 1212 of the conference agreement and sec. 6654 of the Code)

PRESENT LAW

Under present law, the income tax system is designed to ensure that taxpayers pay taxes throughout the year based on their income and deductions. To the extent that tax is not collected through withholding, taxpayers are required to make quarterly estimated payments of tax, the amount of which is determined by reference to the required annual payment. The required annual payment is the lesser of 90 percent of the tax shown on the return or 100 percent of the tax shown on the return for the prior taxable year (110 percent if the adjusted gross income for the preceding year exceeded $150,000). An underpayment results if the required payment exceeds the amount (if any) of the installment paid on or before the due date of the installment. The period of the underpayment runs from the due date of the installment to the earlier of (1) the 15th day of the fourth month following the close of the taxable year or (2) the date on which each portion of the underpayment is made. If a taxpayer fails to pay the required estimated tax payments under the rules, a penalty is imposed in an amount determined by applying the underpayment interest rate to the amount of the underpayment for the period of the underpayment. The penalty for failure to pay estimated tax is the equivalent of interest, which is based on the time value of money.

Taxpayers are not liable for a penalty for the failure to pay estimated tax in certain circumstances. The statute provides exceptions for U.S. persons who did not have a tax liability the preceding year, if the tax shown on the return for the taxable year (or, if no return is filed, the tax), reduced by withholding, is less than

---

[48] For this purpose, the gross receipt test of sec. 448(c) is applied by substituting $15,000,000 for $5,000,000 each place it appears.

$1,000, or the taxpayer is a recently retired or disabled person who satisfies the reasonable cause exception.

HOUSE BILL

No provision.

SENATE AMENDMENT

No provision.

CONFERENCE AGREEMENT

The conference agreement provides that the required annual estimated tax payments of a qualified individual for taxable years beginning in 2009 is not greater than 90 percent of the tax liability shown on the tax return for the preceding taxable year. A qualified individual means any individual if the adjusted gross income shown on the tax return for the preceding taxable year is less than $500,000 ($250,000 if married filing separately) and the individual certifies that at least 50 percent of the gross income shown on the return for the preceding taxable year was income from a small trade or business. For purposes of this provision, a small trade or business means any trade or business that employed no more than 500 persons, on average, during the calendar year ending in or with the preceding taxable year.

Effective date.—The proposal is effective on the date of enactment.

5. Modification of work opportunity tax credit (sec. 1421 of the House bill, sec. 1221 of the Senate amendment, sec. 1221 of the conference agreement, and sec. 51 of the Code)

PRESENT LAW

In general

The work opportunity tax credit is available on an elective basis for employers hiring individuals from one or more of nine targeted groups. The amount of the credit available to an employer is determined by the amount of qualified wages paid by the employer. Generally, qualified wages consist of wages attributable to service rendered by a member of a targeted group during the one-year period beginning with the day the individual begins work for the employer (two years in the case of an individual in the long-term family assistance recipient category).

Targeted groups eligible for the credit

Generally an employer is eligible for the credit only for qualified wages paid to members of a targeted group.

(1) Families receiving TANF

An eligible recipient is an individual certified by a designated local employment agency (e.g., a State employment agency) as being a member of a family eligible to receive benefits under the Temporary Assistance for Needy Families Program ("TANF") for a period of at least nine months, part of which is during the 18-month period ending on the hiring date. For these purposes, members of the family are defined to include only those individuals taken into account for purposes of determining eligibility for the TANF.

(2) Qualified veteran

There are two subcategories of qualified veterans related to eligibility for Food stamps and compensation for a service-connected disability.

Food stamps

A qualified veteran is a veteran who is certified by the designated local agency as a member of a family receiving assistance under a food stamp program under the Food Stamp Act of 1977 for a period of at least three months, part of which is during the 12-month period ending on the hiring date. For these purposes, members of a family are defined to include only those individuals taken into account for purposes of determining eligibility for a food stamp program under the Food Stamp Act of 1977.

Entitled to compensation for a service-connected disability

A qualified veteran also includes an individual who is certified as entitled to compensation for a service-connected disability and: (1) having a hiring date which is not more than one year after having been discharged or released from active duty in the Armed Forces of the United States; or (2) having been unemployed for six months or more (whether or not consecutive) during the one-year period ending on the date of hiring.

Definitions

For these purposes, being entitled to compensation for a service-connected disability is defined with reference to section 101 of Title 38, U.S. Code, which means having a disability rating of 10 percent or higher for service connected injuries.

For these purposes, a veteran is an individual who has served on active duty (other than for training) in the Armed Forces for more than 180 days or who has been discharged or released from active duty in the Armed Forces for a service-connected disability. However, any individual who has served for a period of more than 90 days during which the individual was on active duty (other than for training) is not a qualified veteran if any of this active duty occurred during the 60-day period ending on the date the individual was hired by the employer. This latter rule is intended to prevent employers who hire current members of the armed services (or those departed from service within the last 60 days) from receiving the credit.

(3) Qualified ex-felon

A qualified ex-felon is an individual certified as: (1) having been convicted of a felony under any State or Federal law; and (2) having a hiring date within one year of release from prison or the date of conviction.

(4) Designated community residents

A designated community resident is an individual certified as being at least age 18 but not yet age 40 on the hiring date and as having a principal place of abode within an empowerment zone, enterprise community, renewal community or a rural renewal community. For these purposes, a rural renewal county is a county outside a metropolitan statistical area (as defined by the Office of Management and Budget) which had a net population loss during the five-year periods 1990–1994 and 1995–1999. Qualified wages do not include wages paid or incurred for services performed after the individual moves outside an empowerment zone, enterprise community, renewal community or a rural renewal community.

(5) Vocational rehabilitation referral

A vocational rehabilitation referral is an individual who is certified by a designated local agency as an individual who has a physical or mental disability that constitutes a substantial handicap to employment and who has been referred to the employer while receiving, or after completing: (a) vocational rehabilitation services under an individualized, written plan for employment under a State plan approved under the Rehabilitation Act of 1973; (b) under a rehabilitation plan for veterans carried out under Chapter 31 of Title 38, U.S. Code; or (c) an individual work plan developed and implemented by an employment network pursuant to subsection (g) of section 1148 of the Social Security Act. Certification will be provided by the designated local employment agency upon assurances from the vocational rehabilitation agency that the employee has met the above conditions.

(6) Qualified summer youth employee

A qualified summer youth employee is an individual: (a) who performs services during any 90-day period between May 1 and September 15; (b) who is certified by the designated local agency as being 16 or 17 years of age on the hiring date; (c) who has not been an employee of that employer before; and (d) who is certified by the designated local agency as having a principal place of abode within an empowerment zone, enterprise community, or renewal community (as defined under Subchapter U of Subtitle A, Chapter 1 of the Internal Revenue Code). As with designated community residents, no credit is available on wages paid or incurred for service performed after the qualified summer youth moves outside of an empowerment zone, enterprise community, or renewal community. If, after the end of the 90-day period, the employer continues to employ a youth who was certified during the 90-day period as a member of another targeted group, the limit on qualified first year wages will take into account wages paid to the youth while a qualified summer youth employee.

(7) Qualified food stamp recipient

A qualified food stamp recipient is an individual at least age 18 but not yet age 40 certified by a designated local employment agency as being a member of a family receiving assistance under a food stamp program under the Food Stamp Act of 1977 for a period of at least six months ending on the hiring date. In the case

551

of families that cease to be eligible for food stamps under section
6(o) of the Food Stamp Act of 1977, the six-month requirement is
replaced with a requirement that the family has been receiving
food stamps for at least three of the five months ending on the date
of hire. For these purposes, members of the family are defined to
include only those individuals taken into account for purposes of
determining eligibility for a food stamp program under the Food
Stamp Act of 1977.

(8) Qualified SSI recipient

A qualified SSI recipient is an individual designated by a local
agency as receiving supplemental security income ("SSI") benefits
under Title XVI of the Social Security Act for any month ending
within the 60-day period ending on the hiring date.

(9) Long-term family assistance recipients

A qualified long-term family assistance recipient is an individual certified by a designated local agency as being: (a) a member
of a family that has received family assistance for at least 18 consecutive months ending on the hiring date; (b) a member of a family that has received such family assistance for a total of at least
18 months (whether or not consecutive) after August 5, 1997 (the
date of enactment of the welfare-to-work tax credit [49] if the individual is hired within two years after the date that the 18-month
total is reached; or (c) a member of a family who is no longer eligible for family assistance because of either Federal or State time
limits, if the individual is hired within two years after the Federal
or State time limits made the family ineligible for family assistance.

Qualified wages

Generally, qualified wages are defined as cash wages paid by
the employer to a member of a targeted group. The employer's deduction for wages is reduced by the amount of the credit.

For purposes of the credit, generally, wages are defined by reference to the FUTA definition of wages contained in sec. 3306(b)
(without regard to the dollar limitation therein contained). Special
rules apply in the case of certain agricultural labor and certain
railroad labor.

Calculation of the credit

The credit available to an employer for qualified wages paid to
members of all targeted groups except for long-term family assistance recipients equals 40 percent (25 percent for employment of
400 hours or less) of qualified first-year wages. Generally, qualified
first-year wages are qualified wages (not in excess of $6,000) attrib-
utable to service rendered by a member of a targeted group during
the one-year period beginning with the day the individual began
work for the employer. Therefore, the maximum credit per employee is $2,400 (40 percent of the first $6,000 of qualified first-
year wages). With respect to qualified summer youth employees,

---

[49] The welfare-to-work tax credit was consolidated into the work opportunity tax credit in the
Tax Relief and Health Care Act of 2006, for qualified individuals who begin to work for an employer after December 31, 2006.

the maximum credit is $1,200 (40 percent of the first $3,000 of qualified first-year wages). Except for long-term family assistance recipients, no credit is allowed for second-year wages.

In the case of long-term family assistance recipients, the credit equals 40 percent (25 percent for employment of 400 hours or less) of $10,000 for qualified first-year wages and 50 percent of the first $10,000 of qualified second-year wages. Generally, qualified second-year wages are qualified wages (not in excess of $10,000) attributable to service rendered by a member of the long-term family assistance category during the one-year period beginning on the day after the one-year period beginning with the day the individual began work for the employer. Therefore, the maximum credit per employee is $9,000 (40 percent of the first $10,000 of qualified first-year wages plus 50 percent of the first $10,000 of qualified second-year wages).

In the case of a qualified veteran who is entitled to compensation for a service connected disability, the credit equals 40 percent of $12,000 of qualified first-year wages. This expanded definition of qualified first-year wages does not apply to the veterans qualified with reference to a food stamp program, as defined under present law.

Certification rules

An individual is not treated as a member of a targeted group unless: (1) on or before the day on which an individual begins work for an employer, the employer has received a certification from a designated local agency that such individual is a member of a targeted group; or (2) on or before the day an individual is offered employment with the employer, a pre-screening notice is completed by the employer with respect to such individual, and not later than the 28th day after the individual begins work for the employer, the employer submits such notice, signed by the employer and the individual under penalties of perjury, to the designated local agency as part of a written request for certification. For these purposes, a pre-screening notice is a document (in such form as the Secretary may prescribe) which contains information provided by the individual on the basis of which the employer believes that the individual is a member of a targeted group.

Minimum employment period

No credit is allowed for qualified wages paid to employees who work less than 120 hours in the first year of employment.

Other rules

The work opportunity tax credit is not allowed for wages paid to a relative or dependent of the taxpayer. No credit is allowed for wages paid to an individual who is a more than fifty-percent owner of the entity. Similarly, wages paid to replacement workers during a strike or lockout are not eligible for the work opportunity tax credit. Wages paid to any employee during any period for which the employer received on-the-job training program payments with respect to that employee are not eligible for the work opportunity tax credit. The work opportunity tax credit generally is not allowed for wages paid to individuals who had previously been employed by the employer. In addition, many other technical rules apply.

Expiration

The work opportunity tax credit is not available for individuals who begin work for an employer after August 31, 2011.

HOUSE BILL

In general

The provision creates a new targeted group for the work opportunity tax credit. That new category is unemployed veterans and disconnected youth who begin work for the employer in 2009 or 2010.

An unemployed veteran is defined as an individual certified by the designated local agency as someone who: (1) has served on active duty (other than for training) in the Armed Forces for more than 180 days or who has been discharged or released from active duty in the Armed Forces for a service-connected disability; (2) has been discharged or released from active duty in the Armed Forces during 2008, 2009, or 2010; and (3) has received unemployment compensation under State or Federal law for not less than four weeks during the one-year period ending on the hiring date.

A disconnected youth is defined as an individual certified by the designated local agency as someone: (1) at least age 16 but not yet age 25 on the hiring date; (2) not regularly attending any secondary, technical, or post-secondary school during the six-month period preceding the hiring date; (3) not regularly employed during the six-month period preceding the hiring date; and (4) not readily employable by reason of lacking a sufficient number of skills.

Effective date

The provisions are effective for individuals who begin work for an employer after December 31, 2008.

SENATE AMENDMENT

The Senate amendment is the same as the House bill except that the otherwise applicable definition of unemployed veterans is expanded to include individuals who were discharged or released from active duty in the Armed Forces during the period beginning on September 1, 2001 and ending on December 31, 2010.

CONFERENCE AGREEMENT

The conference agreement follows the House bill and the Senate amendment with one modification. Under this modification an unemployed veteran for purposes of this new targeted group is defined below:

An unemployed veteran is defined as an individual certified by the designated local agency as someone who: (1) has served on active duty (other than for training) in the Armed Forces for more than 180 days or who has been discharged or released from active duty in the Armed Forces for a service-connected disability; (2) has been discharged or released from active duty in the Armed Forces during the five-year period ending on the hiring date; and (3) has received unemployment compensation under State or Federal law for not less than four weeks during the one-year period ending on the hiring date.

For purposes of the disconnected youths, it is intended that a low level of formal education may satisfy the requirement that an individual is not readily employable by reason of lacking a sufficient number of skills. Further, it is intended that the Internal Revenue Service, when providing general guidance regarding the various new criteria, shall take into account the administrability of the program by the State agencies.

6. Clarification of regulations related to limitations on certain built-in losses following an ownership change (sec. 1431 of the House bill, sec. 1281 of the Senate amendment, sec. 1261 of the conference agreement, and sec. 382 of the Code)

PRESENT LAW

Section 382 limits the extent to which a "loss corporation" that experiences an "ownership change" may offset taxable income in any post-change taxable year by pre-change net operating losses, certain built-in losses, and deductions attributable to the pre-change period.[50] In general, the amount of income in any post-change year that may be offset by such net operating losses, built-in losses and deductions is limited to an amount (referred to as the "section 382 limitation") determined by multiplying the value of the loss corporation immediately before the ownership change by the long-term tax-exempt interest rate.[51]

A "loss corporation" is defined as a corporation entitled to use a net operating loss carryover or having a net operating loss carryover for the taxable year in which the ownership change occurs. Except to the extent provided in regulations, such term includes any corporation with a "net unrealized built-in loss" (or NUBIL),[52] defined as the amount by which the fair market value of the assets of the corporation immediately before an ownership change is less than the aggregate adjusted basis of such assets at such time. However, if the amount of the NUBIL does not exceed the lesser of (i) 15 percent of the fair market value of the corporation's assets or (ii) $10,000,000, then the amount of the NUBIL is treated as zero.[53]

An ownership change is defined generally as an increase by more than 50-percentage points in the percentage of stock of a loss corporation that is owned by any one or more five-percent (or great-

---

[50] Sec. 383 imposes similar limitations, under regulations, on the use of carryforwards of general business credits, alternative minimum tax credits, foreign tax credits, and net capital loss carryforwards. Sec. 383 generally refers to sec. 382 for the meanings of its terms, but requires appropriate adjustments to take account of its application to credits and net capital losses.

[51] If the loss corporation had a "net unrealized built-in gain" (or NUBIG) at the time of the ownership change, then the sec. 382 limitation for any taxable year may be increased by the amount of the "recognized built-in gains" (discussed further below) for that year. A NUBIG is defined as the amount by which the fair market value of the assets of the corporation immediately before an ownership change exceeds the aggregate adjusted basis of such assets at such time. However, if the amount of the NUBIG does not exceed the lesser of (i) 15 percent of the fair market value of the corporation's assets or (ii) $10,000,000, then the amount of the NUBIG is treated as zero. Sec. 382(h)(1).

[52] Sec. 382(k)(1).

[53] Sec. 382(h)(3).

er) shareholders (as defined) within a three-year period.[54] Treasury regulations provide generally that this measurement is to be made as of any "testing date," which is any date on which the ownership of one or more persons who were or who become five-percent shareholders increases.[55]

Section 382(h) governs the treatment of certain built-in losses and built-in gains recognized with respect to assets held by the loss corporation at the time of the ownership change. In the case of a loss corporation that has a NUBIL (measured immediately before an ownership change), section 382(h)(1) provides that any "recognized built-in loss" (or RBIL) for any taxable year during a "recognition period" (consisting of the five years beginning on the ownership change date) is subject to the section 382 limitation in the same manner as if it were a pre-change net operating loss.[56] An RBIL is defined for this purpose as any loss recognized during the recognition period on the disposition of any asset held by the loss corporation immediately before the ownership change date, to the extent that such loss is attributable to an excess of the adjusted basis of the asset on the change date over its fair market value on

[54] Determinations of the percentage of stock of any corporation held by any person are made on the basis of value. Sec. 382(k)(6)(C).

[55] See Treas. Reg. sec. 1.382–2(a)(4) (providing that "a loss corporation is required to determine whether an ownership change has occurred immediately after any owner shift, or issuance or transfer (including an issuance or transfer described in Treas. Reg. sec. 1.382–4(d)(8)(i) or (ii)) of an option with respect to stock of the loss corporation that is treated as exercised under Treas. Reg. sec. 1.382–4(d)(2)" and defining a "testing date" as "each date on which a loss corporation is required to make a determination of whether an ownership change has occurred") and Temp. Treas. Reg. sec. 1.382–2T(e)(1) (defining an "owner shift" as "any change in the ownership of the stock of a loss corporation that affects the percentage of such stock owned by any 5-percent shareholder"). Treasury regulations under section 382 provide that, in computing stock ownership on specified testing dates, certain unexercised options must be treated as exercised if certain ownership, control, or income tests are met. These tests are met only if "a principal purpose of the issuance, transfer, or structuring of the option (alone or in combination with other arrangements) is to avoid or ameliorate the impact of an ownership change of the loss corporation." Treas. Reg. sec. 1.382–4(d). Compare prior temporary regulations, Temp. Reg. sec. 1.382–2T(h)(4) ("Solely for the purpose of determining whether there is an ownership change on any testing date, stock of the loss corporation that is subject to an option shall be treated as acquired on any such date, pursuant to an exercise of the option by its owner on that date, if such deemed exercise would result in an ownership change."). Internal Revenue Service Notice 2008–76, I.R.B. 2008–39 (September 29, 2008), released September 7, 2008, provides that the Treasury Department intends to issue regulations modifying the term "testing date" under sec. 382 to exclude any date on or after which the United States acquires stock or options to acquire stock in certain corporations with respect to which there is a "Housing Act Acquisition" pursuant to the Housing and Economic Recovery Act of 2008 (P.L. 110–289). The Notice states that the regulations will apply on and after September 7, 2008, unless and until there is additional guidance. Internal Revenue Service Notice 2008–84, I.R.B. 2008–41 (October 14, 2008), provides that the Treasury Department intends to issue regulations modifying the term "testing date" under sec. 382 to exclude any date as of the close of which the United States owns, directly or indirectly, a more than 50 percent interest in a loss corporation, which regulations will apply unless and until there is additional guidance. Internal Revenue Service Notice 2008–100, 2008–14 I.R.B. 1081 (released October 15, 2008) provides that the Treasury Department intends to issue regulations providing, among other things, that certain instruments acquired by the Treasury Department under the Capital Purchase Program (CPP) pursuant to the Emergency Economic Stabilization Act of 2008 (P.L. 100–343) ("EESA") shall not be treated as stock for certain purposes. The Notice also provides that certain capital contributions made by Treasury pursuant to the CPP shall not be considered to have been made as part of a plan the principal purpose of which was to avoid or increase any sec. 382 limitation (for purposes of section 382(1)(1)). The Notice states that taxpayers may rely on the rules described unless and until there is further guidance; and that any contrary guidance will not apply to instruments (i) held by Treasury that were acquired pursuant to the CCP prior to publication of that guidance, or (ii) issued to Treasury pursuant to the CCP under written binding contracts entered into prior to the publication of that guidance. Internal Revenue Service Notice 2009–14, 2009–7 I.R.B. 1 (January 30, 2009) amplifies and supersedes Notice 2008–100, and provides additional guidance regarding the application of sec. 382 and other provisions of law to corporations whose instruments are acquired by the Treasury Department under certain programs pursuant to EESA.

[56] Sec. 382(h)(2). The total amount of the loss corporation's RBILs that are subject to the section 382 limitation cannot exceed the amount of the corporation's NUBIL.

that date.[57] An RBIL also includes any amount allowable as depreciation, amortization or depletion during the recognition period, to the extent that such amount is attributable to the excess of the adjusted basis of the asset over its fair market value on the ownership change date.[58] In addition, any amount that is allowable as a deduction during the recognition period (determined without regard to any carryover) but which is attributable to periods before the ownership change date is treated as an RBIL for the taxable year in which it is allowable as a deduction.[59]

As indicated above, section 382(h)(1) provides in the case of a loss corporation that has a NUBIG that the section 382 limitation may be increased for any taxable year during the recognition period by the amount of recognized built-in gains (or RBIGs) for such taxable year.[60] An RBIG is defined for this purpose as any gain recognized during the recognition period on the disposition of any asset held by the loss corporation immediately before the ownership change date, to the extent that such gain is attributable to an excess of the fair market value of the asset on the change date over its adjusted basis on that date.[61] In addition, any item of income that is properly taken into account during the recognition period but which is attributable to periods before the ownership change date is treated as an RBIG for the taxable year in which it is properly taken into account.[62]

Internal Revenue Service Notice 2003–65 [63] provides two alternative safe harbor approaches for the identification of built-in items for purposes of section 382(h): the "1374 approach" and the "338 approach."

Under the 1374 approach,[64] NUBIG or NUBIL is the net amount of gain or loss that would be recognized in a hypothetical sale of the assets of the loss corporation immediately before the ownership change.[65] The amount of gain or loss recognized during the recognition period on the sale or exchange of an asset held at the time of the ownership change is RBIG or RBIL, respectively, to the extent it is attributable to a difference between the adjusted basis and the fair market value of the asset on the change date, as described above. However, the 1374 approach generally relies on the accrual method of accounting to identify items of income or deduction as RBIG or RBIL, respectively. Generally, items of income or deduction properly included in income or allowed as a deduction during the recognition period are considered attributable to period

[57] Sec. 382(h)(2)(B).
[58] Id.
[59] Sec. 382(h)(6)(B).
[60] The total amount of such increases cannot exceed the amount of the corporation's NUBIG.
[61] Sec. 382(h)(2)(A).
[62] Sec. 382(h)(6)(A).
[63] 2003–2 C.B. 747.
[64] The 1374 approach generally incorporates rules similar to those of section 1374(d) and the Treasury regulations thereunder in calculating NUBIG and NUBIL and identifying RBIG and RBIL.
[65] More specifically, NUBIG or NUBIL is calculated by determining the amount that would be realized if immediately before the ownership change the loss corporation had sold all of its assets, including goodwill, at fair market value to a third party that assumed all of its liabilities, decreased by the sum of any deductible liabilities of the loss corporation that would be included in the amount realized on the hypothetical sale and the loss corporation's aggregate adjusted basis in all of its assets, increased or decreased by the corporation's section 481 adjustments that would be taken into account on a hypothetical sale, and increased by any RBIL that would not be allowed as a deduction under section 382, 383 or 384 on the hypothetical sale.

before the change date (and thus are treated as RBIG or RBIL, respectively), if a taxpayer using an accrual method of accounting would have included the item in income or been allowed a deduction for the item before the change date. However, the 1374 approach includes a number of exceptions to this general rule, including a special rule dealing with bad debt deductions under section 166. Under this special rule, any deduction item properly taken into account during the first 12 months of the recognition period as a bad debt deduction under section 166 is treated as RBIL if the item arises from a debt owed to the loss corporation at the beginning of the recognition period (and deductions for such items properly taken into account after the first 12 months of the recognition period are not RBILs).[66]

The 338 approach identifies items of RBIG and RBIL generally by comparing the loss corporation's actual items of income, gain, deduction and loss with those that would have resulted if a section 338 election had been made with respect to a hypothetical purchase of all of the outstanding stock of the loss corporation on the change date. Under the 338 approach, NUBIG or NUBIL is calculated in the same manner as it is under the 1374 approach.[67] The 338 approach identifies RBIG or RBIL by comparing the loss corporation's actual items of income, gain, deduction and loss with the items of income, gain, deduction and loss that would result if a section 338 election had been made for the hypothetical purchase. The loss corporation is treated for this purpose as using those accounting methods that the loss corporation actually uses. The 338 approach does not include any special rule with regard to bad debt deductions under section 166.

Section 166 generally allows a deduction in respect of any debt that becomes worthless, in whole or in part, during the taxable year.[68] The determination of whether a debt is worthless, in whole or in part, is a question of fact. However, in the case of a bank or other corporation that is subject to supervision by Federal authorities, or by State authorities maintaining substantially equivalent standards, the Treasury regulations under section 166 provide a presumption of worthlessness to the extent that a debt is charged off during the taxable year pursuant to a specific order of such an authority or in accordance with established policies of such an authority (and in the latter case, the authority confirms in writing upon the first subsequent audit of the bank or other corporation that the charge-off would have been required if the audit had been made at the time of the charge-off). The presumption does not apply if the taxpayer does not claim the amount so charged off as a deduction for the taxable year in which the charge-off takes place. In that case, the charge-off is treated as having been involuntary; however, in order to claim the section 166 deduction in a later taxable year, the taxpayer must produce sufficient evidence to

---

[66] Notice 2003–65, section III.B.2.b.

[67] Accordingly, unlike the case in which a section 338 election is actually made, contingent consideration (including a contingent liability) is taken into account in the initial calculation of NUBIG or NUBIL, and no further adjustments are made to reflect subsequent changes in deemed consideration.

[68] Section 166 does not apply, however, to a debt which is evidenced by a security, defined for this purpose (by cross-reference to section 165(g)(2)(C)) as a bond, debenture, note or certificate or other evidence of indebtedness issued by a corporation or by a government or political subdivision thereof, with interest coupons or in registered form. Sec. 166(e).

show that the debt became partially worthless in the later year or became recoverable only in part subsequent to the taxable year of the charge-off, as the case may be, and to the extent that the deduction claimed in the later year for a partially worthless debt was not involuntarily charged off in prior taxable years, it was charged off in the later taxable year.[69]

The Treasury regulations also permit a bank (generally as defined for purposes of section 581, with certain modifications) that is subject to supervision by Federal authorities, or State authorities maintaining substantially equivalent standards, to make a "conformity election" under which debts charged off for regulatory purposes during a taxable year are conclusively presumed to be worthless for tax purposes to the same extent, provided that the charge-off results from a specific order of the regulatory authority or corresponds to the institution's classification of the debt as a "loss asset" pursuant to loan loss classification standards that are consistent with those of certain specified bank regulatory authorities. The conformity election is treated as the adoption of a method of accounting.[70]

Internal Revenue Service Notice 2008–83,[71] released on October 1, 2008, provides that "[f]or purposes of section 382(h), any deduction properly allowed after an ownership change (as defined in section 382(g)) to a bank with respect to losses on loans or bad debts (including any deduction for a reasonable addition to a reserve for bad debts) shall not be treated as a built-in loss or a deduction that is attributable to periods before the change date."[72] The Notice further states that the Internal Revenue Service and the Treasury Department are studying the proper treatment under section 382(h) of certain items of deduction or loss allowed after an ownership change to a corporation that is a bank (as defined in section 581) both immediately before and after the change date, and that any such corporation may rely on the treatment set forth in Notice 2008–83 unless and until there is additional guidance.

HOUSE BILL

The provision states that Congress finds as follows: (1) The delegation of authority to the Secretary of the Treasury, or his delegate, under section 382(m) does not authorize the Secretary to provide exemptions or special rules that are restricted to particular industries or classes of taxpayers; (2) Internal Revenue Service Notice 2008–83 is inconsistent with the congressional intent in enacting such section 382(m); (3) the legal authority to prescribe Notice 2008–83 is doubtful; (4) however, as taxpayers should generally be able to rely on guidance issued by the Secretary of the Treasury, legislation is necessary to clarify the force and effect of Notice 2008–83 and restore the proper application under the Internal Revenue Code of the limitation on built-in losses following an ownership change of a bank.

---

[69] See Treas. Reg. sec. 1.166–2(d)(1) and (2).
[70] See Treas. Reg. sec. 1.166–2(d)(3); cf. Priv. Let. Rul. 9248048 (July 7, 1992); Tech. Ad. Mem. 9122001 (Feb. 8, 1991).
[71] 2008–42 I.R.B. 2008–42 (Oct. 20, 2008).
[72] Notice 2008–83, section 2.

Under the provision, Treasury Notice 2008–83 shall be deemed to have the force and effect of law with respect to any ownership change (as defined in section 382(g)) occurring on or before January 16, 2009, and with respect to any ownership change (as so defined) which occurs after January 16, 2009, if such change (1) is pursuant to a written binding contract entered in to on or before such date or (2) is pursuant to a written agreement entered into on or before such date and such agreement was described on or before such date in a public announcement or in a filing with the Securities and Exchange Commission required by reason of such ownership change, but shall otherwise have no force or effect with respect to any ownership change after such date.

Effective date.—The provision is effective on the date of enactment.

SENATE AMENDMENT

The Senate amendment is the same as the House bill.

CONFERENCE AGREEMENT

The conference agreement follows the House bill and the Senate amendment.

7. Treatment of certain ownership changes for purposes of limitations on net operating loss carryforwards and certain built-in losses (sec. 1262 of the conference agreement and sec. 382 of the Code)

PRESENT LAW

Section 382 limits the extent to which a "loss corporation" that experiences an "ownership change" may offset taxable income in any post-change taxable year by pre-change net operating losses, certain built-in losses, and deductions attributable to the pre-change period.[73] In general, the amount of income in any post-change year that may be offset by such net operating losses, built-in losses and deductions is limited to an amount (referred to as the "section 382 limitation") determined by multiplying the value of the loss corporation immediately before the ownership change by the long-term tax-exempt interest rate.[74]

A "loss corporation" is defined as a corporation entitled to use a net operating loss carryover or having a net operating loss carryover for the taxable year in which the ownership change occurs. Except to the extent provided in regulations, such term includes

---

[73] Section 383 imposes similar limitations, under regulations, on the use of carryforwards of general business credits, alternative minimum tax credits, foreign tax credits, and net capital loss carryforwards. Section 383 generally refers to section 382 for the meanings of its terms, but requires appropriate adjustments to take account of its application to credits and net capital losses.

[74] If the loss corporation had a "net unrealized built in gain" (or NUBIG) at the time of the ownership change, then the section 382 limitation for any taxable year may be increased by the amount of the "recognized built-in gains" (discussed further below) for that year. A NUBIG is defined as the amount by which the fair market value of the assets of the corporation immediately before an ownership change exceeds the aggregate adjusted basis of such assets at such time. However, if the amount of the NUBIG does not exceed the lesser of (i) 15 percent of the fair market value of the corporation's assets or (ii) $10,000,000, then the amount of the NUBIG is treated as zero. Sec. 382(h)(1).

any corporation with a "net unrealized built-in loss" (or NUBIL),[75] defined as the amount by which the fair market value of the assets of the corporation immediately before an ownership change is less than the aggregate adjusted basis of such assets at such time. However, if the amount of the NUBIL does not exceed the lesser of (i) 15 percent of the fair market value of the corporation's assets or (ii) $10,000,000, then the amount of the NUBIL is treated as zero.[76]

An ownership change is defined generally as an increase by more than 50-percentage points in the percentage of stock of a loss corporation that is owned by any one or more five-percent (or greater) shareholders (as defined) within a three-year period.[77] Treasury regulations provide generally that this measurement is to be made as of any "testing date," which is any date on which the ownership of one or more persons who were or who become five-percent shareholders increases.[78]

HOUSE BILL

No provision.

---

[75] Sec. 382(k)(1).

[76] Sec. 382(h)(3).

[77] Determinations of the percentage of stock of any corporation held by any person are made on the basis of value. Sec. 382(k)(6)(C).

[78] See Treas. Reg. sec. 1.382–2(a)(4) (providing that "a loss corporation is required to determine whether an ownership change has occurred immediately after any owner shift, or issuance or transfer (including an issuance or transfer described in Treas. Reg. sec. 1.382–4(d)(8)(i) or (ii)) of an option with respect to stock of the loss corporation that is treated as exercised under Treas. Reg. sec. 1.382–4(d)(2)" and defining a "testing date" as "each date on which a loss corporation is required to make a determination of whether an ownership change has occurred") and Temp. Treas. Reg. sec. 1.382–2T(e)(1) (defining an "owner shift" as "any change in the ownership of the stock of a loss corporation that affects the percentage of such stock owned by any 5-percent shareholder"). Treasury regulations under section 382 provide that, in computing stock ownership on specified testing dates, certain unexercised options must be treated as exercised if certain ownership, control, or income tests are met. These tests are met only if "a principal purpose of the issuance, transfer, or structuring of the option (alone or in combination with other arrangements) is to avoid or ameliorate the impact of an ownership change of the loss corporation." Treas. Reg. sec. 1.382–4(d). Compare prior temporary regulations, Temp. Reg. sec. 1.382–2T(h)(4) ("Solely for the purpose of determining whether there is an ownership change on any testing date, stock of the loss corporation that is subject to an option shall be treated as acquired on any such date, pursuant to an exercise of the option by its owner on that date, if such deemed exercise would result in an ownership change."). Internal Revenue Service Notice 2008–76, I.R.B. 2008–39 (September 29, 2008), released September 7, 2008, provides that the Treasury Department intends to issue regulations modifying the term "testing date" under section 382 to exclude any date on or after which the United States acquires stock or options to acquire stock in certain corporations with respect to which there is a "Housing Act Acquisition" pursuant to the Housing and Economic Recovery Act of 2008 (P.L. 110–289). The Notice states that the regulations will apply on and after September 7, 2008, unless and until there is additional guidance. Internal Revenue Service Notice 2008–84, I.R.B. 2008–41 (October 14, 2008), provides that the Treasury Department intends to issue regulations modifying the term "testing date" under section 382 to exclude any date as of the close of which the United States owns, directly or indirectly, a more than 50 percent interest in a loss corporation, which regulations will apply unless and until there is additional guidance. Internal Revenue Service Notice 2008–100, 2008–14 I.R.B. 1081 (released October 15, 2008) provides that the Treasury Department intends to issue regulations providing, among other things, that certain instruments acquired by the Treasury Department under the Capital Purchase Program (CPP) pursuant to the Emergency Economic Stabilization Act of 2008 (P.L. 100–343) ("EESA") shall not be treated as stock for certain purposes. The Notice also provides that certain capital contributions made by Treasury pursuant to the CPP shall not be considered to have been made as part of a plan the principal purpose of which was to avoid or increase any section 382 limitation (for purposes of section 382(l)(1)). The Notice states that taxpayers may rely on the rules described unless and until there is further guidance; and that any contrary guidance will not apply to instruments (i) held by Treasury that were acquired pursuant to the CCP prior to publication of that guidance, or (ii) issued to Treasury pursuant to the CCP under written binding contracts entered into prior to the publication of that guidance. Internal Revenue Service Notice 2009–14, 2009–7 I.R.B. 1 (January 30, 2009) amplifies and supersedes Notice 2008–100, and provides additional guidance regarding the application of section 382 and other provisions of law to corporations whose instruments are acquired by the Treasury Department under certain programs pursuant to EESA.

561

No provision.

The conference agreement amends section 382 of the Code to provide an exception from the application of the section 382 limitation. Under the provision, the section 382 limitation that would otherwise arise as a result of an ownership change shall not apply in the case of an ownership change that occurs pursuant to a restructuring plan of a taxpayer which is required under a loan agreement or commitment for a line of credit entered into with the Department of the Treasury under the Emergency Economic Stabilization Act of 2008, and is intended to result in a rationalization of the costs, capitalization, and capacity with respect to the manufacturing workforce of, and suppliers to, the taxpayer and its subsidiaries.[79]

However, an ownership change that would otherwise be excepted from the section 382 limitation under the provision will instead remain subject to the section 382 limitation if, immediately after such ownership change, any person (other than a voluntary employees' beneficiary association within the meaning of section 501(c)(9)) owns stock of the new loss corporation possessing 50 percent or more of the total combined voting power of all classes of stock entitled to vote or of the total value of the stock of such corporation. For purposes of this rule, persons who bear a relationship to one another described in section 267(b) or 707(b)(1), or who are members of a group of persons acting in concert, are treated as a single person.

The exception from the application of the section 382 limitation under the provision does not change the fact that an ownership change has occurred for other purposes of section 382.[80]

Effective date.—The conference agreement applies to ownership changes after the date of enactment.

8. Deferral of certain income from the discharge of indebtedness (sec. 1231 of the Senate amendment, sec. 1231 of the conference agreement, and sec. 108 of the Code)

In general, gross income includes income that is realized by a debtor from the discharge of indebtedness, subject to certain exceptions for debtors in title 11 bankruptcy cases, insolvent debtors, certain student loans, certain farm indebtedness, certain real property business indebtedness, and certain qualified principal residence indebtedness.[81] In cases involving discharges of indebtedness that are excluded from gross income under the exceptions to the general rule, taxpayers generally are required to reduce certain tax attributes, including net operating losses, general business credits,

---

[79] This exception shall not apply in the case of any subsequent ownership change unless such subsequent ownership change also meets the requirements of the exception.

[80] For example, an ownership change has occurred for purposes of determining the testing period under section 382(i)(2).

[81] See sections 61(a)(12) and 108. But see sec. 102 (a debt cancellation which constitutes a gift or bequest is not treated as income to the donee debtor).

minimum tax credits, capital loss carryovers, and basis in property, by the amount of the discharge of indebtedness.[82]

The amount of discharge of indebtedness excluded from income by an insolvent debtor not in a title 11 bankruptcy case cannot exceed the amount by which the debtor is insolvent. In the case of a discharge in bankruptcy or where the debtor is insolvent, any reduction in basis may not exceed the excess of the aggregate bases of properties held by the taxpayer immediately after the discharge over the aggregate of the liabilities of the taxpayer immediately after the discharge.[83]

For all taxpayers, the amount of discharge of indebtedness generally is equal to the excess of the adjusted issue price of the indebtedness being satisfied over the amount paid (or deemed paid) to satisfy such indebtedness.[84] This rule generally applies to (1) the acquisition by the debtor of its debt instrument in exchange for cash, (2) the issuance of a debt instrument by the debtor in satisfaction of its indebtedness, including a modification of indebtedness that is treated as an exchange (a debt-for-debt exchange), (3) the transfer by a debtor corporation of stock, or a debtor partnership of a capital or profits interest in such partnership, in satisfaction of its indebtedness (an equity-for-debt exchange), and (4) the acquisition by a debtor corporation of its indebtedness from a shareholder as a contribution to capital.

Debt-for-debt exchanges

If a debtor issues a debt instrument in satisfaction of its indebtedness, the debtor is treated as having satisfied the indebtedness with an amount of money equal to the issue price of the newly issued debt instrument.[85] The issue price of such newly issued debt instrument generally is determined under sections 1273 and 1274.[86] Similarly, a "significant modification" of a debt instrument, within the meaning of Treas. Reg. sec. 1.1001–3, results in an exchange of the original debt instrument for a modified instrument. In such cases, where the issue price of the modified debt instrument is less than the adjusted issue price of the original debt instrument, the debtor will have income from the cancellation of indebtedness.

If any new debt instrument is issued (including as a result of a significant modification to a debt instrument), such debt instrument will have original issue discount equal to the excess (if any) of such debt instrument's stated redemption price at maturity over its issue price.[87] In general, an issuer of a debt instrument with original issue discount may deduct for any taxable year, with respect to such debt instrument, an amount of original issue discount equal to the aggregate daily portions of the original issue discount for days during such taxable year.[88]

---

[82] Sec. 108(b).
[83] Sec. 1017.
[84] Treas. Reg. sec. 1.61–12(c)(2)(ii). Treas. Reg. sec. 1.1275–1(b) defines "adjusted issue price."
[85] Sec. 108(e)(10)(A).
[86] Sec. 108(e)(10)(B).
[87] Sec. 1273.
[88] Sec. 163(e).

Equity-for-debt exchanges

If a corporation transfers stock, or a partnership transfers a capital or profits interest in such partnership, to a creditor in satisfaction of its indebtedness, then such corporation or partnership is treated as having satisfied its indebtedness with an amount of money equal to the fair market value of the stock or interest.[89]

Related party acquisitions

Indebtedness directly or indirectly acquired by a person who bears a relationship to the debtor described in section 267(b) or section 707(b) is treated as if it were acquired by the debtor.[90] Thus, where a debtor's indebtedness is acquired for less than its adjusted issue price by a person related to the debtor (within the meaning of section 267(b) or 707(b)), the debtor recognizes income from the cancellation of indebtedness. Regulations under section 108 provide that the indebtedness acquired by the related party is treated as new indebtedness issued by the debtor to the related holder on the acquisition date (the deemed issuance).[91] The new indebtedness is deemed issued with an issue price equal to the amount used under regulations to compute the amount of cancellation of indebtedness income realized by the debtor (i.e., either the holder's adjusted basis or the fair market value of the indebtedness, as the case may be).[92] The indebtedness deemed issued pursuant to the regulations has original issue discount to the extent its stated redemption price at maturity exceeds its issue price.

In the case of a deemed issuance under Treas. Reg. sec. 1.108–2(g), the related holder does not recognize any gain or loss, and the related holder's adjusted basis in the indebtedness remains the same as it was immediately before the deemed issuance.[93] The deemed issuance is treated as a purchase of the indebtedness by the related holder for purposes of section 1272(a)(7) (pertaining to reduction of original issue discount where a subsequent holder pays acquisition premium) and section 1276 (pertaining to acquisitions of debt at a market discount).[94]

Contribution of a debt instrument to capital of a corporation

Where a debtor corporation acquires its indebtedness from a shareholder as a contribution to capital, section 118[95] does not apply, but the corporation is treated as satisfying such indebtedness with an amount of money equal to the shareholder's adjusted basis in the indebtedness.

No provision.

---

[89] Sec. 108(e)(8).
[90] Sec. 108(e)(4).
[91] Treas. Reg. sec. 1.108–2(g).
[92] Id.
[93] Treas. Reg. sec. 1.108–2(g)(2).
[94] Id.
[95] Section 118 provides, in general, that in the case of a corporation, gross income does not include any contribution to the capital of the taxpayer.

The provision permits a taxpayer to elect to defer income from cancellation of indebtedness recognized by the taxpayer as a result of a repurchase by (1) the taxpayer or (2) a person who bears a relationship to the taxpayer described in section 267(b) or section 707(b), of a "debt instrument" that was issued by the taxpayer. The provision applies only to repurchases of debt that (1) occur after December 31, 2008, and prior to January 1, 2011, and (2) are repurchases for cash. Thus, for example, the provision does not apply to a debt-for-debt exchange or to any exchange of the taxpayer's equity for a debt instrument of the taxpayer. For purposes of the provision, a "debt instrument" is broadly defined to include any bond, debenture, note, certificate or any other instrument or contractual arrangement constituting indebtedness.

Income from the discharge of indebtedness in connection with the repurchase of a debt instrument in 2009 or 2010 must be included in the gross income of the taxpayer ratably in the eight taxable years beginning with (1) for repurchases in 2009, the second taxable year following the taxable year in which the repurchase occurs or (2) for repurchases in 2010, the taxable year following the taxable year in which the repurchase occurs. The provision authorizes the Secretary of the Treasury to prescribe such regulations as may be necessary or appropriate for purposes of applying the provision.

Effective date.—The provision applies to discharges in taxable years ending after December 31, 2008.

The conference agreement follows the Senate amendment with modifications. The provision permits a taxpayer to elect to defer cancellation of indebtedness income arising from a "reacquisition" of "an applicable debt instrument" after December 31, 2008, and before January 1, 2011. Income deferred pursuant to the election must be included in the gross income of the taxpayer ratably in the five taxable years beginning with (1) for repurchases in 2009, the fifth taxable year following the taxable year in which the repurchase occurs or (2) for repurchases in 2010, the fourth taxable year following the taxable year in which the repurchase occurs.

An "applicable debt instrument" is any debt instrument issued by (1) a C corporation or (2) any other person in connection with the conduct of a trade or business by such person. For purposes of the provision, a "debt instrument" is broadly defined to include any bond, debenture, note, certificate or any other instrument or contractual arrangement constituting indebtedness (within the meaning of section 1275(a)(1)).

A "reacquisition" is any "acquisition" of an applicable debt instrument by (1) the debtor that issued (or is otherwise the obligor under) such debt instrument or (2) any person related to the debtor within the meaning of section 108(e)(4). For purposes of the provision, an "acquisition" includes, without limitation, (1) an acquisition of a debt instrument for cash, (2) the exchange of a debt instrument for another debt instrument (including an exchange resulting from a modification of a debt instrument), (3) the exchange of corporate stock or a partnership interest for a debt instrument, (4) the contribution of a debt instrument to the capital of the issuer, and (5) the complete forgiveness of a debt instrument by a holder of such instrument.

Special rules for debt-for-debt exchanges

If a taxpayer makes the election provided by the provision for a debt-for-debt exchange in which the newly issued debt instrument issued (or deemed issued, including by operation of the rules in Treas. Reg. sec. 1.108–2(g)) in satisfaction of an outstanding debt instrument of the debtor has original issue discount, then any otherwise allowable deduction for original issue discount with respect to such newly issued debt instrument that (1) accrues before the first year of the five-taxable-year period in which the related, deferred discharge of indebtedness income is included in the gross income of the taxpayer and (2) does not exceed such related, deferred discharge of indebtedness income, is deferred and allowed as a deduction ratably over the same five-taxable-year period in which the deferred discharge of indebtedness income is included in gross income.

This rule can apply also in certain cases when a debtor reacquires its debt for cash. If the taxpayer issues a debt instrument and the proceeds of such issuance are used directly or indirectly to reacquire a debt instrument of the taxpayer, the provision treats the newly issued debt instrument as if it were issued in satisfaction of the retired debt instrument. If the newly issued debt instrument has original issue discount, the rule described above applies. Thus, all or a portion of the interest deductions with respect to original issue discount on the newly issued debt instrument are deferred into the five-taxable-year period in which the discharge of indebtedness income is recognized. Where only a portion of the proceeds of a new issuance are used by a taxpayer to satisfy outstanding debt, then the deferral rule applies to the portion of the original issue discount on the newly issued debt instrument that is equal to the portion of the proceeds of such newly issued instrument used to retire outstanding debt of the taxpayer.

Acceleration of deferred items

Cancellation of indebtedness income and any related deduction for original issue discount that is deferred by an electing taxpayer (and has not previously been taken into account) generally is accelerated and taken into income in the taxable year in which the taxpayer: (1) dies, (2) liquidates or sells substantially all of its assets (including in a title 11 or similar case), (3) ceases to do business, or (4) or is in similar circumstances. In a case under title 11 or a similar case, any deferred items are taken into income as of the day before the petition is filed. Deferred items are accelerated in a case under title 11 where the taxpayer liquidates, sells substantially all of its assets, or ceases to do business, but not where a taxpayer reorganizes and emerges from the title 11 case. In the case of a pass thru entity, this acceleration rule also applies to the sale, exchange, or redemption of an interest in the entity by a holder of such interest.

Special rule for partnerships

In the case of a partnership, any income deferred under the provision is allocated to the partners in the partnership immediately before the discharge of indebtedness in the manner such amounts would have been included in the distributive shares of such partners under section 704 if such income were recognized at the time of the discharge. Any decrease in a partner's share of liabilities as a result of such discharge is not taken into account for purposes of section 752 at the time of the discharge to the extent the deemed distribution under section 752 would cause the partner to recognize gain under section 731. Thus, the deemed distribution under section 752 is deferred with respect to a partner to the extent it exceeds such partner's basis. Amounts so deferred are taken into account at the same time, and to the extent remaining in the same amount, as income deferred under the provision is recognized by the partner.

Coordination with section 108(a) and procedures for election

Where a taxpayer makes the election provided by the provision, the exclusions provided by section 108(a)(1)(A), (B), (C), and (D) shall not apply to the income from the discharge of indebtedness for the year in which the taxpayer makes the election or any subsequent year. Thus, for example, an insolvent taxpayer may elect under the provision to defer income from the discharge of indebtedness rather than excluding such income and reducing tax attributes by a corresponding amount. The election is to be made on an instrument by instrument basis; once made, the election is irrevocable. A taxpayer makes an election with respect to a debt instrument by including with its return for the taxable year in which the reacquisition of the debt instrument occurs a statement that (1) clearly identifies the debt instrument and (2) includes the amount of deferred income to which the provision applies and such other information as may be prescribed by the Secretary. The Secretary is authorized to require reporting of the election (and other information with respect to the reacquisition) for years subsequent to the year of the reacquisition.

Regulatory authority

The provision authorizes the Secretary of the Treasury to prescribe such regulations as may be necessary or appropriate for purposes of applying the provision, including rules extending the acceleration provisions to other circumstances where appropriate, rules requiring reporting of the election and such other information as the Secretary may require on returns of tax for subsequent taxable years, rules for the application of the provision to partnerships, S corporations, and other pass thru entities, including for the allocation of deferred deductions.

Effective date.—The provision is effective for discharges in taxable years ending after December 31, 2008.

9. Modifications of rules for original issue discount on certain high yield obligations (sec. 1232 of the conference agreement and sec. 163 of the Code)

PRESENT LAW

In general, the issuer of a debt instrument with original issue discount may deduct the portion of such original issue discount equal to the aggregate daily portions of the original issue discount for days during the taxable year.[96] However, in the case of an applicable high-yield discount obligation (an "AHYDO") issued by a corporate issuer: (1) no deduction is allowed for the "disqualified portion" of the original issue discount on such obligation, and (2) the remainder of the original issue discount on any such obligation is not allowable as a deduction until paid by the issuer.[97]

An AHYDO is any debt instrument if (1) the maturity date on such instrument is more than five years from the date of issue; (2) the yield to maturity on such instrument exceeds the sum of (a) the applicable Federal rate in effect under section 1274(d) for the calendar month in which the obligation is issued and (b) five percentage points, and (3) such instrument has "significant original issue discount."[98] An instrument is treated as having "significant original issue discount" if the aggregate amount of interest that would be includible in the gross income of the holder with respect to such instrument for periods before the close of any accrual period (as defined in section 1272(a)(5)) ending after the date five years after the date of issue, exceeds the sum of (1) the aggregate amount of interest to be paid under the instrument before the close of such accrual period, and (2) the product of the issue price of such instrument (as defined in sections 1273(b) and 1274(a)) and its yield to maturity.[99]

The disqualified portion of the original issue discount on an AHYDO is the lesser of (1) the amount of original issue discount with respect to such obligation or (2) the portion of the "total return" on such obligation which bears the same ratio to such total return as the "disqualified yield" (i.e., the excess of the yield to maturity on the obligation over the applicable Federal rate plus six percentage points) on such obligation bears to the yield to maturity on such obligation.[100] The term "total return" means the amount which would have been the original issue discount of the obligation if interest described in section 1273(a)(2) were included in the 101 stated redemption to maturity.[101] A corporate holder treats the disqualified portion of original issue discount as a stock distribution for purposes of the dividend received deduction.[102]

HOUSE BILL

No provision.

---

[96] Sec. 163(e)(1). For purposes of section 163(e)(1), the daily portion of the original issue discount for any day is determined under section 1272(a) (without regard to paragraph (7) thereof and without regard to section 1273(a)(3)).
[97] Sec. 163(e)(5).
[98] Sec. 163(i)(1).
[99] Sec. 163(i)(2).
[100] Sec. 163(e)(5)(C).
[101] Sec. 163(e)(5)(C)(ii).
[102] Sec. 163(e)(5)(B).

No provision.

The conference agreement adds a provision that suspends the rules in section 163(e)(5) for certain obligations issued in a debt-for-debt exchange, including an exchange resulting from a significant modification of a debt instrument, after August 31, 2008, and before January 1, 2010.

In general, the suspension does not apply to any newly issued debt instrument (including any debt instrument issued as a result of a significant modification of a debt instrument) that is issued for an AHYDO. However, any newly issued debt instrument (including any debt instrument issued as a result of a significant modification of a debt instrument) for which the AHYDO rules are suspended under the provision is not treated as an AHYDO for purposes of a subsequent application of the suspension rule. Thus, for example, if a new debt instrument that would be an AHYDO under present law is issued in exchange for a debt instrument that is not an AHYDO, and the provision suspends application of section 163(e)(5), another new debt instrument, issued during the suspension period in exchange for the instrument with respect to which the rule in section 163(e)(5) was suspended, would be eligible for the relief provided by the provision despite the fact that it is issued for an instrument that is an AHYDO under present law.

In addition, the suspension does not apply to any newly issued debt instrument (including any debt instrument issued as a result of a significant modification of a debt instrument) that is (1) described in section 871(h)(4) (without regard to subparagraph (D) thereof) (i.e., certain contingent debt) or (2) issued to a person related to the issuer (within the meaning of section 108(e)(4)).

The provision provides authority to the Secretary to apply the suspension rule to periods after December 31, 2009, where the Secretary determines that such application is appropriate in light of distressed conditions in the debt capital markets. In addition, the provision grants authority to the Secretary to use a rate that is higher than the applicable Federal rate for purposes of applying section 163(e)(5) for obligations issued after December 31, 2009, in taxable years ending after such date if the Secretary determines that such higher rate is appropriate in light of distressed conditions in the debt capital markets.

Effective date.—The temporary suspension of section 163(e)(5) applies to obligations issued after August 31, 2008, in taxable years ending after such date. The additional authority granted to the Secretary to use a rate higher than the applicable Federal rate for purposes of applying section 163(e)(5) applies to obligations issued after December 31, 2009, in taxable years ending after such date.

10. Special rules applicable to qualified small business stock for 2009 and 2010 (sec. 1241 of the Senate amendment, sec. 1241 of the conference agreement, and sec. 1202 of the Code)

PRESENT LAW

Under present law, individuals may exclude 50 percent (60 percent for certain empowerment zone businesses) of the gain from the sale of certain small business stock acquired at original issue and held for at least five years.[103] The portion of the gain includible in taxable income is taxed at a maximum rate of 28 percent under the regular tax.[104] A percentage of the excluded gain is an alternative minimum tax preference,[105] the portion of the gain includible in alternative minimum taxable income is taxed at a maximum rate of 28 percent under the alternative minimum tax.

Thus, under present law, gain from the sale of qualified small business stock is taxed at effective rates of 14 percent under the regular tax[106] and (i) 14.98 percent under the alternative minimum tax for dispositions before January 1, 2011; (ii) 19.98 percent under the alternative minimum tax for dispositions after December 31, 2010, in the case of stock acquired before January 1, 2001; and (iii) 17.92 percent under the alternative minimum tax for dispositions after December 31, 2010, in the case of stock acquired after December 31, 2000.[107]

The amount of gain eligible for the exclusion by an individual with respect to any corporation is the greater of (1) ten times the taxpayer's basis in the stock or (2) $10 million. In order to qualify as a small business, when the stock is issued, the gross assets of the corporation may not exceed $50 million. The corporation also must meet certain active trade or business requirements.

HOUSE BILL

No provision.

SENATE AMENDMENT

Under the Senate amendment, the percentage exclusion for qualified small business stock sold by an individual is increased from 50 percent (60 percent for certain empowerment zone businesses) to 75 percent.

As a result of the increased exclusion, gain from the sale of qualified small business stock to which the provision applies is

---

[103] Sec. 1202.

[104] Sec. 1(h).

[105] Sec. 57(a)(7). In the case of qualified small business stock, the percentage of gain excluded from gross income which is an alternative minimum tax preference is (i) seven percent in the case of stock disposed of in a taxable year beginning before 2011; (ii) 42 percent in the case of stock acquired before January 1, 2001, and disposed of in a taxable year beginning after 2010; and (iii) 28 percent in the case of stock acquired after December 31, 2000, and disposed of in a taxable year beginning after 2010.

[106] The 50 percent of gain included in taxable income is taxed at a maximum rate of 28 percent.

[107] The amount of gain included in alternative minimum tax is taxed at a maximum rate of 28 percent. The amount so included is the sum of (i) 50 percent (the percentage included in taxable income) of the total gain and (ii) the applicable preference percentage of the one-half gain that is excluded from taxable income.

taxed at effective rates of seven percent under the regular tax[108] and 12.88 percent under the alternative minimum tax.[109]

Effective date.—The provision is effective for stock issued after the date of enactment and before January 1, 2011.

CONFERENCE AGREEMENT

The conference agreement follows the Senate amendment.

11. Temporary reduction in recognition period for S corporation built-in gains tax (sec. 1261 of the Senate amendment, sec. 1251 of the conference agreement, and sec. 1374 of the Code)

PRESENT LAW

A "small business corporation" (as defined in section 1361(b)) may elect to be treated as an S corporation. Unlike C corporations, S corporations generally pay no corporate-level tax. Instead, items of income and loss of an S corporation pass though to its shareholders. Each shareholder takes into account separately its share of these items on its individual income tax return.[110]

A corporate level tax, at the highest marginal rate applicable to corporations (currently 35 percent) is imposed on an S corporation's gain that arose prior to the conversion of the C corporation to an S corporation and is recognized by the S corporation during the recognition period, i.e., the first 10 taxable years that the S election is in effect.[111]

Gains recognized in the recognition period are not built-in gains to the extent they are shown to have arisen while the S election was in effect or are offset by recognized built-in losses. The built-in gains tax also applies to gains with respect to net recognized built-in gain attributable to property received by an S corporation from a C corporation in a carryover basis transaction.[112] The amount of the built-in gains tax is treated as a loss taken into account by the shareholders in computing their individual income tax.[113]

HOUSE BILL

No provision.

SENATE AMENDMENT

The Senate amendment provides that, for any taxable year beginning in 2009 and 2010, no tax is imposed on an S corporation under section 1374 if the seventh taxable year in the corporation's recognition period preceded such taxable year. Thus, with respect to gain that arose prior to the conversion of a C corporation to an

---

[108] The 25 percent of gain included in taxable income is taxed at a maximum rate of 28 percent.

[109] The 46 percent of gain included in alternative minimum tax is taxed at a maximum rate of 28 percent. Forty-six percent is the sum of 25 percent (the percentage of total gain included in taxable income) plus 21 percent (the percentage of total gain which is an alternative minimum tax preference).

[110] Sec. 1366.

[111] Sec. 1374.

[112] Sec. 1374(d)(8). With respect to such assets, the recognition period runs from the day on which such assets were acquired (in lieu of the beginning of the first taxable year for which the corporation was an S corporation). Sec. 1374(d)(8)(B).

[113] Sec. 1366(f)(2).

S corporation, no tax will be imposed under section 1374 after the seventh taxable year the S corporation election is in effect. In the case of built-in gain attributable to an asset received by an S corporation from a C corporation in a carryover basis transaction, no tax will be imposed under section 1374 if such gain is recognized after the date that is seven years following the date on which such asset was acquired.[114]

Effective date.—The provision applies to taxable years beginning after December 31, 2008.

CONFERENCE AGREEMENT

The conference agreement follows the Senate amendment.

12. Broadband internet access tax credit (sec. 1271 of the Senate amendment)

PRESENT LAW

A taxpayer is allowed to recover, through annual depreciation deductions, the cost of certain property used in a trade or business or for the production of income. The amount of the depreciation deduction allowed with respect to tangible property for a taxable year is determined under the modified accelerated cost recovery system ("MACRS").[115] Under MACRS, different types of property generally are assigned applicable recovery periods and depreciation methods. The recovery periods applicable to most tangible personal property (generally tangible property other than residential rental property and nonresidential real property) range from three to 25 years. The depreciation methods generally applicable to tangible personal property are the 200-percent and 150-percent declining balance methods, switching to the straight-line method for the taxable year in which the depreciation deduction would be maximized.

No credit is specifically designed under present law to encourage the development of qualified broadband expenditures.

HOUSE BILL

No provision.

SENATE AMENDMENT

The amendment provides an investment tax credit for "qualified broadband expenditures." Qualified broadband expenditures comprise both "current-generation" and "next-generation" broadband. The provision establishes a 10 percent credit for investment in current-generation broadband in rural and underserved areas. The provision establishes a 20 percent credit for investment in current-generation broadband in unserved areas. The provision establishes a 20 percent credit for investment in next-generation broadband in rural, underserved, unserved, and residential areas. The basis of qualified property must be reduced by the amount of credit received. To qualify for the credit, the qualified broadband

---

[114] Shareholders will continue to take into account all items of gain and loss under section 1366.

[115] Sec. 168.

equipment must be placed in service after December 31, 2008, and before January 1, 2011.

"Current-generation" broadband services are defined as the transmission of signals at a rate of at least 5 million bits per second to the subscriber and at a rate of at least 1 million bits per second from the subscriber or wireless technology transmission of signals at a rate of at least 3 million bits per second to the subscriber and at a rate of at least 768 kilobits per second from the subscriber. "Next-generation" broadband services are defined as the transmission of signals at a rate of at least 100 million bits per second to the subscriber and at a rate of at least 20 million bits per second from the subscriber.

Qualified broadband expenditures means the direct or indirect costs properly taken into account for the taxable year for the purchase or installation of qualified equipment (including upgrades) and the connection of the equipment to a qualified subscriber.

Qualified broadband expenditures include only the portion of the purchase price paid by the lessor, in the case of leased equipment, that is attributable to otherwise qualified broadband expenditures by the lessee. In the case of property that is originally placed in service by a person and that is sold to the taxpayer and leased back to such person by the taxpayer within three months after the date that the property was originally placed in service, the property is treated as originally placed in service by the taxpayer not earlier than the date that the property is used under the leaseback.

A qualified subscriber, with respect to current-generation broadband services, means any nonresidential subscriber maintaining a permanent place of business in a rural, underserved, or unserved area, or any residential subscriber residing in a rural, underserved, or unserved area that is not a saturated market. A qualified subscriber, with respect to next generation broadband services, means any nonresidential subscriber maintaining a permanent place of business in a rural, underserved, or unserved area, or any residential subscriber.

For this purpose, a rural area is a low-income community designated under section 45D which is defined as a population census tract located in either (1) a poverty rate of at least 20 percent or (2) median family income which does not exceed 80 percent of the greater of metropolitan area median family income or statewide median family income (for a non-metropolitan census tract, does not exceed 80 percent of statewide median family income).

An underserved area means a census tract located in an empowerment zone or enterprise community designated under section 1391, or the District of Columbia Enterprise Zone established under section 1400, or a renewal community designated under section 1400E, or a low-income community designated under section 45D.

An unserved area is an area without current-generation broadband service.

A saturated market, for this purpose, means any census tract in which, as of the date of enactment, current generation broadband services have been provided by a single provider to 85 percent or more of the total potential residential subscribers. The services must be usable at least a majority of the time during periods of maximum demand, and usable in a manner substantially the same as services provided through equipment not eligible for the deduction under this provision.

If current- or next-generation broadband services can be provided through qualified equipment to both qualified subscribers and to other subscribers, the provision provides that the expenditures with respect to the equipment are allocated among subscribers to determine the amount of qualified broad broadband expenditures that may be deducted under the provision.

Qualified equipment means equipment that provides current- or next-generation broadband services at least a majority of the time during periods of maximum demand to each subscriber, and in a manner substantially the same as such services are provided by the provider to subscribers through equipment with respect to which no deduction is allowed under the provision. Limitations are imposed under the provision on equipment depending on where it extends, and on certain packet switching equipment, and on certain multiplexing and demultiplexing equipment.

Expenditures generally are not taken into account for purposes of the credit under the provision with respect to property used predominantly outside the United States, used predominantly to furnish lodging, used by a tax-exempt organization (other than in a business whose income is subject to unrelated business income tax), or used by the United States or a political subdivision or by a possession, agency or instrumentality thereof or by a foreign person or entity. The basis of property is reduced by the cost of the property that is taken into account as a deduction under the provision. Recapture rules are provided. The credit is part of the general business credit.

Effective date.—The provision is effective for property placed in service after December 31, 2008.

CONFERENCE AGREEMENT

The conference agreement does not include the Senate amendment provision.

C. FISCAL RELIEF FOR STATE AND LOCAL GOVERNMENTS

1. De minimis safe harbor exception for tax-exempt interest expense of financial institutions and modification of small issuer exception to tax-exempt interest expense allocation rules for financial institutions (secs. 1501 and 1502 of the House bill, secs. 1501 and 1502 of the Senate amendment, secs. 1501 and 1502 of the conference agreement, and sec. 265 of the Code)

PRESENT LAW

Present law disallows a deduction for interest on indebtedness incurred or continued to purchase or carry obligations the interest on which is exempt from tax. [116] In general, an interest deduction is disallowed only if the taxpayer has a purpose of using borrowed funds to purchase or carry tax-exempt obligations; a determination

---

[116] Sec. 265(a).

of the taxpayer's purpose in borrowing funds is made based on all of the facts and circumstances. [117]

Two-percent rule for individuals and certain nonfinancial corporations

In the absence of direct evidence linking an individual taxpayer's indebtedness with the purchase or carrying of tax-exempt obligations, the Internal Revenue Service takes the position that it ordinarily will not infer that a taxpayer's purpose in borrowing money was to purchase or carry tax-exempt obligations if the taxpayer's investment in tax-exempt obligations is "insubstantial." [118] An individual's holdings of tax-exempt obligations are presumed to be insubstantial if during the taxable year the average adjusted basis of the individual's tax-exempt obligations is two percent or less of the average adjusted basis of the individual's portfolio investments and assets held by the individual in the active conduct of a trade or business.

Similarly, in the case of a corporation that is not a financial institution or a dealer in tax-exempt obligations, where there is no direct evidence of a purpose to purchase or carry tax-exempt obligations, the corporation's holdings of tax-exempt obligations are presumed to be insubstantial if the average adjusted basis of the corporation's tax-exempt obligations is two percent or less of the average adjusted basis of all assets held by the corporation in the active conduct of its trade or business.

Financial institutions

In the case of a financial institution, the Code generally disallows that portion of the taxpayer's interest expense that is allocable to tax-exempt interest. [119] The amount of interest that is disallowed is an amount which bears the same ratio to such interest expense as the taxpayer's average adjusted bases of tax-exempt obligations acquired after August 7, 1986, bears to the average adjusted bases for all assets of the taxpayer.

Exception for certain obligations of qualified small issuers

The general rule in section 265(b), denying financial institutions' interest expense deductions allocable to tax-exempt obligations, does not apply to "qualified tax-exempt obligations." [120] Instead, as discussed in the next section, only 20 percent of the interest expense allocable to "qualified tax-exempt obligations" is disallowed. [121] A "qualified tax-exempt obligation" is a tax-exempt obligation that (1) is issued after August 7, 1986, by a qualified small issuer, (2) is not a private activity bond, and (3) is designated by the issuer as qualifying for the exception from the general rule of section 265(b).

---

[117] See Rev. Proc. 72–18, 1972–1 C.B. 740.

[118] Id.

[119] Sec. 265(b)(1). A "financial institution" is any person that (1) accepts deposits from the public in the ordinary course of such person's trade or business and is subject to Federal or State supervision as a financial institution or (2) is a corporation described in section 585(a)(2). Sec. 265(b)(5).

[120] Sec. 265(b)(3).

[121] Secs. 265(b)(3)(A), 291(a)(3) and 291(e)(1).

A "qualified small issuer" is an issuer that reasonably anticipates that the amount of tax-exempt obligations that it will issue
during the calendar year will be $10 million or less. [122] The Code
specifies the circumstances under which an issuer and all subordinate entities are aggregated. [123] For purposes of the $10 million
limitation, an issuer and all entities that issue obligations on behalf of such issuer are treated as one issuer. All obligations issued
by a subordinate entity are treated as being issued by the entity
to which it is subordinate. An entity formed (or availed of) to avoid
the $10 million limitation and all entities benefiting from the de-
vice are treated as one issuer.

Composite issues (i.e., combined issues of bonds for different
entities) qualify for the "qualified tax-exempt obligation" exception
only if the requirements of the exception are met with respect to
(1) the composite issue as a whole (determined by treating the composite issue as a single issue) and (2) each separate lot of obligations that is part of the issue (determined by treating each separate lot of obligations as a separate issue). [124] Thus a composite
issue may qualify for the exception only if the composite issue itself
does not exceed $10 million, and if each issuer benefitting from the
composite issue reasonably anticipates that it will not issue more
than $10 million of tax-exempt obligations during the calendar
year, including through the composite arrangement.

Treatment of financial institution preference items

Section 291(a)(3) reduces by 20 percent the amount allowable
as a deduction with respect to any financial institution preference
item. Financial institution preference items include interest on
debt to tax-exempt obligations acquired after December 31, 1982,
and before August 8, 1986. [125] Section 265(b)(3) treats qualified
tax-exempt obligations as if they were acquired on August 7, 1986.
As a result, the amount allowable as a deduction by a financial institution with respect to interest incurred to carry a qualified tax-
exempt obligation is reduced by 20 percent.

HOUSE BILL

Two-percent safe harbor for financial institutions

The provision provides that tax-exempt obligations issued during 2009 or 2010 and held by a financial institution, in an amount
not to exceed two percent of the adjusted basis of the financial institution's assets, are not taken into account for the purpose of determining the portion of the financial institution's interest expense
subject to the pro rata interest disallowance rule of section 265(b).
For purposes of this rule, a refunding bond (whether a current or
advance refunding) is treated as issued on the date of the issuance
of the refunded bond (or in the case of a series of refundings, the
original bond).

The provision also amends section 291(e) to provide that tax-
exempt obligations issued during 2009 and 2010, and not taken

---

[122] Sec. 265(b)(3)(C).
[123] Sec. 265(b)(3)(E).
[124] Sec. 265(b)(3)(F).
[125] Sec. 291(e)(1).

into account for purposes of the calculation of a financial institution's interest expense subject to the pro rata interest disallowance rule, are treated as having been acquired on August 7, 1986. As a result, such obligations are financial institution preference items, and the amount allowable as a deduction by a financial institution with respect to interest incurred to carry such obligations is reduced by 20 percent.

Modifications to qualified small issuer exception

With respect to tax-exempt obligations issued during 2009 and 2010, the provision increases from $10 million to $30 million the annual limit for qualified small issuers.

In addition, in the case of "qualified financing issue" issued in 2009 or 2010, the provision applies the $30 million annual volume limitation at the borrower level (rather than at the level of the pooled financing issuer). Thus, for the purpose of applying the requirements of the section 265(b)(3) qualified small issuer exception, the portion of the proceeds of a qualified financing issue that are loaned to a "qualified borrower" that participates in the issue are treated as a separate issue with respect to which the qualified borrower is deemed to be the issuer.

A "qualified financing issue" is any composite, pooled or other conduit financing issue the proceeds of which are used directly or indirectly to make or finance loans to one or more ultimate borrowers all of whom are qualified borrowers. A "qualified borrower" means (1) a State or political subdivision of a State or (2) an organization described in section 501(c)(3) and exempt from tax under section 501(a). Thus, for example, a $100 million pooled financing issue that was issued in 2009 could qualify for the section 265(b)(3) exception if the proceeds of such issue were used to make four equal loans of $25 million to four qualified borrowers. However, if (1) more than $30 million were loaned to any qualified borrower, (2) any borrower were not a qualified borrower, or (3) any borrower would, if it were the issuer of a separate issue in an amount equal to the amount loaned to such borrower, fail to meet any of the other requirements of section 265(b)(3), the entire $100 million pooled financing issue would fail to qualify for the exception.

For purposes of determining whether an issuer meets the requirements of the small issuer exception, qualified 501(c)(3) bonds issued in 2009 or 2010 are treated as if they were issued by the 501(c)(3) organization for whose benefit they were issued (and not by the actual issuer of such bonds). In addition, in the case of an organization described in section 501(c)(3) and exempt from taxation under section 501(a), requirements for "qualified financing issues" shall be applied as if the section 501(c)(3) organization were the issuer. Thus, in any event, an organization described in section 501(c)(3) and exempt from taxation under section 501(a) shall be limited to the $30 million per issuer cap for qualified tax exempt obligations described in section 265(b)(3).

Effective date.—The provisions are effective for obligations issued after December 31, 2008.

SENATE AMENDMENT

The Senate amendment is the same as the House bill.

CONFERENCE AGREEMENT

The conference agreement follows the House bill and the Senate amendment.

2. Temporary modification of alternative minimum tax limitations on tax-exempt bonds (sec. 1503 of the House bill, sec. 1503 of the Senate amendment, sec. 1503 of the conference agreement, and secs. 56 and 57 of the Code)

PRESENT LAW

Present law imposes an alternative minimum tax ("AMT") on individuals and corporations. AMT is the amount by which the tentative minimum tax exceeds the regular income tax. The tentative minimum tax is computed based upon a taxpayer's alternative minimum taxable income ("AMTI"). AMTI is the taxpayer's taxable income modified to take into account certain preferences and adjustments. One of the preference items is tax-exempt interest on certain tax-exempt bonds issued for private activities (sec. 57(a)(5)). Also, in the case of a corporation, an adjustment based on current earnings is determined, in part, by taking into account 75 percent of items, including tax-exempt interest, that are excluded from taxable income but included in the corporation's earnings and profits (sec. 56(g)(4)(B)).

HOUSE BILL

The House bill provides that tax-exempt interest on private activity bonds issued in 2009 and 2010 is not an item of tax preference for purposes of the alternative minimum tax and interest on tax exempt bonds issued in 2009 and 2010 is not included in the corporate adjustment based on current earnings. For these purposes, a refunding bond is treated as issued on the date of the issuance of the refunded bond (or in the case of a series of refundings, the original bond).

Effective date.—The provision applies to interest on bonds issued after December 31, 2008.

SENATE AMENDMENT

The Senate amendment is the same as the House bill.

CONFERENCE AGREEMENT

The conference agreement provides that tax-exempt interest on private activity bonds issued in 2009 and 2010 is not an item of tax preference for purposes of the alternative minimum tax and interest on tax exempt bonds issued in 2009 and 2010 is not included in the corporate adjustment based on current earnings. For these purposes, a refunding bond is treated as issued on the date of the issuance of the refunded bond (or in the case of a series of refundings, the original bond).

The conference agreement also provides that tax-exempt interest on private activity bonds issued in 2009 and 2010 to currently refund a private activity bond issued after December 31, 2003, and before January 1, 2009, is not an item of tax preference for purposes of the alternative minimum tax. Also tax-exempt interest on bonds issued in 2009 and 2010 to currently refund a bond issued after December 31, 2003, and before January 1, 2009, is not included in the corporate adjustment based on current earnings.

Effective date.—The provision applies to interest on bonds issued after December 31, 2008.

3. Temporary expansion of availability of industrial development bonds to facilities creating intangible property and other modifications (sec. 1301 of the Senate amendment, sec. 1301 of the conference agreement, and sec. 144(a) of the Code)

PRESENT LAW

Qualified small issue bonds (commonly referred to as "industrial development bonds" or "small issue IDBs") are tax-exempt bonds issued by State and local governments to finance private business manufacturing facilities (including certain directly related and ancillary facilities) or the acquisition of land and equipment by certain farmers. In both instances, these bonds are subject to limits on the amount of financing that may be provided, both for a single borrowing and in the aggregate. In general, no more than $1 million of small-issue bond financing may be outstanding at any time for property of a business (including related parties) located in the same municipality or county. Generally, this $1 million limit may be increased to $10 million if, in addition to outstanding bonds, all other capital expenditures of the business (including related parties) in the same municipality or county are counted toward the limit over a six-year period that begins three years before the issue date of the bonds and ends three years after such date. Outstanding aggregate borrowing is limited to $40 million per borrower (including related parties) regardless of where the property is located.

The Code permits up to $10 million of capital expenditures to be disregarded, in effect increasing from $10 million to $20 million the maximum allowable amount of total capital expenditures by an eligible business in the same municipality or county. However, no more than $10 million of bond financing may be outstanding at any time for property of an eligible business (including related parties) located in the same municipality or county. Other limits (e.g., the $40 million per borrower limit) also continue to apply.

A manufacturing facility is any facility which is used in the manufacturing or production of tangible personal property (including the processing resulting in a change in the condition of such property). Manufacturing facilities include facilities that are directly related and ancillary to a manufacturing facility (as described in the previous sentence) if (1) such facilities are located on the same site as the manufacturing facility and (2) not more than 25 percent of the net proceeds of the issue are used to provide such facilities.[126]

---

[126] The 25 percent restriction was enacted by the Technical and Miscellaneous Tax Act of 1988 because of concern over the scope of the definition of manufacturing facility. See H.R. Rpt. No. 100–795 (1988). The amendment was intended to clarify that while the manufacturing facility definition does not preclude the financing of ancillary activities, the 25 percent restriction was intended to limit the use of bond proceeds to finance facilities other than for "core manufacturing." The conference agreement followed the House bill, which the conference report described as follows: "The House bill clarifies that up to 25 percent of the proceeds of a qualified

No provision.

In general

For bonds issued after the date of enactment and before January 1, 2011, the provision expands the definition of manufacturing facilities to mean any facility that is used in the manufacturing, creation, or production of tangible property or intangible property (within the meaning of section 197(d)(1)(C)(iii)). For this purpose, intangible property means any patent, copyright, formula, process, design, knowhow, format, or other similar item. It is intended to include among other items, the creation of computer software, and intellectual property associated bio-tech and pharmaceuticals.

In lieu of the directly related and ancillary test of present law, the provision provides a special rule for bonds issued after the date of enactment and before January 1, 2011. For these bonds, the provision provides that facilities that are functionally related and subordinate to the manufacturing facility are treated as a manufacturing facility and the 25 percent of net proceeds restriction does not apply to such facilities.[127] Functionally related and subordinate facilities must be located on the same site as the manufacturing facility.

Effective date

The provision is effective for bonds issued after the date of enactment and before January 1, 2011.

The conference agreement follows the Senate amendment.

4. Qualified school construction bonds (sec. 1511 of the House bill, sec. 1521 of the Senate amendment, sec. 1521 of the conference agreement, and new sec. 54F of the Code)

Tax-exempt bonds

Interest on State and local governmental bonds generally is excluded from gross income for Federal income tax purposes if the proceeds of the bonds are used to finance direct activities of these governmental units or if the bonds are repaid with revenues of the governmental units. These can include tax-exempt bonds which finance public schools.[128] An issuer must file with the Internal Revenue Service certain information about the bonds issued in order

---

small issue may be used to finance ancillary activities which are carried out at the manufacturing site. All such ancillary activities must be subordinate and integral to the manufacturing process."

[127] The provision is based in part on a similar rule applicable to exempt facility bonds. Treas. Reg. sec. 1.103–8(a)(3) provides: "(3) Functionally related and subordinate. An exempt facility includes any land, building, or other property functionally related and subordinate to such facility. Property is not functionally related and subordinate to a facility if it is not of a character and size commensurate with the character and size of such facility."

[128] Sec. 103.

for that bond issue to be tax-exempt.[129] Generally, this information return is required to be filed no later than the 15th day of the second month after the close of the calendar quarter in which the bonds were issued.

The tax exemption for State and local bonds does not apply to any arbitrage bond.[130] An arbitrage bond is defined as any bond that is part of an issue if any proceeds of the issue are reasonably expected to be used (or intentionally are used) to acquire higher yielding investments or to replace funds that are used to acquire higher yielding investments.[131] In general, arbitrage profits may be earned only during specified periods (e.g., defined "temporary periods") before funds are needed for the purpose of the borrowing or on specified types of investments (e.g., "reasonably required reserve or replacement funds"). Subject to limited exceptions, investment profits that are earned during these periods or on such investments must be rebated to the Federal Government.

Qualified zone academy bonds

As an alternative to traditional tax-exempt bonds, States and local governments were given the authority to issue "qualified zone academy bonds." [132] A total of $400 million of qualified zone academy bonds is authorized to be issued annually in calendar years 1998 through 2009. The $400 million aggregate bond cap is allocated each year to the States according to their respective populations of individuals below the poverty line. Each State, in turn, allocates the credit authority to qualified zone academies within such State.

A taxpayer holding a qualified zone academy bond on the credit allowance date is entitled to a credit. The credit is includible in gross income (as if it were a taxable interest payment on the bond), and may be claimed against regular income tax and alternative minimum tax liability.

The Treasury Department sets the credit rate at a rate estimated to allow issuance of qualified zone academy bonds without discount and without interest cost to the issuer.[133] The Secretary determines credit rates for tax credit bonds based on general assumptions about credit quality of the class of potential eligible issuers and such other factors as the Secretary deems appropriate. The Secretary may determine credit rates based on general credit market yield indexes and credit ratings. The maximum term of the bond is determined by the Treasury Department, so that the present value of the obligation to repay the principal on the bond is 50 percent of the face value of the bond.

"Qualified zone academy bonds" are defined as any bond issued by a State or local government, provided that (1) at least 95 percent of the proceeds are used for the purpose of renovating, providing equipment to, developing course materials for use at, or training teachers and other school personnel in a "qualified zone

---

[129] Sec. 149(e).
[130] Sec. 103(a) and (b)(2).
[131] Sec. 148.
[132] Sec. 1397E.
[133] Given the differences in credit quality and other characteristics of individual issuers, the Secretary cannot set credit rates in a manner that will allow each issuer to issue tax credit bonds at par.

academy" and (2) private entities have promised to contribute to the qualified zone academy certain equipment, technical assistance or training, employee services, or other property or services with a value equal to at least 10 percent of the bond proceeds.

A school is a "qualified zone academy" if (1) the school is a public school that provides education and training below the college level, (2) the school operates a special academic program in co-operation with businesses to enhance the academic curriculum and increase graduation and employment rates, and (3) either (a) the school is located in an empowerment zone or enterprise community designated under the Code, or (b) it is reasonably expected that at least 35 percent of the students at the school will be eligible for free or reduced-cost lunches under the school lunch program established under the National School Lunch Act.

The arbitrage requirements which generally apply to interest-bearing tax-exempt bonds also generally apply to qualified zone academy bonds. In addition, an issuer of qualified zone academy bonds must reasonably expect to and actually spend 100 percent of the proceeds of such bonds on qualified zone academy property within the three years period that begins on the date of issuance. To the extent less than 100 percent of the proceeds are used to finance qualified zone academy property during the three years spending period, bonds will continue to qualify as qualified zone academy bonds if unspent proceeds are used within 90 days from the end of such three years period to redeem any nonqualified bonds. The three years spending period may be extended by the Secretary if the issuer establishes that the failure to meet the spending requirement is due to reasonable cause and the related purposes for issuing the bonds will continue to proceed with due diligence.

Two special arbitrage rules apply to qualified zone academy bonds. First, available project proceeds invested during the three-year period beginning on the date of issue are not subject to the arbitrage restrictions (i.e., yield restriction and rebate requirements). Available project proceeds are proceeds from the sale of an issue of qualified zone academy bonds, less issuance costs (not to exceed two percent) and any investment earnings on such proceeds. Thus, available project proceeds invested during the three-year spending period may be invested at unrestricted yields, but the earnings on such investments must be spent on qualified zone academy property. Second, amounts invested in a reserve fund are not subject to the arbitrage restrictions to the extent: (1) such fund is funded at a rate not more rapid than equal annual installments; (2) such fund is funded in a manner reasonably expected to result in an amount not greater than an amount necessary to repay the issue; and (3) the yield on such fund is not greater than the average annual interest rate of tax-exempt obligations having a term of 10 years or more that are issued during the month the qualified zone academy bonds are issued.

Issuers of qualified zone academy bonds are required to report issuance to the Internal Revenue Service in a manner similar to the information returns required for tax-exempt bonds.

In general

The provision creates a new category of tax-credit bonds: qualified school construction bonds. Qualified school construction bonds must meet three requirements: (1) 100 percent of the available project proceeds of the bond issue is used for the construction, rehabilitation, or repair of a public school facility or for the acquisition of land on which such a bond-financed facility is to be constructed; (2) the bond is issued by a State or local government within which such school is located; and (3) the issuer designates such bonds as a qualified school construction bond.

National limitation

There is a national limitation on qualified school construction bonds of $11 billion for calendar years 2009 and 2010, respectively. Allocations of the national limitation of qualified school construction bonds are divided between the States and certain large school districts. The States receive 60 percent of the national limitation for a calendar year and the remaining 40 percent of the national limitation for a calendar year is allocated to certain of the largest school districts.

Allocation to the States

Generally allocations are made to the States under the 60 percent allocation according to their respective populations of children aged five through seventeen. However, the Secretary of the Treasury shall adjust the annual allocations among the States to ensure that for each State the sum of its allocations under the 60 percent allocation plus any allocations to large educational agencies within the States is not less than a minimum percentage. A State's minimum percentage for a calendar year is a product of 1.68 and the minimum percentage described in section 1124(d) of the Elementary and Secondary Education Act of 1965 for such State for the most recent fiscal year ending before such calendar year.

For allocation purposes, a State includes the District of Columbia and any possession of the United States. The provision provides a special allocation for possessions of the United States other than Puerto Rico under the 60 percent share of the national limitation for States. Under this special rule an allocation to a possession other than Puerto Rico is made on the basis of the respective populations of individuals below the poverty line (as defined by the Office of Management and Budget) rather than respective populations of children aged five through seventeen. This special allocation reduces the State allocation share of the national limitation otherwise available for allocation among the States. Under another special rule the Secretary of the Interior may allocate $200 million of school construction bonds for 2009 and 2010, respectively, to Indian schools. This special allocation for Indian schools is to be used for purposes of the construction, rehabilitation, and repair of schools funded by the Bureau of Indian Affairs. For purposes of such allocations Indian tribal governments are qualified issuers. The special allocation for Indian schools does not reduce the State allocation share of the national limitation otherwise available for allocation among the States.

If an amount allocated under this allocation to the States is unused for a calendar year it may be carried forward by the State to the next calendar year.

Allocation to large school districts

The remaining 40 percent of the national limitation for a calendar year is allocated by the Secretary of the Treasury among local educational agencies which are large local educational agencies for such year. This allocation is made in proportion to the respective amounts each agency received for Basic Grants under subpart 2 of Part A of Title I of the Elementary and Secondary Education Act of 1965 for the most recent fiscal year ending before such calendar year. Any unused allocation of any agency within a State may be allocated by the agency to such State. With respect to a calendar year, the term large local educational agency means any local educational agency if such agency is: (1) among the 100 local educational agencies with the largest numbers of children aged 5 through 17 from families living below the poverty level, or (2) one of not more than 25 local educational agencies (other than in 1, immediately above) that the Secretary of Education determines are in particular need of assistance, based on a low level of resources for school construction, a high level of enrollment growth, or other such factors as the Secretary of Education deems appropriate. If any amount allocated to large local educational agency is unused for a calendar year the agency may reallocate such amount to the State in which the agency is located.

The provision makes qualified school construction bonds a type of qualified tax credit bond for purposes of section 54A. In addition, qualified school construction bonds may be issued by Indian tribal governments only to the extent such bonds are issued for purposes that satisfy the present law requirements for tax-exempt bonds issued by Indian tribal governments (i.e., essential governmental functions and certain manufacturing purposes).

The provision requires 100 percent of the available project proceeds of qualified school construction bonds to be used within the three-year period that begins on the date of issuance. Available project proceeds are proceeds from the sale of the issue less issuance costs (not to exceed two percent) and any investment earnings on such sale proceeds. To the extent less than 100 percent of the available project proceeds are used to finance qualified purposes during the three-year spending period, bonds will continue to qualify as qualified school construction bonds if unspent proceeds are used within 90 days from the end of such three-year period to redeem bonds. The three-year spending period may be extended by the Secretary upon the issuer's request demonstrating that the failure to satisfy the three-year requirement is due to reasonable cause and the projects will continue to proceed with due diligence.

Qualified school construction bonds generally are subject to the arbitrage requirements of section 148. However, available project proceeds invested during the three-year spending period are not subject to the arbitrage restrictions (i.e., yield restriction and rebate requirements). In addition, amounts invested in a reserve fund are not subject to the arbitrage restrictions to the extent: (1) such fund is funded at a rate not more rapid than equal annual installments; (2) such fund is funded in a manner reasonably expected to result in an amount not greater than an amount necessary to repay the issue; and (3) the yield on such fund is not greater than the average annual interest rate of tax-exempt obligations having a term of 10 years or more that are issued during the month the qualified school construction bonds are issued.

The maturity of qualified school construction bonds is the term that the Secretary estimates will result in the present value of the obligation to repay the principal on such bonds being equal to 50 percent of the face amount of such bonds, using as a discount rate the average annual interest rate of tax-exempt obligations having a term of 10 years or more that are issued during the month the qualified school construction bonds are issued.

As with present-law tax credit bonds, the taxpayer holding qualified school construction bonds on a credit allowance date is entitled to a tax credit. The credit rate on the bonds is set by the Secretary at a rate that is 100 percent of the rate that would permit issuance of such bonds without discount and interest cost to the issuer. The amount of the tax credit is determined by multiplying the bond's credit rate by the face amount on the holder's bond. The credit accrues quarterly, is includible in gross income (as if it were an interest payment on the bond), and can be claimed against regular income tax liability and alternative minimum tax liability. Unused credits may be carried forward to succeeding taxable years. In addition, credits may be separated from the ownership of the underlying bond in a manner similar to the manner in which interest coupons can be stripped from interest-bearing bonds.

Issuers of qualified school construction bonds are required to certify that the financial disclosure requirements and applicable State and local law requirements governing conflicts of interest are satisfied with respect to such issue, as well as any other additional conflict of interest rules prescribed by the Secretary with respect to any Federal, State, or local government official directly involved with the issuance of qualified school construction bonds.

Effective date

The provision is effective for bonds issued after December 31, 2008.

SENATE AMENDMENT

In general

The Senate amendment is the same as the House bill.

National limitation

There is a national limitation on qualified school construction bonds of $5 billion for Calendar years 2009 and 2010, respectively. Also, allocations of the national limitation of qualified school construction bonds are divided between the States with no special allocations to certain large school districts.

Allocation to the States

The allocations are made to the States according to their respective populations of children aged five through seventeen. However, the Secretary of the Treasury shall adjust the annual allocations among the States to ensure that for each State is not less than a minimum percentage. A State's minimum percentage for a calendar year is calculated by dividing (1) the amount the State is eligible to receive under section 1124(d) of the Elementary and Secondary Education Act of 1965 for such State for the most recent fiscal year ending before such calendar year by (2) the amount all States are eligible to received under section 1124(d) of the Elementary and Secondary Education Act of 1965 for such fiscal year, and then multiplying the result by 100.

Allocation to large school districts

No portion of the national limitation for a calendar year is allocated by the Secretary of the Treasury among local educational agencies which are large local educational agencies for such year.

Effective date

The provision is effective for obligations issued after the date of enactment.

CONFERENCE AGREEMENT

In general

The provision creates a new category of tax-credit bonds: qualified school construction bonds. Qualified school construction bonds must meet three requirements: (1) 100 percent of the available project proceeds of the bond issue is used for the construction, rehabilitation, or repair of a public school facility or for the acquisition of land on which such a bond-financed facility is to be constructed; (2) the bond is issued by a State or local government within which such school is located; and (3) the issuer designates such bonds as a qualified school construction bond.

National limitation

There is a national limitation on qualified school construction bonds of $11 billion for calendar years 2009 and 2010, respectively.

Allocation to the States

The national limitation is tentatively allocated among the States in proportion to respective amounts each such State is eligible to receive under section 1124 of the Elementary and Secondary Education Act of 1965 for the most recent fiscal year ending before such calendar year. The amount each State is allocated under the above formula is then reduced by the amount received by any local large educational agency within the State.

For allocation purposes, a State includes the District of Columbia and any possession of the United States. The provision provides a special allocation for possessions of the United States other than Puerto Rico under the national limitation for States. Under this special rule an allocation to a possession other than Puerto Rico is made on the basis of the respective populations of individuals below the poverty line (as defined by the Office of Management and Budget) rather than respective populations of children aged five through seventeen. This special allocation reduces the State allocation share of the national limitation otherwise available for allocation among the States. Under another special rule the Secretary of the Interior may allocate $200 million of school construction bonds for 2009 and 2010, respectively, to Indian schools. This special allocation for Indian schools is to be used for purposes of the construction, rehabilitation, and repair of schools funded by the Bureau of Indian Affairs. For purposes of such allocations Indian tribal governments are qualified issuers. The special allocation for Indian schools does not reduce the State allocation share of the national limitation otherwise available for allocation among the States.

If an amount allocated under this allocation to the States is unused for a calendar year it may be carried forward by the State to the next calendar year.

Allocation to large school districts

Forty percent of the national limitation is allocated among large local educational agencies in proportion to the respective amounts each agency received under section 1124 of the Elementary and Secondary Education Act of 1965 for the most recent fiscal year ending before such calendar year. Any unused allocation of any agency within a State may be allocated by the agency to such State. With respect to a calendar year, the term large local educational agency means any local educational agency if such agency is: (1) among the 100 local educational agencies with the largest numbers of children aged 5 through 17 from families living below the poverty level, or (2) one of not more than 25 local educational agencies (other than in 1, immediately above) that the Secretary of Education determines are in particular need of assistance, based on a low level of resources for school construction, a high level of enrollment growth, or other such factors as the Secretary of Education deems appropriate. If any amount allocated to large local educational agency is unused for a calendar year the agency may reallocate such amount to the State in which the agency is located.

Application of qualified tax credit bond rules

The provision makes qualified school construction bonds a type of qualified tax credit bond for purposes of section 54A. In addition, qualified school construction bonds may be issued by Indian tribal governments only to the extent such bonds are issued for purposes that satisfy the present law requirements for tax-exempt bonds issued by Indian tribal governments (i.e., essential governmental functions and certain manufacturing purposes).

The provision requires 100 percent of the available project proceeds of qualified school construction bonds to be used within the three-year period that begins on the date of issuance. Available project proceeds are proceeds from the sale of the issue less issuance costs (not to exceed two percent) and any investment earnings on such sale proceeds. To the extent less than 100 percent of the available project proceeds are used to finance qualified purposes during the three-year spending period, bonds will continue to qualify as qualified school construction bonds if unspent proceeds are used within 90 days from the end of such three-year period to redeem bonds. The three-year spending period may be extended by the Secretary upon the issuer's request demonstrating that the failure to satisfy the three-year requirement is due to reasonable cause and the projects will continue to proceed with due diligence.

Qualified school construction bonds generally are subject to the arbitrage requirements of section 148. However, available project proceeds invested during the three-year spending period are not subject to the arbitrage restrictions (i.e., yield restriction and rebate requirements). In addition, amounts invested in a reserve fund are not subject to the arbitrage restrictions to the extent: (1) such fund is funded at a rate not more rapid than equal annual installments; (2) such fund is funded in a manner reasonably expected to result in an amount not greater than an amount necessary to repay the issue; and (3) the yield on such fund is not greater than the average annual interest rate of tax-exempt obligations having a term of 10 years or more that are issued during the month the qualified school construction bonds are issued.

The maturity of qualified school construction bonds is the term that the Secretary estimates will result in the present value of the obligation to repay the principal on such bonds being equal to 50 percent of the face amount of such bonds, using as a discount rate the average annual interest rate of tax-exempt obligations having a term of 10 years or more that are issued during the month the qualified school construction bonds are issued.

As with present-law tax credit bonds, the taxpayer holding qualified school construction bonds on a credit allowance date is entitled to a tax credit. The credit rate on the bonds is set by the Secretary at a rate that is 100 percent of the rate that would permit issuance of such bonds without discount and interest cost to the issuer. The amount of the tax credit is determined by multiplying the bond's credit rate by the face amount on the holder's bond. The credit accrues quarterly, is includible in gross income (as if it were an interest payment on the bond), and can be claimed against regular income tax liability and alternative minimum tax liability. Unused credits may be carried forward to succeeding taxable years. In addition, credits may be separated from the ownership of the underlying bond in a manner similar to the manner in which interest coupons can be stripped from interest-bearing bonds.

Issuers of qualified school construction bonds are required to certify that the financial disclosure requirements and applicable State and local law requirements governing conflicts of interest are satisfied with respect to such issue, as well as any other additional conflict of interest rules prescribed by the Secretary with respect to any Federal, State, or local government official directly involved with the issuance of qualified school construction bonds.

Effective date

The provision is effective for obligations issued after the date of enactment.

5. Extend and expand qualified zone academy bonds (sec. 1512 of the House bill, sec. 1522 of the Senate amendment, sec. 1522 of the conference agreement, and sec. 54E of the Code)

PRESENT LAW

Tax-exempt bonds

Interest on State and local governmental bonds generally is excluded from gross income for Federal income tax purposes if the proceeds of the bonds are used to finance direct activities of these governmental units or if the bonds are repaid with revenues of the governmental units. These can include tax-exempt bonds which finance public schools.[134] An issuer must file with the Internal Revenue Service certain information about the bonds issued in order for that bond issue to be tax-exempt.[135] Generally, this information return is required to be filed no later the 15th day of the second month after the close of the calendar quarter in which the bonds were issued.

The tax exemption for State and local bonds does not apply to any arbitrage bond.[136] An arbitrage bond is defined as any bond that is part of an issue if any proceeds of the issue are reasonably expected to be used (or intentionally are used) to acquire high fielding investments or to replace funds that are used to acquire higher yielding investments.[137] In general, arbitrage profits may be earned only during specified periods (e.g., defined "temporary periods") before funds are needed for the purpose of the borrowing or on specified types of investments (e.g., "reasonably required reserve or replacement funds"). Subject to limited exceptions, investment profits that are earned during these periods or on such investments must be rebated to the Federal Government.

Qualified zone academy bonds

As an alternative to traditional tax-exempt bonds, States and local governments were given the authority to issue "qualified zone academy bonds."[138] A total of $400 million of qualified zone academy bonds is authorized to be issued annually in calendar years 1998 through 2009. The $400 million aggregate bond cap is allocated each year to the States according to their respective populations of individuals below the poverty line. Each State, in turn, allocates the credit authority to qualified zone academies within such State.

A taxpayer holding a qualified zone academy bond on the credit allowance date is entitled to a credit. The credit is includible in gross income (as if it were a taxable interest payment on the bond), and may be claimed against regular income tax and alternative minimum tax liability.

The Treasury Department sets the credit rate at a rate estimated to allow issuance qualified zone academy bonds without dis-

---

[134] Sec. 103.
[135] Sec. 149(e).
[136] Sec. 103(a) and (b)(2).
[137] Sec. 148.
[138] See secs. 54E and 1397E.

count and without interest cost to the issuer.[139] The Secretary determines credit rates for tax credit bonds based on general assumptions about credit quality of the class of potential eligible issuers and such other factors as the Secretary deems appropriate. The Secretary may determine credit rates based on general credit market yield indexes and credit ratings. The maximum term of the bond is determined by the Treasury Department, so that the present value of the obligation to repay the principal on the bond is 50 percent of the face value of the bond.

"Qualified zone academy bonds" are defined as any bond issued by a State or local government, provided that (1) at least 95 percent of the proceeds are used for the purpose of renovating, providing equipment to, developing course materials for use at, or training teachers and other school personnel in a "qualified zone academy" and (2) private entities have promised to contribute to the qualified zone academy certain equipment, technical assistance or training, employee services, or other property or services with a value equal to at least 10 percent of the bond proceeds.

A school is a "qualified zone academy" if (1) the school is a public school that provides education and training below the college level, (2) the school operates a special academic program in cooperation with businesses to enhance the academic curriculum and increase graduation and employment rates, and (3) either (a) the school is located in an empowerment zone or enterprise community designated under the Code, or (b) it is reasonably expected that at least 35 percent of the students at the school will be eligible for free or reduced-cost lunches under the school lunch program established under the National School Lunch Act.

The arbitrage requirements which generally apply to interest-bearing tax-exempt bonds also generally apply to qualified zone academy bonds. In addition, an issuer of qualified zone academy bonds must reasonably expect to and actually spend 100 percent or more of the proceeds of such bonds on qualified zone academy property within the three-year period that begins on the date of issuance. To the extent less than 100 percent of the proceeds are used to finance qualified zone academy property during the three-year spending period, bonds will continue to qualify as qualified zone academy bonds if unspent proceeds are used within 90 days from the end of such three-year period to redeem any nonqualified bonds. The three-year spending period may be extended by the Secretary if the issuer establishes that the failure to meet the spending requirement is due to reasonable cause and the related purposes for issuing the bonds will continue to proceed with due diligence.

Two special arbitrage rules apply to qualified zone academy bonds. First, available project proceeds invested during the three-year period beginning on the date of issue are not subject to the arbitrage restrictions (i.e., yield restriction and rebate requirements). Available project proceeds are proceeds from the sale of an issue of qualified zone academy bonds, less issuance costs (not to exceed two percent) and any investment earnings on such proceeds.

---

[139] Given the differences in credit quality and other characteristics of individual issuers, the Secretary cannot set credit rates in a manner that will allow each issuer to issue tax credit bonds at par.

Thus, available project proceeds invested during the three-year spending period may be invested at unrestricted yields, but the earnings on such investments must be spent on qualified zone academy property. Second, amounts invested in a reserve fund are not subject to the arbitrage restrictions to the extent: (1) such fund is funded at a rate not more rapid than equal annual installments; (2) such fund is funded in a manner reasonably expected to result in an amount not greater than an amount necessary to repay the issue; and (3) the yield on such fund is not greater than the average annual interest rate of tax-exempt obligations having a term of 10 years or more that are issued during the month the qualified zone academy bonds are issued.

Issuers of qualified zone academy bonds are required to report issuance to the Internal Revenue Service in a manner similar to the information returns required for tax-exempt bonds.

HOUSE BILL

In general

The provision extends and expands the present-law qualified zone academy bond program. The provision authorizes issuance of up to $1.4 billion of qualified zone academy bonds annually for 2009 and 2010, respectively.

Effective date

The provision applies to obligations issued after December 31, 2008.

SENATE AMENDMENT

The Senate amendment is the same as the House bill.

CONFERENCE AGREEMENT

The conference agreement follows the House bill and the Senate amendment.

6. Build America bonds (sec. 1521 of the House bill, sec. 1531 of the Senate amendment, sec. 1531 of the conference agreement, and new secs. 54AA and 6431 of the Code)

PRESENT LAW

In general

Under present law, gross income does not include interest on State or local bonds. State and local bonds are classified generally as either governmental bonds or private activity bonds. Governmental bonds are bonds the proceeds of which are primarily used to finance governmental functions or which are repaid with governmental funds. Private activity bonds are bonds in which the State or local government serves as a conduit providing financing to nongovernmental persons (e.g., private businesses or individuals). The exclusion from income for State and local bonds does not apply to private activity bonds, unless the bonds are issued for certain permitted purposes ("qualified private activity bonds") and other Code requirements are met.

Private activity bonds

The Code defines a private activity bond as any bond that satisfies (1) the private business use test and the private security or payment test ("the private business test"); or (2) "the private loan financing test." [140]

Private business test

Under the private business test, a bond is a private activity bond if it is part of an issue in which:

1. More than 10 percent of the proceeds of the issue (including use of the bond-financed property) are to be used in the trade or business of any person other than a governmental unit ("private business use"); and

2. More than 10 percent of the payment of principal or interest on the issue is, directly or indirectly, secured by (a) property used or to be used for a private business use or (b) to be derived from payments in respect of property, or borrowed money, used or to be used for a private business use ("private payment test"). [141]

A bond is not a private activity bond unless both parts of the private business test (i.e., the private business use test and the private payment test) are met. Thus, a facility that is 100 percent privately used does not cause the bonds financing such facility to be private activity bonds if the bonds are not secured by or paid with private payments. For example, land improvements that benefit a privately-owned factory may be financed with governmental bonds if the debt service on such bonds is not paid by the factory owner or other private parties.

Private loan financing test

A bond issue satisfies the private loan financing test if proceeds exceeding the lesser of $5 million or five percent of such proceeds are used directly or indirectly to finance loans to one or more nongovernmental persons. Private loans include both business and other (e.g., personal) uses and payments by private persons; however, in the case of business uses and payments, all private loans also constitute private business uses and payments subject to the private business test.

Arbitrage restrictions

The exclusion from income for interest on State and local bonds does not apply to any arbitrage bond. [142] An arbitrage bond is defined as any bond that is part of an issue if any proceeds of the issue are reasonably expected to be used (or intentionally are used) to acquire higher yielding investments or to replace funds that are used to acquire higher yielding investments. [143] In general, arbitrage profits may be earned only during specified periods (e.g., defined "temporary periods") before funds are needed for the pur-

---

[140] Sec. 141.
[141] The 10 percent private business test is reduced to five percent in the case of private business uses (and payments with respect to such uses) that are unrelated to any governmental use being financed by the issue.
[142] Sec. 103(a) and (b)(2).
[143] Sec. 148.

pose of the borrowing or on specified types of investments (e.g., "reasonably required reserve or replacement funds"). Subject to limited exceptions, investment profits that are earned during these periods or on such investments must be rebated to the Federal Government.

Qualified tax credit bonds

In lieu of interest, holders of qualified tax credit bonds receive a tax credit that accrues quarterly. The following bonds are qualified tax credit bonds: qualified forestry conservation bonds, new clean renewable energy bonds, qualified energy conservation bonds, and qualified zone academy bonds.[144]

Section 54A of the Code sets forth general rules applicable to qualified tax credit bonds. These rules include requirements regarding credit allowance dates, the expenditure of available project proceeds, reporting, arbitrage, maturity limitations, and financial conflicts of interest, among other special rules.

A taxpayer who holds a qualified tax credit bond on one or more credit allowance dates of the bond during the taxable year shall be allowed a credit against the taxpayer's income tax for the taxable year. In general, the credit amount for any credit allowance date is 25 percent of the annual credit determined with respect to the bond. The annual credit is determined by multiplying the applicable credit rate by the outstanding face amount of the bond. The applicable credit rate for the bond is the rate that the Secretary estimates will permit the issuance of the qualified tax credit bond with a specified maturiy or redemption date without discount and without interest cost to the qualified issuer.[145] The Secretary determines credit rates for tax credit bonds based on general assumptions about credit quality of the class of potential eligible issuers and such other factors as the Secretary deems appropriate. The Secretary may determine credit rates based on general credit market yield indexes and credit ratings.

The credit is included in gross income and, under regulations prescribed by the Secretary, may be stripped (a separation (including at issuance) of the ownership of a qualified tax credit bond and the entitlement to the credit with respect to such bond).

Section 54A of the Code requires that 100 percent of the available project proceeds of qualified tax credit bonds must be used within the three-year period that begins on the date of issuance. Available project proceeds are proceeds from the sale of the bond issue less issuance costs (not to exceed two percent) and any investment earnings on such sale proceeds. To the extent less than 100 percent of the available project proceeds are used to finance qualified projects during the three-year spending period, bonds will continue to qualify as qualified tax credit bonds if unspent proceeds are used within 90 days from the end of such three-year period to redeem bonds. The three-year spending period may be extended by the Secretary upon the issuer's request demonstrating that the fail-

---

[144] See secs. 54B, 54C, 54D, and 54E.

[145] Given the differences in credit quality and other characteristics of individual issuers, the Secretary cannot set credit rates in a manner that will allow each issuer to issue tax credit bonds at par.

ure to satisfy the three-year requirement is due to reasonable cause and the projects will continue to proceed with due diligence.

Qualified tax credit bonds generally are subject to the arbitrage requirements of section 148. However, available project proceeds invested during the three-year spending period are not subject to the arbitrage restrictions (i.e., yield restriction and rebate requirements). In addition, amounts invested in a reserve fund are not subject to the arbitrage restrictions to the extent: (1) Such fund is funded at a rate not more rapid than equal annual installments; (2) such fund is funded in a manner reasonably expected to result in an amount not greater than an amount necessary to repay the issue; and (3) the yield on such fund is not greater than the average annual interest rate of tax-exempt obligations having a term of 10 years or more that are issued during the month the qualified tax credit bonds are issued.

The maturity of qualified tax credit bonds is the term that the Secretary estimates will result in the present value of the obligation to repay the principal on such bonds being equal to 50 percent of the face amount of such bonds, using as a discount rate the average annual interest rate of tax-exempt obligations having a term of 10 years or more that are issued during the month the qualified tax credit bonds are issued.

HOUSE BILL

In general

The provision permits an issuer to elect to have an otherwise tax-exempt bond treated as a "taxable governmental bond." A "taxable governmental bond" is any obligation (other than a private activity bond) if the interest on such obligation would be (but for this provision) excludable from gross income under section 103 and the issuer makes an irrevocable election to have the provision apply. In determining if an obligation would be tax-exempt under section 103, the credit (or the payment discussed below for qualified bonds) is not treated as a Federal guarantee. Further, the yield on a taxable governmental bond is determined without regard to the credit. A taxable governmental bond does not include any bond if the issue price has more than a de minimis amount of premium over the stated principal amount of the bond.

The holder of a taxable governmental bond will accrue a tax credit in the amount of 35 percent of the interest paid on the interest payment dates of the bond during the calendar year.[146] The interest payment date is any date on which the holder of record of the taxable governmental bond is entitled to a payment of interest under such bond. The sum of the accrued credits is allowed against regular and alternative minimum tax. Unused credit may be carried forward to succeeding taxable years. The credit, as well as the interest paid by the issuer, is included in gross income and the credit may be stripped under rules similar to those provided in section 54A regarding qualified tax credit bonds. Rules similar to those that apply for S corporations, partnerships and regulated in-

---

[146] Original issue discount (OID) is not treated as a payment of interest for purposes of determining the credit under the provision. OID is the excess of an obligation's stated redemption price at maturity over the obligation's issue price (sec. 1273(a)).

vestment companies with respect to qualified tax credit bonds also apply to the credit.

Unlike the tax credit for bonds issued under section 54A, the credit rate would not be calculated by the Secretary, but rather would be set by law at 35 percent. The actual credit that a taxpayer may claim is determined by multiplying the interest payment that the taxpayer receives from the issuer (i.e., the bond coupon payment) by 35 percent. Because the credit that the taxpayer claims is also included in income, the Committee anticipates that State and local issuers will issue bonds paying interest at rates approximately equal to 74.1 percent of comparable taxable bonds. The Committee anticipates that if an issuer issues a taxable governmental bond with coupons at 74.1 percent of a comparable taxable bond's coupon that the issuer's bond should sell at par. For example, if a taxable bond of comparable risk pays a $1,000 coupon and sells at par, then if a State or local issuer issues an equal-sized bond with coupon of $741.00, such a bond should also sell at par. The taxpayer who acquires the latter bond will receive an interest payment of $741 and may claim a credit of $259 (35 percent of $741). The credit and the interest payment are both included in the taxpayer's income. Thus, the taxpayer's taxable income from this instrument would be $1,000. This is the same taxable income that the taxpayer would recognize from holding the comparable taxable bond. Consequently the issuer's bond should sell at the same price as would the taxable bond.

Special rule for qualified bonds issued during 2009 and 2010

A "qualified bond" is any taxable governmental bond issued as part of an issue if 100 percent of the available project proceeds of such issue are to be used for capital expenditures.[147] The bond must be issued after the date of enactment of the provision and before January 1, 2011. The issuer must make an irrevocable election to have the special rule for qualified bonds apply.

Under the special rule for qualified bonds, in lieu of the tax credit to the holder, the issuer is allowed a credit equal to 35 percent of each interest payment made under such bond.[148] If in 2009 or 2010, the issuer elects to receive the credit, in the example above, for the State or local issuer's bond to sell at par, the issuer would have to issue the bond with a $1,000 interest coupon. The taxpayer who holds such a bond would include $1,000 on interest in his or her income. From the taxpayer's perspective the bond is the same as the taxable bond in the example above and the taxpayer would be willing to pay par for the bond. However, under the provision the State or local issuer would receive a payment of $350

---

[147] Under Treas. Reg. sec. 150–1(b), capital expenditure means any cost of a type that is properly chargeable to capital account (or would be so chargeable with a proper election or with the application of the definition of placed in service under Treas. Reg. sec. 1.150–2(c)) under general Federal income tax principles. For purposes of applying the "general Federal income tax principles" standard, an issuer should generally be treated as if it were a corporation subject to taxation under subchapter C of chapter 1 of the Code. An example of a capital expenditure would include expenditures made for the purchase of fiber-optic cable to provide municipal broadband service.

[148] Original issue discount (OID) is not treated as a payment of interest for purposes of calculating the refundable credit under the provision.

for each $1,000 coupon paid to bondholders. (The net interest cost to the issuer would be $650.)

The payment by the Secretary is to be made contemporaneously with the interest payment made by the issuer, and may be made either in advance or as reimbursement. In lieu of payment to the issuer, the payment may be made to a person making interest payments on behalf of the issuer. For purposes of the arbitrage rules, the yield on a qualified bond is reduced by the amount of the credit/payment.

Transitional coordination with State law

As noted above, interest on a taxable governmental bond and the related credit are includible in gross income to the holder for Federal tax purposes. The provision provides that until a State provides otherwise, the interest on any taxable governmental bond and the amount of any credit, determined with respect to such bond shall be treated as being exempt from Federal income tax for purposes of State income tax laws.

Effective date

The provision is effective for obligations issued after the date of enactment.

SENATE AMENDMENT

In general

The Senate amendment is the same as the House bill except that it renames these bonds "Build America Bonds."

The Senate amendment also restricts these bonds to obligations issued before January 1, 2011.

For bonds issued by small issuers,[149] the credit rate is 40 percent instead of 35 percent.

Special rule for qualified bonds issued during 2009 and 2010

The Senate amendment is the same as the House bill, except for bonds issued by small issuers, the credit rate is 40 percent instead of 35 percent.

Transitional coordination with State law

The Senate amendment is the same as the House bill.

Effective date

The Senate amendment is the same as the House bill.

CONFERENCE AGREEMENT

In general

The conference agreement follows the House bill except that it renames these bonds "Build America Bonds."

The conference agreement restricts these bonds to obligations issued before January 1, 2011.

---

[149] Small issuer status is determined generally by reference to the rules of (sec. 148(f)(4)(D)) and increasing the aggregate face amount of all tax-exempt governmental bonds reasonably expected to be issued during the calendar year from $5 million to $30 million.

Special rule for qualified bonds issued during 2009 and 2010

The conference agreement follows the House bill, except that it allows for a reasonably required reserve fund to be funded from bond proceeds.[150]

Transitional coordination with State law

The conference agreement follows the House bill and the Senate amendment.

Effective date

The conference agreement follows the House bill and the Senate amendment.

7. Recovery zone bonds (sec. 1531 of the House bill, sec. 1401 of the Senate amendment, sec. 1401 of the conference agreement, and new secs. 1400U–1, 1400U–2, and 1400U–3 of the Code)

PRESENT LAW

In general

Under present law, gross income does not include interest on State or local bonds. State and local bonds are classified generally as either governmental bonds or private activity bonds. Governmental bonds are bonds the proceeds of which are primarily used to finance governmental functions or which are repaid with governmental funds. Private activity bonds are bonds in which the State or local government serves as a conduit providing financing to nongovernmental persons (e.g., private businesses or individuals). The exclusion from income for State and local bonds does not apply to private activity bonds unless the bonds are issued for certain permitted purposes ("qualified private activity bonds") and other Code requirements are met.

Private activity bonds

The Code defines a private activity bond as any bond that satisfies (1) the private business use test and the private security or payment test ("the private business test"); or (2) "the private loan financing test."[151]

Private business test

Under the private business test, a bond is a private activity bond if it is part of an issue in which:

1. More than 10 percent of the proceeds of the issue (including use of the bond-financed property) are to be used in the trade or business of any person other than a governmental unit ("private business use"); and

2. More than 10 percent of the payment of principal or interest on the issue is, directly or indirectly, secured by (a) property used or to be used for a private business use or (b) to be derived from payments in respect of property, or borrowed

---

[150] Under section 148(d)(2), a bond is an arbitrage bond if the amount of the proceeds from the sale of such issue that is part or any reserve or replacement fund exceeds 10 percent of the proceeds. As such the interest on such bond would not be tax-exempt under section 103 and thus would not be a qualified bond for purposes of the provision.

[151] Sec. 141.

money, used or to be used for a private business use ("private payment test").[152]

A bond is not a private activity bond unless both parts of the private business test (i.e., the private business use test and the private payment test) are met. Thus, a facility that is 100 percent privately used does not cause the bonds financing such facility to be private activity bonds if the bonds are not secured by or paid with private payments. For example, land improvements that benefit a privately-owned factory may be financed with governmental bonds if the debt service on such bonds is not paid by the factory owner or other private parties and such bonds are not secured by the property.

Private loan financing test

A bond issue satisfies the private loan financing test if proceeds exceeding the lesser of $5 million or five percent of such proceeds are used directly or indirectly to finance loans to one or more nongovernmental persons. Private loans include both business and other (e.g., personal) uses and payments to private persons; however, in the case of business uses and payments, all private loans also constitute private business uses and payments subject to the private business test.

Arbitrage restrictions

The exclusion from income for interest on State and local bonds does not apply to any arbitrage bond.[153] An arbitrage bond is defined as any bond that is part of an issue if any proceeds of the issue are reasonably expected to be used (or intentionally are used) to acquire higher yielding investments or to replace funds that are used to acquire higher yielding investments.[154] In general, arbitrage profits may be earned only during specified periods (e.g., defined "temporary periods") before funds are needed for the purpose of the borrowing or on specified types of investments (e.g., "reasonably required reserve or replacement funds"). Subject to limited exceptions, investment profits that are earned during these periods or on such investments must be rebated to the Federal Government.

Qualified private activity bonds

Qualified private activity bonds permit States or local governments to act as conduits providing tax-exempt financing for certain private activities. The definition of qualified private activity bonds includes an exempt facility bond, or qualified mortgage, veterans' mortgage, small issue, redevelopment, 501(c)(3), or student loan bond (sec. 141(e)).

The definition of an exempt facility bond includes bonds issued to finance certain transportation facilities (airports, ports, mass commuting, and high-speed intercity rail facilities); qualified residential rental projects; privately owned and/or operated utility fa-

---

[152] The 10 percent private business test is reduced to five percent in the case of private business uses (and payments with respect to such uses) that are unrelated to any governmental use being financed by the issue.
[153] Sec. 103(a) and (b)(2).
[154] Sec. 148.

cilities (sewage, water, solid waste disposal, and local district heating and cooling facilities, certain private electric and gas facilities, and hydroelectric dam enhancements); public/private educational facilities; qualified green building and sustainable design projects; and qualified highway or surface freight transfer facilities (sec. 142(a)).

In most cases, the aggregate volume of qualified private activity bonds is restricted by annual aggregate volume limits imposed on bonds issued by issuers within each State ("State volume cap"). For calendar year 2007, the State volume cap, which is indexed for inflation, equals $85 per resident of the State, or $256.24 million, if greater. Exceptions to the State volume cap are provided for bonds for certain governmentally owned facilities (e.g., airports, ports, high-speed intercity rail, and solid waste disposal) and bonds which are subject to separate local, State, or national volume limits (e.g., public/private educational facility bonds, enterprise zone facility bonds, qualified green building bonds, and qualified highway or surface freight transfer facility bonds).

Qualified private activity bonds generally are subject to restrictions on the use of proceeds for the acquisition of land and existing property. In addition, qualified private activity bonds generally are subject to restrictions on the use of proceeds to finance certain specified facilities (e.g., airplanes, skyboxes, other luxury boxes, health club facilities, gambling facilities, and liquor stores), and use of proceeds to pay costs of issuance (e.g., bond counsel and underwriter fees). Small issue and redevelopment bonds also are subject to additional restrictions on the use of proceeds for certain facilities (e.g., golf courses and massage parlors).

Moreover, the term of qualified private activity bonds generally may not exceed 120 percent of the economic life of the property being financed and certain public approval requirements (similar to requirements that typically apply under State law to issuance of governmental debt) apply under Federal law to issuance of private activity bonds.

Qualified tax credit bonds

In lieu of interest, holders of qualified tax credit bonds receive a tax credit that accrues quarterly. The following bonds are qualified tax credit bonds: qualified forestry conservation bonds, new clean renewable energy bonds, qualified energy conservation bonds, and qualified zone academy bonds.[155]

Section 54A of the Code sets forth general rules applicable to qualified tax credit bonds. These rules include requirements regarding the expenditure of available project proceeds, reporting, arbitrage, maturity limitations, and financial conflicts of interest, among other special rules.

A taxpayer who holds a qualified tax credit bond on one or more credit allowance dates of the bond during the taxable year shall be allowed a credit against the taxpayer's income tax for the taxable year. In general, the credit amount for any credit allowance date is 25 percent of the annual credit determined with respect to the bond. The annual credit is determined by multiplying the appli-

---

[155] See secs. 54B, 54C, 54D, and 54E.

cable credit rate by the outstanding face amount of the bond. The applicable credit rate for the bond is the rate that the Secretary estimates will permit the issuance of the qualified tax credit bond with a specified maturity or redemption date without discount and without interest cost to the qualified issuer.[156] The Secretary determines credit rates for tax credit bonds based on general assumptions about credit quality of the class of potential eligible issuers and such other factors as the Secretary deems appropriate. The Secretary may determine credit rates based on general credit market yield indexes and credit ratings. The credit is included in gross income and, under regulations prescribed by the Secretary, may be stripped.

Section 54A of the Code requires that 100 percent of the available project proceeds of qualified tax credit bonds must be used within the three-year period that begins on the date of issuance. Available project proceeds are proceeds from the sale of the bond issue less issuance costs (not to exceed two percent) and any investment earnings on such sale proceeds. To the extent less than 100 percent of the available project proceeds are used to finance qualified projects during the three-year spending period, bonds will continue to qualify as qualified tax credit bonds if unspent proceeds are used within 90 days from the end of such three-year period to redeem bonds. The three-year spending period may be extended by the Secretary upon the issuer's request demonstrating that the failure to satisfy the three-year requirement is due to reasonable cause and the projects will continue to proceed with due diligence.

Qualified tax credit bonds generally are subject to the arbitrage requirements of section 148. However, available project proceeds invested during the three-year spending period are not subject to the arbitrage restrictions (i.e., yield restriction and rebate requirements). In addition, amounts invested in a reserve fund are not subject to the arbitrage restrictions to the extent: (1) such fund is funded at a rate not more rapid than equal annual installments; (2) such fund is funded in a manner reasonably expected to result in an amount not greater than an amount necessary to repay the issue; and (3) the yield on such fund is not greater than the average annual interest rate of tax-exempt obligations having a term of 10 years or more that are issued during the month the qualified tax credit bonds are issued.

The maturity of qualified tax credit bonds is the term that the Secretary estimates will result in the present value of the obligation to repay the principal on such bonds being equal to 50 percent of the face amount of such bonds, using as a discount rate the average annual interest rate of tax-exempt obligations having a term of 10 years or more that are issued during the month the qualified tax credit bonds are issued.

---

[156] Given the differences in credit quality and other characteristics of individual issuers, the Secretary cannot set credit rates in a manner that will allow each issuer to issue tax credit bonds at par.

HOUSE BILL

In general

The provision permits an issuer to designate one or more areas as recovery zones. The area must have significant poverty, unemployment, general distress, or home foreclosures, or be any area for which a designation as an empowerment zone or renewal community is in effect. Issuers may issue recovery zone economic development bonds and recovery zone facility bonds with respect to these zones.

There is a national recovery zone economic development bond limitation of $10 billion. In addition, there is a separate national recovery zone facility bond limitation of $15 billion. The Secretary is to separately allocate the bond limitations among the States in the proportion that each State's employment decline bears to the national decline in employment (the aggregate 2008 State employment declines for all States). In turn each State is to reallocate its allocation among the counties (parishes) and large municipalities in such State in the proportion that each such county or municipality's 2008 employment decline bears to the aggregate employment declines for all counties and municipalities in such State. In calculating the local employment decline with respect to a county, the portion of such decline attributable to a large municipality is disregarded for purposes of determining the county's portion of the State employment decline and is attributable to the large municipality only.

For purposes of the provision "2008 State employment decline" means, with respect to any State, the excess (if any) of (i) the number of individuals employed in such State as determined for December 2007, over (ii) the number of individuals employed in such State as determined for December 2008. The term "large municipality" means a municipality with a population of more than 100,000.

Recovery Zone Economic Development Bonds

New section 54AA(h) of the House bill creates a special rule for qualified bonds (a type of taxable governmental bond) issued before January 1, 2011, that entitles the issuer of such bonds to receive an advance tax credit equal to 35 percent of the interest payable on an interest payment date. For taxable governmental bonds that are designated recovery zone economic development bonds, the applicable percentage is 55 percent.

A recovery zone economic development bond is a taxable governmental bond issued as part of an issue if 100 percent of the available project proceeds of such issue are to be used for one or more qualified economic development purposes and the issuer designates such bond for purposes of this section. A qualified economic development purpose means expenditures for purposes of promoting development or other economic activity in a recovery zone, including (1) capital expenditures paid or incurred with respect to property located in such zone, (2) expenditures for public infrastructure and construction of public facilities located in a recovery zone.

The aggregate face amount of bonds which may be designated by any issuer cannot exceed the amount of the recovery zone economic development bond limitation allocated to such issuer.

Recovery Zone Facility Bonds

The provision creates a new category of exempt facility bonds, "recovery zone facility bonds." A recovery zone facility bond means any bond issued as part of an issue if: (1) 95 percent or more of the net proceeds of such issue are to be used for recovery zone property and (2) such bond is issued before January 1, 2011, and (3) the issuer designates such bond as a recovery zone facility bond. The aggregate face amount of bonds which may be designated by any issuer cannot exceed the amount of the recovery zone facility bond limitation allocated to such issuer.

Under the provision, the term "recovery zone property" means any property subject to depreciation to which section 168 applies (or would apply but for section 179) if (1) such property was acquired by the taxpayer by purchase after the date on which the designation of the recovery zone took effect; (2) the original use of such property in the recovery zone commences with the taxpayer; and (3) substantially all of the use of such property is in the recovery zone and is in the active conduct of a qualified business by the taxpayer in such zone. The term "qualified business" means any trade or business except that the rental to others of real property located in a recovery zone shall be treated as a qualified business only if the property is not residential rental property (as defined in section 168(e)(2)) and does not include any trade or business consisting of the operation of any facility described in section 144(c)(6)(B) (i.e., any private or commercial golf course, country club, massage parlor, hot tub facility, suntan facility, racetrack or other facility used for gambling, or any store the principal purpose of which is the sale of alcoholic beverages for consumption off premises).

Subject to the following exceptions and modifications, issuance of recovery zone facility bonds is subject to the general rules applicable to issuance of qualified private activity bonds:

1. Issuance of the bonds is not subject to the aggregate annual State private activity bond volume limits (sec. 146);

2. The restriction on acquisition of existing property does not apply (sec. 147(d));

Effective date

The provision is effective for obligations issued after the date of enactment.

SENATE AMENDMENT

In general

The Senate amendment is the same as the House bill with a modification for allocating the bonds between the States. Under the Senate amendment each State receives a minimum allocation of one percent of the national recovery zone economic development bond limitation and one percent of the national recovery zone facility bond limitation. The remainder of each bond limitation is separately allocated among the States in the proportion that each State's employment decline bears to the national decline in employment (the aggregate 2008 State employment declines for all States).

Recovery Zone Economic Development Bonds

New section 54AA(g) of the Senate amendment creates a special rule for qualified bonds (a type of Build America Bond) issued before January 1, 2011, that entitles the issuer of such bonds to receive an advance tax credit equal to 35 percent of the interest payable on an interest payment date. For Build America Bonds that are designated recovery zone economic development bonds, the applicable percentage is 40 percent. In other respects the Senate amendment is the same as the House bill.

Recovery Zone Facility Bonds

The Senate amendment is the same as the House bill.

Effective date

The Senate amendment is the same as the House bill.

CONFERENCE AGREEMENT

In general

The conference agreement follows the House bill, with a modification for allocating the bond limitations among the States. Under the conference agreement the national recovery zone economic development bond limitation and national recovery zone facility bond limitation are allocated among the States in the proportion that each State's employment decline bears to the national decline in employment (the aggregate 2008 State employment declines for all States).[157] The Secretary is to adjust each State's allocation for a calendar year such that no State receives less than 0.9 percent of the national recovery zone economic development bond limitation and no less than 0.9 percent of the national recovery zone facility bond limitation. The conference agreement also permits a county or large municipality to waive all or part of its allocation of the State bond limitations to allow further allocation within that State. With respect to all other aspects of the allocation of the bond limitations, the conference agreement follows the House bill.

The conference agreement also provides that a "recovery zone" includes any area designated by the issuer as economically distressed by reason of the closure or realignment of a military installation pursuant to the Defense Base Closure and Realignment Act of 1990.

Recovery Zone Economic Development Bonds

The conference agreement follows the House bill, except the issuer of recovery zone economic development bonds is entitled to receive an advance tax credit equal to 45 percent of the interest

---

[157] The Bureau of Labor Statistics prepares data on regional and State employment and unemployment. See e.g., Bureau of Labor Statistics, USDL 09–0093, Regional and State Employment and Unemployment: December 2008 (January 27, 2009) <http://www.bls.gov/news.release/laus.nr0.htm>.

payable on an interest payment date and the conference agreement allows for a reasonably required reserve fund to be funded from the proceeds of a recovery zone economic development bond.

Recovery Zone Facility Bonds

The conference agreement follows the House bill, except "recovery zone property" is defined as any property subject to depreciation to which section 168 applies (or would apply but for section 179) if (1) such property was constructed, reconstructed, renovated, or acquired by purchase by the taxpayer after the date on which the designation of the recovery zone took effect; (2) the original use of such property in the recovery zone commences with the taxpayer; and (3) substantially all of the use of such property is in the recovery zone and is in the active conduct of a qualified business by the taxpayer in such zone.

Effective date

The conference agreement follows the House bill and the Senate amendment.

8. Tribal economic development bonds (sec. 1532 of the House bill, sec. 1402 of the Senate amendment, sec. 1402 of the conference agreement, and new sec. 7871(f) of the Code)

PRESENT LAW

Under present law, gross income does not include interest on State or local bonds.[158] State and local bonds are classified generally as either governmental bonds or private activity bonds. Governmental bonds are bonds the proceeds of which are primarily used to finance governmental facilities or the debt is repaid with governmental funds. Private activity bonds are bonds in which the State or local government serves as a conduit providing financing to nongovernmental persons. For these purposes, the term "nongovernmental person" includes the Federal government and all other individuals and entities other than States or local governments.[159] Interest on private activity bonds is taxable, unless the bonds are issued for certain purposes permitted by the Code and other requirements are met.[160]

Although not States or subdivisions of States, Indian tribal governments are provided with a tax status similar to State and local governments for specified purposes under the Code.[161] Among the purposes for which a tribal government is treated as a State is the issuance of tax-exempt bonds. Under section 7871(c), tribal governments are authorized to issue tax-exempt bonds only if substantially all of the proceeds are used for essential governmental functions.[162]

The term essential governmental function does not include any function that is not customarily performed by State and local governments with general taxing powers. Section 7871(c) further prohibits Indian tribal governments from issuing tax-exempt private

---

[158] Sec. 103.
[159] Sec. 141(b)(6); Treas. Reg. sec. 1.141–1(b).
[160] Secs. 103(b)(1) and 141.
[161] Sec. 7871.
[162] Sec. 7871(c).

activity bonds (as defined in section 141(a) of the Code) with the exception of certain bonds for manufacturing facilities.

Tribal Economic Development Bonds

The provision allows Indian tribal governments to issue "tribal economic development bonds." There is a national bond limitation of $2 billion, to be allocated as the Secretary determines appropriate, in consultation with the Secretary of the Interior. Tribal economic development bonds issued by an Indian tribal government are treated as if such bond were issued by a State except that section 146 (relating to State volume limitations) does not apply.

A tribal economic development bond is any bond issued by an Indian tribal government (I) the interest on which would be tax-exempt if issued by a State or local government but would be taxable under section 7871(c), and (2) that is designated by the Indian tribal government as a tribal economic development bond. The aggregate face amount of bonds that may be designated by any Indian tribal government cannot exceed the amount of national tribal economic development bond limitation allocated to such government.

Tribal economic development bonds cannot be used to finance any portion of a building in which class II or class III gaming (as defined in section 4 of the Indian Gaming Regulatory Act) is conducted, or housed, or any other property used in the conduct of such gaming. Nor can tribal economic development bonds be used to finance any facility located outside of the Indian reservation.

Treasury study

The provision requires that the Treasury Department study the effects of tribal economic development bonds. One year after the date of enactment, a report is to be submitted to Congress providing the results of such study along with any recommendations, including whether the restrictions of section 7871(c) should be eliminated or otherwise modified.

Effective date

The provision applies to obligations issued after the date of enactment.

The Senate amendment is the same as the House bill except the Senate amendment defines a tribal economic development bond as any bond issued by an Indian tribal government (1) the interest on which would be tax-exempt if issued by a State or local government, and (2) that is designated by the Indian tribal government as a tribal economic development bond.

The Senate amendment also clarifies that for purposes of section 141 of the Code, use of bond proceeds by an Indian tribe, or instrumentality thereof, is treated as use by a State.

The conference agreement follows the Senate amendment.

605

9. Pass-through of credits on tax credit bonds held by regulated investment companies (sec. 1541 of the conference agreement and new section 853A of the Code)

PRESENT LAW

In lieu of interest, holders of qualified tax credit bonds receive a tax credit that accrues quarterly. The credit is treated as interest that is includible in gross income. The following bonds are qualified tax credit bonds: qualified forestry conservation bonds, new clean renewable energy bonds, qualified energy conservation bonds, and qualified zone academy bonds.[163] The Code provides that in the case of a qualified tax credit bond held by a regulated investment company, the credit is allowed to shareholders of such company (and any gross income included with respect to such credit shall be treated as distributed to such shareholders) under procedures prescribed by the Secretary.[164] The Secretary has not prescribed procedures for the pass through of the credit to regulated investment company shareholders.

HOUSE BILL

No provision.

SENATE AMENDMENT

No provision.

CONFERENCE AGREEMENT

The conference agreement provides procedures for passing through credits on "tax credit bonds" to the shareholders of an electing regulated investment company. In general, an electing regulated investment company is not allowed any credits with respect to any tax credit bonds it holds during any year for which an election is in effect. The company is treated as having an amount of interest included in its gross income in an amount equal that which would have been included if no election were in effect, and a dividends paid deduction in the same amount is allowed to the company. Each shareholder of the electing regulated investment company is (1) required to include in gross income an amount equal to the shareholder's proportional share of the interest attributable to its credits and (2) allowed such proportional share as a credit against such shareholder's Federal income tax. In order to pass through tax credits to a shareholder, a regulated investment company is required to mail a written notice to such shareholder not later than 60 days after the close of the regulated investment company's taxable year, designating the shareholder's proportionate share of passed-through credits and the shareholder's gross income in respect of such credits.

A tax credit bond means a qualified tax credit bond as defined in section 54A(d), a build America bond (as defined in section 54AA(d)), and any other bond for which a credit is allowable under subpart H of part IV of subchapter A of the Code.

---

[163] See secs. 54B, 54C, 54D, and 54E.
[164] See sec. 54A(h), which also covers real estate investment trusts.

The provision gives the Secretary authority to prescribe the time and manner in which a regulated investment company makes the election to pass through credits on tax credit bonds. In addition, the provision requires the Secretary to prescribe such guidance as may be necessary to carry out the provision, including prescribing methods for determining a shareholder's proportionate share of tax credits.

Effective date.—The provision is applicable to taxable years ending after the date of enactment.

10. Delay in implementation of withholding tax on government contractors (sec. 1541 of the House bill, sec. 1511 of the Senate amendment, sec. 1511 of the conference agreement, and sec. 3402(t) of the Code)

PRESENT LAW

For payments made after December 31, 2010, the Code imposes a withholding requirement at a three-percent rate on certain payments to persons providing property or services made by the Government of the United States, every State, every political subdivision thereof, and every instrumentality of the foregoing (including multi-State agencies). The withholding requirement applies regardless of whether the government entity making such payment is the recipient of the property or services. Political subdivisions of States (or any instrumentality thereof) with less than $100 million of annual expenditures for property or services that would otherwise be subject to withholding are exempt from the withholding requirement.

Payments subject to the three-percent withholding requirement include any payment made in connection with a government voucher or certificate program which functions as a payment for property or services. For example, payments to a commodity producer under a government commodity support program are subject to the withholding requirement. Present law also imposes information reporting requirements on the payments that are subject to withholding requirement.

The three-percent withholding requirement does not apply to any payments made through a Federal, State, or local government public assistance or public welfare program for which eligibility is determined by a needs or income test. The three-percent withholding requirement also does not apply to payments of wages or to any other payment with respect to which mandatory (e.g., U.S.-source income of foreign taxpayers) or voluntary (e.g., unemployment benefits) withholding applies under present law. Although the withholding requirement applies to payments that are potentially subject to backup withholding under section 3406, it does not apply to those payments from which amounts are actually being withheld under backup withholding rules.

The three-percent withholding requirement also does not apply to the following: payments of interest; payments for real property; payments to tax-exempt entities or foreign governments; intra-governmental payments; payments made pursuant to a classified or confidential contract (as defined in section 6050M(e)(3)), and payments to government employees that are not otherwise excludable from the new withholding proposal with respect to the employees' services as employees.

The provision repeals the three-percent withholding requirement on government payments.

Effective date.—The provision is effective on the date of enactment.

The provision delays the implementation of the three percent withholding requirement by one year to apply to payments after December 31, 2011.

Effective date.—The provision is effective on the date of enactment.

The conference agreement follows the Senate amendment.

11. Extend and modify the new markets tax credit (sec. 1403 of the Senate amendment, sec. 1403 of the conference agreement, and sec. 45D of the Code)

Section 45D provides a new markets tax credit for qualified equity investments made to acquire stock in a corporation, or a capital interest in a partnership, that is a qualified community development entity ("CDE").[165] The amount of the credit allowable to the investor (either the original purchaser or a subsequent holder) is (1) a five-percent credit for the year in which the equity interest is purchased from the CDE and for each of the following two years, and (2) a six-percent credit for each of the following four years. The credit is determined by applying the applicable percentage (five or six percent) to the amount paid to the CDE for the investment at its original issue, and is available for a taxable year to the taxpayer who holds the qualified equity investment on the date of the initial investment or on the respective anniversary date that occurs during the taxable year. The credit is recaptured if, at any time during the seven-year period that begins on the date of the original issue of the qualified equity investment, the issuing entity ceases to be a qualified CDE, the proceeds of the investment cease to be used as required, or the equity investment is redeemed.

A qualified CDE is any domestic corporation or partnership: (1) whose primary mission is serving or providing investment capital for low-income communities or low-income persons; (2) that maintains accountability to residents of low-income communities by providing them with representation on any governing board of or any advisory board to the CDE; and (3) that is certified by the Secretary as being a qualified CDE. A qualified equity investment means stock (other than nonqualified preferred stock) in a corporation or a capital interest in a partnership that is acquired directly

---

[165] Section 45D was added by section 121(a) of the Community Renewal Tax Relief Act of 2000, Pub. L. No. 106–554 (2000).

from a CDE for cash, and includes an investment of a subsequent purchaser if such investment was a qualified equity investment in the hands of the prior holder. Substantially all of the investment proceeds must be used by the CDE to make qualified low-income community investments. For this purpose, qualified low-income community investments include: (1) capital or equity investments in, or loans to, qualified active low-income community businesses; (2) certain financial counseling and other services to businesses and residents in low-income communities; (3) the purchase from another CDE of any loan made by such entity that is a qualified low-income community investment; or (4) an equity investment in, or loan to, another CDE.

A "low-income community" is a population census tract with either (1) a poverty rate of at least 20 percent or (2) median family income which does not exceed 80 percent of the greater of metropolitan area median family income or statewide median family income (for a non-metropolitan census tract, does not exceed 80 percent of statewide median family income). In the case of a population census tract located within a high migration rural county, low-income is defined by reference to 85 percent (rather than 80 percent) of statewide median family income. For this purpose, a high migration rural county is any county that, during the 20-year period ending with the year in which the most recent census was conducted, has a net out-migration of inhabitants from the county of at least 10 percent of the population of the county at the beginning of such period.

The Secretary has the authority to designate "targeted populations" as low-income communities for purposes of the new markets tax credit. For this purpose, a "targeted population" is defined by reference to section 103(20) of the Riegle Community Development and Regulatory Improvement Act of 1994 (12 U.S.C. 4702(20)) to mean individuals, or an identifiable group of individuals, including an Indian tribe, who (A) are low-income persons; or (B) otherwise lack adequate access to loans or equity investments. Under such Act, "low-income" means (1) for a targeted population within a metropolitan area, less than 80 percent of the area median family income; and (2) for a targeted population within a non-metropolitan area, less than the greater of 80 percent of the area median family income or 80 percent of the statewide non-metropolitan area median family income.[166] Under such Act, a targeted population is not required to be within any census tract. In addition, a population census tract with a population of less than 2,000 is treated as a low-income community for purposes of the credit if such tract is within an empowerment zone, the designation of which is in effect under section 1391, and is contiguous to one or more low-income communities.

A qualified active low-income community business is defined as a business that satisfies, with respect to a taxable year, the following requirements: (1) at least 50 percent of the total gross income of the business is derived from the active conduct of trade or business activities in any low-income community; (2) a substantial portion of the tangible property of such business is used in a low-

---

[166] 12 U.S.C. sec. 4702(17) (defines "low-income" for purposes of 12 U.S.C. sec. 4702(20)).

income community; (3) a substantial portion of the services performed for such business by its employees is performed in a low-income community; and (4) less than five percent of the average of the aggregate unadjusted bases of the property of such business is attributable to certain financial property or to certain collectibles.

The maximum annual amount of qualified equity investments is capped at $3.5 billion per year for calendar years 2006 through 2009. Lower caps applied for calendar years 2001 through 2005.

HOUSE BILL

No provision.

SENATE AMENDMENT

For calendar years 2008 and 2009, the Senate amendment increases the maximum amount of qualified equity investments by $1.5 billion (to $5 billion for each year). The Senate amendment requires that the additional amount for 2008 be allocated to qualified CDEs that submitted an allocation application with respect to calendar year 2008 and either (1) did not receive an allocation for such calendar year, or (2) received an allocation for such calendar year in an amount less than the amount requested in the allocation application. The Senate amendment also provides alternative minimum tax relief for equity investment allocations subject to the 2009 annual limitation.

Effective date.—The provision is effective on the date of enactment.

CONFERENCE AGREEMENT

The conference agreement generally follows the Senate amendment but does not provide for any alternative minimum tax relief.

D. ENERGY INCENTIVES

1. Extension of the renewable electricity production credit (sec. 1601 of the House bill, sec. 1101 of the Senate amendment, sec. 1101 of the conference agreement, and sec. 45 of the Code)

PRESENT LAW

In general

An income tax credit is allowed for the production of electricity from qualified energy resources at qualified facilities (the "renewable electricity production credit").[167] Qualified energy resources comprise wind, closed-loop biomass, open-loop biomass, geothermal energy, solar energy, small irrigation power, municipal solid waste, qualified hydropower production, and marine and hydrokinetic renewable energy. Qualified facilities are, generally, facilities that generate electricity using qualified energy resources. To be eligible for the credit, electricity produced from qualified energy resources at qualified facilities must be sold by the taxpayer to an unrelated person.

[167] Sec. 45. In addition to the renewable electricity production credit, section 45 also provides income tax credits for the production of Indian coal and refined coal at qualified facilities.

Credit amounts and credit period

In general

The base amount of the electricity production credit is 1.5 cents per kilowatt-hour (indexed annually for inflation) of electricity produced. The amount of the credit was 2.1 cents per kilowatt-hour for 2008. A taxpayer may generally claim a credit during the 10-year period commencing with the date the qualified facility is placed in service. The credit is reduced for grants, tax-exempt bonds, subsidized energy financing, and other credits.

Credit phaseout

The amount of credit a taxpayer may claim is phased out as the market price of electricity exceeds certain threshold levels. The electricity production credit is reduced over a 3-cent phaseout range to the extent the annual average contract price per kilowatt-hour of electricity sold in the prior year from the same qualified energy resource exceeds 8 cents (adjusted for inflation; 11.8 cents for 2008).

Reduced credit periods and credit amounts

Generally, in the case of open-loop biomass facilities (including agricultural livestock waste nutrient facilities), geothermal energy facilities, solar energy facilities, small irrigation power facilities, landfill gas facilities, and trash combustion facilities placed in service before August 8, 2005, the 10-year credit period is reduced to five years, commencing on the date the facility was originally placed in service. However, for qualified open-loop biomass facilities (other than a facility described in section 45(d)(3)(A)(i) that uses agricultural livestock waste nutrients) placed in service before October 22, 2004, the five-year period commences on January 1, 2005. In the case of a closed-loop biomass facility modified to co-fire with coal, to co-fire with other biomass, or to co-fire with coal and other biomass, the credit period begins no earlier than October 22, 2004.

In the case of open-loop biomass facilities (including agricultural livestock waste nutrient facilities), small irrigation power facilities, landfill gas facilities, trash combustion facilities, and qualified hydropower facilities the otherwise allowable credit amount is 0.75 cent per kilowatt-hour, indexed for inflation measured after 1992 (1 cent per kilowatt-hour for 2008).

Other limitations on credit claimants and credit amounts

In general, in order to claim the credit, a taxpayer must own the qualified facility and sell the electricity produced by the facility to an unrelated party. A lessee or operator may claim the credit in lieu of the owner of the qualifying facility in the case of qualifying open-loop biomass facilities and in the case of closed-loop biomass facilities modified to co-fire with coal, to co-fire with other biomass, or to co-fire with coal and other biomass. In the case of a poultry waste facility, the taxpayer may claim the credit as a lessee or operator of a facility owned by a governmental unit.

For all qualifying facilities, other than closed-loop biomass facilities modified to co-fire with coal, to co-fire with other biomass, or to co-fire with coal and other biomass, the amount of credit a taxpayer may claim is reduced by reason of grants, tax-exempt bonds, subsidized energy financing, and other credits, but the reduction cannot exceed 50 percent of the otherwise allowable credit. In the case of closed-loop biomass facilities modified to co-fire with coal, to co-fire with other biomass, or to co-fire with coal and other biomass, there is no reduction in credit by reason of grants, tax-exempt bonds, subsidized energy financing, and other credits.

The credit for electricity produced from renewable resources is a component of the general business credit.[168] Generally, the general business credit for any taxable year may not exceed the amount by which the taxpayer's net income tax exceeds the greater of the tentative minimum tax or 25 percent of so much of the net regular tax liability as exceeds $25,000. However, this limitation does not apply to section 45 credits for electricity or refined coal produced from a facility (placed in service after October 22, 2004) during the first four years of production beginning on the date the facility is placed in service.[169] Excess credits may be carried back one year and forward up to 20 years.

Qualified facilities

Wind energy facility

A wind energy facility is a facility that uses wind to produce electricity. To be a qualified facility, a wind energy facility must be placed in service after December 31, 1993, and before January 1, 2010.

Closed-loop biomass facility

A closed-loop biomass facility is a facility that uses any organic material from a plant which is planted exclusively for the purpose of being used at a qualifying facility to produce electricity. In addition, a facility can be a closed-loop biomass facility if it is a facility that is modified to use closed-loop biomass to co-fire with coal, with other biomass, or with both coal and other biomass, but only if the modification is approved under the Biomass Power for Rural Development Programs or is part of a pilot project of the Commodity Credit Corporation.

To be a qualified facility, a closed-loop biomass facility must be placed in service after December 31, 1992, and before January 1, 2011. In the case of a facility using closed-loop biomass but also co-firing the closed-loop biomass with coal, other biomass, or coal and other biomass, a qualified facility must be originally placed in service and modified to co-fire the closed-loop biomass at any time before January 1, 2011.

A qualified facility includes a new power generation unit placed in service after October 3, 2008, at an existing closed-loop biomass facility, but only to the extent of the increased amount of electricity produced at the existing facility by reason of such new unit.

---

[168] Sec. 38(b)(8).
[169] Sec. 38(c)(4)(B)(ii).

Open-loop biomass (including agricultural livestock waste nutrients) facility

An open-loop biomass facility is a facility that uses open-loop biomass to produce electricity. For purposes of the credit, open-loop biomass is defined as (1) any agricultural livestock waste nutrients or (2) any solid, nonhazardous, cellulosic waste material or any lignin material that is segregated from other waste materials and which is derived from:

- forest-related resources, including mill and harvesting residues, precommercial thinnings, slash, and brush;
- solid wood waste materials, including waste pallets, crates, dunnage, manufacturing and construction wood wastes, and landscape or right-of-way tree trimmings; or
- agricultural sources, including orchard tree crops, vineyard, grain, legumes, sugar, and other crop by-products or residues.

Agricultural livestock waste nutrients are defined as agricultural livestock manure and litter, including bedding material for the disposition of manure. Wood waste materials do not qualify as open-loop biomass to the extent they are pressure treated, chemically treated, or painted. In addition, municipal solid waste, gas derived from the biodegradation of solid waste, and paper which is commonly recycled do not qualify as open-loop biomass. Open-loop biomass does not include closed-loop biomass or any biomass burned in conjunction with fossil fuel (co-firing) beyond such fossil fuel required for start up and flame stabilization.

In the case of an open-loop biomass facility that uses agricultural livestock waste nutrients, a qualified facility is one that was originally placed in service after October 22, 2004, and before January 1, 2009, and has a nameplate capacity rating which is not less than 150 kilowatts. In the case of any other open-loop biomass facility, a qualified facility is one that was originally placed in service before January 1, 2011. A qualified facility includes a new power generation unit placed in service after October 3, 2008, at an existing open-loop biomass facility, but only to the extent of the increased amount of electricity produced at the existing facility by reason of such new unit.

Geothermal facility

A geothermal facility is a facility that uses geothermal energy to produce electricity. Geothermal energy is energy derived from a geothermal deposit that is a geothermal reservoir consisting of natural heat that is stored in rocks or in an aqueous liquid or vapor (whether or not under pressure). To be a qualified facility, a geothermal facility must be placed in service after October 22, 2004, and before January 1, 2011.

Solar facility

A solar facility is a facility that uses solar energy to produce electricity. To be a qualified facility, a solar facility must be placed in service after October 22, 2004, and before January 1, 2006.

Small irrigation facility

A small irrigation power facility is a facility that generates electric power through an irrigation system canal or ditch without any dam or impoundment of water. The installed capacity of a qualified facility must be at least 150 kilowatts but less than five megawatts. To be a qualified facility, a small irrigation facility must be originally placed in service after October 22, 2004, and before October 3, 2008. Marine and hydrokinetic renewable energy facilities, described below, subsume small irrigation power facilities after October 2, 2008.

Landfill gas facility

A landfill gas facility is a facility that uses landfill gas to produce electricity. Landfill gas is defined as methane gas derived from the biodegradation of municipal solid waste. To be a qualified facility, a landfill gas facility must be placed in service after October 22, 2004, and before January 1, 2011.

Trash combustion facility

Trash combustion facilities are facilities that use municipal solid waste (garbage) to produce steam to drive a turbine for the production of electricity. To be a qualified facility, a trash combustion facility must be placed in service after October 22, 2004, and before January 1, 2011. A qualified trash combustion facility includes a new unit, placed in service after October 22, 2004, that increases electricity production capacity at an existing trash combustion facility. A new unit generally would include a new burner/boiler and turbine. The new unit may share certain common equipment, such as trash handling equipment, with other pre-existing units at the same facility. Electricity produced at a new unit of an existing facility qualifies for the production credit only to the extent of the increased amount of electricity produced at the entire facility.

Hydropower facility

A qualifying hydropower facility is (1) a facility that produced hydroelectric power (a hydroelectric dam) prior to August 8, 2005, at which efficiency improvements or additions to capacity have been made after such date and before January 1, 2011, that enable the taxpayer to produce incremental hydropower or (2) a facility placed in service before August 8, 2005, that did not produce hydroelectric power (a nonhydroelectric dam) on such date, and to which turbines or other electricity generating equipment have been added after such date and before January 1, 2011.

At an existing hydroelectric facility, the taxpayer may claim credit only for the production of incremental hydroelectric power. Incremental hydroelectric power for any taxable year is equal to the percentage of average annual hydroelectric power produced at the facility attributable to the efficiency improvement or additions of capacity determined by using the same water flow information used to determine an historic average annual hydroelectric power production baseline for that facility. The Federal Energy Regulatory Commission will certify the baseline power production of the facility and the percentage increase due to the efficiency and capacity improvements.

Nonhydroelectric dams converted to produce electricity must be licensed by the Federal Energy Regulatory Commission and meet all other applicable environmental, licensing, and regulatory requirements.

For a nonhydroelectric dam converted to produce electric power before January 1, 2009, there must not be any enlargement of the diversion structure, construction or enlargement of a bypass channel, or the impoundment or any withholding of additional water from the natural stream channel.

For a nonhydroelectric dam converted to produce electric power after December 31, 2008, the nonhydroelectric dam must have been (1) placed in service before October 3, 2008, (2) operated for flood control, navigation, or water supply purposes and (3) did not produce hydroelectric power on October 3, 2008. In addition, the hydroelectric project must be operated so that the water surface elevation at any given location and time that would have occurred in the absence of the hydroelectric project is maintained, subject to any license requirements imposed under applicable law that change the water surface elevation for the purpose of improving environmental quality of the affected waterway. The Secretary, in consultation with the Federal Energy Regulatory Commission, shall certify if a hydroelectric project licensed at a nonhydroelectric dam meets this criteria.

Marine and hydrokinetic renewable energy facility

A qualified marine and hydrokinetic renewable energy facility is any facility that produces electric power from marine and hydrokinetic renewable energy, has a nameplate capacity rating of at least 150 kilowatts, and is placed in service after October 2, 2008, and before January 1, 2012. Marine and hydrokinetic renewable energy is defined as energy derived from (1) waves, tides, and currents in oceans, estuaries, and tidal areas; (2) free flowing water in rivers, lakes, and streams; (3) free flowing water in an irrigation system, canal, or other manmade channel, including projects that utilize nonmechanical structures to accelerate the flow of water for electric power production purposes; or (4) differentials in ocean temperature (ocean thermal energy conversion). The term does not include energy derived from any source that uses a dam, diversionary structure (except for irrigation systems, canals, and other man-made channels), or impoundment for electric power production.

Summary of credit rate and credit period by facility type

TABLE 1.—SUMMARY OF SECTION 45 CREDIT FOR ELECTRICITY PRODUCED FROM CERTAIN RENEWABLE RESOURCES

Eligible electricity production activity	Credit amount for 2008 (cents per kilowatt-hour)	Credit period for facilities placed in service on or before August 8, 2005 (years from placed-in-service date)	Credit period for facilities placed in service after August 8, 2005 (years from placed-in-service date)
Wind	2.1	10	10
Closed-loop biomass	2.1	[1] 10	10

TABLE 1.—SUMMARY OF SECTION 45 CREDIT FOR ELECTRICITY PRODUCED FROM CERTAIN RENEWABLE RESOURCES—Continued

Eligible electricity production activity	Credit amount for 2008 (cents per kilo-watt-hour)	Credit period for fa-cilities placed in service on or before August 8, 2005 (years from placed-in-service date)	Credit period for fa-cilities placed in service after August 8, 2005 (years from placed-in-service date)
Open-loop biomass (including agricultural livestock waste nutrient facilities)	1.0	[2] 5	10
Geothermal	2.1	5	10
Solar (pre-2006 facilities only)	2.1	5	10
Small irrigation power	1.0	5	10
Municipal solid waste (including landfill gas facilities and trash combustion facilities)	1.0	5	10
Qualified hydropower	1.0	N/A	10
Marine and hydrokinetic	1.0	N/A	10

[1] In the case of certain co-firing closed-loop facilities, the credit period begins no earlier than October 22, 2004.
[2] For certain facilities placed in service before October 22, 2004, the five-year credit period commences on January 1, 2005.

Taxation of cooperatives and their patrons

For Federal income tax purposes, a cooperative generally computes its income as if it were a taxable corporation, with one exception: the cooperative may exclude from its taxable income distributions of patronage dividends. Generally, a cooperative that is subject to the cooperative tax rules of subchapter T of the Code [170] is permitted a deduction for patronage dividends paid only to the extent of net income that is derived from transactions with patrons who are members of the cooperative.[171] The availability of such deductions from taxable income has the effect of allowing the cooperative to be treated like a conduit with respect to profits derived from transactions with patrons who are members of the cooperative.

Eligible cooperatives may elect to pass any portion of the credit through to their patrons. An eligible cooperative is defined as a cooperative organization that is owned more than 50 percent by agricultural producers or entities owned by agricultural producers. The credit may be apportioned among patrons eligible to share in patronage dividends on the basis of the quantity or value of business done with or for such patrons for the taxable year. The election must be made on a timely filed return for the taxable year and, once made, is irrevocable for such taxable year.

HOUSE BILL

The provision extends for three years (generally, through 2013; through 2012 for wind facilities) the period during which qualified facilities producing electricity from wind, closed-loop biomass, open-loop biomass, geothermal energy, municipal solid waste, and qualified hydropower may be placed in service for purposes of the electricity production credit. The provision extends for two years (through 2013) the placed-in-service period for marine and hydrokinetic renewable energy resources.

The provision also makes a technical amendment to the definition of small irrigation power facility to clarify its integration into the definition of marine and hydrokinetic renewable energy facility.

---

[170] Secs. 1381–1383.
[171] Sec. 1382.

Effective date.—The extension of the electricity production credit is effective for property placed in service after the date of enactment. The technical amendment is effective as if included in section 102 of the Energy Improvement and Extension Act of 2008.

The Senate amendment is the same as the House bill.

The conference agreement follows the House bill and the Senate amendment.

2. Election of investment credit in lieu of production tax credits (sec. 1602 of the House bill, sec. 1102 of the Senate amendment, sec. 1102 of the conference agreement, and secs. 45 and 48 of the Code)

Renewable electricity credit

An income tax credit is allowed for the production of electricity from qualified energy resources at qualified facilities.[172] Qualified energy resources comprise wind, closed-loop biomass, open-loop biomass, geothermal energy, solar energy, small irrigation power, municipal solid waste, qualified hydropower production, and marine and hydrokinetic renewable energy. Qualified facilities are, generally, facilities that generate electricity using qualified energy resources. To be eligible for the credit, electricity produced from qualified energy resources at qualified facilities must be sold by the taxpayer to an unrelated person. The credit amounts, credit periods, definitions of qualified facilities, and other rules governing this credit are described more fully in section D.1 of this document.

Energy credit

An income tax credit is also allowed for certain energy property placed in service. Qualifying property includes certain fuel cell property, solar property, geothermal power production property, small wind energy property, combined heat and power system property, and geothermal heat pump property.[173] The amounts of credit, definitions of qualifying property, and other rules governing this credit are described more fully in section D.3 of this document.

The House bill allows the taxpayer to make an irrevocable election to have certain qualified facilities placed in service in 2009 and 2010 be treated as energy property eligible for a 30-percent investment credit under section 48. For this purpose, qualified facilities are facilities otherwise eligible for the section 45 production tax credit (other than refined coal, Indian coal, and solar facilities) with respect to which no credit under section 45 has been allowed.

---

[172] Sec. 45. In addition to the electricity production credit, section 45 also provides income tax credits for the production of Indian coal and refined coal at qualified facilities.
[173] Sec. 48.

A taxpayer electing to treat a facility as energy property may not claim the production credit under section 45.

Effective date.—The provision applies to facilities placed in service after December 31, 2008.

SENATE AMENDMENT

The Senate amendment is similar to the House bill, but with a modification with respect to the placed in service period that determines eligibility for the election. Under the Senate amendment, facilities are eligible if placed in service during the extension period of section 45 as provided in the Senate amendment (generally, through 2013; through 2012 for wind facilities), and with respect to which no credit under section 45 has been allowed.

CONFERENCE AGREEMENT

The conference agreement generally follows the Senate amendment. Property eligible for the credit is tangible personal or other tangible property (not including a building or its structural components), and with respect to which depreciation or amortization is allowable but only if such property is used as an integral part of the qualified facility. For example, in the case of a wind facility, the conferees intend that only property eligible for five-year depreciation under section 168(e)(3)(b)(vi) is treated as credit-eligible energy property under the election.

3. Modification of energy credit [174] (sec. 1603 of the House bill, sec. 1103 of the Senate amendment, sec. 1103 of the conference agreement, and sec. 48 of the Code)

PRESENT LAW

In general

A nonrefundable, 10-percent business energy credit [175] is allowed for the cost of new property that is equipment that either (1) uses solar energy to generate electricity, to heat or cool a structure, or to provide solar process heat, or (2) is used to produce, distribute, or use energy derived from a geothermal deposit, but only, in the case of electricity generated by geothermal power, up to the electric transmission stage. Property used to generate energy for the purposes of heating a swimming pool is not eligible solar energy property.

The energy credit is a component of the general business credit. [176] An unused general business credit generally may be carried back one year and carried forward 20 years. [177] The taxpayer's basis in the property is reduced by one-half of the amount of the credit claimed. For projects whose construction time is expected to equal or exceed two years, the credit may be claimed as progress expenditures are made on the project, rather than during the year

---

[174] Additional provisions that (1) allow section 45 facilities to elect to be treated as section 48 energy property, and (2) allow section 45 and 48 facilities to elect to receive a grant from the Department of the Treasury rather than the section 45 production credit or the section 48 energy credit, are described in sections D.2 and D.4 of this document.

[175] Sec. 48.

[176] Sec. 38(b)(1).

[177] Sec. 39.

the property is placed in service. The credit is allowed against the alternative minimum tax for credits determined in taxable years beginning after October 3, 2008.

Property financed by subsidized energy financing or with proceeds from private activity bonds is subject to a reduction in basis for purposes of claiming the credit. The basis reduction is proportional to the share of the basis of the property that is financed by the subsidized financing or proceeds. The term "subsidized energy financing" means financing provided under a Federal, State, or local program a principal purpose of which is to provide subsidized financing for projects designed to conserve or produce energy.

Special rules for solar energy property

The credit for solar energy property is increased to 30 percent in the case of periods prior to January 1, 2017. Additionally, equipment that uses fiber-optic distributed sunlight to illuminate the inside of a structure is solar energy property eligible for the 30-percent credit.

Fuel cells and microturbines

The energy credit applies to qualified fuel cell power plants, but only for periods prior to January 1, 2017. The credit rate is 30 percent.

A qualified fuel cell power plant is an integrated system composed of a fuel cell stack assembly and associated balance of plant components that (1) converts a fuel into electricity using electrochemical means, and (2) has an electricity-only generation efficiency of greater than 30 percent and a capacity of at least one-half kilowatt. The credit may not exceed $1,500 for each 0.5 kilowatt of capacity.

The energy credit applies to qualifying stationary microturbine power plants for periods prior to January 1, 2017. The credit is limited to the lesser of 10 percent of the basis of the property or $200 for each kilowatt of capacity.

A qualified stationary microturbine power plant is an integrated system comprised of a gas turbine engine, a combustor, a recuperator or regenerator, a generator or alternator, and associated balance of plant components that converts a fuel into electricity and thermal energy. Such system also includes all secondary components located between the existing infrastructure for fuel delivery and the existing infrastructure for power distribution, including equipment and controls for meeting relevant power standards, such as voltage, frequency and power factors. Such system must have an electricity-only generation efficiency of not less than 26 percent at International Standard Organization conditions and a capacity of less than 2,000 kilowatts.

Geothermal heat pump property

The energy credit applies to qualified geothermal heat pump property placed in service prior to January 1, 2017. The credit rate is 10 percent. Qualified geothermal heat pump property is equipment that uses the ground or ground water as a thermal energy source to heat a structure or as a thermal energy sink to cool a structure.

Small wind property

The energy credit applies to qualified small wind energy property placed in service prior to January 1, 2017. The credit rate is 30 percent. The credit is limited to $4,000 per year with respect to all wind energy property of any taxpayer. Qualified small wind energy property is property that uses a qualified wind turbine to generate electricity. A qualifying wind turbine means a wind turbine of 100 kilowatts of rated capacity or less.

Combined heat and power property

The energy credit applies to combined heat and power ("CHP") property placed in service prior to January 1, 2017. The credit rate is 10 percent.

CHP property is property: (1) that uses the same energy source for the simultaneous or sequential generation of electrical power, mechanical shaft power, or both, in combination with the generation of steam or other forms of useful thermal energy (including heating and cooling applications); (2) that has an electrical capacity of not more than 50 megawatts or a mechanical energy capacity of no more than 67,000 horsepower or an equivalent combination of electrical and mechanical energy capacities; (3) that produces at least 20 percent of its total useful energy in the form of thermal energy that is not used to produce electrical or mechanical power, and produces at least 20 percent of its total useful energy in the form of electrical or mechanical power (or a combination thereof); and (4) the energy efficiency percentage of which exceeds 60 percent. CHP property does not include property used to transport the energy source to the generating facility or to distribute energy produced by the facility.

The otherwise allowable credit with respect to CHP property is reduced to the extent the property has an electrical capacity or mechanical capacity in excess of any applicable limits. Property in excess of the applicable limit (15 megawatts or a mechanical energy capacity of more than 20,000 horsepower or an equivalent combination of electrical and mechanical energy capacities) is permitted to claim a fraction of the otherwise allowable credit. The fraction is equal to the applicable limit divided by the capacity of the property. For example, a 45 megawatt property would be eligible to claim 15/45ths, or one-third, of the otherwise allowable credit. Again, no credit is allowed if the property exceeds the 50 megawatt or 67,000 horsepower limitations described above.

Additionally, the provision provides that systems whose fuel source is at least 90 percent open-loop biomass and that would qualify for the credit but for the failure to meet the efficiency standard are eligible for a credit that is reduced in proportion to the degree to which the system fails to meet the efficiency standard. For example, a system that would otherwise be required to meet the 60-percent efficiency standard, but which only achieves 30-percent efficiency, would be permitted a credit equal to one-half of the otherwise allowable credit (i.e., a 5-percent credit).

The House bill eliminates the credit cap applicable to qualified small wind energy property. The House bill also removes the rule that reduces the basis of the property for purposes of claiming the credit if the property is financed in whole or in part by subsidized energy financing or with proceeds from private activity bonds.

Effective date.—The provision applies to periods after December 31, 2008, under rules similar to the rules of section 48(m) of the Code (as in effect on the day before the enactment of the Revenue Reconciliation Act of 1990).

The Senate amendment is the same as the House bill.

The conference agreement follows the House bill and the Senate amendment.

4. Grants for specified energy property in lieu of tax credits (secs. 1604 and 1721 of the House bill, secs. 1104 and 1603 of the conference agreement, and secs. 45 and 48 of the Code)

Renewable electricity production credit

An income tax credit is allowed for the production of electricity from qualified energy resources at qualified facilities (the "renewable electricity production credit").[178] Qualified energy resources comprise wind, closed-loop biomass, open-loop biomass, geothermal energy, solar energy, small irrigation power, municipal solid waste, qualified hydropower production, and marine and hydrokinetic renewable energy. Qualified facilities are, generally, facilities that generate electricity using qualified energy resources. To be eligible for the credit, electricity produced from qualified energy resources at qualified facilities must be sold by the taxpayer to an unrelated person. The credit amounts, credit periods, definitions of qualified facilities, and other rules governing this credit are described more fully in section D.1 of this document.

Energy credit

An income tax credit is also allowed for certain energy property placed in service. Qualifying property includes certain fuel cell property, solar property, geothermal power production property, small wind energy property, combined heat and power system property, and geothermal heat pump property.[179] The amounts of credit, definitions of qualifying property, and other rules governing this credit are described more fully in section D.3 of this document.

The provision authorizes the Secretary of Energy to provide a grant to each person who places in service during 2009 or 2010 en-

---

[178] Sec. 45. In addition to the renewable electricity production credit, section 45 also provides income tax credits for the production of Indian coal and refined coal at qualified facilities.
[179] Sec. 48.

ergy property that is either (1) an electricity production facility otherwise eligible for the renewable electricity production credit or (2) qualifying property otherwise eligible for the energy credit. In general, the grant amount is 30 percent of the basis of the property that would (1) be eligible for credit under section 48 or (2) comprise a section 45 credit-eligible facility. For qualified microturbine, combined heat and power system, and geothermal heat pump property, the amount is 10 percent of the basis of the property.

It is intended that the grant provision mimic the operation of the credit under section 48. For example, the amount of the grant is not includable in gross income. However, the basis of the property is reduced by fifty percent of the amount of the grant. In addition, some or all of each grant is subject to recapture if the grant eligible property is disposed of by the grant recipient within five years of being placed in service.[180]

Nonbusiness property and property that would not otherwise be eligible for credit under section 48 or part of a facility that would be eligible for credit under section 45 is not eligible for a grant under the provision. The grant may be paid to whichever party would have been entitled to a credit under section 48 or section 45, as the case may be.

Under the provision, if a grant is paid, no renewable electricity credit or energy credit may be claimed with respect to the grant eligible property. In addition, no grant may be awarded to any Federal, State, or local government (or any political subdivision, agency, or instrumentality thereof) or any section 501(c) tax-exempt entity.

The provision appropriates to the Secretary of Energy the funds necessary to make the grants. No grant may be made unless the application for the grant has been received before October 1, 2011.

Effective date.—The provision is effective on date of enactment.

No provision.

The conference agreement generally follows the House bill with the following modifications. The conference agreement clarifies that qualifying property must be depreciable or amortizable to be eligible for a grant. The conference agreement also permits taxpayers to claim the credit with respect to otherwise eligible property that is not placed in service in 2009 and 2010 so long as construction begins in either of those years and is completed prior to 2013 (in the case of wind facility property), 2014 (in the case of other renewable power facility property eligible for credit under section 45), or 2017 (in the case of any specified energy property described in section 48). The conference agreement also provides that the grant program be administered by the Secretary of the Treasury.

---

[180] Section 1604 of the House bill.

5. Expand new clean renewable energy bonds (sec. 1611 of the
House bill, sec. 1111 of the Senate amendment, sec. 1111 of the
conference agreement, and sec. 54C of the Code)

New Clean Renewable Energy Bonds

New clean renewable energy bonds ("New CREBs") may be
issued by qualified issuers to finance qualified renewable energy facilities.[181] Qualified renewable energy facilities are facilities that:
(1) qualify for the tax credit under section 45 (other than Indian
coal and refined coal production facilities), without regard to the
placed-in-service date requirements of that section; and (2) are
owned by a public power provider, governmental body, or cooperative electric company.

The term "qualified issuers" includes: (1) public power providers; (2) a governmental body; (3) cooperative electric companies;
(4) a not-for-profit electric utility that has received a loan or guarantee under the Rural Electrification Act; and (5) clean renewable
energy bond lenders. The term "public power provider" means a
State utility with a service obligation, as such terms are defined in
section 217 of the Federal Power Act (as in effect on the date of
the enactment of this paragraph). A "governmental body" means
any State or Indian tribal government, or any political subdivision
thereof. The term "cooperative electric company" means a mutual
or cooperative electric company (described in section 501(c)(12) or
section 1381(a)(2)(C)). A clean renewable energy bond lender means
a cooperative that is owned by, or has outstanding loans to, 100 or
more cooperative electric companies and is in existence on February 1, 2002 (including any affiliated entity which is controlled by
such lender).

There is a national limitation for New CREBs of $800 million.
No more than one third of the national limit may be allocated to
projects of public power providers, governmental bodies, or cooperative electric companies. Allocations to governmental bodies and cooperative electric companies may be made in the manner the Secretary determines appropriate. Allocations to projects of public
power providers shall be made, to the extent practicable, in such
manner that the amount allocated to each such project bears the
same ratio to the cost of such project as the maximum allocation
limitation to projects of public power providers bears to the cost of
all such projects.

New CREBs are a type of qualified tax credit bond for purposes of section 54A of the Code. As such, 100 percent of the available project proceeds of New CREBs must be used within the
three-year period that begins on the date of issuance. Available
project proceeds are proceeds from the sale of the bond issue less
issuance costs (not to exceed two percent) and any investment
earnings on such sale proceeds. To the extent less than 100 percent
of the available project proceeds are used to finance qualified
projects during the three-year spending period, bonds will continue
to qualify as New CREBs if unspent proceeds are used within 90
days from the end of such three-year period to redeem bonds. The

---

[181] Sec. 54C.

three-year spending period may be extended by the Secretary upon the qualified issuer's request demonstrating that the failure to satisfy the three-year requirement is due to reasonable cause and the projects will continue to proceed with due diligence.

New CREBs generally are subject to the arbitrage requirements of section 148. However, available project proceeds invested during the three-year spending period are not subject to the arbitrage restrictions (i.e., yield restriction and rebate requirements). In addition, amounts invested in a reserve fund are not subject to the arbitrage restrictions to the extent: (1) such fund is funded at a rate not more rapid than equal annual installments; (2) such fund is funded in a manner reasonably expected to result in an amount not greater than an amount necessary to repay the issue; and (3) the yield on such fund is not greater than the average annual interest rate of tax-exempt obligations having a term of 10 years or more that are issued during the month the New CREBs are issued.

As with other tax credit bonds, a taxpayer holding New CREBs on a credit allowance date is entitled to a tax credit. However, the credit rate on New CREBs is set by the Secretary at a rate that is 70 percent of the rate that would permit issuance of such bonds without discount and interest cost to the issuer.[182] The Secretary determines credit rates for tax credit bonds based on general assumptions about credit quality of the class of potential eligible issuers and such other factors as the Secretary deems appropriate. The Secretary may determine credit rates based on general credit market yield indexes and credit ratings.[183]

The amount of the tax credit is determined by multiplying the bond's credit rate by the face amount of the holder's bond. The credit accrues quarterly, is includible in gross income (as if it were an interest payment on the bond), and can be claimed against regular income tax liability and alternative minimum tax liability. Unused credits may be carried forward to succeeding taxable years. In addition, credits may be separated from the ownership of the underlying bond similar to how interest coupons can be stripped for interest-bearing bonds.

An issuer of New CREBs is treated as meeting the "prohibition on financial conflicts of interest" requirement in section 54A(d)(6) if it certifies that it satisfies (i) applicable State and local law requirements governing conflicts of interest and (ii) any additional conflict of interest rules prescribed by the Secretary with respect to any Federal, State, or local government official directly involved with the issuance of New CREBs.

HOUSE BILL

In general

The provision expands the New CREBs program. The provision authorizes issuance of up to an additional $1.6 billion of New CREBs.

---

[182] Given the differences in credit quality and other characteristics of individual issuers, the Secretary cannot set credit rates in a manner that will allow each issuer to issue tax credit bonds at par.
[183] See Internal Revenue Service, Notice 2009–15, Credit Rates on Tax Credit Bonds, 2009–6 I.R.B. 1 (January 22, 2009).

Effective date

The provision applies to obligations issued after the date of enactment.

The Senate amendment is the same as the House bill.

The conference agreement follows the House bill and the Senate amendment.

6. Expand qualified energy conservation bonds (sec. 1612 of the House bill, sec. 1112 of the Senate amendment, sec. 1112 of the conference agreement, and sec. 54D of the Code)

Qualified energy conservation bonds may be used to finance qualified conservation purposes.

The term "qualified conservation purpose" means:

1. Capital expenditures incurred for purposes of reducing energy consumption in publicly owned buildings by at least 20 percent; implementing green community programs; rural development involving the production of electricity from renewable energy resources; or any facility eligible for the production tax credit under section 45 (other than Indian coal and refined coal production facilities);

2. Expenditures with respect to facilities or grants that support research in: (a) development of cellulosic ethanol or other nonfossil fuels; (b) technologies for the capture and sequestration of carbon dioxide produced through the use of fossil fuels; (c) increasing the efficiency of existing technologies for producing nonfossil fuels; (d) automobile battery technologies and other technologies to reduce fossil fuel consumption in transportation; and (E) technologies to reduce energy use in buildings;

3. Mass commuting facilities and related facilities that reduce the consumption of energy, including expenditures to reduce pollution from vehicles used for mass commuting;

4. Demonstration projects designed to promote the commercialization of: (a) green building technology; (b) conversion of agricultural waste for use in the production of fuel or otherwise; (c) advanced battery manufacturing technologies; (D) technologies to reduce peak-use of electricity; and (d) technologies for the capture and sequestration of carbon dioxide emitted from combusting fossil fuels in order to produce electricity; and

5. Public education campaigns to promote energy efficiency (other than movies, concerts, and other events held primarily for entertainment purposes).

There is a national limitation on qualified energy conservation bonds of $800 million. Allocations of qualified energy conservation bonds are made to the States with sub-allocations to large local governments. Allocations are made to the States according to their respective populations, reduced by any sub-allocations to large local governments (defined below) within the States. Sub-allocations to large local governments shall be an amount of the national qualified energy conservation bond limitation that bears the same ratio to the amount of such limitation that otherwise would be allocated to the State in which such large local government is located as the population of such large local government bears to the population of such State. The term "large local government" means: any municipality or county if such municipality or county has a population of 100,000 or more. Indian tribal governments also are treated as large local governments for these purposes (without regard to population).

Each State or large local government receiving an allocation of qualified energy conservation bonds may further allocate issuance authority to issuers within such State or large local government. However, any allocations to issuers within the State or large local government shall be made in a manner that results in not less than 70 percent of the allocation of qualified energy conservation bonds to such State or large local government being used to designate bonds that are not private activity bonds (i.e., the bond cannot meet the private business tests or the private loan test of section 141).

Qualified energy conservation bonds are a type of qualified tax credit bond for purposes of section 54A of the Code. As a result, 100 percent of the available project proceeds of qualified energy conservation bonds must be used for qualified conservation purposes. In the case of qualified conservation bonds issued as private activity bonds, 100 percent of the available project proceeds must be used for capital expenditures. In addition, qualified energy conservation bonds only may be issued by Indian tribal governments to the extent such bonds are issued for purposes that satisfy the present law requirements for tax-exempt bonds issued by Indian tribal governments (i.e., essential governmental functions and certain manufacturing purposes).

Under present law, 100 percent of the available project proceeds of qualified energy conservation bonds to be used within the three-year period that begins on the date of issuance. Available project proceeds are proceeds from the sale of the issue less issuance costs (not to exceed two percent) and any investment earnings on such sale proceeds. To the extent less than 100 percent of the available project proceeds are used to finance qualified conservation purposes during the three-year spending period, bonds will continue to qualify as qualified energy conservation bonds if unspent proceeds are used within 90 days from the end of such three-year period to redeem bonds. The three-year spending period may be extended by the Secretary upon the issuer's request demonstrating that the failure to satisfy the three-year requirement is due to reasonable cause and the projects will continue to proceed with due diligence.

Qualified energy conservation bonds generally are subject to the arbitrage requirements of section 148. However, available project proceeds invested during the three-year spending period are not subject to the arbitrage restrictions (i.e., yield restriction and rebate requirements). In addition, amounts invested in a reserve fund are not subject to the arbitrage restrictions to the extent: (1) such fund is funded at a rate not more rapid than equal annual installments; (2) such fund is funded in a manner reasonably expected to result in an amount not greater than an amount necessary to repay the issue; and (3) the yield on such fund is not greater than the average annual interest rate of tax-exempt obligations having a term of 10 years or more that are issued during the month the qualified energy conservation bonds are issued.

The maturity of qualified energy conservation bonds is the term that the Secretary estimates will result in the present value of the obligation to repay the principal on such bonds being equal to 50 percent of the face amount of such bonds, using as a discount rate the average annual interest rate of tax-exempt obligations having a term of 10 years or more that are issued during the month the qualified energy conservation bonds are issued.

As with other tax credit bonds, the taxpayer holding qualified energy conservation bonds on a credit allowance date is entitled to a tax credit. The credit rate on the bonds is set by the Secretary at a rate that is 70 percent of the rate that would permit issuance of such bonds without discount and interest cost to the issuer.[184] The Secretary determines credit rates for tax credit bonds based on general assumptions about credit quality of the class of potential eligible issuers and such other factors as the Secretary deems appropriate. The Secretary may determine credit rates based on general credit market yield indexes and credit ratings.[185] The amount of the tax credit is determined by multiplying the bond's credit rate by the face amount on the holder's bond. The credit accrues quarterly, is includible in gross income (as if it were an interest payment on the bond), and can be claimed against regular income tax liability and alternative minimum tax liability. Unused credits may be carried forward to succeeding taxable years. In addition, credits may be separated from the ownership of the underlying bond similar to how interest coupons can be stripped for interest-bearing bonds.

Issuers of qualified energy conservation bonds are required to certify that the financial disclosure requirements that applicable State and local law requirements governing conflicts of interest are satisfied with respect to such issue, as well as any other additional conflict of interest rules prescribed by the Secretary with respect to any Federal, State, or local government official directly involved with the issuance of qualified energy conservation bonds.

HOUSE BILL

In general

The provision expands the present-law qualified energy conservation bond program. The provision authorizes issuance of an additional $2.4 billion of qualified energy conservation bonds. The provision expands eligibility for these tax credit bonds to include loans and grants for capital expenditures as part of green commu-

---

[184] Given the difference in credit quality and other characteristics of individual issuers, the Secretary cannot set credit rates in a manner that will allow each issuer to issue tax credit bonds at par.

[185] See Internal Revenue Services, Notice 2009–15, Credit Rates on Tax Credit Bonds, 2009–6 I.R.B. 1 (January 22, 2009).

nity programs. For example, this expansion will enable States to issue these tax credit bonds to finance loans and/or grants to individual homeowners to retrofit existing housing. The use of bond proceeds for such loans and grants will not cause such bond to be treated as a private activity bond for purposes of the private activity bond restrictions contained in the qualified energy conservation bond provisions.

Effective date

The provision is effective for bonds issued after the date of enactment.

SENATE AMENDMENT

In general

The provision expands the present-law qualified energy conservation bond program. The provision authorizes issuance of an additional $2.4 billion of qualified energy conservation bonds. The provision clarifies that capital expenditures to implement green community programs, includes grants, loans and other repayment mechanisms for capital expenditures to implement such programs.

Effective date

The provision is effective for bonds issued after the date of enactment.

CONFERENCE AGREEMENT

In general

The provision expands the present-law qualified energy conservation bond program. The provision authorizes issuance of an additional $2.4 billion of qualified energy conservation bonds. Also, the provision clarifies that capital expenditures to implement green community programs includes grants, loans and other repayment mechanisms to implement such programs. For example, this expansion will enable States to issue these tax credit bonds to finance retrofits of existing private buildings through loans and/or grants to individual homeowners or businesses, or through other repayment mechanisms. Other repayment mechanisms can include periodic fees assessed on a government bill or utility bill that approximates the energy savings of energy efficiency or conservation retrofits. Retrofits can include heating, cooling, lighting, water-saving, storm water-reducing, or other efficiency measures.

Finally, the provision clarifies that any bond used for the purpose of providing grants, loans or other repayment mechanisms for capital expenditures to implement green community programs is not treated as a private activity bond for purposes of determining whether the requirement that not less than 70 percent of allocations within a State or large local government be used to designate bonds that are not private activity bonds (sec. 54D(e)(3)) has been satisfied.

Effective date

The conference agreement follows the House bill and the Senate amendment.

7. Modification to high-speed intercity rail facility bonds (sec. 1504 of the Senate amendment, sec. 1504 of the conference agreement, and sec. 142(i) of the Code)

In general

Under present law, gross income does not include interest on State or local bonds. State and local bonds are classified generally as either governmental bonds or private activity bonds. Governmental bonds are bonds the proceeds of which are primarily used to finance governmental functions or which are repaid with governmental funds. Private activity bonds are bonds in which the State or local government serves as a conduit providing financing to nongovernmental persons (e.g., private businesses or individuals). The exclusion from income for State and local bonds does not apply to private activity bonds unless the bonds are issued for certain permitted purposes ("qualified private activity bonds") and other Code requirements are met.

High-speed rail

An exempt facility bond is a type of qualified private activity bond. Exempt facility bonds can be issued for high-speed intercity rail facilities. A facility qualifies as a high-speed intercity rail facility if it is a facility (other than rolling stock) for fixed guideway rail transportation of passengers and their baggage between metropolitan statistical areas. The facilities must use vehicles that are reasonably expected to operate at speeds in excess of 150 miles per hour between scheduled stops and the facilities must be made available to members of the general public as passengers. If the bonds are to be issued for a nongovernmental owner of the facility, such owner must irrevocably elect not to claim depreciation or credits with respect to the property financed by the net proceeds of the issue.

The Code imposes a special redemption requirement for these types of bonds. Any proceeds not used within three years of the date of issuance of the bonds must be used within the following six months to redeem such bonds.

Seventy-five percent of the principal amount of the bonds issued for high-speed rail facilities is exempt from the volume limit. If all the property to be financed by the net proceeds of the issue is to be owned by a governmental unit, then such bonds are completely exempt from the volume limit.

No provision.

In general

The provision modifies the requirement that high-speed intercity rail transportation facilities use vehicles that are reasonably expected to operate at speeds in excess of 150 miles per hour. Instead, under the provision such facilities must use vehicles capable of attaining a maximum speed in excess of 150 miles per hour.

Effective date

The provision is effective for obligations issued after the date of enactment.

The conference agreement follows the Senate amendment.

8. Extension and modification of credit for nonbusiness energy property (sec. 1621 of the House bill, sec. 1121 of the Senate amendment, sec. 1121 of the conference agreement, and sec. 25C of the Code)

Section 25C provides a 10-percent credit for the purchase of qualified energy efficiency improvements to existing homes. A qualified energy efficiency improvement is any energy efficiency building envelope component (1) that meets or exceeds the prescriptive criteria for such a component established by the 2000 International Energy Conservation Code as supplemented and as in effect on August 8, 2005 (or, in the case of metal roofs with appropriate pigmented coatings, meets the Energy Star program requirements); (2) that is installed in or on a dwelling located in the United States and owned and used by the taxpayer as the taxpayer's principal residence; (3) the original use of which commences with the taxpayer; and (4) that reasonably can be expected to remain in use for at least five years. The credit is nonrefundable.

Building envelope components are: (1) insulation materials or systems which are specifically and primarily designed to reduce the heat loss or gain for a dwelling; (2) exterior windows (including skylights) and doors; and (3) metal or asphalt roofs with appropriate pigmented coatings or cooling granules that are specifically and primarily designed to reduce the heat gain for a dwelling.

Additionally, section 25C provides specified credits for the purchase of specific energy efficient property. The allowable credit for the purchase of certain property is (1) $50 for each advanced main air circulating fan, (2) $150 for each qualified natural gas, propane, or oil furnace or hot water boiler, and (3) $300 for each item of qualified energy efficient property.

An advanced main air circulating fan is a fan used in a natural gas, propane, or oil furnace originally placed in service by the taxpayer during the taxable year, and which has an annual electricity use of no more than two percent of the total annual energy use of the furnace (as determined in the standard Department of Energy test procedures).

A qualified natural gas, propane, or oil furnace or hot water boiler is a natural gas, propane, or oil furnace or hot water boiler with an annual fuel utilization efficiency rate of at least 95.

Qualified energy-efficient property is: (1) an electric heat pump water heater which yields energy factor of at least 2.0 in the standard Department of Energy test procedure, (2) an electric heat pump which has a heating seasonal performance factor (HSPF) of at least 9, a seasonal energy efficiency ratio (SEER) of at least 15, and an energy efficiency ratio (EER) of at least 13, (3) a central air conditioner with energy efficiency of at least the highest efficiency tier established by the Consortium for Energy Efficiency as in effect on Jan. 1, 2006,[186] (4) a natural gas, propane, or oil water heater which has an energy factor of at least 0.80 or thermal efficiency of at least 90 percent, and (5) biomass fuel property.

Biomass fuel property is a stove that burns biomass fuel to heat a dwelling unit located in the United States and used as a principal residence by the taxpayer, or to heat water for such dwelling unit, and that has a thermal efficiency rating of at least 75 percent. Biomass fuel is any plant-derived fuel available on a renewable or recurring basis, including agricultural crops and trees, wood and wood waste and residues (including wood pellets), plants (including aquatic plants, grasses, residues, and fibers).

Under section 25C, the maximum credit for a taxpayer with respect to the same dwelling for all taxable years is $500, and no more than $200 of such credit may be attributable to expenditures on windows.

The taxpayer's basis in the property is reduced by the amount of the credit. Special proration rules apply in the case of jointly owned property, condominiums, and tenant-stockholders in cooperative housing corporations. If less than 80 percent of the property is used for nonbusiness purposes, only that portion of expenditures that is used for nonbusiness purposes is taken into account.

For purposes of determining the amount of expenditures made by any individual with respect to any dwelling unit, there shall not be taken into account expenditures which are made from subsidized energy financing. The term "subsidized energy financing" means financing provided under a Federal, State, or local program a principal purpose of which is to provide subsidized financing for projects designed to conserve or produce energy.

The credit applies to expenditures made after December 31, 2008 for property placed in service after December 31, 2008, and prior to January 1, 2010.

HOUSE BILL

The House bill raises the 10 percent credit rate to 30 percent. Additionally, all energy property otherwise eligible for the $50, $100, or $150 credits is instead eligible for a 30 percent credit on expenditures for such property.

The House bill additionally extends the provision for one year, through December 31, 2010. Finally, the $500 lifetime cap (and the $200 lifetime cap with respect to windows) is eliminated and replaced with an aggregate cap of $1,500 in the case of property placed in service after December 31, 2008 and prior to January 1, 2011.

The present law rule related to subsidized energy financing is eliminated.

Effective date.—The provision is effective for taxable years beginning after December 31, 2008.

---

[186] The highest tier in effect at this time was tier 2, requiring SEER of at least 15 and EER of at least 12.5 for split central air conditioning systems and SEER of at least 14 and EER of at least 12 for packaged central air conditioning systems.

SENATE AMENDMENT

The Senate amendment is similar to the House bill, but modifies the efficiency standards for qualifying property.

Specifically, the Senate amendment updates the building insulation requirements to follow the prescriptive criteria of the 2009 International Energy Conservation Code. Additionally, qualifying exterior windows, doors, and skylights must have a U-factor at or below 0.30 and a seasonal heat gain coefficient ("SHGC") at or below 0.30.

Electric heat pumps must achieve the highest efficiency tier of Consortium for Energy Efficiency, as in effect on January 1, 2009. These standards are a SEER greater than or equal to 15, EER greater than or equal to 12.5, and HSPF greater than or equal to 8.5 for split heat pumps, and SEER greater than or equal to 14, EER greater than or equal to 12, and HSPF greater than or equal to 8.0 for packaged heat pumps.

Central air conditioners must achieve the highest efficiency tier of Consortium for Energy Efficiency, as in effect on January 1, 2009. These standards are a SEER greater than or equal to 16 and EER greater than or equal to 13 for split systems, and SEER greater than or equal to 14 and EER greater than or equal to 12 for packaged systems.

Natural gas, propane, or oil water heaters must have an energy factor greater than or equal to 0.82 or a thermal efficiency of greater than or equal to 90 percent. Natural gas, propane, or oil water boilers must achieve an annual fuel utilization efficiency rate of at least 90. Qualified oil furnaces must achieve an annual fuel utilization efficiency rate of at least 90.

Lastly, the requirement that biomass fuel property have a thermal efficiency rating of at least 75 percent is modified to be a thermal efficiency rating of at least 75 percent as measured using a lower heating value.

Effective date.—The provision is generally effective for taxable years beginning after December 31, 2008. The provisions that alter the efficiency standards of qualifying property, other than biomass fuel property, apply to property placed in service after December 31, 2009. The modification with respect to biomass fuel property is effective for taxable years beginning after December 31, 2008.

CONFERENCE AGREEMENT

The conference agreement follows the Senate amendment, with the exception that the new efficiency standards for qualifying property, other than those for biomass fuel property, apply to property placed in service after the date of enactment.

9. Credit for residential energy efficient property (sec. 1622 of the House bill, sec. 1122 of the Senate amendment, sec. 1122 of the conference agreement, and sec. 25D of the Code)

PRESENT LAW

Section 25D provides a personal tax credit for the purchase of qualified solar electric property and qualified solar water heating property that is used exclusively for purposes other than heating swimming pools and hot tubs. The credit is equal to 30 percent of qualifying expenditures, with a maximum credit of $2,000 with respect to qualified solar water heating property. There is no cap with respect to qualified solar electric property.

Section 25D also provides a 30 percent credit for the purchase of qualified geothermal heat pump property, qualified small wind energy property, and qualified fuel cell power plants. The credit for geothermal heat pump property is capped at $2,000, the credit for qualified small wind energy property is limited to $500 with respect to each half kilowatt of capacity, not to exceed $4,000, and the credit for any fuel cell may not exceed $500 for each 0.5 kilowatt of capacity.

The credit with respect to all qualifying property may be claimed against the alternative minimum tax.

Qualified solar electric property is property that uses solar energy to generate electricity for use in a dwelling unit. Qualifying solar water heating property is property used to heat water for use in a dwelling unit located in the United States and used as a residence if at least half of the energy used by such property for such purpose is derived from the sun.

A qualified fuel cell power plant is an integrated system comprised of a fuel cell stack assembly and associated balance of plant components that (1) converts a fuel into electricity using electrochemical means, (2) has an electricity-only generation efficiency of greater than 30 percent. The qualified fuel cell power plant must be installed on or in connection with a dwelling unit located in the United States and used by the taxpayer as a principal residence.

Qualified small wind energy property is property that uses a wind turbine to generate electricity for use in a dwelling unit located in the U.S. and used as a residence by the taxpayer.

Qualified geothermal heat pump property means any equipment which (1) uses the ground or ground water as a thermal energy source to heat the dwelling unit or as a thermal energy sink to cool such dwelling unit, (2) meets the requirements of the Energy Star program which are in effect at the time that the expenditure for such equipment is made, and (3) is installed on or in connection with a dwelling unit located in the United States and used as a residence by the taxpayer.

The credit is nonrefundable, and the depreciable basis of the property is reduced by the amount of the credit. Expenditures for labor costs allocable to onsite preparation, assembly, or original installation of property eligible for the credit are eligible expenditures.

Special proration rules apply in the case of jointly owned property, condominiums, and tenant-stockholders in cooperative housing corporations. If less than 80 percent of the property is used for nonbusiness purposes, only that portion of expenditures that is used for nonbusiness purposes is taken into account.

For purposes of determining the amount of expenditures made by any individual with respect to any dwelling unit, there shall not be taken into account expenditures which are made from subsidized energy financing. The term "subsidized energy financing" means financing provided under a Federal, State, or local program a principal purpose of which is to provide subsidized financing for projects designed to conserve or produce energy.

The credit applies to property placed in service prior to January 1, 2017.

The House bill eliminates the credit caps for solar hot water, geothermal, and wind property and eliminates the reduction in credits for property using subsidized energy financing.

Effective date.—The provision applies to taxable years beginning after December 31, 2008.

The Senate amendment is the same as the House bill.

The conference agreement follows the House bill and the Senate amendment.

10. Temporary increase in credit for alternative fuel vehicle refueling property (sec. 1623 of the House bill, sec. 1123 of the Senate amendment, sec. 1123 of the conference agreement, and sec. 30C of the Code)

Taxpayers may claim a 30-percent credit for the cost of installing qualified clean-fuel vehicle refueling property to be used in a trade or business of the taxpayer or installed at the principal residence of the taxpayer.[187] The credit may not exceed $30,000 per taxable year per location, in the case of qualified refueling property used in a trade or business and $1,000 per taxable year per location, in the case of qualified refueling property installed on property which is used as a principal residence.

Qualified refueling property is property (not including a building or its structural components) for the storage or dispensing of a clean-burning fuel or electricity into the fuel tank or battery of a motor vehicle propelled by such fuel or electricity, but only if the storage or dispensing of the fuel or electricity is at the point of delivery into the fuel tank or battery of the motor vehicle. The use of such property must begin with the taxpayer.

Clean-burning fuels are any fuel at least 85 percent of the volume of which consists of ethanol, natural gas, compressed natural gas, liquefied natural gas, liquefied petroleum gas, or hydrogen. In addition, any mixture of biodiesel and diesel fuel, determined without regard to any use of kerosene and containing at least 20 percent biodiesel, qualifies as a clean fuel.

Credits for qualified refueling property used in a trade or business are part of the general business credit and may be carried back for one year and forward for 20 years. Credits for residential qualified refueling property cannot exceed for any taxable year the difference between the taxpayer's regular tax (reduced by certain other credits) and the taxpayer's tentative minimum tax. Gen-

---

[187] Sec. 30C.

erally, in the case of qualified refueling property sold to a tax-exempt entity, the taxpayer selling the property may claim the credit.

A taxpayer's basis in qualified refueling property is reduced by the amount of the credit. In addition, no credit is available for property used outside the United States or for which an election to expense has been made under section 179.

The credit is available for property placed in service after December 31, 2005, and (except in the case of hydrogen refueling property) before January 1, 2011. In the case of hydrogen refueling property, the property must be placed in service before January 1, 2015.

HOUSE BILL

For property placed in service in 2009 or 2010, the provision increases the maximum credit available for business property to $200,000 for qualified hydrogen refueling property and to $50,000 for other qualified refueling property. For nonbusiness property, the maximum credit is increased to $2,000. In addition, the credit rate is increased from 30 percent to 50 percent, except in the case of hydrogen refueling property.

Effective date.—The provision is effective for taxable years beginning after December 31, 2008.

SENATE AMENDMENT

The Senate amendment is the same as the House bill, except that it adds interoperability, public access, and other standards to qualified refueling property that is used for recharging electric or hybrid-electric motor vehicles.

CONFERENCE AGREEMENT

The conference agreement follows the House bill.

11. Recovery period for depreciation of smart meters (sec. 1124 of the Senate amendment)

PRESENT LAW

A taxpayer generally must capitalize the cost of property used in a trade or business and recover such cost over time through annual deductions for depreciation or amortization. Tangible property generally is depreciated under the modified accelerated cost recovery system ("MACRS"), which determines depreciation by applying specific recovery periods, placed-in-service conventions, and depreciation methods to the cost of various types of depreciable property.[188] The class lives of assets placed in service after 1986 are generally set forth in Revenue Procedure 87–56.[189] Present law provides a 10-year recovery period [190] and the 150-percent declining balance method [191] be used for smart meters.

---

[188] Sec. 168.

[189] 1987–2 C.B. 674 (as clarified and modified by Rev. Proc. 88–22, 1988–1 C.B. 785). Assets included in class 49.14, describing assets used in the transmission and distribution of electricity for sale and related land improvements, are assigned a class life of 30 years and a recovery period of 20 years.

[190] Sec. 168(e)(3)(D)(iii).

[191] Sec. 168(b)(2)(C).

A qualified smart electric meter means any time-based meter and related communication equipment which is placed in service by a taxpayer who is a supplier of electric energy or a provider of electric energy services and which is capable of being used by the taxpayer as part of a system that (1) measures and records electricity usage data on a time-differentiated basis in at least 24 separate time segments per day; (2) provides for the exchange of information between the supplier or provider and the customer's smart electric meter in support of time-based rates or other forms of demand response; and (3) provides data to such supplier or provider so that the supplier or provider can provide energy usage information to customers electronically; and (4) provides all commercial and residential customers of such supplier or provider with net metering.[192] The term "net metering" means allowing a customer a credit, if any, as complies with applicable Federal and State laws and regulations, for providing electricity to the supplier or provider.

HOUSE BILL

No provision.

SENATE AMENDMENT

The provision provides a 5-year recovery period and 200 percent declining balance method for any qualified smart electric meter placed in service before January 1, 2011.

Effective date.—The provision is effective for property placed in service after the date of enactment.

CONFERENCE AGREEMENT

The conference agreement does not include the Senate amendment provision.

12. Energy research credit (sec. 1631 of the House bill and sec. 1131 of the Senate amendment)

PRESENT LAW

General rule

A taxpayer may claim a research credit equal to 20 percent of the amount by which the taxpayer's qualified research expenses for a taxable year exceed its base amount for that year.[193] Thus, the research credit is generally available with respect to incremental increases in qualified research.

A 20-percent research tax credit is also available with respect to the excess of (1) 100 percent of corporate cash expenses (including grants or contributions) paid for basic research conducted by universities (and certain nonprofit scientific research organizations) over (2) the sum of (a) the greater of two minimum basic research floors plus (b) an amount reflecting any decrease in nonresearch giving to universities by the corporation as compared to such giving during a fixed-base period, as adjusted for inflation. This separate

---

[192] Sec. 168(i)(18).
[193] Sec. 41.

credit computation is commonly referred to as the university basic research credit.[194]

Finally, a research credit is available for a taxpayer's expenditures on research undertaken by an energy research consortium. This separate credit computation is commonly referred to as the energy research credit. Unlike the other research credits, the energy research credit applies to all qualified expenditures, not just those in excess of a base amount.

The research credit, including the university basic research credit and the energy research credit, expires for amounts paid or incurred after December 31, 2009.[195]

Computation of allowable credit

Except for energy research payments and certain university basic research payments made by corporations, the research tax credit applies only to the extent that the taxpayer's qualified research expenses for the current taxable year exceed its base amount. The base amount for the current year generally is computed by multiplying the taxpayer's fixed-base percentage by the average amount of the taxpayer's gross receipts for the four preceding years. If a taxpayer both incurred qualified research expenses and had gross receipts during each of at least three years from 1984 through 1988, then its fixed-base percentage is the ratio that its total qualified research expenses for the 1984–1988 period bears to its total gross receipts for that period (subject to a maximum fixed-base percentage of 16 percent). All other taxpayers (so-called start-up firms) are assigned a fixed-base percentage of three percent.[196]

In computing the credit, a taxpayer's base amount cannot be less than 50 percent of its current-year qualified research expenses.

To prevent artificial increases in research expenditures by shifting expenditures among commonly controlled or otherwise related entities, a special aggregation rule provides that all members of the same controlled group of corporations are treated as a single taxpayer.[197] Under regulations prescribed by the Secretary, special rules apply for computing the credit when a major portion of a trade or business (or unit thereof) changes hands, under which qualified research expenses and gross receipts for periods prior to the change of ownership of a trade or business are treated as transferred with the trade or business that gave rise to those expenses and receipts for purposes of recomputing a taxpayer's fixed-based percentage.[198]

---

[194] Sec. 41(e).

[195] Sec. 41(h).

[196] The Small Business Job Protection Act of 1996 expanded the definition of start-up firms under section 41(c)(3)(B)(i) to include any firm if the first taxable year in which such firm had both gross receipts and qualified research expenses began after 1983. A special rule (enacted in 1993) is designed to gradually recompute a start-up firm's fixed-base percentage based on its actual research experience. Under this special rule, a start-up firm is assigned a fixed-base percentage of three percent for each of its first five taxable years after 1993 in which it incurs qualified research expenses. A start-up firm's fixed-base percentage for its sixth through tenth taxable years after 1993 in which it incurs qualified research expenses is a phased-in ratio based on the firm's actual research experience. For all subsequent taxable years, the taxpayer's fixed-base percentage is its actual ratio of qualified research expenses to gross receipts for any five years selected by the taxpayer from its fifth through tenth taxable years after 1993. Sec. 41(c)(3)(B).

[197] Sec. 41(f)(1).

[198] Sec. 41(f)(3).

Alternative incremental research credit regime

Taxpayers are allowed to elect an alternative incremental research credit regime.[199] If a taxpayer elects to be subject to this alternative regime, the taxpayer is assigned a three-tiered fixed-base percentage (that is lower than the fixed-base percentage otherwise applicable under present law) and the credit rate likewise is reduced.

Generally, for amounts paid or incurred prior to 2007, under the alternative incremental credit regime, a credit rate of 2.65 percent applies to the extent that a taxpayer's current-year research expenses exceed a base amount computed by using a fixed-base percentage of one percent (i.e., the base amount equals one percent of the taxpayer's average gross receipts for the four preceding years) but do not exceed a base amount computed by using a fixed-base percentage of 1.5 percent. A credit rate of 3.2 percent applies to the extent that a taxpayer's current-year research expenses exceed a base amount computed by using a fixed-base percentage of 1.5 percent but do not exceed a base amount computed by using a fixed-base percentage of two percent. A credit rate of 3.75 percent applies to the extent that a taxpayer's current-year research expenses exceed a base amount computed by using a fixed-base percentage of two percent. Generally, for amounts paid or incurred after 2006, the credit rates listed above are increased to three percent, four percent, and five percent, respectively.[200]

An election to be subject to this alternative incremental credit regime can be made for any taxable year beginning after June 30, 1996, and such an election applies to that taxable year and all subsequent years unless revoked with the consent of the Secretary of the Treasury. The alternative incremental credit regime terminates for taxable years beginning after December 31, 2008.

Alternative simplified credit

Generally, for amounts paid or incurred after 2006, taxpayers may elect to claim an alternative simplified credit for qualified research expenses.[201] The alternative simplified research credit is equal to 12 percent (14 percent for taxable years beginning after December 31, 2008) of qualified research expenses that exceed 50 percent of the average qualified research expenses for the three preceding taxable years. The rate is reduced to six percent if a taxpayer has no qualified research expenses in any one of the three preceding taxable years.

An election to use the alternative simplified credit applies to all succeeding taxable years unless revoked with the consent of the Secretary. An election to use the alternative simplified credit may not be made for any taxable year for which an election to use the alternative incremental credit is in effect. A transition rule applies which permits a taxpayer to elect to use the alternative simplified credit in lieu of the alternative incremental credit if such election is made during the taxable year which includes January 1, 2007.

---

[199] Sec. 41(c)(4).
[200] A special transition rule applies for fiscal year 2006–2007 taxpayers.
[201] A special transition rule applies for fiscal year 2006–2007 taxpayers.

The transition rule applies only to the taxable year which includes that date.

Eligible expenses

Qualified research expenses eligible for the research tax credit consist of: (1) in-house expenses of the taxpayer for wages and supplies attributable to qualified research; (2) certain time-sharing costs for computer use in qualified research; and (3) 65 percent of amounts paid or incurred by the taxpayer to certain other persons for qualified research conducted on the taxpayer's behalf (so-called contract research expenses).[202] Notwithstanding the limitation for contract research expenses, qualified research expenses include 100 percent of amounts paid or incurred by the taxpayer to an eligible small business, university, or Federal laboratory for qualified energy research.

To be eligible for the credit, the research not only has to satisfy the requirements of present-law section 174 (described below) but also must be undertaken for the purpose of discovering information that is technological in nature, the application of which is intended to be useful in the development of a new or improved business component of the taxpayer, and substantially all of the activities of which constitute elements of a process of experimentation for functional aspects, performance, reliability, or quality of a business component. Research does not qualify for the credit if substantially all of the activities relate to style, taste, cosmetic, or seasonal design factors.[203] In addition, research does not qualify for the credit: (1) if conducted after the beginning of commercial production of the business component; (2) if related to the adaptation of an existing business component to a particular customer's requirements; (3) if related to the duplication of an existing business component from a physical examination of the component itself or certain other information; or (4) if related to certain efficiency surveys, management function or technique, market research, market testing, or market development, routine data collection or routine quality control.[204] Research does not qualify for the credit if it is conducted outside the United States, Puerto Rico, or any U.S. possession.

Relation to deduction

Under section 174, taxpayers may elect to deduct currently the amount of certain research or experimental expenditures paid or incurred in connection with a trade or business, notwithstanding the general rule that business expenses to develop or create an asset that has a useful life extending beyond the current year must be capitalized.[205] However, deductions allowed to a taxpayer under section 174 (or any other section) are reduced by an amount equal

---

[202] Under a special rule, 75 percent of amounts paid to a research consortium for qualified research are treated as qualified research expenses eligible for the research credit (rather than 65 percent under the general rule under section 41(b)(3) governing contract research expenses) if (1) such research consortium is a tax-exempt organization that is described in section 501(c)(3) (other than a private foundation) or section 501(c)(6) and is organized and operated primarily to conduct scientific research, and (2) such qualified research is conducted by the consortium on behalf of the taxpayer and one or more persons not related to the taxpayer. Sec. 41(b)(3)(C).

[203] Sec. 41(d)(3).

[204] Sec. 41(d)(4).

[205] Taxpayers may elect 10-year amortization of certain research expenditures allowable as a deduction under section 174(a). Secs. 174(f)(2) and 59(e).

to 100 percent of the taxpayer's research tax credit determined for the taxable year.[206] Taxpayers may alternatively elect to claim a reduced research tax credit amount under section 41 in lieu of reducing deductions otherwise allowed.[207]

The House bill creates a new 20 percent credit for all qualified energy research expenses paid or incurred in 2009 or 2010. Qualified energy research expenses are qualified research expenses related to the fields of fuel cells and battery technology, renewable energy, energy conservation technology, efficient transmission and distribution of electricity, and carbon capture and sequestration.

Effective date.—The provision is effective for taxable years beginning after December 31, 2008.

The Senate amendment is the same as the House bill, except that it adds expenses related to renewable fuels research to the list of qualified energy research expenses.

The conference agreement does not include either the House bill or the Senate amendment provision.

13. Modification of credit for carbon dioxide sequestration (sec. 1141 of the Senate amendment, sec. 1131 of the conference agreement, and sec. 45Q of the Code)

A credit of $20 per metric ton is available for qualified carbon dioxide captured by a taxpayer at a qualified facility and disposed of by such taxpayer in secure geological storage (including storage at deep saline formations and unminable coal seams under such conditions as the Secretary may determine).[208] In addition, a credit of $10 per metric ton is available for qualified carbon dioxide that is captured by the taxpayer at a qualified facility and used by such taxpayer as a tertiary injectant (including carbon dioxide augmented waterflooding and immiscible carbon dioxide displacement) in a qualified enhanced oil or natural gas recovery project. Both credit amounts are adjusted for inflation after 2009.

Qualified carbon dioxide is defined as carbon dioxide captured from an industrial source that (1) would otherwise be released into the atmosphere as an industrial emission of greenhouse gas, and (2) is measured at the source of capture and verified at the point or points of injection. Qualified carbon dioxide includes the initial deposit of captured carbon dioxide used as a tertiary injectant but does not include carbon dioxide that is recaptured, recycled, and reinjected as part of an enhanced oil or natural gas recovery project process. A qualified enhanced oil or natural gas recovery project is a project that would otherwise meet the definition of an enhanced

---

[206] Sec. 280C(c).
[207] Sec. 280C(c)(3).
[208] Sec. 45Q.

oil recovery project under section 43, if natural gas projects were included within that definition.

A qualified facility means any industrial facility (1) which is owned by the taxpayer, (2) at which carbon capture equipment is placed in service, and (3) which captures not less than 500,000 metric tons of carbon dioxide during the taxable year. The credit applies only with respect to qualified carbon dioxide captured and sequestered or injected in the United States [209] or one of its possessions.[210]

Except as provided in regulations, credits are attributable to the person that captures and physically or contractually ensures the disposal, or use as a tertiary injectant, of the qualified carbon dioxide. Credits are subject to recapture, as provided by regulation, with respect to any qualified carbon dioxide that ceases to be recaptured, disposed of, or used as a tertiary injectant in a manner consistent with the rules of the provision.

The credit is part of the general business credit. The credit sunsets at the end of the calendar year in which the Secretary, in consultation with the Administrator of the Environmental Protection Agency, certifies that 75 million metric tons of qualified carbon dioxide have been captured and disposed of or used as a tertiary injectant.

HOUSE BILL

No provision.

SENATE AMENDMENT

The provision requires that carbon dioxide used as a tertiary injectant and otherwise eligible for a $10 per metric ton credit must be sequestered by the taxpayer in permanent geological storage in order to qualify for such credit. The Senate amendment also clarifies that the term permanent geological storage includes oil and gas reservoirs in addition to unminable coal seams and deep saline formations. In addition, the Senate amendment requires that the Secretary of the Treasury consult with the Secretary of Energy and the Secretary of the Interior, in addition to the Administrator of the Environmental Protection Agency, in promulgating regulations relating to the permanent geological storage of carbon dioxide.

Effective date.—The provision is effective for carbon dioxide captured after the date of enactment.

CONFERENCE AGREEMENT

The conference agreement follows the Senate amendment.

---

[209] Sec. 638(1).
[210] Sec. 638(2).

641

14. Modification of the plug-in electric drive motor vehicle credit (secs. 1151 and 1152 of the Senate amendment, secs. 1141 through 1144 of the conference agreement, and secs. 30B and 30D of the Code)

PRESENT LAW

Alternative motor vehicle credit

A credit is available for each new qualified fuel cell vehicle, hybrid vehicle, advanced lean burn technology vehicle, and alternative fuel vehicle placed in service by the taxpayer during the taxable year.[211] In general, the credit amount varies depending upon the type of technology used, the weight class of the vehicle, the amount by which the vehicle exceeds certain fuel economy standards, and, for some vehicles, the estimated lifetime fuel savings. The credit generally is available for vehicles purchased after 2005. The credit terminates after 2009, 2010, or 2014, depending on the type of vehicle. The alternative motor vehicle credit is not allowed against the alternative minimum tax.

Plug-in electric drive motor vehicle credit

A credit is available for each qualified plug-in electric drive motor vehicle placed in service. A qualified plug-in electric drive motor vehicle is a motor vehicle that has at least four wheels, is manufactured for use on public roads, meets certain emissions standards (except for certain heavy vehicles), draws propulsion using a traction battery with at least four kilowatt-hours of capacity, and is capable of being recharged from an external source of electricity.

The base amount of the plug-in electric drive motor vehicle credit is $2,500, plus another $417 for each kilowatt-hour of battery capacity in excess of four kilowatt-hours. The maximum credit for qualified vehicles weighing 10,000 pounds or less is $7,500. This maximum amount increases to $10,000 for vehicles weighing more than 10,000 pounds but not more than 14,000 pounds, to $12,500 for vehicles weighing more than 14,000 pounds but not more than 26,000 pounds, and to $15,000 for vehicles weighing more than 26,000 pounds.

In general, the credit is available to the vehicle owner, including the lessor of a vehicle subject to lease. If the qualified vehicle is used by certain tax-exempt organizations, governments, or foreign persons and is not subject to a lease, the seller of the vehicle may claim the credit so long as the seller clearly discloses to the user in a document the amount that is allowable as a credit. A vehicle must be used predominantly in the United States to qualify for the credit.

Once a total of 250,000 credit-eligible vehicles have been sold for use in the United States, the credit phases out over four calendar quarters. The phaseout period begins in the second calendar quarter following the quarter during which the vehicle cap has been reached. Taxpayers may claim one-half of the otherwise allowable credit during the first two calendar quarters of the phaseout period and twenty-five percent of the otherwise allowable credit

---
[211] Sec. 30B.

during the next two quarters. After this, no credit is available. Regardless of the phase-out limitation, no credit is available for vehicles purchased after 2014.

The basis of any qualified vehicle is reduced by the amount of the credit. To the extent a vehicle is eligible for credit as a qualified plug-in electric drive motor vehicle, it is not eligible for credit as a qualified hybrid vehicle under section 30B. The portion of the credit attributable to vehicles of a character subject to an allowance for depreciation is treated as part of the general business credit; the nonbusiness portion of the credit is allowable to the extent of the excess of the regular tax over the alternative minimum tax (reduced by certain other credits) for the taxable year.

HOUSE BILL

No provision.

SENATE AMENDMENT

Credit for electric drive low-speed vehicles, motorcycles, and three-wheeled vehicles

The Senate amendment creates a new 10-percent credit for low-speed vehicles, motorcycles, and three-wheeled vehicles that would otherwise meet the criteria of a qualified plug-in electric drive motor vehicle but for the fact that they are low-speed vehicles or do not have at least four wheels. The maximum credit for such vehicles is $4,000. Basis reduction and other rules similar to those found in section 30 apply under the provision. The new credit is part of the general business credit. The new credit is not available for vehicles sold after December 31, 2011.

Credit for converting a vehicle into a plug-in electric drive motor vehicle

The Senate amendment also creates a new 10-percent credit, up to $4,000, for the cost of converting any motor vehicle into a qualified plug-in electric drive motor vehicle. To be eligible for the credit, a qualified plug-in traction battery module must have a capacity of at least 2.5 kilowatt-hours. In the case of a leased traction battery module, the credit may be claimed by the lessor but not the lessee. The credit is not available for conversions made after December 31, 2012.

Modification of plug-in electric drive motor vehicle credit

The Senate amendment modifies the plug-in electric drive motor vehicle credit by increasing the 250,000 vehicle limitation to 500,000. It also modifies the definition of qualified plug-in electric drive motor vehicle to exclude low-speed vehicles.

Effective date.—The Senate amendment is generally effective for vehicles sold after December 31, 2009. The credit for plug-in vehicle conversion is effective for property placed in service after December 31, 2008, in taxable years beginning after such date.

CONFERENCE AGREEMENT

The conference agreement follows the Senate amendment with substantial modifications.

643

Credit for electric drive low-speed vehicles, motorcycles, and three-wheeled vehicles

With respect to electric drive low-speed vehicles, motorcycles, and three-wheeled vehicles, the conference agreement follows the Senate amendment with the following modifications. Under the conference agreement, the maximum credit available is $2,500. The conference agreement also makes other technical changes.

Credit for converting a vehicle into a plug-in electric drive motor vehicle

With respect to plug-in vehicle conversions, the conference agreement follows the Senate amendment but increases the minimum capacity of a qualified battery module to four kilowatt-hours, changes the effective date to property placed in service after the date of enactment, and eliminates the credit for plug-in conversions made after December 31, 2011. The conference agreement also removes the rule permitting lessors of battery modules to claim the plug-in conversion credit.

Modification of the plug-in electric drive motor vehicle credit

The conference agreement modifies the plug-in electric drive motor vehicle credit by limiting the maximum credit to $7,500 regardless of vehicle weight. The conference agreement also eliminates the credit for low speed plug-in vehicles and for plug-in vehicles weighing 14,000 pounds or more.

The conference agreement replaces the 250,000 total plug-in vehicle limitation with a 200,000 plug-in vehicles per manufacturer limitation. The credit phases out over four calendar quarters beginning in the second calendar quarter following the quarter in which the manufacturer limit is reached. The conference agreement also makes other technical changes.

The changes to the plug-in electric drive motor vehicle credit are effective for vehicles acquired after December 31, 2009.

Treatment of alternative motor vehicle credit as a personal credit allowed against the alternative minimum tax

The conference agreement provides that the alternative motor vehicle credit is a personal credit allowed against the alternative minimum tax. The provision is effective for taxable years beginning after December 31, 2008.

15. Parity for qualified transportation fringe benefits (sec. 1251 of the Senate amendment, sec. 1151 of the conference agreement, and sec. 132 of the Code)

PRESENT LAW

Qualified transportation fringe benefits provided by an employer are excluded from an employee's gross income for income tax purposes and from an employee's wages for payroll tax purposes.[212] Qualified transportation fringe benefits include parking, transit passes, vanpool benefits, and qualified bicycle commuting reimbursements. Up to $230 (for 2009) per month of employer-provided

---

[212] Code secs. 132(f), 3121(b)(2), 3306(b)(16), and 3401(a)(19).

parking is excludable from income. Up to $120 (for 2009) per month of employer-provided transit and vanpool benefits are excludable from gross income. These amounts are indexed annually for inflation, rounded to the nearest multiple of $5. No amount is includible in the income of an employee merely because the employer offers the employee a choice between cash and qualified transportation fringe benefits. Qualified transportation fringe benefits also include a cash reimbursement by an employer to an employee. However, in the case of transit passes, a cash reimbursement is considered a qualified transportation fringe benefit only if a voucher or similar item which may be exchanged only for a transit pass is not readily available for direct distribution by the employer to the employee.

HOUSE BILL

No provision.

SENATE AMENDMENT

The provision increases the monthly exclusion for employer-provided transit and vanpool benefits to the same level as the exclusion for employer-provided parking.

Effective date.—The provision is effective for months beginning on or after date of enactment. The proposal does not apply to tax years beginning after December 31, 2010.

CONFERENCE AGREEMENT

The conference agreement follows the Senate amendment.

16. Credit for investment in advanced energy property (sec. 1302 of the Senate amendment, sec. 1302 of the conference agreement, and new sec. 48C of the Code)

PRESENT LAW

An income tax credit is allowed for the production of electricity from qualified energy resources at qualified facilities.[213] Qualified energy resources comprise wind, closed-loop biomass, open-loop biomass, geothermal energy, solar energy, small irrigation power, municipal solid waste, qualified hydropower production, and marine and hydrokinetic renewable energy. Qualified facilities are, generally, facilities that generate electricity using qualified energy resources.

An income tax credit is also allowed for certain energy property placed in service. Qualifying property includes certain fuel cell property, solar property, geothermal power production property, small wind energy property, combined heat and power system property, and geothermal heat pump property.[214]

In addition to these, numerous other credits are available to taxpayers to encourage renewable energy production and energy conservation, including, among others, credits for certain biofuels,

---

[213] Sec. 45. In addition to the electricity production credit, section 45 also provides income tax credits for the production of Indian coal and refined coal at qualified facilities.
[214] Sec. 48.

plug-in electric vehicles, and energy efficient appliances, and for improvements to heating, air conditioning, and insulation.

No credit is specifically designed under present law to encourage the development of a domestic manufacturing base to support the industries described above.

No provision.

The Senate amendment establishes a 30 percent credit for investment in qualified property used in a qualified advanced energy manufacturing project. A qualified advanced energy project is a project that re-equips, expands, or establishes a manufacturing facility for the production: (1) property designed to be used to produce energy from the sun, wind, or geothermal deposits (within the meaning of section 613(e)(2)), or other renewable resources; (2) fuel cells, microturbines, or an energy storage system for use with electric or hybrid-electric motor vehicles; (3) electric grids to support the transmission of intermittent sources of renewable energy, including storage of such energy; (4) property designed to capture and sequester carbon dioxide; (5) property designed to refine or blend renewable fuels (but not fossil fuels) or to produce energy conservation technologies (including energy-conserving lighting technologies and smart grid technologies; or (6) other advanced energy property designed to reduce greenhouse gas emissions as may be determined by the Secretary.

Qualified property must be depreciable (or amortizable) property used in a qualified advanced energy project. Qualified property does not include property designed to manufacture equipment for use in the refining or blending of any transportation fuel other than renewable fuels. The basis of qualified property must be reduced by the amount of credit received.

Credits are available only for projects certified by the Secretary of Treasury, in consultation with the Secretary of Energy. The Secretary of Treasury must establish a certification program no later than 180 days after date of enactment, and may allocate up to $2 billion in credits.

In selecting projects, the Secretary may consider only those projects where there is a reasonable expectation of commercial viability. In addition, the Secretary must consider other selection criteria, including which projects (1) will provide the greatest domestic job creation; (2) will provide the greatest net impact in avoiding or reducing air pollutants or anthropogenic emissions of greenhouse gases; (3) have the greatest readiness for commercial employment, replication, and further commercial use in the United States; (4) will provide the greatest benefit in terms of newness in the commercial market; (5) have the lowest levelized cost of generated or stored energy, or of measured reduction in energy consumption or greenhouse gas emission; and (6) have the shortest project time from certification to completion.

Each project application must be submitted during the three-year period beginning on the date such certification program is established. An applicant for certification has two years from the date the Secretary accepts the application to provide the Secretary with evidence that the requirements for certification have been met. Upon certification, the applicant has five years from the date of issuance of the certification to place the project in service. Not later than six years after the date of enactment of the credit, the Secretary is required to review the credit allocations and redistribute any credits that were not used either because of a revoked certification or because of an insufficient quantity of credit applications.

Effective date.—The provision is effective on the date of enactment.

CONFERENCE AGREEMENT

The conference agreement follows the Senate amendment with the following modifications. The conference agreement increases by $300 million (to $2.3 billion) the amount of credits that may be allocated by the Secretary. The conference agreement expands the list of qualifying advance energy projects to include projects designed to manufacture any new qualified plug-in electric drive motor vehicle (as defined by section 30D(c)), any specified vehicle (as defined by section 30D(f)(2)), or any component which is designed specifically for use with such vehicles, including any electric motor, generator, or power control unit. The conference agreement also replaces the third and fourth project selection criteria with a requirement that the Secretary, in addition to the remaining criteria, consider projects that have the greatest potential for technological innovation and commercial deployment.

In addition, the conference agreement shortens to two years the period during which project applications may be submitted, shortens to one year the period during which the project applicants must provide evidence that the certification requirements have been met, and shortens to three years the period during which certified projects must be placed in service. The conference agreement also shortens the period after which the Secretary must review the credit allocations from six to four years. Finally, the conference agreement clarifies that only tangible personal property and other tangible property (not including a building or its structural components) is credit-eligible.

17. Incentives for manufacturing facilities producing plug-in electric drive motor vehicles and components (sec. 1303 of the Senate amendment)

PRESENT LAW

Depreciation rules

A taxpayer is allowed to recover through annual depreciation deductions the cost of certain property used in a trade or business or for the production of income. The amount of the depreciation deduction allowed with respect to tangible property for a taxable year is determined under the modified accelerated cost recovery system ("MACRS"). Under MACRS, different types of property generally are assigned applicable recovery periods and depreciation methods. The recovery periods applicable to most tangible personal property range from 3 to 25 years. The depreciation methods generally applicable to tangible personal property are the 200-percent and 150-percent declining balance methods, switching to the straight-line method for the taxable year in which the taxpayer's depreciation deduction would be maximized.

Bonus depreciation

For property placed in service in calendar year 2009, an additional first-year depreciation deduction is available equal to 50 percent of the adjusted basis of qualified property.[215] The additional first-year depreciation deduction is allowed for both regular tax and alternative minimum tax ("AMT") purposes.[216] Certain other rules and limitations apply.

Election to claim additional research or minimum tax credits in lieu of claiming bonus depreciation

Corporations otherwise eligible for bonus depreciation under section 168(k) may elect to claim additional research or minimum tax credits in lieu of claiming depreciation under section 168(k) for "eligible qualified property" placed in service after March 31, 2008.[217] A corporation making the election forgoes the depreciation deductions allowable under section 168(k) and instead increases the limitation under section 38(c) on the use of research credits or section 53(c) on the use of minimum tax credits.[218] The increases in the allowable credits are treated as refundable for purposes of this provision. The depreciation for qualified property is calculated for both regular tax and AMT purposes using the straight-line method in place of the method that would otherwise be used absent the election under this provision.

The research credit or minimum tax credit limitation is increased by the bonus depreciation amount, which is equal to 20 percent of bonus depreciation[219] for certain eligible qualified property that could be claimed absent an election under this provision. Generally, eligible qualified property included in the calculation is bonus depreciation property that meets the following requirements: (1) the original use of the property must commence with the taxpayer after March 31, 2008; (2) the taxpayer must purchase the property either (a) after March 31, 2008, and before January 1, 2009, but only if no binding written contract for the acquisition is in effect before April 1, 2008,[220] or (b) pursuant to a binding written contract which was entered into after March 31, 2008, and be-

---

[215] Sec. 168(k). The additional first-year depreciation deduction is subject to the general rules regarding whether an item is deductible under section 162 or instead is subject to capitalization under section 263 or section 263A.

[216] However, the additional first-year depreciation deduction is not allowed for purposes of computing earnings and profits.

[217] Sec. 168(k)(4). In the case of an electing corporation that is a partner in a partnership, the corporate partner's distributive share of partnership items is determined as if section 168(k) does not apply to any eligible qualified property and the straight line method is used to calculate depreciation of such property.

[218] Special rules apply to an applicable partnership.

[219] For this purpose, bonus depreciation is the difference between (i) the aggregate amount of depreciation for all eligible qualified property determined if section 168(k)(1) applied using the most accelerated depreciation method (determined without regard to this provision), and shortest life allowable for each property, and (ii) the amount of depreciation that would be determined if section 168(k)(1) did not apply using the same method and life for each property.

[220] In the case of passenger aircraft, the written binding contract limitation does not apply.

fore January 1, 2009;[221] and (3) the property must be placed in service after March 31, 2008, and before January 1, 2009 (January 1, 2010 for certain longer-lived and transportation property).

The bonus depreciation amount is limited to the lesser of: (1) $30 million, or (2) six percent of the sum of research credit carryforwards from taxable years beginning before January 1, 2006 and minimum tax credits allocable to the adjusted minimum tax imposed for taxable years beginning before January 1, 2006. All corporations treated as a single employer under section 52(a) are treated as one taxpayer for purposes of the limitation, as well as for electing the application of this provision.

Credit for plug-in vehicles

A credit is available for each qualified plug-in electric drive motor vehicle placed in service. A qualified plug-in electric drive motor vehicle is a motor vehicle that has at least four wheels, is manufactured for use on public roads, meets certain emissions standards (except for certain heavy vehicles), draws propulsion using a traction battery with at least four kilowatt-hours of capacity, and is capable of being recharged from an external source of electricity.

The base amount of the plug-in electric drive motor vehicle credit is $2,500, plus another $417 for each kilowatt-hour of battery capacity in excess of four kilowatt-hours. The maximum credit for qualified vehicles weighing 10,000 pounds or less is $7,500. This maximum amount increases to $10,000 for vehicles weighing more than 10,000 pounds but not more than 14,000 pounds, to $12,500 for vehicles weighing more than 14,000 pounds but not more than 26,000 pounds, and to $15,000 for vehicle weighing more than 26,000 pounds.

In general, the credit is available to the vehicle owner, including the lessor of a vehicle subject to lease. If the qualified vehicle is used by certain tax-exempt organizations, governments, or foreign persons and is not subject to a lease, the seller of the vehicle may claim the credit so long as the seller clearly discloses to the user in a document the amount that is allowable as a credit. A vehicle must be used predominantly in the United States to qualify for the credit.

Once a total of 250,000 credit-eligible vehicles have been sold for use in the United States, the credit phases out over four calendar quarters. The phaseout period begins in the second calendar quarter following the quarter during which the vehicle cap has been reached. Taxpayers may claim one-half of the otherwise allowable credit during the first two calendar quarters of the phaseout period and twenty-five percent of the otherwise allowable credit during the next two quarters. After this, no credit is available. Regardless of the phase-out limitation, no credit is available for vehicles purchased after 2014.

The basis of any qualified vehicle is reduced by the amount of the credit. To the extent a vehicle is eligible for credit as a qualified plug-in electric drive motor vehicle, it is not eligible for credit

---

[221] Special rules apply to property manufactured, constructed, or produced by the taxpayer for use by the taxpayer.

as a qualified hybrid vehicle under section 30B. The portion of the credit attributable to vehicles of a character subject to an allowance for depreciation is treated as part of the general business credit; the nonbusiness portion of the credit is allowable to the extent of the excess of the regular tax over the AMT (reduced by certain other credits) for the taxable year.

HOUSE BILL

No provision.

SENATE AMENDMENT

The Senate amendment permits taxpayers to elect to expense one hundred percent of the cost of any electric drive motor vehicle manufacturing facility property placed in service before 2012 and fifty percent of the cost of such property placed in service after 2011 and before 2015. For purposes of this election, qualified property is property which is a facility or a portion of a facility used for the production of any new qualified plug-in electric drive motor vehicle [222] or any eligible component. Eligible components are any battery, any electric motor or generator, or any power control unit which is designed specifically for use with a new qualified plug-in electric drive motor vehicle.

The original use of any qualified property must begin with the taxpayer. In the case of dual use property, the amount of cost eligible to be expensed is reduced by the total cost of the facility multiplied by the percentage of property expected to be produced that is not qualified property.

The Senate amendment permits taxpayers to waive this election in favor of a loan equal to thirty-five percent of the amount eligible to be expensed under the general provision. The loan is in the form of a senior note, with a 20-year term and an interest rate payable at the applicable Federal rate, issued by the taxpayer to the Secretary of Treasury and secured by the qualified manufacturing property. Upon repayment of the loan, the taxpayer's tax liability limitations are increased for the research credit [223] and the alternative minimum tax credit [224] by the amount of the loan.

Effective date.—The provision is effective for taxable years beginning after the date of enactment.

CONFERENCE AGREEMENT

The conference agreement does not include the Senate amendment provision.

---

[222] As defined by section 30D(c).
[223] Sec. 38(c).
[224] Sec. 53(c).

E. OTHER PROVISIONS

1. Application of certain labor standards to projects financed with certain tax-favored bonds (sec. 1701 of the House bill, sec. 1901 of the Senate amendment, and sec. 1601 of the conference agreement)

PRESENT LAW

The United States Code (Subchapter IV of Chapter 31 of Title 40) applies a prevailing wage requirement to certain contracts to which the Federal Government is a party.

HOUSE BILL

The provision provides that Subchapter IV of Chapter 31 of Title 40 of the U.S. Code shall apply to projects financed with the proceeds of:

1. any qualified clean renewable energy bond (as defined in sec. 54C of the Code) issued after the date of enactment;

2. any qualified energy conservation bond (as defined in sec. 54D of the Code) issued after the date of enactment;

3. any qualified zone academy bond (as defined in sec. 54E of the Code) issued after the date of enactment;

4. any qualified school construction bond (as defined in sec. 54F of the Code); and

5. any recovery zone economic development bond (as defined in sec. 1400U–2 of the Code).

Effective date.—The provision is effective on the date of enactment.

SENATE AMENDMENT

The Senate amendment is the same as the House bill except it makes a technical correction to change "qualified clean renewable energy bond" to "new clean renewable energy bond."

CONFERENCE AGREEMENT

The conference agreement follows the Senate amendment.

2. Increase in the public debt limit (sec. 1902 of the Senate amendment and sec. 1604 of the conference agreement)

PRESENT LAW

The statutory limit on the public debt is $11,315,000,000,000.

HOUSE BILL

No provision.

SENATE AMENDMENT

The Senate amendment increases the statutory limit on the public debt by $825,000,000,000 to $12,140,000,000,000.

Effective date.—The provision is effective on the date of enactment.

CONFERENCE AGREEMENT

The conference agreement increases the statutory limit on the public debt by $789,000,000,000 to $12,104,000,000,000.

Effective date. The provision is effective on the date of enactment.

3. Failure to redeem certain securities from the United States (sec. 6021 of the Senate amendment)

PRESENT LAW

An employer generally may deduct reasonable compensation for personal services as an ordinary and necessary business expense. Section 162(m) (relating to remuneration expenses for certain executives that are in excess of $1 million) and section 280G (relating to excess parachute payments) provide explicit limitations on the deductibility of certain compensation expenses in the case of corporate employers, and section 4999 imposes an additional tax of 20 percent on the recipient of an excess parachute payment. The Emergency Economic Stabilization Act of 2008 ("EESA") limits the amount of payments that may be deducted as reasonable compensation by certain financial institutions that receive financial assistance from the United States pursuant to the troubled asset relief program ("TARP") established under EESA by modifying the section 162(m) and section 280G limits. EESA also provided nontax rules relating to the compensation that is payable by such a financial institution (the "TARP executive compensation rules").

HOUSE BILL

No provision.

SENATE AMENDMENT

In general

The provision amends the TARP executive compensation rules to limit payment of "excessive bonuses" to "covered individuals" by financial institutions whose preferred stock was purchased by the United States using funds provided under TARP. Excessive bonuses are defined as the portion of an "applicable bonus payment" made to a covered individual in excess of $100,000.

An applicable bonus payment is any bonus payment that is (1) paid, or payable, for services performed by a covered individual in a tax year of the financial institution ending in 2008, and (2) the amount of which was communicated to the covered individual at some time between January 1, 2008, and January 31, 2009, or was based on a resolution of the financial institution's board of directors and adopted before the end of the financial institution's 2008 taxable year. For purposes of determining an applicable bonus, any bonus payments that relate to a taxable year prior to 2008, but which are wholly or partially contingent on the performance of services in the 2008 taxable year, are disregarded. In addition, any conditions on 2008 bonuses that require the covered individual to perform services in a subsequent taxable year are also disregarded (e.g., if a 2008 bonus is dependent on the performance of services

in 2009, the bonus is still considered to be an applicable bonus if
it meets all of the other requirements for such status).

The definition of bonus includes discretionary payments for
services provided that are in addition to amounts payable for regular services performed and is payable in cash or property other
than (1) the stock of the financial institution or (2) an interest in
a troubled asset (within the meaning of EESA) held directly or indirectly by the financial institution. Bonuses do not include com-
missions, welfare and fringe benefits, or expense reimbursements.

A covered individual is any director, officer, or other employee
of a financial institution or its controlled group of corporations.[225]

Stock redemption

If a financial institution pays one or more excessive bonuses to
one or more covered individuals, the financial institution must redeem from the government an amount of preferred stock equal to
the aggregate amount of all excessive bonuses paid or payable to
such covered individual or individuals. The redemption obligation
exists notwithstanding any otherwise applicable restrictions on the
redeemability of the preferred stock. The preferred stock must be
redeemed by the later of: 120 days after date of enactment (for excessive bonuses that had already been paid) or the day before the
excessive bonus (or a portion thereof) is paid.

Excise tax

An excise tax is imposed on any financial institution that pays
one or more excessive bonuses but does not redeem its preferred
stock from the government in a timely manner. The tax is equal
to 35 percent of the amount of preferred stock that the financial
institution should have redeemed from the government (i.e., the
amount of the excessive bonus). For example, if a financial institution granted a 2008 bonus of $1 million to its chief executive offi-
cer, and the financial institution did not redeem $900,000 worth of
preferred stock from the United States, it must pay a tax of
$315,000 ($1 million minus $100,000 times 35 percent). Once a fi-
nancial institution pays the 35 percent tax, the institution is no
longer required to redeem from the government an amount of preferred stock equal to the amount of the excessive bonus. That is,
a financial institution that pays an excessive bonus must either redeem stock or pay an excise tax on that bonus but it will not be
required to do both for any single bonus.

Payment of the excise tax does not have any effect on otherwise applicable agreements to redeem preferred stock purchased by
the Federal Government using funds provided by TARP.

Effective Date

The provision applies to a failure to redeem preferred stock
that occurs after the date of enactment.

---

[225] Members of a controlled group of corporations are determined as provided under section
52(a).

CONFERENCE AGREEMENT

The conference agreement does not include the Senate amendment provision.

F. TRADE RELATED PROVISIONS

1. TRADE ADJUSTMENT ASSISTANCE [226]

I. OVERVIEW

The conference report amends the Trade Act of 1974 ("the Trade Act") to reauthorize trade adjustment assistance ("TAA"), to extend trade adjustment assistance to service workers, communities, firms, and farmers, and for other purposes.

II. HOUSE BILL

No provision.

III. SENATE BILL

First, the Senate bill amends section 245(a) of the Trade Act of 1974 to extend the authorization for the TAA for Workers program until December 31, 2010. Second, the proposal amends section 246(b)(1) of the Trade Act of 1974 to extend the authorization for Alternative Trade Adjustment Assistance program by two years. Third, the proposal amends section 256(b) of the Trade Act of 1974 to extend the authorization for the TAA for Firms program until December 31, 2010. Fourth, the proposal amends section 298(a) of the Trade Act of 1974 to extend the TAA for Farmers program until December 31, 2010. Fifth, the proposal amends section 285 of the Trade Act of 1974 to extend the overall termination date of the TAA programs until December 31, 2010. Sixth, the proposal provides that these amendments shall have an effective date of January 1, 2008. Seventh, the proposal includes a Sense of the Senate that a TAA for Communities program should be revived.

IV. CONFERENCE REPORT

A. PART I—TRADE ADJUSTMENT ASSISTANCE FOR WORKERS

1. SUBPART A—TRADE ADJUSTMENT ASSISTANCE FOR SERVICE SECTOR WORKERS

Extension of Trade Adjustment Assistance to Service Sector and Public Agency Workers; Shifts in Production (Section 1701 (amending Sections 221, 222, 231, 244, and 247 of the Trade Act of 1974))

Present Law

Section 222 of the Trade Act provides trade adjustment assistance to workers in a firm or an appropriate subdivision of a firm if (1) a significant number or proportion of the workers in the firm or subdivision have become (or are threatened to become) totally or

---

[226] Descriptions prepared by the majority staffs of the House Committee on Ways and Means and the Senate Committee on Finance.

partially separated; (2) the firm produces an article; and (3) the separation or threat of same is due to trade with foreign countries.

There are three ways to demonstrate the connection between job separation and trade. The Secretary of Labor ("the Secretary") must determine either (1) that increased imports of articles "like or directly competitive" with articles produced by the firm have contributed importantly to the separation and to an absolute decrease in the firm's sales or production, or both; (2) that the workers' firm has shifted its production of articles "like or directly competitive" with articles produced by the firm to a trade agreement partner of the United States or a beneficiary country under the Andean Trade Preference Act, the African Growth and Opportunity Act, or the Caribbean Basin Economic Recovery Act; or (3) that the firm has shifted production of such articles to another country and there has been or is likely to be an increase in imports of like or directly competitive articles.

Section 222 of the Trade Act also provides TAA to adversely affected secondary workers. Eligible secondary workers include (1) secondary workers that supply directly to another firm component parts for articles that were the basis for a certification of eligibility for TAA benefits; and (2) downstream workers that were affected by trade with Mexico or Canada.

When the Department investigates workers' petitions, it requires firms and customers to certify the questionnaires that the workers' firm and the firm's customers submit. Present law also authorizes the Secretary to use subpoenas to obtain information in the course of its investigation of a petition. The law provides for the imposition of criminal and civil penalties for providing false information and failing to disclose material information, but the penalties apply only to petitioners.

Explanation of Provision

The provision would amend section 222 of the Trade Act to expand the availability of TAA to include workers in firms in the services sector. Like workers in firms that produce articles, workers in firms that supply services would be eligible for TAA if a significant number or proportion of the workers have become (or are threatened to become) totally or partially separated, and if increased imports of services "contributed importantly" to the workers' separation or threat of separation.

As with articles, there would be three ways for service sector workers to demonstrate that they are eligible for TAA. First, TAA would be available if increased imports of services like or directly competitive with services supplied by the firm have contributed importantly to the separation and to an absolute decrease in the firm's sales or production, or both. Second, TAA would be available in "shift in supply" ("service relocation") scenarios, if the workers' firm or subdivision established a facility in a foreign country to supply services like or directly competitive with the services supplied by the trade-impacted workers. Third, TAA would be available in "foreign contracting" scenarios, if the workers' firm or subdivision acquired from a service supplier in a foreign country services like or directly competitive with the services that the trade-impacted workers had supplied. In each scenario, the relevant activity would need to have contributed importantly to the workers' separation or threat of separation.

The provision also expands the "shift in production" prong of present law by eliminating the requirement in section 222 that the shift be to a trade agreement partner of the United States or a country that benefits from a unilateral preference program. Under the modified provision, if workers are separated because their firm shifts production from a domestic facility to any foreign country, the separated workers would potentially be eligible for TAA. Additionally, there would be no requirement to demonstrate separately that the shift was accompanied by an increase of imports of products like or directly competitive with those produced by the workers' firm or subdivision.

The provision also amends section 222 to make workers at public agencies eligible for TAA. Under the modified provision, if a public agency acquires services from a foreign country that are like or directly competitive with the services that the public agency supplies, and if the acquisition contributed importantly to the workers' separation or threat thereof, the workers would be able to seek TAA benefits.

The provision also amends section 222 to expand the universe of adversely affected secondary workers that could be eligible for TAA. First, the provision adds firms that supply testing, packaging, maintenance, and transportation services to the list of downstream producers whose workers potentially are eligible for TAA. Second, workers at firms that supply services used in the production of articles or in the supply of services would also become potentially eligible for benefits. Third, the provision permits downstream producers to be eligible for TAA if the primary firm's certification is linked to trade with any country, not just Canada or Mexico. The provision requires the Secretary to obtain information that the Secretary determines necessary to make certifications from workers' firms or customers of workers' firms through questionnaires and in such other manner as the Secretary considers appropriate. The provision also permits the Secretary to seek additional information from other sources, including (1) officials or employees of the workers' firm; (2) officials of customers of the firm; (3) officials of unions or other duly recognized representatives of the petitioning workers; and (4) one-stop operators. The provision states that the Secretary shall require a firm or customer to certify all information obtained through questionnaires, as well as other information that the Secretary relies upon in making a determination under section 223, unless the Secretary has a reasonable basis for determining that the information is accurate and complete.

The provision states that the Secretary shall require a worker's firm or a customer of a worker's firm to provide information by subpoena if the firm or customer fails to provide the information within 20 days after the date of the Secretary's request, unless the firm or customer demonstrates to the Secretary's satisfaction that the firm or customer will provide the information in a reasonable period of time. The Secretary retains the discretion to issue a subpoena sooner than 20 days if necessary. The provision also establishes standards for the protection of confidential business information submitted in response to a request made by the Secretary.

The provision amends the penalties provision in section 244 of the Trade Act to cover persons, including persons who are employed by firms and customers, who provide information during an investigation of a worker's petition.

Finally, the provision amends section 247 of the Trade Act to add definitions for certain key terms and makes various conforming changes to sections 221 and 222.

Reasons for Change

Most service sector workers presently are ineligible for TAA benefits because of a statutory requirement that the workers must have been employed by a firm that produces an "article." Of the 800 TAA petitions denied in FY2006, almost half were denied for this reason. Most of the denied service-related petitions came from two service industries: business services (primarily computer-related) and airport-related services (e.g., aircraft maintenance). In April 2006, the Department of Labor issued a regulation expanding TAA eligibility to software workers that partially, but not fully, addresses the service worker coverage issue. See GAO Report 07–702. The provision fully addresses the issue by making service sector workers eligible for TAA on equivalent terms to workers at firms that produce articles.

The provision expands the "shift in production" prong of present law for similar reasons. Under present law, a worker whose firm relocates to China is not necessarily eligible for TAA; such worker must also show that the relocation to China will result in increased imports into the United States. In contrast, a worker whose firm relocates to a country with which the United States has a trade agreement (e.g., Mexico, Israel, Chile) does not need to show increased imports. The provision eliminates this disparate treatment by making TAA benefits available in both scenarios on the same terms.

Present law also fails to cover foreign contracting scenarios, where a company closes a domestic operation and contracts with a company in a foreign country for the goods or services that had been produced in the United States. For example, if a U.S. airline lays off a number of its U.S.-based maintenance personnel and contracts with an independent aircraft maintenance company in a foreign country, the laid off personnel are not covered under present law, even if they lost their jobs because of foreign competition. The Conferees believe such workers should be potentially eligible for TAA benefits.

Similarly, the Conferees believe that workers who supply services at public agencies should be treated the same as their private-sector counterparts: if such workers are laid off because their employer contracts with a supplier in a foreign country for the services that the workers had supplied, the workers should be able to seek TAA benefits.

The provision provides that in cases involving production or service relocation or foreign contracting, a group of workers (including workers in a public agency) may be certified as eligible for adjustment assistance if the shift "contributed importantly" to such workers' separation or threat of separation. This requirement is identical to the existing causal link requirement in section

222(a)(2)(A)(iii), which establishes the criteria for certifying workers on the basis of "increased imports."

The Conferees understand that the Department of Labor has interpreted the "contributed importantly" requirement in section 222(a)(2)(A)(iii) to mean that imports must have been a factor in the layoffs or threat thereof. Or, in other words, under present law the Secretary of Labor will certify a group of workers as eligible for assistance if the facts demonstrate a causal nexus between increased imports and the workers' separation or threat thereof. The Conferees approve of the Department's interpretation of the "contributed importantly" requirement and expect that the Department will continue to apply it in future cases involving increased imports. Similarly, the Conferees also understand that the existing language in section 222(a)(2)(B) addressing production relocation contains an implicit causation requirement. Thus, the Department has required production relocation under section 222(a)(2)(B) to be a factor in the workers' separation or threat thereof. The provision makes the requirement explicit. The Conferees emphasize that by making the "contributed importantly" requirement in section 222(a)(2)(B) explicit, no change in the Department's administration of cases involving production relocation is intended. The Conferees expect that this change in section 222 would not affect the outcomes that the Department has been reaching under present law in such cases, and will not alter outcomes in future cases. Thus, as has been the case, if the Department finds that production relocation was a factor in the layoff (or threat thereof) of a group of workers in the United States, the Conferees expect that the Secretary will certify such workers as eligible for adjustment assistance.

Finally, with respect to certifications involving production or service relocations or foreign contracting, the Conferees recognize that there may be delays in time between when the domestic layoffs (or threat of layoffs) occur, and when the production or service relocation or foreign contracting occurs. The Conferees intend that the Department of Labor certify petitions where there is credible evidence that production or service relocation or foreign contracting will occur, and when the other requirements of the statute are met. Such evidence could include the conclusion of a contract relating to foreign production of the article, supply of services, or acquisition of the article or service at issue; the construction, purchase, or renting of foreign facilities for the production of the article, supply of the service, or acquisition of the article or service at issue; or certified statements by a duly authorized representative at the workers' firm that the firm intends to engage in production or service relocation or foreign contracting. The Conferees are aware of concerns that the Secretary may rely on inaccurate information in making its determinations, including when denying certification of petitions. The provision addresses these concerns by requiring the Secretary to obtain certifications of all information obtained from a firm or customer through questionnaires as well as other information from a firm or customer that the Secretary relies upon in making a determination under section 223, unless the Secretary has a reasonable basis for determining that the information is accurate and complete.

The Conferees are also aware of concerns that some firms and customers fail to respond to the Secretary's requests for information or provide inaccurate or incomplete information. The subpoena, confidentiality of information, and penalty language included in this provision are designed to address these problems.

The provision would also apply if the Secretary needs to obtain information from a customer's customer, such as in an investigation involving component part suppliers.

Effective Date

The provision goes into effect upon expiration of the 90-day period beginning on the date of enactment of this Act, and applies to petitions filed on or after that date.

Group Eligibility—Component Parts (Section 1701 (amending Section 222 of the Trade Act of 1974))

Present Law

Under present law, U.S. suppliers of inputs (i.e., component parts) may be certified for TAA benefits only pursuant to the secondary workers provision of section 222(b), which requires that the downstream producer have employed a group of workers that received TAA certification. Thus, for example, domestic producers of taconite have been unable to obtain certification for TAA benefits when downstream producers of steel slab have not obtained certification. Additionally, U.S. suppliers of inputs have been unable to obtain certification for TAA benefits in situations in which there is a shift in imports from articles incorporating their inputs to articles incorporating inputs produced outside the United States.

Explanation of Provision

The provision allows for the certification of workers in a firm when imports of the finished article incorporating inputs produced outside the United States that are like or directly competitive with imports of the finished article produced using U.S. inputs have increased and the firm has met the other criteria for certification, including a significant number of workers being totally or partially separated, a decrease in sales or production, and the increase in imports has contributed importantly to the workers' separation.

For example, under the new provision, workers in a U.S. fabric plant may be certified if the U.S. firm sold fabric to a Honduran apparel manufacturer for production of apparel subsequently imported into the United States and (1) the Honduran apparel manufacturer ceased purchasing, or decreased its purchasing, of fabric from the U.S. producer and, instead, used fabric from another country; or (2) imports of apparel from another country using non-U.S. fabric that are like or directly competitive with imports of Honduran apparel using U.S. fabric have increased.

Prior to certification, the Department of Labor would also have to determine that the firm met the other statutory requirements for certification, including that a significant number of workers had been totally or partially separated, or are threatened to become totally or partially separated, the sales or production of the petitioning fabric firm had decreased, and the increased imports of apparel using non-U.S. fabric had contributed importantly to that decrease and to the workers' separation or threat thereof.

Likewise, workers in a U.S. picture tube manufacturing plant that sells picture tubes to a Mexican television manufacturer for production of televisions subsequently imported into the United States would be certified under section 222 if the U.S. manufacturer's sales or production of picture tubes decreased and (1) the manufacturer of televisions located in Mexico switched to picture tubes produced in another country; or (2) imports of televisions from another country using non-U.S. picture tubes that are like or directly competitive with imports of Mexican televisions using U.S. picture tubes have increased.

As in the apparel example above, prior to certification, the Department of Labor would also have to determine that the picture tube firm met the other statutory requirements for certification, including that a significant number of workers had been totally or partially separated, or are threatened to become totally or partially separated, the sales or production of the petitioning picture tube firm had decreased, and the increased imports of televisions using non-U.S. picture tubes had contributed importantly to that decrease and to the workers' separation or threat thereof.

Reasons for Change

Section 222(a) is being amended to provide improved TAA coverage for U.S. suppliers of inputs, and to address situations where suppliers of component parts have been unable to obtain certification for TAA benefits because of gaps in coverage under present law.

The amended language is broad enough to encompass both the situation in which the input producer's customer switches to inputs produced outside the United States, and the situation in which the input producer's customer is displaced by a third country producer, because both situations may equally impact the sales or production of the domestic input producer.

Additionally, for purposes of section 222(a)(2)(A)(ii)(III), as in other instances, when company-specific data is unavailable, the Secretary may reasonably rely on such aggregate data or such other information as the Secretary deems appropriate.

As reflected in the examples above, the Conferees intend that the Secretary of Labor should interpret the term component parts, as used in section 222(a)(2)(A)(ii)(III), flexibly. For example, the Conferees intend that uncut fabric would be considered to be a component part of apparel for purposes of this provision, even though, for purposes of other trade laws, U.S. Customs and Border Protection might not consider such fabric to be a component part.

Effective Date

The provision goes into effect upon expiration of the 90-day period beginning on the date of enactment of this Act, and applies to petitions filed on or after that date.

Separate Basis for Certification (Section 1702 (amending Section 222 of the Trade Act of 1974))

Present Law

There is no provision in present law.

Explanation of Provision

The provision amends section 222(c) of the Trade Act by providing that a petition filed under section 221 of the Trade Act on behalf of a group of workers in a firm, or appropriate subdivision of a firm, meets the requirements of subsection 222(a) of the Trade Act if the firm is publicly identified by name by the U.S. International Trade Commission ("ITC") as a member of a domestic industry in (1) an affirmative determination of serious injury or threat thereof in a global safeguard investigation under section 202(b)(1) of the Trade Act; (2) an affirmative determination of market disruption or threat thereof in a China safeguard investigation under section 421(b)(1) of the Trade Act; or (3) an affirmative final determination of material injury or threat thereof in an antidumping or countervailing duty investigation under section 705(b)(1)(A) or 735(b)(1)(A) of the Tariff Act of 1930 (19 U.S.C. 1671d(b)(1)(A) and 1673d(b)(1)(A)), but only if the petition is filed within 1 year of the date that notice of the affirmative ITC determination is published in the Federal Register (or, in the case of a global safeguard investigation under section 202(b)(1), a summary of the report submitted to the President by the ITC under section 202(f)(1) is published in the Federal Register under section 202(f)(3)) and the workers on whose behalf such petition was filed have become totally or partially separated from such workers' firm within either that 1-year period or the 1-year period preceding the date of such publication.

Reasons for Change

The Conferees note that the provision allows workers in firms publicly identified by name in certain ITC investigations to be eligible for adjustment assistance on the basis of an affirmative injury determination by the ITC under certain circumstances, and without an additional determination by the Secretary of Labor that either increased imports of a like or directly competitive article contributed importantly to such workers' separation or threat of separation (and to an absolute decline in the sales or production, or both, of such workers' firm or subdivision), or that a shift in production of articles contributed importantly to such workers' separation or threat of separation.

In order for workers to avail themselves of this provision, the petition must be filed with the Secretary (and with the Governor of the State in which such workers' firm or subdivision is located) within 1 year of the date of publication in the Federal Register of the applicable notice from the ITC and the workers on whose behalf such petition was filed must have become totally or partially separated from such workers' firm within either that 1-year period or the 1-year period preceding such date of publication.

If a petition is filed on behalf of such workers more than 1 year after the date that the applicable notice from the ITC is published in the Federal Register, it will remain necessary for the Secretary of Labor to investigate the petition and determine that the statutory criteria for certifying such workers in section 222 are satisfied.

Effective Date

The provision goes into effect upon expiration of the 90-day period beginning on the date of enactment of this Act, and applies to petitions filed on or after that date.

Determinations by the Secretary of Labor (Section 1703 (amending Section 223 of the Trade Act of 1974))

Present Law

The Secretary is required to investigate petitions filed by workers and determine whether such workers are eligible for TAA benefits. A summary of such group eligibility determination, together with the Secretary's reasons for making the determination, must be promptly published in the Federal Register. Similarly, a termination of a certification, together with the Secretary's reasons for the termination, must be promptly published in the Federal Register.

Explanation of Provision

This section requires the Secretary to publish (1) a summary of a group eligibility determination, together with the Secretary's reasons for the determination; and (2) a certification termination, together with the Secretary's reasons for the termination, promptly on the Department's website (as well as in the Federal Register). The section also requires the Secretary to establish standards for investigating petitions, and criteria for making determinations. Moreover, the Secretary is required to consult with the Senate Committee on Finance ("Senate Finance Committee") and the Committee on Ways and Means of the House of Representatives ("House Committee on Ways and Means") 90 days prior to issuing a final rule on the standards.

Reasons for Change

To improve accountability, transparency, and public access to this information, the Secretary should be required to post (1) a summary of a group eligibility determination, together with the Secretary's reasons for the determination; and (2) a certification termination, together with the Secretary's reasons for the termination, promptly on the Department's website (as well as in the Federal Register). The Secretary also should have objective and transparent standards for investigating petitions, and criteria for the basis on which an eligibility determination is made. The Secretary should consult with Senate Finance and House Ways and Means to ensure the intent of Congress is accurately reflected in such standards.

Effective Date

The provision goes into effect upon expiration of the 90-day period beginning on the date of enactment of this Act, and applies to petitions filed on or after that date.

Monitoring and Reporting Relating to Service Sector (Section 1704 (amending Section 282 of the Trade Act of 1974))

Present Law

Present law requires the Secretaries of Commerce and Labor to establish and maintain a program to monitor imports of articles into the United States, including (1) information concerning changes in import volume; (2) impacts on domestic production; and (3) impacts on domestic employment in industries producing like or competitive products. Summaries must be provided to the Adjustment Assistance Coordinating Committee, the ITC, and Congress.

Explanation of Provision

The provision is renamed "Trade Monitoring and Data Collection." The provision requires the Secretaries of Commerce and Labor to monitor imports of services (in addition to articles). To address data limitations, the provision requires the Secretary of Labor, not later than 90 days after enactment, to collect data on impacted service workers (by State, industry, and cause).

Finally, it requires the Secretary of Commerce, in consultation with the Secretary of Labor, to report to Congress, not later than one year after enactment, on ways to improve the timeliness and coverage of data regarding trade in services.

Reasons for Change

Existing data on trade in services are sparse. Because of the increases in trade in services, the Conferees believe that it is critical that the government collect data on imports of services and the impact of these imports on U.S. workers. Such information will be useful when considering any further refinement of TAA that Congress may contemplate. More generally, the additional data will give U.S. businesses and workers insight into trade in services, helping them better compete in the global marketplace.

Effective Date

The provision goes into effect on the date of enactment of this Act.

2. SUBPART B—INDUSTRY NOTIFICATIONS FOLLOWING CERTAIN AFFIRMATIVE DETERMINATIONS

Notifications following certain affirmative determinations (Section 1711 (amending Section 224 of the Trade Act of 1974))

Present Law

Present law includes a provision requiring the ITC to notify the Secretary of Labor when it begins a section 201 global safeguard investigation. The Secretary must then begin an investigation of (1) the number of workers in the relevant domestic industry; and (2) whether TAA will help such workers adjust to import competition. The Secretary of Labor must submit a report to the President within 15 days of the ITC's section 201 determination. The Secretary's report must be made public and a summary printed in the Federal Register.

Explanation of Provision

The provision expands the notification requirement to instruct the ITC to notify the Secretary of Labor and the Secretary of Commerce, or the Secretary of Agriculture when dealing with agricultural commodities, when it issues an affirmative determination of injury or threat thereof under sections 202 or 421 of the Trade Act, an affirmative safeguard determination under a U.S. trade agreement, or an affirmative determination in a countervailing duty or dumping investigation under sections 705 or 735 of the Tariff Act of 1930. Additionally, the provision requires the President to notify the Secretaries of Labor and Commerce upon making an affirmative determination in a safeguard investigation relating to textile and apparel articles. Whenever an injury determination is made, the Secretary of Labor must notify employers, workers, and unions of firms covered by the determination of the workers' potential eligibility for TAA benefits and provide them with assistance in filing petitions. Similarly, the Secretary of Commerce must notify firms covered by the determination of their potential eligibility for TAA for Firms and provide them with assistance in filing petitions, and the Secretary of Agriculture must do the same for investigations involving agricultural commodities.

Reasons for Change

A significant hurdle to ensuring that workers and firms avail themselves of TAA benefits is the lack of awareness about the program. In situations like these, where the ITC has made a determination that a domestic industry has been injured as a result of trade, giving notice to the workers and firms in that industry of TAA's potential benefits is warranted.

Effective Date

The provision goes into effect upon expiration of the 90-day period beginning on the date of enactment of this Act, and applies to petitions filed on or after that date.

Notification to Secretary of Commerce (Section 1712 (amending Section 225 of the Trade Act of 1974))

Present Law

Under present law, the Secretary of Labor must provide workers with information about TAA and provide whatever assistance is necessary to help petitioners apply for TAA. The Secretary must also reach out to State Vocational Education Boards and their equivalent agencies, as well as other public and private institutions, about affirmative group certification determinations and projections of training needs.

The Secretary must also notify each worker who the State has reason to believe is covered by a group certification in writing via U.S. Mail of the benefits available under TAA. If the worker lost his job before group certification, then the notice occurs at the time of certification. If the worker lost her job after group certification, then the notice occurs at the time the worker loses her job. The Secretary must also publish notice in the newspapers circulating in the area where the workers reside.

Explanation of Provision

The provision requires the Secretary of Labor, upon issuing a certification, to notify the Secretary of Commerce of the identity of the firms covered by a certification.

Reasons for Change

Firms employing workers certified as eligible for TAA benefits may not be aware that they may be eligible for assistance under the TAA for Firms program. Requiring the Secretary of Labor to notify the Secretary of Commerce when workers at a firm are certified as TAA eligible will help put these firms on notice of their potential TAA for Firms eligibility.

Effective Date

The provision goes into effect upon expiration of the 90-day period beginning on the date of enactment of this Act, and applies to petitions filed on or after that date.

3. SUBPART C—PROGRAM BENEFITS

Qualifying requirements for workers (Section 1721 (amending Section 231 of the Trade Act of 1974))

Present Law

Present law authorizes a worker to receive TAA income support (known as "Trade Readjustment Allowance" or "TRA") for weeks of unemployment that begin 60 days after the date of filing the petition on which certification was granted.

To qualify for TAA benefits, a worker must have (1) lost his job on or after the trade impact date identified in the certification, and within two years of the date of the certification determination; (2) been employed by the TAA certified firm for at least 26 of the 52 weeks preceding the layoff; and (3) earned at least $30 or more a week in that employment. A worker must qualify for, and exhaust, his State unemployment compensation ("UC") benefits before receiving a weekly TRA.

Further, to receive TRA, a worker must be enrolled in an approved training program by the later of 8 weeks after the TAA petition was certified, or 16 weeks after job loss (the "8/16" deadline). The 8/16 deadline can be extended in certain limited circumstances. Workers may also receive limited waivers of the 8/16 training enrollment deadline.

Present law provides for waivers in the following circumstances: (1) the worker has been or will be recalled by the firm; (2) the worker possesses marketable skills; (3) the worker is within 2 years of retirement; (4) the worker cannot participate in training because of health reasons; (5) training enrollment is unavailable; or (6) training is not reasonably available to the worker (nothing suitable, no reasonable cost, no training funds).

Waivers last 6 months, unless the Secretary determines otherwise, and will be revoked if the basis for the waiver no longer exists. States have the authority to issue waivers. By regulation, State and local agencies must "review" the waivers every thirty days.

If a worker fails to begin training or has stopped participating in training without justifiable cause or if the worker's waiver is revoked, the worker will receive no income support until the worker begins or resumes training.

Explanation of Provision

The provision amends existing law to change the date on which a worker can receive TAA income support from 60 days from the date of the petition to the date of certification. The provision strikes the 8/16 rule and extends the deadline for trade-impacted workers. If a worker lost his job before the certification, then the worker has 26 weeks from the date of certification to enroll in training. If the worker lost his job after certification, he has 26 weeks from the date he lost his job to enroll in training.

The provision also gives the Secretary the authority to waive the new 26-week training enrollment deadline if a worker was not given timely notice of the deadline.

The provision clarifies that the "marketable skills" training waiver may apply to workers who have post-graduate degrees from accredited institutions of higher education. The provision requires the State to review training waivers 3 months after such waiver is issued, and every month thereafter.

Reasons for Change

The Conferees believe that the 60-day rule makes little sense and leads to the following scenario: a worker laid off well before certification could exhaust his unemployment insurance and yet have to wait to receive the trade readjustment assistance to which the worker was otherwise entitled.

The Government Accountability Office, the Department of Labor, the states, and workers' advocacy groups have criticized the 8/16 deadline as being too short. First, these deadlines often occur while the worker is still on traditional UI (most workers receive up to 26 weeks of State UI compensation). During those 26 weeks, most workers are actively engaged in a job search and are not focused on retraining. Forcing workers to enroll in training at such an early stage can discourage active job search. Second, typically, a worker decides to consider training only after an extended period of unsuccessful job searching. Under present law, workers are only beginning to consider training options close to the 8/16 deadline, and often make hurried decisions about training merely to preserve their TAA eligibility. Third, when large numbers of certified workers are laid off all at once, it can be difficult for TAA administrators to perform adequate training assessments and meet the 8/16 deadline. See GAO Report 04–1012. Therefore, extending the enrollment deadlines to the later of 26 weeks after layoff or certification would provide a reasonable period for a worker to search for employment and consider training options, as well as for the State to assess workers and meet the enrollment deadlines.

While recognizing the necessity of waivers in certain circumstances, states have identified the monthly review of waivers to be burdensome. Many states have complained that processing the sheer volume of waivers requires significant administrative time and cost. For example, according to GAO, 59,375 waivers were issued in 2005 (and 60,948 in 2004). The new requirement that waivers be reviewed initially three months rather than one month after they are issued reduces the administrative burden while continuing to provide for appropriate review, thus allowing the State to ensure the worker continues to qualify for the waiver. The provision does not require a review of waivers issued on the basis that an adversely affected worker is within two years of being eligible for Social Security benefits or a private pension. The status of such workers is unlikely to change and thus, automatic review of their waivers is a waste of resources. States still retain the discretion to review such waivers if circumstances warrant. When a worker has failed to meet the training enrollment deadline through no fault of his own, the Conferees believe that there should be redress. Under present law, there is none. The Department of Labor has acknowledged that this is a problem.

Effective Date

The provision goes into effect upon expiration of the 90-day period beginning on the date of enactment of this Act, and applies to petitions filed on or after that date.

Weekly amounts (Section 1722 (amending Section 232 of the Trade Act of 1974))

Present Law

TRA is the income support that workers receive weekly. It is equal to the worker's weekly UI benefit. TRA is divided into two main periods: "Basic TRA" and "Additional TRA." Under present law, because of the operation of State UI laws, workers who are in training and working part-time run the risk of resetting their UI benefits (and their TRA benefit) at the lower part-time level which would leave them with insufficient income support to continue with training.

Explanation of Provision

The provision amends existing law to (1) disregard, for purposes of determining a worker's weekly TRA amount, earnings from a week of work equal to or less than the worker's most recent unemployment insurance benefits where the worker is working part-time and participating in full-time training; and (2) ensure that workers will retain the amount of income support provided initially under TRA even if a new UI benefit period (with a lower weekly amount) is established due to the worker obtaining part-time or short-term full-time employment.

Reasons for Change

The Conferees believe that the disincentive to combining full-time training and part-time work needs to be removed so that workers who might not otherwise be in training, but for the additional income they earn working part-time, are not excluded from the program.

Effective Date

The provision goes into effect upon expiration of the 90-day period beginning on the date of enactment of this Act, and applies to petitions filed on or after that date.

Limitations on Trade Readjustment Allowances; Allowances for Extended Training and Breaks in Training (Section 1723 (amending Section 233(a) of the Trade Act of 1974))

Present Law

Basic TRA is available for 52 weeks minus the number of weeks of unemployment insurance for which the worker was eligible (usually 26 weeks). Basic TRA must be used within 104 weeks after the worker lost his job (130 weeks for workers requiring remedial training). Any Basic TRA not used in that period is foregone.

Additional TRA is available for up to 52 more weeks if the worker is enrolled in and participating in training. The worker receives Additional TRA only for weeks in training. A worker on an approved break in training of 30 days or less is considered to be participating in training and therefore eligible for TRA during that period. Additional TRA must otherwise be used over a consecutive period (e.g., 52 consecutive weeks).

Participation in remedial training makes a worker eligible for up to 26 more weeks of TRA.

Explanation of Provision

The provision increases the number of weeks for which a worker can receive Additional TRA from 52 to 78 and expands the time within which a worker can receive such Additional TRA from 52 weeks to 91 weeks.

Reasons for Change

The Conferees believe that the program must provide incentives for eligible workers to participate in long term training, such as a two-year Associate's degree, a nursing certification, or completion of a four-year degree (if that four-year degree was previously initiated or if the worker will complete it using non-TAA funds).

Typically, workers cannot participate in a training program without TAA income support. Thus, because many workers exhaust at least some of their basic TRA while they seek another job instead of beginning training, they are limited to shorter-term training options, both practically and because training approvals are usually tied to the period of TRA eligibility. The purpose of the additional 26 weeks of income support, for a total of 78 weeks of additional TRA, is to provide an opportunity for workers to engage in long term training that might not have otherwise been a viable option.

The Conferees note that the Department of Labor's practice is to approve, before training begins, a training program consisting of a course or related group of courses designed for an individual to meet a specific occupational goal. 20 CFR 617.22(f)(3)(i). Nothing in this section is intended to change current Department of Labor practice. The additional 26 weeks of income support are intended to provide more options for long term training at the time when this individual training program is designed and approved.

In short, the new, additional income support is available only for workers in long term training.

The Conferees note that, at the same time, it is not their intent to limit the Secretary's ability, in certain, limited circumstances, to modify a worker's training program where the Secretary determines that the current training program is no longer appropriate for the individual.

Effective Date

The provision goes into effect upon expiration of the 90-day period beginning on the date of enactment of this Act, and applies to petitions filed on or after that date.

Special Rules for Calculation of Eligibility Period (Section 1724 (amending Section 233 of the Trade Act of 1974))

Present Law

There is no provision in present law.

Explanation of Provision

The provision states that periods during which an administrative or judicial appeal of a negative determination is pending will not be counted when calculating a worker's eligibility for TRA. Moreover, the provision also grants justifiable cause authority to the Secretary to extend certain applicable deadlines concerning receipt of Basic and Additional TRA. Further, the provision allows workers called up for active duty military or full-time National Guard service to restart the TAA enrollment process after completion of such service.

The provision also strikes the 210-day rule, which mandates that a worker is not eligible for additional TRA payments if the worker has not applied for training 210 days from certification or job loss, whichever is later.

Reasons for Change

The Conferees believe that tolling of deadlines is necessary; otherwise judicial relief obtained from a successful court challenge would be meaningless, as the decision of the court will inevitably take place after the TAA program eligibility deadlines have passed. The Department of Labor provides for similar tolling in its present and proposed regulations.

Similarly, the Conferees believe that affording the Secretary flexibility in instances where a worker is ineligible through no fault of her own is consistent with the spirit of the program and will help ensure that workers get the retraining they need. The amendment permits the Secretary to extend the periods during which trade readjustment allowances may be paid to an individual if there is justifiable cause. The provision does not increase the amount of such allowances that are payable. The Conferees intend that the justifiable cause extension should allow the Secretary equitable authority to address unforeseen circumstances, such as a health emergency. The 210-day deadline is superseded by the 8/16 deadline in current law, the new 26/26 enrollment deadlines under these amendments, and the requirement that a worker be in training to receive additional TRA.

Effective Date

The provision goes into effect upon expiration of the 90-day period beginning on the date of enactment of this Act, and applies to petitions filed on or after that date.

Application of State Laws and Regulations on Good Cause for Waiver of Time Limits or Late Filing of Claims (Section 1725 (amending Section 234 of the Trade Act of 1974))

Present Law

A State's unemployment insurance laws apply to a worker's claims for TRA.

Explanation of Provision

The provision makes a State's "good cause" law, regulations, policies, and practices applicable when the State is making determinations concerning a worker's claim for TRA or other adjustment assistance.

Reasons for Change

Most States have "good cause" laws allowing the waiver of a statutory deadline when the deadline was missed because of agency error or for other reasons where the claimant was not at fault. These good cause laws apply to administration of State UI laws. The Department of Labor, by regulation, has precluded application of State good cause laws to TAA. This prohibition unjustifiably penalizes workers who miss a deadline through no fault of their own.

Effective Date

The provision goes into effect upon expiration of the 90-day period beginning on the date of enactment of this Act, and applies to petitions filed on or after that date.

Employment and Case Management Services; Administrative Expenses and Employment and Case Management Services (Sections 1726 and 1727 (amending Section 235 of the Trade Act of 1974))

Present Law

Present law requires the Secretary of Labor to make "every reasonable effort" to secure services for affected workers covered by a certification including "counseling, testing, and placement services" and "[s]upportive and other services provided for under any other Federal law," including WIA one-stop services. Typically, the Secretary provides these services through agreements with the States.

Explanation of Provision

The provisions require the Secretary and the States to, among other things (1) perform comprehensive and specialized assessments of enrollees' skill levels and needs; (2) develop individual employment plans for each impacted worker; and (3) provide enrollees with (a) information on available training and how to apply for such training, (b) information on how to apply for financial aid, (c) information on how to apply for such training, (d) short-term prevocational services, (e) individual career counseling, (f) employment statistics information, and (g) information on the availability of supportive services.

The provision requires the Secretary, either directly or through the States (through cooperating agreements), to make the employment and case management services described in section 235 available to TAA eligible workers. TAA eligible workers are not required to accept or participate in such services, however, if they choose not to do so.

These provisions provide for each State to receive funds equal to 15 percent of its training funding allocation on top of its training fund allocation. Not more than two-thirds of these additional funds may be used to cover administrative expenses, and not less than one-third of such funds may be used for the purpose of providing employment and case management services, as defined under section 235. Finally, the section provides for an additional $350,000 to be provided to each State annually for the purpose of providing employment and case management services. With respect to these latter funds, States may decline or otherwise return such funds to the Secretary.

Reasons for Change

States incur costs to administer the TAA program, including for processing applications and providing employment and case management services. While appropriators customarily provide the Department of Labor with administrative funds equal to 15 percent of the total training funds for disbursement to the States, the Conferees believe that this practice should be codified, with the changes discussed above.

The Conferees believe that the employment services and case management funding provided for in this section should be in addition to, and not offset, any funds that the State would otherwise receive under WIA or any other program.

Effective Date

The provision goes into effect upon expiration of the 90-day period beginning on the date of enactment of this Act, and applies to petitions filed on or after that date.

Training Funding (Section 1728 (amending Section 236 of the Trade Act of 1974))

Present Law

The total amount of annual training funding provided for under present law is $220,000,000. During the year, if the Secretary determines that there is inadequate funding to meet the demand for training, the Secretary has the authority to decide how to apportion the remaining funds to the States.

Based on internal department policy, at the beginning of each fiscal year, the Department of Labor allocates 75 percent of the training funds to States based on each State's training expenditures and the average number of training participants over the previous 2½ years. The previous year's allocation serves as a floor. The Department of Labor also has a "hold harmless" policy that ensures that each State's initial allocation can be no less than 85 percent of its initial allocation in the previous year. The Department of Labor holds the remaining 25 percent in reserve to distribute to States throughout the year according to need; most of the remaining funds are disbursed at the end of the fiscal year. States have 3 years to spend their federal funds. If the funds are not spent, the money reverts back to the General Treasury.

Under present law, the Secretary shall approve training if (1) there is no suitable employment; (2) the worker would benefit from appropriate training; (3) there is a reasonable expectation of employment following training (although not necessarily immediately available employment); (4) the approved training is reasonably available to the worker; (5) the worker is qualified for the training; and (6) training is suitable and available at a reasonable cost. "Insofar as possible," the Secretary is supposed to ensure the provision of training on the job. Training will be paid for directly by the Secretary or using vouchers.

One of the statutory criteria for approval of training is that the worker be qualified to undertake and complete such training. The statute doesn't specifically address how the income support available to a worker is to be considered in determining the length of training the worker is qualified to undertake. Another of the statutory training approval criteria is that the training is available at a reasonable cost. The statute doesn't specifically address if funds other than those available under TAA may be considered in making this determination.

Explanation of Provision

The provision strikes the obsolete requirement that the Secretary of Labor shall "assure the provision" of training on the job.

This provision increases the training cap from $220,000,000 to $575,000,000 in FY2009 and FY2010, prorated for the period beginning October 1, 2010 and ending December 31, 2010. The provision requires the Secretary to make an initial distribution of training funds to the States as soon as practicable after the beginning of the fiscal year based on the following criteria: (1) the trend in numbers of certified workers; (2) the trend in numbers of workers participating in training; (3) the number of workers enrolled in training; (4) the estimated amount of funding needed to provide approved training; and (5) other factors the Secretary determines are appropriate. The provision specifies that initial distribution of training funds to a State may not be less than 25 percent of the initial distribution to that State in the previous fiscal year.

The provision requires the Secretary to establish procedures for the distribution of the funds held in reserve, which may include the distribution of such funds in response to requests made by States in need of additional training funds. The provision also requires the Secretary to distribute 65 percent of the training funds in the initial distribution, and to distribute at least 90 percent of training funds for a particular fiscal year by July 15 of that fiscal year.

The provision directs the Secretary to decide how to distribute funds if training costs will exceed available funds.

The provision would specify that in determining if a worker is qualified to undertake and complete training, the training may be approved for a period that is longer than the period for which TRA is available if the worker demonstrates the financial ability to complete the training after TRA is exhausted. It is intended that financial ability means the ability to pay living expenses while in TAA-funded training after the period of TRA eligibility.

The provision would specify that in determining whether the costs of training are reasonable, the Secretary may consider whether other public or private funds are available to the worker, but may not require the worker to obtain such funds as a condition for approval of training. This means, for example, that if a training program would be determined not to have a reasonable cost if only the use of TAA training funds were considered, the Secretary may consider the availability of other public and private funds to the worker. If the worker voluntarily commits to using such funds to supplement the TAA training funds to pay for the training program, the training program may be approved. However, the Secretary may not require the worker to use the other public or private funds where the costs of the training program would be reasonable using only TAA training funds.

Finally, the provision requires the Secretary to issue regulations in consultation with the Senate Finance Committee and the House Committee on Ways and Means.

Reasons for Change

The Conferees believe that the training cap needs to be increased for two reasons. First, more funding is needed to cover the expanded group of TAA eligible workers because of changes made elsewhere in the bill (e.g., coverage of service workers, expanded coverage of manufacturing workers). Second, during high periods of TAA usage, the existing training funding has proved to be insufficient. Some states have run out of training funds, resulting in some States freezing enrollment of eligible workers in training. See GAO–04–1012.

As the GAO has documented, there are significant problems with the Department's method of allocating training funds. The primary problem is that the Department of Labor's method of allocation appears to result in insufficient funds for some States. This appears to be occurring because of the Department's reliance on historical usage and a "hold harmless" policy. In particular, States that were experiencing heavy layoffs at the time the initial allocation formula was implemented may no longer be experiencing layoffs at the same rate, but still receive significant allocations from the Department. In contrast, a State experiencing relatively few layoffs several years ago may now have far greater numbers of layoffs, but still receive a limited amount in its distribution. In short, the allocation that States receive at the beginning of the fiscal year may not reflect their present demand for training services. The provision addresses these problems by lowering the "hold harmless" provision to 25 percent, requiring initial and subsequent distributions to be based on need, and by requiring that 90 percent of the funds be allocated by July 15 of each fiscal year. Additionally, the Conferees expect the Secretary to distribute the remaining funds as soon as possible after that date.

In order to facilitate the approval of longer-term training, the Conferees intend to ensure that the period of approved training is not necessarily limited to the duration of TRA. Where the worker demonstrates the ability to pay living expenses while in TAA funded training after TRA is exhausted, such training should be approved if the other training approval criteria are also met.

The Conferees intend to ensure that training programs that would otherwise not be approved under TAA due to costs may be approved if a worker voluntarily commits to using supplemental public or private funds to pay a portion of the costs.

It is also the intent that, together, these amendments to the training approval criteria allow training to be approved for a period that is longer than the period for which TRA and TAA-funded training is available if the worker demonstrates the financial ability to pay living expenses and pay for the additional training costs using other funds after TRA and the TAA-funded training are exhausted.

Effective Date

The provision increasing the training cap goes into effect upon the date of enactment of this Act. The provisions relating to training fund distribution procedures go into effect October 1, 2009. The other provisions in this section go into effect upon expiration of the 90-day period beginning on the date of enactment of this Act, and apply to petitions filed on or after that date.

Prerequisite Education, Approved Training Programs (Section 1729 (amending Section 236 of the Trade Act of 1974))

Present Law

Under present law, approvable training includes employer-based training (on-the-job training/customized training), training approved under the Workforce Investment Act of 1998, training approved by a private industry council, any remedial education program, any training program whose costs are paid by another federal or State program, and any other program approved by the Secretary. Additionally, remedial training is approvable and participation in such training makes a worker eligible for up to 26 more weeks of TAA-related income support.

Explanation of Provision

The provision clarifies that existing law allows training funds to be used to pay for apprenticeship programs, any prerequisite education required to enroll in training, and training at an accredited institution of higher education (such as those covered by 102 of the Higher Education Act), including training to obtain or complete a degree or certification program (where completion of the degree or certification can be reasonably expected to result in employment). The provision also prohibits the Secretary from limiting training approval to programs provided pursuant to the Workforce Investment Act of 1998.

The provision offers up to an additional 26 weeks of income support while workers take prerequisite training or remedial training necessary to enter a training program. A worker may enroll in remedial training or prerequisite training, or both, but may not receive more than 26 weeks of additional income support.

Reasons for Change

Present law does not explicitly state whether TAA training funds may be used to obtain a college or advanced degree. Some States have interpreted this silence to preclude enrollment in a two-year community college or four-year college or university as a training option, even where a TAA participant was working towards completion of a degree prior to being laid off. The Conferees believe that States should be encouraged to approve the use of training funds by TAA enrollees to obtain training or a college or advanced degree, including degrees offered at two-year community colleges and four-year colleges or universities.

While a worker can obtain additional income support while participating in remedial training, there is no corollary support for workers participating in prerequisite training (e.g., individuals enrolling in nursing usually need basic science prerequisites, which are not considered qualifying remedial training). States have requested additional income support for workers who participate in prerequisite training.

The Conferees believe that while WIA-approved training is an approvable TAA training option, it should not be the only one that TAA enrollees are authorized to pursue. The Conferees are concerned that some States have restricted training opportunities to those approved under WIA. According to the Congressional Research Service, many community colleges, for instance, do not get WIA certification because of its costly reporting requirements. To limit TAA training opportunities in this way unacceptably curbs the scope of training that TAA enrollees might elect to participate in and potentially impairs their ability to get retrained and reemployed.

Effective Date

The provision goes into effect upon expiration of the 90-day period beginning on the date of enactment of this Act, and applies to petitions filed on or after that date.

Pre-Layoff and Part-Time Training (Section 1730 (amending Section 236 of the Trade Act of 1974))

Present Law

Present law does not permit pre-layoff or part-time training.

Explanation of Provision

This provision specifies that the Secretary may approve training for a worker who (1) is a member of a group of workers that has been certified as eligible to apply for TAA benefits; (2) has not been totally or partially separated from employment; and (3) is determined to be individually threatened with total or partial separation. Such training may not include on-the-job training, or customized training unless such customized training is for a position other than the worker's current position.

Additionally, the provision permits the Secretary to approve part-time training, but clarifies that a worker enrolled in part-time training is not eligible for a TRA.

Reasons for Chance

This provision explicitly establishes Congress' intent that workers be eligible to receive pre-layoff and part-time training.

Effective Date

The provision goes into effect upon expiration of the 90-day period beginning on the date of enactment of this Act, and applies to petitions filed on or after that date.

On-the-Job Training (Section 1731 (amending Section 236 of the Trade Act of 1974))

Present Law

Current law provides that the Secretary may approve on-the-job training ("OJT"), but does not govern the content of acceptable OJT.

Explanation of Provision

This provision permits the Secretary to approve OJT for any adversely affected worker if the worker meets the training requirements, and the Secretary determines the OJT (1) can reasonably lead to employment with the OJT employer; (2) is compatible with the worker's skills; (3) will allow the worker to become proficient in the job for which the worker is being trained; and (4) the State determines the OJT meets necessary requirements. The Secretary may not enter into contracts with OJT employers that exhibit a pattern of failing to provide workers with continued long-term employment and adequate wages, benefits, and working conditions as regular employees.

Reasons for Change

The provision incorporates requirements to ensure OJT is effective. Specifically, OJT must be (1) reasonably expected to lead to suitable employment; (2) compatible with the workers' skills; and (2) include a State-approved benchmark-based curriculum. Moreover, the provision is intended to prevent employers from treating workers participating in OJT differently in terms of wages, benefits, and working conditions from regular employees who have worked a similar period of time and are doing the same type of work.

Effective Date

The provision goes into effect upon expiration of the 90-day period beginning on the date of enactment of this Act, and applies to petitions filed on or after that date.

Eligibility for Unemployment Insurance and Program Benefits While in Training (Section 1732 (amending Section 236 of the Trade Act of 1974))

Present Law

Current law states that a worker may not be deemed ineligible for UI (and thus, TAA) if they are in training or leave unsuitable work to enter training.

Explanation of Provision

The provision states that a worker will not be ineligible for UI or TAA if the worker (1) is in training, even if the worker does not meet the requirements of availability for work, active work search, or refusal to accept work under Federal and State UI law; (2) leaves work to participate in training, including temporary work during a break in training; or (3) leaves OJT that did not meet the requirements of this Act within 30 days of commencing such training.

Reasons for Change

The Conferees are concerned that confusion in present UI law surrounding a worker's decision to quit work to enter training and the ramifications of that decision from a UI eligibility perspective may preclude a worker from being able to participate in TAA training. The provision is meant to eliminate that confusion.

Effective Date

The provision goes into effect upon expiration of the 90-day period beginning on the date of enactment of this Act, and applies to petitions filed on or after that date.

Job Search and Relocation Allowances (Section 1733 (amending Section 237 of the Trade Act of 1974))

Present Law

The Secretary may grant an application for a job search allowance where (1) the allowance will help the totally separated worker find a job in the United States; (2) suitable employment is not available in the local area; and (3) the application is filed by the later of (a) 1 year from separation, (b) 1 year from certification, or (c) 6 months after completing training (unless the worker received a waiver, in which case the worker must file by the later of one year after separation or certification). A worker may be reimbursed for 90 percent of his job search costs, up to $1,250.

The Secretary may grant an application for a relocation allowance where: (1) the allowance will assist a totally separated worker relocate within the United States; (2) suitable employment is not available in the local area; (3) the affected worker has no job at the time of relocation; (4) the worker has found suitable employment that may reasonably be expected to be of long-term duration; (5) the worker has a bona fide offer of employment; and (6) the worker filed the application the later of (a) 425 days from separation, (b) 425 days from certification, or (c) 6 months after completing training (unless the worker received a waiver, in which case the worker must file by the later of 425 days after separation or certification). A worker may be reimbursed for 90 percent of his relocation costs plus a lump sum payment of three times the worker's weekly wage up to $1,250.

Explanation of Provision

The provision reimburses 100 percent of a worker's job search expenses, up to $1,500, and 100 percent of a worker's relocation expenses, and increases the additional lump sum payment for relocation to a maximum of $1,500. It also strikes the provision in existing law under which a worker who has completed training but who received a prior training waiver has a shorter period to apply for a job search allowance and relocation allowance than other workers who have completed training.

Reasons for Change

The Conferees believe that the job search and relocation allowances need to be increased to reflect the cost of inflation and the cost and difficulty a worker faces when looking for work and taking a job outside the worker's local community.

The Conferees believe that workers completing training should have the same periods after training to apply for job search and relocation allowances irrespective of whether a worker received a waiver from the enrollment in training requirements prior to undertaking and completing the training. This period allows workers a reasonable opportunity to obtain the same assistance as other workers needed to find and relocate to a new job after being trained.

Effective Date

The provision goes into effect upon expiration of the 90-day period beginning on the date of enactment of this Act, and applies to petitions filed on or after that date.

4. SUBPART D—REEMPLOYMENT TRADE ADJUSTMENT ASSISTANCE PROGRAM

Reemployment Trade Adjustment Assistance Program (Section 1741 (amending Section 246 of the Trade Act of 1974))

Present Law

The Trade Act of 2002 created a demonstration project for alternative trade adjustment assistance for older workers (ATAA or "wage insurance"). Through this program, some workers who are eligible for TAA and reemployed at lower wages may receive a partial wage subsidy. Under the program, States use Federal funds provided under the Trade Act to pay eligible workers up to 50 percent of the difference between reemployment wages and wages at the time of separation. Eligible workers may not earn more than $50,000 in reemployment wages, and total payments to a worker may not exceed $10,000 during a maximum period of two years. In addition to having been certified for TAA, such workers must be at least 50 years of age, obtain full-time reemployment with a new firm within 26 weeks of separation from employment, and have been separated from a firm that is specifically certified for ATAA.

When considering certification of a firm for ATAA, the Secretary of Labor considers whether a significant number of workers in the firm are 50 years of age or older and possess skills that are not easily transferable. ATAA beneficiaries may not receive TAA benefits other than the Health Coverage Tax Credit (HCTC).

Explanation of Provision

The provision renames ATAA "reemployment TAA." The provision eliminates the requirement that a group of workers (in addition to individuals) be specifically certified for wage insurance in addition to TAA certification. The provision eliminates the current-law requirement that a worker must find employment within 26 weeks of being laid off to be eligible for the wage insurance benefit, and replaces it with a requirement that the clock on the two-year duration of the benefit begin at the sooner of exhaustion of regular unemployment benefits or reemployment, allowing initial receipt of the wage insurance benefit at any point during that two-year period. The provision allows workers to shift from receiving a TRA, while training, to receiving reemployment TAA, while employed, at any point during the two-year period. The provision increases the limit on wages in eligible reemployment from $50,000 a year to $55,000 a year. Similarly, it increases the maximum wage insurance benefit (over two years) from up to $10,000 to up to $12,000.

The provision lifts the restriction on wage insurance recipients' participation in TAA-funded training. It also permits workers reemployed less than full-time, but at least 20 hours a week, and in approved training, to receive the wage insurance benefit (which would be prorated if the worker is reemployed for fewer hours compared to previous employment).

Reasons for Change

The Conferees believe that the reemployment TAA, or wage insurance, program is a potentially beneficial option for many older workers, but it includes unnecessary barriers to participation. The Conferees believe that changes to section 246 of the Trade Act will make the wage insurance program a more viable option for many more potentially interested workers. Inflation has lessened the maximum value of the available benefit, and increasing personal, nominal, median income has lowered the share of workers eligible to participate in the program. Several other requirements make the program inaccessible and unattractive.

Findings from the Government Accountability Office (GAO) highlight the need to reform specific aspects of the program. First, the 26-week reemployment deadline was cited by the GAO as one of "two key factors [that] limit participation." The GAO went on to note that "[o]fficials in States [the GAO] visited said that one of the greatest obstacles to participation was the requirement for workers to find a new job within 26 weeks after being laid off. For example, according to officials in one State, 80 percent of participants who were seeking wage insurance but were unable to obtain it failed because they could not find a job within the 26-week period. The challenges of finding a job within this time frame may be compounded by the fact that workers may actually have less than 26 weeks to secure a job if they are laid off prior to becoming certified for TAA. For example, a local caseworker in one State [the GAO] visited said that "the 26 weeks had passed completely before a worker was certified for the benefit." Additionally, the GAO found that automatically certifying workers for the wage insurance benefit would cut the Department of Labor's workload and promote program participation. Currently, workers opting for wage insurance must also surrender eligibility for TAA-funded training and be reemployed full-time. The provision eliminates these restrictions.

The Conferees believe that eliminating the 26-week deadline for reemployment, eliminating the need for firms to be certified for wage insurance, eliminating the prohibition on wage insurance beneficiaries receiving TAA-funded training, and allowing part-time workers and former TRA recipients access to the wage insurance benefit should make the wage insurance program more accessible and attractive.

Effective Date

The provision goes into effect upon expiration of the 90-day period beginning on the date of enactment of this Act, and applies to petitions filed on or after that date.

5. SUBPART E—OTHER MATTERS

Office of Trade Adjustment Assistance (Section 1751 (amending Subchapter C of chapter 2 of title II of the Trade Act of 1974))

Present Law

The TAA for Workers program is currently operated by the Employment and Training Administration at the Department of Labor.

Explanation of Provision

The provision creates an Office of Trade Adjustment Assistance headed by an administrator who shall report directly to the Deputy Assistant Secretary for Employment and Training Administration. Under the provision, the administrator will be responsible for overseeing and implementing the TAA for Workers program and carrying out functions delegated to the Secretary of Labor, including: making group certification determinations; providing TAA information and assisting workers and others assisting such workers prepare petitions or applications for program benefits (including health care benefits); ensuring covered workers receive Section 235 employment and case management services; ensuring States comply with the terms of their Section 239 agreements; advocating for workers applying for benefits; and operating a hotline that workers and employers may call with questions about TAA benefits, eligibility requirements, and application procedures.

The provision requires the administrator to designate an employee of the Department with appropriate experience and expertise to receive complaints and requests for assistance, resolve such complaints and requests, compile basic information concerning the same, and carry out other tasks that the Secretary specifies.

Reasons for Change

It is the view of the Conferees that creating an Office of Trade Adjustment Assistance in the Department of Labor with primary accountability for the management and performance of the TAA for Workers program will improve the program's operation.

The creation of the Office of Trade Adjustment Assistance should not interfere with the coordination of services provided by TAA, the National Emergency Grant program, and Department of Labor Rapid Response services.

Effective Date

The provision goes into effect upon expiration of the 90-day period beginning on the date of enactment of this Act.

Accountability of State Agencies; Collection and Publication of Program Data; Agreements with States (Section 1752 (amending Section 239 of the Trade Act of 1974))

Present Law

Present law gives the Secretary of Labor the authority to delegate to the States through agreements many aspects of TAA implementation, including responsibilities to (1) receive applications for TAA and provide payments; (2) make arrangements to provide certain employment services through other Federal programs; and (3) issue waivers. It also mandates that any agreement entered into shall include sections requiring that the provision of TAA services and training be coordinated with the provision of Workforce Investment Act (WIA) services and training. In carrying out its responsibilities, each State must notify workers who apply for UI about TAA, facilitate early filing for TAA benefits, advise workers to apply for training when they apply for TRA, and interview affected workers as soon as possible for purposes of getting them into training. States must also submit to the Department of Labor information like that provided under a WIA State plan.

Explanation of Provision

The provision requires the Secretary, either directly or through the States (through cooperating agreements), to make the employment and case management services described in the amended section 235 available to TAA eligible workers. TAA eligible workers are not required to accept or participate in such services, however, if they choose not to do so.

The provision requires States and cooperating State agencies to implement effective control measures and to effectively oversee the operation and administration of the TAA program, including by monitoring the operation of control measures to improve the accuracy and timeliness of reported data.

The provision also requires States and cooperating State agencies to report comprehensive performance accountability data to the Secretary, on a quarterly basis.

Reasons for Change

To ensure that the employment and case management services described in the amended section 235 are made available to TAA enrollees as required under that section, the Conferees believe that it is necessary to incorporate those obligations into the agreements that the Department of Labor enters into with each of the States concerning the administration of TAA.

Effective Date

The provision goes into effect upon expiration of the 90-day period beginning on the date of enactment of this Act, and applies to petitions filed on or after that date.

Verification of Eligibility for Program Benefits (Section 1753 (amending Section 239 of the Trade Act of 1974))

Present Law

There is no provision in present law.

Explanation of Provision

Section 1753 requires a State to re-verify the immigration status of a worker receiving TAA benefits using the Systematic Alien Verification for Entitlements (SAVE) Program (42 U.S.C. 1320b–7(d)) if the documentation provided during the worker's initial verification for the purposes of establishing the worker's eligibility for unemployment compensation would expire during the period in which that worker is potentially eligible to receive TAA benefits.

The section also requires the Secretary to establish procedures to ensure that the re-verification process is implemented properly and uniformly from State to State.

Reasons for Change

This provision is intended to ensure that workers maintain a satisfactory immigration status while receiving benefits. This section was included for the purposes of the TAA program only and should not be extended to other programs.

Effective Date

The provision goes into effect upon expiration of the 90-day period beginning on the date of enactment of this Act, and applies to petitions filed on or after that date.

Collection of Data and Reports; Information to Workers (Section 1754 (amending Subchapter C of chapter 2 of title II of the Trade Act of 1974))

Present Law

Present law does not contain statutory language requiring the collection of data or performance goals and the TAA program has suffered a history of problems with its performance data that has undermined the data's credibility and limited their usefulness. Most of the outcome data reported in a given program year actually reflects participants who left the program up to 5 calendar quarters earlier. In addition, as of FY 2006, the Department of Labor does not consistently report TAA data by State or industry or by services or benefits received.

While the Department of Labor has taken some steps aimed at improving performance data, the data remain suspect and fail to capture outcomes for some of the program's participants, and many participants are not included in the final outcomes at all.

Explanation of Provision

The provision would require the Secretary of Labor to implement a system for collecting data on all workers who apply for or receive TAA. The system must include the following data classified by State, industry, and nationwide totals: number of petitions; number of workers covered; average processing time for petitions; a breakdown of certified petitions by the cause of job loss (increased imports etc.); the number of workers receiving benefits under any aspect of TAA (broken down by type of benefit); the average time during which workers receive each type of benefit; the number of workers enrolled in training, classified by type of training; the average duration of training; the number and type of training waiver granted; the number of workers who complete and do not complete training; data on outcomes, including the sectors in which workers are employed after receiving benefits; and data on rapid response activities.

The provision would also require, by December 15 of each year, the Secretary to provide to the Senate Finance Committee and the House Committee on Ways and Means a report that includes a summary of the information above, information on distributions of training funds under section 236(a)(2), and any recommendations on whether changes to eligibility requirements, benefits, or training funding should be made based on the data collected. Those data must be made available to the public on the Department of Labor's website in a searchable format and must be updated quarterly.

Reasons for Change

The Conferees believe that valuable information on TAA and its impact is neither being collected nor being made publicly available. This, in turn, inhibits the ability of Congress to perform its oversight responsibilities and, if necessary, to refine and improve the program, its performance, and worker outcomes. Additionally, the Conferees believe that all of the data that the Department of Labor gathers should be made available and posted on its website in a searchable format. This will enhance the accountability of the TAA program and the Department of Labor, not just to Congress, but to the American people as well.

Effective Date

The provision goes into effect on the date of enactment of this Act.

Fraud and recovery of overpayments (Section 1755 (amending Section 243(a)(1) of the Trade Act of 1974))

Present Law

An overpayment of TAA benefits may be waived if, in accordance with the Secretary's guidelines, the payment was made without fault on the part of such individual, and requiring such repayment would be contrary to "equity and good conscience."

683

Explanation of Provision

The provision states that the Secretary shall waive repayment if the overpayment was made without fault on the part of such individual and if repayment "would cause a financial hardship for the individual (or the individual's household, if applicable) when taking into consideration the income and resources reasonably available to the individual or household and other ordinary living expenses of the individual or household."

Reasons for Change

The Conferees believe that the Department of Labor has adopted a very strict standard for issuing overpayment waivers. In particular, 20 CFR 617.55(a)(2)(ii)(C) defines equity and good conscience to require "extraordinary and lasting financial hardship" that would "result directly" in the "loss of or inability to obtain minimal necessities of food, medicine, and shelter for a substantial period of time" and "may be expected to endure for the foreseeable future." The Conferees understand that no worker has met this strict waiver standard. In including standard statutory waiver language in TAA, there is no indication that Congress intended to make waivers impossible to secure. To the contrary, the Conferees believe that Congress intended that overpaid individuals who are without fault and unable to repay their TAA overpayments should have a reasonable opportunity for waivers of the requirement to return those overpayments. The provision clarifies this intent.

Effective Date

The provision goes into effect upon expiration of the 90-day period beginning on the date of enactment of this Act, and applies to petitions filed on or after that date.

Sense of Congress on Application of Trade Adjustment Assistance (Section 1756 (amending Chapter 5 of title II of the Trade Act of 1974))

Present Law

There is no provision in present law.

Explanation of Provision

The provision expresses the Sense of Congress that the Secretaries of Labor, Commerce, and Agriculture should apply the provisions of their respective trade adjustment assistance programs with the utmost regard for the interests of workers, firms, communities, and farmers petitioning for benefits.

Reasons for Change

Courts reviewing determinations by the Department of Labor regarding certification for trade adjustment assistance have stated that the Department is obliged to conduct its investigations with "utmost regard for the interests of the petitioning workers." See, e.g., Former Employees of Komatsu Dresser v. United States Secretary of Labor, 16 C.I.T. 300, 303 (1992) (citations omitted). The courts have explained that such statements flow from the ex parte nature of the Department's certification process (as opposed to a judicial or quasi-judicial proceeding) and the remedial purpose of the trade adjustment assistance program. This section reflects such statements and extends them to the firms, farmers, and communities programs.

Effective Date

The provision goes into effect upon expiration of the 90-day period beginning on the date of enactment of this Act, and applies to petitions filed on or after that date.

Consultations in Promulgation of Regulations (Section 1757 (amending Section 248 of the Trade Act of 1974))

Present Law

The Secretary is required to prescribe necessary regulations.

Explanation of Provision

This provision requires the Secretary to consult with the Senate Finance Committee and the House Committee on Ways and Means 90 days prior to the issuance of a final rule or regulation.

Reasons for Change

Requiring that the Secretary consult with the relevant committees 90 days prior to the issuance of a final rule or regulations will help ensure that such rules and regulations reflect Congress' intent.

Effective Date

The provision goes into effect upon expiration of the 90-day period beginning on the date of enactment of this Act, and applies to petitions filed on or after that date.

B. PART II—TRADE ADJUSTMENT ASSISTANCE FOR FIRMS

Trade Adjustment Assistance for Firms (Section 1761–1767 (amending Sections 251, 254, 255, 256, 257, and 258 of the Trade Act of 1974))

Present Law

A firm may file a petition for certification with the Secretary of Commerce. Upon receipt of the petition, the Secretary shall publish a notice in the Federal Register that the petition has been received and is being investigated. The petitioner, or anyone else with a substantial interest, may request a public hearing concerning the petition.

To be certified to receive TAA benefits, a firm must show (1) a "significant" number of workers became or are threatened to become totally or partially separated; (2) sales or production of an article, or both, decreased absolutely, or sales or production, or both, of an article that accounted for not less than 25 percent of the total production or sales of the firm during the 12-month period preceding the most recent 12-month period for which data are available have decreased absolutely; and (3) increased imports of competing articles "contributed importantly" to the decline in sales, production, and/or workforce.

A firm certified under section 251 has two years in which to file an adjustment assistance application, which must include an economic adjustment proposal.

In deciding whether to approve an application, the Secretary of Commerce must determine that the proposal (1) is reasonably calculated "to materially contribute" to the economic adjustment of the firm; (2) gives adequate consideration to the interests of the firm's workers; and (3) demonstrates that the firm will use its own resources for adjustment.

Criminal and civil penalties are applicable for, among other things, making false statements or failing to disclose material facts. However, the penalties do not cover the acts and omissions of customers or others responding to queries made in the course of an investigation of a firm's petition.

The Secretary must make its decisions within 60 days.

Explanation of Provision

The provision makes service sector firms potentially eligible for benefits under the TAA for Firms program. It also expands the look back so that all firms can use the average of one, two, or three years of sales or production data, as opposed to one year, to show that the firm's sales, production, or both, have decreased absolutely or that the firm's sales, production, or both of an article or service that accounts for at least 25 percent of its total production, or sales have decreased absolutely.

In determining eligibility, the provision makes clear that the Secretary may use data from the preceding 36 months to determine an increase in imports, and may determine that increased imports exist if customers accounting for a significant percentage of the decline in a firm's sales or production certify that their purchases of imported articles or services have increased absolutely or relative to the acquisition of such articles or services from suppliers in the United States.

The provision requires the Secretary of Commerce, upon receiving information from the Secretary of Labor that the workers of a firm are TAA-covered, to notify the firm of its potential TAA eligibility.

The provision requires the Secretary of Commerce to provide grants to intermediary organizations to deliver TAA benefits. The provision requires the Secretary to endeavor to align the contracting schedules for all such grants by 2010, and to provide annual grants to the intermediary organizations thereafter. The provision requires the Secretary to develop a methodology to ensure prompt initial distribution of a portion of the funds to each of the intermediary organizations, and to determine how the remaining funds will be allocated and distributed to them. The Secretary must develop the methodology in consultation with the Senate Finance Committee and the House Committee on Ways and Means.

The provision amends the penalties provision in section 259 to cover entities, including customers, providing information during an investigation of a firm's petition. Additionally, the provision requires the Secretary of Commerce to submit an annual report demonstrating the operation, effectiveness, and outcomes of the TAA for Firms program to the Senate Finance Committee and the

House Committee on Ways and Means, and to make the report available to the public. The methodology for the distribution of funds to the intermediary organizations shall include criteria based on the data in the report. The provision creates rules relating to the disclosure of confidential business information included in this annual report.

Reasons for Change

Most service sector firms are currently ineligible for the TAA for Firms program because of a statutory requirement that the workers must have been employed by a firm that produces an "article." In an era when 80 percent of U.S. workers are employed in the service sector, the Conferees believe service sector firms should be eligible for TAA.

The Conferees also note that firms currently have a limited "look back" under existing law, which unfairly restricts their ability to show that increased imports are hurting their businesses.

Because data is not always readily available to demonstrate an increase in imports of articles or services, or to show how such increased imports compete with the articles or services of a particular firm, the Conferees believe that the Secretary should be able to utilize information from the customers of a firm that account for a significant percentage of the decline in the firm's sales or production to verify these customers have increased their imports of the relevant articles or services, either absolutely or relative to their purchases from domestic suppliers.

Since a firm may not know that it could be eligible for TAA benefits, despite the fact that workers at the firm have qualified for the TAA for workers program, the Conferees believe it is important to give these firms notice of their potential eligibility for TAA benefits.

The Conferees are concerned that at present, the Economic Development Administration (EDA) is entering into contracts with intermediary organizations that vary in length. Thus, the contracts begin and end at different times during the year. The provision requires the Secretary of Commerce to provide grants to intermediary organizations to deliver TAA benefits and, to the maximum extent practicable, that contracts with such organizations be for 12 month periods and have the same beginning and end dates. The Conferees will leave it to the discretion of the Secretary to determine the appropriate 12 month contract cycle.

The Conferees also believe that the methodology for distributing funds to intermediary organizations should be based in part on their performance, the number of firms they serve, and the outcomes of firms completing the program. The Secretary of Commerce should consult Congress before finalizing such methodology.

The Conferees understand that some customers provide inaccurate or incomplete information in response to questionnaires posed by the Secretary. The penalty language included in this provision is designed to address this problem.

Effective Date

The provision goes into effect upon expiration of the 90-day period beginning on the date of enactment of this Act, and applies to petitions filed on or after that date.

Extension of Authorization of Trade Adjustment Assistance for Firms (Section 1764)

Present Law

The authorization of the TAA for Firms program expired on December 31, 2007. The program is currently authorized at $16 million per year.

Explanation of Provision

The provision reauthorizes the program through December 31, 2010, and increases its funding to $50 million per year for fiscal years 2009 and 2010, and prorates such funding for the period beginning October 1, 2010 and ending December 31, 2010. Of that amount, $350,000 is set aside each year to fund full-time TAA for Firms positions at the Department of Commerce, including a director of the TAA for Firms program.

Reasons for Change

The Conferees believe that the TAA for Firms program has been underfunded, as at least $15 million in approved projects lack funding. Additionally, the Firms team at the Department of Commerce lacks adequate full-time staff to administer the program.

Effective Date

The provision goes into effect upon expiration of the 90-day period beginning on the date of enactment of this Act, and applies to petitions filed on or after that date.

C. PART III—TRADE ADJUSTMENT ASSISTANCE FOR COMMUNITIES

Trade Adjustment Assistance for Communities (Section 1771–1773)

Present Law

There is no provision in present law.

Explanation of Provision

The provision creates a Trade Adjustment Assistance for Communities program that will allow a community to apply for designation as a community affected by trade. A community may receive such designation from the Secretary of Commerce if the community demonstrates that (1) the Secretary of Labor has certified a group of workers in the community as eligible for TAA for Workers benefits, the Secretary of Commerce has certified a firm in the community as eligible for TAA for Firms benefits, or a group of agricultural producers in the community has been certified to receive benefits under the TAA for Farmers and Fishermen program; and (2) the Secretary determines that the community is significantly affected by the threat to, or the loss of, jobs associated with that certification. The Secretary of Commerce must notify the community and the Governor of the State in which the community is located upon making an affirmative determination that the community is affected by trade.

The Secretary of Commerce shall provide technical assistance to a community affected by trade to assist the community to (1) diversify and strengthen its economy; (2) identify impediments to economic development that result from the impact of trade; and (3) develop a community strategic plan to address economic adjustment and workforce dislocation in the community. The Secretary of Commerce shall also identify Federal, State and local resources available to assist the community, and ensure that Federal assistance is delivered in a targeted, integrated manner. The Secretary shall establish an Interagency Community Assistance Working Group to assist in coordinating the Federal response.

A community affected by trade may develop a strategic plan for the community's economic adjustment and submit the plan to the Secretary. The plan should be developed, to the extent possible, with participation from local, county, and State governments, local firms, local workforce investment boards, labor organizations, and educational institutions. The plan should include an analysis of the economic development challenges facing the community and the community's capacity to achieve economic adjustment to these challenges; an assessment of the community's long-term commitment to the plan and the participation of community members; a description of projects to be undertaken by the community; a description of educational opportunities and future employment needs in the community; and an assessment of the funding required to implement the strategic plan.

Of the funds appropriated, the Secretary of Commerce may award up to $25 million in grants to assist the community in developing a strategic plan.

The provision authorizes $150 million in discretionary grants to be awarded by the Secretary of Commerce. An eligible community may apply for a grant from the Secretary to implement a project or program included in the community's strategic plan. Grants may not exceed $5 million. The Federal share of the grant may not exceed 95 percent of the cost of the project and the community's share is an amount not less than 5 percent. Priority shall be given to grant applications submitted by small and medium-sized communities.

Educational institutions may also apply for Community College and Career Training grants from the Secretary of Labor. Grant proposals must include information regarding (1) the manner in which the grant will be used to develop or improve an education or training program suited to workers eligible for the TAA for Workers program; (2) the extent to which the program will meet the needs of the workers in the community; (3) the extent to which the proposal fits into a community's strategic plan or relates to a Sector Partnership Grant received by the community; and (4) any previous experience of the institution in providing programs to workers eligible for TAA. Educational institutions applying for a grant must also reach out to employers in the community to assess current deficiencies in training and the future employment opportunities in the community.

The provision authorizes $40 million in discretionary grants to be awarded by the Secretary of Labor for the Community College and Career Training Grant program. Priority shall be given to grant applications submitted by eligible institutions that serve communities that the Secretary of Commerce has certified under section 273.

The provision also establishes a Sector Partnership Grant program that allows the Secretary of Labor to award industry or sector partnership grants to facilitate efforts of the partnership to strengthen and revitalize industries. The partnerships shall consist of representatives of an industry sector; local county, or State government; multiple firms in the industry sector; local workforce investment boards established under section 117 of the Workforce Investment Act of 1998 (29 U.S.C. 2832); local labor organizations, including State labor federations and labor-management initiatives, representing workers in the community; and educational institutions.

The provision authorizes $40 million in discretionary grants to be awarded by the Secretary of Labor for the Sector Partnership Grant program. The Sector Partnership Grants may be used to help the partnerships identify the skill needs of the targeted industry or sector and any gaps in the available supply of skilled workers in the community impacted by trade; develop strategies for filling the gaps; assist firms, especially small- and medium-sized firms, in the targeted industry or sector increase their productivity and the productivity of their workers; and assist such firms to retain incumbent workers.

Reasons for Change

The TAA for Workers program provides assistance to individual workers who lose their jobs because of trade with foreign countries. The program does not, however, provide broader assistance when the closure or downsizing of a key industry, company, or plant creates severe economic challenges for an entire community impacted by trade. The Conferees believe there is a need for additional programs and incentives to assist such communities. Accordingly, the provision creates a TAA for Communities program to provide a coordinated Federal response to eligible communities by identifying Federal, State and local resources and helping such communities to access available Federal assistance.

The provision does not establish precise criteria for determining when a particular community is impacted by trade. In the view of the Conferees, this determination is better left to the discretion of the Secretary of Commerce, who can evaluate specific facts in specific cases. As a general matter, the Conferees believe the Secretary should review the underlying certification(s) that provide a basis for a community's application and evaluate the potential impact of the job losses (or threat thereof) associated with such certification(s) on the broader community, given the community's overall economic situation. The Conferees intend for the Secretary to focus grants on communities facing the most difficult hardships, to the extent practicable.

The Conferees believe small- and medium-sized communities, and in particular, those in rural areas where the manufacturing sector has historically been a significant employer, would benefit from the technical assistance and grants available through this program. Such communities have been disproportionately impacted by the adverse effects of trade, where some lumber mills, factories and call centers, for instance, have scaled back operations or closed entirely in response to increased trade and globalization.

The Conferees do not intend for the preference for such communities to result in all grants, or the majority of grants, going to such communities to the exclusion of other impacted communities.

Effective Date

The provision goes into effect upon expiration of the 90-day period beginning on the date of enactment of this Act.

Authorization of Appropriations for Trade Adjustment Assistance for Communities (Section 1772)

Present Law

There is no provision in present law.

Explanation of Provision

The provision authorizes $150,000,000 to the Secretary of Commerce for each of fiscal years 2009 and 2010, and $37,500,000 for the period beginning October 1, 2010 through December 31, 2010 to carry out the TAA for Communities program.

The provision authorizes $40,000,000 to the Secretary of Labor for each of fiscal years 2009 and 2010, and $10,000,000 for the period beginning October 1, 2010 through December 31, 2010 to carry out the Community College and Career Training Grant Program.

The provision authorizes $40,000,000 to the Secretary of Labor for each of fiscal years 2009 and 2010, and $10,000,000 for the period beginning October 1, 2010 through December 31, 2010 to carry out the Sector Partnership Grant Program.

Effective Date

The provision goes into effect on the date of enactment of this Act.

D. PART IV—TRADE ADJUSTMENT ASSISTANCE FOR FARMERS

Trade Adjustment Assistance for Farmers (Section 1781–1786 (amending sections 291, 292, 293, 296 and 297 of the Trade Act of 1974))

Present Law

A group of agricultural producers or their representative may file a petition for certification with the Secretary of Agriculture. Upon receipt of the petition, the Secretary shall publish a notice in the Federal Register that the petition has been received and is being investigated. The petitioner, or anyone else with a substantial interest, may request a public hearing concerning the petition.

To be certified to receive TAA benefits under this chapter, the group of producers must show (1) that the national average price of the agricultural commodity in the most recent marketing year is less than 80 percent of the national average price for the commodity for the 5 previous marketing years, and (2) that increased imports of articles like or directly competitive with the commodity contributed importantly to the decline in price.

A group of producers certified under Section 291 has one year to receive TAA benefits, but may apply to be re-certified for a second year of benefits if the group can show a further 20 percent price decline in the national average price of the commodity, and that imports continued to contribute importantly to that decline.

To qualify to receive benefits, individual agricultural producers that are covered by a certified petition must show (1) that the individual producer produced the qualified commodity; and (2) the net income of the producer has decreased. Producers meeting these criteria are eligible to participate in an initial technical assistance course, and to receive cash benefits, not to exceed $10,000, based on their production and the decline in price for the commodity. Where available, the producer may also attend more intensive technical assistance.

Explanation of Provision

The provision defines an agricultural commodity producer, for the purpose of the TAA for Farmers program, to include fishermen, as well as farmers.

The provision allows a group of producers to petition the Secretary based on a 15 percent decline in price, value of production, quantity of production, or cash receipts for the commodity, rather than a 20 percent decline in price. The provision shortens the look back period, from an average of 5 years to an average of the national average price for the previous three year period. Petitioning producers must also show that imports contributed importantly to the decline in price, production, value of production, or cash receipts.

Once the Secretary certifies a group of commodity producers for TAA, individual producers can qualify for benefits if the producer shows (1) that they are producers of the commodity; and (2) that the price received, quantity of production, or value of production for the commodity has decreased.

Producers deemed eligible to receive benefits by the Secretary are eligible to receive initial technical assistance, and may opt to receive intensive technical assistance, which consists of a series of courses designed for producers of the certified commodity. Upon completion of the series of courses, the producer develops an initial business plan which (1) reflects the skills gained by the producer during the courses; and (2) demonstrates how the producer intends to apply these skills to the producer's farming or fishing operation. Upon approval by the Secretary of the business plan described above, the producer is entitled to receive up to $4,000 to implement the business plan or to assist in the development of a long-term business plan.

Producers who complete an initial business plan may choose to receive assistance to develop a long-term business adjustment plan. The Secretary must review the plan to ensure that it (1) will contribute to the economic adjustment of the producer; (2) considers the interests of the producer's employees, if any; and (3) demonstrates that the producer has sufficient resources to implement the plan. If the Secretary approves the plan, the producer is eligible to receive up to $8,000 to implement the long-term business plan.

Once a petition is certified for the group of producers, qualifying producers are eligible for benefits for a 36-month period. A producer may not receive more than $12,000 in any 36-month period to develop and implement business plans under the program.

The provision allows fishermen and aquaculture producers who are otherwise eligible to receive TAA benefits to demonstrate increased imports based on imports of farm-raised or wild-caught fish or seafood, or both.

Reasons for Change

The Conferees believe that the 20 percent price decline currently required for a group of producers to be certified under the TAA for Farmers program is too high, and creates an unnecessary barrier for producers to qualify for TAA benefits. Further, producers and the Department of Agriculture were concerned that the current five-year look back period was too long and burdensome for producers.

Additionally, since net farm income is a function of many factors, it has proven very difficult for producers to show the required decline in net income, even when the price for specific commodities had declined significantly. Several disputes regarding whether producers met the net income test were taken to the U.S. Court of International Trade, resulting in significant administrative expense for both the producers and the Department of Agriculture.

The Conferees believe that demonstrating a decline in the production or price of the commodity facing import competition is a better measure of the impact of trade on the individual producer, rather than net income. The provision would allow farmers to demonstrate that either their production decisions or price received for the qualified commodity were affected.

The Conferees also believe that the focus of the TAA for Farmers program should be adjustment assistance, rather than cash benefits. Under the current program, most producers received only initial technical assistance, with little opportunity for additional curricula. The Conferees believe that all producers eligible for TAA benefits should receive more thorough technical assistance and the opportunity for individualized business planning, with financial assistance provided to help the producer implement the business plans.

Further, technical assistance should be provided by the Department of Agriculture through the National Institute on Food and Agriculture ("NIFA"), which may choose to make grants to land grant universities and other outside organizations to assist in the development and delivery of technical assistance. NIFA (formerly the Cooperative State Research, Education, and Extension Service) delivers technical assistance under the current Farmers program, and had successfully developed curricula to respond to producers' adjustment needs.

The Conferees believe that the current one-year limit to obtain TAA benefits unnecessarily limits producers' ability to access technical assistance, particularly when farmers and fishermen must spend significant portions of each year in the fields or at sea. Extending the eligibility period to 36 months will allow producers to take advantage of all the benefits offered, and will eliminate the need for the current burdensome recertification process.

The Conferees believe that fishermen and aquaculture producers who are otherwise eligible for TAA should be able to demonstrate an increase in imports of like or directly competitive products without regard to whether those imported products were wild-caught or farm-raised. Current law allows these producers to apply for benefits based on imports of farm raised fish and seafood only.

The Conferees expect that the Department of Agriculture will fully fund and operate the TAA for Farmers and Fishermen program for the full duration of each fiscal year for which it is authorized.

Effective Date

The provision goes into effect upon expiration of the 90-day period beginning on the date of enactment of this Act, and applies to petitions filed on or after that date.

Extension of Authorization and Appropriation for Trade Adjustment Assistance for Farmers (Section 1787 (amending Section 298 of the Trade Act of 1974))

Present Law

The authorization and appropriation for the TAA for Farmers program expired on December 31, 2007. The program is currently authorized at $90 million per year.

Explanation of Provision

This provision reauthorizes the program through December 30, 2010, and maintains its funding at $90 million per year for fiscal years 2009 and 2010. The provision further provides funding on a prorated basis for the period beginning October 1, 2010, and ending December 31, 2010.

Effective Date

The provision goes into effect on the date of enactment of this Act.

E. PART V—GENERAL PROVISION

Government Accountability Office Report (Section 1793)

Present Law

There is no provision in present law.

Explanation of Provision

The provision requires the Comptroller General of the United States to prepare and submit a report to the Senate Finance Committee and the House Committee on Ways and Means on the operation and effectiveness of these amendments to chapters 2, 3, 4, and 6 of the Trade Act no later than September 30, 2012.

Reasons for Change

It is critical that GAO review and evaluate the TAA program to assess the changes made by this legislation to ensure that they have improved the effectiveness, operation, and performance of the program.

Effective Date

The provision goes into effect on the date of enactment of this Act.

2. CUSTOMS AND BORDER PROTECTION COLLECTIONS [227]

I. OVERVIEW

The conference report prevents U.S. Customs and Border Protection ("CBP") from collecting over $92 million in antidumping and countervailing duties that CBP collected on imports from Canada and Mexico between 2001 and 2005, and later distributed to U.S. companies that petitioned the U.S. Government for relief.

II. HOUSE BILL

No provision

III. SENATE AMENDMENT

Section 1801 of the American Recovery and Reinvestment Act of 2009, as passed by the Senate, has four sections. First, it prohibits the Secretary of Homeland Security, or any other person, from requiring repayment of, or in any other way recouping, duties that were (1) distributed pursuant to the Continued Dumping and Subsidy Offset Act of 2000 ("CDSOA"); (2) assessed and paid on imports of goods from Canada and Mexico; and (3) distributed on or after January 1, 2001, and before January 1, 2006. Second, it prohibits CBP from offsetting any current or future duty distributions on goods from countries other than Canada and Mexico in an attempt to recoup duties described above. Third, the provision requires CBP to refund any such duty repayments or recoupments it has already received. Further, it requires CBP to fully distribute any duties it is withholding as an offset against current or future duty distributions. Fourth, the provision clarifies that CBP is not prohibited from collecting payments resulting from (1) false statements or other misconduct by a recipient of a duty payment or (2) re-liquidation of entries with respect to which duty payments were made.

IV. CONFERENCE REPORT

The conferees adopted the Senate provision. The conferees do not intend this provision to amend the antidumping or countervailing duty laws of the United States.

---

[227] Description prepared by the majority staffs of the House Committee on Ways and Means and the Senate Committee on Finance.

695

TITLE II OF DIVISION B

ASSISTANCE FOR UNEMPLOYED WORKERS AND STRUGGLING FAMILIES

CONFERENCE DOCUMENT

H.R. 1

TABLE OF CONTENTS

Assistance for Unemployed Workers and Struggling Families   1
  Short Title (House bill Section 2000; Senate bill Section 2000; Conference agreement Section 2000)   1
  Subtitle A—Unemployment Insurance   1
    Extension of Emergency Unemployment Compensation Program Benefits (House bill Sec. 2001; Senate bill Sec. 2001; Conference agreement Sec. 2001)   1
    Increase in Unemployment Compensation Benefits (House bill Sec. 2002; Senate bill Sec. 2002; Conference agreement Sec. 2002)   2
    Special Transfers for Unemployment Compensation Modernization (House bill Sec. 2003; Senate bill Sec. 2003; Conference agreement Sec. 2003)   3
    Temporary Assistance for States with Advances (House bill n.a.; Senate bill Sec. 2004; Conference agreement Sec. 2004)   5
    Full Federal Funding of Extended Unemployment Compensation for a Limited Period (House bill n.a.; Senate bill n.a.; Conference agreement Sec. 2005)   6
    Temporary Increase in Extended Unemployment Benefits under the Railroad Unemployment Insurance Act (House bill n.a.; Senate bill n.a.; Conference agreement Sec. 2006)   7
  Subtitle B—Assistance for Vulnerable Individuals   8
    Emergency Fund for TANF Program (House bill Section 2101; Senate bill Sec. 2101; Conference agreement Sec. 2101)   8
    Extension of Supplemental Grants (House bill n.a.; Senate bill Sec. 2102; Conference Agreement Sec. 2102).   9
    Clarification of Authority of States to Use TANF Funds Carried over From Prior Years To Provide TANF Benefits and Services (House bill n.a.; Senate bill Sec. 2103; Conference Agreement Sec. 2103)   10
    Temporary Resumption of Prior Child Support Law (House bill Sec. 2103; Senate bill Sec. 2104; Conference agreement Sec. 2104)   10
    One-Time Emergency Payments to Certain Social Security, Supplemental Security Income, Railroad Retirement, Veterans Beneficiaries, and Certain Government Retirees (House bill Sec. 2102; Senate bill Sec. 1601; Conference agreement sections 2201 and 2202).   11

ASSISTANCE FOR UNEMPLOYED WORKERS AND STRUGGLING FAMILIES

Short Title (House bill Section 2000; Senate bill Section 2000; Conference agreement Section 2000)

Current Law

No provision.

House Bill

The "Assistance for Unemployed Workers and Struggling Families Act."

Senate Bill

Same as the House bill.

Conference Agreement

The conference agreement is the same as the House and Senate bills.

SUBTITLE A—UNEMPLOYMENT INSURANCE

Extension of Emergency Unemployment Compensation Program Benefits (House bill Sec. 2001; Senate bill Sec. 2001; Conference agreement Sec. 2001)

Current Law

Title IV, Emergency Unemployment Compensation, of the Supplemental Appropriations Act, 2008 (Public Law 110–252; 26 U.S.C. 3304 note) as amended by the Unemployment Compensation Act of 2008 (Public Law 110–449) created a temporary emergency unemployment compensation program (EUC08). The program ends on the week ending on or before March 31, 2009. No compensation under the program is payable for any week beginning after August 27, 2009. Funds in the extended unemployment compensation account (EUCA) of the unemployment trust fund (UTF) are used for financing EUC08 payments. State administration funds are made from the employment security administration account (ESAA). Compensation for EUC08 payments to former employees of nonprofits and governments are from the general fund of the Treasury.

House Bill

The duration of the EUC08 program would extend through the week ending on or before December 31, 2009. No benefits would be payable for any week beginning after May 31, 2010. The extension would be financed through the general fund of the Treasury. The funds would not need to be repaid.

Senate Bill

Same provision.

Conference Agreement

The conference agreement includes the identical provisions of the House and Senate bills.

Increase in Unemployment Compensation Benefits (House bill Sec. 2002; Senate bill Sec. 2002; Conference agreement Sec. 2002)

Current Law

No such provision. Federal law does not provide formulas, floors, or ceilings of regular weekly State unemployment compensation amounts. In general, the States set weekly benefit amounts as a fraction of the individual's average weekly wage up to some State-determined maximum. Some States include dependents' allowances in addition to the underlying benefit.

House Bill

The provision would create an additional, federally-funded $25 weekly benefit that would be available to all individuals receiving regular unemployment compensation (UC) benefits. All the provisions of section 2002 would also apply to regular UC, extended benefits (EB), and EUC08 benefits. It would require States to not take the additional compensation into consideration when determining regular UC benefits (including any dependants' allowances). The additional benefit would be payable either at the same time and in the same manner as any regular UC payable for the week involved or payable separately but on the same weekly basis as any regular compensation otherwise payable. States would not be allowed to alter the method governing the computation of UC under State law in such a manner that the weekly benefit amount would be less than the benefit amount that would have been payable under State law as of December 31, 2008. Funding for the additional benefit would be appropriated from the general fund of the Treasury, without fiscal year limitation. The funds would not be required to be repaid.

States would pay the additional compensation to individuals once the State entered into an agreement with the Labor Secretary and ending before January 1, 2010. The additional compensation would be "grandfathered" for individuals who had not exhausted the right to regular compensation as of January 1, 2010. No additional compensation would be payable for any week beginning after June 30, 2010.

The additional benefit would be disregarded in considering the amount of income of any individual for any purposes under Medicaid and SCHIP.

Senate Bill

Same provision.

Conference Agreement

The conference agreement includes the identical provisions of the House and Senate bills.

Special Transfers for Unemployment Compensation Modernization (House bill Sec. 2003; Senate bill Sec. 2003; Conference agreement Sec. 2003)

Current Law

Section 903 of the Social Security Act (SSA) describes the set of conditions under which funds are transferred to eligible State unemployment accounts from the federal accounts in the Unemployment Trust Fund (UTF) when those federal account balances exceed certain levels. Transfers of excess funds in the UTF to State accounts are called Reed Act distributions. No Reed Act distributions are expected in the next 5 years.

Section 903(a)(2)(B) of the SSA describes the manner in which the distribution of Reed Act funds occurs. Funds are distributed to the State UTF accounts based on the State's share of estimated federal unemployment taxes (excluding reduced credit payments) made by the State's employers.

Unemployment Insurance Policy Letter 44–97, which interpreted section 5401 of P.L. 105–33, the Balanced Budget Act of 1997, says that States are not required to offer an alternative base period (ABP) in determining eligibility for UC benefits.

While federal laws and regulations provide broad guidelines on UC coverage, eligibility, and benefit determination, the specifics of regular UC benefits are determined by each State through State laws and regulations.

House Bill

The House bill would provide a special transfer of UTF funds from the federal unemployment account (FUA) of up to $7 billion to the State accounts within the UTF as "incentive payments" for changing or already having in place certain State UC laws. The maximum incentive payment allowable for a State would be calculated using the methods required by the Reed Act if a distribution were to have occurred on October 1, 2008.

One-third of the maximum payment would be contingent on State law calculating the base period by either:

(A) allowing use of a base period that includes the most recently completed calendar quarter before the start of the benefit year for the purpose of determining UC eligibility; or

(B) providing that, in the case of an individual who would not otherwise be UC-eligible under State law, eligibility shall be determined using a base period that includes the most recently completed calendar quarter.

The remaining 2/3 of the incentive payment would be contingent on qualifying for the first 1/3 payment and the applicable State law containing at least two of the following four provisions:

(A) No denial of UC under State law provisions relating to availability for work, active search for work, or refusal to accept work solely because the individual is seeking only part-time work. States may exclude an individual if the majority of the weeks of work in the individual's base period do not include part-time work. The Labor Secretary would define part-time.

(B) No UC disqualification for separation from employment if it is for compelling family reasons. These reasons must include (i) domestic violence, (ii) illness or disability of an immediate family member, and (iii) the need to accompany a spouse to a place from where it is impractical to commute and due to a change in location of the spouse's employment. The Labor Secretary would define immediate family member.

(C) Weekly UC continues for individuals who have exhausted all rights to regular benefits but are enrolled and making satisfactory progress in a State-approved training program or in a job training program authorized under the Workforce Investment Act of 1998. The benefit must be for at least an additional 26 weeks and be equivalent to the previously calculated UC benefit (including dependents' allowances) for the most recent benefit year. The training program must prepare the individual for entry into a "high-demand" occupation.

(D) UC Dependents' allowances are provided to all individuals with a dependent (as defined by State law) at a level equal to at least $15 per dependent per week. The aggregate limit on dependents' allowances must be not less than the lesser of $50 or 50% of the weekly benefit amount for the benefit year.

Within 60 days after enactment, the Labor Secretary may prescribe (by regulation or otherwise) information required in relation to the compliance of the modernization requirements. The Labor Secretary would have 30 days after receiving a complete application to determine if modernization incentives are payable to the State.

The Labor Secretary, while determining if State law meets the requirements for an incentive payment, would disregard any State law provisions that are not currently effective as permanent law or are subject to a discontinuation under certain circumstances. Once the Treasury Secretary has been notified of the certification of the incentive payment, the appropriate transfer to the State account would occur within seven days. State law provisions which are to take effect within 12 months after the date of their certification would be considered to be in effect for the purposes of certification. States must be eligible for certification under section 303 [of the Social Security Act] and under section 3304 of the Federal Unemployment Tax Act (FUTA) [section 3304 of the Internal Revenue Code of 1986].

Applications submitted before enactment or after the latest date necessary (as determined by the Labor Secretary) will not be considered in order to ensure that all incentive payments are made before October 1, 2011. Incentive payments may be used only for the payment of UC benefits and dependents' allowances. An exception is made if the State appropriates the funds for administrative expenses. Funds that satisfy this exception may be used for the administration of UC law and for public employment offices.

The Treasury Secretary would be required to reserve $7 billion for incentive payments in the Federal Unemployment Account (FUA) of the UTF. Any amount so reserved for which the Secretary of the Treasury has not received a certification under the proposed paragraph (4)(B) of the bill by the deadline determined by the Secretary of Labor shall become unrestricted regarding its use as part of the FUA upon the close of fiscal year 2011.

The bill would transfer a total of $500 million from the federal employment security administration account (ESAA) to the States' accounts in the UTF within 30 days of enactment. Each State's transfers would be calculated using the methods required by the Reed Act if a distribution were to have occurred on October 1, 2008. Any amount transferred to a State account as a result of this $500 million transfer would be required to be used by the State agency of such State only in (A) payment of expenses incurred through carrying out of the purposes in State law required to receive the incentive payments, (B) improved outreach to individuals who might be eligible for regular UC by virtue of the changes in State law, (C) improvement of unemployment benefit and unemployment tax operations, including responding to increased demand for unemployment compensation, and (D) staff-assisted reemployment services for UC claimants.

Senate Bill

Same as the House bill, except that the Senate bill does not explicitly give the Secretary of Labor the ability to define part-time work.

The Senate bill would require that all payments be made before October 1, 2010 (rather than October 1, 2011) except in those States where the first day of the first regularly scheduled session of the State legislature following enactment begins after December 31, 2010. Those States' payments would be made before October 1, 2011.

Conference Agreement

The conference agreement follows the House bill with two exceptions.

If in a training program (option C under the qualifying conditions of the remaining 2/3 incentive payment), the agreement would allow States to not pay UC benefit if the individual is receiving stipends or other training allowances. Under the same training program option, the agreement would also allow States to opt to take any deductible income (as determined under State law) into account and offset the UC payment.

Temporary Assistance for States with Advances (House bill n.a.; Senate bill Sec. 2004; Conference agreement Sec. 2004)

Current Law

Section 1202(b) of the Social Security Act (42 U.S.C. 1322(b)) requires that States are charged interest on new loans that are not repaid by the end of the fiscal year in which they were obtained. The interest rate on the loans is the same rate as that paid by the federal government on State reserves in the UTF for the quarter ending December 31 of the preceding year, but not higher than 10% per annum. States may not pay the interest directly or indirectly from funds in their State account with the UTF.

Section 1202(b)(2) allows a State to borrow funds without interest from the FUA during the year if the State repays the loans by September 30 of the calendar year in which the advances were made. No loans may be made in October, November, or December of the calendar year of such an interest-free loan. Otherwise, the "interest-free" loan will accrue interest charges.

House Bill

No provision.

Senate Bill

The Senate bill would temporarily waive interest payments and the accrual of interest on advances to State unemployment funds by amending section 1202(b) of the Social Security Act. The interest payments that come due from the time of enactment of the proposal until December 31, 2010 would be deemed to have been made by the State. No interest on advances accrues during the period.

Conference Agreement

The conference agreement follows the Senate bill.

Full Federal Funding of Extended Unemployment Compensation for a Limited Period (House bill n.a.; Senate bill n.a.; Conference agreement Sec. 2005)

Current Law

The Extended Benefit (EB) program, established by the Federal-State Extended Unemployment Compensation Act of 1970 (EUCA), P.L. 91–373 (26 U.S.C. 3304, note), may extend receipt of unemployment benefits (extended benefits) at the State level if certain economic situations exist within the State.

Extended benefits (EB) are funded half (50%) by the federal government through its account for that purpose in the UTF; States fund the other half (50%) through their State accounts in the UTF.

Individual eligibility for EB payments, among other matters, requires that the worker has exhausted all rights to regular UC benefits and be within the State-determined benefit year (generally within 52 weeks of first claiming regular UC eligibility) when a State's EB program becomes active on account of economic conditions.

States that do not require a one-week UC waiting period, or have an exception for any reason to the waiting period, must pay 100% of the first week of EB (rather than 50%). P.L. 110–449, the Unemployment Compensation Extension Act of 2008, suspended this waiting week requirement from the time of its enactment until the week ending on or before December 8, 2009.

House Bill

No provision.

Senate Bill

No provision.

Conference Agreement

The conference agreement would temporarily alter Federal-State funding ratios. Extended benefits would be 100% federally financed from the date of enactment through January 1, 2010.

The agreement also would temporarily allow States to ignore benefit year calculations but instead base EB eligibility upon having qualified for and exhausted EUC08 benefits, disregarding benefit year calculations as long as the EB period fell between the date of enactment and before January 1, 2010.

The agreement would allow States to opt to grandfather those workers who received EUC08 payments and exhausted them on or after January 1, 2010. Those workers would be eligible to receive EB payments based on EUC08 exhaustion and disregarding benefit year determinations until the week ending on or before June 1, 2010.

The agreement would continue the temporary suspension of the waiting week requirement for federal funding until the week ending before May 30, 2010.

Temporary Increase in Extended Unemployment Benefits under the Railroad Unemployment Insurance Act. (House bill n.a.; Senate bill n.a.; Conference agreement Sec. 2006)

Current Law

The Railroad Unemployment Insurance Act (45 U.S.C. 351–369) provides up to 26 weeks of normal unemployment benefits for railroad employees. It also provides up to 13 weeks of extended benefits for railroad employees with 10 or more years of service.

House Bill

No provision.

Senate Bill

No provision.

Conference Agreement

The conference agreement would temporarily increase the duration of extended unemployment benefits for railroad workers. The agreement would add an additional 13 weeks to the maximum amount of time railroad workers may receive extended unemployment benefits, allowing for up to 26 weeks of extended benefits in addition to the 26 weeks of normal benefits provided under current law.

The agreement would apply to all qualifying railroad employees, regardless of their years of service (i.e., it would apply to those with fewer than 10 years of service, who do not qualify for extended benefits under current law). The provision would apply to employees who received normal unemployment benefits during the benefit year beginning July 1, 2008 and ending June 30, 2009. No extended benefits under this bill would begin after December 31, 2009.

The agreement would appropriate $20 million from the general fund of the Treasury to cover the cost of the additional extended unemployment benefits. Subsection 2006(b) would provide an additional $80,000 for administering the additional benefits. If the additional extended benefits were to reach $20 million in cost before December 31, 2009, the additional benefits would terminate.

SUBTITLE B—ASSISTANCE FOR VULNERABLE INDIVIDUALS

Emergency Fund for TANF Program (House bill Section 2101; Senate bill Sec. 2101; Conference agreement Sec. 2101)

Current Law

TANF Recession-Related Funds. The 1996 welfare reform established a contingency fund under the Temporary Assistance for Needy Families (TANF) block grant. To qualify for contingency dollars, States must spend under the TANF program a sum of their own dollars equal to their pre-TANF FY1994 spending and meet a test of economic need. Economic need is established by either: (1) Supplemental Nutrition Assistance Program (SNAP, formerly known as food stamps) participation for the most recent three months for which data are available that is at least 10% higher than it was during the corresponding three-month period in either

FY1994 or FY1995; or (2) a three-month average unemployment rate of at least 6.5% and that equals or exceeds 110% of the rate measured in the corresponding three-month period in either of the previous two years. Eligible expenditures above the pre-TANF level are matched at the Medicaid (Federal Medical Assistance Percentage or FMAP) rate. A state's annual contingency fund grant is capped at 20% of its basic TANF block grant. The 1996 welfare law appropriated $2 billion to the contingency fund. At the beginning of FY2009, about $1.3 billion remained in the contingency fund. The contingency fund is available to the 50 States and the District of Columbia. The Commonwealth of Puerto Rico, Guam, the Virgin Islands, and tribes operating tribal TANF programs are not eligible for contingency funds.

TANF Caseload Reduction Credit. TANF established federal work participation standards, which are numerical performance standards that States must meet or be subject to a financial penalty. A State must meet two standards—the all family standard of 50% and the two-parent standard of 90%. These standards may be met either by engaging participants in creditable activities or through reductions in the cash welfare caseload. States are given a caseload reduction credit toward the standards of one percentage point for each percent decline in the caseload from FY2005 to the preceding fiscal year. Under current law, the caseload reduction credit for FY2009 is based on caseload change from FY2005 to FY2008; the credit for FY2010 will be based on caseload change from FY2005 to FY2009; the caseload reduction credit for FY2011 will be based on caseload change from FY2005 to FY2010.

House Bill

TANF Recession Funds. The House bill retains the current TANF contingency fund and creates a new, temporary emergency contingency fund for FY2009 and FY2010. States with increased cash welfare caseloads under TANF or separate State programs funded with TANF State maintenance of effort dollars are eligible for capped grants from the fund. Also eligible are States with increased short-term non-recurrent benefit expenditures or increased subsidized employment expenditures under TANF and separate State programs. The fund reimburses States for 80% of the increased expenditures on basic assistance (cash welfare), short-term non-recurrent benefits, or subsidized employment in TANF and separate State programs, up to a cap. Increased caseloads and expenditures are measured on a quarterly basis, comparing each quarter in FY2009 and FY2010 to the corresponding quarter in the base years of FY2007 and FY2008. The applicable base period for a State varies depending on whichever results in the greatest increase for each State for the cash assistance caseload and by expenditure category.

Total combined State grants from the current law contingency fund and the emergency contingency fund are limited to 25% of a State's basic block grant. The emergency fund is appropriated such sums as necessary (no national funding cap, but total funding is limited by individual State caps discussed above). Puerto Rico, Guam, and the Virgin Islands are eligible for emergency contingency funds.

Caseload Reduction Credit. The House bill gives States an optional measuring period for the caseload reduction credit that would apply to the FY2010 and FY2011 standards. States would have the option to measure caseload reduction from FY2005 to either FY2007 or FY2008 when determining the caseload reduction credit toward the TANF work participation standards for those two years.

Senate Bill

The Senate bill includes all the provisions of the House bill, with modifications. The Senate bill caps the appropriation to the TANF emergency contingency fund at $3 billion. For the Commonwealth of Puerto Rico, Guam, and the Virgin Islands, any payments from the emergency contingency fund are excluded from the overall limit on federal funding for public assistance programs, including TANF, that applies to these jurisdictions. The Senate bill also gives States an optional measuring period for the caseload reduction credit for the FY2009 standards, allowing States to measure caseload reduction from FY2005 to FY2007 for that year.

Conference Agreement

The conference agreement follows the House and Senate bills, with some modifications. It sets the appropriation for the emergency contingency fund at $5 billion. The cap on each State's grant is modified, from a cap on each year's grant, to a cap on cumulative grants over the two years that the emergency fund will operate. Cumulative, combined grants from the existing contingency fund and the emergency fund are limited to 50% of a state's annual basic block grant for FY2009 and FY2010.

The agreement also makes tribes that operate tribal TANF programs eligible for the emergency fund. Tribes will be able to access the fund in the same manner as the States, and are similarly limited to cumulative emergency fund grants equal to 50% of its annual tribal family assistance grant.

The agreement follows the Senate bill for the temporary modifications to the caseload reduction credit. It also clarifies that all temporary provisions will be repealed. The emergency fund is repealed as of October 1, 2010. The change to the caseload reduction credit is repealed as of October 1, 2011.

Extension of Supplemental Grants (House bill n.a.; Senate bill Sec. 2102; Conference Agreement Sec. 2102).

Current Law

TANF provides supplemental grants to 17 States that met historical criteria of low federal grants for welfare per poor person and/or high population growth. Supplemental grants total $319 million, but are set to expire at the end of FY2009.

House Bill

No provision.

Senate Bill

The Senate bill extends supplemental grants through FY2010.

Conference Agreement

The conference agreement includes the Senate provision, extending supplemental grants through FY2010.

Clarification of Authority of States to Use TANF Funds Carried Over From Prior Years To Provide TANF Benefits and Services (House bill n.a.; Senate bill Sec. 2103; Conference Agreement Sec. 2103)

Current Law

States and tribes may reserve unused TANF funds without fiscal year limit. However, the use of these reserves is restricted to providing assistance (essentially cash welfare).

House Bill

No provision.

Senate Bill

Allows States to use reserve TANF funds for any TANF benefit, service, or activity.

Conference Agreement

The conference agreement includes the Senate provision.

Temporary Resumption of Prior Child Support Law (House bill Sec. 2103; Senate bill Sec. 2104; Conference agreement Sec. 2104)

Current Law

The federal government reimburses each State 66% of its expenditures on Child Support Enforcement (CSE) activities. The federal government also provides States with an incentive payment to encourage them to operate effective CSE programs. Federal law requires States to reinvest CSE incentive payments back into the CSE program or related activities. P.L. 109–171 (the Deficit Reduction Act of 2005) prohibited federal matching/reimbursement of CSE incentive payments that are reinvested in the CSE program.

House Bill

The House bill requires HHS to temporarily provide federal matching funds on CSE incentive payments that States reinvest back into the CSE program. This means that CSE incentive payments that are/were received by States and reinvested in the CSE program can be used to draw down federal funds. Federal matching funds for CSE incentive payments are to be provided for FY2009 and FY2010 (i.e., from October 1, 2008 through September 30, 2010).

Senate Bill

Same as the House bill, except that federal matching funds for CSE incentive payments are to be provided for the period October 1, 2008 through December 31, 2010 (i.e., from October 1, 2008 through December 31, 2010).

Conference Agreement

The conference agreement follows the House bill.

One-Time Emergency Payments to Certain Social Security, Supplemental Security Income, Railroad Retirement, Veterans Beneficiaries, and Certain Government Retirees (House bill Sec. 2102; Senate bill Sec. 1601; Conference agreement sections 2201 and 2202).

SECTION 2201. ECONOMIC RECOVERY PAYMENTS TO RECIPIENTS OF SOCIAL SECURITY, SUPPLEMENT SECURITY INCOME, RAILROAD RETIREMENT BENEFITS, AND VETERANS DISABILITY COMPENSATION OR PENSION BENEFITS.

Current Law

Title II of the Social Security Act authorizes cash benefits for retired and disabled workers and their dependents and survivors under the Old Age and Survivors Insurance (OASI) and Disability Insurance (DI) programs. Title XVI of the Social Security Act authorizes monthly cash benefits for blind and disabled persons and persons age 65 or over who have limited income and resources under the Supplemental Security Income (SSI) program.

The Railroad Retirement Act of 1974 authorizes cash benefits for retired and disabled railroad workers and their dependents and survivors.

Title 38 of the United States Code authorizes cash benefits for certain veterans and their dependents and survivors.

Current law does not authorize any one-time emergency payments for any of these programs.

Under Title II of the Social Security Act, a person is eligible for Social Security benefits only if he or she has insured status as the result of sufficient employment that was covered by the Social Security system and for which Social Security payroll taxes were paid. Federal employees hired before 1983 were covered by the Civil Service Retirement System (CSRS) and, unless they were eligible for the CSRS-Offset or elected to enroll in the Federal Employees Retirement System (FERS), they are not eligible for Social Security benefits on the basis of their federal service. In addition, some state and local government employees are not covered by the Social Security system and thus are not eligible for Social Security benefits on the basis of their public service.

Current law does not authorize any one-time tax credit for government retirees who are not eligible for Social Security benefits.

House Bill

The House bill authorizes a one-time emergency payment to be made to SSI recipients. This payment must be made by the Social Security Administration (SSA) at the earliest practical date and no more than 120 days after enactment of the law. The amount of this one-time emergency payment would be equal to the average monthly amount of federal SSI benefits paid to an individual (approximately $456) or a married couple (approximately $637) in the most recent month for which data are available.

To be eligible for the one-time emergency payment, a person must be eligible for an SSI benefit, other than a personal needs allowance, for at least one day during the month of the payment. A person who was eligible for an SSI benefit, other than a personal needs allowance, for at least one day during the two-month period preceding the month of the emergency payment and their SSI eligibility ended during the two-month period solely because their income exceeded the SSI income guidelines is also eligible for the one-time emergency payment.

Only persons who are determined by the Commissioner of Social Security in calendar year 2009 to fall into one of the categories described above are eligible for the emergency payment. Thus, a person who is awarded SSI benefits anytime after 2009 would not be eligible for the emergency payment, even if he or she is awarded benefits retroactive to a date before the date of the emergency payment.

The one-time emergency payment would be protected from garnishment and assignment and would not be considered income in the month of receipt and the following 6 months for the purposes of determining eligibility of the recipient (or the recipient's spouse or family) for any means-tested program funded entirely or in part with federal funds.

The House bill provides an appropriation of such sums as may be necessary to carry out this section, including any administrative costs associated with the payment.

Senate Bill

The Senate bill provides for a one-time economic recovery payment of $300 to adult Social Security (Old Age and Survivors Insurance and Disability Insurance) and Railroad Retirement beneficiaries, Supplemental Security Income (SSI) recipients, and veterans receiving compensation or pension benefits from the Department of Veterans Affairs.

The economic recovery payment would be made by the Secretary of the Treasury after eligible beneficiaries are identified by the Social Security Administration (SSA), the Railroad Retirement Board, and the Department of Veterans Affairs. Payments are to be made at the earliest practicable date and in no event later than 120 days after enactment.

To be eligible for the economic recovery payment, a person must have been during the three-month period prior to the month of the enactment: an adult Social Security Old Age and Survivors Insurance (OASI) or Disability Insurance (DI) beneficiary (including adults eligible for child's benefits on the basis of as disability that began before the age of 22, persons eligible under transitional insured status, and persons eligible under special rules for uninsured persons over the age of 72), an adult Railroad Retirement or disability beneficiary (including dependents, survivors, and disabled adult children), a veterans pension or compensation beneficiary, or an SSI recipient (excluding persons who only receive a personal needs allowance).

The Senate bill requires that economic recovery payment recipients live in the United States or its territories. The Senate bill prohibits any person from receiving more than one economic recovery payment regardless of whether the individual is entitled to, or eligible for, more than one benefit or cash payment under this section.

The Senate bill prohibits the payment of an economic recovery payment to any Social Security beneficiary or person eligible for Social Security benefits paid by the Railroad Retirement Board, or SSI recipient, if, for the most recent month of the three-month period prior to enactment the person's benefits were not payable due to his or her status as a prisoner, inmate in a public institute, illegal alien, or fugitive felon.

The bill prohibits an economic recovery payment to any veterans compensation or pension beneficiary if, for the most recent month of the three-month period prior to enactment, the person's benefits were not payable due to his or her status as a prisoner or fugitive felon. It also prohibits the payment of an economic recovery payment to any person who dies before the date he or she is certified as eligible to receive a payment.

The bill limits the applicability of the economic recovery payments to retroactive beneficiaries by providing that no payment may be made for any reason after December 31, 2010.

The economic recovery payment would not be considered income in the month of receipt and the following 9 months for the purposes of determining eligibility of the recipient (or the recipient's spouse or family) for any means-tested program funded entirely or in part with federal funds. The payment would not be considered income for the purposes of taxation and would be protected from garnishment and assignment. However, the payment could be used to collect debts owed to the federal government. Electronic payments and payments to representative payees and fiduciaries would be authorized.

The Senate bill provides additional appropriations for the period from fiscal year 2009 through fiscal year 2011 in the amounts of: $57,000,000 to the Department of the Treasury; $90,000,000 to the SSA; $1,000,000 to the Railroad Retirement Board; and $7,200,000 to the Department of Veterans Affairs for administrative expenses associated with the one-time economic recovery payment. Of the money appropriated to the Department of Veterans Affairs, $100,000 shall be for the Information Systems Technology Account and $7,100,000 for general expenses related to the administration of the economic recovery payment. It also appropriates to the Department of the Treasury such sums as may be necessary for making economic recovery payments.

The Senate bill provides that the amount of a person's Making Work Pay tax credit authorized by Section 1001 of Division A of the Senate bill would be offset by the amount of any economic recovery payment that person receives.

Conference Agreement

The conference agreement follows the Senate bill, with some modifications. The conference agreement directs the Secretary of the Treasury to disburse a onetime Economic Recovery Payment of $250 to adults who were eligible for Social Security benefits, Railroad Retirement benefits, or veteran's compensation or pension benefits; or individuals who were eligible for Supplemental Security

Income (SSI) benefits (excluding individuals who receive SSI while in a Medicaid institution). Only individuals who were eligible for one of the four programs for any of the three months prior to the month of enactment shall receive an Economic Recovery Payment.

The provision stipulates that Economic Recovery Payments will only be made to individuals whose address of record is in 1 of the 50 states, the District of Columbia, Puerto Rico, Guam, the United States Virgin Islands, American Samoa, or the Northern Mariana Islands.

An individual shall only receive one $250 Economic Recovery Payment under this section regardless of whether the individual is eligible for a benefit from more than one of the four federal programs. If the individual is also eligible for the "Making Work Pay" credit from Section 1001, that credit shall be reduced by the Economic Recovery Payment made under this section.

Individuals who are otherwise eligible for an Economic Recovery Payment will not receive a payment if their federal program benefits have been suspended because they are in prison, a fugitive, a probation or parole violator, have committed fraud, or are no longer lawfully present in the United States.

The provision directs the Commissioner of Social Security, the Railroad Retirement Board, and the Secretary of Veterans Affairs to provide the Secretary of the Treasury with information and data to send the payments to eligible individuals and to disburse the payments.

The provision provides that the Economic Recovery Payments shall not be taken into account as income, or taken into account as resources for the month of receipt and the following 9 months, for purposes of determining the eligibility of such individual or any other individual for benefits or assistance, or the amount or extent of benefits or assistance, under any Federal program or under any State or local program financed in whole or in part with Federal funds.

The provision provides that Economic Recovery Payments shall not be considered gross income for income tax purposes and that the payments are protected by the assignment and garnishment provisions of the four federal benefit programs. The payments will be subject to the Treasury Offset Program.

The provision stipulates that if an individual who is eligible for an Economic Recovery Payment has a representative payee, the payment shall be made to the representative payee and the entire payment shall only be used for the benefit of the individual who is entitled to the Economic Recovery Payment.

The provision appropriates the following amounts for FY2009 through FY2011: to the Secretary of the Treasury, $131 million for administrative costs to carry out the provisions of this section and the new Section 36A (the Making Work Pay credit); to the Commissioner of Social Security, such funds as are necessary to make the payments and $90 million to carry out the provisions of this section; to the Railroad Retirement Board, such funds as are necessary to make the payments and $1.4 million to carry out the provisions of this section; and to the Secretary of Veterans Affairs, such funds as are necessary to make the payments, $100,000 for the Information Systems Technology account and $7,100,000 to the General Operating Expenses account.

The Secretary of the Treasury shall commence making payments as soon as possible, but no later than 120 days after the date of enactment. No Economic Recovery Payments shall be made after December 31, 2010.

SECTION 2202. SPECIAL CREDIT FOR CERTAIN GOVERNMENT RETIREES.

Current Law

No provision.

House Bill

No provision.

Senate Bill

No provision.

Conference Agreement

The conference agreement creates a $250 credit ($500 for a joint return where both spouses are eligible) against income taxes owed for tax year 2009 for individuals who receive a government pension or annuity from work not covered by Social Security, and were not eligible to receive a payment under section 2201. If the individual is also eligible for the "Making Work Pay" credit from Section 1001, that credit shall be reduced by the credit made under this section. Each tax return on which this credit is claimed must include the social security number of the taxpayer (in the case of a joint return, the social security number of at least one spouse).μ The provision states that the credit under this section shall be a refundable credit.

The provision provides that any credit or refund allowed or made by this provision shall not be taken into account as income and shall not be taken into account as resources for the month of receipt and the following two months for purposes of determining the eligibility of such individual or any other individual for benefits or assistance, or the amount or extent of benefits or assistance, under any Federal program or under any State or local program financed in whole or in part with Federal funds.

The provision is effective on the date of enactment.

TITLE III—HEALTH INSURANCE ASSISTANCE

A. ASSISTANCE FOR COBRA CONTINUATION COVERAGE (SEC. 3002(A) OF THE HOUSE BILL, SEC. 3001 OF THE SENATE AMENDMENT, SEC. 3001 OF THE CONFERENCE AGREEMENT, AND SEC. 4980B AND NEW SECS. 139C, 6432, AND 6720C OF THE CODE)

PRESENT LAW

In general

The Code contains rules that require certain group health plans to offer certain individuals ("qualified beneficiaries") the opportunity to continue to participate for a specified period of time in the group health plan ("continuation coverage") after the occurrence of certain events that otherwise would have terminated such participation ("qualifying events").[228] These continuation coverage rules are often referred to as "COBRA continuation coverage" or "COBRA," which is a reference to the acronym for the law that added the continuation coverage rules to the Code.[229]

The Code imposes an excise tax on a group health plan if it fails to comply with the COBRA continuation coverage rules with respect to a qualified beneficiary. The excise tax with respect to a qualified beneficiary generally is equal to $100 for each day in the noncompliance period with respect to the failure. A plan's noncompliance period generally begins on the date the failure first occurs and ends when the failure is corrected. Special rules apply that limit the amount of the excise tax if the failure would not have been discovered despite the exercise of reasonable diligence or if the failure is due to reasonable cause and not willful neglect.

In the case of a multiemployer plan, the excise tax generally is imposed on the group health plan. A multiemployer plan is a plan to which more than one employer is required to contribute, that is maintained pursuant to one or more collective bargaining agreements between one or more employee organizations and more than one employer, and that satisfies such other requirements as the Secretary of Labor may prescribe by regulation. In the case of a plan other than a multiemployer plan (a "single employer plan"), the excise tax generally is imposed on the employer.

Plans subject to COBRA

A group health plan is defined as a plan of, or contributed to by, an employer (including a self-employed person) or employee organization to provide health care (directly or otherwise) to the employees, former employees, the employer, and others associated or formerly associated with the employer in a business relationship, or their families. A group health plan includes a self-insured plan. The term group health plan does not, however, include a plan under which substantially all of the coverage is for qualified long-term care services.

The following types of group health plans are not subject to the Code's COBRA rules: (1) a plan established and maintained for its employees by a church or by a convention or association of churches which is exempt from tax under section 501 (a "church plan"); (2) a plan established and maintained for its employees by the Federal government, the government of any State or political subdivision thereof, or by any instrumentality of the foregoing (a "governmental plan");[230] and (3) a plan maintained by an employer that normally employed fewer than 20 employees on a typical busi-

---

[228] Sec. 4980B.

[229] The COBRA rules were added to the Code by the Consolidated Omnibus Budget Reconciliation Act of 1985, Pub. L. No. 99–272. The rules were originally added as Code sections 162(i) and (k). The rules were later restated as Code section 4980B, pursuant to the Technical and Miscellaneous Revenue Act of 1988, Pub. L. No. 100–647.

[230] A governmental plan also includes certain plans established by an Indian tribal government.

ness day during the preceding calendar year[231] (a "small employer plan").

Qualifying events and qualified beneficiaries

A qualifying event that gives rise to COBRA continuation coverage includes, with respect to any covered employee, the following events which would result in a loss of coverage of a qualified beneficiary under a group health plan (but for COBRA continuation coverage): (1) death of the covered employee; (2) the termination (other than by reason of such employee's gross misconduct), or a reduction in hours, of the covered employee's employment; (3) divorce or legal separation of the covered employee; (4) the covered employee becoming entitled to Medicare benefits under title XVIII of the Social Security Act; (5) a dependent child ceasing to be a dependent child under the generally applicable requirements of the plan; and (6) a proceeding in a case under the U.S. Bankruptcy Code commencing on or after July 1, 1986, with respect to the employer from whose employment the covered employee retired at any time.

A "covered employee" is an individual who is (or was) provided coverage under the group health plan on account of the performance of services by the individual for one or more persons maintaining the plan and includes a self-employed individual. A "qualified beneficiary" means, with respect to a covered employee, any individual who on the day before the qualifying event for the employee is a beneficiary under the group health plan as the spouse or dependent child of the employee. The term qualified beneficiary also includes the covered employee in the case of a qualifying event that is a termination of employment or reduction in hours.

Continuation coverage requirements

Continuation coverage that must be offered to qualified beneficiaries pursuant to COBRA must consist of coverage which, as of the time coverage is being provided, is identical to the coverage provided under the plan to similarly situated non-COBRA beneficiaries under the plan with respect to whom a qualifying event has not occurred. If coverage under a plan is modified for any group of similarly situated non-COBRA beneficiaries, the coverage must also be modified in the same manner for qualified beneficiaries. Similarly situated non-COBRA beneficiaries means the group of covered employees, spouses of covered employees, or dependent children of covered employees who (i) are receiving coverage under the group health plan for a reason other than pursuant to COBRA, and (ii) are the most similarly situated to the situation of the qualified beneficiary immediately before the qualifying event, based on all of the facts and circumstances.

The maximum required period of continuation coverage for a qualified beneficiary (i.e., the minimum period for which continuation coverage must be offered) depends upon a number of factors, including the specific qualifying event that gives rise to a qualified beneficiary's right to elect continuation coverage. In the case of a qualifying event that is the termination, or reduction of hours, of

---

[231] If the plan is a multiemployer plan, then each of the employers contributing to the plan for a calendar year must normally employ fewer than 20 employees during the preceding calendar year.

a covered employee's employment, the minimum period of coverage that must be offered to the qualified beneficiary is coverage for the period beginning with the loss of coverage on account of the qualifying event and ending on the date that is 18 months [232] after the date of the qualifying event. If coverage under a plan is lost on account of a qualifying event but the loss of coverage actually occurs at a later date, the minimum coverage period may be extended by the plan so that it is measured from the date when coverage is actually lost.

The minimum coverage period for a qualified beneficiary generally ends upon the earliest to occur of the following events: (1) the date on which the employer ceases to provide any group health plan to any employee, (2) the date on which coverage ceases under the plan by reason of a failure to make timely payment of any premium required with respect to the qualified beneficiary, and (3) the date on which the qualified beneficiary first becomes (after the date of election of continuation coverage) either (i) covered under any other group health plan (as an employee or otherwise) which does not include any exclusion or limitation with respect to any preexisting condition of such beneficiary or (ii) entitled to Medicare benefits under title XVIII of the Social Security Act. Mere eligibility for another group health plan or Medicare benefits is not sufficient to terminate the minimum coverage period. Instead, the qualified beneficiary must be actually covered by the other group health plan or enrolled in Medicare. Coverage under another group health plan or enrollment in Medicare does not terminate the minimum coverage period if such other coverage or Medicare enrollment begins on or before the date that continuation coverage is elected.

Election of continuation coverage

The COBRA rules specify a minimum election period under which a qualified beneficiary is entitled to elect continuation coverage. The election period begins not later than the date on which coverage under the plan terminates on account of the qualifying event, and ends not earlier than the later of 60 days or 60 days after notice is given to the qualified beneficiary of the qualifying event and the beneficiary's election rights.

Notice requirements

A group health plan is required to give a general notice of COBRA continuation coverage rights to employees and their spouses at the time of enrollment in the group health plan.

An employer is required to give notice to the plan administrator of certain qualifying events (including a loss of coverage on account of a termination of employment or reduction in hours) generally within 30 days of the qualifying event. A covered employee or qualified beneficiary is required to give notice to the plan administrator of certain qualifying events within 60 days after the event. The qualifying events giving rise to an employee or beneficiary no-

---

[232] In the case of a qualified beneficiary who is determined, under Title II or XVI of the Social Security Act, to have been disabled during the first 60 days of continuation coverage, the 18 month minimum coverage period is extended to 29 months with respect to all qualified beneficiaries if notice is given before the end of the initial 18 month continuation coverage period.

tification requirement are the divorce or legal separation of the covered employee or a dependent child ceasing to be a dependent child under the terms of the plan. Upon receiving notice of a qualifying event from the employer, covered employee, or qualified beneficiary, the plan administrator is then required to give notice of COBRA continuation coverage rights within 14 days to all qualified beneficiaries with respect to the event.

Premiums

A plan may require payment of a premium for any period of continuation coverage. The amount of such premium generally may not exceed 102 percent[233] of the "applicable premium" for such period and the premium must be payable, at the election of the payor, in monthly installments.

The applicable premium for any period of continuation coverage means the cost to the plan for such period of coverage for similarly situated non-COBRA beneficiaries with respect to whom a qualifying event has not occurred, and is determined without regard to whether the cost is paid by the employer or employee. The determination of any applicable premium is made for a period of 12 months (the "determination period") and is required to be made before the beginning of such 12 month period.

In the case of a self-insured plan, the applicable premium for any period of continuation coverage of qualified beneficiaries is equal to a reasonable estimate of the cost of providing coverage during such period for similarly situated non-COBRA beneficiaries which is determined on an actuarial basis and takes into account such factors as the Secretary of Treasury prescribes in regulations. A self-insured plan may elect to determine the applicable premium on the basis of an adjusted cost to the plan for similarly situated non-COBRA beneficiaries during the preceding determination period.

A plan may not require payment of any premium before the day which is 45 days after the date on which the qualified beneficiary made the initial election for continuation coverage. A plan is required to treat any required premium payment as timely if it is made within 30 days after the date the premium is due or within such longer period as applies to, or under, the plan.

Other continuation coverage rules

Continuation coverage rules which are parallel to the Code's continuation coverage rules apply to group health plans under the Employee Retirement Income Security Act of 1974 (ERISA).[234] ERISA generally permits the Secretary of Labor and plan participants to bring a civil action to obtain appropriate equitable relief to enforce the continuation coverage rules of ERISA, and in the case of a plan administrator who fails to give timely notice to a participant or beneficiary with respect to COBRA continuation coverage, a court may hold the plan administrator liable to the partici-

---

[233] In the case of a qualified beneficiary whose minimum coverage period is extended to 29 months on account of a disability determination, the premium for the period of the disability extension may not exceed 150 percent of the applicable premium for the period.

[234] Secs. 601 to 608 of ERISA.

pant or beneficiary in the amount of up to $110 a day from the date of such failure.

Although the Federal government and State and local governments are not subject to the Code and ERISA's continuation coverage rules, other laws impose similar continuation coverage requirements with respect to plans maintained by such governmental employers.[235] In addition, many States have enacted laws or promulgated regulations that provide continuation coverage rights that are similar to COBRA continuation coverage rights in the case of a loss of group health coverage. Such State laws, for example, may apply in the case of a loss of coverage under a group health plan maintained by a small employer.

HOUSE BILL

Reduced COBRA premium

The provision provides that, for a period not exceeding 12 months, an assistance eligible individual is treated as having paid any premium required for COBRA continuation coverage under a group health plan if the individual pays 35 percent of the premium.[236] Thus, if the assistance eligible individual pays 35 percent of the premium, the group health plan must treat the individual as having paid the full premium required for COBRA continuation coverage, and the individual is entitled to a subsidy for 65 percent of the premium. An assistance eligible individual is any qualified beneficiary who elects COBRA continuation coverage and satisfies two additional requirements. First, the qualifying event with respect to the covered employee for that qualified beneficiary must be a loss of group health plan coverage on account of an involuntary termination of the covered employee's employment. However, a termination of employment for gross misconduct does not qualify (since such a termination under present law does not qualify for COBRA continuation coverage). Second, the qualifying event must occur during the period beginning September 1, 2008 and ending with December 31, 2009 and the qualified beneficiary must be eligible for COBRA continuation coverage during that period and elect such coverage.

An assistance eligible individual can be any qualified beneficiary associated with the relevant covered employee (e.g., a dependent of an employee who is covered immediately prior to a qualifying event), and such qualified beneficiary can independently elect COBRA (as provided under present law COBRA rules) and independently receive a subsidy. Thus, the subsidy for an assist-

---

[235] Continuation coverage rights similar to COBRA continuation coverage rights are provided to individuals covered by health plans maintained by the Federal government. 5 U.S.C. sec. 8905a. Group health plans maintained by a State that receives funds under Chapter 6A of Title 42 of the United States Code (the Public Health Service Act) are required to provide continuation coverage rights similar to COBRA continuation coverage rights for individuals covered by plans maintained by such State (and plans maintained by political subdivisions of such State and agencies and instrumentalities of such State or political subdivision of such State). 42 U.S.C. sec. 300bb-1.

[236] For this purpose, payment by an assistance eligible individual includes payment by another individual paying on behalf of the individual, such as a parent or guardian, or an entity paying on behalf of the individual, such as a State agency or charity. Further, the amount of the premium used to calculate the reduced premium is the premium amount that the employee would be required to pay for COBRA continuation coverage absent this premium reduction (e.g. 102 percent of the "applicable premium" for such period).

ance eligible individual continues after an intervening death of the covered employee.

Under the provision, any subsidy provided is excludible from the gross income of the covered employee and any assistance eligible individuals. However, for purposes of determining the gross income of the employer and any welfare benefit plan of which the group health plan is a part, the amount of the premium reduction is intended to be treated as an employee contribution to the group health plan. Finally, under the provision, notwithstanding any other provision of law, the subsidy is not permitted to be considered as income or resources in determining eligibility for, or the amount of assistance or benefits under, any public benefit provided under Federal or State law (including the law of any political subdivision).

Eligible COBRA continuation coverage

Under the provision, continuation coverage that qualifies for the subsidy is not limited to coverage required to be offered under the Code's COBRA rules but also includes continuation coverage required under State law that requires continuation coverage comparable to the continuation coverage required under the Code's COBRA rules for group health plans not subject to those rules (e.g., a small employer plan) and includes continuation coverage requirements that apply to health plans maintained by the Federal government or a State government. Comparable continuation coverage under State law does not include every State law right to continue health coverage, such as a right to continue coverage with no rules that limit the maximum premium that can be charged with respect to such coverage. To be comparable, the right generally must be to continue substantially similar coverage as was provided under the group health plan (or substantially similar coverage as is provided to similarly situated beneficiaries) at a monthly cost that is based on a specified percentage of the group health plan's cost of providing such coverage.

The cost of coverage under any group health plan that is subject to the Code's COBRA rules (or comparable State requirements or continuation coverage requirement under health plans maintained by the Federal government or any State government) is eligible for the subsidy, except contributions to a health flexible spending account.

Termination of eligibility for reduced premiums

The assistance eligible individual's eligibility for the subsidy terminates with the first month beginning on or after the earlier of (1) the date which is 12 months after the first day of the first month for which the subsidy applies, (2) the end of the maximum required period of continuation coverage for the qualified beneficiary under the Code's COBRA rules or the relevant State or Federal law (or regulation), or (3) the date that the assistance eligible individual becomes eligible for Medicare benefits under title XVIII of the Social Security Act or health coverage under another group health plan (including, for example, a group health plan maintained by the new employer of the individual or a plan maintained by the employer of the individual's spouse). However, eligibility for coverage under another group health plan does not terminate eligibility for the subsidy if the other group health plan provides only dental, vision, counseling, or referral services (or a combination of the foregoing), is a health flexible spending account or health reimbursement arrangement, or is coverage for treatment that is furnished in an on-site medical facility maintained by the employer and that consists primarily of first-aid services, prevention and wellness care, or similar care (or a combination of such care).

If a qualified beneficiary paying a reduced premium for COBRA continuation coverage under this provision becomes eligible for coverage under another group health plan or Medicare, the provision requires the qualified beneficiary to notify, in writing, the group health plan providing the COBRA continuation coverage with the reduced premium of such eligibility under the other plan or Medicare. The notification by the assistance eligible individual must be provided to the group health plan in the time and manner as is specified by the Secretary of Labor. If an assistance eligible individual fails to provide this notification at the required time and in the required manner, and as a result the individual's COBRA continuation coverage continues to be subsidized after the termination of the individual's eligibility for such subsidy, a penalty is imposed on the individual equal to 110 percent of the subsidy provided after termination of eligibility.

This penalty only applies if the subsidy in the form of the premium reduction is actually provided to a qualified beneficiary for a month that the beneficiary is not eligible for the reduction. Thus, for example, if a qualified beneficiary becomes eligible for coverage under another group health plan and stops paying the reduced COBRA continuation premium, the penalty generally will not apply. As discussed below, under the provision, the group health plan is reimbursed for the subsidy for a month (65 percent of the amount of the premium for the month) only after receipt of the qualified beneficiary's portion (35 percent of the premium amount). Thus, the penalty generally will only arise when the qualified beneficiary continues to pay the reduced premium and does not notify the group health plan providing COBRA continuation coverage of the beneficiary's eligibility under another group health plan or Medicare.

Special COBRA election opportunity

The provision provides a special 60-day election period for a qualified beneficiary who is eligible for a reduced premium and who has not elected COBRA continuation coverage as of the date of enactment. The 60-day election period begins on the date that notice is provided to the qualified beneficiary of the special election period. However, this special election period does not extend the period of COBRA continuation coverage beyond the original maximum required period (generally 18 months after the qualifying event) and any COBRA continuation coverage elected pursuant to this special election period begins on the date of enactment and does not include any period prior to that date. Thus, for example, if a covered employee involuntarily terminated employment on September 10, 2008, but did not elect COBRA continuation coverage and was not eligible for coverage under another group health plan,

718

the employee would have 60 days after date of notification of this new election right to elect the coverage and receive the subsidy. If the employee made the election, the coverage would begin with the date of enactment and would not include any period prior to that date. However, the coverage would not be required to last for 18 months. Instead the maximum required COBRA continuation coverage period would end not later than 18 months after September 10, 2008.

The special enrollment provision applies to a group health plan that is subject to the COBRA continuation coverage requirements of the Code, ERISA, Title 5 of the United States Code (relating to plans maintained by the Federal government), or the Public Health Service Act ("PHSA").

With respect to an assistance eligible individual who elects coverage pursuant to the special election period, the period beginning on the date of the qualifying event and ending with the day before the date of enactment is disregarded for purposes of the rules that limit the group health plan from imposing pre-existing condition limitations with respect to the individual's coverage.[237]

Reimbursement of group health plans

The provision provides that the entity to which premiums are payable (determined under the applicable COBRA continuation coverage requirement)[238] shall be reimbursed by the amount of the premium for COBRA continuation coverage that is not paid by an assistance eligible individual on account of the premium reduction. An entity is not eligible for subsidy reimbursement, however, until the entity has received the reduced premium payment from the assistance eligible individual. To the extent that such entity has liability for income tax withholding from wages[239] or FICA taxes[240] with respect to its employees, the entity is reimbursed by treating the amount that is reimbursable to the entity as a credit against its liability for these payroll taxes.[241] To the extent that such amount exceeds the amount of the entity's liability for these payroll taxes, the Secretary shall reimburse the entity for the excess directly. The provision requires any entity entitled to such reimbursement to submit such reports as the Secretary of the Treasury may require, including an attestation of the involuntary termination of employment of each covered employee on the basis of whose termination entitlement to reimbursement of premiums is

---

[237] Section 9801 provides that a group health plan may impose a pre-existing condition exclusion for no more than 12 months after a participant or beneficiary's enrollment date. Such 12-month period must be reduced by the aggregate period of creditable coverage (which includes periods of coverage under another group health plan). A period of creditable coverage can be disregarded if, after the coverage period and before the enrollment date, there was a 63-day period during which the individual was not covered under any creditable coverage. Similar rules are provided under ERISA and PHSA.

[238] Applicable continuation coverage that qualifies for the subsidy and thus for reimbursement is not limited to coverage required to be offered under the Code's COBRA rules but also includes continuation coverage required under State law that requires continuation coverage comparable to the continuation coverage required under the Code's COBRA rules for group health plans not subject to those rules (e.g., a small employer plan) and includes continuation coverage requirements that apply to health plans maintained by the Federal government or a State government.

[239] Sec. 3401.

[240] Sec. 3102 (relating to FICA taxes applicable to employees) and sec. 3111 (relating to FICA taxes applicable to employers).

[241] In determining any amount transferred or appropriated to any fund under the Social Security Act, amounts credited against an employer's payroll tax obligations pursuant to the provision shall not be taken into account.

claimed, and a report of the amount of payroll taxes offset for a reporting period and the estimated offsets of such taxes for the next reporting period. This report is required to be provided at the same time as the deposits of the payroll taxes would have been required, absent the offset, or such times as the Secretary specifies.

Notice requirements

The notice of COBRA continuation coverage that a plan administrator is required to provide to qualified beneficiaries with respect to a qualifying event under present law must contain, under the provision, additional information including, for example, information about the qualified beneficiary's right to the premium reduction (and subsidy) and the conditions on the subsidy, and a description of the obligation of the qualified beneficiary to notify the group health plan of eligibility under another group health plan or eligibility for Medicare benefits under title XVIII of the Social Security Act, and the penalty for failure to provide this notification. The provision also requires a new notice to be given to qualified beneficiaries entitled to a special election period after enactment. In the case of group health plans that are not subject to the COBRA continuation coverage requirements of the Code, ERISA, Title 5 of the United States Code (relating to plans maintained by the Federal government), or PHSA, the provision requires that notice be given to the relevant employees and beneficiaries as well, as specified by the Secretary of Labor. Within 30 days after enactment, the Secretary of Labor is directed to provide model language for the additional notification required under the provision. The provision also provides an expedited 10-day review process by the Department of Labor, under which an individual may request review of a denial of treatment as an assistance eligible individual by a group health plan.

Regulatory authority

The provision provides authority to the Secretary of the Treasury to issue regulations or other guidance as may be necessary or appropriate to carry out the provision, including any reporting requirements or the establishment of other methods for verifying the correct amounts of payments and credits under the provision. For example, the Secretary of the Treasury might require verification on the return of an assistance eligible individual who is the covered employee that the individual's termination of employment was involuntary. The provision directs the Secretary of the Treasury to issue guidance or regulations addressing the reimbursement of the subsidy in the case of a multiemployer group health plan. The provision also provides authority to the Secretary of the Treasury to promulgate rules, procedures, regulations, and other guidance as is necessary and appropriate to prevent fraud and abuse in the subsidy program, including the employment tax offset mechanism.

Reports

The provision requires the Secretary of the Treasury to submit an interim and a final report regarding the implementation of the premium reduction provision. The interim report is to include information about the number of individuals receiving assistance, and the total amount of expenditures incurred, as of the date of the report. The final report, to be issued as soon as practicable after the last period of COBRA continuation coverage for which premiums are provided, is to include similar information as provided in the interim report, with the addition of information about the average dollar amount (monthly and annually) of premium reductions provided to such individuals. The reports are to be given to the Committee on Ways and Means, the Committee on Energy and Commerce, the Committee on Health, Education, Labor and Pensions and the Committee on Finance.

Effective date

The provision is effective for premiums for months of coverage beginning on or after the date of enactment. However, it is intended that a group health plan will not fail to satisfy the requirements for COBRA continuation coverage merely because the plan accepts payment of 100 percent of the premium from an assistance eligible employee during the first two months beginning on or after the date of enactment while the premium reduction is being implemented, provided the amount of the resulting premium overpayment is credited against the individual's premium (35 percent of the premium) for future months or the overpayment is otherwise repaid to the employee as soon as practical.

SENATE AMENDMENT

The Senate amendment is the same as the House bill with certain modifications. The amount of the COBRA premium reduction (or subsidy) is 50 percent of the required premium under the Senate amendment (rather than 65 percent as provided under the House bill).

In addition, a group health plan is permitted to provide a special enrollment right to assistance eligible individuals to allow them to change coverage options under the plan in conjunction with electing COBRA continuation coverage. Under this special enrollment right, the assistance eligible individual must only be offered the option to change to any coverage option offered to employed workers that provides the same or lower health insurance premiums than the individual's group health plan coverage as of the date of the covered employee's qualifying event. If the individual elects a different coverage option under this special enrollment right in conjunction with electing COBRA continuation coverage, this is the coverage that must be provided for purposes of satisfying the COBRA continuation coverage requirement. However the coverage plan option into which the individual must be given the opportunity to enroll under this special enrollment right does not include the following: a coverage option providing only dental, vision, counseling, or referral services (or a combination of the foregoing); a health flexible spending account or health reimbursement arrangement; or coverage for treatment that is furnished in an on-site medical facility maintained by the employer and that consists primarily of first-aid services, prevention and wellness care, or similar care (or a combination of such care).

Effective date.—The provision is effective for months of coverage beginning after the date of enactment. In addition, the Senate amendment specifically provides rules for reimbursement of an assistance eligible individual if such individual pays 100 percent of the premium required for COBRA continuation coverage for any month during the 60-day period beginning on the first day of the first month after the date of enactment. The person who receives the premium overpayment is permitted to provide a credit to the assistance eligible individual for the amount overpaid against one or more subsequent premiums (subject to the 50-percent payment rule) for COBRA continuation coverage, but only if it is reasonable to believe that the credit for the excess will be used by the assistance eligible individual within 180 days of the individual's overpayment. Otherwise, the person must make a reimbursement payment to the individual for the amount of the premium overpayment within 60 days of receiving the overpayment. Further, if as of any day during the 180-day period it is no longer reasonable to believe that the credit will be used during that period by the assistance eligible individual (e.g., the individual ceases to be eligible for COBRA continuation coverage), payment equal to the remainder of the credit outstanding must be made to the individual within 60 days of such day.

CONFERENCE AGREEMENT

In general

The conference agreement generally follows the House bill. Thus, as under the House bill, the rate of the premium subsidy is 65 percent of the premium for a period of coverage. However, the period of the premium subsidy is limited to a maximum of 9 months of coverage (instead of a maximum of 12 months). As under the House bill and Senate amendment, the premium subsidy is only provided with respect to involuntary terminations that occur on or after September 1, 2008, and before January 1, 2010.

The conference agreement includes the provision in the Senate amendment that permits a group health plan to provide a special enrollment right to assistance eligible individuals to allow them to change coverage options under the plan in conjunction with electing COBRA continuation coverage.[242] This provision only allows a group health plan to offer additional coverage options to assistance eligible individuals and does not change the basic requirement under Federal COBRA continuation coverage requirements that a group health plan must allow an assistance eligible individual to choose to continue with the coverage in which the individual is enrolled as of the qualifying event.[243] However, once the election of the other coverage is made, it becomes COBRA continuation coverage under the applicable COBRA continuation provisions. Thus, for example, under the Federal COBRA continuation coverage provisions, if a covered employee chooses different coverage pursuant to being provided this option, the different coverage elected must generally be permitted to be continued for the applicable required period (generally 18 months or 36 months, absent an event that permits coverage to be terminated under the Federal COBRA con-

[242] An employer can make this option available to covered employees under current law.
[243] All references to "Federal COBRA continuation coverage" mean the COBRA continuation coverage provisions of the Code, ERISA, and PHSA.

tinuation provisions) even though the premium subsidy is only for nine months.

The conference agreement adds an income threshold as an additional condition on an individual's entitlement to the premium subsidy during any taxable year. The income threshold applies based on the modified adjusted gross income for an individual income tax return for the taxable year in which the subsidy is received (i.e., either 2009 or 2010) with respect to which the assistance eligible individual is the taxpayer, the taxpayer's spouse or a dependent of the taxpayer (within the meaning of section 152 of the Code, determined without regard to sections 152(b)(1), (b)(2) and (d)(1)(B)). Modified adjusted gross income for this purpose means adjusted gross income as defined in section 62 of the Code increased by any amount excluded from gross income under section 911, 931, or 933 of the Code. Under this income threshold, if the premium subsidy is provided with respect to any COBRA continuation coverage which covers the taxpayer, the taxpayer's spouse, or any dependent of the taxpayer during a taxable year and the taxpayer's modified adjusted gross income exceeds $145,000 (or $290,000 for joint filers), then the amount of the premium subsidy for all months during the taxable year must be repaid. The mechanism for repayment is an increase in the taxpayer's income tax liability for the year equal to such amount. For taxpayers with adjusted gross income between $125,000 and $145,000 (or $250,000 and $290,000 for joint filers), the amount of the premium subsidy for the taxable year that must be repaid is reduced proportionately.

Under this income threshold, for example, an assistance eligible individual who is eligible for Federal COBRA continuation coverage based on the involuntary termination of a covered employee in August 2009 but who is not entitled to the premium subsidy for the periods of coverage during 2009 due to having income above the threshold, may nevertheless be entitled to the premium subsidy for any periods of coverage in the remaining period (e.g. 5 months of coverage) during 2010 to which the subsidy applies if the modified adjusted gross income for 2010 of the relevant taxpayer is not above the income threshold.

The conference report allows an individual to make a permanent election (at such time and in such form as the Secretary of the Treasury may prescribe) to waive the right to the premium subsidy for all periods of coverage. For the election to take effect, the individual must notify the entity (to which premiums are reimbursed under section 6432(a) of the Code) of the election. This waiver provision allows an assistance eligible individual who is certain that the modified adjusted gross income limit prevents the individual from being entitled to any premium subsidy for any coverage period to decline the subsidy for all coverage periods and avoid being subject to the recapture tax. However, this waiver applies to all periods of coverage (regardless of the tax year of the coverage) for which the individual might be entitled to the subsidy. The premium subsidy for any period of coverage cannot later be claimed as a tax credit or otherwise be recovered, even if the individual later determines that the income threshold was not exceeded for a relevant tax year. This waiver is made separately by each qualified beneficiary (who could be an assistance eligible individual) with respect to a covered employee.

Technical changes

The conference agreement makes a number of technical changes to the COBRA premium subsidy provisions in the House bill. The conference agreement clarifies that a reference to a period of coverage in the provision is a reference to the monthly or shorter period of coverage with respect to which premiums are charged with respect to such coverage. For example, the provision is effective for a period of coverage beginning after the date of enactment. In the case of a plan that provides and charges for COBRA continuation coverage on a calendar month basis, the provision is effective for the first calendar month following date of enactment.

The conference agreement specifically provides that if a person other than the individual's employer pays on the individual's behalf then the individual is treated as paying 35 percent of the premium, as required to be entitled to the premium subsidy. Thus, the conference agreement makes clear that, for this purpose, payment by an assistance eligible individual includes payment by another individual paying on behalf of the individual, such as a parent or guardian, or an entity paying on behalf of the individual, such as a State agency or charity.

The conference agreement clarifies that, for the special 60 day election period for a qualified beneficiary who is eligible for a reduced premium and who has not elected COBRA continuation coverage as of the date of enactment provided in the House bill, the election period begins on the date of enactment and ends 60 days after the notice is provided to the qualified beneficiary of the special election period. In addition, the conference agreement clarifies that coverage elected under this special election right begins with the first period of coverage beginning on or after the date of enactment. The conference agreement also extends this special COBRA election opportunity to a qualified beneficiary who elected COBRA coverage but who is no longer enrolled on the date of enactment, for example, because the beneficiary was unable to continue paying the premium.

The conference agreement clarifies that a violation of the new notice requirements is also a violation of the notice requirements of the underlying COBRA provision. As under the House bill, a notice must be provided to all individuals who terminated employment during the applicable time period, and not just to individuals who were involuntarily terminated.

As under the House bill, coverage under a flexible spending account ("FSA") is not eligible for the subsidy. The conference agreement clarifies that a FSA is defined as a health flexible spending account offered under a cafeteria plan within the meaning of section 125 of the Code.[244]

As under the House bill, there is a provision for expedited review, by the Secretary of Labor or Health and Human Services (in

---

[244] Other FSA coverage does not terminate eligibility for coverage. Coverage under another group Health Reimbursement Account ("HRA") will not terminate an individual's eligibility for the subsidy as long as the HRA is properly classified as an FSA under relevant IRS guidance. See Notice 2002–45, 2002–2 CB 93.

consultation with the Secretary of the Treasury), of denials of the premium subsidy. Under the conference agreement, such reviews must be completed within 15 business days (rather than 10 business days as provided in the House bill) after receipt of the individual's application for review. The conference agreement is intended to give the Secretaries the flexibility necessary to make determinations within 15 business days based upon evidence they believe, in their discretion, to be appropriate. Additionally, the conference agreement intends that, if an individual is denied treatment as an assistance eligible individual and also submits a claim for benefits to the plan that would be denied by reason of not being eligible for Federal COBRA continuation coverage (or failure to pay full premiums), the individual would be eligible to proceed with expedited review irrespective of any claims for benefits that may be pending or subject to review under the provisions of ERISA 503. Under the conference agreement, either Secretary's determination upon review is de novo and is the final determination of such Secretary.

The conference agreement clarifies the reimbursement mechanism for the premium subsidy in several respects. First, it clarifies that the person to whom the reimbursement is payable is either (1) the multiemployer group health plan, (2) the employer maintaining the group health plan subject to Federal COBRA continuation coverage requirements, and (3) the insurer providing coverage under an insured plan. Thus, this is the person who is eligible to offset its payroll taxes for purposes of reimbursement. It also clarifies that the credit for the reimbursement is treated as a payment of payroll taxes. Thus, it clarifies that any reimbursement for an amount in excess of the payroll taxes owed is treated in the same manner as a tax refund. Similarly, it clarifies that overstatement of reimbursement is a payroll tax violation. For example, IRS can assert appropriate penalties for failing to truthfully account for the reimbursement. However, it is not intended that any portion of the reimbursement is taken into account when determining the amount of any penalty to be imposed against any person, required to collect, truthfully account for, and pay over any tax under section 6672 of the Code.

It is intended that reimbursement not be mirrored in the U.S. possessions that have mirror income tax codes (the Commonwealth of the Northern Mariana Islands, Guam, and the Virgin Islands). Rather, the intent of Congress is that reimbursement will have direct application to persons in those possessions. Moreover, it is intended that income tax withholding payable to the government of any possession (American Samoa, the Commonwealth of the Northern Mariana Islands, the Commonwealth of Puerto Rico, Guam, or the Virgin Islands) (in contrast with FICA withholding payable to the U.S. Treasury) will not be reduced as a result of the application of this provision. A person liable for both FICA withholding payable to the U.S. Treasury and income tax withholding payable to a possession government will be credited or refunded any excess of (1) the amount of FICA taxes treated as paid under the reimbursement rule of the provision over (2) the amount of the person's liability for those FICA taxes.

Effective date

The provision is effective for periods of coverage beginning after the date of enactment. In addition, specific rules are provided in the case of an assistance eligible individual who pays 100 percent of the premium required for COBRA continuation coverage for any coverage period during the 60-day period beginning on the first day of the first coverage period after the date of enactment. Such rules follow the Senate amendment.

B. EXTENSION OF MINIMUM COBRA CONTINUATION COVERAGE (SEC. 3002(b) OF THE HOUSE BILL)

PRESENT LAW

A covered employee's termination of employment (other than for gross misconduct), whether voluntary or involuntary, is a COBRA qualifying event.[245] A covered employee's reduction in hours of employment, whether voluntary or involuntary, is also a COBRA qualifying event if the reduction results in a loss of employer sponsored group health plan coverage.[246]

The minimum length of coverage continuation that must be offered to a qualified beneficiary depends upon a number of factors, including the specific qualifying event that gives rise to a qualified beneficiary's right to elect coverage continuation. In the case of a qualifying event that is the termination, or reduction of hours, of a covered employee's employment, the minimum period of coverage that must be offered to each qualified beneficiary generally must extend until 18 months after the date of the qualifying event.[247] Under certain circumstances, however, the coverage continuation period can be extended up to a maximum total of 36 months. For example, if a second qualifying event occurs within the initial 18 month continuation period the initial period will be extended up to an additional 18 months (for a total of 36 months) for qualified beneficiaries other than the covered employee. Similarly, if a qualified beneficiary is determined to be disabled for purposes of Social Security during the first 60 days of the initial 18 month continuation coverage period, the initial 18 month period may be extended up to an additional 11 months (for a total of 29 months) for the disabled beneficiary and all of his or her covered family members. If a second qualifying event then occurs during the additional 11 month coverage period, the continuation period may be extended for another seven months, for a total of 36 months of continuation coverage.

HOUSE BILL

The provision amends section 4980B(f)(2)(B) to provide extended COBRA coverage periods for covered employees who qualify for COBRA continuation coverage due to termination of employment or reduction in hours and who (a) are age 55 or older, or (b) have 10 or more years of service with the employer, at the time of

---

[245] Sec. 4980B(f)(3)(B); Treas. Reg. 54.4980B–4.
[246] Sec. 4980(f)(3)(B).
[247] Sec. 4980B(f)(2)(B)(i)(I). If coverage under a plan is lost on account of a qualifying event but the loss of coverage actually occurs at a later date, the minimum coverage period may be extended by the plan so that it is measured from the date when coverage is actually lost.

the qualifying event. Such individuals would be permitted to continue their COBRA coverage until the earlier of enrollment for Medicare benefits under title XVIII of the Social Security Act, becomes covered under another group health plan (described in section 4980B(f)(2)(B)(iv)), or termination of all health plans sponsored by the employer offering the COBRA coverage. The extended coverage period would apply to all qualified beneficiaries of the covered employee.

The provision makes parallel changes to ERISA and PHSA.

Effective date.—The provision is effective for periods of coverage which would (without regard to any amendments made by the provision) end on or after the date of enactment.

SENATE AMENDMENT

No provision.

CONFERENCE AGREEMENT

The conference agreement does not include the House bill provision.

C. Modify the Health Coverage Tax Credit (Secs. 1899 to 1899L of the Conference Agreement and Secs. 35, 4980B, 7527, and 9801 of the Code)

PRESENT LAW

In general

Under the Trade Act of 2002,[248] in the case of taxpayers who are eligible individuals, a refundable tax credit is provided for 65 percent of the taxpayer's premiums for qualified health insurance of the taxpayer and qualifying family members for each eligible coverage month beginning in the taxable year. The credit is commonly referred to as the health coverage tax credit ("HCTC"). The credit is available only with respect to amounts paid by the taxpayer. The credit is available on an advance basis.[249]

Qualifying family members are the taxpayer's spouse and any dependent of the taxpayer with respect to whom the taxpayer is entitled to claim a dependency exemption. Any individual who has other specified coverage is not a qualifying family member.

Persons eligible for the credit

Eligibility for the credit is determined on a monthly basis. In general, an eligible coverage month is any month if, as of the first day of the month, the taxpayer (1) is an eligible individual, (2) is covered by qualified health insurance, (3) does not have other specified coverage, and (4) is not imprisoned under Federal, State, or local authority.[250] In the case of a joint return, the eligibility re-

---

[248] Pub. L. No. 107–210 (2002).

[249] An individual is eligible for the advance payment of the credit once a qualified health insurance costs credit eligibility certificate is in effect. Sec. 7527. Unless otherwise indicated, all "section" references are to the Internal Revenue Code of 1986, as amended.

[250] An eligible month must begin after November 4, 2002. This date is 90 days after the date of enactment of the Trade Act of 2002, which was August 6, 2002.

quirements are met if at least one spouse satisfies the requirements.

An eligible individual is an individual who is (1) an eligible TAA recipient, (2) an eligible alternative Trade Adjustment Assistance ("TAA") recipient, or (3) an eligible Pension Benefit Guaranty Corporation ("PBGC") pension recipient.

An individual is an eligible TAA recipient during any month the individual (1) is receiving for any day of such month a trade readjustment allowance [251] or who would be eligible to receive such an allowance but for the requirement that the individual exhaust unemployment benefits before being eligible to receive an allowance and (2) with respect to such allowance, is covered under a certification issued under subchapter A or D of chapter 2 of title II of the Trade Act of 1974. An individual is treated as an eligible TAA recipient during the first month that such individual would otherwise cease to be an eligible TAA recipient.

An individual is an eligible alternative TAA recipient during any month if the individual (1) is a worker described in section 246(a)(3)(B) of the Trade Act of 1974 who is participating in the program established under section 246(a)(1) of such Act, and (2) is receiving a benefit for such month under section 246(a)(2) of such Act. An individual is treated as an eligible alternative TAA recipient during the first month that such individual would otherwise cease to be an eligible TAA recipient.

An individual is a PBGC pension recipient for any month if he or she (1) is age 55 or over as of the first day of the month, and (2) is receiving a benefit any portion of which is paid by the PBGC. The IRS has interpreted the definition of PBGC pension recipient to also include certain alternative recipients and recipients who have received certain lump-sum payments on or after August 6, 2002. A person is not an eligible individual if he or she may be claimed as a dependent on another person's tax return.

An otherwise eligible taxpayer is not eligible for the credit for a month if, as of the first day of the month, the individual has other specified coverage. Other specified coverage is (1) coverage under any insurance which constitutes medical care (except for insurance substantially all of the coverage of which is for excepted benefits) [252] maintained by an employer (or former employer) if at least 50 percent of the cost of the coverage is paid by an employer [253] (or former employer) of the individual or his or her

---

[251] The eligibility rules and conditions for such an allowance are specified in chapter 2 of title II of the Trade Act of 1974. Among other requirements, payment of a trade readjustment allowance is conditioned upon the individual enrolling in certain training programs or receiving a waiver of training requirements.

[252] Excepted benefits are: (1) coverage only for accident or disability income or any combination thereof; (2) coverage issued as a supplement to liability insurance; (3) liability insurance, including general liability insurance and automobile liability insurance; (4) worker's compensation or similar insurance; (5) automobile medical payment insurance; (6) credit-only insurance; (7) coverage for on-site medical clinics; (8) other insurance coverage similar to the coverages in (1)–(7) specified in regulations under which benefits for medical care are secondary or incidental to other insurance benefits; (9) limited scope dental or vision benefits; (10) benefits for long-term care, nursing home care, home health care, community-based care, or any combination thereof; and (11) other benefits similar to those in (9) and (10) as specified in regulations; (12) coverage only for a specified disease or illness; (13) hospital indemnity or other fixed indemnity insurance; and (14) Medicare supplemental insurance.

[253] An amount is considered paid by the employer if it is excludable from income. Thus, for example, amounts paid for health coverage on a salary reduction basis under an employer plan

Continued

spouse or (2) coverage under certain governmental health programs. Specifically, an individual is not eligible for the credit if, as of the first day of the month, the individual is (1) entitled to benefits under Medicare Part A, enrolled in Medicare Part B, or enrolled in Medicaid or SCHIP, (2) enrolled in a health benefits plan under the Federal Employees Health Benefit Plan, or (3) entitled to receive benefits under chapter 55 of title 10 of the United States Code (relating to military personnel). An individual is not considered to be enrolled in Medicaid solely by reason of receiving immunizations.

A special rule applies with respect to alternative TAA recipients. For eligible alternative TAA recipients, an individual has other specified coverage if the individual is (1) eligible for coverage under any qualified health insurance (other than coverage under a COBRA continuation provision, State-based continuation coverage, or coverage through certain State arrangements) under which at least 50 percent of the cost of coverage is paid or incurred by an employer of the taxpayer or the taxpayer's spouse or (2) covered under any such qualified health insurance under which any portion of the cost of coverage is paid or incurred by an employer of the taxpayer or the taxpayer's spouse.

Qualified health insurance

Qualified health insurance eligible for the credit is: (1) COBRA continuation [254] coverage; (2) State-based continuation coverage provided by the State under a State law that requires such coverage; (3) coverage offered through a qualified State high risk pool; (4) coverage under a health insurance program offered to State employees or a comparable program; (5) coverage through an arrangement entered into by a State and a group health plan, an issuer of health insurance coverage, an administrator, or an employer; (6) coverage offered through a State arrangement with a private sector health care coverage purchasing pool; (7) coverage under a State-operated health plan that does not receive any Federal financial participation; (8) coverage under a group health plan that is available through the employment of the eligible individual's spouse; and (9) coverage under individual health insurance if the eligible individual was covered under individual health insurance during the entire 30-day period that ends on the date the individual became separated from the employment which qualified the individual for the TAA allowance, the benefit for an eligible alternative TAA recipient, or a pension benefit from the PBGC, whichever applies.[255]

Qualified health insurance does not include any State-based coverage (i.e., coverage described in (2)–(7) in the preceding paragraph), unless the State has elected to have such coverage treated as qualified health insurance and such coverage meets certain re-

---

are considered paid by the employer. A rule aggregating plans of the same employer applies in determining whether the employer pays at least 50 percent of the cost of coverage.

[254] COBRA continuation is defined in section 9832(d)(1).

[255] For this purpose, "individual health insurance" means any insurance which constitutes medical care offered to individuals other than in connection with a group health plan. Such term does not include Federal- or State-based health insurance coverage.

quirements.[256] Such State coverage must provide that each qualifying individual is guaranteed enrollment if the individual pays the premium for enrollment or provides a qualified health insurance costs eligibility certificate and pays the remainder of the premium. In addition, the State-based coverage cannot impose any pre-existing condition limitation with respect to qualifying individuals. State-based coverage cannot require a qualifying individual to pay a premium or contribution that is greater than the premium or contribution for a similarly situated individual who is not a qualified individual. Finally, benefits under the State-based coverage must be the same as (or substantially similar to) benefits provided to similarly situated individuals who are not qualifying individuals.

A qualifying individual is an eligible individual who seeks to enroll in the State-based coverage and who has aggregate periods of creditable coverage[257] of three months or longer, does not have other specified coverage, and who is not imprisoned. In general terms, creditable coverage includes health care coverage without a gap of more than 63 days. Therefore, if an individual's qualifying coverage were terminated more than 63 days before the individual enrolled in the State-based coverage, the individual would not be a qualifying individual and would not be entitled to the State-based protections. A qualifying individual also includes qualified family members of such an eligible individual.

Qualified health insurance does not include coverage under a flexible spending or similar arrangement or any insurance if substantially all of the coverage is for excepted benefits.

Other rules

Amounts taken into account in determining the credit may not be taken into account in determining the amount allowable under the itemized deduction for medical expenses or the deduction for health insurance expenses of self-employed individuals. Amounts distributed from a medical savings account or health savings accounts are not eligible for the credit. The amount of the credit available through filing a tax return is reduced by any credit received on an advance basis. Married taxpayers filing separate returns are eligible for the credit; however, if both spouses are eligible individuals and the spouses file separate returns, then the spouse of the taxpayer is not a qualifying family member.

The Secretary of the Treasury is authorized to prescribe such regulations and other guidance as may be necessary or appropriate to carry out the credit provision.

COBRA

The Consolidated Omnibus Reconciliation Act of 1985 ("COBRA") requires that a group health plan must offer continuation coverage to qualified beneficiaries in the case of a qualifying event. An excise tax under the Code applies on the failure of a

---

[256] For guidance on how a State elects a health program to be qualified health insurance for purposes of the credit, see Rev. Proc. 2004–12, 2004–1 C.B. 528.

[257] Creditable coverage is determined under the Health Insurance Portability and Accountability Act. Sec. 9801(c).

group health plan to meet the requirement.[258] Qualifying events include the death of the covered employee, termination of the covered employee's employment, divorce or legal separation of the covered employee, and certain bankruptcy proceedings of the employer. In the case of termination from employment, the coverage must be extended for a period of not less than 18 months. In certain other cases, coverage must be extended for a period of not less than 36 months. Under such period of continuation coverage, the plan may require payment of a premium by the beneficiary of up to 102 percent of the applicable premium for the period.

HOUSE BILL

No provision.

SENATE AMENDMENT

No provision.[259]

CONFERENCE AGREEMENT

Increase in credit percentage amount

The provision increases the amount of the HCTC to 80 percent of the taxpayer's premiums for qualified health insurance of the taxpayer and qualifying family members.

Effective date.—The provision is effective for coverage months beginning on or after the first day of the first month beginning 60 days after date of enactment. The increased credit rate does not apply to months beginning after December 31, 2010.

Payment for monthly premiums paid prior to commencement of advance payment of credit

The provision provides that the Secretary of the Treasury shall make one or more retroactive payments on behalf of certified individuals equal to 80 percent of the premiums for coverage of the taxpayer and qualifying family members for qualified health insurance for eligible coverage months occurring prior to the first month for which an advance payment is made on behalf of such individual. The amount of the payment must be reduced by the amount of any payment made to the taxpayer under a national emergency grant pursuant to section 173(f) of the Workforce Investment Act of 1998 for a taxable year including such eligible coverage months.

Effective date.—The provision is effective for eligible coverage months beginning after December 31, 2008. The Secretary of the Treasury, however, is not required to make any payments under the provision until after the date that is six months after the date of enactment. The provision does not apply to months beginning after December 31, 2010.

TAA recipients not enrolled in training programs eligible for credit

The provision modifies the definition of an eligible TAA recipient to eliminate the requirement that an individual be enrolled in

---

[258] Sec. 4980B.
[259] The Senate amendment did not amend the HCTC, but section 1701 of the Senate amendment provided for a temporary extension of the Trade Adjustment Assistance Program (generally until December 31, 2010). Certain beneficiaries of this program are eligible for the HCTC.

training in the case of an individual receiving unemployment compensation. In addition, the provision clarifies that the definition of an eligible TAA recipient includes an individual who would be eligible to receive a trade readjustment allowance except that the individual is in a break in training that exceeds the period specified in section 233(e) of the Trade Act of 1974, but is within the period for receiving the allowance.

Effective date.—The provision is effective for months beginning after the date of enactment in taxable years ending after such date. The provision does not apply to months beginning after December 31, 2010.

TAA pre-certification period rule for purposes of determining whether there is a 63-day lapse in creditable coverage

Under the provision, in determining if there has been a 63-day lapse in coverage (which determines, in part, if the State-based consumer protections apply), in the case of a TAA-eligible individual, the period beginning on the date the individual has a TAA-related loss of coverage and ending on the date which is seven days after the date of issuance by the Secretary (or by any person or entity designated by the Secretary) of a qualified health insurance costs credit eligibility certificate (under section 7527) for such individual is not taken into account.

Effective date.—The provision is effective for plan years beginning after the date of enactment. The provision does not apply to plan years beginning after December 31, 2010.

Continued qualification of family members after certain events

The provision provides continued eligibility for the credit for family members after certain events. The rule applies in the case of (1) the eligible individual becoming entitled to Medicare, (2) divorce and (3) death.

In the case of a month which would be an eligible coverage month with respect to an eligible individual except that the individual is entitled to benefits under Medicare Part A or enrolled in Medicare Part B, the month is treated as an eligible coverage month with respect to the individual solely for purposes of determining the amount of the credit with respect to qualifying family members (i.e., the credit is allowed for expenses paid for qualifying family members after the eligible individual is eligible for Medicare). Such treatment applies only with respect to the first 24 months after the eligible individual is first entitled to benefits under Medicare Part A or enrolled in Medicare Part B.

In the case of the finalization of a divorce between an eligible individual and the individual's spouse, the spouse is treated as an eligible individual for a period of 24 months beginning with the date of the finalization of the divorce. Under such rule, the only family members that may be taken into account with respect to the spouse as qualifying family members are those individuals who were qualifying family members immediately before such divorce finalization.

In the case of the death of an eligible individual, the spouse of such individual (determined at the time of death) is treated as an eligible individual for a period of 24 months beginning with the date of death. Under such rule, the only qualifying family members that may be taken into account with respect to the spouse are those individuals who were qualifying family members immediately before such death. In addition, any individual who was a qualifying family member of the decedent immediately before such death [260] treated as an eligible individual for a period of 24 months beginning with the date of death, except that in determining the amount of the HCTC only such qualifying family member may be taken into account.

Effective date.—The provision is effective for months beginning after December 31, 2009. The provision does not apply to months that begin after December 31, 2010.

Alignment of COBRA coverage

The maximum required COBRA continuation coverage period is modified by the provision with respect to certain individuals whose qualifying event is a termination of employment or a reduction in hours. First, in the case of such a qualifying event with respect to a covered employee who has a nonforfeitable right to a benefit any portion of which is paid by the PBGC, the maximum coverage period must end not earlier than the date of death of the covered employee (or in the case of the surviving spouse or dependent children of the covered employee, not earlier than 24 months after the date of death of the covered employee). Second, in the case of such a qualifying event where the covered employee is a TAA eligible individual as of the date that the maximum coverage period would otherwise terminate, the maximum coverage period must extend during the period that the individual is a TAA eligible individual.

Effective date.—The provision is effective for periods of coverage that would, without regard to the provision, end on or after the date of enactment, provided that the provision does not extend any periods of coverage beyond December 31, 2010.

Addition of coverage through voluntary employees' beneficiary associations

The provision expands the definition of qualified health insurance by including coverage under an employee benefit plan funded by a voluntary employees' beneficiary association ("VEBA", as defined in section 501(c)(9)) established pursuant to an order of a bankruptcy court, or by agreement with an authorized representative, as provided in section 1114 of title 11, United States Code.

Effective date.—The provision is effective on the date of enactment. The provision does not apply with respect to certificates of eligibility issued after December 31, 2010.

Notice requirements

The provision requires that the qualified health insurance costs credit eligibility certificate provided in connection with the advance payment of the HCTC must include (1) the name, address, and telephone number of the State office or offices responsible for

---

[260] In the case of a dependent, the rule applies to the taxpayer to whom the personal exemption deduction under section 151 is allowable.

providing the individual with assistance with enrollment in qualified health insurance, (2) a list of coverage options that are treated as qualified health insurance by the State in which the individual resides, (3) in the case of a TAA-eligible individual, a statement informing the individual that the individual has 63 days from the date that is seven days after the issuance of such certificate to enroll in such insurance without a lapse in creditable coverage, and (4) such other information as the Secretary may provide.

Effective date.—The provision is effective for certificates issued after the date that is six months after the date of enactment. The provision does not apply to months beginning after December 31, 2010.

Survey and report on enhanced health coverage tax credit program

Survey

The provision requires that the Secretary of the Treasury must conduct a biennial survey of eligible individuals containing the following information:

1. In the case of eligible individuals receiving the HCTC (including those participating in the advance payment program (the "HCTC program")) (A) demographic information of such individuals, including income and education levels, (B) satisfaction of such individuals with the enrollment process in the HCTC program, (C) satisfaction of such individuals with available health coverage options under the credit, including level of premiums, benefits, deductibles, cost-sharing requirements, and the adequacy of provider networks, and (D) any other information that the Secretary determines is appropriate.

2. In the case of eligible individuals not receiving the HCTC (A) demographic information on each individual, including income and education levels, (B) whether the individual was aware of the HCTC or the HCTC program, (C) the reasons the individual has not enrolled in the HCTC program, including whether such reasons include the burden of process of enrollment and the affordability of coverage, (D) whether the individual has health insurance coverage, and, if so, the source of such coverage, and (E) any other information that the Secretary determines is appropriate.

Not later than December 31 of each year in which a survey described above is conducted (beginning in 2010), the Secretary of the Treasury must report to the Committee on Finance and the Committee on Health, Education, Labor, and Pensions of the Senate and the Committee on Ways and Means and the Committee on Education and Labor of the House of Representatives the findings of the most recent survey.

Report

Not later than October 1 of each year (beginning in 2010), the Secretary of the Treasury must report to the Committee on Finance and the Committee on Health, Education, Labor, and Pensions of the Senate and the Committee on Ways and Means and the Committee on Education and Labor of the House of Representatives the following information with respect to the most recent taxable year ending before such date:

1. In each State and nationally (A) the total number of eligible individuals and the number of eligible individuals receiving the HCTC, (B) the total number of such eligible individuals who receive an advance payment of the HCTC through the HCTC program, (C) the average length of the time period of participation of eligible individuals in the HCTC program, and (D) the total number of participating eligible individuals in the HCTC program who are enrolled in each category of qualified health insurance with respect to each category of eligible individuals.

2. In each State and nationally, an analysis of (A) the range of monthly health insurance premiums, for self-only coverage and for family coverage, for individuals receiving the benefit of the HCTC and (B) the average and median monthly health insurance premiums, for self-only coverage and for family coverage, for individuals receiving the HCTC with respect to each category of qualified health insurance.

3. In each State and nationally, an analysis of the following information with respect to the health insurance coverage of individuals receiving the HCTC who are enrolled in State-based coverage: (A) deductible amounts, (B) other out-of-pocket cost-sharing amounts, and (C) a description of any annual or lifetime limits on coverage or any other significant limits on coverage services or benefits. The information must be reported with respect to each category of coverage.

4. In each State and nationally, the gender and average age of eligible individuals who receive the HCTC in each category of qualified health insurance with respect to each category of eligible individuals.

5. The steps taken by the Secretary of the Treasury to increase the participation rates in the HCTC program among eligible individuals, including outreach and enrollment activities.

6. The cost of administering the HCTC program by function, including the cost of subcontractors, and recommendations on ways to reduce the administrative costs, including recommended statutory changes.

7. After consultation with the Secretary of Labor, the number of States applying for and receiving national emergency grants under section 173(f) of the Workforce Investment Act of 1998, the activities funded by such grants on a State-by-State basis, and the time necessary for application approval of such grants.

Other non-revenue provisions

The provision also authorizes appropriations for implementation of the revenue provisions of the provision and provides grants under the Workforce Investment Act of 1998 for purposes related to the HCTC.

GAO study

The provision requires the Comptroller General of the United States to conduct a study regarding the HCTC to be submitted to Congress no later than March 31, 2010. The study is to include an analysis of (1) the administrative costs of the Federal government with respect to the credit and the advance payment of the credit and of providers of qualified health insurance with respect to providing such insurance to eligible individuals and their families, (2) the health status and relative risk status of eligible individuals and qualified family members covered under such insurance, (3) participation in the credit and the advance payment of the credit by eligible individuals and their qualifying family members, including the reasons why such individuals did or did not participate and the effects of the provision on participation, and (4) the extent to which eligible individuals and their qualifying family members obtained health insurance other than qualifying insurance or went without insurance coverage. The provision provides the Comptroller General access to the records within the possession or control of providers of qualified health insurance if determined relevant to the study. The Comptroller General may not disclose the identity of any provider of qualified health insurance or eligible individual in making information available to the public.

EFFECTIVE DATE

The provision is generally effective upon the date of enactment, except as otherwise noted above.

TITLE IV—HEALTH INFORMATION TECHNOLOGY

Subtitle C—Incentives for the Use of Health Information Technology 1
Part II—Medicare Program 1
    Incentives for Eligible Professionals. (House bill Sec. 4311; Senate bill Sec. 4201; Conference agreement Sec. 4201) 1
    Incentives for Hospitals. (House bill Sec. 4312; Senate bill Sec. 4202; Conference agreement Sec. 4202) 1
    Treatment Of Payments And Savings; Implementation Funding. (House bill Sec. 4313; Senate bill Sec. 4203; Conference agreement Sec. 4203) 1
    Study on Application of HIT Payment Incentives For Providers Not Receiving Other Incentive Payments. (House bill Sec. 4314; Senate bill Sec. 4205; Conference agreement Sec. 4204) 1
    Study on Availability of Open Source Health Information Technology Systems. (Senate bill Sec. 4206) 1
Part III—Medicaid Funding 1
    Medicaid Provider HIT Adoption and Operation Payments; Implementation Funding. (House bill Sec. 4321; Senate bill Sec. 4211; Conference agreement Sec. 4211) 1
    Medicaid Nursing Home Grant Program. (House bill Sec. 4322) 1
Subtitle E—Miscellaneous Medicare Provisions 1
    Moratoria on Certain Medicare Regulations. (House bill Sec. 4501; Senate bill Sec. 4204; Conference agreement Sec. 4301) 1
    Long-term Care Hospital Technical Corrections. (House bill Sec. 4502; Conference agreement Sec. 4302) 1

Part II—Medicare Program

INCENTIVES FOR ELIGIBLE PROFESSIONALS. (HOUSE BILL SEC. 4311; SENATE BILL SEC. 4201; CONFERENCE AGREEMENT SEC. 4101)

CURRENT LAW

There are several current legislative and administrative initiatives to promote the use of Health Information Technology (HIT) and Electronic Health Records (EHRs) in the Medicare program. The Medicare Modernization Act of 2003 (MMA; P.L. 108–173) established a timetable for the Centers for Medicare and Medicaid Services (CMS) to develop e-prescribing standards, which provide for the transmittal of such information as eligibility and benefits for the transmittal of such information as eligibility and benefits (including formulary drugs), information on the drug being prescribed and other drugs listed in the patient's medication history (including drug-drug interactions), and information on the availability of lower-cost, therapeutically appropriate alternative drugs. CMS issued a set of foundation standards in 2005, then piloted and tested additional standards in 2006, several of which were part of a 2008 final rule. The final Medicare e-prescribing standards, which become effective on April 1, 2009, apply to all Part D sponsors, as well as to prescribers and dispensers that electronically transmit prescriptions and prescription-related information about Part D drugs prescribed for Part D eligible individuals. The MMA did not require Part D drug prescribers and dispensers to e-prescribe. Under its provisions, only those who choose to e-prescribe must comply with the new standards. However, the Medicare Improvement for Patients and Providers Act of 2008 (MIPPA; P.L. 110–275) included an e-prescribing mandate and authorized incentive bonus payments for e-prescribers between 2009 and 2013. Beginning in 2012, payments will be reduced for those who fail to e-prescribe.

CMS is administering a number of additional programs to promote EHR adoption. The MMA mandated a three-year pay-for-performance demonstration in four states (AR, CA, MA, UT) to encourage physicians to adopt and use EHR to improve care for chronically ill Medicare patients. Physicians participating in the Medicare Care Management Performance (MCMP) demonstration receive bonus payments for reporting clinical quality data and meeting clinical performance standards for treating patients with certain chronic conditions. They are eligible for an additional incentive payment for using a certified EHR and reporting the clinical performance data electronically.

CMS has developed a second demonstration to promote EHR adoption using its Medicare waiver authority. The five-year Medicare EHR demonstration is intended to build on the foundation created by the MCMP program. It will provide financial incentives to as many as 1,200 small- to medium-sized physician practices in 12 communities across the country for using certified EHRs to improve quality, as measured by their performance on specific clinical quality measures. Additional bonus payments will be made based on the number of EHR functionalities a physician group has incorporated into its practice.

The Tax Relief and Health Care Act of 2006 (P.L. 109–432) established a voluntary physician quality reporting system, including an incentive payment for Medicare providers who report data on quality measures. The Medicare Physician Quality Reporting Initiative (PQRI) was expanded by the Medicare, Medicaid, and SCHIP Extension Act of 2007 (P.L. 110–173) and by MIPPA, which authorized the program indefinitely and increased the incentive that eligible physicians can receive for satisfactorily reporting quality measures. In 2009, eligible physicians may earn a bonus payment equivalent to 2.0% of their total allowed charges for covered Medicare physician fee schedule services. The PQRI quality measures include a structural measure that conveys whether a physician has and uses an EHR.

HOUSE BILL

The House bill would add an incentive payment to certain eligible professionals for the adoption and "meaningful use," defined below, of a certified EHR system. Professionals eligible for the incentive payments are those who participate in Medicare and who are defined under Sec. 1861(r) of the Social Security Act.

Incentive payments. The amount of EHR incentive payments that eligible providers could receive would be capped, based on the amount of Medicare-covered professional services furnished during the year in question, and the total possible amount of the incentive payment would decrease over time. The bill permits a rolling implementation period, with cohorts starting in 2011, 2012, and 2013, respectively, being eligible for the entire five years of incentives. For example, incentives that start in 2011 would continue through 2015, while those that begin in 2012 would run through 2016 and those starting in 2013 would run through 2017.

For the first calendar year of the designated period described above, the limit would be $15,000. Over the next four calendar years, the total possible amount would decrease respectively by year to $12,000, $8,000, $4,000, and $2,000. The phase-down is different for eligible professionals first adopting EHR after 2013. For these eligible providers, the limit on the amount of the incentive payment would equal the limit in the first payment year for someone whose first payment year is 2013. For example, if the first payment year is after 2014 then the limit on the incentive payments for that year would be $12,000 rather than $15,000. The EHR incentive payments for professionals would not be available to a hospital-based eligible physician, such as a pathologist, anesthesiologist or emergency physician who furnishes substantially all such services in a hospital setting using the hospital's facilities and equipment, including computer equipment. However, health IT incentive payments are made available to hospitals in Sec. 4312.

The payments could be in the form of a single consolidated payment or in periodic installments, as determined by the Secretary. The Secretary would establish rules to coordinate the limits on the incentive payments for eligible professionals who provide covered professional services in more than one practice. The Secretary would seek to avoid duplicative requirements from federal and state governments to demonstrate meaningful use of certified EHR technology under the Medicare and Medicaid programs. The Secretary would be allowed to adjust the reporting periods in order to carry out this clause.

Meaningful use. For purposes of the EHR incentive payment, an eligible professional would be treated as a "meaningful user" of EHR technology if the eligible professional meets the following three criteria: (1) the eligible professional demonstrates to the satisfaction of the Secretary that during the period the professional is using a certified EHR technology in a meaningful manner, which would include the use of electronic prescribing as determined to be appropriate by the Secretary; (2) the eligible professional demonstrates to the satisfaction of the Secretary that during such period such certified EHR technology is connected in a manner that provides, in accordance with law and standards applicable to the exchange of information, for the electronic exchange of health information to improve the quality of health care, such as promoting care coordination; and (3) the eligible professional submits information on clinical quality measures.

The Secretary could provide for the use of alternative means for meeting the above requirements in the case of an eligible professional furnishing covered professional services in a group practice (as defined by the Secretary). The Secretary would seek to improve the use of electronic health records and health care quality by requiring more stringent measures of meaningful use over time.

Clinical quality measures. The Secretary would select the clinical quality measures and other measures but must be consistent with the following: (1) the Secretary would provide preference to clinical quality measures that have been endorsed by the consensus-based entity regarding performance measurement with which the Secretary has a contract under Sec. 1890(a) of the Social Security Act; and (2) prior to any measure being selected for the purposes of this provision, the Secretary would publish the measure in the Federal Register and provide for a period of public comment. The Secretary could not require the electronic reporting of information on clinical quality measures unless the Secretary has the capacity to accept the information electronically, which may be on a pilot basis. In selecting the measures and in establishing the form and manner for reporting these measures, the Secretary would seek to avoid redundant or duplicative reporting otherwise required, including reporting under the physician quality reporting initiative.

A professional could satisfy the demonstration requirement above through means specified by the Secretary, which may include the following: (1) an attestation; (2) the submission of claims with appropriate coding (such as a code indicating that a patient encounter was documented using certified EHR technology); (3) a survey response; (4) reporting the clinical quality and other measures mentioned above; and (5) other means specified by the Secretary. Notwithstanding other provisions of law that place restrictions on the use of Part D data, the Secretary could use data regarding drug claims submitted for purposes of determining payment under Part D for purposes of determining the EHR incentive payments under this legislation.

Payment adjustments. Fee schedule payments to eligible professionals would be adjusted under certain conditions. For covered professional services furnished by an eligible professional during 2016 or any subsequent payment year, if the professional is not a meaningful EHR user during the previous year's reporting period, the fee schedule amount would be reduced to 99% in 2016, 98% in 2017, and 97% in 2018 and in each subsequent year.

For 2019 and each subsequent year, if the Secretary finds that the proportion of eligible professionals who are meaningful EHR users is less than 75%, the applicable fee schedule amount would be decreased by 1 percentage point from the applicable percent in the preceding year, but in no case would the applicable percent be less than 95%.

Hardship exemption. The Secretary could, on a case-by-case basis, exempt an eligible professional from the application of the payment adjustment above if the Secretary determines, subject to annual renewal, that being a meaningful EHR user would result in a significant hardship, such as in the case of an eligible professional who practices in a rural area without sufficient Internet access. In no case would an eligible professional be granted such an exemption for more than five years.

Medicare Advantage. In general, Medicare incentives created under this section are not available to Medicare Advantage (MA) plans, and both the payments and penalties made under this section are exempt from the MA benchmark determinations. However, the legislation establishes conditions under which the EHR bonus payments and penalties for the adoption and meaningful use of certified EHR technology would apply to certain HMO-affiliated eligible professionals. In general, with respect to eligible professionals in a qualifying MA organization for whom the organization attests to the Secretary as meaningful users of EHR, the incentive payments and adjustments would apply in a similar manner as they apply to other eligible professionals. Incentive payments would be made to, and payment adjustments would apply to, the qualifying organizations. With respect to a qualifying MA organization, an eligible professional would be an eligible professional who (i) is employed by the organization or is employed by or is a partner of an entity that through contract furnishes at least 80% of the entity's patient care services to enrollees of the organization; and furnishes at least 80% of the professional services of the eligible professional to enrollees of the organization; and (ii) furnishes, on average, at least 20 hours per week of patient care services. For these MA-affiliated eligible professionals, the Secretary would determine the incentive payments which should be similar to the payments that would have been available to the professionals under FFS.

To avoid duplication of payments, if an eligible professional is both an MA-affiliated professional and eligible for the maximum payment under the fee-for-service program (FFS), the payment incentive would be made only under FFS. Otherwise, the incentive payment would be made to the plan. The Secretary would develop a process to ensure that duplicate payments are not made. A qualifying MA organization would specify a year (not earlier than 2011) that would be treated as the first payment year for all eligible professionals with respect to the MA organization.

In applying the applicable percentage payment adjustment to MA-affiliated eligible professionals, instead of the payment adjustment being an applicable percent of the fee schedule amount for a year, the payment adjustment to the payment to the MA organization would be a proportional amount based on the payment adjustment applicable to FFS providers and the fraction of the organization's eligible professionals who are not meaningfully using EHRs.

SENATE BILL

The Senate bill is mostly the same as the House bill, but with the following exceptions. The Senate bill does not provide for any incentive payments to eligible professionals who first adopt EHR in 2014 or in subsequent years but does provide a greater incentive for early adoption of EHR, with payments of $18,000 if the first payment year under the EHR incentive program is 2011 or 2012.

Certain rural eligible providers would receive larger incentive payments in the Senate bill. The incentive payment would be increased by 25% if the provider predominantly serves beneficiaries in a rural area designated as a health professional shortage area.

Under the Senate bill, the Secretary would also be given the authority to deem providers who satisfy state requirements for demonstrating meaningful use of EHR technology as meeting the criteria for meaningful use under the Medicare EHR incentive program. No similar authority or provision is included in the House bill.

The incentive adjustment (penalty) would begin a year earlier in 2015 under the Senate bill as opposed to 2016 in the House bill. The schedule of reductions over time in the applicable percentage also reflects this difference, so that the applicable percent under the Senate bill would be 99% in 2015, 98% in 2016, and 97% in 2017.

With respect to the application of the incentive payment program to managed care organizations, the Senate bill differs from the House bill in two areas. First, the Senate bill applies a slightly different requirement to determine an eligible professional. Under the Senate bill, a professional who furnishes at least 75% (vs. 80% in the House bill) of his or her professional services to enrollees of the managed care organization and who also met the additional criteria noted above would be eligible for this incentive program. Second, the Senate bill includes a cap on large managed care organizations that limits incentive payments to no more than 5,000 eligible professionals of the organization in recognition of economies of scale in such organizations. This difference is also reflected in the payment adjustment penalty calculation in the Senate bill.

The Senate bill would require that the names, business addresses, and business phone numbers of each qualifying managed care organization and the associated eligible professionals receiving EHR incentive payments be posted on the CMS website in an easily understandable format.

Finally, the Senate bill would require the HHS Secretary to provide assistance to eligible professionals, Medicaid providers, and eligible hospitals located in rural or other medically underserved areas to successfully choose, implement, and use certified EHR technology. To the extent practicable, the assistance would be through entities that have expertise in this area.

CONFERENCE AGREEMENT

With regard to eligible professionals, the conference agreement includes provisions from the House and Senate bills.

The conference agreement provides eligible professionals who show meaningful use of an EHR in 2011 or 2012 with incentive payments of $18,000 in the first year; provides no payment incentives after 2016; and does not provide incentive payments to eligible professionals who first adopt an EHR in 2015 or subsequent years.

Incentive payments would be increased by 10% if the provider predominately serves beneficiaries in any area designated as a health professional shortage area. The conference agreement mirrors the Senate bill in that payment adjustments for eligible professionals not demonstrating meaningful use of an EHR would begin in 2015.

The conference agreement, like the House and Senate-passed bills, prohibits payments to hospital-based professionals (because such professionals are generally expected to use the EHR system of that hospital). This policy does not disqualify otherwise eligible professionals merely on the basis of some association or business relationship with a hospital. Common examples of such arrangements include professionals who are employed by a hospital to work in an ambulatory care clinic or billing arrangements in which physicians submit claims to Medicare together with hospitals or other entities. The change in the conference agreement clarifies that this test will be based on the setting in which a provider furnishes services rather than any billing or employment arrangement between a provider and hospital or other provider entity.

For MA organizations, the conference agreement reflects the Senate bill with the following exceptions. The agreement requires MA-affiliated professionals to provide 80 percent of their Medicare services to the enrollees of the qualifying MA organization and removes the payment incentive cap on eligible professionals affiliated with health maintenance organizations. It also extends the language of limitations on review for eligible professionals to professionals eligible under the managed care section and makes several technical corrections.

In addition, the conference report requires the Secretary to report to Congress on methods of making payment incentives and adjustments with respect to eligible professionals who (1) contract with one or more MA organizations or with intermediary organizations that contracts with one or more MA organizations and (2) are not eligible for incentive payments under this legislation. The report is due to Congress within 120 days of enactment and shall include recommendations for legislation as appropriate. The agreement reflects the Congress's intent to provide payment incentives and adjustments towards the meaningful use of certified EHRs with respect to all physicians who treat Medicare patients without regard to practice organization.

INCENTIVES FOR HOSPITALS. (HOUSE BILL SEC. 4312; SENATE BILL SEC. 4202; CONFERENCE AGREEMENT SEC. 4102)

CURRENT LAW

Medicare pays acute care hospitals using a prospectively determined payment for each discharge. These payment rates are increased annually by an update factor that is established, in part, by the projected increase in the hospital market basket (MB) index. However, starting in FY2007, hospitals that do not submit required quality data will have the applicable MB percentage reduced by two percentage points. The reduction would apply for that year and would not be taken into account in subsequent years. Currently, Medicare's payments to acute care hospitals under the inpatient prospective payment system (IPPS) are not affected by the adoption of EHR technology. Critical access hospitals (CAHs) receive cost-plus reimbursement under Medicare. Under current law, Medicare reimburses CAHs at 101% of their Medicare costs. These reimbursements include payments for Medicare's share of CAH expenditures on health IT, plus an additional 1%.

The bill would establish incentives, starting in FY2011, within Medicare's IPPS for eligible hospitals that are meaningful EHR users. Generally, these hospitals would receive diminishing additional payments over a four-year period. Starting in FY2016, eligible hospitals that do not become meaningful EHR users could receive lower payments because of reductions to their annual MB updates.

Incentive payments. Subject to certain limitations, each qualified hospital would receive an incentive payment calculated as the sum of a base amount ($2 million) added to its discharge related payment, which would then be multiplied by its Medicare's share. These payments would be reduced over a four-year transition period. A qualified hospital would receive $200 for each discharge paid under the inpatient prospective payment system (IPPS) starting with its 1,150th discharge through its 23,000th discharge.

A hospital's Medicare share would be calculated according to a specified formula. The numerator would equal inpatient bed days attributable to individuals for whom a Part A payment may be made, either under traditional Medicare or for those who are enrolled in Medicare Advantage (MA) organizations. The denominator would equal the total number of inpatient bed days in the hospital adjusted by a hospital's share of charges attributed to charity care. Specifically, the hospital's total days would be multiplied by a fraction calculated by dividing the hospital's total charges minus its charges attributed to charity care by its total charges. If a hospital's charge data on charity care is not available, the Secretary would be required to use the hospital's uncompensated care data which may be adjusted to eliminate bad debt. If hospital data to construct the charity care factor is unavailable, the fraction would be set at one. If hospital data necessary to include MA days is not available, that component of the formula would be set at zero.

The legislation establishes a four-year incentive payment transition schedule. A hospital that is a meaningful EHR user would receive the full amount of the incentive payment in its first payment year; 75% of the amount in its second payment year; 50% of the amount in its third payment year; and finally, 25% of the amount in its fourth payment year. The first payment year for a meaningful EHR user would be FY2011 or, alternatively, the first fiscal year for which an eligible hospital would qualify for an incentive payment. Hospitals that first qualify for the incentive payments after FY2013, would receive incentive payments on the transition schedule as if their first payment year is FY2013. Hospitals that become meaningful EHR users after FY2015 would not receive incentive payments. The incentive payments may be made as a single consolidated payment or may be made as periodic payments, as determined by the Secretary.

Meaningful use. An eligible hospital would be treated as a meaningful EHR user if it demonstrates that it uses certified EHR technology in a meaningful manner and provides for the electronic exchange of health information (in accordance with applicable legal standards) to improve the quality of care. A hospital would satisfy the demonstration requirements through an attestation; the submission of appropriately coded claims; a survey response; EHR reporting on certain measures; or other means specified by the Secretary.

Clinical quality measures. EHR measures would include clinical quality measures and other measures selected by the Secretary. Prior to implementation, the measures would be published in the Federal Register and subject to public comment. The electronic reporting of the clinical quality measures would not be required unless the Secretary has the capacity to accept the information electronically, which may be on a pilot basis. When establishing the measures, the Secretary shall provide preference to clinical quality measures that have been selected for the Reporting Hospital Quality Data for Annual Payment Update program (RHQDAPU) established at 1886(b)(3)(B)(viii) of the Social Security Act or that have been endorsed by the entity with a contract with the Secretary under Sec. 1890(a), which is currently the National Quality Forum. The Secretary shall seek to avoid redundant measures or duplicative reporting. Not withstanding restrictions placed on the use and disclosure of Medicare Part D information, the Secretary would be able to use data regarding drug claims.

Miscellaneous. There would be no administrative or judicial review of the determination of any incentive payment or payment update adjustment (described subsequently), including, the determination of a meaningful EHR user, the determination of the measures, or the determination of an exception to the payment update adjustment.

The Secretary would post listings of the eligible hospitals that are meaningful EHR users or that are subject to the penalty and other relevant data on the CMS website. Hospitals would have the opportunity to review the other relevant data prior to the data being made publicly available.

Penalties. Starting in FY2016, eligible IPPS hospitals that do not submit the required quality data would be subject to a 25% reduction in their annual update, rather than the 2 percentage point reduction under current law. Those hospitals that are not meaningful EHR users would be subject to a reduction in their annual MB update for the remaining three-quarters of the update. This reduction would be implemented over a three-year period. In FY2016, one-quarter of the update will be at risk for quality reporting and one-quarter at risk for meaningful use of EHR. In FY2017, one-quarter of the update will be at risk for quality reporting and one-half will be at risk for meaningful use of EHR. In FY2018 and subsequent years, one-quarter of the update will be at risk for quality reporting and three-quarters will be at risk for meaningful use of EHR. These reductions would apply only to the fiscal year involved and would not be taken into account in subsequent fiscal years. Starting in FY2016, payments to acute care hospitals that are not meaningful EHR users in a state operating under a Medicare waiver under section 1814(b)(3) of the Social Security Act would be subject to comparable aggregate reductions. The state would be required to report its payment adjustment methodology to the Secretary.

Hardship exemption. The Secretary would be able to exempt certain IPPS hospitals from these payment adjustments for a fiscal year if the Secretary determines that requiring a hospital to be a meaningful EHR user during that year would result in significant hardship, such as a hospital in a rural area without adequate Internet access. Such determinations would be subject to annual renewal. In no case would a hospital be granted an exemption for more than five years.

Medicare Advantage. In general, Medicare incentives created under this section are not available to Medicare Advantage (MA) plans and the payments made under this section are exempt from the benchmark determinations. However, payment incentives and penalties would be established for certain qualifying MA organizations to ensure maximum capture of relevant data relating to Medicare beneficiaries. An eligible hospital would be one that is under common corporate governance with a qualifying MA organization and serves enrollees in an MA plan offered by the organization. The Secretary would be required to determine incentive payment amounts similar to the estimated amount in the aggregate that would be paid if the hospital services had been payable under Part A as described above. The Secretary would be required to avoid duplicative EHR incentive payments to hospitals. If an eligible hospital under Medicare Part C was also eligible for EHR incentive payments under Medicare Part A, and for which at least 33% of hospital discharges (or bed days) were covered under Medicare Part A, the EHR incentive payment would only be made under Part A and not Part C. If fewer than 33% of discharges are covered under Part A, the Secretary would be required to develop a process to ensure that duplicative payments were not made and to collect data from MA organizations to ensure against duplicative payments.

If one or more eligible hospitals under a common corporate governance with a qualifying MA Health Maintenance Organization are not meaningful EHR users, the incentive payment to the organization would be reduced by a specified percentage. The percentage is defined as 100% minus the product of (a) the percentage point reduction to the payment update for the period described above and (b) the Medicare hospital expenditure proportion. This hospital expenditure proportion is defined as the Secretary's estimate of the portion of expenditures under Parts A and B that are not attributable to this part, that are attributable to expenditures for inpatient hospital services. The Secretary would be required to apply the payment adjustment based on a methodology specified by the Secretary, taking into account the proportion of eligible hospitals or discharges from eligible hospitals that are not meaningful EHR users for the period.

SENATE BILL

The Senate bill is largely the same as the House bill, but with the following differences. First, instead of a fixed amount per discharge, a qualified hospital would receive $200 per discharge for the 1,150th through the 9,200th discharge, $100 per discharge for the 9,201st through the 13,800th discharge, and $60 per discharge for the 13,801st through the 23,000th discharge. Second, the Senate bill would include CAHs as eligible hospitals, and limit the total amount of payments to a CAH for all payment years to $1.5 million. CAHs would continue to also receive their cost-plus reimbursement available under current law. Third, the penalties would begin a year earlier in FY2015; in the House bill the penalties begin in FY2016. Fourth, beginning in FY2015, a CAH that is not a meaningful EHR user would have its Medicare reimbursement rate as a percentage of its Medicare costs reduced to the following: FY2015, 100.66%; FY2016, 100.33%; FY2017 and each subsequent fiscal year, 100%. The Secretary would be permitted, on a case-by-case basis, to exempt a CAH from the penalties due to significant hardship. Finally, the Senate bill would require that the names, business addresses, and business phone numbers of each qualifying MA organization receiving EHR incentive payments be posted on the CMS website in an easily understandable format.

CONFERENCE AGREEMENT

The Conference Agreement follows the House bill, but with the following differences. First, the Conference agreement includes bonus payments for CAHs that are meaningful users of EHR technology. These bonus payments are capped at an enhanced Medicare share of 101 percent of those reasonable costs that are normally subject to depreciation and that are for the purchase of certified EHR. The enhanced Medicare share will equal the Medicare share calculated for 1886(d) hospitals, for EHR bonuses, including an adjustment for charity care, plus an additional 20 percentage points, except that the Medicare share may not exceed 100 percent. CAHs that are meaningful users of EHR technology will be able to expense these costs in a single payment year and receive prompt interim payments, rather than receiving reimbursement over a multi-year depreciation schedule. Beginning in 2011, if a CAH is a meaningful EHR user, they are eligible for four consecutive years of these bonuses, regardless of the year they meet the meaningful user standard, except that a CAH cannot get bonuses after 2015, similar to the bonus timeframe for a 1886(d) hospital. CAHs will continue to receive cost-plus reimbursement for their remaining costs, such as for ongoing maintenance or other costs that are not subject to depreciation. This cost-plus reimbursement continues beyond the bonus period, consistent with current law. Normal cost reporting rules would apply for the purchase of certified EHR technology until the CAH becomes a meaningful EHR user. CAHs are eligible for the same hardship exemption that is available to 1886(d) hospitals. Second, the conference agreement adopts the Senate's penalty schedule for both 1886(d) hospitals and CAHs. Third, the conference agreement includes the Senate provision requiring CMS to post information about qualifying MA hospitals on the website. Fourth, the conference agreement clarifies which provisions are subject to limitations on review for hospitals and extends appropriate limitations to CAHs and MA hospitals.

TREATMENT OF PAYMENTS AND SAVINGS; IMPLEMENTATION FUND-
ING. (HOUSE BILL SEC. 4313; SENATE BILL SEC. 4203; CON-
FERENCE AGREEMENT SEC. 4103)

CURRENT LAW

Physician and outpatient services provided under Medicare
Part B are financed through a combination of beneficiary premiums, deductibles, and federal general revenues. In general, Part
B beneficiary premiums are set to equal 25% of estimated program
costs for the aged, with federal general revenues accounting for the
remainder. The Part B premium fluctuates along with total Part B
expenditures.

Absent specific legislation to exempt premiums from policy effects, the recent growth in expenditures for physician services, led
by the increase in imaging and diagnostic services, generally results in premium increases to cover the beneficiaries 25% share of
total expenditures. While an individual's Social Security payment
cannot decrease from one year to the next as a result of an increase
in the Part B premium (except for those subject to the income-re-
lated premium), current law does permit the entire cost-of-living
(COLA) increase to be consumed by Medicare premium increases.

MIPPA established the Medicare Improvement Fund (MIF),
available to the Secretary to make improvements under the original fee-for-service program under parts A and B for Medicare beneficiaries.

For FY2009 through FY2013, the Secretary of Health and
Human Services would transfer $140 million from the Federal Hos-
pital Insurance Trust Fund and the Federal Supplementary Medical Insurance Trust Fund to the CMS Program Management Account. The amounts drawn from the funds would be in the same
proportion as for Medicare managed care payments (Medicare Advantage), that is, in a proportion that reflects the relative weight
that benefits under part A and under part B represent of the actuarial value of the total benefits.

HOUSE BILL

The House bill would exempt spending under this title from
the annual amount of Medicare physician expenditures used to calculate the Part B premium; beneficiaries would be held harmless
from potential premium increases due to the increased Part B expenditures that result from this added payment. Further, the bill
would authorize the transfer of funds from the Treasury to the
Supplementary Medical Insurance (Part B) Trust Fund to cover the
amount of EHR payment incentives that would otherwise be offset
by Part B premiums.

The bill would modify the purposes of the Medicare Improvement Fund by allowing the monies to be used to adjust Medicare
part B payments to protect against projected shortfalls due to any
increase in the conversion factor used to calculate the Medicare
Part B fee schedule.

The amount in the fund in FY2014, after taking into account
the transfer directed by this section, would be modified to be
$22.29 billion. For FY2020 and each subsequent fiscal year, the
amount in the fund would be the Secretary's estimate, as of July

1 of the fiscal year, of the aggregate reduction in Medicare expenditures directly resulting from the penalties imposed as a result of various Medicare providers not using HIT in a meaningful fashion. To implement the provisions in and amendments made by this section, $60 million for each of FY2009 through FY2015 and $30 million for each succeeding fiscal year through FY2019 would be appropriated to the Secretary for the CMS Program Management Account. The amounts appropriated would be available until expended.

SENATE BILL

The premium hold-harmless provisions in the Senate bill are identical to those in the House. However, the Senate bill does not include the provisions regarding the Medicare Improvement Fund including the transfers of aggregate reductions resulting from the penalties into the MIF. The two bills also differ in the funding amounts to CMS for implementation. Whereas the House bill would appropriate $60 million for each of FY2009–FY2015 and $30 million for FY2016 through FY2019, the Senate bill would appropriate $100 million for each of FY2009–FY2015 and $45 million for FY2016 through FY2018.

CONFERENCE AGREEMENT

The conference agreement includes the premium hold-harmless, as well as changes contained in the House bill to the Medicare Improvement Fund. The agreement also appropriates $100 million in FY2009–FY2015 and $45 million in FY 2016.

STUDY ON APPLICATION OF HIT PAYMENT INCENTIVES FOR PROVIDERS NOT RECEIVING OTHER INCENTIVE PAYMENTS. (HOUSE BILL SEC. 4314; SENATE BILL SEC. 4205; CONFERENCE AGREEMENT SEC. 4104)

CURRENT LAW

No current law.

HOUSE BILL

The House bill would require the Secretary to conduct a study to determine whether payment incentives to implement and use qualified HIT should be made available to health care providers who are receiving minimal or no payment incentives or other funding under this Act, including from Medicare or Medicaid, or any other funding. These health care providers could include skilled nursing facilities, home health agencies, hospice programs, laboratories, federally qualified health centers, and non-physician professionals.

The study would include an examination of the following: (1) the adoption rates of qualified HIT by such health care providers; (2) the clinical utility of HIT by such health care providers; (3) whether the services furnished by such health care providers are appropriate for or would benefit from the use of such technology; (4) the extent to which such health care providers work in settings that might otherwise receive an incentive payment or other fund-

748

ing under this Act, Medicare or Medicaid, or otherwise; (5) the potential costs and the potential benefits of making payment incentives and other funding available to such health care providers; and (6) any other issues the Secretary deems to be appropriate. The Secretary would be required to submit a report to Congress on the findings and conclusions of the study by June 30, 2010.

SENATE BILL

Same provision.

CONFERENCE AGREEMENT

The conference report includes the study contained in the House and Senate bills on providing incentive payments to encourage use of health IT to providers who are receiving minimal or no payment incentives or other funding under this Act. It also includes a study in Section 4206 of the Senate bill on the availability of open source health IT systems.

STUDY ON AVAILABILITY OF OPEN SOURCE HEALTH INFORMATION TECHNOLOGY SYSTEMS. (SENATE BILL SEC. 4206)

CURRENT LAW

No provision.

HOUSE BILL

No provision.

SENATE BILL

The Senate bill would require the Secretary, in consultation with other federal agencies, to study and report to Congress by October 1, 2010, on the availability of open source HIT systems to safety net providers.

CONFERENCE AGREEMENT

This study is included in Section 4104 of the conference agreement.

Part III—Medicaid Funding

MEDICAID PROVIDER HIT ADOPTION AND OPERATION PAYMENTS; IMPLEMENTATION FUNDING. (HOUSE BILL SEC. 4321; SENATE BILL SEC. 4211; CONFERENCE AGREEMENT SEC. 4201)

CURRENT LAW

The federal government pays a share of every state's spending on Medicaid services and program administration. The federal match for administrative expenditures does not vary by state and is generally 50%, but certain functions receive a higher amount. Section 1903(a)(3) of the Social Security Act authorizes a 90% match for expenditures attributable to the design, development, or installation of mechanized claims processing and information retrieval systems—referred to as Medicaid Management Information Systems (MMISs)—and a 75% match for the operation of MMISs

749

that are approved by the Secretary of Health and Human Services (HHS). A 50% match is available for non-approved MMISs under Section 1903(a)(7). In order to receive payments under Section 1903(a) for the use of automated data systems in the administration of their Medicaid programs, states are required under Section 1903(r) to have an MMIS that meets specified requirements and that the Secretary has found (among other things) is compatible with the claims processing and information retrieval systems used in the administration of the Medicare program.

State expenditures to encourage the purchase, adoption, and use of electronic health records do not receive federal financial participation, nor do State expenditures for the operation and maintenance of such systems.

The House Bill would amend Title XIX of the Social Security Act to authorize a 100% Federal match for a portion of payments to encourage the adoption of EHR technology (including support services and maintenance) to certain Medicaid providers who meet certain requirements. The state must prove to the Secretary that allowable costs are paid directly to the provider without any deduction or rebate; that the provider is responsible for payment of the EHR technology costs not provided for; and, that for costs not associated with purchase and initial implementation, the provider certifies meaningful use of the EHR technology. Finally, the certified EHR technology should be compatible with state or Federal administrative management systems.

Eligible providers would include physicians, nurse mid-wives, and nurse practitioners who are not hospital-based, and who have patient volume of at least 30% attributable to Medicaid patients. In order to qualify as a Medicaid provider, the professional would have to waive any right to Medicare EHR incentive payments for professionals detailed in the bill. This group of providers would be eligible for a payment equal to 85% of their net allowable technology costs. However, the allowable costs for the purchase and initial implementation of EHR technology cannot exceed $25,000 or include costs over a period of more than 5 years. Annual allowable costs not associated with initial implementation or purchase of the EHR technology could not exceed $10,000 per year or be made over a period of more than 5 years. Aggregate allowable costs for these eligible professionals, after application of the 85% adjustment, could not exceed $63,750.

Acute care hospitals with at least 10% Medicaid patient volume would be eligible for payments, as would children's hospitals of any Medicaid patient volume. Payments to hospitals would be limited to amounts analogous to those specified for eligible hospitals in Medicare in Section 4312. The payment limit for such hospitals is calculated as a base amount plus an amount related to the total number of discharges for such a hospital. The hospital's patient share attributable to Medicaid is then multiplied by that amount to calculate the limit of the payment an eligible hospital can receive. Unlike the Medicare hospital amount, the Medicaid hospital amount in the House bill is available, subject to State administration, without restriction as to the schedule of payments over time. That amount may not exceed the total amount described above.

Rural health clinics and Federally-Qualified Health Centers with at least 30% patient volume attributable to Medicaid patients would also be eligible for a payment for the costs of adoption and use of certified EHR technology, limited to amounts to be determined by the Secretary.

In counting towards patient volume thresholds, patients in Medicaid managed care plans are to be counted equivalently to other individuals in Medicaid in all circumstances. Individuals enrolled in optional Medicaid expansion programs financed through title XXI of the Social Security Act also must be counted.

Because the payments to eligible professionals would be sufficient to cover most or all of the costs of acquiring and operating a certified EHR, providers eligible under for both Medicare and Medicaid payments are required to choose one. The Secretary would be required to ensure that eligible professionals do not receive payments from both Medicare and Medicaid. The Secretary would also be instructed to attempt to avoid duplicative requirements for Federal and state governments to demonstrate meaningful use of EHR technology under Medicaid and Medicare, and may deem demonstration of meaningful use of certified EHRs in Medicare to be sufficient for demonstration of meaningful use of such technology in Medicaid.

By contrast, hospital limitations for Medicare and Medicaid are assessed on a proportional basis depending upon a hospital's patient volume from each payer, so hospitals could receive funding from both sources.

The House bill would authorize a 90% Federal match for payment to the states for administrative expenses related to EHR technology payments. In order for a state to receive the match it must show that: it is using the funds provided for these purposes to administer these systems including tracking of meaningful use by providers; conducting adequate oversight of meaningful use of the systems; and pursuing initiatives to encourage the adoption of certified EHR technology to promote health care quality and the appropriate exchange of information.

The House bill would appropriate $40 million for each of FY2009 through FY2015 and $20 million for each succeeding fiscal year through FY2019 to the Centers for Medicare & Medicaid Services for the costs of administering the provisions of this section.

SENATE BILL

The Senate bill is very similar to the House bill, with the following differences. First, in measuring meaningful use, which may include the reporting of clinical quality measures, a State would be required to ensure that populations with unique needs, such as children, are appropriately addressed. Second, rural health clinics and Federally-Qualified Health Centers that have at least 30% of their patient volume attributable to Medicaid patients would face a somewhat higher required contribution to the costs of adoption and use of certified EHRs. Finally, the Senate bill would require that the Secretary submit a report to Congress no later than July

1, 2012, that details the process developed to ensure coordination of the different health information technology program payments.

CONFERENCE AGREEMENT

The Conference agreement mirrors both the House-passed and Senate-passed bills. Across all eligible provider categories, the conference agreement provides Medicaid incentives towards the use of certified EHR technology based on a provider's involvement in the Medicaid program or other care for the uninsured and low-income populations. In addition to payment incentives for eligible professionals and hospitals contained in both bills, the agreement also provides for expanded funding to pediatricians, federally qualified health clinics (FQHCs), rural health clinics (RHCs), and physician assistants in physician assistant-led rural health clinics.

Specifically, eligible pediatricians with 20 to 30 percent patient volume attributable to patients receiving assistance through Medicaid would be eligible to receive up to two-thirds of the amount of eligible professionals with 30 percent patient volume attributable to such individuals (approximately $42,500 over a period of six years).

Federally qualified health centers and rural health clinics would be able to count additional patients towards the 30 percent qualifying threshold for Medicaid payments, including Medicaid patients; individuals receiving assistance through the Children's Health Insurance Program; individuals receiving charity care; and individuals receiving care for which payment is made on a sliding scale basis according to a patient's ability to pay. In addition, FQHCs and RHCs would be paid an amount for the adoption and use of certified EHRs proportional to the number of eligible professionals practicing predominantly in such settings according to the payment amounts determined for other eligible professionals (typically, up to $63,750 in federal contributions over a period of six years).

Additionally, the conference agreement provides that physician assistants practicing in RHCs and FQHCs that are led by physician assistants may receive Medicaid payments related to certified EHRs, provided that the facility meets the 30% facility threshold described above.

Like both the House-passed and Senate-passed bills, the conference agreement provides for up to $63,750 in federal contributions towards the adoption, implementation, upgrade, maintenance, and operation of certified EHR technology for eligible professionals. Up to 85% of $25,000, or $21,250, subject to a cap on average allowable costs, would be provided to eligible professionals to aid in adopting, implementing, and upgrading certified EHR systems. And up to 85% of $10,000, or $8,500, would be provided to eligible professionals for purposes of operation and maintenance of such systems over a period of up to 5 years.

Payments to hospitals would be limited to amounts analogous to those specified for eligible hospitals in Medicare in Section 4102. The payment limit for such hospitals is calculated as a base amount plus an amount related to the total number of discharges for such a hospital. The hospital's patient share attributable to Medicaid is then multiplied by that amount to calculate the limit of the payment an eligible hospital can receive. Relative to both the House and Senate-passed bills, the conference agreement provides additional specificity on the spending limitations for eligible hospitals in Medicaid. States may not pay more than 50% of the aggregate amount to a hospital in any year, and must spread payments to hospitals out over at least three years (contingent on demonstration of meaningful use of certified electronic health records).

Like both the House-passed and Senate-passed bills, the conference agreement prohibits payments to hospital-based professionals (because such professionals are generally expected to use the EHR system of that hospital). This policy does not disqualify otherwise eligible professionals merely on the basis of some association or business relationship with a hospital. Common examples of such arrangements include professionals who are employed by a hospital to work in an ambulatory care clinic or billing arrangements in which physicians submit claims to Medicare together with hospitals or other entities. The conference agreement clarifies that this test will be based on the setting in which a provider furnishes services rather than any billing or employment arrangement between a provider and hospital or other provider entity.

The agreement requires coordination of payments to eligible professionals with Medicare payments under sections 1848(o) and 1853(l) in order to assure no duplication of funding. The provision requires that such coordination include, to the extent practicable, a data matching process between State Medicaid agencies and the CMS using national provider numbers. The Congress intends that such process be used to identify providers who have received funding from either Medicare or Medicaid so as to prevent such providers from accessing incentives in the other program.

MEDICAID NURSING HOME GRANT PROGRAM. (HOUSE BILL SEC. 4322)

CURRENT LAW

No provision.

HOUSE BILL

The House bill would authorize the appropriation of $600, to remain available until expended, for the Secretary to establish a Medicaid grant program for the purpose of making incentive payments, through States, to nursing facilities to encourage the meaningful use of certified EHR technology in nursing facilities. The program would require nursing facilities to engage in quality improvement programs in addition to demonstrating meaningful use of certified EHR technology. The Secretary would be authorized to award grants to not more than 10 states. Incentive payments would cover up to 90% of a facility's EHR adoption and operation costs.

SENATE BILL

No provision.

No provision.

Subtitle E—Miscellaneous Medicare Provisions

MORATORIA ON CERTAIN MEDICARE REGULATIONS. (HOUSE BILL SEC. 4501; SENATE BILL SEC. 4204; CONFERENCE AGREEMENT SEC. 4301)

(a) Delay in phase out of Medicare hospice budget neutrality adjustment factor during Fiscal Year 2009

CURRENT LAW

The prospective payment methodology for hospice was established in 1983. This prospective payment system (PPS) pays hospices according to the general type of care provided to a beneficiary on a daily basis. This rate attempts to adjust for geographic differences through a wage index adjustment. The current hospice wage index methodology was implemented in 1997 through the rulemaking process. The hospice wage index is updated annually and based upon the most current hospital wage data and any changes to the Office of Management and Budget's (OMB) Metropolitan Statistical Areas (MSA) definitions. Prior to this date, the wage adjustment used a hospice wage index based upon 1981 hospital data collected by the Bureau of Labor Statistics (BLS). The change in 1997 was intended to improve the data used to account for disparities in geographic location and improve accuracy, reliability, and equity of Medicare payments to hospices across the country.

When the data source used to adjust hospice payments for differences in the cost of labor across geographic area was changed in 1997 from the BLS data to the hospital wage data, a budget neutrality adjustment factor (BNAF) was instituted as part of the payment system. The BNAF prevents participating hospices from experiencing reductions in total payments as a result of the wage data change. The BNAF increases payments to those hospices that would otherwise experience a payment reduction by boosting hospice payments to these providers by amounts that would make overall payments budget neutral to the levels they would have received had the BLS based wage adjustment data been used. On August 8, 2008, in a final rule, published by HHS, the BNAF would be phased-out over three years, beginning with a 25% reduction in FY2009, an additional 50% reduction (totaling 75%) in FY2010, and a final 100%, or elimination, in FY2011. The phase-out of the BNAF went into effect on October 1, 2008.

HOUSE BILL

The House bill would require that the Secretary not phase-out or eliminate the budget neutrality adjustment factor before October 1, 2009. The hospice wage index used for FY2009 would be recomputed as if there had been no reduction in the budget neutrality factor.

754

SENATE BILL

No provision.

CONFERENCE AGREEMENT

The Conference Agreement recedes to the House provision. The Conferees do not anticipate extending this provision as they expect the hospice community to seek a permanent fix in the annual rule-making cycle for Medicare hospice payments.

(b) Non-application of phased-out Indirect Medical Education (IME) adjustment factor for Fiscal Year 2009

CURRENT LAW

Medicare sets separate per discharge payment rates to cover the costs for depreciation, interest, rent and other property-related expenses in acute care hospitals. Due to a regulatory change implemented by the Centers for Medicare and Medicaid Services (CMS), Medicare's indirect medical education (IME) adjustment in its capital inpatient prospective payment system (IPPS) is scheduled to be phased out over a 2-year period starting in FY2009. In FY2009, teaching hospitals will receive half of the IME adjustment in Medicare's capital IPPS; in FY2010 and in subsequent years, the capital IME adjustment will be eliminated.

HOUSE BILL

The FY2009 adjustment to 50% of the capital IME adjustment would not be implemented. Medicare payments would be recomputed for discharges after October 1, 2008. The elimination of capital IME in FY2010 would not be affected. To implement this provision, $2 million would be transferred from Medicare's Federal Hospital Insurance Trust Fund into the CMS Program Management Account for FY2009.

SENATE BILL

The Senate bill includes the same IME adjustment provision, but without implementation funding.

CONFERENCE AGREEMENT

The Conference Agreement recedes to the House provision. The Conferees do not anticipate extending this provision as they expect the hospital community to seek a permanent fix in the annual IPPS rulemaking cycle.

LONG-TERM CARE HOSPITAL TECHNICAL CORRECTIONS. (HOUSE BILL SEC. 4502; CONFERENCE AGREEMENT SEC. 4302)

CURRENT LAW

Long-term care hospitals (LTCHs) are generally defined as hospitals that have an average Medicare inpatient length of stay greater than 25 days. LTCHs are designed to provide extended medical and rehabilitative care for patients who are clinically complex and have multiple acute or chronic conditions.

Starting October 1, 2004, CMS established limits on the number of discharged Medicare patients that an LTCH hospital-within-hospital (HwH) or satellite LTCH could admit from its co-located host hospital. In general, CMS applied a payment adjustment for discharges in excess of a 25% threshold that an LTCH HwH or satellite admitted from its co-located host hospital. After that threshold had been reached, generally, the LTCH would receive a lower payment for subsequent patient admissions that had been discharged from the host hospital. The adjustment was not applied to "grandfathered" HwHs or "grandfathered" LTCH satellites. Beginning in rate year 2008, CMS extended the 25% threshold payment adjustment for discharges from co-located host hospitals to grandfathered HwHs and LTCH satellite facilities. CMS also extended the 25% threshold payment adjustment to LTCH discharges admitted from hospitals with which the LTCH or satellite facility was not co-located, also referred to as freestanding LTCHs. The regulatory policy setting forth the payment adjustment policy for referrals from co-located hospitals is in 42 CFR 412.534. The regulatory policy setting forth the payment adjustment policy for referrals from non-co-located hospitals is in 42 CFR 412.536.

The Medicare, Medicaid and SCHIP Extension Act of 2007 (MMSEA) provided for a three-year delay for grandfathered LTCH HwHs of the 25% threshold for discharges admitted from a co-located host (42 CFR 412.534). MMSEA also provided for a three-year delay for grandfathered LTCH HwHs and freestanding LTCHs of the 25% threshold payment adjustment for referrals from non-co-located hospitals (42 CFR 412.536). These provisions in MMSEA became effective for cost reporting periods beginning on or after December 29, 2007.

MMSEA also increased the patient percentage thresholds from 25% to 50% for certain LTCH HwH and non-grandfathered satellite discharges admitted from a co-located hospital (CFR 412.534), and from 50% to 75% for certain LTCH HwH and satellite discharges admitted from a co-located rural, MSA-dominant, or urban single hospital for a three-year period. These provisions were effective for cost reporting periods beginning on or after December 29, 2007.

MMSEA provided a three-year moratorium on new LTCHs or satellite LTCHs, with exceptions for an LTCH that, as of the date of enactment: (1) began its qualifying payment period as an LTCH; (2) had binding written agreements and had expended a certain percent of estimated cost or dollar amount for the purpose of construction, renovation, lease or demolition; and, (3) had an approved certificate of need from a State where one is required.

HOUSE BILL

The House bill would align the start date of the three-year delay in the implementation of the 25% patient threshold adjustment for referrals from non-co-located facilities for freestanding LTCHs and grandfathered HwHs with the original effective date for the phase-in of this regulatory policy. This new effective date is July 1, 2007. The bill also would align the start date of the three-year delay in the implementation of the 25% patient threshold for referrals from co-located hospitals with the original effective date for the phase-in of this regulatory policy (at 42 CFR

412.534(g)). The new effective date is October 1, 2007. For grand-fathered LTCH satellite facilities, the effective date is July 1, 2007.
The bill would clarify that the 3-year delay from the 25% threshold policy for referrals from non-co-located facilities applies to LTCH or LTCH satellites that are co-located with an entity that is a provider-based, off-campus location of a subsection (d) hospital which did not provide 1886(d) services at the off-campus location. It also clarifies that grandfathered satellite facilities receive the same relief as non-grandfathered satellites from 42 CFR 412.534 pertaining to applicable patient percentage thresholds.

The bill would clarify that the exception from the LTCH mora-torium applies to LTCHs with certificates of need for bed expan-sions prior to date of enactment but no earlier than April 1, 2005.

SENATE BILL

No provision.

CONFERENCE AGREEMENT

The Conference Agreement recedes to the House provision.

TITLE V—STATE FISCAL RELIEF

SEC. 5000. PURPOSES (SEC. 5000 OF THE SENATE BILL)

CURRENT LAW

No provision.

HOUSE BILL

No provision.

SENATE BILL

The Senate bill sets forth the purposes of the State Fiscal Re-lief title as: (1) to provide fiscal relief to states in a period of eco-nomic downturn, and (2) to protect and maintain state Medicaid programs during a period of economic downturn, including by help-ing to avert cuts to provider payment rates and benefits or services, and to prevent constrictions of income eligibility requirements for such programs, but not to promote increases in such requirements.

CONFERENCE AGREEMENT

The conference agreement follows the Senate bill.

SEC. 5001. TEMPORARY INCREASE OF MEDICAID FMAP (SEC. 5001 OF THE HOUSE BILL; SEC. 5001 OF THE SENATE BILL)

CURRENT LAW

The federal medical assistance percentage (FMAP) is the rate at which states are reimbursed by the federal government for most Medicaid service expenditures. It is based on a formula that pro-vides higher reimbursement to states with lower per capita in-comes relative to the national average (and vice versa); it has a statutory minimum of 50% and maximum of 83%. Exceptions to the FMAP formula have been made for certain states and situations.

For example, the District of Columbia's Medicaid FMAP is set in statute at 70%, and the territories have FMAPs set at 50% (they are also subject to federal spending caps). During the last economic downturn under the Jobs and Growth Tax Relief Reconciliation Act of 2003 (P.L. 108–27), all states received a temporary increase in Medicaid FMAPs for the last two quarters of FY2003 and the first three quarters of FY2004 as part of a fiscal relief package. In addition to Medicaid, the FMAP is used in determining the federal share of certain other programs (e.g., foster care and adoption assistance under Title IV–E of the Social Security Act) and serves as the basis for calculating an enhanced FMAP that applies to the Children's Health Insurance Program.

HOUSE BILL

The House bill provides a temporary adjustment FMAP during a recession adjustment period that begins with the first quarter of FY2009 and runs through the first quarter of FY2011. The House provision would hold all states harmless from any scheduled decline in their regular FMAPs, provide all states with an across-the-board increase of 4.9 percentage points, and provide high unemployment states with an additional increase. It would also allow each territory to choose between an FMAP increase of 4.9 percentage points along with a 10% increase in its spending cap, or its regular FMAP along with a 20% increase in its spending cap. It is estimated that the House provision would provide about half of its spending via the hold harmless and across-the-board increases, and about half via the unemployment-related increase which is targeted to the states hit hardest by job loss.

States would be evaluated on a quarterly basis for the additional unemployment-related FMAP increase, which would equal a percentage reduction in the state share. The percentage reduction would be applied to the state share after the hold harmless increase and before the 4.9 percentage point increase. For example, after applying the 4.9 point increase provided to all states, a state with a regular FMAP of 50% (state share of 50%) would have an FMAP of 54.90%. If the state share were further reduced by 6%, the state would receive an additional FMAP increase of 3 points (50 * 0.06 = 3). The state's total FMAP increase would be 7.9 points (4.9 + 3 = 7.9), providing an FMAP of 57.90%.

The additional unemployment-related FMAP increase would be based on a state's unemployment rate in the most recent 3-month period for which data are available (except for the first two and last two quarters of the recession adjustment period, for which the 3-month period would be specified) compared to its lowest unemployment rate in any 3-month period beginning on or after January 1, 2006. The criteria would be as follows:

- unemployment rate increase of at least 1.5 but less than 2.5 percentage points = 6% reduction in state share;
- unemployment rate increase of at least 2.5 but less than 3.5 percentage points = 12% reduction in state share; and
- unemployment rate increase of at least 3.5 percentage points = 14% reduction in state share.

If a state qualifies for the additional unemployment-related FMAP increase and later has a decrease in its unemployment rate, its percentage reduction in state share could not decrease until the fourth quarter of FY2010 (for most states, this corresponds with the first quarter of SFY2011). If a state qualifies for the additional unemployment-related FMAP increase and later has an increase in its unemployment rate, its percentage reduction in state share could increase.

The full amount of the temporary FMAP increase would only apply to Medicaid (excluding disproportionate share hospital payments). A portion of the temporary FMAP increase (hold harmless plus 4.9 percentage points) would apply to Title IV–E foster care and adoption assistance. States would be required to maintain their Medicaid eligibility standards, methodologies, and procedures as in effect on July 1, 2008, in order to be eligible for the increase. They would be prohibited from depositing or crediting the additional federal funds paid as a result of the temporary FMAP increase to any reserve or rainy day fund. States would also be required to ensure that local governments do not pay a larger percentage of the state's nonfederal Medicaid expenditures than otherwise would have been required on September 30, 2008.

SENATE BILL

Similar to the House provision, the Senate provision would hold all states harmless from any decline in their regular FMAPs. However, it would provide a larger across-the-board increase of 7.6 percentage points and a smaller unemployment-related increase. It would apply the 7.6 percentage point increase and raise the territories' spending caps in the territories by 15.2%. It is estimated that the Senate provision would provide about 80% of its spending via the hold harmless and across-the-board increases, and about 20% via the unemployment-related increase.

As in the House provision, the Senate provision would calculate the unemployment-related increase as a percentage reduction in the state share. However, the percentage reduction would be applied to the state share after both the hold harmless increase and the across-the-board increase of 7.6 percentage points. The Senate provision would evaluate states based on the same unemployment data, except that it would not specify the three-month period to be used for the first two and last two quarters of the temporary FMAP increase. The criteria would be as follows: unemployment rate increase of at least 1.5 but less than 2.5 percentage points = 2.5% reduction in state share; increase of at least 2.5 but less than 3.5 percentage points = 4.5% reduction; increase of at least 3.5 percentage points = 6.5% reduction. Like the House provision, a state's percentage reduction could increase over time as its unemployment rate increases, but it would not be allowed to decrease until the last quarter of FY2010.

Unlike the House provision, the Senate provision would not apply the temporary FMAP increase to expenditures for individuals who are eligible for Medicaid because of an increase in a state's income eligibility standards above what was in effect on July 1, 2008. It would also prohibit states from receiving the temporary increase if they are not in compliance with existing requirements for prompt payment of health care providers under Medicaid and would extend this requirement to nursing facilities. States would be required to report to the Secretary of HHS on their compliance with such requirements. Otherwise, the Senate provision is similar to the House provision.

CONFERENCE AGREEMENT

The conference agreement follows the Senate bill with modifications. The across-the-board increase in FMAP would be 6.2 percentage points. The reductions in state share for states with increases in unemployment rates would be 5.5%, 8.5%, and 11.5%. These percent reductions would be applied against the state share after the hold harmless reduction and after an across-the-board increase of 3.1 percentage points. Each territory would be allowed to choose between an FMAP increase of 6.2 percentage points along with a 15% increase in its spending cap, or its regular FMAP along with a 30% increase in its spending cap. It is estimated that the conference agreement would provide about 65% of its spending via the hold harmless and across-the-board increases, and about 35% via the unemployment-related increase.

The conference agreement would also prohibit states from receiving the temporary increase if they are not in compliance with existing requirements for prompt payment of practitioners under Medicaid and would extend this requirement to nursing facilities and hospitals. States would be required to report to the Secretary of HHS on their compliance with such requirements.

SEC. 5001(f)(2). COMPLIANCE WITH PROMPT PAY REQUIREMENTS
(SEC. 3304 OF THE SENATE BILL)

CURRENT LAW

Under SSA Sec. 1902(a)(37)(A) states are to reimburse providers for services within 30 days of the receipt of a reimbursement claim. State Medicaid programs are to reimburse providers for 90% of claims submitted for payment within 30 days of receipt of the claim. Medicaid also is to process and pay 99% of claims within 90 days from the date of receipt of such claims. These requirements allow states additional time to process claims that are inaccurate, incomplete, or otherwise cannot be processed in a timely manner.

HOUSE BILL

No provision.

SENATE BILL

Under this provision, for states to qualify for the temporary enhanced FMAP funding under section 5001, states would have to meet current prompt payment requirements under section 1902(a)(37)(A), as well as a temporary extension of those requirements to nursing facilities, which are not currently subject to the prompt pay requirements in title XIX.

CONFERENCE AGREEMENT

The conference agreement follows the Senate bill with modifications to the reporting requirements, to temporarily extend application of the prompt pay requirements to hospitals, and to provide a grace period before states become ineligible for increased FMAP as a result of failure to comply with the requirements as relate to nursing facilities and hospitals.

SEC. 5002. TEMPORARY INCREASE IN DSH ALLOTMENTS DURING RECESSION (SEC. 5006 OF THE HOUSE BILL; SEC. 5002 OF THE SENATE BILL)

CURRENT LAW

Medicaid law requires that states make Medicaid payment adjustments for hospitals that serve a disproportionate share of low-income patients with special needs. Payments to these hospitals known as disproportionate share hospital (DSH) payments, are specifically defined in Medicaid law. They are subject to aggregate annual state-specific limits on federal financial participation. States are required to provide an annual report to the Secretary describing the payment adjustments made to each DSH hospital.

HOUSE BILL

This provision would increase states' FY2009 annual Disproportionate Share Hospital (DSH) allotments by 2.5% above the allotment they would have received in FY2009 under current law. In addition, states' DSH allotments in FY2010 would be equal to the FY2009 DSH allotment (with the adjustment) increased by 2.5%. After FY2010, states' annual DSH allotments would be determined as under current law. If, under current law, states' annual DSH allotments are higher in either FY 2009 or FY 2010 than they would have been with the 2.5% adjustment, then states would receive the higher DSH allotments without the recession adjustment.

SENATE BILL

Under this provision, states that reported to the Health and Human Services Secretary, as of August 31, 2009, FY2006 total (federal and state) DSH allotments of less than 3% of the state's total state plan medical assistance expenditures would receive special DSH allotments established under the Medicare Modernization Act of 2003 (MMA, P.L. 108–391). This new provision may affect the number of states that are determined to be low-DSH states since the provision would rely on a different base year than that used under MMA. Under this provision, low-DSH states would receive the following revised DSH allotments:
- for FY2009, the DSH allotment would be the FY2008 DSH allotment increased by 16%;
- for FY2010, the DSH allotment would be the FY2009 DSH allotment increased by 16%;
- for the first quarter of FY2011(through December 31, 2010), the DSH allotment would be ¼ of the DSH allotment for FY2010 increased by 16%;
- for the remainder of FY2011 (January 1, 2011–September 30, 2011), the DSH allotment would be ¾ of the FY2010 DSH allotment for each qualified state without the changes contained in this provision;

• for FY2012, qualified states' DSH allotments would be FY2010 DSH allotment (as if this provision had not been enacted);
• for FY2013 and subsequent years, qualified states would receive the DSH allotment for the previous fiscal year with an inflation adjustment, as described in the Social Security Act (SSA), Section 1923(f)(5).

CONFERENCE AGREEMENT

The conference agreement follows the House provision.

SEC. 5003. MORATORIA ON CERTAIN MEDICAID FINAL REGULATIONS (SEC. 5002 OF THE HOUSE BILL; SEC. 5002 OF THE SENATE BILL)

CURRENT LAW

In 2007 and 2008, the Centers for Medicare and Medicaid Services (CMS) issued seven Medicaid regulations that generated controversy during the 110th Congress. To address concerns with the impact of the regulations, Congress passed a law that imposed moratoria on six of the Medicaid regulations until April 1, 2009 (excluding the rule on outpatient hospital facility and clinic services). The seven Medicaid regulations covered the following Medicaid areas:

• Graduate Medical Education,
• Cost Limit for Public Providers,
• Rehabilitation Services,
• Targeted Case Management,
• School-Based Services,
• Provider Taxes, and
• Outpatient Hospital Services.

HOUSE BILL

This provision would extend the moratoria on the first six regulations beyond April 1, 2009, when the current moratoria expire, to July 1, 2009. The regulations covered under the extension would include: (1) Graduate Medical Education, (2) Cost Limit for Public Providers, (3) Rehabilitative Services, (4) Targeted Case Management, (5) School-Based Services, and (6) Provider Taxes. In addition, this provision would specifically prohibit the Health and Human Services Secretary from taking any action until after June 30, 2009 (through regulation, regulatory guidance, use of federal payment audit procedures, or other administrative action, policy, or practice, including Medical Assistance Manual transmittal or state Medicaid director letter) to implement a final regulation covering Outpatient Hospital facility services.

SENATE BILL

No provision.

CONFERENCE AGREEMENT

The conference agreement follows the House bill with a modification limiting the application of the moratoria to the four regulations that have been published as final: (1) Targeted Case Management, (2) School-Based Services, (3) Provider Taxes, and (4) Outpatient Hospital Services. The conference agreement also states the sense of the Congress that the Secretary of HHS should not promulgate as final the proposed regulations relating to Graduate Medical Education, Cost Limit for Public Providers, and Rehabilitative Services.

SEC. 5004. EXTENSION OF TRANSITIONAL MEDICAL ASSISTANCE (TMA) (SEC. 5003 OF THE HOUSE BILL; SEC. 3101 OF THE SENATE BILL)

CURRENT LAW

States are required to continue Medicaid benefits for certain low-income families who would otherwise lose coverage because of changes in their income. This continuation is called transitional medical assistance (TMA). Federal law permanently requires four months of TMA for families who lose Medicaid eligibility due to increased child or spousal support collections, as well as those who lose eligibility due to an increase in earned income or hours of employment. However, Congress expanded work-related TMA under Section 1925 of the Social Security Act in 1988, requiring states to provide at least six, and up to 12, months of coverage. Since 2001, these work-related TMA requirements have been funded by a series of short-term extensions, most recently through June 30, 2009.

To qualify for work-related TMA under Section 1925, a family must have received Medicaid in at least three of the six months preceding the month in which eligibility is lost and have a dependent child in the home. During the initial 6-month period of TMA, states must provide the same benefits the family was receiving, although this requirement may be met by paying a family's premiums, deductibles, coinsurance, and similar costs for employer-based health coverage. An additional 6-month extension of TMA (for a total of up to 12 months) is available for families who continue to have a dependent child in the home, who meet reporting requirements, and whose average gross monthly earnings (less work-related child care costs) are below 185% of the federal poverty line. States may impose a premium, limit the scope of benefits, and use an alternative service delivery system during the second six months of TMA.

HOUSE BILL

The provision would extend work-related TMA under Section 1925 for 18 months through December 31, 2010. The provision also would give States the flexibility to extend an initial eligibility period of 12 months of Medicaid coverage to families transitioning from welfare to work, in which case the additional 6-month extension would not apply. The House bill also gives states the option of waiving the requirement that a family must have received Medicaid in at least three of the last six months in order to qualify.

Under the House provision, states would be required to collect and submit to the Secretary of Health and Human Services (and make publicly available) information on average monthly enrollment and participation rates for adults and children under work-related TMA; states would also be required to collect and submit

763

information on the number and percentage of children who become ineligible for work-related TMA, but who continue to be eligible under another Medicaid eligibility category or who are enrolled in the Children's Health Insurance Program.

SENATE BILL

The Senate bill is the same as the House bill.

CONFERENCE AGREEMENT

The conference agreement follows the House and Senate bills.

SEC. 5005. EXTENSION OF THE QUALIFYING INDIVIDUAL (QI) PROGRAM (SEC. 3201 OF THE SENATE BILL)

CURRENT LAW

Certain low-income individuals who are aged or have disabilities, as defined under the Supplemental Security Income (SSI) program, and who are eligible for Medicare, are also eligible to have their Medicare Part B premiums paid for by Medicaid under the Medicare Savings Program (MSP). Eligible groups include Qualified Medicare Beneficiaries (QMBs), Specified Low-Income Medicare Beneficiaries (SLMBs), and Qualifying Individuals (QIs). QMBs have incomes no greater than 100% of the federal poverty level (FPL) and assets no greater than $4,000 for an individual and $6,000 for a couple. SLMBs meet QMB criteria, except that their incomes are greater than 100% of FPL but do not exceed 120% FPL. QIs meet the QMB criteria, except that their income is between 120% and 135% of FPL. Further, they are not otherwise eligible for Medicaid. The QI program is currently slated to terminate December 2009.

In general, Medicaid payments are shared between federal and state governments according to a matching formula. Unlike the QMB and SLMB programs, the QI program is paid 100% by the federal government from the Part B Trust fund. The total amount of federal QI spending is limited each year and allocated among the states. States are required to cover only the number of people that would bring their annual spending on these population groups to their allocation levels. For the period beginning on January 1, 2009 and ending on September 30, 2009, the total allocation amount for all states was $350 million. For the period that begins on October 1, 2009 and ends on December 31, 2009, the total allocation is $150 million.

HOUSE BILL

No provision.

SENATE BILL

This provision would extend the QI program an additional year from December 2009 to December 2010. It establishes specific funding limits:
• from January 1, 2010, through September 30, 2010, the total allocation amount would be $412.5 million, and

• from October 1, 2010, through December 31, 2010, the total allocation amount would be $150 million.

CONFERENCE AGREEMENT

The conference agreement follows the Senate bill.

SEC. 5006(A), (B), (C). PROTECTIONS FOR INDIANS UNDER MEDICAID AND CHIP (SEC. 5004 OF THE HOUSE BILL; SEC. 3301 OF THE SENATE BILL)

CURRENT LAW

Premiums and Cost Sharing. In Medicaid, premiums and enrollment fees generally are prohibited for most beneficiaries. Nominal premiums and enrollment fees specified in regulations may be imposed on selected groups (e.g., medically needy, certain families qualifying for transitional Medicaid, pregnant women and infants with income over 150% FPL). Premiums and enrollment fees can exceed these nominal amounts for other selected groups (e.g., certain workers with disabilities and individuals covered under Section 1115 demonstrations).

Service-related cost-sharing (e.g., deductibles, copayments, coinsurance) is prohibited for selected groups (e.g., children under 18, pregnant women) and for selected benefits (e.g., hospice care, emergency services, family planning services and supplies). For most other groups and services, nominal cost-sharing amounts specified in regulations may be applied at state option. For other selected groups (e.g., workers with disabilities and individuals covered under Section 1115 demonstrations), cost-sharing can exceed nominal amounts.

The Deficit Reduction Act of 2005 (P.L. 109–171) added a new Medicaid state option for alternative premiums and cost-sharing for certain subgroups. Applicable maximum amounts vary by income level (as a percent of the federal poverty level). Special rules apply to prescription drugs and to non-emergency services provided in hospital emergency rooms.

Indians are not explicitly exempted from cost-sharing and premium charges in Medicaid. When an Indian Medicaid beneficiary receives services from a contract health services (CHS) provider, Medicaid pays for the service. Any copayment that Medicaid does not pay must be paid by the Indian Health Service (IHS) or the Tribe from its CHS budget, since the CHS provider may not bill the Indian patient. The practical effect of this is simply to reduce the amount of appropriated funds available for health care from IHS or CHS for Tribes that already lack sufficient resources. CHIP programs are already prohibited from imposing cost-sharing on eligible Indians.

Eligibility Determinations under Medicaid and CHIP. The federal Medicaid statute defines more than 50 eligibility pathways. For some pathways, states are required to apply an assets test. For other pathways, assets tests are a state option. When assets tests apply, some pathways give states flexibility to define specific assets that are to be counted and which can be disregarded. For other pathways, primarily for people qualifying on the basis of having a disability or who are elderly, assets tests are required. States generally follow asset guidelines specified for the Supplementary Security Income (SSI) program. Medicaid also defines the rules for the counting of certain assets. Under SSI law, several types of assets are excluded, including: (1) any land held in trust by the United States for a member of a federally-recognized tribe, or any land held by an individual Indian or tribe and which can only be sold, transferred, or otherwise disposed of with the approval of other individuals, his or her tribe, or an agency of the federal government; and (2) certain distributions (including land or an interest in land) received by an individual Alaska Native or descendant of an Alaska Native from an Alaska Native Regional and Village Corporation pursuant to the Alaska Native Claims Settlement Act. Most other property is required to be counted. There is no similar provision in current CHIP law.

Estate Recovery. The Omnibus Budget Reconciliation Act of 1993 requires all states to recover property and assets of deceased Medicaid beneficiaries for the cost of certain services provided by Medicaid. At a minimum, states must seek recovery for certain services provided, including nursing home care, services provided by an intermediate care facility for the mentally retarded or other similar medical institutions, and Medicaid payments to Medicare for cost-sharing related benefits. The state has discretion to recover further assets to cover the costs for all Medicaid services provided to the beneficiary. The state also has the authority to grant an exemption if the recovery would place undue hardship against the estate. The Secretary specifies the standards for a state hardship waiver for Medicaid estate recovery purposes.

HOUSE BILL

Premiums and Cost Sharing. The provision would specify that no enrollment fee, premium or similar charge, and no deduction, co-payment, cost-sharing, or similar charge shall be imposed against an Indian who receives Medicaid-coverable services or items directly from the Indian Health Service (IHS), an Indian Tribe (IT), Tribal Organization (TO), or Urban Indian Organization (UIO), or through referral under the contract health services (CHS) program. In addition, Medicaid payments due to the IHS, an IT, TO, or UIO, or to a health care provider through referral under the CHS program for providing services to a Medicaid-eligible Indian, could not be reduced by the amount of any enrollment fee, premium or similar charge, as well as any cost-sharing or similar charge that would otherwise be due from an Indian, if such charges were permitted. A rule of construction would specify that nothing in this provision could be construed as restricting the application of any other limitations on the imposition of premiums or cost-sharing that may apply to a Medicaid-enrolled Indian. This language would also add Indians receiving services through Indian entities to the list of individuals exempt from paying premiums or cost-sharing under the DRA option for alternative premiums and cost-sharing under Medicaid. The effective date of this provision would be October 1, 2009.

Eligibility Determinations under Medicaid and CHIP. The provision would prohibit consideration of four different classes of property from resources in determining Medicaid eligibility of an Indian. These classes include: (1) property, including real property and improvements, that is held in trust (subject to federal restrictions or otherwise under the supervision of the Secretary of the Interior), located on a reservation, including any federally recognized Indian Tribes reservation, Pueblo, or Colony, including former reservations in Oklahoma, Alaska Native regions established by the Alaska Native Claims Settlement Act (ANCSA), and Indian allotments on or near a reservation as designated and approved by the Bureau of Indian Affairs; (2) for any federally recognized Tribe not described in the first class, property located within the most recent boundaries of a prior federal reservation; (3) ownership interests in rents, leases, royalties, or usage rights related to natural resources, including extraction of natural resources or harvesting of timber, other plants and plant products, animals, fish, and shellfish, resulting from the exercise of federally protected rights; and (4) ownership interest in or usage rights to items not covered in the previous classes that have unique religious, spiritual, traditional, or cultural significance or rights that support subsistence or a traditional life style according to applicable tribal law or custom. This provision is modeled on the provisions of the Centers for Medicare & Medicaid Services (CMS) State Medicaid Manual that exempt the same type of Indian property from Medicaid estate recovery. The House bill would also apply this new language to CHIP in the same manner in which it applies to Medicaid.

Estate Recovery. The provision would provide that certain income, resources, and property would remain exempt from Medicaid estate recovery if they were exempted under Section 1917(b)(3) of the Social Security Act (allowing the Secretary to specify standards for a state hardship waiver of asset criteria) under instructions regarding Indian tribes and Alaskan Native Villages as of April 1, 2003. The provision also would allow the Secretary to provide for additional estate recovery exemptions for Indians under Medicaid.

SENATE BILL

Same as House bill, except that these provisions would sunset on December 31, 2010. The Senate bill did not specify an effective date for the premiums and cost sharing provision, meaning those provisions would take effect upon enactment.

CONFERENCE AGREEMENT

The conference agreement follows the Senate bill with modifications for the provisions to be permanently effective July 1, 2009.

SEC. 5006(d). RULES APPLICABLE UNDER MEDICAID AND CHIP TO MANAGED CARE ENTITIES WITH RESPECT TO INDIAN ENROLLEES AND INDIAN HEALTH CARE PROVIDERS AND INDIAN MANAGED CARE ENTITIES (SEC. 3302 OF THE SENATE BILL)

CURRENT LAW

Section 1903(m)(1) of Title XIX defines: (1) the term Medicaid managed care organization (MCO), (2) requirements regarding accessibility of services for Medicaid MCO beneficiaries vis-a-vis non-MCO Medicaid beneficiaries within the area served by the MCO; (3) solvency standards in general and specific to different types of organizations; and (4) the duties and functions of the Secretary with respect to the status of an organization as a Medicaid MCO.

Section 1905(t) of Title XIX defines another type of managed care arrangement called primary care case management (PCCM). Under such arrangements, states contract with primary care case managers who are responsible for locating, coordinating and monitoring covered primary care (and other services stipulated in contracts) provided to all individuals enrolled in such PCCM programs.

Title XIX contains a number of additional provisions regarding managed care under Medicaid. Section 1932(a)(5) specifies rules regarding the provision of information about managed care to beneficiaries and potential enrollees. Such information must be in an easily understood form, and must address the following topics: (1) who providers are and where they are located, (2) enrollee rights and responsibilities, (3) grievance and appeal procedures, (4) covered items and services, (5) comparative information for available MCOs regarding benefits, cost-sharing, service area and quality and performance, and (6) information on benefits not covered under managed care arrangements. In addition, Section 1932(d)(2)(B) requires managed care entities to distribute marketing materials to their entire service areas.

Sections 1903(m) and 1932 provide cross-referencing definitions for the term "Medicaid managed care organization." Under Title XIX, section 1932(a)(2)(C) stipulates the rules regarding Indian enrollment in Medicaid managed care. A state may not require an Indian (as defined in Section 4(c) of the Indian Health Care Improvement Act (IHCIA) to enroll in a managed care entity unless the entity is one of the following (and only if such entity is participating under the plan): (1) the IHS, (2) an IHP operated by an Indian tribe or tribal organization pursuant to a contract, grant, cooperative agreement, or compact with the IHS pursuant to the Indian Self-Determination Act, or (3) an urban IHP operated by a UIO pursuant to a grant or contract with the IHS pursuant to Title V of IHCIA.

In general, Federally Qualified Health Centers (FQHCs) are paid on a per visit basis, using a prospective payment system that takes into account costs incurred and changes in the scope of services provided. Per visit payment rates are also adjusted annually by the Medicare Economic Index applicable to primary care services. When an FQHC is a participating provider with a Medicaid managed care entity (MCE), the state must make supplemental payments to the center in an amount equal to any difference between the rate paid by the MCE and the per visit amount determined under the prospective payment system.

HOUSE BILL

No provision.

SENATE BILL

Under this provision, Medicaid managed care contracts with Managed Care Entities (MCEs) and Primary Care Case Management (PCCMs) companies would be required to meet certain conditions relating to access for Indian Medicaid beneficiaries in order to receive Medicaid payments, including:

- MCEs and PCCMs would need to demonstrate that the number of participating Indian health care providers was sufficient to ensure timely access to covered Medicaid managed care services for eligible enrollees, and
- MCEs and PCCMs would need to agree to pay Indian health care providers (IHPs) at rates equal to the rates negotiated between these organizations and the provider involved, or, if such a rate has not been negotiated, at a rate that is not less than the level and amount of payment which the MCE or PCCM would make for services rendered by a participating non-Indian health care provider.

In addition, this provision would specify that MCEs and PCCMs must agree to make prompt payment, as required under Medicaid rules for all providers, to participating Indian health care providers, and states would be prohibited from waiving requirements relating to assurance that payments are consistent with efficiency, economy, and quality.

Further, this provision would apply special payment provisions to certain Indian health care providers that are Federally Qualified Health Centers (FQHCs). For non-participating Indian FQHCs that provide covered Medicaid managed care services to Indian MCE enrollees, the MCE must pay a rate equal to the payment that would apply to a participating non-Indian FQHC. When payments to such participating and non-participating providers by an MCE for services rendered to an Indian enrollee with the MCE are less than the rate under the state plan, the state must pay such providers the difference between the rate and the MCE payment. Likewise, if the amount paid to a non-FQHC Indian provider (whether or not the provider participates with the MCE) is less than the rate that applies under the state plan, the state must pay the difference between the applicable rate and the amount paid by MCEs. Under this provision, Indian Medicaid MCEs would be permitted to restrict enrollment to Indians and to members of specific tribes in the same manner as IHPs may restrict the delivery of services to such Indians and tribal members.

Finally, the provision would apply specific sections affecting Medicaid to the CHIP program, including (1) Section 1932(a)(2)(C) in current law regarding enrollment of Indians in Medicaid managed care (e.g., states cannot require Indians to enroll in a MCE unless the entity is the IHS, certain IHPs operated by tribes or tribal organizations, or certain urban IHPs operated by Urban Indian Organizations (UIOs), and (2) the new Section 1932(h) as described above.

CONFERENCE AGREEMENT

The conference agreement follows the Senate bill with a modification deleting the sunset date clarifying that Indian Medicaid MCEs would be permitted to restrict enrollment to Indians but not to members of specific tribes, and clarifying access standards in states where there are no Indian providers. The provision would be effective July 1, 2009.

SEC. 5006(e). CONSULTATION ON MEDICAID, CHIP, AND OTHER HEALTH CARE PROGRAMS FUNDED UNDER THE SOCIAL SECURITY ACT INVOLVING INDIAN HEALTH PROGRAMS AND URBAN INDIAN ORGANIZATIONS (SEC. 5005 OF THE HOUSE BILL; SEC. 3303 OF THE SENATE BILL)

CURRENT LAW

There are no provisions in current Medicaid or CHIP statutes regarding a Tribal Technical Advisory Group (TTAG) within the Centers for Medicare and Medicaid Services (CMS), the federal agency that oversees the Medicare, Medicaid and CHIP programs. CMS currently maintains a TTAG for consultation on matters relating to Indian health care, but it is not codified in law.

HOUSE BILL

The provision would require the Secretary to maintain within CMS a Tribal TAG, previously established in accordance with requirements of a charter dated September 30, 2003. The provision also would require that the TAG include a representative of the UIOs and IHS. The UIO representative would be deemed an elected official of a tribal government for the purposes of applying Section 204(b) of the Unfunded Mandates Reform Act of 1995, which exempts elected tribal officials from the Federal Advisory Committee Act for certain meetings with federal officials.

The provision would also require states in which one or more IHPs or UIOs provide health services to establish a process for obtaining advice on a regular, on-going basis from designees of IHPs and UIOs regarding Medicaid law and its direct effects on those entities. This process must include seeking advice prior to submission of state Medicaid plan amendments, waiver requests or proposed demonstrations likely to directly affect Indians, IHPs, or UIOs. This process may include appointment of an advisory panel and of a designee of IHPs and UIOs to the Medicaid medical care advisory committee advising the state on its state Medicaid plan. The provision would also apply this new language to CHIP in the same manner in which it applies to Medicaid. Finally, the provision would prohibit construing these amendments as superseding existing advisory committees, working groups, guidance or other advisory procedures established by the Secretary or any state with respect to the provision of health care to Indians.

SENATE BILL

This provision is similar to the House provision. Both versions would require the Secretary to maintain within CMS a Tribal Technical Advisory Group (TTAG), previously established in accordance with requirements of a charter dated September 30, 2003. The provision also would require that the TTAG include a IHS representative. Unlike the House bill, however, under this provision in S.Amdt. 570, the TTAG also would include a representative of a national urban Indian Health organization, rather than a representative of the UIOs. The non-application of Federal Advisory Committee Act (FACA) would still hold for a representative of a national UIO.

CONFERENCE AGREEMENT

The conference agreement follows the Senate bill with a modification deleting the sunset date. The provision would be effective July 1, 2009.

SEC. 5007. FUNDING FOR OVERSIGHT AND IMPLEMENTATION (SEC. 5004 OF THE SENATE BILL)

CURRENT LAW

The Office of Inspector General (OIG) of the Department of Health and Human Services is responsible for ensuring program integrity of over 300 programs in the Department, including the Medicaid program. The OIG's program integrity activities are funded through a combination of discretionary appropriations and mandatory funding through the Health Care Fraud and Abuse Control Program. The Centers for Medicare & Medicaid Services (CMS) in the Department of Health and Human Services administers the Medicaid program at the federal level. These administrative activities are funded through discretionary appropriations.

HOUSE BILL

No provision.

SENATE BILL

Under this provision, the Health and Human Services Office of the Inspector General (HHS OIG) is to receive $31.25 million to ensure the proper expenditure of federal Medicaid funds. These funds are appropriated from any money in the Treasury not otherwise appropriated and are available throughout the recession period (defined as October 1, 2008 through December 31, 2010). Amounts appropriated under this provision would be available until September 30, 2012, without further appropriation, and would be in addition to any other amounts appropriated or made available to HHS OIG.

CONFERENCE AGREEMENT

The conference agreement follows the Senate bill with a modification. The funds for the HHSOIG would be appropriated in FY2009 and would be available for expenditure until September 30, 2011. The conference agreement would also appropriate $5 million in FY2009 to CMS for the implementation and oversight of the state fiscal relief provisions relating to Medicaid. These funds would remain available until expended.

SEC. 5008. GAO STUDY AND REPORT REGARDING STATE NEEDS DURING PERIODS OF NATIONAL ECONOMIC DOWNTURN (SEC. 5005 OF THE SENATE BILL)

CURRENT LAW

No provision.

HOUSE BILL

No provision.

Under this provision, the Comptroller General of the United States, would study the current (as of the date of enactment of the legislation) economic recession as well as previous national economic downturns since 1974. GAO would develop recommendations to address states' needs during economic recessions, including the past and projected effects of temporary increases in the federal medical assistance percentage (FMAP) during these recessions. By April 1, 2011, GAO would submit a report to appropriate congressional committees that would include the following:

- Recommendations for modifying the national economic downturn assistance formula for temporary Medicaid FMAP adjustments (a "countercyclical FMAP," as described in GAO report number, GAO–07–97), to improve the effectiveness of the countercyclical FMAP for addressing states' needs during national economic downturns:
  - what improvements are needed to identify factors to begin and end the application of a countercyclical FMAP;
  - how to adjust the amount of a countercyclical FMAP to account for state and regional variations; and
  - how a countercyclical FMAP could be adjusted to better account for actual Medicaid costs incurred by states during economic recessions.
- Analysis of the impact on states of recessions, including declines in private health insurance benefits coverage; declines in state revenues; and maintenance and growth of caseloads under Medicaid, CHIP, or any other publicly funded programs that provide health benefits coverage to state residents.

CONFERENCE AGREEMENT

The conference agreement follows the Senate bill.

PAYMENT OF MEDICARE LIABILITY TO STATES AS A RESULT OF THE SPECIAL DISABILITY WORKLOAD PROJECT (SEC. 5003 OF THE SENATE BILL)

CURRENT LAW

No provision.

HOUSE BILL

No provision.

SENATE BILL

Under this provision, within three months after enactment of this law, the Secretary, in consultation with the Commissioner of Social Security, would negotiate an agreement on a payment amount to be made to each state for the Medicare Special Disability Workload (SDW) project. Payments to states would be subject to certain conditions:

- states would waive the right to file or be a part of any civil action in any federal or state court where payment was sought for liability related to the Medicare SDW project;

- states would release the federal government from any further claims for reimbursement of state expenditures arising from the SDW project;
    - states that are parties to civil actions in any federal or state court seeking reimbursement for the SDW project, would be ineligible to receive payment under this provision while such action is pending or if it is resolved in a state's favor.

In negotiating with states, the Secretary and SSA Commissioner would use the most recent federal data available, including estimates, to determine the amount of payment to be offered to each state that elects to enter into an agreement with the Secretary. The payment methodology would consist of the following factors:

- the number of SDW cases that were eligible for benefits under Medicare and the month when these cases initially became eligible;
    - the applicable non-federal share of Medicaid expenditures made by states during the period these cases were eligible; and
    - other factors determined appropriate by the Secretary and the SSA Commissioner in consultation with states.

However, as a condition of payment under a negotiated agreement for SDW cases, states would not be required to submit individual paid Medicaid claims data.

To make payments to states for the SDW project, $3 billion would be appropriated for FY2009 from money in the treasury not otherwise appropriated. Aggregate payments to states could not exceed $3 billion. Payments to states would be provided within four months from the date of enactment of ARRA.

An SDW case would be defined as an individual determined by the SSA Commissioner to have been eligible for benefits under Title II of the SSA for a period during which such benefits were not provided to the individual and who was, during all or part of such period, enrolled in Medicaid.

CONFERENCE AGREEMENT

The conference agreement follows the House bill.

TITLE VI—BROADBAND TECHNOLOGY OPPORTUNITIES PROGRAM

HOUSE BILL

Section 6001 of the House bill directs the National Telecommunications and Information Administration ("NTIA") to develop and maintain a broadband inventory map of the United States that identifies and depicts broadband service availability and capability and directs the NTIA to make the map accessible on the NTIA's website no later than 2 years after the date of enactment of this Act. It authorizes the creation of grant programs for the deployment of wireless and wireline broadband infrastructure to be administered by the NTIA. It also authorizes a state to submit a priority report to the NTIA that identifies the geographic areas within that state that have greatest need for new or additional telecommunications infrastructure. A state may not identify areas encompassing more than 20% of that state's population.

Section 6002 of the House bill authorizes the NTIA to award wireless deployment grants and broadband deployment grants to eligible entities for the non-recurring costs of deploying broadband infrastructure in qualified urban, suburban, and rural areas. Section 6002 directs the NTIA to seek to distribute wireless grants, to the extent possible, so that 25% of the available funds go to "unserved areas" for basic wireless voice services and 75% to "underserved areas" for advanced wireless broadband services. It also directs that the NTIA shall seek to distribute broadband deployment grants, to the extent possible, so that 25% of the available funds go to "unserved areas" for basic broadband services and 75% to "underserved areas" for advanced broadband services. Section 6002 directs the NTIA to establish certain grant requirements, including that grant recipients are not unjustly enriched by the program, adhere to the FCC's August 5, 2005, broadband Internet policy statement, operate networks on an open access basis, and adhere to a build out schedule.

Section 6002 of the House bill sets forth the requirements of the grant application and grant selection criteria. The NTIA is required to consider certain public policy goals (e.g., public safety benefits and enhancement of computer ownership or literacy) before awarding grants. It requires the NTIA to coordinate with the FCC and to consult with other agencies as necessary. Section 6002 requires the NTIA to submit an annual report to Congress assessing the impact of the grants on the policy objectives and criteria contained in this Section and grants the NTIA authority to prescribe rules as necessary to implement this Section. Section 6002 also contains definitions of terms used in this Section, and directs the FCC to develop definitions for the terms unserved, underserved, and open access.

Section 6002 defines "basic broadband service" as a service delivering data to the end user at a speed of at least 5 megabits per second downstream and 1 megabit per second upstream. The term "advanced broadband service" means a service capable of delivering at least 45 megabits per second downstream and 15 megabits per second upstream. The term advanced wireless broadband service means a service capable of delivering at least 3 megabits downstream and 1 megabit upstream.

Section 6003 of the House bill requires the FCC to, not later than one year after the date of enactment of this section, develop and submit to Congress a report containing a national broadband plan and specifies what the plan should include.

SENATE BILL

Section 201 of the Senate bill authorizes the NTIA to create a grant program entitled the Broadband Technology Opportunity Program to award competitive grants to State and local governments, nonprofits, and public-private partnerships to: (1) accelerate broadband deployment in unserved and underserved areas and to strategic institutions that are likely to create jobs or provide significant public benefits; (2) increase sustained broadband adoption;

and (3) upgrade technology and capacity for public safety entities and at public computing centers, which are a key source of access to the Internet for lower income users, such as libraries and community colleges.

Section 201 gives the NTIA the authority to impose grant conditions with regard to interconnection and nondiscrimination requirements that apply to facilities funded in part by this program, regardless of who operates those facilities.

Section 201 also (1) imposes a 20-percent match requirement for grants, which may be satisfied by the grant applicant or any third-party partnering with the grant applicant, and may be waived only under special circumstances; (2) requires specific commitments from grantees on scheduled progress for meeting the goals of the grant; (3) requires that grant applications show that the proposed broadband deployment would not occur during the grant period without this Federal investment; (4) requires quarterly reporting by any entity receiving funds regarding how funds are spent and progress meeting the schedule, as well as quarterly reporting to Congress by Federal agencies making grants regarding how funds are being spent; (5) requires strong public transparency regarding how funds are spent under the program and grantees' progress fulfilling specific commitments to deploy facilities, increase broadband adoption or deploy computer infrastructure; and (6) empowers the NTIA to revoke funding in any case of misspending, and to recapture funds in certain circumstances.

CONFERENCE AGREEMENT

Summary

The Conference substitute retains the general structure and language of the Senate bill, while incorporating a series of amendments related to the priorities of the House.

Section 6001. Section 6001 establishes the Broadband Technology Opportunities Program within the NTIA. The Conferees intend that the NTIA has discretion in selecting the grant recipients that will best achieve the broad objectives of the program. The Conferees also intend that the NTIA select grant recipients that it judges will best meet the broadband access needs of the area to be served, whether by a wireless provider, a wireline provider, or any provider offering to construct last-mile, middle-mile, or long haul facilities. The Conferees intend that the NTIA award grants serving all parts of the country, including rural, suburban, and urban areas. The Conferees intend that the NTIA seek to ensure, to the extent practicable, that grant funds be used to assist infrastructure investments that would not otherwise be made by the entity applying, or, secondarily, that might not be made as quickly.

Part of the program is directed towards competitive grants for innovative programs to encourage sustainable adoption of broadband service in particular by vulnerable populations. The Conferees note the success of such programs in several States, and hope that these grantees will be involved in aggregating demand, ensuring community involvement, and fostering useful technology applications, thereby stimulating economic growth and job creation.

Eligible Entities. The Conference substitute creates a new, broad definition of entities that are eligible to receive grants. It is the intent of the Conferees that, consistent with the public interest and purposes of this section, as many entities as possible be eligible to apply for a competitive grant, including wireless carriers, wireline carriers, backhaul providers, satellite carriers, public-private partnerships, and tower companies.

Grant Distribution Considerations and Broadband Speeds. The Conference substitute inserts a new Section 6001(h) that incorporates several of the grant distribution considerations from the House bill. In particular, new Section 6001(h)(3) requires the NTIA to consider whether a grant applicant is a socially and economically disadvantaged small business, as defined under the Small Business Act.

New Section 6001(h)(2)(*B*) also requires the NTIA to consider whether an application will result in the greatest possible broadband speeds being delivered to consumers. While the House bill had included specific speed thresholds that an applicant must have met to be eligible for a grant, the substitute requires only that the NTIA consider the speeds that would be delivered to consumers in awarding grants. The Conferees are mindful that a specific speed threshold could have the unintended result of thwarting broadband deployment in certain areas. The Conferees are also mindful that the construction of broadband facilities capable of delivering next-generation broadband speeds is likely to result in greater job creation and job preservation than projects centered on current-generation broadband speeds. Therefore, the Conferees instruct the NTIA to seek to fund, to the extent practicable, projects that provide the highest possible, next-generation broadband speeds to consumers.

Broadband Policy Statement. The Conference substitute inserts the House language that requires grant recipients to adhere to the principles contained in the Federal Communications Commission's Broadband Policy Statement.

National Broadband Plan. The Conference substitute adopts the House language on the creation of a national broadband plan, with some minor modifications.

Federal/State Cooperation. Section 6001(c) directs the NTIA to consult with States on: (1) the identification of unserved and underserved areas within their borders; and (2) the allocation of grants funds to projects affecting each State. The Conferees recognize that States have resources and a familiarity with local economic, demographic, and market conditions that could contribute to the success of the broadband grant program. States are encouraged to coalesce stakeholders and partners, assess community needs, aggregate demand for services, and evaluate demand for technical assistance. The Conferees therefore expect and intend that the NTIA, at its discretion, will seek advice and assistance from the States in reviewing grant applications, as long as the NTIA retains the sole authority to approve the awards. The Conferees further intend that the NTIA will, in its discretion, assist the States in post-grant monitoring to ensure that recipients comply fully with the terms and conditions of their grants.

Definitions. The substitute does not define such terms as "unserved area" "underserved areas" and "broadband." The Conferees instruct the NTIA to coordinate its understanding of these terms with the FCC, so that the NTIA may benefit from the FCC's considerable expertise in these matters. In defining "broadband service," the Conferees intend that the NTIA take into consideration the technical differences between wireless and wireline networks, and consider the actual speeds that broadband networks are able to deliver to consumers under a variety of circumstances.

TITLE VII—LIMITS ON EXECUTIVE COMPENSATION

A. EXECUTIVE COMPENSATION OVERSIGHT (SECS. 6001 TO 6006 OF THE SENATE AMENDMENT AND SEC. 7001 OF THE CONFERENCE AGREEMENT)

PRESENT LAW

An employer generally may deduct reasonable compensation for personal services as an ordinary and necessary business expense. Section 162(m) (relating to remuneration expenses for certain executives that are in excess of $1 million) and section 280G (relating to excess parachute payments) provide explicit limitations on the deductibility of certain compensation expenses in the case of corporate employers, and section 4999 imposes an additional tax of 20 percent on the recipient of an excess parachute payment. The Emergency Economic Stabilization Act of 2008 ("EESA") limits the amount of payments that may be deducted as reasonable compensation by certain financial institutions ("TARP recipients") that receive financial assistance from the United States pursuant to the troubled asset relief program ("TARP") established under EESA by modifying the section 162(m) and section 280G limits. EESA also provided non-tax rules relating to the compensation that is payable by such a financial institution (the "TARP executive compensation rules").

HOUSE BILL

No provision.

SENATE AMENDMENT

The provision modifies and expands the present law non-tax TARP executive compensation rules. The modifications include: (1) expanding the requirement of recovery of a bonus, retention award, or incentive compensation paid to a senior executive officer based on statements of earnings, revenues, gains, or other criteria that are found to be materially inaccurate to the next 20 most highly compensated employees of a TARP recipient; (2) expanding the prohibition on the payment of golden parachute payments from senior executive officers to the next five most highly compensated employees of the TARP recipient, and defining the term "golden parachute payment" as any payment to a senior executive officer for departure from a company for any reason, except for payments for services performed or benefits accrued; and (3) prohibiting a TARP recipient from paying or accruing any bonus, retention award, or incentive compensation to at least the 25 most highly compensated employees; and (4) prohibiting any compensation plan that would encourage manipulation of the reported earnings of a TARP recipient to enhance the compensation of any of its employees. The provision also provides rules relating to the compensation committees of TARP recipients, nonbinding shareholder votes on executive compensation payable by a TARP recipient, and the adoption by TARP recipients of policies regarding luxury expenditures such as entertainment, aviation, and office renovation expenses.

CONFERENCE AGREEMENT

The conference agreement follows the Senate amendment with several modifications. Among the modifications are (1) a rule that provides that financial assistance under TARP is not treated as outstanding for a period in which the United States only holds warrants to purchase common stock of the TARP recipient; (2) rules that phase-in the restriction on bonuses, retention awards, and other incentive compensation by the amount of financial assistance received by the entity receiving TARP assistance, and that permit compensation to be paid in the form of restricted stock; and (3) and a directive to the Secretary of the Treasury to review compensation paid to senior executive officers and the next 20 most highly compensated employees of an entity receiving TARP assistance before the date of enactment to determine whether such payments were inconsistent with the provision, the TARP, or public interest.

TAX COMPLEXITY ANALYSIS

Section 4022(b) of the Internal Revenue Service Reform and Restructuring Act of 1998 (the "IRS Reform Act") requires the staff of the Joint Committee on Taxation (in consultation with the Internal Revenue Service and the Treasury Department) to provide a tax complexity analysis. The complexity analysis is required for all legislation reported by the Senate Committee on Finance, the House Committee on Ways and Means, or any committee of conference if the legislation includes a provision that directly or indirectly amends the Internal Revenue Code and has widespread applicability to individuals or small businesses. For each such provision identified by the staff of the Joint Committee on Taxation a summary description of the provision is provided along with an estimate of the number and type of affected taxpayers, and a discussion regarding the relevant complexity and administrative issues.

Following the analysis of the staff of the Joint Committee on Taxation are the comments of the IRS and Treasury regarding each of the provisions included in the complexity analysis.

1. MAKE WORK PAY CREDIT

SUMMARY DESCRIPTION OF THE PROVISION

The provision creates a refundable tax credit for taxable years beginning in 2009 and 2010 equal to the lesser of (1) 6.2 percent of an individual's earned income or (2) $400 ($800 in the case of a joint return). The credit is phased out at a rate of two percent of the eligible individual's modified adjusted gross income above $75,000 ($150,000 in the case of a joint return).

It is estimated that the provision will affect in excess of 100 million individual tax returns.

DISCUSSION

The provision will require additional paperwork for taxpayers and additional processing burdens for IRS. It is expected that taxpayers will need to complete additional worksheets and or forms to compute the amount of the credit. Taxpayers may also wish to adjust their income tax withholding by filing the appropriate forms before the end of 2009. The IRS is anticipated to revise income tax withholding schedules and publish new schedules. These revised income tax withholding schedules should be designed to reduce taxpayers' income tax withheld for each remaining pay period in the remainder of 2009 so that the full benefit of the provision is reflected in the income tax withholding schedules during the balance of 2009.

2. EXTENSION OF ALTERNATIVE MINIMUM TAX RELIEF FOR INDIVIDUALS

SUMMARY DESCRIPTION OF THE PROVISION

The provision increases the individual AMT exemption amount for taxable years beginning in 2009 to $70,950 in the case of married individuals filing a joint return and surviving spouses; $46,700 in the case of other unmarried individuals; and $35,475 in the case of married individuals filing separate returns. In addition, for taxable years beginning in 2009, the provision allows an individual to offset the entire regular tax liability and alternative minimum tax liability by the nonrefundable personal credits.

NUMBER OF AFFECTED TAXPAYERS

It is estimated that the provision will affect approximately 25 million individual tax returns.

DISCUSSION

Many individuals will not have to compute their alternative minimum tax and file the IRS forms relating to that tax.

3. SPECIAL ALLOWANCE FOR CERTAIN PROPERTY ACQUIRED DURING 2009

SUMMARY DESCRIPTION OF THE PROVISION

The provision extends the additional first-year depreciation deduction for one year, generally through 2009 (through 2010 for certain longer-lived and transportation property).

NUMBER OF AFFECTED TAXPAYERS

It is estimated that more than 10 percent of small businesses will be affected by the provision.

DISCUSSION

It is not anticipated that small businesses will have to keep additional records due to this provision, nor will additional regulatory guidance be necessary to implement this provision. It is not anticipated that the provision will result in an increase in disputes between small businesses and the IRS. However, small businesses will have to perform additional analysis to determine whether property qualifies for the provision. In addition, for qualified property, small businesses will be required to perform additional calculations to determine the proper amount of allowable depreciation. Complexity may also be increased because the provision is temporary. For example, different tax treatment will apply for identical equipment based on the acquisition and placed in service date. Further, the Secretary of the Treasury is expected to have to make appropriate revisions to the applicable depreciation tax forms.

4. PREMIUM ASSISTANCE FOR COBRA BENEFITS

SUMMARY DESCRIPTION OF THE PROVISION

The provision reimburses employers providing COBRA continuation health coverage to employees to the extent of 65 percent of the premium amount for up to nine months and requires the eligible individual to pay 35 percent of the premium. The program is mandatory for employers required to offer COBRA continuation health coverage. Eligible individuals must have a qualifying event between September 1, 2008 and December 31, 2009, and must have been terminated involuntarily. Firms providing COBRA benefits will be able to allow those electing COBRA to choose from other insurance options at the time of the qualifying event, and firms will be able to contribute to the individual portion of the premium. Lastly, the benefit phases out for single taxpayers with modified adjusted gross incomes between $125,000 and $145,000 ($250,000 and $290,000 for joint filers) for the taxable year.

Employers will pay reduced payroll taxes in the aggregate amount of 65 percent of the premium for all individuals who opt into the provision, or, if COBRA subsidy exceeds payroll taxes, employers will be reimbursed directly through a program established by the Department of Treasury. COBRA continuation health coverage for this purpose includes not only coverage that applies to private, nongovernmental employers with 20 or more employees but also coverage rules that apply to Federal and State and local governmental employers pursuant to Federal law, and to State law mandates that apply to small employers (employers with less than 20 employees) and other employers not covered by Federal law, provided that such State law mandates require an employer or other entity to offer comparable continuation health coverage. The social security trust fund is held harmless from payroll tax offsets that are permitted under the program.

NUMBER OF AFFECTED TAXPAYERS

It is estimated that more than 10 percent of small businesses will be affected by the provision.

DISCUSSION

This provision will require additional processing by the IRS in three areas; accounting, income eligibility and provision enforcement. First, for all firms with eligible employees, the firm must deduct that amount from their payroll taxes, so IRS must be aware of the number of employees eligible for the reimbursement and the average monthly premium at the firm to properly assess the amount of the deduction from payroll taxes. The Department of the Treasury must then transfer the appropriate amount of funds back into the social security trust fund. All employers bound by COBRA or COBRA-type legislation described above, and who terminate individuals from employment between September 1, 2008, and December 31, 2009, are affected by this provision. In addition, firms are permitted to collect full premiums from individuals for 60 days in accordance with their current premium billing cycles, but must then credit back the difference in later payments or if later payments are insufficient to credit back all funds, the employer will submit payment to the individual. The IRS must also distinguish between the 65 percent of subsidy contribution mandated and any optional firm contribution to the remaining 35 percent of premium.

Second, the income eligibility provision in the bill limits eligibility for the modified adjusted gross income limit of the provision phasing out between $125,000 and $145,000 for single filers ($250,000 and $290,000 for joint filers) for the taxable year. While individuals may waive the subsidy if they believe their earnings will exceed the limit, if an individual accepts the subsidy and earns over the limit the individual will be responsible for paying the subsidy back to Treasury. For married individuals filing separately, if any family member is over the single modified adjusted gross income limit of $125,000, the entire non-subsidized portion (this accounts for the phase out) must be repaid. This clause requires IRS to match the incomes of spouses filing separately and determine if the modified adjusted gross income of either spouse disqualifies both for the subsidy received. Children not claimed as dependents, however, who are still on family plans have their incomes excluded from this limitation.

Third, the IRS must create rules and regulations to prevent fraud and abuse of this provision. For example, taxpayers may be required to provide evidence of eligibility for the subsidy including evidence of involuntary separation from work, which can include attestation from the former employer or certification from state unemployment insurance agencies. If a premium assistance eligible individual becomes eligible for other group coverage while receiving premium assistance, that individual must forfeit the subsidy or face a penalty and the IRS must attempt to prevent individuals from claiming the subsidy while eligible for other group coverage either through a spouse or through a new employer.

COMPLIANCE WITH CLAUSE 9 OF RULE XXI (EARMARKS)

Pursuant to clause 9 of rule XXI of the Rules of the House of Representatives, neither this conference report nor the accompanying joint statement of managers contains any congressional

781

earmarks, limited tax benefits, or limited tariff benefits as defined in clause 9(e), 9(f), or 9(g) of rule XXI.

DAVID OBEY,
CHARLES RANGEL,
HENRY WAXMAN,
Managers on the Part of the House.

DANIEL K. INOUYE,
MAX BAUCUS,
HARRY REID,
Managers on the Part of the Senate.

○